Alexander the Great, Julius Caesar, Genghis Khan, and Adolf Hitler tried to take over the world. All of them failed. Yet an illiterate desert prophet and his followers hammered together an empire eleven times the size of the conquests of Alexander the Great, five times the size of the Roman Empire, and seven times the size of the United States. The biggest empire in history. How did Muhammad pull it off? And how does his success threaten you and me?

The
MUHAMMAD
Code

How a Desert Prophet Brought You
ISIS, al Qaeda, and Boko Haram
or
How Muhammad Invented Jihad

by Howard Bloom

Feral House
2016

10 9 8 7 6 5 4 3 2 1

Published by
Feral House
1240 W. Sims Way #124
Port Townsend, WA 98368
www.feralhouse.com

Edited by Laura Smith
Cover and book design by John Hubbard / EMKS.fi
Printed and bound in the United States of America

FERALHOUSE.COM

Table of Contents

Introduction

RIGHTEOUSNESS IN ISLAM comes from following Muhammad's footsteps. And those footsteps are, alas, violent, imperialist, colonialist, sadistic, and genocidal. Muhammad's story, the story at the heart of Islam, is the subject of this book.

Millions of Muslims interpret Islam as a religion of tolerance, pluralism, and peace. I have many Muslim friends. Many. And none of them follow Muhammad's pattern. None of them are violent, imperialist, sadistic, and genocidal.

The Sheikh who made Dubai what it is today and who doubles as the prime minister of the United Arab Emirates named a race horse after one of my books. Bless him. The former development minister of Dubai, a current member of Dubai's ruling council, now runs Dubai's $33 billion sovereign real estate empire. His company built the world's tallest building. He has gone in front of the Arabian Business and Economic Forum, of which he's a co-founder, and has told the leading businessmen of the Arab world that one of my books contains the future of Dubai. The eleventh president of India, Dr. Abdul P.J. Kalam, a Muslim, called that same book "a visionary creation." When I was asked to create a two-day intensive program for business leaders called "Reperceiving Leadership," that request came from one of the world's 57 Islamic nations, Malaysia. And the ten CEOs and General Managers to whom I gave the program were all Muslims. Every one of them.

My biggest fan is a Muslim atheist who splits his time between Islamabad in Pakistan, where he's the trainer to the stars of the national cricket team, and Dubai, where he's established that city's most expensive training establishment. I wrote the promotional materials for his Dubai business when he first started it. Because I believe in him as much as he believes in me.

I not only appear regularly on Saudi and Iranian TV, but my producer at Saudi TV is dear to my heart.

One day in roughly 2000, after my howardbloom.net website had gone up, I was perplexed to discover that I was getting a steady trickle of hits from Saudi Arabia and the United Arab Emirates. Why was I attracting these hits? Was it because I was being stalked? "No," said the man who calls himself my "Muslim brother," the therapist who helped save me when I was in deep trouble from 1998 to 2002. "Don't you understand," he said, "there are university professors teaching in Saudi Arabia and the UAE. They can't open their mouths about their real feelings. You are speaking for them."

What does he mean? Muhammad's example of murderous intolerance toward dissidents threatens all of my Muslim friends. It is the example on which the people of ISIS, al Qaeda, and Boko Haram have modeled their lives. In fact, it is their excuse for mass murder and war crimes. And that militancy kills far more Muslims than it kills Westerners.

To be blunt, I have kept the names of some of my Muslim friends out of this introduction because to reveal them in this book would threaten at the very least vicious disapproval from their families and at the most death.

But ISIS, al Qaeda, and Boko Haram are not unique. The war they wage against the world...and against the moderates in their own community... is just the latest manifestation of a violent conflict that has gone on since 623 A.D. A world war that's been in motion for nearly 1,400 years. To understand that war, and to understand the danger that my moderate Muslim friends and yours are in, you have to understand one of history's most astonishing stories. A story that has had more impact than the lives of Alexander the Great, Julius Caesar, and Napoleon combined. You have to understand the life of the one true prophet of Allah, the one true source of holiness and virtue in Islam, Muhammad.

What's Sex Have to do With It?

IN THE FALL OF 2014, a Saudi fighter for the Islamic State, ISIS, in Al-Shaddadi, Syria, bought a female slave in the market, a 34-year-old Yazidi captive. He raped her over and over again. Why else do you buy a female slave? Then he purchased a second sex slave. This one was a 12-year-old girl. And suddenly the handcuffs of the Saudi fighter's lust came off. Said the 34-year-old sex slave after she escaped, the ISIS fighter raped the 12-year-old youngster "for days on end despite heavy bleeding."[10] The 34-year-old escapee says with a mixture of despair and disgust, "He destroyed her body. She was badly infected. The fighter kept coming and asking me, 'Why does she smell so bad?' And I said, she has an infection on the inside, you need to take care of her."[11]

"'She's just a little girl,' pleaded the 34-year-old. But the ISIS fighter answered: 'No. She's not a little girl. She's a slave. And she knows exactly how to have sex.'" Then he added something vital: "And having sex with her pleases God." So the fighter never provided medical care. Instead, he prostrated himself on the floor next to the adolescent girl's bed, prayed to Allah, then mounted the child over and over again. Each time when he was finished, he laid himself out on the floor again and prayed. We do not know the end of the story. We do not know if Allah the merciful, Allah the compassionate ever answered the prayers with healing. And, frankly, we do not know if the fighter even bothered to pray for such a thing.

This was just one of many stories told by those who managed to escape. Those who managed to slip away from the new institutions of sexual slavery that ISIS crowed proudly about in cover lines on its October 11, 2014, issue of its glossy magazine *Dābiq* with the proud words, "The Revival of Slavery Before the Hour."[12] What's the Hour? It's the Muslim equivalent of Christianity's rapture, it's the arrival of the day of judgement. And why was *Dābiq* so proud of "the revival of slavery"? Sexual slavery?

The leader of the Islamic State is Abu Bakr al-Baghdadi. Abu Bakr Al-Baghdadi was born Ibrahim al-Badri in 1971 in a city of 349,000 inhabitants, Samarra, a city 77 miles north of Baghdad with claims to holiness.[13] Baghdadi's father taught "Koranic recitation" in a local mosque. But his family traced its lineage all the way back to the Prophet Muhammad. The Brookings Institution says that the young al-Baghdadi was "an introvert with a passion for religion and soccer."[14] You can tell which passion was dominant by the nickname pinned on him: "The Believer." Baghdadi studied religious texts with zeal, began teaching children to chant the Qur'an as a teenager, and even in his youth bawled out those he felt were straying from the strict practices of Islam.

Baghdadi hoped to attend law school at the University of Baghdad in 1996, but his high school grades were too low. So he signed up at Baghdad's Saddam University for Islamic Studies and went for a master's degree in Qur'anic recitation. Then he went for a doctorate. Meanwhile, Baghdadi had a mentor who had fought in the war to drive the Soviet Union out of Afghanistan, Muhammad Hardan.[15] The anti-Russian warriors of Afghanistan were supported and trained by a strange triumvirate: the United States, Saudi Arabia, and China.[16] This backing did not earn these three nations any loyalty. The so-called "freedom fighters," the Muslims from all over the Islamic world who battled in Afghanistan, fashioned a violently anti-Western, anti-superstate organization, al Qaeda. Under his mentor Hardan, al-Baghdadi entered the Muslim Brotherhood and gravitated to its most mil-itant wing,[17] a wing that wanted to imitate the first forefathers of Islam, the "companions of the prophet." Among other things, those "companions" had picked up the banner of global conquest when the Prophet died in 632 A.D. And they had conquered the core of the biggest empire in history, an empire 11 times the size of the conquests of Alexander the Great, five times the size of the Roman Empire, and seven times the size of the United States.

The first three generations of Muslims are referred to as the salaf, the "ancestors," the "forefathers."[18] And the extremists within the Muslim Brotherhood who were determined to emulate these ancestors were called Salafists.[19] They were men dedicated to their founding fathers' style of vio-lence and warfare. Abu Bakr al-Baghdadi would eventually go on to found ISIS. And, invoking his descent from Muhammad, he would declare himself the Caliph, the ruler of a new power destined to take over the Earth, the Islamic State.

But ISIS' military approach, its jihad against all non-Muslim powers, would not be Abu Bakr al-Baghdadi's only contribution to the 21st century. By 2004, al-Baghdadi had two wives and six children.[20] And the facts give the impression that he wanted more. Much more.

Here's the story of Baghdadi's sexual aims as told to London's *Daily Mail Online* by what the *Mail* calls "al-Baghdadi's personal sex slave," Muna. Muna was 16 years old with blue eyes. She was a Yazidi, a member of a group that believes the world is controlled by seven angels. During her interviews, a face-veil covered everything but her eyes, intense and beautiful eyes that the *Mail* calls "penetrating."

Thousands[21] of Yazidi women were taken prisoner in August 2014 in the siege of Iraq's Mount Sinjar. Yes, thousands. Later in 2014, 61 of these women, girls ranging from nine years old to 22, were gathered at a captured Christian building in Mosul, a building that Muna calls "a white palace … between the mountain and the sea."[22] For what purpose? " To be "sold at the slave market." Says Muna, the average age of the girls gathered to be sold as property—sexual property—"was 15."

Muna was apparently chosen…for what she may not have known. In the words of the *Mail*, she was "held for two nights under the guard of five militants at a property in ISIS' de facto capital Raqqa, Baghdadi himself turned up at around 10 p.m. on August 15 last year." That's August 15, 2014. With Baghdadi was his bodyguard and son-in-law, a 30-year-old Kurd from the Iraqi city of Kirkuk named Mansour. Muna was taken to a two-story house in Raqqa's center, a house where Baghdadi lived with a number of wives that had by now gone up from two to three, plus his three daughters, and three sons. Baghdadi's oldest daughter was married to his Kurdish bodyguard, Mansour. And, says Muna, "The wives were always worse than Baghdadi. They were always telling the children that they were lazy and beating them." But the children were not the wives' only targets. The wives would force the sex slaves to clean and do household chores. And while these teenagers labored, the wives and their six children would humiliate and make fun of them.[23]

But the men were even worse. Says Muna, one of the first things Baghdadi explained to his sex slaves was that they should forget their old life. Why? It no longer existed. Recalls Muna, Baghdadi "would always tell us: Forget your father and your brothers. We have killed them. And we have married off your mothers and sisters. Forget them."[24] Baghdadi explained these deaths to make a point. The women were now totally dependent on the whims of the men who owned them. And totally in the hands of Islam.

Baghdadi spent time with Muna. But you'll have to judge whether that time was an indication of compassion. Baghdadi's first move? He showed Muna a complete and detailed film of the beheading of an American, journalist James Foley.[25] It was a video in which a British-born ISIS member, Jihadi John, Muhammad Emwazi, wielded the knife. As Muna recalls, "There was a journalist, an American journalist, and there was a man dressed all in black. ...He killed the journalist. He beheaded him[26]. ... (Al-Baghdadi) showed us this on the laptop, and they said to me, 'If you don't convert to Islam, this will happen to you—we will behead all of you.'"[27] Then Baghdadi tried to convert Muna to Islam. "'You have two choices,' they said. 'Convert to Islam. Or die like this.'"[28] Why? Said Baghdadi, Muna was an infidel. Her only way to make it to heaven was to convert to the "nice and clean" religion of Islam. Baghdadi was very explicit about who had ordered the killing of Foley. He had. And according to the *Mail*, "The implication was clear, Muna said. Convert to Islam or die a brutal death like James Foley."[29]

The day after Muna joined the Baghdadi household, the building next door was flattened by an airstrike.[30] So Baghdadi, his family, and his entire entourage moved. Then, ten days later, the family and its entourage apparently moved again, to Syria's Aleppo. Or, as the *Mail* puts it, Muna was moved from one location to another "to be abused at Baghdadi's convenience." Sexually abused.

Things at al-Baghdadi's households, where Muna was kept, were a bit odd. Baghdadi and his family loved expensive watches and ate takeout every night so that the wives would neither have to cook and nor to go out in public. Baghdadi was big on watches. Says Muna, Baghdadi gave one of his wives, an American we'll meet later, Kayla Mueller, a watch to lay claim to her as one of his wives. "It was a normal watch, but it was so expensive. ... He also gifted his other wives the same kind of watch."[31] Baghdadi slept late, got up at 10 a.m., and stayed awake until midnight.[32] Says Muna, "Sometimes, he would talk to us ... but then we wouldn't see him for days. We didn't know where he had gone."[33] Baghdadi kept his distance from mobile phones, knowing that Western intelligence services could use a phone to get a bead on his location. He was particularly concerned about drones. As Muna explains it, "He did not use a telephone. He was afraid that the aircraft would know his location."[34] And from him, says Muna, "there were no kind words."[35] Very much like the prophet himself. Very much like Muhammad. But we'll get to Muhammad in a bit.

One night in Aleppo, Muna tried to escape. The attempt did not work out well. ISIS guards caught her. "We got the key [to the house] and unlocked the door. We ran and ran ... we saw a house just outside Aleppo ... and there was an Arab woman. She said, 'Come in, come in. I will help you and bring you to Iraq.' ... She said ... she would help us, but then she called Abu Bakr al-Baghdadi."[36] Baghdadi assigned himself the task of punishing her. Says the *Mail*, "he beat her all over her body with a belt and garden hose, leaving her body covered in bruises. Telling her she 'belongs to the Islamic State,' the terror chief also slapped her in the face until her nose bled and beat her around the face with cables and wooden sticks." "They beat us all over our bodies," Muna recalls. "We were completely black from the beating. They beat us with everything: cables, belts and wooden sticks." Muna emphasizes that "(Al-Baghdadi) hit me (with a) garden hose and (a) belt. Then he slapped my face and my nose bled."[37] In attacking her face, Baghdadi was breaking the rules set forth in an ISIS pamphlet on how to deal with sex slaves. That pamphlet says, "It is permissible to beat the female slave as a [form of] darb ta'deeb [disciplinary beating], [but] it is forbidden to [use] darb al-takseer [literally, breaking beating], [darb] al-tashaffi [beating for the purpose of achieving gratification], or [darb] al-ta'dheeb [torture beating]. Further, it is forbidden to hit the face."[38]

But that was not the only beating Muna received at the hands of ISIS' founder. Says the *Mail*, "Muna said one beating from Baghdadi was so brutal that it left her with a dislocated shoulder and her friend with bone fractures in the face."

"Al-Baghdadi told us, 'We beat you because you ran away from us. We chose you to convert to our religion. We chose you. You belong to the Islamic State.'"[39] Was Baghdadi implying that being chosen as a slave, and a sexual slave at that, was an honor? What Muna didn't know was the identity of her master. He turned out to be Abu Bakr al-Baghdadi, the caliph of the Islamic State.[40]

After her escape attempt, Baghdadi disposed of Muna. He sent her to a prison for women in Raqqa. It was there that she met a blondish 25-year-old from Prescott, Arizona,[41] Kayla Mueller, another potential sex toy who had been captured over a year earlier, on August 3, 2013. Who was Kayla Mueller? She was a dedicated human rights activist from Prescott, Arizona, with a special interest in the Muslim world. In high school, she'd been a member of the Save Darfur Coalition.[42] What was the major crime in Darfur?

Camel-riding Arab militia men, Muslim militia men, supported by the government in the North of Sudan, galloped southwest to attack Darfur's black[43] Fur, Masalit, and Zaghawa villages and to kill and mutilate as many men as possible. But these camel-mounted warriors were also famed for something else: rape. Influential Muslim professor of Political Science and African Studies at the State University of New York at Binghamton, Ali Mazrui, reports a phrase that was common in the Sudan: "I am going south—to bring into the world 40 more Arabs before I die!"[44] Rape was the means to achieve this population expansion.

While Mueller was in school at Northern Arizona University, she organized the university's chapter of Amnesty International and a chapter of STAND, a national anti-genocide group. When she graduated college in 2009 after a mere two-and-a-half years,[45] she worked in northern India and the Middle East, then went back to the USA, where she worked in an AIDS clinic by day and a women's shelter by night. Finally, Kayla returned to the Middle East, heading for the border between Syria and Turkey to join a group called Support to Life that helped refugees fleeing the Syrian Civil War. When Mueller briefly returned home, she told a Kiwanis Club meeting that "Syrians are dying by the thousands, and they're fighting just to talk about the rights we have." But her sympathy for the Syrian refugees would be her undoing.

Mueller had a 32-year-old Syrian boyfriend, photographer Omar Alkhani. Omar had committed to driving a medical worker from Turkey to Syria's Aleppo province (also known as Halab).[46] The medical worker needed a ride to a Spanish Doctors Without Borders hospital—a dangerous trip through a hot zone in the Syrian Civil War. Mueller begged Alkhani to take her with him.[47] But after dropping off the medical worker in Syria, things went bad. Very bad. Kayla and Omar were ambushed by men carrying guns. The Qur'an says about unbelievers, "capture them and besiege them, and prepare for them each and every ambush."[48] Ambush was what snagged Kayla Mueller.

Omar, Kayla's photographer boyfriend,[49] tried to protect the Arizona native by saying that Mueller was his wife.[50] But when the gunmen quizzed Kayla, they promised that if she told the truth they would let her go (war is deception, says Muhammad—but more about that later). Kayla spilled the beans on her unmarried status. So the fighters decided that she was marriage material. Marriage jihadist style. The sort of marriage we call rape. The ISIS fighters interrogated Alkhani, Kayla's boyfriend, then, when they discovered that he was a Sunni Muslim, they let him go. Who ended up as Mueller's husband? Abu Bakr al-Baghdadi, the new Khalifah,[51] the new Caliph of the Islamic State. In Baghdadi's mind was probably Muhammad's example of "marrying" the wives of the chiefs of tribes, a move that followed in the footsteps of the great conquerors of history.[52] But first, the ISIS warriors pulled out Mueller's fingernails. Then they "converted" her to Islam.

Muna met Mueller in the woman's prison in Raqqa. "The first time I entered the room," says Muna, "I saw Kayla. I thought she was Yazidi, so I spoke in Kurdish to her. She told me, 'I don't understand,' so I spoke to her in Arabic. ... I told her I am a Yazidi girl from Sinjar and I was captured by Daesh (ISIS)." Adds Muna, "After that we stayed together and became like sisters."[53] Conditions for Muna and Kayla were not luxurious. "There was so little room (in the cell), and it was dark, with no power. It was summer and it was so hot." The menu was even less appealing. Says CNN, "bread and cheese in the morning, and rice or macaroni at night."[54] What's worse, it was "just a little bit, and we were starving."[55]

Then Mueller, Muna, and a third sex slave, a Yazidi named Susan, were taken together to a home in Raqqa's suburbs, the home of a very important man, Abu Sayyaf.[56] Abu Sayyaf, a Tunisian, was one of Abu Bakr al-Baghdadi's best friends. But he was more. He was Abu Bakr al-Baghdadi's deputy, the deputy in charge of the sale of the gas and oil that brought ISIS revenues of between one million[57] and three million dollars a day.[58] Yes, between one and three million dollars. Per day. Muna, Mueller, and three other Yazidi sex slaves were guarded by five fighters and kept hanging for two nights. One of these young girls was then "married" to Abu Sayyaf,[59] the owner of the house. Very convenient. Another was "married" to the man with the job of bringing new Yazidi girls to the Sayyaf household.[60] And at 10 p.m. on August 15, 2014, who showed up in Abu Sayyaf's home? Abu Bakr al-Baghdadi. The leader of ISIS. The caliph of a group committed to building a one-world empire, a global empire of Islam. But we're getting ahead of ourselves.

Sayyaf's home wasn't much of an improvement over the jail. Says Britain's *The Independent*, who interviewed a 14-year-old Yazidi sex slave, "according to those held captive, many Yazidi women passed through the house on their way to being given as 'presents' or sold to Isis fighters."[61] For what purpose? Rape. Why was one house Rape Central? One of Abu Sayyaf's wives was the organizer of the sex trade in ISIS. An extraordinarily complex sex trade. But more about that in a minute. Abu Bakr al-Baghdadi was a frequent visitor at the Abu Sayyaf household. So frequent that he had his own room.

And when al-Baghdadi first showed up after the arrival of Muna and Kayla Mueller, Mueller was summoned to a tête-à-tête with the Caliph in that room. Baghdadi's first move was apparently his usual ploy—showing the grisly video of the beheading of James Foley with every sawing of the blade into the throat of a living, pain-sensing man. Recalls Muna, "When Kayla came back to us, we asked her, 'Why are you crying?' And Kayla told us al-Baghdadi said: 'I am going to marry you by force and you are going to be my wife. If you refuse, I will kill you.'"[62]

There were many more visits from al-Baghdadi. Each time, Abu Sayyaf came to fetch Mueller and take her to al-Baghdadi's room in the house. Says another of the escaped sex slaves, "I saw him often, he came there often. And every time he came, he took Kayla away. She would always come back after."[63] But Kayla didn't come back calm and composed. In fact, Mueller often came back in tears.

Though Abu Bakr al-Baghdadi apparently told Kayla in September that he would take her as his wife "by force," he did not consummate the "marriage" until October. Then he prostrated himself on the floor, prayed, and "repeatedly raped Kayla in front of Muna," says the *Mail*, then prostrated himself on the floor and prayed once again.[64] Reported Muna of Kayla's reaction, "She was afraid and she didn't resist as he would beat her, she said." More than that, says Muna, "She said her friend James Foley had already been beheaded and she feared suffering the same fate." Continues Muna, "I saw him rape her three or four times and they told us that anybody who runs away, including Kayla, would be killed... Kayla did not know" that the man invading her body over and over again "was the Caliph, but she knew he was important." Over and over again when Kayla was summoned to Baghdadi's room, said Muna, "when Kayla returned in the morning she was crying and said she'd been raped."

Because she was his "wife," one account says that Baghdadi forced Mueller to wear a hijab, a garment that covers the head and chest. But, in fact, Mueller had been wearing a hijab voluntarily even before she was captured... to hide her foreign features.[65] Muna explains why Baghdadi made this voluntary bit of clothing obligatory: "Al-Baghdadi married her ... she was his wife. He did not allow his friend Abu Sayyaf to see her face. Always she had to wear the niqāb [face veil]."[66] And the Caliph personally gave Mueller Qur'an lessons.

If Mueller was his wife, why did Baghdadi not relocate her to his own home, where his three previous wives and his six children lived? Why did he keep her at the home of his deputy and best friend? Because Abu Bakr al-Baghdadi, the leader of the most merciless warriors on Earth, was afraid of his wives. Muna recalls that the lady of the Sayyaf household, "Umm Sayyaf [Abu Sayyaf's wife] told Kayla that Baghdadi's wives did not know he had been married to her." And Baghdadi was "terrified" that his other wives would find out about Kayla and cause trouble.[67]

What was sex with a rapist, a profoundly religious rapist, like? The two Yazidi former sex slaves who talked to the press were as discreet as possible and avoided the sexual details. But *The New York Times'* Rukmini Callimachi gives us a hint in her description of what another escaped Yazidi sex slave, a girl held for 11 months before she escaped, told her.[68] The girl was only 12 years old, with a waist so small, says Callimachi, that you could encircle it with your two hands. Her ISIS rapist began by explaining to his 12-year-old captive that the Qur'an says that raping young girls is a holy deed. He then tied her hands and put a gag in her mouth, got down on the floor, prayed, then, to use Callimachi's euphemism, got on top of her. Says the girl, "I kept telling him it hurts—please stop." His response? "He told me that according to Islam he is allowed to rape an unbeliever. He said that by raping me, he is drawing closer to God."[69] Another escapee, a 15-year-old Yazidi, recalls that her rapist said the same thing in slightly different words. Words that are revealing. "He said that raping me is his prayer to God. I said to him, 'What you're doing to me is wrong, and it will not bring you closer to God.'[70] And he said, 'No, it's allowed. It's halal.'"[71] Another 15-year-old who became the possession of an ISIS fighter in his twenties said, "He kept telling me this is Ibadah."[72] Meaning that having sex with an unwilling non-Muslim is a form of worship.

Explains *The New York Times'* Callimachi, the leadership of ISIS elevates and celebrates "each sexual assault as spiritually beneficial, even virtuous."[73]

In a letter Kayla Mueller wrote and gave to French captives that ISIS released from captivity, the Arizona native said she had "formed a bond of love and support," but not with Baghdadi, with her fellow sexual captives. Trying to reassure her parents, she wrote, "I am not breaking down and I will not give in no matter how long it takes." She apparently didn't confess that to save her life, she'd converted to Islam. And her parents are very defensive on the issue. Perhaps Mueller was using one of Muhammad's favorite weapons of war—deception.

The forced sex between al-Baghdadi and Kayla Mueller continued. On one occasion, "Kayla told me specifically ... 'Abu Bakr al-Baghdadi raped me.' (She said he raped her) four times."[74] But there was more in store for Muna.

"Al-Baghdadi told us [sex slaves], 'I did this to Kayla. And what I did to Kayla, I will do to you. On Friday. On Friday it will be your time.'"

Says Muna about Mueller's brutal sexual experiences at Baghdadi's hands, "When I heard what Kayla told me, I wanted to escape. I told Kayla to escape with me, but Kayla refused. She told me about the American journalist who was beheaded, and she said, 'If I escape, they will behead me.'"[75]

"The first time I told her I would escape, she said, 'Don't run away. If they catch you, they will surely kill you.' But I told her, 'No. I saw what Abu Bakr al-Baghdadi did to you. I saw how you suffered. I saw how much pain you were in. I will escape whatever way I can.'"[76]

On October 8, 2014, Muna and her friend and fellow sex slave Susan sprung what would be Muna's second escape.[77] Said Muna, "One night me and Susan told Kayla we were planning to run away but she said the last time you guys tried to escape you were captured and beaten. This time they will kill you." Nonetheless, "'Susan and I insisted on running away and told Kayla to come with us. But she said her friend [James Foley] had already been beheaded and she feared suffering the same fate." "There was one window in our room," Muna recalls. "It was a little broken. We kept pushing it and pushing it until there was a small space."[78] Then Muna and Susan got out through that space, no matter how small. And they ran. "We didn't know where we were going. We just prayed to God. Prayed for God to help us, to end our suffering. We didn't know where to go, we had no plan … we just ran in any direction."[79] When ISIS fighters shot at them in the dark, they crawled. The pair continued on foot for three hours, putting as much distance as they could between themselves and their "owner." "We saw all the houses had no electricity, there was no power except for one house," she remembers. "I told (my friend), 'We are going to go to that house and ask for help. … ISIS always turns off the electricity because of air strikes, (so) we should choose that house.'"[80] Apparently the people of the house were kind to these two runaways. Muna was able to contact Kurdish forces, who got her out of ISIS territory and brought her together with a brother whom ISIS had not killed, despite al-Baghdadi's claims to the contrary. Muna informed the *Mail* that her next step would be to join the flood of Muslim refugees to Europe—a flood of a million people in 2015. She hoped to make it to Germany.

Meanwhile, the American, Kayla Mueller, spent one-and-a-half years in captivity. Then ISIS claims Mueller was killed along with Abu Sayyaf in a Jordanian airstrike on February 10, 2015.[81] But Muna says, "I don't believe she was killed in an airstrike."[82] The Pentagon asserts that Mueller was killed by ISIS, and that American special forces attacked the Abu Sayyaf home on May 16, 2015[83] after Mueller was dead. There the Americans captured computers,[84] USB sticks,[85] papers and one of Sayyaf's wives, the wife who the *Christian Science Monitor* reports "had organized the sex trade during Mueller's captivity." That wife, Umm Sayyaf, explained a great deal when she was interrogated by American Special Forces,[86] including the concept that Abu Bakr al-Baghdadi "owned" Kayla Mueller. Then Umm Sayyaf was turned over to the Iraqi Kurds to be tried.

Concludes Muna about Mueller, "she was such a close friend to me—more than a sister. I loved Kayla."

*   *   *

What sort of sexual operation was Abu Sayyaf's wife Umm Sayyaf running? A very big one. One based on implementing what the *New York Times* calls "a Theology of Rape."

Says the *New York Times*' Rukmini Callimachi, a Romanian-American journalist, "The Islamic State has developed a detailed bureaucracy of sex slavery, including sales contracts notarized by the ISIS-run Islamic courts."[87] Writes Ms. Callimachi, "A growing body of internal policy memos and theological discussions has established guidelines for slavery, including a lengthy how-to manual issued by the Islamic State Research and Fatwa Department." When they are captured, the women are separated from their sons, their husbands, and their fathers. The men are transported to a distant field, herded like sheep to a predetermined location, told to lie down, then are finished off with a spray of machine gun bullets. The women are gathered in warehouses, a "network" of holding pens, often located in public buildings. For example, 1,300 Yazidi girls were housed in the huge banquet room of Mosul's Galaxy Wedding Hall, a luxury location with marble floors.[88] Others were housed at Mosul's Directory of Youth building or at one of the palaces built for Iraq's longtime dictator Saddam Hussein. Some of these warehouses included viewing rooms, where the sex-slaves-to-be could be displayed for potential buyers. But first, the women were inventoried. At the Galaxy Wedding Hall, for example, three Islamic State fighters showed up and demanded that the women stand up one at a time, that each one "state her first, middle and last name, her age, her hometown, whether she was married, and if she had children."[89] The women could be kept in places like the Galaxy, shelved like a manufacturer's inventory, for months. When it came time to transport them, there were waiting lines of buses in the parking lot, a fleet of buses with curtained windows, curtains to close the girls off and to prevent men on the sidewalks or in passing cars from seeing their tempting faces. The buses were traveling versions of the harems of bygone eras of Islamic imperialism. If the girls refused to leave when the buses arrived, they were dragged out by their hair. Then men haggled over them. The youngest and prettiest were sold first. The older women were often forced to wait for months before they were bought. Helping the trade along were wholesalers, men who bought women in batches, sat each one down on a couch with a sign announcing that she was slave girl number one, slave girl number two, etc. then took photographs and used the photos to tempt buyers.[90]

Where did these strange practices come from? Was American president Barack Obama right when he said this was a perversion of Islam?[91] Or are the Qur'anic scholars of ISIS right? Is raping unbelievers a holy act?

What's the gold standard of holiness? The life of Muhammad. Does Muhammad's life justify driving female children, teenagers, and women "like sheep by the edge of the sword"?[92] Surely not. Or does it?

You be the judge.

The Tree That's Watered With Blood

"Islam is a tree that feeds on blood and grows
on severed limbs."[93]
—A young Egyptian in 1987 to the makers
of Grenada TV's *The Sword of Islam*

IN THE LATE FALL AND EARLY WINTER of 2015, ISIS—the Islamic State of Iraq and Syria—was playing a hot hand. American president Barack Obama was trying to convince the American public that his steady campaign of bombing and aerial drone assassinations was "degrading" ISIS, slowly but surely depriving ISIS of leadership and territory. For example, the President went to the Pentagon on December 13, 2015, met with his war cabinet for two hours, then gave an eight-minute speech in which he declared that ISIS "has lost about 40 percent of the populated areas it once controlled in Iraq and it will lose more. ...The Iraqi forces are now fighting their way deeper into Ramadi, they are working to encircle Fallujah and cut off ISIL's supply routes into Mosul."[94] Sounds like progress, right?

But ISIS wanted to make a point. That any attack upon it will be avenged. And, more important, that it has a long-term goal: global conquest. That God has guaranteed that this conquest will someday be achieved. And that to do its conquering, ISIS is required by Allah, yes, by God himself, to rouse terror in the hearts of unbelievers far and wide, particularly in the West. Or, to put it in the words of ISIS' online magazine *Dābiq*, God himself has set ISIS the task of "terrorizing, massacring, and humiliating the enemies of Allah."[95] To what end? To make sure that the Islamic State's one-world government, its Caliphate, its Khilafah, will "continue to expand further until its shade covers the entire earth, all the lands where the day and night reach."[96] Why? Because "the earth belongs to Allah"[97] and "Allah has promised those who have believed among you and done righteous deeds that He will surely grant them succession to authority upon the Earth."[98] Authority: that means dominance, control, rule...absolute rule. The kind of rule that appeared in Abu Bakr al-Baghdadi's use of sex slaves.

ISIS made these points with blood. In a five-week period, from October 31, 2015, to December 2, 2015, ISIS, its followers, and its "waliyats," its foreign provinces, killed over 710 people—Russians, Frenchmen, Californians, Nigerians, and one Japanese.[99]

On October 31, 2015, a Russian passenger plane, Metrojet Flight 9268, was carrying 224 Russian, Ukrainian, and Belorussian vacationers—men, women and children—from the Egyptian resort city of Sharm el Sheikh to St. Petersburg, Russia. Over the desert of Sinai, the Airbus A321-231 exploded, killing everyone on board.[100] Brags ISIS, this was revenge for Russia's September 2015 decision to carry out air strikes on ISIS' turf in Syria. Or, as ISIS' online magazine *Dābiq* puts it:

> And so after having discovered a way to compromise the security at the Sharm el-Sheikh International Airport and resolving to bring down a plane belonging to a nation in the American-led Western coalition against the Islamic State, the target was changed to a Russian plane. A bomb was smuggled onto the airplane, leading to the deaths of 219 Russians and 5 other crusaders only a month after Russia's thoughtless decision.

To hammer home just how far it could reach into your life and mine, *Dābiq* showed a picture of the bomb that had brought the plane down. It was in a harmless-looking can of Schweppes Gold, a carbonated malt beverage with pineapple flavoring made in Egypt.[101]

Thirteen days after the downing of the Russian jet, on November 13, 2015, ISIS says it pulled off an "invasion." An invasion of "the capital of prostitution and obscenity, the carrier of the banner of the Cross in Europe."[102] To be more specific, ISIS achieved what it called "the Blessed Paris Invasion on the French Crusaders."[103] ISIS operatives attacked six Parisian locations—the Bataclan concert hall "where," says ISIS, "hundreds of apostates had gathered in a profligate prostitution party."[104] Plus four restaurants, and France's national soccer stadium, or, as ISIS puts it, "the Stade de France during the match between the Crusader German and French teams, where the fool of France, François Hollande [France's prime minister], was present." Each location was thronged with innocent civilians. The result? ISIS killed 130 people and injured 368. In Paris, the City of Light.

Who were the attackers? First of all, there were only eight of them. Eight men accomplishing what it took others entire army battalions to achieve. Or, as ISIS puts it, "eight brothers wrapped in explosive belts and armed with machine rifles."[105] Explains ISIS in *Dābiq*, these were "youths who divorced the world" who "went to their enemy seeking to be killed in the cause of

Allah"[106] The goal of these "dear knights of Muhammad the Conqueror?"[107] Terror, massacre, and humiliation,[108] to "cast in the hearts of the Crusaders horror in the middle of their land,"[109] and "to put the nose of His [Allah's] enemies in the ground."[110]

Then, 19 days later, on December 2, 2015, came an unexpected bonus to ISIS' cause. A six-foot-tall, 28-year-old Muslim health inspector born in Chicago, Illinois,[111] and his wife, a 29-year-old born in Pakistan to a wealthy, politically influential, land-owning family,[112] left their six-month-old baby with the husband's mother[113] and went to a Christmas party at the Inland Regional Center in San Bernardino, California, a party thrown by the husband's employer, the San Bernardino County Public Health Department.[114] But this husband and wife were not bearing gifts. They were carrying two combat assault rifles, two handguns,[115] and 1,600 rounds of ammunition.[116] When they left the party, 14 people were dead and 21 were injured.[117] During the shooting, yes, during the shooting, the wife, Tashfeen Malik, took time out to leave a pledge of allegiance to ISIS' leader, its Caliph, Abu Bakr al-Baghdadi,[118] on Facebook. The pledge read: "We pledge allegiance to Khalifa bu bkr al bhaghdadi al quraishi."

But that was just the tip of the iceberg—these were only the attacks that the Western media covered. 7,712 miles away from San Bernardino, in Nigeria, another army of jihadists had also declared its allegiance to Abu Bakr al-Baghdadi and ISIS. This jihadist army's name was Boko Haram. Which roughly translated means "Western education is cursed, poisonous, and forbidden." In less than three months—from September 27, 2015, to December 16, 2015—Boko Haram had carried out eight attacks, killing 345. In fact, *The New York Times*,[119] the *Atlantic*,[120] London's *Guardian*,[121] and a slew of other Western media outlets had declared Boko Haram "The World's Deadliest Terrorist Group." These publications were reporting on the data in the *Terrorism Index 2015*, a report from The Institute for Economics and Peace.[122] ISIS' main operation, the new report declared, had only killed 6,073 people in 2014. But Boko Haram, the "Islamic State's West Africa province (ISWAP),"[123] had killed a whopping 6,644. That's 38 percent more than all the Americans who died in our ten-year-long Iraq War.[124]

And even that was not the end of it. *Dābiq*'s issue number 12, published on November 18, 2015, bragged about ten more military attacks it had carried out in a mere two months, attacks in lands stretching the 5,582 miles from Africa to India and Bangladesh. Attacks whose targets were Italian, Japanese, Lebanese, Iraqis, and Russians. What's more, *Dābiq* asserted that "These operations are merely a selection of the numerous operations that the Islamic State has conducted on various fronts across many regions over the course of the last two months."[125]

Dābiq also mentioned in an off-hand way that if it played its cards right, it might not have to "blow up any dirty bombs in Manhattan."[126] It might tempt the West into an apocalyptic showdown in the Iraqi town of Dābiq, a final battle that would bring the end of time and the day of judgement.

Explained *Dābiq*, "the tree of this Ummah," the tree of the people of Islam, "is not watered except by the blood of its martyrs."[127] And by the "filthy blood"[128] of those who do not believe in Allah and His one true prophet, Muhammad.

Barack Obama declared that he had degraded ISIS. ISIS disagreed. In *Dābiq*, it declared that "The Islamic State not only remained in Iraq, it had spread to the Arabian Peninsula, Sham [Syria], North and West Africa, Khurasan [Afghanistan and Turkmenistan], al-Qawqaz [the Caucasus— Georgia, Armenia, and Azerbaijan], and elsewhere."[129] And *Dābiq* added, "May Allah keep the Islamic State remaining and expanding."[130]

Where did ISIS and Boko Haram get the idea that the path to world domination has been mapped out by God? And where did they get the notion that to conquer the globe, God demands "terrorizing, massacring, and humiliating"?

The answer is in the life of Muhammad.

Why I Am Writing This Book...

And Why I Am Writing It To You

BEFORE WE GET TO THE REAL DEAL, to Muhammad, the One True Prophet of God, a word of full disclosure. I am heavily biased when it comes to militant Islam. Militant Islam says that I should be killed. Why? I believe in tolerance, pluralism, and freedom of speech. Not just mild freedom of speech, but extreme freedom of speech—the right to say the outrageous, the rebellious, and the heretical. To militant Islam these "fake concepts"[131] of "freedom,"[132] "democracy,"[133] and "human rights"[134] are a slap in the face of God. They are Satanic lies. But there's more. I am an atheist, a secular scientific thinker, and... even worse...a Jew. Muhammad did not take kindly to Jews. Said Muhammad, "Whoever of the Jews falls into your hands, kill him."[135] And, "The Hour will not be established until you fight with the Jews, and the stone behind which a Jew will be hiding will say, 'O Muslim! There is a Jew hiding behind me, so kill him.'"[136]

My introduction to militant Islam came in 1962. My parents and grandparents were Zionists—people who wished ardently for the right of Jews to return to a homeland that appears in a flood of Hebrew prayers, the Promised Land, the Hebrew territory from which Jews were expelled over and over again and which the Jews stubbornly rebelled to retake in 66 A.D., 133 A.D., 351 A.D., 438 A.D., and 614 A.D.[137] Those Jews, my ancestors, settled in Israel in 1200 B.C., then battled the biggest imperialists of one historic era after another to stay there: the Assyrians in 701 B.C.,[138] the Babylonians in 586 B.C.,[139] and the Romans in 66 A.D.[140] and 135 A.D.[141] In 70 A.D. the Romans destroyed the Jewish temple in Jerusalem, confiscated lands from Jewish owners, imposed a harsh new punitive tax,[142] and forced many of the city's Jews to flee. In 132 A.D., after a three-year armed revolt, Rome had had it. It expelled the Jews from Judea, sent many of them to another traditionally Jewish territory, the Galilee, replaced them with non-Jews, and exported masses of Jews as slaves.[143] The Jewish remnants scattered across the face of the Mediterranean world, from Libya[144] to Spain[145] and France.[146] Yet Jews insistently trickled back into what they considered their native land again, and by 636 A.D.,[147] Arab historians say these Hebrew returnees and the Jews still on the land of Judea had built 41 cities[148] in what is today called Palestine and Israel. Then in 637 A.D. came an imperialist force that made the Romans look like pipsqueaks, a violent, militaristic, colonialist empire on its way to becoming the largest in the history of the planet—one of the few imperial powers still around in today's world and still in a mood for conquest: the empire of Islam. According to the ninth-century Muslim historian Abu Al-Abbas Al-Baladhuri,[149] the armies of Islam wiped those 41 Jewish cities off the face of the map. For the next 1,312 years,[150] Jews would end their springtime holiday Passover dinner with the phrase "Next year in Jerusalem."

Zionists like my grandparents and parents were proud of the fact that Jews had continued to live in Israel in every century[151]—often by the hundreds of thousands.[152] And that in the 19th and 20th century, Jewish returnees had drained the malarial swamps, had run irrigation lines to the deserts, and had made this slice of miserable Turkish land one-sixth the size of New York State[153] into a garden, a rich farmland. To my grandparents and parents, Zionism meant establishing a Jewish state and teaching our Arab brethren how to turn the vast and barren two billion acres[154] under Arab control into a land with trees, groves, and valleys abundant in harvests.

In 1962, when I was 19 years old, my father offered to send me for a year to Israel, a country a mere 14 years old. Israel had kibbutzim—one of the most radical forms of social experiment on the planet. These were socialist agricultural communities in which the land and goods were held in common by roughly 350 adults. The children were raised together by loving child-care experts, the meals were made in a communal kitchen and eaten in a communal dining hall, and the laundry was done by a communal laundry staff. As a result, when they finished their day of farming, parents could romp with their kids for hours, free from the worry of nagging their children to clean up their bedrooms, and free from the need to shop and cook a meal.

My dad's offer sounded good. I wanted to see if 19th- and 20th-century thinkers were right…if by changing the structure of society you could change human nature and wipe away greed, gripes, and violence. The kibbutz was a laboratory of social change. So I said yes.

To prep myself, I hitchhiked from my hometown, Buffalo, New York, down to Pennsylvania's Swarthmore College, where I had friends, and spent a month in the library studying peoples of the Middle East like the Natufians of 11,000 years ago, and the Nabataeans, a little-known culture who invented a system of terraced irrigation[155] that allowed them to successfully farm the deserts of southern Israel and the surrounding lands from 312 B.C. to 105 A.D.[156]

Then one day, I had a shock. In the back of a library file of miscellaneous materials on the Middle East, I found several English-language pamphlets printed by the Arab League, a coalition of 12 leading Arab governments.[157] The pamphlets tried to reach people like you and me with an extremely urgent clarification of historical errors. First off, the Holocaust, the mass murder of six million Jews by Germany's Nazis, was a charade, a hoax. It never happened. Second, World War II had not been a confrontation started by the Germans in an effort to take over the world on behalf of a blond and blue-eyed master race. It had been started by Jews out to win the sympathy of the world and to establish the state of Israel. Third, Adolph Hitler had not been a Jew-hater. To the contrary. He'd been a Jewish puppet, a Jewish creation set in motion, once again, to achieve the establishment of a so-called Jewish homeland.

The villains behind these radical misunderstandings of history were those clever liars, those people out to dominate the world, those folks the Qur'an said that Allah had turned into "apes and swine"[158]—pigs and monkeys—the Jews...my family and me.

One of my aunts had managed to survive the Holocaust's concentration camps. Another relative, one of my cousins, had lost her parents, her brothers, and her sisters, and had been saved by a Catholic farm family in Poland. The rest of my family in Europe, the Shebshelovitzes of Riga, Latvia, and the Wechelefskys of Belarus, had disappeared utterly. I was under the impression that the Holocaust had been real. Very real. But the Arab League wanted me—and you—to believe otherwise.

This was one of my first introductions to the fact that another culture can have a radically different system of thought, a radically different way of seeing the world. It was also my introduction to Islamic anti-Semitism.

Where did this hatred of Jews come from? There are fewer Jews on the planet than the inhabitants of just one Muslim city, Cairo.[159] And there are 23 Islamic cities with populations of over three million.[160] Or, to put it differently, there are 123 Muslims for every Jew on this Earth. Did the officials of the Arab League seriously imagine that a tribe so absurdly small could manipulate the mind of the German volk, the mass mind of the German people, and could plan and promote one of the biggest wars in history? If I was to understand just how different the world looked through the lens of another culture, I might as well study a culture that made hatred of me a central preoccupation.

For the next four decades I studied the instinctual underpinnings of war, creativity, and genocide. For the next four decades I studied mass behavior, from the mass behavior of quarks, nucleons, and galaxies, to the mass behavior of reptiles, chimps, rats, birds, fish, bacteria, and human beings. And for the next four decades I used the culture of Islam as a test case, a supreme living specimen in which to watch the instinctual forces of history at work. But living specimens can be dangerous.

Why an Ayatollah Wants to Rule the World

IN 1979, THE AYATOLLAH RUHOLLAH KHOMEINI toppled the Shah of Iran and started a disturbing new form of government. The Ayatollah made blunt statements about a new genocide in the making, an all-out war of true Muslims to "obliterate"[161] those of us who refuse to believe. Meanwhile, there were numerous indications that Islam would soon have nuclear weapons. And the words of the Qur'an called out over and over again that "slaughter is better than tumult and oppression"[162]—slaughter is better than unbelief. What's more, the weapon God most often used in the Qur'an to punish those who disdained His message was fire. Not just any fire. But "the fire whose fuel is Men and Stones."[163] This phrase seemed to eerily hint that God was telling his followers to use the atomic bomb.

The Western press paid no attention to the Ayatollah's blizzard of pronouncements that "Muslims have no alternative… to an armed holy war against profane governments. …Holy war means the conquest of all non-Muslim territories."[164] They paid no attention to the fact that the Ayatollah's words are still[165] considered gospel in 2017, when Iran has built a uranium enrichment industry that appears able to produce the key materials for nuclear weapons. And they paid little attention to the fact that when Iran signed an agreement that we were told limited its nuclear weapons capability—the JCPOA, the Joint Comprehensive Plan of Action[166]—a nuclear weapons limitation is not what Iran felt the agreement guaranteed. Iran believed that the agreement granted its nuclear program an official right to exist from the United Nations.[167]

In 1989, I entered four months of negotiations with George Crile, a producer at *60 Minutes*. The goal? To warn America that while it slumbered in complacency, a new enemy was plotting its destruction. That new enemy was militant Islam. Jihadist Islam. In the end, I put together a 40-page, single-spaced document for Crile with quotes from the Ayatollah, from activists in Lebanon's Hezbollah, and from a wide variety of other Muslim sources indicating that the fall of Western civilization was militant Islam's goal and that any means—even nuclear means—were permissible. I tried to get a very alien way of thinking across to Crile. A way of thinking that makes total sense once you know its premises. A way of thinking that tells idealists— would-be savers of the human race—that their only way to save you, me, and George Crile may be mass murder.

Finally, Crile took me to dinner with his wife (who had been named the editor of *Premiere*, the film magazine, earlier that day) and his assistant. The dossier I'd put together of militant Islamic statements and their meaning had scared his assistant witless. But Crile was charming...and aloof. Would he cover the threat of militant Islam? He wouldn't say. The next day he flew to Saudi Arabia. When he returned, he gave his answer. No. No reason, just no.

Then Crile wrote a book—*Charlie Wilson's War*. About what? About militant Islam. But about militant Islam as a creation of the CIA! Crile was accurate in his portrayal of the way that the U.S. had funded, armed, and trained what would eventually become al Qaeda. But Crile was wrong in his sense of history. He made the We-Did-It mistake—the assumption that only Westerners are sufficiently powerful to work the levers of history. The racist assumption that all non-Westerners are pygmies and victims. He implied that modern Islamic civilization is so weak and American civilization so all-powerful that a nearly 1,400-year-old movement—militant Islam—is a recent genie conjured from a bottle by American intelligence agents.

That view can be fatal.

Time to Get Serious—The Punch of 9/11

[We] have struck them blows that will not quickly be forgotten, and they have taught them lessons which are still seared on their skin, and they are still convulsing from the pains of these lessons—lessons which lowered their flags to half-mast and shook their feet and confused their thoughts until fright wormed its way into their joints, and the worm of despair bored into their bones. It could not be otherwise, for our heroes massacred them, to the point where they saw the cowardice of the American soldier. "O young Islamic man in Iraq and in all Muslim countries, you who are perplexed and seeking life, you who yearn to come to the aid of the religion of Allah, you who offer your life to your Lord, here is guidance to the right path, here is wisdom and probity, here is the ecstasy of self-sacrifice and the pleasure of Jihad."[168]

—Abu Musab al-Zarqawi

FOUR YEARS LATER, IN 1993, Muslim militants made their first attempt to topple the World Trade Center. They detonated a Ryder rental truck packed with 1,500 pounds of explosives in the Trade Center's basement parking lot, a bomb that killed six people, injured a thousand, penetrated five underground floors, but did not topple the Twin Towers.[169] In 2001, the militants were more successful. Islamic fighters commandeered four passenger jets, flew two of them into the World Trade Center's boxy skyscrapers, flew another into the Pentagon, and were prevented by the passengers of the fourth plane from destroying yet another Washington target. I stood on my roof in Park Slope, Brooklyn, and watched as the Twin Towers of the World Trade Center in lower Manhattan burned and collapsed.

It was agonizing. For 12 years I'd been trying to warn of attacks of this kind. So had others. One of my books, *The Lucifer Principle: A Scientific Expedition Into the Forces of History*, used Islam as one example of how ideas, social groups, biological self-destruct mechanisms, and battles for status shape your fate and mine. Two Amazon.com reviewers called *The Lucifer*

Principle the book that had predicted 9/11. A Muslim Amazon.com reviewer said the book was his new source of truth, his new "Bible."[170]

Another book I'd written and published before 9/11, *Global Brain: The Evolution of Mass Mind From the Big Bang to the 21st Century*, had focused on the way subcultures battle to take over the mass mind of a society. One chapter had zeroed in on a man only a handful of others had paid attention to, Osama bin Laden. A Pakistani Muslim reader called *Global Brain* the only book that tells it like it is about militant Islam. Yet, like other watchmen at the gates, I'd utterly failed to get my warnings across.

I did not want to fail again. So I set aside my work in the science of mass behavior and focused full-time on the puzzles of militant Islam.

*   *   *

Militant Islamic history is extremely hard to follow. The 4,000 pages I'd compiled on the topic were jumbled like jigsaw puzzle pieces. They refused to tell a coherent story. So when I was asked to give a speech I called "Islam's War to Save the West" at the New York Military Affairs Symposium in 2004, I spent six months compiling a 159-page timeline of militant Islam from its beginning in the seventh century to the present, a timeline complete with a world map showing the reach of militant Islam's colonialism and imperialism, a colonialism invisible to us because of its astonishing success as an indigenous culture-eraser and new-culture-shaper.

The armies and merchants of Islam, the map revealed, had achieved something you and I are never told about. These Muslims had pieced together the biggest empire in world history—11 times the size of the conquests of Alexander the Great, five times the size of the Roman Empire, and seven times the size of the United States. The timeline finally gave the story of this extraordinary colonialist crusade, pinpointing 2,156 key battles in the 1,380-year-long Islamic fight for conquest.

But I was stymied by yet another puzzle.

The Osama Riddle

I'D COMPLETED A COMPILATION of every public statement ever made by Osama bin Laden, intending to publish it in book form, then realized that to the average Western reader Osama's words were gibberish. Bin Laden spoke brilliantly on behalf of his militant beliefs. But he referred over and over again to a historical weave of names, places, and events I could not track down. For example, he referred to places with obscure names, names that in some cases didn't even appear in any English-language encyclopedia—Assam, Fatani and Ogadin.[171] He referred to "knights of Muhammad the conqueror"[172] and the causes they fought for using names of ancient heroes and events that weren't traceable on Google and didn't show up in Western or modern Muslim histories of the Middle East. He referred to a past that gave a powerful but mysterious foundation to his militant Islamic thought. What was this history? Why couldn't I find it? Why was it not in the books I dug up in Islamic bookstores or in English-language Islamic websites? Why was it not in the Western histories of Islam? Why wasn't it part of your basic education and mine?

My computer file of research materials on Islam kept growing. And I was tapped more than 20 times to go on national radio as an expert commentator on Islam's nuclear capabilities, on the Iraq War of 2003, on the jihadist bombings in London and Madrid in 2004 and 2005, on the Muslim riots in France in 2005, on America's showdown with Iran in 2006, on the hanging of Saddam Hussein in 2006, on the Arab Spring of 2010 and 2011, on Iran's messianic Islamic beliefs and on a string of other events in which militant Islam fought—or defended itself from—the West. But I didn't have the answers to a trio of basic questions—what's the organizing key to the history of militant Islam? What's the story of its foundation and rise? And why has Islam outdone every other form of colonialism and imperialism on the planet?

For four years, I hunted for the key that would unlock Osama's use of historical allusions. Then I finally found it. The key was hidden in plain sight. And it unlocked everything from the mystery of militant Islam's use of sex to its picture of a New World Order for which the pious have struggled for more than a thousand years and for which they must continue to battle this year and next. This hidden key also hinted at what militant Islam might do in the coming months, and how those efforts, if they succeed, will utterly change your life and mine. I'd discovered the key to The Muhammad Code—the story of the life of Muhammad.

More specifically, I'd discovered the key to understanding the mind of Osama bin Laden, Abu Bakr al-Baghdadi, and of militant Muslims from Iran to Indonesia and from Trinidad to Dearborn, Michigan. That key lay in something I'd avoided studying for nearly 40 years because I did not want my biases to get in the way of clear thinking. The key was in Muhammad's extremely clever use of Jews.

But before we get to Muhammad's story—and the vital role the Jews played in his life—let's take a minute out to examine the powers that Muhammad harnessed in remarkable ways. The forces of history.

The Krazy Glue of the Crowd—The Founder Effect

"The history of what man has accomplished in this world, is at bottom the history of the great men who have worked here."
　　　— Carlyle[173]

"Great men hallow a whole people and lift up all who live in their time."
　　　— Sidney Smith[174]

"Man is not the creature of circumstances. Circumstances are the creatures of men."
　　　— Benjamin Disraeli

"National historical memory—or amnesia—can have concrete political consequences. ...As long as [the] young...have positive feelings toward a murderous dictator who institutionalized terror throughout their country, they are unlikely to mobilize behind calls for greater justice, human rights, or transparency—factors critical to... transformation into a modern democratic society."
　　　— Sarah E. Mendelson and Theodore P. Gerber on 21st-century Russian youths' idealization of Josef Stalin[175]

RUTH BENEDICT, ONE OF THE FOUNDING mothers of anthropology, says that every culture has a personality. Every culture suppresses some emotions and favors others.[176] In her classic book *Patterns of Culture* she shows how the Dobu of Southeastern New Guinea in the early 20th century did everything in their power to make their children—and their adults—aggressive and violent. To the Dobu, says Benedict, "All existence is cut-throat competition, and every advantage is gained at the expense of a defeated rival."[177] To make matters worse, the Dobu idealize those who make sure that "this competition... is secret and treacherous."[178] When a Dobu has a problem, he handles his frustration by picking out a victim and "projecting his misery upon him." He soothes his woes by dishing out punishment.

To the Zunis in the Colorado region of New Mexico, on the other hand, Benedict says the ideal human is "incorrigibly mild... [free] from any forms of social exploitation or of social sadism."[179] As Benedict and her friend, lover,[180] and fellow anthropologist Margaret Mead illustrated with many another example, some cultures encourage rage and some encourage sensitivity.[181] Some encourage the brutal and some encourage the gentle.

How likely is it that these differences in culture come from the personality of a demanding or a relaxed founder? Can one tribe's sin be another's pleasure because each tribe carries the marks of a different founder's obsessions? Can some founders be better than others at remaking a people totally... remaking their chosen tribe so powerfully that the stamp of the founder remains alive long after the founder has gone to his grave? If a founder wants to rule his people for thousands of years after his death, how would he go about it? And if some founders are more effective than others, how does Muhammad rank in the competition to outdo the forces of death and change?

Ruth Benedict's work in her *Patterns of Culture*[182] hints that indeed a culture can be a reflection of its founder's personality.[183] If the founder is a frowning, angry man, the culture he establishes may impose frowns and fury for centuries to come. If the founder is a man of smiles and delight, the culture he molds is more likely to encourage youngsters and adults to smile and enjoy life. Plato is even more explicit than Benedict. He doesn't just hint that the character of a society is determined by the personality of the man who leads it. Plato is outright convinced that the personality of the leader stamps itself on the society he leads. An ignorant leader can make a good people evil, he says. And a wise, intelligent leader can make an ordinary group of followers good.[184]

Plato and Benedict would have been pleased to know that studies of monkeys have borne them out. The impact of a leader on the personality of a group seems built into our instinctual base, our animal roots. In troops of Japanese macaques, an innovative leader can spread new practices through the group in hours. But a conservative monkey leader, a dictatorial defender of the traditions he's inherited or created, can force his group to reject opportunities that glitter with potential. In the Minoo Valley near Osaka, Japan, for example, a dominant male monkey, a macaque, came up with a radical innovation: eating wheat. His new breakthrough spread rapidly to the dominant adult females in his entourage—the influential lady aristocrats who hung out in his hallowed presence. From there it moved to the infants who played around those dominant females' feet. Wheat-eating then spread to the lower-class playmates of the privileged kids and to the mothers of those they played with. Within four hours, wheat-eating had permeated the entire troop.[185] Innovations spreading from the bottom up, on the other hand, could take years to get to the top...if they ever got anywhere at all.[186] All this is in a group with an open-minded leader.

But what happens in macaque troops if the leader snarls at new practices? In Takagoyama, Japan, experimenters handed persimmons—high-energy treats—to lower-class males and to youngsters who had been shoved out to the boundaries of the troop. These macaques knew how good persimmons were. They stole them whenever possible from local farming gardens. But the leader punished every group member who dared accept this lush food directly from the hands of the experimenters. And he meted out his punishment violently. His severity was highly effective. In a time so short that the researchers called it "sudden," none of the monkeys would touch a persimmon offered by a human being.[187]

In Takasakiyama, Japan, another macaque leader, Jupiter, laid down a cultural pattern that encouraged bullying, beating, and humiliating females. But when Jupiter grew old and died, the new leader—Titan—abolished this extreme emphasis on anti-female aggression. He also shifted the times, destinations, and other ways of wandering—the "pattern of nomadism"—of the group and even changed the time of day the troop ate.[188]

The impact of a macaque leader on the culture of his troop was so obvious in these studies that the Japanese researchers were forced to use a word that was considered taboo among animal researchers back in the 1950s and 1960s, when these meticulous observations were made. Leadership, the Japanese experimenters said, made a huge difference. And one factor in the leader's "influence," wrote the researchers, was the top monkey's "so-called 'personality.'"[189]

When the stamp a leader puts on a group outlasts him, especially when it outlasts him for generations, it takes on a form that goes far beyond what Japan's macaque-investigators observed. It shifts into a pattern that biology demigod Ernst Mayer put on the scientific map, a pattern that appears at numerous levels in the world of living things. In genetics and population biology, Mayr calls it "the founder effect."[190] A group of founders goes off to start its own group and stamps its peculiar genetic limitations and gifts—its unique genetic character—on the entire population it founds.[191]

In the world of human culture, the founder effect would theoretically mean that the personality of a founding father can be as central to the emotional twists he passes on as are his pronouncements, his ideas. But does the founder effect really apply to human societies? How often is the personality of a culture determined by the personality of its founder? Experts in organizational culture like MIT's Edgar H. Schein and like the 170 scholars who participated in the ten-year-long GLOBE study of leadership in 62 worldwide cultures say that the answer is very often. Very often indeed.[192]

One of those who proves their point is Shaka Zulu. In 1781,[193] there were a mere 1,500 Zulus,[194] and they weren't particularly warlike. Far from it. Their occasional battles were lackluster affairs.[195] They and their enemies stood on either side of a barrier like a stream, insulted each other, and occasionally tossed a spear until, finally, someone was injured. Then the tribe that inflicted the wound declared itself victorious,[196] and everyone went home. When pitted against a dead serious militant enemy, the Zulus lost. Every time!

One man totally transformed the character and spirit of this people. His name was Shaka. Shaka was a bitter and brutal youngster whose primary pleasure in life came from organizing men to kill. Shaka's mother, a disdainful, argumentative daughter of a Zulu chief, had an illicit affair with the head of a nearby clan—the eLangeni—and became pregnant. Her own people, the Zulu, despised her for this outrage. So her lover installed her in his own village, but that didn't stop the scandal. Not one whit. Everyone in the eLangeni settlement turned up their noses at her.

When her belly swelled with her unborn child, the villagers joked that she was growing large because she had an intestinal beetle—a shaka. Her son, derisively named Shaka after the alleged beetle, grew up the butt of jokes, unwanted by either tribe. eLangeni kids picked on him mercilessly, doing everything their fertile little imaginations could conceive to humiliate him. We'll soon see how similar problems shaped the early life of Muhammad.

Culture-founders are often those who turn catastrophe into opportunity. Shaka was among them. When famine struck the eLangeni, no one wanted to give scarce food to those they loathed. So the eLangeni threw Shaka and his mother out of their kraal—out of their stockaded village—leaving the pair to die of starvation.[197] But Shaka and his mom lived. In fact, Shaka grew up to be 6'3", powerfully built, and marvelously inventive at one particular art: the art of killing. The standard weapon in Shaka's South African neighborhood was a long spear thrown from overhead. Shaka had the audacity to dramatically shorten its shaft, to increase the size of its blade, to strengthen it, and to turn it into an underhand stabbing weapon.

Shaka also did away with the old practice of standing at a distance from the enemy and only occasionally tossing a weapon. His idea of combat was brutally face-to-face and chest-to-chest. In fact, he came up with a trick that could only work in close contact, a way of using a shield as an offensive weapon. You hook your shield under the corner of the shield of your opponent, yank quickly, spin your opponent around, then jab your vicious stabbing weapon, a weapon the length of a bayonet, into the man's temporarily exposed side. Shaka's new spear was named for the sucking sound it made as you pulled it out of your victim, iKlwa.

When Shaka felled a man, he added a touch that may have sprung from the thrill he felt in killing, but that would soon become yet another weapon, a terror-spreader. Shaka shouted a blood-curdling victory cry, a cry perfect for the founder of what would soon be a greedy, expansionist and imperialist culture: "Ngadla," "I have eaten." Muhammad would do something similar.

Despite his role as an outcast, Shaka proved a master at creating the seeds of new military techniques. He boosted his speed and stability by tossing away the slippery sandals worn by traditional warriors. Shaka ran barefoot until his soles hardened so that he could sprint over stones, briars, and any other obstacles in his path. Then, equipped with his breakthrough techniques, he joined the army of the local militant empire builder, Dingiswayo, and became a battlefield nightmare of a kind South Africa had never seen.

Dingiswayo was so impressed by Shaka's killing abilities that he rewarded this strange new warrior with a huge promotion. The warlord sent Shaka back to the Zulus who had rejected him and his mother. But Shaka didn't merely come back to the Zulus as an honored citizen. Dingiswayo gave Shaka the ultimate revenge. He made Shaka the tribe's new chief.

How did Shaka handle this position of authority? First, he consolidated his hold by murdering everyone who had ever insulted him or his mother. Then he reorganized the tribe's psyche... and its military. To make it clear that this was a tribe that would be reborn in a new image, in the image of Shaka, and to make it plain that the tribe would be reborn or else, Shaka ordered the Zulus to destroy their old kraal and to build a new one. He demoted all the young men who were about to graduate from youth to adult status, and he militarized the society. He divided all the men into fighting units, then began something few Zulus had ever seen before. He armed his reluctant new followers with the short spears he'd devised, with new shields larger and stiffer than the old ones, and drilled his troops in the battlefield maneuvers he had invented, practicing the techniques until his men dropped. Literally.

From now on Zulu adult males would not just be summertime warriors. They'd be full-time, disciplined mass murderers—a culture shift of a kind that would also be crucial to Muhammad. The days of disorganized milling about on a field, staring at an enemy a hundred feet away, and occasionally lobbing a half-hearted spear were over. So were the days of declaring victory after one flesh wound and going home. From now on every adult male was either an expert at close-quarter killing ...or he was dead.

What did this give Shaka? One of Africa's most ferocious standing armies.[198] But that was just the beginning of Shaka's genius at creating new forms of social organization. Shaka trained his troops mercilessly, making them soldiers in a powerfully unified, army-ant-like social structure. He divided his men into four tactical units whose precise coordination, training, and discipline was critical. First in battle came "the chest," a main body that attacked the enemy face to face, pinned it down, and prevented its escape. Then came "the horns," flanks that raced out on either side and surrounded the enemy in a pincer movement. Finally there were "the loins," a reserve that sat behind the battlefield with its back to the fighting to prevent its emotional involvement from draining its energy. The loins were a backup, a fail-safe mechanism sent into battle to close any gaps or to shore up any weaknesses.

Shaka had introduced something southern African Bantu people had seldom seen before: sophisticated military strategy. Tactics. To execute military tactics, it helps to have a militarily motivated people, a murder-motivated people, a people whose personality apes that of a leader like Shaka.

Zulus were not that kind of folks when Shaka first took them over. But they sure as hell were by the time he was finished. Shaka insisted, for example, that his troops do what he'd done when he was out in the wilderness honing his newly invented killing skills. He made his fighters toss away their sandals and run barefoot. Yes, not walk but run. Run as fast, as hard, and as long as they could.

Not everyone was pleased with the idea of exposing his bare feet to the sharp stones, roots, and thorns of South Africa's pathways. So Shaka instituted a simple procedure for weeding out those without the guts to run barefoot. He had an open area scattered with thorns, then ordered his men to dance barefoot on this specially prepared ground. Anyone who didn't look as if he was thoroughly concentrating on his dance steps—anyone who even winced with pain—was executed.[199] In other words, Shaka kept those he could mold to his own style and killed those whose personalities did not lend themselves to an imitation of his bitter determination and absolute ferocity.

One result: by the time Shaka was finished, his troops could cover 50 miles barefoot in a single day. Napoleon's troops, who had been in action just a few years earlier in Europe, were considered miracles of modern swiftness because they could cover 25 to 30 miles. But that was a mere *half* of the speed of Shaka's troops.[200]

Shaka was delighted to discover that by the time he was finished, his men were so disgusted with peace and so in love with war that their kraals had to be built at many a spear's throw from each other.[201] If those kraals weren't separated by enough space, the men in each would do their best to bash the blood and brains out of their overly close neighbors in the kraal next door.[202]

The eLangeni—the tribe who had made Shaka's life miserable when he was young—woke up one morning and found their kraal surrounded.[203] Expecting the usual lenient treatment meted out by the half-hearted Zulu warriors they'd known in the past, they surrendered without a fight... something that also happened often in Muhammad's career as a military commander. And as we'll soon see in the life of Muhammad, surrender doesn't always bring mercy. Mercy was a quality Shaka Zulu squelched in his men and apparently strangled utterly in himself.

Shaka lined up the eLangeni men and picked out those who had mocked him when he was a child. He gave presents of oxen to the few who had been kind to his mother. Then he asked those he'd rewarded to stick around and see how the new culture he was crafting handled those who had not been so generous to their new lord and master. Every one of the men who'd spat on and made fun of Shaka when he was a kid was paraded to the high fence surrounding the kraal and impaled on its stakes. Shaka ordered that the victims be left dangling, tortured and alive, like frantically flipping live fish on an upright shish kebob skewer, for the 14 hours of a long, hot day. At nightfall he ended the misery of the miscreants by commanding that the fence be set on fire, barbecuing the men hanging from its shafts.[204] Barbecuing them alive.

At this point the Zulu army was still microscopic. It consisted of a mere 350 men. But its regimented and brutal members were a whole new kind of people—a people formed in the image of their leader.

The form of warfare Shaka was about to roll out would be as psychologically brilliant as it was physically unique. It was designed to shatter not just the weapons and bones, but the confidence of his enemies. In his first major battle, with the Butelezi, Shaka introduced one of his psyche-smashing maneuvers. The warriors on his front line bunched close together and carried their shields with the edges facing the enemy so they looked like a minuscule force as they approached the foe. The chests of the Butelezi swelled with arrogance and disdain at the sight of this puny Zulu mini-gang. Then Shaka's men suddenly fanned out. Troops who had been hidden behind the vanguard appeared as if from nowhere, and all of Shaka's soldiers turned their shields suddenly with their broad fronts facing the enemy. The pitifully undersized Zulu force now seemed to have tripled in size in a flick. The cocky Butelezi's hearts sank. Shaka had counted on this shock value and on the panic it produced to help him win.[205] In other words, Shaka was an expert at the manipulation of an emotion that we'll later see was critical to both the military and peacetime strategies of Muhammad—terror, a fear so overwhelming that it shakes loose the very roots of the soul.

The result of this battle? What historian Donald L. Morris, the teller of the tale in his book *The Washing of the Spears*, calls "a triumphant vindication" for Shaka's innovations. Shaka reduced the Butelezi to "a bloody welter."[206]

Shaka was ruthless at enforcing obedience and absolute conformity to the pattern of personality he'd laid out for his new group. Wherever he went, his retinue came complete with executioners who kept their king happy by snapping a dozen necks or by dashing a couple of skulls nearly every day.[207] It didn't take much to get you killed in the presence of his majesty. If you sneezed while Shaka ate or if you made him laugh when he was trying to look serious, that was it. You were dead before you had a chance to take your next breath. This brutality wasn't just handy for maintaining decorum in Shaka's immediate vicinity. Word spread, and the string of murders for mere nothings kept people near and far in line.

The result: conquests that built an empire of millions, one of the biggest empires in the history of Black Africa, an empire that at first utterly defeated the Victorian British despite the Brits' cannons, rifles, and superb organization, an empire molded in the image of one man and of his peculiarly violent personality, Shaka Zulu.

Is the case of Shaka Zulu and of the brutal culture he molded in his own image an accidental anecdote, a rare case, the exception to the rule? Do culture-founders really stamp their own character on their chosen people?

Can the founder's legacy be the source of one culture's emphasis on kindness and another's emphasis on killing, one culture's emphasis on caring and another's on harshness? Can it make some into barbarians and others a bit less barbaric? Think of Moses, Buddha, Jesus, Lenin, Mao, and Korea's Kim Il-sung.[208] Each of these culture-founders decreed that some emotions were good and others were unacceptable. Each tried to stamp his most intense personal values into a society. And each succeeded.

In his book *The Nuer Conquest: The Structure and Development of an Expansionist System*,[209] social scientist Raymond C. Kelly has worked with every science at his disposal, including mathematical modeling, to understand militarism and expansionism. His case study focuses on another African culture out for nonstop conquest, the Nuer of the southern Sudan, a tribe that, in the 19th century, nearly destroyed an individualistic neighboring tribe that couldn't get its military act together, the Dinka. Kelly tries to get at the heart of the imperialist, "expansionist" impulse—the push to constantly seize new territory. He and evolutionary biologist David Sloan Wilson, who has analyzed Kelly's work and written about it in three books,[210] come to a strange conclusion. The violent lust to take new land at any expense does not come from genes, say Wilson[211] and Kelly. And it doesn't come from material need. It comes from mere whiffs of nothing, from ideas.[212] It comes from what Kelly calls "aspirations" built into the Nuer culture, aspirations to territorial wealth that Kelly says can never be filled,[213] aspirations that, if left to their own devices, would gladly take over the grasslands of the entire planet... then would still hunger for more.

Here's how this perpetual hunger for conquest works. Among the Nuer, to outdo your neighbors you have to have more cattle than they do. To have more cattle, you need more land. So you go out with your fellow warriors, clobber a neighbor from another tribe, drive him off his fields, and conquer more territory.[214] You put a few cows and bulls into the new pasture land and let them multiply. Meanwhile, your neighbors do the same. By the time you're both finished, you have a lot more cattle. This should put you ahead. But it doesn't. Why? Because your neighbor has more cattle too. So to outdo that goddamned neighbor, you either have to go out to grab more land so you can cultivate more cattle...or you have to live in humiliation and shame.

Where do these aspirations, these standards against which men and women measure their pride or their mortification, come from? What Kelly doesn't explore is the role of founders in establishing hungry teams of ideas, hungry teams of memes.

What the heck are memes? The word meme comes to us courtesy of an evolutionary thinker and zoologist at Oxford University named Richard Dawkins. In 1976, Dawkins published a landmark book, *The Selfish Gene*.[215] Dawkins took us back to the beginning of life 4.1 billion[216] years ago and invited us to imagine a primordial puddle. In that bit of water, Dawkins imagined an early megamolecule learning two new tricks. The first—how to gather a gang of smaller molecules and self-assemble. Then something even more remarkable: to grab hold of more stray molecules, line them up in just the right way, and make a copy of itself. Megamolecules that made copies of themselves would live on for generation after generation. They would be capable of something God demanded in the Old Testament. They'd be fruitful and multiply like the stars in the skies.

Dawkins called these self-copying megamolecules "replicators." Genes, said, Dawkins, are one of the two most potent forms of replicators on the planet. Look what they've managed to assemble—8.7 million[217] species of bacteria, plants, animals, and you and me! The second form of replicator wouldn't appear on the scene until life had been around on this planet replicating for roughly four billion years. When man arose, a new form of puddle appeared...the puddle of the human mind. And in the rich broth of consciousness, a new replicator appeared. Ideas self-assembled. Folks got together and tried to get others to hum the tunes they had just snapped together in their own heads. They tried to get others to go along with their ideas. And they tried to badger, bully, or seduce others into sharing their techniques and beliefs. Ideas, tunes, techniques, and beliefs were all replicators—things that tried to make copies of themselves. Those that made the most copies thrived and survived. They were, said Dawkins, like mind viruses. The most successful spread like a contagion. Some were so good at copying themselves and overcoming the shredding power of time that they remain alive today in the minds of all 7.3 billion[218] people on this planet. Ideas like language, laws, and religion.

Memes are the magic bullet that would make Muhammad one of the most influential men in the history of life. A man who outdid Shaka Zulu and the Nuer in ways so extraordinary that his followers consider them miracles of Allah. But those miracles are based on such tenacious and successful replicators, such tenacious and successful memes, that they've outdone the imperial conquests of Julius Caesar, Genghis Khan, Napoleon, and of Western imperialism at its peak. What's more, those memes influence—and threaten—your way of life and mine today. Muhammad's memes, in fact, are out to replace the memes we hold dear—human rights, gender equality, freedom of speech, freedom of religion, democracy, pluralism, and tolerance. Only time will tell if our memes have the stick-to-it-iveness to survive or if Muhammad's memes will take over your life and mine.

Memes gave Muhammad's chosen people an astounding advantage over the Nuer and the Zulus. How? The violence of both the Zulu and the Nuer was stopped in 1910 by yet another militant, expansionist, imperialist group that tried to replicate and to expand the sway of its memes by making war for centuries. This world-grabbing empire looked back to founders like a resolute peacenik named Jesus and to the democratic, pluralist legacy of a "Glorious Revolution" in 1688. It was the Empire of England.

The British would also someday take Islamic territory. But they would hold it only briefly. And they would prove utterly incapable of yanking out Muslim memes and replacing them entirely with British replicators, British ideas. What's more, Islam would show signs of reversing Britain's victories in a snap of historical time. Militant Islam, in fact, would brag in the 20th and 21st century that it was about to take over Britain itself. How in the world did this reversal happen? Why did Muhammad's memes prove so resistant to removal? And why did they show the power to do what the Nuer ways of thought and the ideas of Shaka Zulu could not achieve—out-expand the greatest empires on Earth? How, in fact, did the ideas of Muhammad and his Founder Effect give Islam a head start in the competition to take over yet another new puddle that would emerge in the 20th and 21st century—the puddle of a globalized world?

A Prophet Is Born

HOW DOES A MAN BORN in a distant desert found a movement that outdoes every expansionist and colonialist culture in the history of humankind? How does that man give birth to a movement that does something Western scholars like Harvard's Caroline Elkins call impossible—winning hearts and minds. Winning them so completely that the conquered peoples refuse to give up the beliefs that were imposed on their ancestors by the deliberate and systematic use of military tactics we would call "war crimes" and "atrocities"?

The story begins over three hundred years before the birth of Muhammad, a time when the superpowers of the world were in a situation very similar to ours today—they were racked by indecision, under attack by outsiders, and, in one important case, crumbling like Roquefort cheese.

* * *

History did a lot to soften the turf for the rise of Islam. In 410 A.D. the barbarian Alaric led his Visigoths in the sack of Rome. The result was a long, slow slide of the Roman Empire into chaos. Europe turned from a paradise into a scrap-heap oozing blood. Roughly half of Western Europe's population died of starvation or plague. In the West, it was the beginning of the Dark Ages.

Things seemed to be going far better in the East. In 324 A.D. a Roman Emperor, Constantine, transformed an ancient Greek city that straddled the waters dividing Europe from Asia into a capital he called *Nova Roma*, the New Rome. We know that city better by its original Greek name, Byzantium, and by a name honoring the Emperor who lifted its stature, Constantinople. Six years after Constantine's facelift, he named Byzantium the new capital of the Roman Empire. So, in a sense, Rome didn't fall when Alaric entered its gates to literally rape and pillage. It moved. The city of Byzantium fought hard to keep the Western properties of its Empire—the Roman Empire. In some cases it succeeded. In some, it failed. Because of those failures, the Western Roman Empire—especially the 2,200-mile-long northern coast of Africa—remained shaky, a shakiness that would eventually help the armies of Islam. But the New Rome, Byzantium, managed to hold on to the Eastern half of the Roman Empire…and to keep it in one piece.

That was not as comforting as it sounds. In the East, the New Rome, Byzantium, was up against another superpower, the Empire of Persia. The Persian Empire was as land-hungry as Rome—the new Rome. And its credentials for conquest were even more august. The Persians had been masters of lands from India to Egypt in the days when Herodotus was writing Western civilization's first history, around 440 B.C. In those days, Rome was just a pip with a minor squeak. Nine hundred and ninety years later, in 550 A.D. or so, the Persians and the New Romans, the Byzantines, had worn each other into exhaustion in a nonstop battle for the domination of Syria, Egypt, and Asia Minor.

I'd like to say that both the New Romans and the Persians dismissed the desert fleas of the Arab Peninsula as insignificant barbarians. But that would be an exaggeration. In fact, as we'll see further on, the emperors of the New Rome and of Persia didn't even seem to know that the Arabs existed. This ignorance would also someday play into Muhammad's hands. In part, because the Arabs, like many of history's overlooked barbarians, used war as what Islamic biographer Muhammad Abdul Hai would someday call a "hobby."[219] They loved to fight, to kill, to raid, to take revenge for minor slights, and to run off with the spoils—some old clothes and a camel or sheep.

Those who pursue hobbies obsessively sometimes become remarkably good at the skills they practice…another fact that Muhammad would eventually turn to good advantage.

A few peculiar events in the wild wastes of the Arab desert also paved the way for Muhammad's arrival on the scene. The year was 552 A.D.[220] It was the Year of the Elephant. No, this wasn't China, and years in the deserts where the Arabs made their home were not normally named after pigs, bears, and mice. But this year, there was a struggle over the religious soul of the Arab heartland, a struggle that would involve an animal with a trunk where its nose should have been.

The Red Sea divides Arabia from Africa by only 17 miles at its narrowest point. On the Arab side was Yemen. On the African side were the paths that led the one hundred miles south to Ethiopia. Ethiopia was not the mousy little nation we view it as today. The Persian religious thinker Mani listed it as one of the four great powers of its time, along with Rome, Persia, and China.[221] For roughly two hundred years, Ethiopia had been Christian.[222] For at least five hundred years, Ethiopia and Yemen had been trade partners.[223] And since 520 A.D.,[224] only 30 years earlier, the Ethiopians had actually ruled Southern Arabia, including Yemen. So the Ethiopians decided to bring a little holiness to their newly acquired land. They set up a church in the Yemeni city of Sanaa, the sort of massive church designed to attract converts.

In 552 A.D., a citizen of a city deep in the mountainous deserts six hundred miles away took offense on behalf of the ragtag idols of his fathers, snuck into Sanaa one night, and vandalized the brand new Ethiopian church, defiling it to the best of his ability. The church-defiler came from a trading town with a name that would eventually be known around the world—Mecca. At the time, however, Mecca was the desert equivalent of Chillicothe, Ohio—a town of nearly total anonymity. The Christian governor of Yemen—the man who ruled Yemen on behalf of Ethiopia—was not at all pleased with the vandalism perpetrated by this desert hick. He sent a military force equipped with the mega-mobile-terror-weapon of the day, elephants,[225] to take revenge on the Meccans by destroying Mecca's holy building, the Kaaba.

According to Meccan poets, a god named Allah didn't care for having his headquarters in Mecca assaulted, even if that headquarters was filled with the shabby idols of gods from the deserts hither and yon. Allah sent in His air force—birds carrying molten rocks, rocks the birds dropped with absolute precision on the heads of the Ethiopian troops, burning holes from the top of their heads to their nether ends, literally boring the Ethiopian soldiers to death, and eliminating the Ethiopian army.

The Meccans quickly turned this holy victory to their advantage. Up until now, the Arabs had observed a sacred period of "holy months," roughly 40 days in which war was forbidden and in which the tribes of the neighborhood set out on what they called the Hajj. Each tribe made the rounds of three distant sacred sites, staying 20 days in the first destination, ten days in the second, and eight days in the third, performing holy rituals to keep the gods of these hamlets, their hills, and their rocks happy, setting up fairs, and trading with the tribes in whose vicinity the sacred sites were located.[226] This holy ramble was the great commercial integrator, idea exchanger, and new-wife-finder of the day.

Now, with the Victory of the Bored Ethiopians under their turbans, the Meccans aimed for a monopoly over the Holy perambulation business, for a monopoly over religious tourism. The Meccans declared that *their* sacred site, the Kaaba, was more sacred than ever, that only they were holy enough to lead rituals in it, and that only Mecca was good enough to be the town to which folks should come to worship and to trade. The Meccans added that "We are the sons of Abraham, men of honour, governors of the house of Allah, inhabitants of Mecca. No Arab has such virtue as we, nor such dignity as we."[227]

The Meccans must have been far better at wheeling, dealing, and self-promotion than history tells us. They succeeded in their aim, establishing Mecca as the deity's only hot spot and themselves as the only men holy enough to handle the ceremonies that pleased the gods. To top it off, the Meccan opportunists laid down an interesting set of new sacred rules. When you came to Mecca, you couldn't bring your own food. You had to buy food from the Meccans. You couldn't wear your old clothes. You had to buy new ones from, guess who? The Meccans.

The Meccans would, however, make an exception for you if you were rich and showed up in a really expensive outfit. When you finished your holy perambulations around the Kaaba you had to leave your clothes behind and never touch them again.[228] Don't worry, the Meccans took good care of your garments. Neat way to clean up, isn't it? These lucrative religious innovations would pump money into Mecca's coffers for the next 1,465 years.[229]

In the year 571 A.D., 19 years after The Year of the Elephant, for all practical purposes, nothing happened. Or did it? According to one Islamic source, "most of the idols at the Ka'ba toppled over; the palace of the Sassanid Emperor shook and cracked, and its 14 pinnacles collapsed; the small lake of Sawa in Persia sank into the earth, and the fire which was worshipped by the Magians [followers of the sixth-century B.C. prophet of flame and darkness, Zoroaster] at Istakhrabad and had been lit continually for a thousand years was extinguished."[230] To put it differently, an obscure baby was born into an obscure family in an obscure town on an ordinary Monday.[231, 232] The town was our old friend Mecca, the village that had recently motivated several elephants to take a six-hundred-mile walk into the vast nowhere of the Arabian Peninsula in the deserts that today belong to Saudi Arabia. Mecca, as we've seen, had two major industries: trade and religion. It was a way station on the route from Yemen to Syria, Jordan, Israel, and Palestine. This may not sound like much, but Yemen's position on the Indian Ocean made it a contact point for trade with the two biggest exporting nations of the day, China and India—lands whose goods were so high-end that they were consistently referred to in the world literature of the day as "treasures." What's more, the Yemenis were not just masters of the import business. They raised the plants that produced perfumes and air fresheners like frankincense and myrrh.[233] The sixth century A.D. was one of the smelliest eras in history. Something nice to sniff, especially on festive occasions—from feasts to funerals—could give you a nasal vacation worth a fortune. No wonder Yemen was Mecca's source of merchandise.

What was at the other end of the Meccans' business operations? Where were the customers to whom the Meccans carried the goods of Yemen? Syria, Jordan, Israel, and Palestine, outlets to the ultra-rich consumer empires of the Persians and the Romans. Outlets to the Mediterranean Sea.

Living in a broiled and bland, make-your-own-sandstorm center like Mecca wasn't much.[234] But every poison is a miracle cure awaiting its moment of reinvention. To survive from one month to the next in the deserts of Arabia, you had to be fairly good at camel-wrangling. Camels were great for making war among the dunes. But what else could you do with animals so nasty that they hiss? The seagoing Arabs of the Indian Ocean,[235] roughly six hundred miles away, had invented ships that carried cargo in mass quantities—up to 30 tons.[236] Cross a Red Sea vessel with an Indian cargo boat and you get a hybrid called a dhow,[237] a mistress of the Eastern seas that can haul Indian and Chinese cargo by the ton to Yemen. But there was a catch: Ships need water. The stretch of crunching brown silicon between the Indian Ocean and the swatch of Greater Syria that the Meccans traded with had no rivers. At best it had a few watering holes, oases[238] like Mecca. Carrying goods by ship was impossible. So how could you transport goods from Yemen overland in mass quantities? How could you carry big loads of "frankincense, silk, precious metals and leather"?[239] By harnessing the strange-humped beasts of the desert and stringing them together in caravans.

Hence the name "ship of the desert." Not to be confused with a "ship off the old block." However, there was an old block in Mecca. And, thanks to the new approach to the Hajj that the Meccans had invented roughly 20 years before Muhammad's birth, that old block was now as profitable as the camel-caravan-based transport business. The cube we're talking about was a big, black meteoric stone in a day when stones were popularly associated with gods. The Meccans made the most of this strangely geometric blob of rock by associating it with every god in the neighborhood—and every god in the 2.1 million or so surrounding square kilometers. Which means that every tribe in and out of sight kept the idol of its deity in a sugar-cube-shaped

Meccan building in which the naturally squared-off meteoric stone was housed—the Kaaba (Arabic for "cube").[240] Then, once a year, the rabblers and scrabblers of the sands tried to restrain themselves from muggings and plunder for four months,[241] hang on to a period of precarious peace, and make pilgrimages to visit the gods of their fathers, or at least to visit the 360 or so wooden and stone effigies thereof housed in Mecca's Kaaba. So Mecca may have been a flyspeck among the dunes, but it was a flyspeck that evaded eradication thanks to the profits of commerce—commerce in goods, and commerce in gods. What's more, there was a saying in the neighborhood that the Arabs were so good at these feeble industries that they could "turn a grain of sand into a nugget of gold."[242] This was the Mecca into which Muhammad was born.

In 577 A.D., when Muhammad was six years old, his mother took him 280 miles from Mecca to her hometown[243] Medina,[244] a "city" of only a thousand inhabitants originally founded by Jews,[245] a city that would someday save Muhammad from assassination and would prove crucial to the rise of Islam. And a city whose oldest citizens, its Jews, would play a critical role in the next 1,400 years of Muslim history. It may have been in Medina that Muhammad became obsessed with the God of the Old Testament, with the Jewish holy book the Torah, and with the Jewish story of the universe and mankind, from creation to Noah, to Abraham, to Moses, and to the Jewish hope that someday a prophet would arise who would save the Hebrews from perpetual humiliation at the hands of mightier nations, a prophet who would prove to be a Messiah. All these would be crucial ideas to Muhammad, memes he would adopt and knit together in surprising and often ominous new ways. But all that was in the future.

On the way back from Medina, Muhammad's mother died. Which meant that Muhammad's childhood in Mecca would set him apart from other children. His father had died before he was born. When his mother died,[246] he became an orphan. Kids are not kind to those whose background is odd or disadvantaged. Just look at what happened to Shaka Zulu. There's also evidence that kids made fun of Muhammad.[247] The result? Muhammad was apparently a loner, possibly even a loner with a persecution complex. According to one of his Islamic biographers, Sarwat Saulat, he "was a boy of a serious nature he did not play with the boys of the streets, kept himself aloof from idolatry and never took wine."[248] Muhammad was a sober, stern, and serious kid.

But when Muhammad was still a child of eight, he was beset by other challenges. In 579 A.D., his loss of relatives continued—and continued to disadvantage him. His grandfather died. That grandfather, according to Islamic tradition, had been one of Mecca's leaders. The granddad's position at the top of the heap put Muhammad's family, the Hashem,[249] at the pinnacle of power and prestige within their tribe, the Quraysh. But that power and prestige disappeared utterly when Muhammad's grandfather was no longer around to defend the family's position. Instead a rival family, the Banu Umayya, shoved Muhammad's Hashem clan to the bottom of the heap.[250]

That humiliation, too, would shape history. Someday Muhammad would reverse this loss and would gain power over the very people who had humiliated him and his clan—the Banu Umayya. He would subjugate the Banu Umayya with a new approach to violence and to psychological manipulation. But the Banu Umayya would once again turn the tables and take over something far bigger and more prophetable—sorry, profitable—than mere pecking order prestige in Mecca. The Banu Umayya would become the keeper of Muhammad's legacy. A legacy that would go global.

Muhammad Sees Empire

IN 579 A.D., WHEN MUHAMMAD'S grandfather died, his uncle, Abu Talib, the new head of Muhammad's Banu Hashim[251] clan, took over as his foster parent, sticking by him for the next 40 years.[252] This was yet another disadvantage. Abu Talib apparently didn't have the clout of Muhammad's grandfather. In fact, he was so poor that at one point he couldn't feed his own sons.[253] The one thing he did have was the strength of character to defend Muhammad from attack.[254] And Muhammad would continue to be attacked for the next 35 years.

In 581 A.D., Muhammad turned 11 and, like other kids his age in Mecca, became a shepherd and grazed goats.[255] But keeping goats company would not prove to be Muhammad's calling. When Muhammad turned 12, the youngster forced his uncle, Abu Talib, to slip him into the commercial and entrepreneurial currents that plugged Mecca into the larger world, the world of the superpowers—Persia and Rome. Abu Talib was going on a trading expedition, a caravan, to the Roman[1] province of Syria.[256] And Abu Talib had no intention of taking his nephew. But Muhammad begged and begged, then finally held on to his uncle's neck and refused to let go.[257] Abu Talib gave in, and Muhammad began his indoctrination into Mecca's major business, long-distance trade, with his first trip to a land of big-city sophistication. The patch of Roman territory Muhammad traveled to was al-Sham,[258] yes, the Sham of ISIS, "The Islamic State of Iraq and al-Sham." Al-Sham, "Greater Syria," was a land that included modern Syria, Jordan, Lebanon, Israel, and

---

1. Keep in mind that to the folks of the time—including the young Muhammad—Byzantium was the new Rome, and Byzantium's empire was the Roman Empire, period. It's we who insist on the silly and demeaning tactic of calling territories like sixth-century A.D. Syria parts of "the Byzantine Empire." See the argument for Byzantium as the New Rome in: Edward Gibbon. *The Decline and Fall of the Roman Empire—Volume III*. New York: The Modern Library, New York, or, for a shorter version, Byzantine Empire. *Encyclopædia Britannica*, from Encyclopædia Britannica Deluxe Edition 2005 CD. Copyright © 1994–2004 Encyclopædia Britannica, Inc. May 30, 2004.

Palestine.[259] It was the most intensely Christian and Jewish territory on the face of the Earth. Greater Syria was the birthplace of Judaism, the location of the traditional Jewish "promised land"—Israel, Judaea, and Samaria. It was also the cradle of Christianity—the location of Jesus' birth and life, of St. Paul's conversion to Christianity on the road to Damascus (the famous incident in which Paul was blinded by a divine light and fell off his ass), and was the home base of the apostles and the fathers of the church.

In addition to meaning "Greater Syria," al-Sham, the destination of Muhammad's first trip beyond the Arab deserts, meant "Damascus"[260]—the sophisticated Syrian city. Damascus was a bustling trade metropolis where radically different cultures met and mingled. The city had traded hands between the Byzantine and the Persian Empires and was riddled with Byzantine and Persian influences.[261] It was a junction on the Silk Road that carried silks, furs, cotton, spices, and peppers overland from Malaysia, Indonesia, China, and India to the Mediterranean.[262] Damascus was also a key entrepôt on the King's Highway, the 1,500-year-old trade route that carried goods and pilgrims from Egypt to Syria and Iraq. Topping all that, Damascus was a hive of Christianity. The city was filled with pilgrims, churches, monks, monasteries, monastic cells, and monastic towers—towers up to 60 feet high with monastic cells on their tops to advertise the willingness of monks to sacrifice their material lives for Christ.[263]

One of Muhammad's chief biographers, Muhammad Haykal, is convinced that "it was in al Sham that" Muhammad "came to know of Byzantine and Christian history and heard of the Christians' scriptures."[264] These were things Muhammad would never forget. When the pedal hit the metal, they would turn him into a globalist.

Ten years later, from his 21st to his 24th year, Muhammad got his first taste of what biographer Muhammad Abdul Hai calls the Arab "hobby": war. An intertribal conflict broke out for four years running, and Muhammad's tribe was caught up in it. At first, the conflict appeared to be a mere nothing, just a persistent scuffle of the kind that the Arabs used for sport—two clans battling each other until they grew tired of the fight, reached an agreement, and the winning tribe paid the losers blood money for the dead. In this four-year-long affair, the War of the Wicked, Muhammad collected the arrows fired at his tribe by the enemies and handed them to his uncle to present to the more important warriors, who fired them back in the other direction.[265] But over time, the war impoverished the Meccans, lowered them in the eyes of their neighbors and made them vulnerable to raids. So the warring tribes got together for dinner and concluded a truce. Muhammad was one of those at the dinner who swore to uphold the peace agreement.[266] Muhammad would later upscale the nature of war—and of alliances—among the Arabs dramatically.

In 594 A.D., when Muhammad hit the age of 23, he lucked out. He was too poor to marry. But the most successful businessperson in Mecca was a woman—the 40-year-old Khadija, a widow who'd already had two husbands[267] die out from under her. Khadija didn't need a husband with money. Like Muhammad's uncle, Abu Talib, Khadija was in the trade and transport profession. Like his uncle, she was a traveler who had seen the world beyond the desert. But unlike Muhammad's uncle, Khadija was a highly skilled and ridiculously successful practitioner of commerce.[268] She had inherited a rich transport business from her father, then had apparently expanded it. According to the hadith collection of Mulla Muhammad Baqir, the *Bihār al-Anwār*, "she had more than 80,000 camels. Her business interests extended up to Ethiopia and Egypt."[269] Khadija was an entrepreneurial organizer, always on the prowl for talented men she could send on trade missions. The result: she was the wealthiest woman in Mecca.[270] She'd amassed a fortune bigger than those of all the other members of Muhammad's extended tribe, the Quraysh,[271] combined. Meanwhile, Muhammad had earned a reputation for honesty.[272] If you were going on a business trip and wanted to leave your goods with someone trustworthy, everyone in town knew that Muhammad was your man. Or so says Islamic tradition.

Khadija decided to test Muhammad's reputation. She hired the 23-year-old Muhammad to travel on her behalf to Syria, carrying and selling her merchandise. She loaned Muhammad one of her male slaves to keep him company, to help him lug things, and to spy on him. Muhammad's powers as a salesman and his skills at bargaining were apparently above average… though it was his "honesty and fair dealings" that Islamic biographers like Sarwat Saulat try to stress. Muhammad returned from Syria with a handsome profit.[273] And Khadija's slave reported to her privately that Muhammad hadn't skimmed any of the proceeds off for himself.[274] A rare quality.

So in 595 A.D., Khadija made Muhammad an offer he could easily have refused. She asked him to marry her. The future prophet was only 25 years old and Khadija was 40. But Khadija was offering Muhammad a jackpot—access to all of her wealth and slaves. So Muhammad said yes. Once the marriage was consummated, the groom made a noble decision. He set all of Khadija's slaves free.[275] That move would later prove critical when

Muhammad needed followers for a new way of thinking and behaving. But we'll get to that later. Muhammad summed up his marriage to Khadija like this: "When I was poor she [Khadija] enriched me and when they called me a liar, she supported my mission."[276] Muhammad's career was about to be catapulted to a higher level by a powerful, supportive, and brainy woman. It's ironic that the religion he would found would eventually reduce women to invisibility.

*   *   *

The first 11 years of Muhammad's marriage were so uneventful that they've nearly disappeared from history. Khadija gave birth to seven children.[277] Two of them died early in life. More important, Khadija had a Christian cousin, a man who Muhammad's first biographer, the eighth-century scholar Ibn Ishaq, says was "well versed in sacred and profane literature"[278]—the literature of the Christians and the Jews. When Khadija and her cousin discussed the people Muhammad had met on his first trade trip to Syria for Khadija, they suspected that some of the strangers may have been angels sent to protect Muhammad. This was the first hint of more things to come—Muhammad's one-of-a-kind relationship with God.

Meanwhile in 606 A.D., when Muhammad was 26 years old, he showed signs of a new skill: a talent for social organization. The Kaaba—the cube-shaped building that housed the wooden idols of the gods of tribes for hundreds of miles around, the building that attracted the lucrative pilgrimage business—was damaged by rain. The Meccans wanted to rebuild it, but were terrified that if they laid a hand on the Kaaba's divine cube-shaped meteoric stone and the timbers of the building that housed it, the gods would strike them dead. They allowed one brave citizen, al-Walid, to do what no one else dared. Walid grabbed a pickaxe and demolished an entire section of the Kaaba's wall. The Meccans waited breathlessly until the next morning to see if Walid would survive the wrath of the gods. When Walid woke up alive and went back to demolishing walls, the men of the tribes of Mecca breathed a sigh of relief and pitched in to join him.

But once the old building was gone and the new building erected, there was a problem. The sacred black stone—the cube-shaped meteorite—had to be put in place in the new building, and every tribe wanted the honor of completing this last and most holy of tasks. The tribes quarreled for four days, began to form factions, and started muttering about war. Who would save Mecca from civil strife? And how?

One elder suggested that the arguing crowd let whoever walked through the door next act as umpire and decide the matter. Surprise, surprise. The next man to come through the door was...Muhammad. Muhammad asked for a cloak, put the black stone on it, and said, "Let every group take hold of a part of the cloak." The tribesmen each gripped a bit of the cloak's fringe and lifted the stone to the height of its resting place. And Muhammad himself slid the stone from the cloak onto its base. All earned the honor of elevating the stone![279] Did this mean that Muhammad had a gift for uniting men in new ways? And a gift for compromise? We shall have to see.

609 A.D. was the year that would change the world...literally. In the ninth month of each year, the month of Ramadan, Muhammad followed the Meccan religious tradition of taking his family into the mountains above town, secluding himself in a cave, then praying and meditating.[280] All kinds of shenanigans were going on back in town, forms of behavior that Muhammad despised. According to biographer Sarwat Saulat, there was a laundry list of sins: "idolatry, dishonesty, murder, civil strife, gambling, robbery, usury, and drinking of wine."[281] During his Ramadan retreat, Muhammad was asleep in his cave when he was sideswiped by an odd experience. He dreamed that a massive and indistinct force came to him carrying a brocade coverlet with words stitched into it, then ordered him to "recite, to read." In his sleep, Muhammad admitted that he was illiterate:[282] "I cannot read,"[283] he said. But the force wouldn't take no for an answer. Muhammad felt himself being crushed three times so hard that "I thought it was death." "What can I read?[284]" pleaded Muhammad finally, caving in to stop the pain.[285] Said the voice of the force, "Read in the name of thy lord who... created man from a clot. Read: And thy Lord is the Most Bounteous." These words and a few more stuck with Muhammad as though "they had been graven on my heart."[286] They also convinced him that he'd turned overnight into either a mystic poet or a lunatic, two sorts of humans he despised.[287]

Rather than be ridiculed by his fellow Meccans as a madman, Muhammad trekked up into the mountains to find a convenient cliff from which he could fling himself "and gain rest."[288] But a man showed up like the Jolly Green Giant, straddling the horizon with his torso in the sky, his feet planted on the ground, and with wings outstretched from one end of the sky to the other.[289] This oversized apparition spanned the horizon no matter which way Muhammad turned his head. Said the super-sized humanoid, "Oh, Muhammad, thou art the apostle of God and I am Gabriel." Muhammad stopped still in his tracks.

Meanwhile, his wife, Khadija, was worried and sent out servants to find her missing spouse. The servants brought back a seriously shaken man. Sitting at Khadija's thigh, Muhammad told his wife that he thought he was losing it. "None of God's creatures was more hateful to me than an (ecstatic) poet or a man possessed," he said, "I could not even look at them."[290] Yet that was the level of delusion to which he felt he'd sunk. Khadija reassured Muhammad that God would never implant madness in a man so honest and kind.

But beneath her soothing manner, Khadija, too, must have been disturbed. When the family returned home from the mountains, Khadija gathered her robes about her[291] and paid a visit to her cousin the Christian, the man schooled in the Jewish Torah and in the Christian Gospels. The cousin came up with the perfect face-saving solution. Muhammad's visions were not a humiliation, he said, they were a promotion. Explained the cousin, "the law of Moses has been bestowed on him and he is the prophet of this nation!"[292] Exactly which nation the cousin was talking about was unclear.

That was it. A new calling. In 610 A.D. Muhammad started his career in prophecy. For its first three years, it was at best a home business, a mom-and-pop cottage industry. Muhammad's first convert was just a few inches away in his bed—Khadija, his wife. Doesn't sound like much, but with Khadija signed up as a believer, Muhammad had her fortune as funding. Convert number two was a newly arrived[293] house guest, Muhammad's ten-year-old nephew. Abu Talib, Muhammad's uncle and guardian, had been too strapped financially during a famine to continue taking care of his two sons, including his younger son, Ali.[294] Muhammad, flush with Khadija's money, had taken over the task and Ali had moved in to Muhammad's home. Now the ten-year-old signed up eagerly as a follower of Muhammad's still rudimentary belief system. But Muhammadanism would have a tougher time with adults. Abu Talib, Ali's father and one of the men closest to Muhammad, gave the self-styled spokesperson for Allah a turndown, explaining, "I cannot abandon the religion of my forefathers."[295] Then came a big score, an actual jump outside the immediate household—Muhammad's good-natured and popular best friend, the merchant Abu Bakr. And Abu Bakr pulled in five new converts: Uthman, al-Zubayr, Abdur-Rahman, Sad bin Abu Waqqas, and Talha. Among these were some of the heavyweights who would play a role in militant Islam's blitzkrieg of the Middle East, Africa, and Asia. But there would be many difficulties to overcome before Islam could pull that blitzkrieg off.

It took three years, but by 613 A.D. Muhammad's new religion, Islam, which Sarwat Saulat says means "the religion of obedience, peace, and security"[296] had taken shape in Muhammad's mind. The angel Gabriel taught Muhammad how to wash up five times a day, then to pray.[297] God, Allah, revealed enough scriptures to Muhammad to fill a small Qur'an. The big He in the sky drove home a core belief: "Anyone who does not admit the existence of God or believes in polytheism is a rebel. This was the real and true religion of Adam, the first man, of Abraham, of Moses, and of Jesus."[298] In other words, God told Muhammad that the religion of the Jews and the Christians was distorted, dishonest, and corrupt, but that He, the Most Gracious Most Merciful,[299] was going to hand Muhammad the REAL religion that the Jews and Christians should follow.

What's more, by 613 A.D. Muhammad had worked out his way of introducing himself to strangers: "I am an apostle from Allah to you and command you to adore Allah and not to bestow this adoration on any other; to renounce the worship of idols; to believe me, His apostle, and to defend me that I may explain to you the revelation with which Allah has sent me."[300] He was asking a lot. That may be why the new belief system, still limited to a hidden existence in Muhammad's house, had only worked its way up to 40 believers.

So God sent Muhammad the word that it was time to get serious. It was time to go public. Very public. Or, as God put it, it was time to "publish that which thou hast been commanded."[301] But Muhammad couldn't read or write and the printing press hadn't been invented. What's more, God was very specific. Start by warning "thy closest relatives."[302] So Muhammad followed God's instructions, gathered the clans of the Quraysh, and said, "O children of Ka'ab Ibn Lu'ay, save yourselves from Hell. O children of Murrah lbn Ka'ab, save yourselves from Hell. O children of Hashim, save yourselves from Hell."[303] How? Basically, by doing anything and everything Muhammad demanded.[304] After those cheerful words, Muhammad went to one of the highest soap-boxes around, the sacred Mount of Safa, a hill topped with the idol of the goddess Na'ila.[305] He asked the people of Mecca to gather 'round, then gave his equivalent of the Sermon on the Mount, a speech that showed just how dramatically Islam would be a religion of fear, not a religion of love:

> Would you believe me if I tell you that a large army was hidden
> behind this hill ready to attack you? Well, if you think so, I ask you
> to believe in one God, and if you refuse to do so God will give you
> severe punishment.[306]

With these uplifting words, Muhammad lost his audience, who promptly headed for just about any part of town where Muhammad wasn't standing.[307] One reason for this instant departure: much as the Meccans loved mocking their fellow humans—and they did—they preferred to laugh[308] about Muhammad behind his back. But the laughing would not last.

Why be laughed at for taking an inch when you can be hated for stealing a mile? For the next six years, from 613 A.D. to 619 A.D., Muhammad took his religion a giant step forward. He turned it, says Sarwat, into "a call to create a whole new society, free from all evils and exploitations, on the basis of Divine guidance."[309] This didn't go down well with the Meccans in power, those who benefitted from the existing status quo. Says Muhammad's first biographer, Ibn Ishaq, when Muhammad insulted their idols, the folks at the top, "accused him of seeking power, denied his revelation, and united to injure him."[310] Then came the heavy-duty persecution. Depending on whose version of the story you listen to, and there's only one left: the Muslim version. Which goes like this. Something rather hard to gather together on the planet Earth of the year 613 A.D. or so—a group of Muhammad's followers—went out to a valley to pray. A group of something not quite so hard to find—idol-fearing Meccans—came across the Muhammadans, insulted them, and "provoked them to fight."[311] One of the Muslims, a bloke named Sad, clobbered one of the Meccans with the jaw of a camel, a natural lever long and hefty enough to kill someone. In this case, the Meccan victim was only injured. But Ibn Ishaq notes a critical fact: this was "the first blood shed in Islam."[312] It wouldn't be the last. Far from it.

The Meccans tried to figure out how to handle the trouble Muhammad was causing. He was undermining the fabric of society. And he was doing it big-time. Said one of the Meccans, Muhammad "has come with words … which separate a man from his father or from his brother, or from his wife, or from his family."[313] So the Meccans made a singularly poor decision. The annual Holy Months had arrived, the time when everyone within hundreds of miles had to schlep to Mecca to amble around the Kaaba, to honor the idols, and to trade. The Meccan elders took up a position by the roadside, stopped every incoming visitor, and warned him about Muhammad and his antisocial poison. The move backfired. Without knowing it, the elders had just given Muhammad something he'd never had before—a public relations campaign. Word of Muhammad spread far and wide.

So the Meccans tried to convince Muhammad to return to his position as a respectable member of the community. They offered him money. They offered to make him a prince. They offered to make him a king. They asked him to produce a few miracles to prove that his claims of prophecy were legit. Nothing worked.[314] So the Meccans turned to cruder techniques of cult-deprogramming. One believer's uncle tied his nephew up hand and foot, beat him with ropes, locked him in a room, and told him he'd stay there until he agreed to leave the Muhammad-cult and return to his senses.[315] The Muhammadan didn't abandon his wild and crazy belief in Muhammad and his preachings. Another uncle of a believer tossed his cult-ridden nephew into a room filled with choking smoke. When yet another convert announced in public that he was switching over to the Muhammad sect, the public responded by beating him up. Others were beaten, then locked up without food and water until they couldn't stand it and did more than merely abjure Muhammad. They promised to worship a dung beetle.[316]

To the extent that Islam was catching on, it was doing best with the poor and with the slaves. And it was the slaves who got the really heavy-duty de-Muhammadification treatment. The desert sands outside of Mecca heated up like a hamburger grill when the sun hit them. The master of one black Muslim slave forced his victim's back down on this searing desert surface at noon, when the heat would have charred a slice of camel liver into solid carbon, tied him in place, then loaded the slave's chest with a huge stone to pin him down and to make sure that he baked evenly.[317] The slave refused to leave the Muhammad cult. So the master took another approach. He tied a rope around the broiled slave's neck, then took advantage of a powerful motive force—adolescent boys, some of whom are always up for a joyride. The slave owner asked the boys if they'd oblige him by dragging the sautéed slave "from one corner of town to the other."[318] The slave could barely talk, but he still managed to spit out the Muslim catchphrase, "God is one."[319] Finally Abu Bakr, Muhammad's best friend and second male convert, offered the owner a trade—a black slave of his own—in exchange for the cooked and dragged Muslim slave, and gained the charbroiled Muslim his freedom.[320]

Another slave was beaten into unconsciousness, wakened, then beaten again. To make matters worse, his father was battered, bloodied, and bruised, and his mother was run through with a lance. This cocktail-toothpick treatment was fatal to the unfortunate old woman. Another slave got an even more decisive detoxification. He was spread out on burning coals until the melted fat of his body finally cooled the embers. By then, he was presumably dead.[321] But Muhammad himself was untouched. No one dared cross his uncle and his uncle's allies.[322]

In the deserts of Mecca, even bad publicity is good publicity. All this persecution spread the word of Islam and its essential messages, and kept new converts trickling in.[323]

In 615 A.D., Muhammad made a move that would someday gain his system of belief half a continent. Muhammad got one group of believers out of the firing line by telling them to take refuge in Africa—in the Christian superpower of Ethiopia.[324] News of Islam inched its way through tiny portions of the Ethiopian population and fired up curiosity. So 20 Christians took the long trip from Ethiopia to Mecca to check out the self-proclaimed "Apostle of Allah" for themselves. When Muhammad recited the Qu'ran to them they cried, they believed, and they apparently converted.[325] This took Islam international for the first time. But it was only a nano-preview of the international surprises Islam would spring a mere 20 years down the line.

For the next three years, from 615 A.D. to 618 A.D., the Meccans tried to choke Islam before it could get more threatening. Their tourniquet of choice? Economic sanctions. They banned all trade with the Muslims, ruling out even the sale of food to Muhammad's followers. The goal was what Muhammad's biographer Muhammad Haykal calls "boycott, isolation, and starvation."[326] Meanwhile five Meccans amused themselves by mocking Muhammad. They wouldn't get away with this insult for long. Allah tapped Muhammad's shoulder to deliver one of the revelations—one of the direct communiqués from God the Merciful, the Compassionate—that now popped into Muhammad's life on a regular basis. These bulletins would someday be collected in the Qur'an. The message, in this case, concerned the five wise guys who were making fun of Muhammad. "They will know," says Allah. In other words, they'll get the message. But what message and how would they get it?

Gabriel stood by Muhammad's side when the five wise guys were worshipping by circling the Kaaba. One of the jokers was hit by a green leaf in the face and went blind. Gabriel pointed to the stomach of another, his stomach swelled[2] and he died. Gabriel pointed to a wound on the heel of the third man who had dared to make fun of Muhammad. The scar that covered the wound opened and killed him. Three taunters down, two to go! Then Gabriel did something normally only worms and contortionists can pull off. He pointed to the sole of the fourth target's foot. A thorn penetrated the sole and killed the guy. For his final act, Gabriel pointed to the head of the fifth

2. Technically, this unfortunate was stricken with "dropsy," a form of edema.

mocker, which "began to ferment with poison,"[327] a poison that sent the cut-up directly to the new home of his four co-mockers, hell. The lesson? It's handy to have a merciful and compassionate God on your side. And sometimes the fact that He shows His mercy and compassion by killing can give you a competitive edge.

Then came two strokes of bad luck. In 619 A.D., Muhammad's two protectors, Khadija, his venture capitalist, and Abu Talib, his uncle and his muscle,[328] died.[329] Things had been bad in Mecca for the Muslims, and now Muhammad was afraid they'd get worse. So Ibn Ishaq tells us that the fledgling Prophet set out on a trip to "al-Taif [the nearest city of importance] in search of aid and protection."[330] He didn't get it. In fact, the inhabitants of al-Taif set their slaves upon him, cursing him, shouting at him, and driving him to take refuge in an orchard.[331] Muhammad, says Ibn Ishaq, was in despair. Nonetheless, to give himself extra ammunition, he worked out a minor variation on his opening line: "I am an apostle from Allah to you and command you to adore Allah and not to bestow this adoration on any other; to renounce the worship of idols; to believe me, His apostle, and to defend me that I may explain to you the revelation with which Allah has sent me."[332]

And he tried another tack, the export market. Mecca still had its trade fairs, events that attracted the visits of tribes from great distances.[333] If your neighbors won't buy your spiel, why not try it out on strangers? Especially ones who've shown up in a buying mood? So Muhammad tried winning over the tourists. In the process, he met the folks from Medina, a hamlet 280 miles up the road, the town to which his mother had taken him when he was six.[334] And he lucked out. The Medinaites seemed far more interested in what he had to say than most of the folks at home.

But on the home front things were worse than ever. The Meccans had come to the end of their rope. Once simply playing practical jokes and mocking Muhammad had been enough. Like the day a bunch of Meccan pranksters slid a camel fetus or a camel's guts, depending on whose account you're reading, down the back of Muhammad's robes. But those days were over. Now the Meccans planned to solve their unwanted prophet problem by doing away with its cause, Muhammad. Muhammad got wind of this scheme, and hot-footed it out of town with his best friend and first adult convert, Abu Bakr—a man who would someday be rewarded for his loyalty with conquests beyond most men's dreams. The two headed the 280 miles to Medina, leaving behind another convert, Muhammad's 21-year-old cousin Ali. And Ali did something brave. He slept in Muhammad's bed that night, setting himself up as a decoy. It turned out that the rumor of Muhammad's assassination was true. A gang of Meccans intent on murder entered Muhammad's home in the middle of the night armed to the teeth. But when they peeled back the covers to give them a clear aim at their victim, all they found was Ali. Killing Muhammad's relatives was not what they had in mind. So they gave up. Thank Allah.

Over the next days, Ali followed Muhammad's instructions and, says Ibn Ishaq, "returned all the goods which people had entrusted to the keeping of the apostle." Despite the plots against him, writes Ibn Ishaq, "there was not a man in Mecca who had property about which he was anxious who did not deposit it with Muhammad because of his renowned truthfulness and honesty."[335] With this last act taken care of, Ali left for Medina to join up with Muhammad and Abu Bakr. The Meccans would someday rue their mercy. Ali would soon become one of Islam's greatest slayers, a man who would hone his blade on the bodies of Meccans.

A handful of other followers joined Muhammad in Medina. The year was 622 A.D. Note it well. This year of the relocation of the Allah operation, known as the hejirah, would become year zero on the Islamic calendar. It was the point Muslims would come to regard as the beginning of history. All that came before 622 would be considered jahiliyya—the years of darkness, when chaos, ignorance, idol worship, and evil ruled mankind. What would banish that black and endless night of humanity? The light that Muhammad bore like a lantern. The light of Islam.

*　*　*

Meanwhile, tribal wars were a constant. One of Muhammad's Islamic biographers, Sarwat Saulat, thinks this strife went against Muhammad's grain. "The Prophet," he says, "was by his nature a human[e] and peace-loving person... [who] hated war."[336] Muhammad's life in Medina would tend to argue otherwise.

How Muhammad Built Militant Islam

WHAT DOES THIS ALL AMOUNT TO? In 622 A.D., when it looked as if Muhammad was about to be murdered in his hometown, Mecca, he and a handful of believers fled 280 miles through wild hills and desert to a tiny city with only a thousand inhabitants—most of them Jews[337]—Medina. There Muhammad and the Meccans who followed him lived on the food and lodging provided by their Medinaite hosts.

Those hosts were generous as could be. But in the long run, house guests become a burden. And their hosts long to kick them out. How would Muhammad insure that his hosts, the Ansar,[338] the helpers, would continue to house his crew?

Muhammad instinctively knew the biologically built-in rules of clever collectives, from bacterial societies and the immune system to human societies: he who gets gets more. He who loses is left out. Muhammad needed camels, sheep, land, date palms, oases, slaves, swords, and armor.[339] He needed these things to feed his followers, to give them the best weapons, and to give them pecking-order status, to give them prestige.[340] He needed consumer goods to make sure that the meme-team he preached would spread. He needed wealth and earthly possessions to build solidarity in the Muslim community. And he needed luxuries and the good things in life to pay his Medinaite hosts back for housing and supporting his "believers."

How would he manage to get his hands on these riches? What was he best equipped for? The hobby of the desert—killing. War. A constant stream of military wins. And how do you guarantee that you'll win? You pick on the little guy. You pick on someone who is helpless. Or someone who doesn't expect you to attack him.

The first technique that the One True Prophet chose to score wins and to bring in booty, to bring in loot, was simple: raid passing caravans then divvy up the loot.[341] Take advantage of the fact that these caravans were lightly guarded[342] and that the tradition of the desert was to give them safe passage.[343] God himself backed Muhammad in this switch to a murderous policy, this switch of Islam from a mere belief system to a military structure. As the Qur'an says, "Allah made it binding on the Muslims to fight in His way. Warfare is ordained for you, though you dislike it."[344] This revelation would prove vital to Islam's next 1,400 years.

war like (handwritten annotation)

Muhammad led his desert raids literally dressed to kill. As one of the most influential Islamic scholars of the 20th century, the Ayatollah Khomeini, put it, Muhammad "would place a helmet on his blessed head, don his coat of chain mail, and gird on a sword."[345] Ibn Ishaq, who wrote the first and most definitive Islamic biography of Muhammad just 150 years after Muhammad's death, explains that to down foes at a distance,[346] Muhammad also carried a bow and a full arrow case.[347] And Muhammad would eventually have nine swords in his personal weapons collection, many of them stripped from the hands and bodies of slain enemies.[348] But that would come later.

Jihad ordained (handwritten annotation)

624 A.D. was the year of what Ibn Ishaq calls the "Permission to Wage War," the permission to make Jihad.[349] Or, as Allah puts it in the Qur'an, "To those against whom war is made permission is given (to fight)."[350] There was one small problem. No one was making war against Muhammad and his followers. At least not yet. Despite this technicality, Allah offered the Muslims and their Medinaite helpers a special treat. Mecca, the Muslims' hometown, had humiliated the Prophet and his first followers. Now a Meccan camel caravan bringing home the profits of a luxury-goods transport mission to Syria[351] was about to pass near Medina. The owners of this caravan and of its cargo of treasure were Mecca's leading citizens, the folks whose ridicule and threats had turned Muhammad into a fugitive. This was a brilliant opportunity for plunder[352]... and for revenge.[353]

When Muhammad and his followers attacked the string of Meccan cargo camels, one of the caravan's leaders, a Meccan aristocrat, sent home for help. An army of a thousand men, seven hundred camels, and one hundred cavalry horses[354] heeded the caravan's call for military backup. This forced Muhammad to switch from mere raiding to full-scale war.[355]

According to Muhammad's Islamic biographers, the Muslims "were in a difficult test, they were going to face their own brothers, sons and relatives"[356]—they were about to go toe-to-toe with the people they'd grown up with back home in Mecca. And Muhammad was apparently gut-wrenchingly scared. He prayed his heart out, but his words were haunted by fear of defeat:

"O Allah, bring about what Thou hast promised to me. O Allah, if this small band of Muslims is destroyed, Thou will not be worshipped on this earth."[357]

Despite Muhammad's fears, one Islamic biographer says proudly, "The Messenger of Allah fought fiercely. He fought closely with the enemy and none was braver that day."[358] One of Islam's most prolific historians, the ninth-century scholar Muhammad ibn Jarir al-Tabari,[359] makes it plain that "The Messenger of God [Muhammad] killed many...at Badr."[360]

Though it wasn't easy, the untried army of Islam slammed the Meccans into "a back-breaking defeat."[361] And, like any other ancient soldiers, raiders, or pirates, Muhammad's troops stripped the corpses of the men they killed,[362] taking everything of value for themselves. The clothes, armor, and weapons stripped from just one downed man could be sold back in Medina for enough money to buy a small date palm grove.[363] It could elevate a man from poverty to wealth.

Even the Prophet participated in the gory plunder. Al-Tabari explains that Muhammad snatched a prized camel from one of his slain enemies at Badr, the "Mahri dromedary on which he used to go on raids."[364] Among the other spoils the Prophet grabbed was a sword that would become legendary for its magic powers—the sword of Dhu al-Faqar,[365] ripped from the body of "a pagan who died in the battle of Badr."[366] This captured weapon would eventually become "the most famous sword of Islam."[367]

To insult those he'd defeated, Muhammad had the bodies of his slain enemies tossed down the mouth of a deep well.[368] Meanwhile, Muhammad's men went on a rampage against the Meccans who still lived, cutting off legs, hands, arms, and heads as they hacked still living men to death. One Muslim fighter, Abdul-Rahman, encountered an old friend from Mecca among those who'd been unable to flee. The friend promised Abdul-Rahman a fortune in ransom if Rahman would spare his life and the life of his son. The Muslim fighter did his best to honor the man's wishes, but, to use his words, his fellow Muslims "formed a ring round us, and I tried to protect him, but a man struck off the leg of the son of Ummaya and he fell to the ground. Then Ummaya uttered a cry such as I had never heard before. I said to him, 'Save thyself. I can no longer help thee,' and the people fell upon them with their swords and killed them both." Ibn Ishaq adds a scarcely necessary conclusion: "the slaughter was great."[369]

But when it came to the few captives left alive, Muhammad was merciful. He had only two prisoners beheaded.[370] One of them, a former neighbor, asked Muhammad plaintively, "Who will look after my children,

Muhammad?"[371] The Prophet answered with a vicious "hellfire" and had the man's head hacked off.[372] Muhammad allowed the others to be ransomed. And each captive warrior too poor to pay ransom was forced to teach ten Muslims to read,[373] then was released.[374] Through this battle, the Battle of Badr,[375] Allah revealed a vital meme-hook, a meme's way of guaranteeing that it forever anchors a grappling iron in new minds. Allah set an example of what would happen to those who refuse Islam. He established what one Islamic source calls "the first installment of punishment for...denying the invitation to Islam."[376]

kill the infidel

Keep the phrase "punishment for...denying the invitation to Islam" in mind. It will come in handy later in this story.

Allah also delivered three other critical messages for the future, three other reproductive tricks of the Islamic meme, three other experiments Muhammad and his followers would test on behalf of Islam's rapidly evolving mass mind:

1. "It behoveth not a prophet that he should have captives until he hath greatly slaughtered in the land.'"[377]
2. "Allah guarantees that He will admit the Mujahid [the Muslim fighter] into Paradise if he is killed, otherwise He will return him to his home safely with rewards and war booty."[378]
3. And, in the words of Muhammad, "The head of...Islam... is the jihad."[379]

definitely not a peaceful religion

The Birth of the Meme Police

"Founders usually have a major impact on how the group defines and solves its external problem of surviving and growing, and how it will internally organize itself and integrate its own efforts. ... Since they started the group, they tend to impose their assumptions on the group and to cling to them until such time as they become unworkable or the group fails and breaks up. As new members and leaders come into the group, the founder's assumptions and beliefs will gradually be modified, but they will always have the biggest impact on what will ultimately be the group's culture."

—Edgar H. Schein,[380] specialist in organizational culture at MIT's Sloan School of Management

WHY WAS MUHAMMAD'S MOTLEY CREW of followers able to whomp the marrow out of the Meccans, a tribe with many generations of experience in warfare? One small part of the answer may come from prayer. Not from the powers of Allah, not from the will of God that prayer allegedly draws down to Earth. But from the ritual of prayer that Muhammad had adopted in roughly 621 A.D., the year before his relocation to Medina. It was a practice Muhammad had gotten either from the people of Yemen, the Sabeans,[381] or from Allah himself, depending on which account you trust.

In 621 A.D., three years before the Battle of Badr, Muhammad had experienced one of his strangest encounters with God—a face-to-face meeting in heaven. As Muhammad told the story in one of the Hadith[382]—the holy compilations of eyewitness accounts of Muhammad's life—he was lying down when "someone came to me and cut my body open from" his throat to his pubic bone. Muhammad explains that his heart was taken out and "was washed and filled (with belief)" from a golden bowl "and then returned to its original place."[383] But that was mere preparation. "Then," says Muhammad, "a white animal which was smaller than a mule and bigger than a donkey was brought to me."[384] On that white beast, Muhammad was taken on a tour by the angel Gabriel, a tour that climbed upward through the seven levels of heaven. At each level, Muhammad met a figure from religious history, most of them from the history of the Jews and the Christians—Adam, John the Prophet, Jesus, Joseph, Aaron, Moses, Abraham, and an Arab prophet, Idris. In the seventh heaven, Muhammad reports, "the prayers were enjoined on me: They were fifty prayers a day."[385] That's a whopping number. Then Muhammad, Gabriel, and the white beast began their descent to earth. On their return trip through the sixth heaven, Muhammad ran into Moses. As Muhammad recalls, "I passed by Moses who asked (me), 'What have you been ordered to do?' I replied, 'I have been ordered to offer fifty prayers a day.' Moses said, 'Your followers cannot bear fifty prayers a day, and by Allah, I have tested people before you, and I have tried my level best with Bani Israel (in vain). Go back to your Lord and ask for reduction to lessen your followers' burden.'"[386] So Muhammad turned the white beast around, headed back up to the seventh heaven, and asked God himself, Allah, for a reduction. Allah generously lowered the number of prayers per day to 40. But when Muhammad descended to the sixth heaven and ran into Moses again, Moses said the number of prayers was still more than followers could bear. So Muhammad went back upward and got a reduction to 30. Moses still thought this was too much. So Muhammad trekked back upward and got a reduction to five. Moses was still not happy. But Muhammad was afraid to go back for another bargaining session with Allah. He told Moses, "I have requested so much of my Lord that I feel ashamed, but I am satisfied now and surrender to Allah's Order."[387]

That's how Islam got its five prayers a day. But what does this have to do with the strength of Muhammad's followers in battle? More than you might think.

Military victory requires heavy-duty conformity enforcement. It requires discipline, obedience, and daily practice at working in sync with your fellow fighters. When men make choreographed muscular movements together over and over again, it gives them an enduring bond. It pulls them together tightly as components in a cohesive social group,[388] cells in a superorganism. The historian William McNeill, in his book *Keeping Together in Time: Dance and Drill in Human History*,[389] calls this social glue "muscular bonding."

Islam's five group-prayers a day are among Muhammad's cleverest meme-hooks, his most innovative conformity enforcers. They are also one of the Five Pillars of Islam.[390] Five times a day, 35 times a week, 1,825 times a year, men are required to gather in ranks and to show their absolute submission to Muhammad's revelations. "Submission" is one of the key meanings of the word

"Islam."[391] The faithful line up in rows, spread their prayer rugs, get down on their knees, and move as a single unit, pressing their foreheads to the ground, and bowing in unison to just one place, Mecca.[392] Says the Muslim website islamreligion.com, "The prayer connects the believers to God and the qibla connects the believers to one another. It has been said that if one could observe all the Muslims" in the world "at prayer we would be able to see lines of worshippers bowing and prostrating" all over the globe "like the petals of a flower opening and closing in unison."[393] Muslims in prayer are not just a disciplined unit isolated in a single mosque. They are following a central timetable whose orders circle the planet. Today that central timetable is available on your smartphone as an app.

Could these be practice sessions for the synchronized movements of soldiers in battle, soldiers all focused on one central goal? Could they train men who may never meet each other to operate in unison? Could they prepare men for the massively parallel processed coordination of peace and war, including modern urban guerrilla war, war with no central commander but with the centering and guidance of a powerful meme team, the form of warfare that would reveal itself in the Islamic "terrorism" of the early 21st century?

Here's a clue that the answer may be yes. Your prayers are most acceptable to Allah if you gather in a prayer group called a jama'ah,[394] a unity,[395] a community, or a party, a form of organization that shows up often in terrorist groups like the New York- and Pakistan-based Jamaat-ul-Fuqra[396] and the Asian-Pacific Jemaah Islamiyah.[397]

In many societies, ritual is practice for vital social activities. Polynesian men, for example, perform dance rituals in which they make movements that ape the coordinated paddling they have to do when taking their sleek boats out on the open sea to fish.[398] Anthropologist Mary Douglas believes that almost all the rituals of religion are exercises for the social reflexes that keep a culture together,[399] practice for what my book *The Genius of the Beast* calls the "infrastructure of habit." Like the practice for obedience to bureaucratic authority that Douglas feels underlies Catholic ritual. Are Islamic prayer rituals, too, preparation for coordination in peace and war? Or is that notion racist paranoia? Let's go back to Muhammad's story and see.

When we left off many pages ago, the year was 624 A.D. Only two years had passed since Muhammad had fled Mecca in fear for his life. Now, he'd trounced the Meccans in a bloody victory at the Battle of Badr and had added insult to injury by dumping the bodies of some of Mecca's most distinguished citizens in a well. He'd taken a big risk and had made the sort of "screw you" gesture, the sort of pecking order challenge, that can get you and your group obliterated.

So making the right decisions about how to assemble Muhammad's embryonic society would be vital to Islam's survival. Among the questions ahead of Muhammad and his God were these: to what extent would Islam use persuasion and to what extent would it use coercion as it assembled the first community of Islam? To what extent would it use words and to what extent would it use weapons? To what extent would it use fear and to what extent would it use passion, pleasure, stimulation, and imagination? To what extent would it use conformity and to what extent would it use diversity? What collective personality would Muhammad and his God, Allah, create? And how would they go about it?

When the Prophet was still glorying in his victory at the Battle of Badr, he made a decision that would stain Islam for generations to come. He chose the face of fierceness. He picked the path of military dictatorship. He picked the path of totalitarianism. Like Shaka Zulu, he chose to kill the opposition.

Muhammad's first step when he set out on the return trip from Badr to Medina, the town of a thousand where he and his followers were holed up, was a meme-campaign, a pecking-order propaganda offensive. He sent two messengers ahead of him, messengers "to bring the good news of victory granted to him by God and the killing of"[400] many a Meccan. To increase the pecking-order punch of this bulletin, the couriers listed the names of the distinguished Meccans they had killed.[401]

A poet in the audience—Ka'b—heard these names and was horrified. According to Ibn Ishaq, Muhammad's first biographer, Ka'b said, "Is this true? Did Muhammad actually kill these... men?"[402] "Those were the nobles of Arabia, the kings of mankind. By God, if Muhammad has vanquished these people, the interior of the earth is a better dwelling than the top of it."[403] Recounts Ibn Ishaq, the alarmed rhymer "left the town and went to Mecca"[404] 280 miles away. When he arrived, Ka'b recited "verses in which he bewailed the Quraysh who were thrown into the pit after having been slain at Badr."[405] One of Ka'b's verses read,

> Badr's mill ground out the blood of its people
> At events like Badr you should weep and cry.
> ...How many noble, handsome men,
> The refuge of the homeless were slain
> Liberal when the stars gave no rain.[406]

How many benefactors of Arab society had Muhammad killed and tossed into a pit as if they were garbage?

In Muhammad's eyes, these verses and Ka'b's trip to Mecca made the poet an enemy of God, one "who has hurt Allah and His Apostle."[407] "Who," he asked, "will rid me of"[408] this offending bard?

Two potential assassins stepped forward, but they were not just run-of-the-mill killers. One considered himself the poet's brother.[409] The other was his foster brother.[410] Neither shuddered at the idea of hacking a close family member to death. The only thing bothering them was whether they'd be forced to commit a Muslim sin. "O apostle of God," said one of the volunteers, "we shall have to tell lies."[411] Muhammad answered with a cold-hearted line he would use more than once as he rose in power: "Say what you like. You are absolved in the matter."[412] Dishonesty was permissible when it came to protecting "the religion of truth."[413] One face of the new culture's personality had just been revealed. One of its core memes had just been set in place. Lie to an enemy of God.

The two killers went to their brother the poet's house in the middle of the night and stood outside shouting to him to come out.[414] The poet woke suddenly, "jumping up in the bedsheet."[415] His wife was terrified. Don't worry. It's just my brother and my foster brother, said the poet.[416] This didn't calm his spouse, who swore that the voices outside were dripping with blood.[417] But Ka'b, the poet, spoke the words of a noble soul: "A generous man should respond to a call at night even if invited to be killed."[418]

Ka'b's words were prophetic. When he got outside, his brother and foster brother complimented Ka'b on the pomade in his hair and asked if they could smell it. Ka'b tilted his head, and one of the brothers grabbed the hair on both of Ka'b's temples tightly and shouted to his partner, "Smite the enemy of God!"[419] The two stabbed, pummeled, and sliced at their brother with their swords, but Ka'b's strength held up. What's more, he roared so loudly that lights went on in all the houses in the neighborhood.

It was time to finish the killing and get out before anyone could show up to stop the execution. One of the killers gave up on his sword, grabbed his dagger and, he says, "thrust it into the lower part" of Ka'b's body then "bore down upon it until I reached his genitals, and the enemy of God fell to the ground."[420]

Ka'b, the "enemy of God," was dead.

How did the killers feel about their deed? How did they feel about killing someone they had known all of their lives, someone with whom they shared close family ties? They were exultant. They extemporized poetry—a common practice in the Arab society of the day—bragging that they'd snuck up on Ka'b in the middle of the night and had used deception and dishonesty to snuff out his life. "Sword in hand we cut him down," said the poetry, "Ka'b's brother...beguiled him and brought him down with guile."[421] In other words, Ka'b's brothers killed the poet using lies and trickery. "Guile"—lies and trickery—would become a key tactic when it came to attacking those outside the circle of the devout, outside the circle of Islam. Someday it would be used on you and me.

prophetic

depraved religion

* * *

The next morning, when the brothers reported their accomplishment to Muhammad and word spread, many other followers of Muhammad spouted their own rap-like poetry to celebrate the murder. Crowed the Muslim rappers, the killers who'd fought an unarmed man, two against one, were "bold as lions." The cowardly killing was an act of courage, said the exuberant poets, because the killers were "seeking victory for the religion of their prophet."[422] Thus was murder "for the religion of the prophet" elevated to a virtue of the highest degree—one mark of the cultural strategies that would still be at work among extremists and jihadists in today's society.

The killing of Ka'b, the poet, could conceivably have been justified. Ka'b was encouraging an enemy. But this was just the beginning of Muhammad's clampdown on freedom of speech, his newest contribution to the evolving Muslim social structure, his policy of killing dissidents.

Said the Prophet to his men, "Fight everyone in the way of God and kill those who do not believe in God."[423] One of the next on the hit list was the leader of the Meccans. Muhammad sent two loyalists to sneak into Mecca and kill the city's leading citizen, Abu Sufyan. But one of the pair of assassins was recognized when he wormed his way back into his hometown, and was remembered as a longtime troublemaker. His name was Amr. When the Meccans spotted Amr, they rushed him before he could do any harm.[424]

But this did not deprive Amr of the privilege of "killing those who do not believe in God."[425] Amr and his companion ran out of town and hid in a cave. While Amr was laying low, he had a stroke of luck. A one-eyed shepherd with a single sheep came into Amr's cave to rest. Amr and the shepherd compared family backgrounds, found they had mutual friends, and carried on a schmoozy conversation. Then the shepherd did something he probably considered harmless. Before going to sleep, Amr reports, "he lay down beside me and lifting up his voice began to sing:

> I won't be a Muslim as long as I live,
> Nor heed to their religion give.[426]

Amr brags about how lustily he carried out Muhammad's order to do away with anyone who does "not believe in God."[427] "As soon as the *badu* [desert dweller][428] was asleep and snoring, I got up and killed him in a more horrible way than any man has [ever] been killed. I put the end of my bow in his sound eye, then I bore down on it until I forced it out at the back of his neck."[429] Note the sheer pride in killing someone with whom you have found common threads, someone you have pretended to befriend.

Then came more lessons in killing those who disagreed with Islam, more murders, including the assassination by night of a wealthy and influential Jew, Abu Rafi, "the chief of the Jews of Khaibar."[430] Abu Rafi's crime? The usual: dissent. In Muhammad's opinion, Abu Rafi was "inciting people against him."[431] What's more, Abu Rafi had supported Ka'b the poet.[432] But the story is told in unbeatable detail by al-Tabari, one of the two earliest chroniclers of Muhammad's life. Here's how al-Tabari phrases it: "The Messenger of God," Muhammad, "sent some of the Ansar, the hosts and helpers of the Muslims"

> against Abu Rafi' the Jew, who was in the Hijaz. Abu Rafi' used to injure and wrong the Messenger of God. He lived in his stronghold in the Hijaz. When the Muslim party drew close to it, as the sun was setting and the people were bringing their flocks back, … [the commander of the group Muhammad had sent to perform the assassination] said to the others, "Stay where you are, and I will go and ingratiate myself with the doorkeeper, in the hope of gaining entrance." He went forward, and when he was close to the door, he wrapped himself up in his cloak as though he were relieving himself. Everybody else had gone in, and the doorkeeper called to him, "You there, if you want to come in, come in, because I want to shut the door." "I went in," he said, "and hid myself in a donkey pen.
>
> When everybody had come in, the man shut the door and hung up the keys on a wooden peg. I went to the keys, took them, and opened the door. Abu Rafi' had company that evening in some upper rooms, and when his guests left I went up to him. Every time I

opened a door, I shut it again behind me from inside, saying to myself, 'If they become aware of me, they will not be able to reach me before I kill him.' When I reached him, he was in a dark room along with his family. As I did not know where he was in the room, I said, 'Abu Rafi'!' and he said, 'Who is that?' I rushed toward the sound and gave him a blow with my sword, but I was in a state of confusion and did not achieve anything. He gave a shout, and I left the room but remained close at hand. I then went in again and said, 'What was that noise, Abu Rafi'?' 'God damn it,' he said, 'there is a man in the house who has just struck me with his sword.' Then I hit him and covered him with wounds, but I could not kill him, so I thrust the point of my sword into his stomach until it came out through his back. At that, I knew that I had killed him, and I opened the doors one by one until I reached a flight of stairs. Thinking that I had reached the ground, I put my foot out but fell into a moonlit night and broke my leg. I bound it up with my turban and moved on. Finally, finding myself sitting by the door, I said to myself, 'By God, I will not leave tonight until I know whether I have killed him or not.' When the cock crowed, the announcer of his death stood upon the wall and said, 'I announce the death of Abu Rafi', the profit-maker of the people of Hijaz.' I went to my companions and said, 'Deliverance! God has killed Abu Rafi'.' Then I went to the Prophet and told him, and he said, 'Stretch out your leg!' When I stretched it out, he stroked it, and it was as though I had never had anything wrong with it."[433]

This death upset a 120-year-old fellow Jew in Medina, who sang a verse praising the upright behavior of the clan of the victim.[434] Abu Afak's verses bore no criticism of Muhammad or of Islam. They were simply words of lamentation for the death of a decent man. But Muhammad was not pleased.

Using his usual wording, Muhammad called for a volunteer. "Who," he asked, "will deal with this rascal for me?" The man who took on the challenge went by night and found Abu Afak sleeping out in the open in his yard.[435] Says the Islamic historian Ibn Sa'd, the killer "placed the sword on his [victim's] liver and pressed it till it reached his bed."[436] The next day the assassin sang celebratory verses advertising the glory of what he'd done. In those triumphant lines he let his listeners know that he'd killed a man too old to defend himself and had done it in the most cowardly of ways, a way that was becoming a Muslim trademark—sneaking up on the victim in his sleep:[437] "You gave the lie to God's religion...", said the murderer. The punishment for this offense? A Muslim[438] "gave you a thrust in the night saying 'Take that Abu Afak in spite of your age!'"[439]

Next on the hit list was a mother of five, a mother still suckling an infant. Her sin was showing what the earliest Muslim historians called "disaffection" with all the bloodshed in her neighborhood. In her poetry, she dared warn that it was a bad idea to hang around with a leader whose hobby seemed to be "the killing of your chiefs." Do you follow him, her poetry said, simply to grab your share of the plunder that comes in after his violent raids on passing caravans? Are you making the mistake of following this "stranger who is none of yours" out of sheer greed, "like a hungry man waiting for a cook's broth"?[440] Then the poetess suggested that Muhammad be treated the way he was treating others:

> Is there no man of pride who would attack him by surprise
> And cut off the hopes of those who expect aught from him?[441]

Reports the first biographer of Muhammad, Ibn Ishaq, "When the apostle heard what she had said" he repeated his usual line, 'Who will rid me of Marwan's daughter?'"[442] The response to this by now familiar phrase was instant. One of Muhammad's followers[443] went to the poetess' house in the middle of the night, found her with her five "children...sleeping around her," felt in the dark to find the baby suckling at her breast, laid the baby aside on the bed, then rammed "his sword in her chest till it pierced up to her back."[444]

When the murder was complete, all was not well in the killer's heart. He was worried that God would punish him for this cowardly act. Says Ibn Ishaq, the assassin went to Muhammad first thing in the morning to ask if he'd brought the wrath of the Almighty down on his head. Not at all, said Muhammad, "You have helped God and His apostle."[445] What's more, explained Muhammad, ending a life in the name of Allah is a trivial matter, even if the victim is a mother of five. Declared Muhammad, "Two goats won't butt their heads together about her."[446] A killing in the name of Islam is so inconsequential that it won't even rile farm animals...much less bring down the fury of Allah. Muhammad had just added another key conviction to his growing weave of cultural concepts, his weave of memes—killing a critic of Islam is nothing to get upset about. In fact, it's the default mode. It should be automatic. And it's glorious. More about that default mode in a minute.

Muhammad's brutality achieved its purpose. At first, the clan of the poetess was in an uproar over her murder.[447] But Muhammad sent the killer to bully her kids. "Withstand me if you can," he told the orphans, "don't keep me waiting."[448] The daughter of Marwan's extended family got the message: don't complain, threaten, or criticize Islam. Convert or risk a bloody death. Says Ibn Ishaq, "The day after Bint Marwan was killed the men of" her tribe "became Muslims." Why did they switch to a God that had done away with their mother? Answers Ibn Ishaq, "They saw the power of Islam."[449]

Murder was proving to be an effective recruitment strategy for the infant social structure of Islam.

Everybody Needs a Nerd

> The Jews, who are the nation of pigs and monkeys, are nothing but a source of evil, corruption, tribulation and war. Hatred against the Muslims is inherited by every generation of Jews who in turn teach it to their children. Our enmity and hostility against them is based on our faith. The Jews have never and will never lower the banner of war against us Muslims; it is a war between truth and falsehood, belief and disbelief. It is a war between the truth of Islaam and the falsehood of Judaism. The Jews will never stop adding fuel to the fire of war, nor will they ever stop plotting against us. Whenever the fire of one battle is extinguished, they light another. ... all their men should be beheaded, their properties be seized and distributed among the Muslims and... their women and offspring be held captive. ... This is the judgment of Allaah with regard to the Jews.
>
> —Shaykh 'Abdul-'Azeez Al-Qaari[450]
> Imam of Masjid Quba and professor of Tafsir Quranic recitation at the Islamic University of Medina

BEAR WITH ME WHILE I GIVE YOU a story from my 1995 book *The Lucifer Principle*. You'll need it as a tool. Here goes. Ready?

Researcher Richard Savin-Williams spent a season watching summer campers interact. In June, the bunkmates met for the first time. For roughly an hour, the campers felt each other out, probing each other's strengths and weaknesses, deciding who would be friends with whom. Then they quickly sorted themselves into a superorganism with a head, limbs and a tail. One camper became the "alpha male," the dominant individual, the group leader. Another became the "bully," a big, strong brute nobody particularly liked. A third became the "joker," everybody's goodnatured sidekick. And one became the "nerd," the unathletic, overlyeager sort that everyone else felt free to kick around. ...Each boy had taken his place in a kind of preordained social blueprint.

Just how preordained that blueprint was and how much of his potential each boy had to sacrifice to assume his role became clear when another researcher tried an experiment. The scientist assembled a cabin composed entirely of "leaders," boys who had been dominant, "alpha" males in their old groups. Very quickly, the new cluster sorted itself out according to the familiar pattern. One of the leaders took charge. Another became the bully. A third became the group joker. And one of the formerly commanding lads even became the new group's nerd.

Yes, one of the former cocky, powerful leaders became the equivalent of a runt chicken in a barnyard, the miserable creature everyone else feels free to peck. But back to our text:

When the researchers went through the scientific literature to find other data related to their work, they discovered that studies of Chicago gangs in the 1920s had shown these long-gone groups arranging themselves according to an almost identical unconscious plan. The gangmembers of a bygone era also had their leaders, bullies, jokers and nerds.

Each individual took up a position in the superorganism's unfolding structure. And each shaped his personality to fit the spot he landed in.[451]

The point? Every gang has its leader, its bully, its joker, and its nerd. The same is true in the pecking order of societies, the pecking order of nations, and the pecking order of civilizations. Every pecking order needs its scapegoats, its victims, its easy targets. Every pecking order needs its nerds. Muhammad would take advantage of this fact. In spades.

*   *   *

Why are nerds so important? Why would they be crucial to the growth of Islam in its early days? And why would they be central to reviving Islam's strength 1,312 years later? Because they're vital to social solidarity,[452] to keeping the gang from tearing itself apart when it runs into tough sledding. And they're vital to something equally important, to the group's confidence. To its sense that it can whup the stuffing out of others.

The role of the nerd in gluing a group together and upping its sense of superiority goes all the way back to our animal past. It's built into the primitive parts of our brain. Give one lab animal a hard time, and he takes out his woes on another animal smaller than he is. He mauls the lesser animal ferociously. We know this from research on the Frustration Aggression Hypothesis, research that began in 1939 at Yale.[453] But how does the principle of taking your problems out on someone (or some-rat) else work when you've got more than just one rodent with a problem? How does it work when you've got a troubled group or gang?

If you put seven rats on an electrified grid and turn up the current, the pain is intense. Do the rats huddle together and give each other comfort? Do they become kinder, more compassionate, and more caring? Not on your life. The maddened animals quickly feel out which is the weakest among them. Then the six strongest turn on their most feeble hot-plate-mate, and maul him. Viciously.[454] The gang finds its scapegoat. It finds its nerd!!

Nerds are so important that if you remove the animal who's being beaten, battered, and abused, you don't stop the rain of battering. A group deprived of its scapegoat simply picks the weakest animal left in the bunch and begins the nerd-bashing all over again. Nerd-bashing is, says primatologist Frans de Waal, a primal, potent, and apparently biologically built-in bonding mechanism.[455]

Picking on the helpless doesn't do anything to lower the hot plate's temperature. But apparently it eases the pain. And it transforms a negative into a positive. Evidence indicates it ups testosterone levels and turns a moment of shared torment into a cement that bonds the six strongest rats together.[456] Yes, violence against the weakest among you can bring your group together. It can provide social cohesion. Mother Nature can be appallingly cruel. And so could Muhammad.

In 624 A.D. Muhammad found his nerd, his scapegoat, his easy target. He found the demon-that-bonds...he found an enemy. An enemy too small to fight back. But that's not all. This was a demon that, when attacked, would deliver up rich rewards. Especially once Muhammad learned how to use his scapegoat to best advantage.

*   *   *

Muhammad's successful Battle of Badr had just ended, and the Prophet's murders of protesters, poets, and satirists had done their job.[457] They'd "cast terror" into the hearts of the citizens of Medina. Specifically, says Muhammad's first biographer, Ibn Ishaq, they'd "cast terror among the Jews, and there was no Jew in Medina who did not fear for his life."[458] The "fear" "instilled in the Jews" was so great, says the Muslim biographer Muhammad Haykal, "that none of them dared leave his house."[459] Why were the Jews in particular frightened by the string of political assassinations? Like many a dissident before and after them, the murdered male poets, Ka'b and the 120-year-old Abu Afak, were Jewish. So were Abu Rafi', the man with the stronghold in the Hijaz, and Marwan's daughter, the assassinated poetess with five children.

The morning after the murder of the poet Ka'b, the Prophet took a giant step beyond individual killings and called for genocide. "Whoever of the Jews falls into your hands," he said, "kill him."[460] The result? According to ibn Ishaq,

> "Thereupon …Mas'ud leapt upon …Sunayna, a Jewish merchant with whom…[he] had social and business relations and killed him. … [His older brother, who wasn't a follower of Muhammad] began to beat him, saying, 'You enemy of God, [why] did you kill him when much of the fat on your belly comes from his wealth?' Muhayissa answered, 'Had the one who ordered me to kill him [Muhammad] ordered me to kill you I would have cut your head off. …[His older brother] replied, 'By God, if Muhammad had ordered you to kill me would you have killed me?' He [the younger brother] said, 'Yes, by God, had he ordered me to cut off your head I would have done so.' He [the older brother] exclaimed, 'By God, a religion which can bring you to this is marvelous!' and he became a Muslim."[461]

From that moment on, the Jews would play a special role in Islamic history. So would the "marvelous" appeal of killing.

* * *

Muhammad rapidly discovered that Jews could be used for more than mere practice in homicide. In 624 A.D., he was running low on cash.[462] So the Prophet staged a provocation. He went to the marketplace of a tribe of Jewish jewelers and goldsmiths[463] on the outskirts of Medina, the Banu Qaynuqa, and demanded that the Jews convert to Islam or face "the vengeance" with which Allah had slaughtered the losers in the Battle of Badr.[464] The Jewish Banu Qaynuqa refused to switch religions[465] and tried to tough it out. Said their leaders, "O, Muhammad, ...do not deceive yourself because you encountered a people with no knowledge of war and got the better of them; for by God if we fight you, you will find that we are real men."[466]

With that statement, Muhammad claimed that the Jews had declared war[467] and besieged the quarters of the jewelers and of their families for 15 days.[468] The Jewish tribe was not able to live up to its brave words and surrendered unconditionally.[469]

The minute the Jews gave up, says the classic Muslim historian al-Tabari, Muhammad "wanted to kill them."[470] Horrified by Muhammad's zeal for mass murder, a chief of one of the local Medina tribes—one of the tribes who had ponied up the cost of hosting the Muslims and who had fought alongside Muhammad and his followers in their risky camel-caravan raids[471]—demanded that Muhammad treat the Jewish captives well. They were, he said, his allies.[472]

Muhammad turned his back on this Medinaite aristocrat and pointedly ignored him. So the tribal leader grabbed Muhammad by "the collar of the apostle's robe."[473] To quote the ninth-century Islamic historian al-Tabari:

> "The Messenger of God said, 'Let me go!'—he was so angry that they could see shadows in his face. Then he said, 'Damn you, let me go! He [the tribal leader calling for mercy] replied, 'No, by God, I will not let you go until you treat my mawali [friends and allies[474]] well. Four hundred men without armour and three hundred with coats of mail, who defended me from the Arab and the non-Arab alike, and you would mow them down in a single morning? By God I do not feel safe and am afraid of what the future may have in store."[475]

That fear would prove to be prophetic. But Muhammad was forced to give up his publicly announced project of killing all the Jews, and finally spat an answer to the local chief, "You can have them.[476] ...Let them go; may Allah curse them, and may he curse" you.[477]

But merely letting the Jews go free was not enough for the Prophet of Mercy.[478] Says al-Tabari, Muhammad went back on his word and "gave orders to expel" the Jews.[479] He ordered an ethnic cleansing.

Though Muhammad had gained a reputation for honesty in his early days as a trader, double-dealing with Jews was apparently OK. How can we tell? Allah provided Muhammad with a hefty bonus for breaking his word. Says al-Tabari, "God gave their [the Jews'] property as booty to his Messenger [Muhammad] and the Muslims."[480] This holy gift of loot included weapons, goldsmithing tools,[481] and in all likelihood a small treasure of gold.

What's more, it wasn't really Muhammad who uprooted an entire tribe from their homes and "decreed exile for them."[482] It was God. Explains the Qur'an, "Allah...is He who got out the Unbelievers among the People of the Book from their homes.... They thought that their fortresses would defend them from Allah! But the (wrath of) Allah came to them from quarters from which they little expected (it) and cast terror into their hearts..... "[483] The Qur'an follows up this assertion with a threat that resounds to our very day: "Take warning then o ye with eyes (to see)! If anyone resists Allah verily Allah is severe in Punishment."[484]

The lesson wasn't lost on Muhammad. Trouncing an easy target, a scapegoat, can give you wealth, standing, and solidarity. And pounding your scapegoat in theatrically brutal ways can frighten the pants off of bigger targets...a strategic insight Muhammad would use to its utmost three years later.

*   *   *

But first came further lessons in the creative use of nerds and scapegoats. In 625 A.D. Muhammad would fight—and lose—the Battle of Uhud, a battle in which the wives of the victorious Meccans would make anklets, necklaces, and pendants out of the ears and noses of the defeated Muslim corpses.[485] Defeat is dangerous. Allies flee from a group that's lowered to the bottom of the pecking order. And the Muslims were about to take a pecking-order tumble. A big one. One that would force Muhammad to create one of his most powerful innovations.

The Value of Rigged Victories

> "The leaders of our religion were all soldiers,
> commanders and warriors. ...They killed. ... This idea
> of turning the other cheek has been wrongly attributed
> to Jesus (peace be unto him); it is those barbaric
> imperialists that have attributed it to him. Jesus was
> a prophet, and no prophet can be so illogical."[486]
> —Ayatollah Khomeini,
> the founding father of today's Iran

MUHAMMAD HAD ESTABLISHED the collective personality of his people, a personality that would call for justice, charity, and care for the poor—as long as those poor, those widows and orphans, were obedient Muslims. These were important memes. But Muhammad's "complete system of life"[487] would also encourage five less admirable emotions:

- anger, a word that shows up 63 times[488] in just one of the Hadith—one of the six holy books of eyewitness accounts of Muhammad's life. The characters who show the most anger in the Hadith are Muhammad...and God.
- Fear, a word that shows up 126 times.[489]
- Punishment—the word "punish" shows up 284 times.[490]
- Obedience—"obey" appears 141 times.[491]
- and fighting—"fight" pops up 291 times.[492]

Muhammad was a harsh man creating a harsh culture. But his severity wasn't entirely his choice. He needed it to survive in a hostile world. Which brings us back to our story. In 625 A.D.,[493] one year after the Battle of Badr, the Meccans, grieving over their losses, put on their helmets, donned their armor, strapped on their swords, and headed toward Medina bent on revenge[494] against the holy gang-leader they called "the highwayman."[495] The women of Mecca, deeply embittered over the loss of their husbands, fathers, and brothers at the Battle of Badr, came to stand in the back of the battlefield and literally cheer their men on.

This would be the Prophet's second full-scale battle. And Muhammad was up for the challenge. "It is not fitting that a Prophet who has put on his armour should put it aside until he has fought,"[496] he said. But Muhammad didn't win this battle. Far from it. And his loss would lead to one of the greatest recruiting tools in the history of belief systems.

Muhammad stationed his troops with their backs to a mountain—the mountain of Uhud. But this position had a critical weakness. Behind the Muslims was a pass through which they could easily be attacked from the rear. But Muhammad was no dummy. He positioned 50 archers to block this gorge, then turned his attention to the enemy.[497]

Early in the battle, Muhammad's troops drove their foes into what looked like a panicky retreat. Since plunder is one of the rewards of violence, especially for makers of jihad,[498] Muhammad's men stopped to pluck as many clothes,[499] arms, and treasures as they could from the bodies and from the abandoned equipment of the fleeing enemy. But the archers stationed at the pass realized that all of the good stuff would be gone long before they could get to it. So they ran down to the battlefield to scoop up their share of the prizes before the battlefield could be picked clean.[500] This was a big mistake. The enemy cavalry doubled around, threaded through the abandoned pass, and descended on Muhammad's troops from the rear.

Muhammad was only 44 years old,[501] but he was overweight, was weakening with age, and was born down by the two coats of mail he'd donned before the battle.[502] None of that reduced his appetite for bloodshed. He fired arrow after arrow at the Meccans until his bow broke.[503] Then he was hit in the face with a rock that smashed both of his front teeth, drove two links of his helmet's iron strap deep into his cheek,[504] knocked him off his feet, and sent the blood pouring down his cheeks and chin.[505] "How can a people prosper who have stained their prophet's face with blood,"[506] he complained angrily.

A rumor that the Prophet had been killed spread among the fighters of Islam, and the Muslim soldiers lost their nerve, panicked, and fled. After most of the Muslims had left the field, one of the Meccan enemies discovered that the Prophet was still alive and charged on his horse toward Muhammad, determined to finish what the rock had begun.

Muhammad, weak and tottering, but with a legendary grip of steel,[507] rammed a spear at the attacker's neck and sent him tumbling from his horse's back with a wound that would kill him shortly after the battle was over.[508] Despite this gory gesture, the Muslims lost the battle, and lost it ignominiously.

To celebrate their victory and to literally taste revenge, the women of the Meccans, who had stood behind their men playing drums and cheerleading them on during the fight, went through the battlefield cutting the ears and noses off of Muslim corpses and turning "them into anklets, collars" and "pendants."[509] One cut the liver out of the corpse of one of Muhammad's uncles, Hamza,[510] Islam's first military commander, whose ferocity in caravan raids and in battle against the Meccans[511] had earned him the nickname The Lion of Islam. The Meccan matriarch chewed on The Lion of Islam's liver, tried to swallow it, found it too tough, and was forced to spit it out.[512] But she made her point. The beaten Muslims were too weak to stop this gruesome humiliation.

This is the world in which Islam was born. The brutality of the Arab desert's culture, along with Muhammad's humorless, rigid, kill-'em-if-they-sneeze personality, may explain why early Islam was one heck of a mean meme.

But Muhammad would derive a brilliant meme-hook from this defeat.

*　*　*

At Uhud many of Muhammad's troops had become discouraged and lain down their arms or had fled the battlefield.[513] What's worse, they'd abandoned Muhammad on the field of battle and had left him to fend for himself with only six bodyguards.[514] How could Muhammad make sure this never happened again? How could he insure that his men would stand their ground even if it meant certain death? At this crucial point, Allah came to the rescue. He gave Muhammad a new meme-hook, a startlingly original one. Those who stand firm in battle, who charge under impossible circumstances, who refuse to retreat, who kill no matter what the obstacle, and who are killed while "fighting in the cause of Allah,"[515] said Allah, will be rewarded with something that's worth more than earthly booty. They'll be given a prize conceived by a clever meme—a towering position in an invisible world. They'll be martyrs and will go to paradise.[516] But that's not all.

Explained Muhammad, "When your brethren were smitten at the battle of Uhud, Allah put their spirits in the crops of green birds which go down to the rivers of Paradise, eat its fruit and nestle in lamps of gold in the shade of the Throne [of Allah]."[517] But rivers, fruits, and lamps are boring. The paradise of the Christians was one of the most sleep-inducing retirement homes the world had ever seen. Or not seen, as the case may be. You woke up in the morning, grabbed your harp, gathered with others on a cloud, and sang God's praises. All day long. What an unendurable way to spend eternity. What a hell in the clouds. Muhammad needed something more, something whose motivational power would be intense and overwhelming. Something that would rouse men to a fever. A killing fever. What could that something possibly be?

How about women. Girls. Virgins. Sex. That's where innovation came in. Major innovation. Muhammad said that "chairs made of pearl are arranged for the martyrs and the maidens with big lustrous eyes will get down from their upstairs rooms... Which are made of green emerald and red ruby."[518] These "large-eyed maidens"[519] will be more delicious than anything you've ever seen on Earth.[520] They will be "beautiful,"[521] "full-breasted,"[522] "eternally young," with "wide and beautiful/lovely eyes"[523] and "eyes like pearls."[524] Yet they will look at you with "modest gazes."[525] In fact, they will look only at you and no other man. Or, as the Muslim website Islam The True Religion of One God puts it, quoting from holy scriptures:

> The Houris (hoors/hoor al-Ayn) have variously been described as being "chaste females," "restraining their glances," "modest gaze," "wide and beautiful/lovely eyes," "like pearls," "untouched / with hymen unbroken by sexual intercourse," "virgins," "non-menstruating/ urinating/defecating and child-free," "voluptuous/full-breasted," "with large, round breasts which are not inclined to hang," "companions of equal age"... "pure," "beautiful," "white," "revirginating," [and of] "splendid beauty."[526]

What's more, these heavenly girls will be "hairless except the eyebrows and the head"[527] and "so beautiful, pure and transparent [that] the marrow of the bones of their legs will be seen through the bones and the flesh."[528] Then there's the number of girls you'll receive. The precise total has been controversial, but the imam of the Sacred Mosque in Mecca, Usaamah Khayyaat, reassures you that you "will have seventy-two Women of Paradise."[529] Hot diggity.

Yes, Muhammad did it. He added a new incentive to an old idea—paradise. He offered intercourse in the cushiest place around—the palace of God. He crafted the first *Playboy* centerfold heaven. Or, to put it in offensive but accurate language, Muhammad put pussy in paradise.

All those girls you couldn't get on Earth? All those girls who ignored you. All those girls whose fathers thought you were trash. All those girls whose bride price you couldn't afford? Forget them. Girls beyond your highest dreams were available to you in the halls of heaven. Every sexual fantasy you'd ever imagined would become a reality in the palace of Allah.

And how do you get an express ticket to this lust-engorged paradise? "Paradise lies in the shadows of the swords."[530] You kill and are killed in battle. Specifically, you kill unbelievers.

Worldviews can concoct remarkable fantasies. And those fantasies can produce astonishing deeds. Deeds that a mere 20 years later would change the world. But back to Muhammad's pickle—how to wipe out the stain of defeat at Uhud.

There was one more answer near at hand. Pick on the nerds! Muhammad claimed that God had whispered a message in his ear—that the Jewish Banu Nadir tribe a walking distance from Medina planned to kill him by rolling a stone from a roof above him while he sat with his back to a wall.[531] When a Jewish leader, Huyayy, was told that Muhammad was using this fantasy as a pretext in Medina to recruit every able-bodied male for a full-scale military assault on his tribe, he sloughed it off as "a clever trick of Muhammad's."[532] He didn't believe that the Muslims could be roused to battle by a mere imagined assassination attempt.

But Huyayy was wrong. When there was an opportunity to get rich by stealing other people's goods, even the flimsiest excuse would do. Especially when those other people were too small in number to resist. Muhammad roused the men of Medina to a righteous fury, then "ordered them [the believers in Islam] to prepare for war and to march against"[533] the Banu Nadir. The men of the Muslim community strapped on their armor, their bows, their arrow cases, and their swords and marched off to the exurb of Medina that housed the unsuspecting Jewish clan.

To quote Ibn Ishaq, when Muhammad and his army approached their homes:

> "The Jews took refuge in their forts and the apostle ordered that the palm trees should be cut down and burnt, and they [the besieged Banu Nadir] called out to him, 'Muhammad, you have prohibited wanton destruction and blamed those guilty of it. Why then are you cutting and burning down our palm trees?'[534]

The Qur'an supplies the answer. It says about the vandalism, "Whether ye cut down (o ye Muslims!) the tender palm trees or ye left them standing on their roots it was by leave of Allah and in order that He might cover with shame the rebellious transgressors. ... Allah gives power to His apostles over any He pleases: and Allah has power over all things."[535] In other words, God cut down the trees using the Muslims as his saws and axes. He did it to humiliate the Jews. And God could do far more damage to anyone he wished, including, way, way down the line, you and me. Al-Tabari picks up the story from there.

> "The Messenger of Allah besieged the Banu Nadir for fifteen days
> until he had reduced them to a state of utter exhaustion"[536]

The Jews had allies who had sworn to come to their defense in affairs of this kind. But the rules of social learning machines, the rules of group IQs, drive allies away from losers. Social learning machines work on rules called Darwinian algorithms. Darwinian algorithms are one of the key tools we use to make supercomputers smart. We construct neural nets in these computers. Then we power those nets with Darwinian algorithms. The result is artificial intelligence.

In a neural net, clusters of nodes compete for resources and attention. The groups of nodes that show they have a handle on the problem of the moment are showered with resources, with electrical current and with active connections to others.[537] These active connections are the machine equivalent of popularity and influence. The nodes that show they don't have a clue are shunned. They are deprived of resources and, most important, stripped of attention, influence and allies. A line from Jesus sums up the Darwinian algorithm perfectly: "To he who hath it shall be given. From he who hath not, even what he hath shall be taken away."[538] That's one of the cruelest statements in the New Testament.

You can see this vicious Darwinian learning algorithm at work in the pecking order among barnyard chickens. The chicken who is on top gets attention.[539] She's popular. What's more, others copy her. She has influence. But she who is on the bottom gets attention only when some superior chicken wants someone to peck. Someone to torture and humiliate. We shun losers. And we flock to winners. That's the learning machine rule at work.

So when none of their allies appeared to help the Jews, "God cast terror," Muhammad's favorite emotion, "into their hearts."[540] The Jews of the Banu Nadir gave up without resistance. Says Ibn Ishaq, they pleaded for a simple ethnic cleansing instead of the alternative, genocide. "They asked the apostle to deport them and to spare their lives on condition that they could retain all of their property which they could carry on their camels, except their armour, and he [Muhammad] agreed."[541]

The Jews tried to carry away as many of their possessions as they could under the circumstances.[542] Says Ibn Ishaq, "Men were destroying their houses down to the lintel of the door which they put upon the back of their camels."[543] And they were forced to accept this mass expulsion with as much dignity as they could muster. The Jews put their families on their camels' backs, and "carried off the women and children and property with tambourines and pipes and singing-girls playing behind them. ...(They went) with such pomp and splendour as had never been seen from any tribe in their day."[544] Good for them.

This act of nerd-bashing produced a hefty payoff: a reversal of the abject state Muhammad and his men had been in when they were trounced and humiliated at the Battle of Uhud. Bonanza number one: the Banu Nadir "left their property to Muhammad and it became his personal possession, which he could dispose of as he wished."[545] That property included items of tremendous value to a prophet of war—"weapons and mail coats" and rich oases.[546] The income from the Jews' date palms alone supported Muhammad's "dependents for the whole year...[and] whatever was saved from it was spent." For what? For "horses and weapons."[547]

Bonus number two: bragging rights. The right to crow with all your might over the glory of your violence. Like 1990s gangsta rappers, the Arabs of Muhammad's time were renowned for their poetry. It's in poetry that they advertised the prizes that come to those who intimidate or kill in the name of Allah. And it's in poetry that they warned about the losses of those who refuse to knuckle under. After the ethnic cleansing of the Banu Nadir, one Muslim warrior, his chest puffed up with pride, recited these lofty verses about obeying the will of what he calls "God the Kind, God the Most Kind"[548]:

> Oh you who foolishly threaten him [Muhammad]
> ...Do you not fear the basest punishment
> ...That you may be thrown beneath his swords
> As Ka'b al-Ashraf [the Jewish poet] was
> ...When...He [Allah] sent down Gabriel with a gracious revelation
> To His servant [Muhammad] about his killing.[549]

Another exultant warrior crowed enthusiastically about Islam's payoff to the greedy—loot and plunder:

> "The spoil which God gave the apostle from the people of the towns [the Jews] belongs to God and His apostle. What the Muslims gallop against with horses and camels and what is captured by force of

arms belongs to God and his apostle...and what the apostle gives you take."[550]

The subtext of all this ancient Islamic poetry and prose was simple. It was a key meme that militant Muslims would use for the next 1,400 years. God gives money, goods, and sex—a subject we'll get even further into in a minute— to those who are willing to kill in the name of Allah. God delivers the goods to those who make war. He delivers the profit of plunder to those who murder on his behalf. As the Qur'an puts it, "with Allah are profits and spoils abundant."[551] What's more, God adds a bonus. He gives the hormonal boost that exalts a winner. He gives the glee of victory. He gives a boost of testosterone.[552] God also grants the ultimate learning-machine prize—a lift in the pecking order, a lift in power, in prestige, and in influence.

Part of that pecking-order lift would come from a sense of superiority to a permanent class of underdogs and enemies: the Jews. Jews would remain Islam's nerds, its easy targets and one of its key sources of bonding, cohesion, and social glue, for the next 1,400 years.

No, Islam's anti-Semitism did not begin with the founding of modern Israel in 1948. It started with Muhammad.

*   *   *

Meanwhile, the Jews of the Banu Nadir took refuge in Syria and in the town of Khaibar.[553] But Khaibar and Syria too would soon be threatened by the advance of a new picture of the invisible world, by the advance of a new social learning machine, by the hunger of a new superorganism eager to compete in the pecking order of groups, a new superorganism driven by a new team of memes. Khaibar and Syria would soon be utterly changed by the advance of militant Islam.

Off With Their Heads

"The person who governs the Muslim community
must always have its interests at heart and not his own.
This is why Islam has put so many people to death:
to safeguard the interests of the Muslim community.
Islam has obliterated many tribes because they were
sources of corruption and harmful to the welfare of
Muslims."

—Ayatollah Khomeini, the founding father of today's
Islamic Republic of Iran[554]

AFTER TWO ETHNIC cleansings and a call for genocide issued by the Prophet himself, the Jews got the message:[555] they'd become a permanent target. And if they didn't do something about it they'd become an arrow-mulched bull's-eye. According to one Islamic biographer, A.S. Muhammad Abdul Hai, the latest group of Hebrews that the Prophet tossed out of their homes in Medina, the Banu Nadir,[556] working from their refugee camp in Khaibar, "hatched a dire conspiracy against Muslims. They instigated nearby tribes against Muslims and made Quraysh [the leading tribe of Muhammad's hometown, Mecca] agree for a battle,"[557] a battle to wipe out Islam utterly.[558]

In fact, it appears that the Meccans were eager to attack the Muslims with or without Jewish instigation. One Meccan leader looked forward to the fight with relish. Making "an end of Muhammad and his men," he said, would bring "immortal fame."[559] He'd turn out to be wrong. Dead wrong.

The Muslims got wind of the Meccan attack weeks in advance, and couldn't figure out how to deal with it.[560] Then one of Muhammad's followers, a Persian, came up with a bright idea. He recommended that Muhammad protect his men from face-to-face combat by using a Persian defensive ploy—digging a trench to shield Medina and the forces of Islam. Muhammad took an iron pickaxe[561] and hacked out the first chunks of soil and rock himself.[562] Then the Prophet put three thousand of his followers and allies to work digging the remainder of the 15-foot-deep, almost three-and-a-half-mile-long defensive ditch,[563] a ditch it took 20 days to complete.[564] After the trench was finished, the Meccan attackers finally showed up, allegedly accompanied by ten thousand black mercenaries, three tribes of allies,[565] and a contingent of Jewish soldiers.[566] The Meccans and their coalition troops soon discovered that even with their camels and horses, trying to cross the Muslim trench set them up for easy slaughter.[567] So the Meccans pitched camp outside the trench and laid siege to Medina.

For nearly a month, the "war" bogged down in stalemate.[568] Thanks to the trench, there was very little serious fighting. But there were also no fresh supplies. The Muslims and their allies in Medina ran low on food and were close to starvation. But the attackers, the Meccan "unbelievers," were not doing that well either. They had difficulty finding food in the desert. Says Ibn Ishaq, their "horses and camels were dying." And the weather proved to be far less than friendly. A blast of bitterly cold wind put out the Meccans' fires, "upset their cooking pots and overthrew their tents."[569] Or, as the Qur'an puts it:[570] "the grace of Allah ...sent against them a hurricane."[571]

The leader of the Meccans couldn't take it anymore. He said, "You can see the violence of the wind which leaves us neither cooking pots, nor fire, nor tents to count on. Be off, for I am going."[572] With that he walked to his camel, which was hunkered down to avoid the wind, "mounted it, and beat it so it got up on its...legs,"[573] then trotted back to Mecca. Thus ended what went down in history as the Battle of the Trench.[574] Chalk up another victory for Allah!

But there are no spoils and no booty in a victory in which few men face combat and in which only six Muslims and three Meccans[575] are killed.[576] For Muhammad that lack of loot was a serious problem. How do you supply your troops, give them prizes, and raise your prestige when your triumph consists in freezing the enemy with a freak of the weather, exhausting them, and convincing them to go back home? How do you prove that Allah delivers the goods, that, in the words of the Qur'an, "those who strive and fight hath He distinguished above those who sit (at home) by a special reward"[577] and that "Allah will swiftly reward those who (serve him)"[578]? You return to your strategy for automatic wins. You go back to picking on your nerds. So in 627 A.D., Muhammad moved his war against the Jews into higher gear...this time in a bid for an even higher material payoff.

Muhammad got the ball rolling by telling his followers that the Jews were "a people without understanding...transformed into apes and swine...racing each other in sin and rancor.... Evil indeed are their works."[579] The Prophet added that, in fact, Islam's very ability to affect history would depend on a slaughter of Hebrews. "The Hour will not be established," he said, "until you fight with the Jews, and the stone behind which a Jew will be hiding will say, 'O Muslim! There is a Jew hiding behind me, so kill him.'"[580]

Then Muhammad explained that when he'd returned from the loot-less Battle of the Trench to the house of one of his wives,[581] had laid down his arms, and had taken a bath,[582] Allah the Most Benevolent, the Most Merciful[583] had sent a figure in an embroidered gold turban riding up to the house where Muhammad was cleaning up.[584] The visitor "on a white mule with a brocade-covered saddle"[585] was the angel Gabriel, who the Prophet said had told him to stop lazing around, to put his armor back on,[586] and to attack the richest people in the neighborhood, a town of Jewish leather specialists[587] called the Banu Quraiza. As an added incentive, Gabriel promised that "I, too, will attack the Jews and shake them out of their homes."

To show how deeply Allah was committed to this assault, Muhammad said that God had promised to augment the Muslim forces with a troop of armed angels.[588]

Harnessing the restlessness of soldiers who'd been bored by a long and nearly eventless siege, Muhammad ordered his troops to gather together again and to stride off on a fast march[589] with no time out even for the obligatory afternoon Muslim prayer session.[590] In addition, say the Hadith, the dust rose in the streets of Medina as "Gabriel's regiment," the promised regiment of killer angels, marched through.[591] When the combined force of men and angels approached the fortifications of the Jewish village, the angel Gabriel rode out ahead of the vanguard, still on his "white mule with a brocade-covered saddle ...to shake their fortresses and cast terror into their lives."[592] (Note that word "terror." It will prove important.)

Then came Muhammad's turn. As Ibn Ishaq puts it, "The Messenger approached the Jews and said, 'You brothers of monkeys, has God disgraced you and brought his vengeance upon you?' They replied, 'Oh ...[Muhammad], you are not a barbarous person.'"[593] Muhammad did his best to prove the Jews wrong. He opened a 25-day siege[594] of the Banu Quraiza's village.

This is where Islam's conformity enforcement comes in handy. It's difficult to outlast an enemy in a siege. It's tough when you're surrounded and the enemy is separated from you by a ditch. It's even tougher when you're surrounding someone else, when you're separated by walls, and when the open landscape constantly tempts your forces to give up and go home. Poorly disciplined troops, troops that haven't been conformity-enforced by lining up in ranks to say prayers five times a day, are likely to cut and run. But Muhammad's warriors, schooled in absolute submission ("Islam"), absolute obedience, and coordinated effort, were prepped for lengthy military struggles by their dictatorial belief system. They could outlast those they chose to attack.

Outlasting the Jews worked wonders. Says Ibn Ishaq, "God cast terror into their hearts....They felt sure that the apostle would not leave them until he had made an end of them."[595] And they would prove to be right.

After a night in which the women and children wept[596] from dusk until daylight, the Jews decided to "surrender to the apostle's judgement"[597] and threw themselves on Muhammad's mercy. But they were counting on the wrong man. A tribe of Muslims with close ties to the Jews asked Muhammad to do what he had done for other Jewish tribes—spare the Jews' lives and settle for a simple ethnic cleansing.[598] This seemed logical for a Prophet who insisted that he spoke in the name of "Allah, the Merciful, the Compassionate."[599] But this is not how Muhammad, the paragon of Islamic "clemency, love and kindness,"[600] handled the lives that Allah had placed in his hands. According to one Islamic biographer, Muhammad Haykal, Muhammad had concluded before the war even began that "The Banu Qurayzah...must be completely destroyed."[601] The result was what Ibn Ishaq calls a "massacre."[602] Explains the eighth-century biographer:

> worst brutality against Jews
>
> "They [the Jews of the Banu Quraiza] surrendered, and the apostle confined them in Medina.... Then the apostle went out to the market of Medina (which is still its market today) and dug trenches in it. Then he sent for them and struck off their heads in those trenches as they were brought out to him in batches. ...There were 600 or 700 in all, though some put the figure as high as 800 or 900. As they were being taken out in batches to the apostle they asked [their leader]...what he thought would be done with them. He replied, 'Will you never understand? Don't you see that the summoner never stops and those who are taken do not return? By Allah, it is death!' This went on until the apostle made an end of them."[603]

Worry not. Muhammad did not soil his hands with the neck slicing. "He sat down," says al-Tabari, "and Ali and al-Zubayr began cutting off their heads in his presence."[604]

Some of the wives, mothers, and sisters of these captives apparently were forced to watch the head-chopping. Says Muhammad's favorite wife, Aisha, "Only one of their women was killed. She was actually with me and was talking with me and laughing immoderately as the apostle was killing her men in the market when suddenly an unseen voice called her name. 'Good heavens,' I cried, 'what is the matter?' 'I am to be killed,' she replied. ... She was taken away and beheaded. ...I shall never forget my wonder at her good spirits and her loud laughter when all the time she knew that she would be killed."[605]

Then, says Ibn Ishaq, came the goodies. Muhammad "was a very sea of generosity to us."[606] "The Prophet divided the wealth, wives, and children of the Banu Qurayza [Jews] among the Muslims."[607] Boasted one of the Muslim warriors who partook of the spoils:

> War has left to us
> The best gift of our bounteous Lord;
> High white forts and resting places for camels where
> Palms are black and milk is plentiful.
> ...And horses swift as wolves...
> Now guarding the tribesman's cattle,
> Now slaying the enemy and returning with the spoil[608]

One thing is clear. To this warrior, Allah was a god of war. No wonder; the Qur'an calls the mass murder of the Banu Quraiza and its aftermath the epitome of Allah's generosity, "His kindness to" the Muslims.[609] "With Allah are profits and spoils abundant"[610] indeed.

What's more, one of the Muslim warriors bragged something very new in his rap-like poetry after the defeat of the Banu Qurayza Jews,

> We have a prophet, a true helper,
> By whom we can conquer all men.[611]

Two decades later, those words would take on more meaning than the man who uttered them could possibly have imagined.

Sex and Violence—Party Time for Genes

THE TALE OF THE VICTORY OVER the Banu Qurayza told by the Hadith and by the Muslim biographers rapidly turns sexual: "The Messenger of God selected for himself from" the women of the slaughtered Jews a choice beauty,[612] "Rayhanah...and she remained his concubine" for the rest of his life.[613] The rest of the captured women and children were given out as slaves to the others who had "fought in the way of Allah."

This was one of many victories in which Allah saved his best sex prizes for Muhammad,[614] a man with strong carnal appetites. Muhammad coupled with women of all ages, but the holy books of Islam, the Hadith, explain that he had a special "liking for the virgins and for fondling them"[615] and for "a young girl so that you might play with her and she with you."[616] Allah was extraordinarily open-handed in the sexual gifts he showered on Muhammad,

> O prophet! We have made lawful to thee thy wives to whom thou hast paid their dowers; and those whom thy right hand possesses out of the prisoners of war whom Allah has assigned to thee; and daughters of thy paternal uncles and aunts and daughters of thy maternal uncles and aunts who migrated (from Mecca) with thee; and any believing woman who dedicates her soul to the Prophet if the Prophet wishes to wed her this only for thee and not for the Believers (at large).[617]

Note the phrase "those whom thy right hand possesses." Possessing "captives" with the "right hand" is a code-phrase for rape or sex by any means possible.[618] Since every child begotten by sex imposed on a sexual plaything, a "slave girl," must be raised as a Muslim, this form of sexual abuse was considered a legitimate way to spread the truth of Allah.[619] As modern Islamic historian Ali Mazrui puts it, Islam's "culture of procreation...[is] a strategy for 'multiplying in the name of Allah.' Procreation itself," he says, "can be counted as a form of jihad."[620]

Adds Mazrui, "The Muslim ummah (global community of Muslims) is allowed to expand by divine intervention and biological impregnation."[621] In other words, forced sex is a legitimate way to spread a picture of the invisible world, to spread a weave of memes. No wonder ISIS' sexual abusers of 12-year-old girls feel they are performing a holy deed.

War, its spoils, its sexual rewards, and divvying them up would become so fundamental to militant Islam's meme team that the Qur'an has an entire chapter on the subject—chapter eight. It's called "The Spoils of War, The Booty."[622] That chapter is based in large part on the example Muhammad set after the murder of the Banu Quraiza.[623] To repeat one of militant Islam's most potent meme-hooks, "with Allah are profits and spoils abundant."[624]

Why was a supply of sex slaves so important to this holy jackpot?

Why were even those Muslims who died fighting in the way of Allah[625] showered with sexual prizes: the famous "seventy-two Women of Paradise"[626] "so beautiful, pure and transparent that the marrow of the bones of their legs will be seen through the bones and the flesh"?[627]

Because sexual slavery filled a need so deep that anthropologist Napoleon Chagnon found it 7,982 miles away from Arabia, on the border between Argentina and Brazil. The 200-village, 30,000-person[628] tribe that Chagnon studied in the Amazon and Orinoco River basin hints that we may have a biologically built-in strategy, a primal instinct left over from our hunter-gatherer days, days long before the dawn of civilization. The tribe Chagnon studied was the Yanomamo, otherwise known as the "fierce people." The Yanomamo raided neighboring villages in order to kill a man or two and make off with the village's girls and women. The attackers were eager to steal as many girls and women as possible.[629] But the Yanomamo were not alone.

Capturing women as sex slaves had also been important to the earliest Romans. According to legend, sometime around 750 B.C.[630] when the Roman founders were putting together the beginnings of a city, they had recruited plenty of men but very few women. What's more, the men were, says Livy, "an obscure and lowly rabble...whether freemen or slaves who were interested in change." The Romans had made themselves unpopular by forming their "throng of all sorts without distinction" into an army "so strong," says Livy, "that it was a match for any of the neighboring nations in war."[631] So when the Romans sent messages to neighboring tribes asking for young women, brides, in exchange for alliance, the tribes turned these hairy, sweaty, and potentially dangerous city-founders down. The Romans switched to another tack. They declared a new holiday, Consualia, a festival of Neptune Equester, Neptune the god of horses and of horse races, and invited the neighbors in to see "a spectacle...an exhibition splendid and calculated to raise expectation."[632] Then, when the neighbors were distracted by holy sporting events[633]—probably chariot races—the Romans abducted and raped all of the young women that the Sabines had brought along to see the show. The Sabine husbands, fathers, and brothers fled. And, it is said, the Romans slowly won these captured women over to their cause. The event is known to history as the "Rape of the Sabine Women."[634] Does it sound a bit like sex slavery? And like ISIS' caliph Abu Bakr al-Baghdadi trying to convert his unwilling "wife," Kayla Mueller, and his sex slaves to Islam?

Why did sex prove such a powerful motivator in Muhammad's new religion? Because genes reproduce gleefully in new wombs. And memes—religions, ideas, and worldviews—reproduce with equal glee in the minds of the children those new wombs produce. So the hunger of genes and memes—the hunger of replicators—whisper, shout, and scream in the holy books of Islam.

Turning Instinct Into Tradition

Crafting a Permanent Nerd

MUHAMMAD HAD GOTTEN ACROSS his message. When you can't win in any other way, pick on a Jew. But he was about to shape the instinctual itch to attack scapegoats into an even more potent military strategy: using atrocities against Jews to attract allies and, more important, to terrify bigger targets— non-Jewish targets—into surrendering without a fight.

The Prophet's real goal was to take over the reins of the town in which he'd grown up, the town that had humiliated him, the town from which he'd fled, and the town that had the holiest site[635] in the mountainous strip of Arab desert called the Hijaz. That town was Mecca, the religious and camel caravan center in a strip of desert and mountains so difficult to cross that it was called "the Barrier."[636] But beating the Meccans wouldn't be easy. Muhammad had tried it in the Battle of Badr and had done well. He had tried it again in the Battle of Uhud and had failed miserably. Then he had racked up a questionable victory in the Battle of the Trench. How could Muhammad conquer Mecca without a fight? How could he use his favorite weapon, terror, to bring Mecca to its knees? And how could he generate that terror by using the pick-on-the-little-guy strategy? How could he take Mecca by using his nerds?

Ninety-five miles away[637] from Muhammad's base, Medina, was a re-markable town, a town that belonged to Muhammad's favorite walking wallets, the Jews. Called Khaibar, this community was nestled in the valleys between tall cliffs. It was rich in date palms, wheat, orchards,[638] jewelers,[639] armor-crafters, weapons-makers, and wealthy merchants.[640] Says one of the 20th century's most prominent Muslim biographers of Muhammad, Mohammad Haykal, "The masses of Jews living in Khaibar were the stron-gest [and] the richest...of all the peoples of Arabia."[641] Ibn Ishaq, Muhammad's very first Muslim biographer, writing in the eighth century, adds that Khaibar was "the garden of the Hijaz...the principal town of"[642] its portion of the Arabian Peninsula.[643] Khaibar was a perfect target for what Muhammad had in mind—scaring the robes off the town fathers of Mecca.

The citizens of Khaibar were sitting ducks. They had no idea a Muslim "raid" was coming. Ibn Ishaq quotes the recollections of one of Muhammad's soldiers, who explained that Muhammad's army arrived at Khaibar by night, set up camp, then marched just after dawn[644] with their leaders, including Muhammad, riding war horses.[645] "We met the workers of Khaibar coming out in the morning with their spades and baskets. When they saw the apostle and the army they cried, 'Muhammed with his force,' and turned tail and fled."[646]

How did Muhammad feel about taking a people he was at peace with by surprise? Apparently wonderful. When the unarmed farmers of Khaibar ran in panic, Muhammad "rode… through the lane of Khaibar quickly… and… when he entered the town"[647] gave out a mighty "Allah Akbar! Khaibar is destroyed. When we arrive in a people's square it is a bad morning for those who have been warned [to convert to Islam]."[648] Just to make his message clear—and to set an example for 1,400 years of Muslim conquerors to come—Muhammad repeated his blood-curdling war cry…"Allah Akbar," "God is great"…three times.[649]

The Muslim army besieged Khaibar for 20 days.[650] The fighting was bloody. Ibn Ishaq describes a model soldier, a "leader glorious, [a] knight ever ready"[651] like this: "Stepping into the breach, he cut heads to pieces."[652] One of the participants in Muhammad's battles said that Muslim "swords… cut off every arm and skull with their blows."[653]

Ali, Muhammad's nephew and son-in-law, the man who had substituted for Muhammad in his bed when assassins had arrived, confronted one Jewish defender who was wearing a stone helmet and "a safflower-dyed Yemeni neck protector."[654] Ali had gone from poverty to riches thanks to war plunder, so he was as just as fashionable. He "was wearing a suit of reddish purple whose fringes were of two colors, white and red."[655] But expensive clothes didn't get in the way of the matter of the day—gore. "Ali struck" his opponent "a swift blow that split the stone [helmet], the neck protector, and his head and landed in his rear teeth."[656]

When the Jews of Khaibar gave up, Muhammad "had already taken all their property,"[657] but he wanted more. He wanted their money—their savings, their jewelry, and their cash. The keeper of Khaibar's treasury—one of the city's most prominent leaders, a man whose prestige will come up in a sexual context in a few pages—refused to tell where the town's valuables were hidden. Muhammad confronted this problem with his usual compassion and mercy. He told one of his warriors, Zubayr, "Torture him until you extract what he has."[658]

What on-the-spot torment did Zubayr improvise? "He kindled fire with flint and steel on" the Jewish leader's "chest until he was nearly dead."[659] Ibn Ishaq doesn't tell us whether the tortured Jewish dignitary ever gave Muhammad the location of the town's treasury. He simply says that "the apostle delivered" the half-dead victim to a Muslim soldier who "struck off his head."[660]

Why are details like this important? The Islamic empire's worldview insists that following in Muhammad's footsteps is essential to a righteous life. Strict Islam insists on remaining true to the examples that the Prophet and his companions set in the seventh century.

Other peoples, says Islam, have been given the authentic word of God. Allah has sent mankind over 25 true prophets.[661] And every people that's received God's truth, God's chosen ideas, the words in the Qur'an and in the Hadith, has perverted the gift of divine truth. How? By reinterpreting Allah's message to fit the circumstances of the day. That reinterpretation has turned the truth from a heavenly blessing to a Satanic perversion.

Only the empire of Islam, the Islamic ummah, has known how to preserve God's word. Only the Muslims have looked unflinchingly backward to the life of Muhammad and to his words and deeds. Only the Muslims have studied Muhammad's utterances and his actions to find answers to every question from how to make war to how to wipe yourself when you defecate.[662] So the Prophet's examples have played a major role in shaping the militant Islam of the last 13 centuries...including our century. Islam is the ultimate cult of personality. It's the Founder Effect.

As Abubakar Shekau, the leader of Nigeria's Boko Haram—a group that invades college dormitories in the middle of the night and kills students by the hundreds—put it in a video he released May 14, 2014:[663]

> This is what our leader [Muhammad] said.... We will die killing and slaughtering them [Christians and all other unbelievers], if you meet infidels in battlefield brethren, just harvest their necks; Allah said it and not Shekau. Cut out their necks until the time that you will get majority over infidels of the world.

But harvesting heads is just one of the glories dictated by Allah through the actions of his Prophet. Muhammad's example, says Shekau, means that the slaughter can't end until

> After we have killed, killed, killed and get fatigue and wondering on what to do with smelling of their corpses, smelling of Obama, Bush, Putin and [Nigerian president Goodluck] Jonathan.

Why all the people that Shekau says laughingly that he has "slaughtered in the cause of Islam"?

> Infidels have no value. ... Any infidel is a sheep to be sold.[664]

Where does Shekau get these ideas? He explains proudly, "It is Quran that said so." And he adds something crucial: "I will not model anyone except Prophet."[665] I will not, he says, follow any role model but Muhammad.

Islam's worldview, including its examples from the life of Muhammad, is likely to prove a potent shaper of the actions of militant, extremist, and even mainstream Muslim groups long after Abubakar Shekau and Boko Haram are forgotten. Muhammad's life embodies a philosophy that you and I can't afford to ignore. But back to our story.

The Jews of Khaibar who remained alive once the mayhem ended agreed to give 50% of the yield of their farms each year to the Muslims,[666] supplying food that would nourish Islam's troops...allowing the soldiers of Islam to leave their day jobs and to remain permanently mobilized for war.[667] As Julius Caesar says in his *Conquest of Gaul*,[668] full-time soldiers, soldiers who fight nearly every day, can whip part-time fighters any day of the week. But giving Muhammad a standing army, a permanently mobilized killing machine, was just the tip of what evolutionary biologists call "the resources"—the plunder and payoff, the "profits and spoils"[669] of jihad.

The bonanza Khaibar yielded to the embryonic Muslim empire was one of the biggest Muhammad and his raiders had ever seized. It was so ample that it made the 1,800 men Muhammad had led in battle richer than ever before.[670] The booty included donkeys, horses, sheep, cows, camels, chickens,[671] gardens, rich food, lace, and clothing[672]—a highly prized luxury even if it was slightly used. The food may sound inconsequential to us, but it meant everything to at least one of the clans that had marched with Muhammad. They were so hungry that their strength had gone. To them receiving "the richest food in Khaibar" was literally a godsend, a battle-prize that Ibn Ishaq says Allah gave specifically to feed this starving group.[673] This bit of just-in-time nourishment was one more proof that "to he who hath it shall be given." One more proof of the Darwinian algorithm that turns groups into learning machines. We shun losers. And we flock to winners. He who can gather riches also gathers allies.

Then there was the land. Just two of Khaibar's valleys were big enough to divide into 1,800 shares. Muhammad's men got not just the real estate, but a half-share of the crops these orchards and fields would yield for years to come. To top it off, Muhammad gave out a staggering number of loads of wheat, barley, and dates. One of the men under him who had been helpful in negotiating the surrender of nearby towns got 30 loads of barley and 30 loads of dates.[674]

Muhammad's family made out even better. Says Ibn Ishaq, Muhammad "gave his daughter Fatima 200 loads"[675] of dates and apportioned 700 loads "to his own wives."[676] Then Muhammad gave his wives 180 loads of wheat.[677]

As usual, mere material goods were not enough. Islam was a masterful satisfier of what Richard Dawkins calls selfish genes.[678] And Islam was a masterful collector of new wombs in which those genes could incubate. Says Ibn Ishaq, "The women of Khaibar were distributed among the Muslims."[679] And Muhammad set down rules for their use. He prohibited "carnal intercourse"[680] with pregnant captives. And he said that "it is not lawful for a man who believes in Allah" to have sex with one of his new slave girls or slave women "until he made sure she was in a state of cleanness."[681] A few sentences after issuing rules for the use and abuse of captured women, the Prophet gave out edicts on the employment of captured animals and clothing—ordering that no one remove a steed or a garment from the pool of booty, ride the animal to exhaustion or wear the clothing out, then return it to the pool in unusable condition.[682] The prophet implicitly lowered the captive women to the rank of animals by including them in this list.

Then there were the trophies won in Islam's picture of the invisible world—its picture of eternity in heaven or hell. Even those who died fighting on the Muslim side got sexual prizes. A hired servant of the Jews who had turned on his employers mere hours before the battle began and had fought on the side of the Muslims was killed by a stone. Despite the fact that the servant had never had a chance to participate in the prayers demanded by Islam, Muhammad said, "He has with him now his two wives from the dark-eyed houris [the virgins of paradise]."[683]

The fantasy of a paradise oozing sex was a cheap way to give out big prizes. But it worked.

Captured women did more than slake sexual appetites. They added to your prestige. Another fighter wanted a woman named Safiya, but Muhammad[684] insisted on taking her for himself and gave Safiya's two female cousins to the warrior who had initially claimed her.[685] Why did Muhammad want this particular captive? Pecking order stature. Prestige.

When Muhammad first saw Safiya, she was not at her prettiest. She was led out of Khaibar past the bodies of her beheaded husband and her husband's friends. Driven wild with grief, she shrieked and slapped her face and poured dust on her head. When the apostle saw her he said, "Take this she-devil away from me."[686]

Despite his distaste for her howls, Muhammad

> Gave orders that Safiya was to be put behind him and threw his mantle over her, so that the Muslims knew he had chosen her for himself.[687]

Then the prophet showed something rare—a moment of pity. Muhammad turned to the Muslim fighter who had led Safiya and another Jewish woman out of the fortifications and into their new role as slaves, concubines, or unwilling brides. "Had you no compassion," he barked at his companion, "when you brought two women past their dead husbands?"[688]

In Safiya's case, sexual appetite and empire-building went hand in hand. When she calmed down, Safiya[689] was more than merely attractive. She was still in her teens,[690] and, equally important, she was "the lady of the Banu Qurayzah and Banu al Nadir" and "the daughter of their king."[691] She was also the wife of the leader whom Muhammad's henchmen had tortured in an attempt to find the Jews' treasures. She was a queen.

So Muhammad ordered that Safiya be made "beautiful and combed"[692] and "passed the night with her"[693] in one of his tents, thus marrying her within hours of her husband's beheading. Whether Safiya went into Muhammad's tent willingly or unwillingly, the biographers don't bother to say. If she went against her will, we would call her treatment at the hand of Muhammad "rape."

And that kind of institutionalized rape would ripple down the paths of history. In his May 2015 videotape, Abubakar Shekau, leader of Boko Haram, a group that, like ISIS, has murdered husbands, fathers, and brothers and taken the dead men's women as sex slaves by the thousands, boasted:

I will marry out a female at 12; I will do same for a nine-year-old girl
like it was done on my mother Aisha and wife of Prophet

In this, Shekau referred to the example of Muhammad, who became engaged to his favorite wife, Aisha, when she was six. However, Muhammad waited patiently and did not consummate the marriage until Aisha was nine.[694] But that's not the point. Back to what else Shekau learned from Muhammad's example of how to treat women taken in battle.

I am the one that captured your girls and I will sell them in the market. Yes, I will sell the girls... people, I am selling the girls like Allah said until we soak the ground of Nigeria with infidels blood.... There is slavery in Islam, don't be deceive about United Nations [human rights].... Are daughters of slaves not slaves? It is Quran that said so, There are slaves in Islam, you should know this, Prophet Muhammed took slaves himself during Badr war.[695]

This is where the tail end of a quote you've seen above becomes relevant:

After we have killed, killed, killed and get fatigue and wondering on what to do with smelling of their corpses, smelling of Obama, Bush, Putin and Jonathan...It is [former Nigerian President Goodluck] Jonathan's daughter that I will imprison; nothing will stop this until you convert.[696]

What inspires these disturbing words? Among other things, the sexual enslavement—the forced "marriage"—of the queen of the Khaibar Jews, Safiya. One of the prophet's Muslim chroniclers, former Egyptian Minister of Education Muhammad Haykal, explains proudly that in raping Safiya, Muhammad followed "the example of the great conquerors who married the daughters and wives of the kings whom they had conquered."[697]

A conqueror is not a normal role model for the sort of prophet we're accustomed to. In fact, prophets like Buddha[698] and Jesus[699] loathed war. But the words "conquer" and "conquest" appear 95 times in just one of Islam's holy books, one of the Hadith, the compilations of eyewitness accounts of Muhammad's life.[700] By contrast, the words "conquer" and "conqueror" don't show up in another bloody and genocidal book, the Old Testament, at all.[701] Muhammad's model of war and conquest would soon become very normal for those following in the Prophet's footsteps.

One other thing would become normal: The conviction that, as Mohammad Haykal—who was a former high-level Egyptian politician and mainstream newspaper editor[702]—puts it, "there could be no peace with the Jews as long as they were not thoroughly destroyed."[703]

The Top Predator Trick

"You must become so notorious for bad things that when you come into an area people will tremble in their sandals. Anyone can do beatings and starve people. I want your unit to find new ways of torture so terrible that the screams will frighten even crows from their nests and if the person survives he will never again have a night's sleep."

—Hafiz Sadiqulla Hassani, reporting on the instructions he allegedly received from his former boss, the commandant of Afghanistan's Secret Police under the Taliban, 2001

WHEN A BARBARIAN TRIBE—a tribe without big cities and without urban sophistication, a tribe that specializes in violence, a tribe that's expert in weapons use and in raiding, a tribe that practices the techniques of war month after month and year after year, a tribe that elevates killing to a virtue, and a tribe that idealizes its mass murderers—goes up against a settled community, a community that's built a civilization, the barbarian tribe all too often wins. Why?

If this were a just universe, it should be the other way around. The civilized, those who contribute the most to the enrichment of human lives, should be the victors. The civilized should have the sharpest, most sophisticated mass minds. The civilized should trounce the rabble and carry on their business in peace. But that's not the way it happens. Instead, human history is littered with the results of one of the nastiest of Mother Nature's tricks.

Why would Islam prove capable of overcoming loftily sophisticated societies? Because Islam was about to take advantage of an open niche in the global social system, a power vacuum that opens in the biological ecosystems of the ocean, the forest, the field, and in the world of human beings. That open slot was the opportunity to become top predator.

*   *   *

In roughly 1900, when he was still a child, Norway's Thorleif Schjelderup-Ebbe got into a strange habit: counting the number of pecks that the chickens in his family's flock landed on each other and who pecked whom. By the time he was ready to write his Ph.D. dissertation in 1918, Schjelderup-Ebbe had close to 20 years of data. And that data demonstrated something strange.

Chickens in a barnyard are not egalitarian. They have a strict hierarchy. At the top is a chicken who gets special privileges. All others step aside when she goes to the trough. She is the first to eat. And she can peck any other chicken in the group. Then comes chicken number two. She is the second to eat. And she can peck anyone in the flock with one notable exception. She cannot peck the top chicken. Then comes chicken number three, chicken number four, and so on. Each one cannot peck the chickens above her on the social ladder. But each has free rein to peck the chickens below. Finally, there's the bottom chicken, a chicken everyone is free to peck but who is free to peck no one. Schjelderup-Ebbe called this a "peck order," a pecking order, a dominance hierarchy.

The chicken on the bottom is the nerd.

Pecking order squabbles don't just take place between beasts. They take place between nations. And they organize entire ecosystems. At the top in a natural ecosystem is not a Prophet, a Pope, a conqueror, or a king. It's a meat-eater and killing machine called the top predator.[7] A top predator is the descendant of the replicators in the Earth's primordial seas roughly 4.1 billion years ago,[705] replicators that invented a shortcut to gathering the goods they needed to make copies themselves.

If you're on the bottom or middle of an ecological food chain, you spend a lot of your time nosing around trying to find stuff to eat. And once you've swallowed your food, you may need a huge and energy-consuming gut to turn it from seaweed, leaves, and grass to muscle mass, to meat. The bellies of cows, goats, sheep, camels, giraffes, llamas, buffalo, deer, wildebeest, and antelopes, for example, contain stomachs with four separate chambers. These poor animals have to take the time to eat their food twice. On the first go-round, the beasts yank, mash, and grind the grasses of the fields with their lips and teeth. They swallow these tough blades of greenery and deposit them temporarily in the first two caverns of their four-chambered stomachs—caverns called the rumen and reticulum. There the grass blades are saturated with saliva. Then the easy-to-get-at nutrients—the starches—are dissolved by digestive enzymes.[706] And the resulting natural Gatorade is sent to the two back-end stomach chambers for final processing.

But the much tougher fibers are kept on hold in the stomach's two preliminary processing chambers, the rumen and the reticulum, until the animal gets a substantial dollop of spare time. Then the beast brings the ball of stems, stalks, and remaining greenery back up into its mouth for a second bout of chewing. This burdensomely long second pass at grinding, slicing and mashing is known as rumination, the food-processing technique from which these animals get their name: ruminants.

Even after an acid bath and a second go at chewing, when the twice-mulched food is returned to the four chambers of the stomach, it's still too tough for the cow, camel, antelope, or sheep to digest on its own. The ruminant needs the aid of massive bacterial and protist colonies in its four-fold stomach to wring the fuel it needs from the grasses it eats... and re-eats.[707]

If you're a top predator you do not take this long and difficult route to nourishment. Instead you pounce on others who've already gathered the ingredients you need, then you feast on the treasure they've managed to pre-assemble as protein...as rumps, loins, and ribs. You gorge on the nutrients your victims have packed into their meat. The predatory strategy is a shortcut to riches. And with riches you can ride the social learning machine others have created, making the collective intelligence of those you prey upon work for you.

Or, to put it in human terms, why build a civilization from scratch when you can take over the helm of a civilization that others have spent hundreds of years piecing together? And, while you're at it, why not go further and hijack a whole bunch of civilizations? Predation is efficient. It also often sews what it swallows together in new ways.

Top predators in the world of humans have advantages others lack. They focus on the glory of killing and war. They aren't held back by what us settled folk call scruples. When the Jews of the Banu Quraiza had held out for over three weeks against Muhammad, they concluded that extending the war would give Muhammad an excuse to exterminate them utterly. So the Jews weighed their options. Said their leader, the men of the Banu Quraiza had three choices.

CHOICE ONE: reject the Torah, the holy book of the Jewish people, and accept[708] Muhammad as a legitimate...and final...prophet. This is like asking Christians to shred the New Testament and to toss away their belief in Jesus. The Jews answered that they "will never abandon the law of the Torah."[709]

CHOICE TWO: "Kill our wives and children and send men with their swords drawn to Muhammad and his companions leaving no encumbrances behind us.... If we conquer we can acquire other wives and children."[710] The Jews replied, "Should we kill these poor creatures? What would be the good of life when they were dead?"[711]

And CHOICE THREE: try to "take Muhammad and his companions by surprise."[712] How? By attacking on a Saturday, a day consecrated to rest. The Jews refused to "profane" their Sabbath.[713]

These are scruples. Because the men of the Banu Quraiza refused to abandon these scruples, they lost their heads.

A second advantage of barbarians is often their delight in war and their distaste for peace. The Vikings loved hacking and chopping their fellow humans so mightily that their version of paradise was a Valhalla[714] in which they woke up every morning, donned their armor and their weapons, then rode to the battlefield and spent the day glorying in the pleasures of combat, in the thrill of lopping off arms and legs, in the delights of their favorite sport, killing.

Many of the Christian Crusaders loved fighting so much that when they had to abandon the killing fields of the Holy Land, they went off looking for other pagans they could slice into submission—and found them in the as-yet-unchristianized Slavic tribes of Prussia.[715]

These are just a few of the reasons why nomadic peoples who luxuriate in the use of weapons, why enthusiastic removers of limbs and of lives, often go down in history despite their atrocities.

But there's more. Some top predators suture together the civilizations they conquer in new ways. The Indo-Europeans were brutal tribes who went out in military bands, besieged cities, and probably killed the men and children, then took the women as sex toys and wives.[716] They were nasty, brutal, and illiterate. But they spread from China to Scandinavia and left us our language. The Vikings terrorized and blitzkrieged the Holy Roman Empire, brutalized—and revitalized—Normandy, upgraded England,[717] and did the same for Eastern Europe and Western fringe of Asia, where the Norse raiders established the nucleus of an entirely new empire, a gaggle of princedoms that some say got its name from the Vikings' russet hair, a gaggle that would slowly evolve into the Empire of Russia.[718]

The violent, nomadic Mongols conquered the Chinese Empire and killed 25 million[719] Chinese. Then they introduced paper money, standardized China's weights and measures, and established massive free-trade zones in Asia.[720] The barbarians known as the Manchu ruled China from 1644 to 1911. These Manchu invaders took China to greater heights than it had ever seen before, giving it control over 13 million square kilometers of land,[721] including an island China wants back today—Taiwan.[722] In addition, the barbarian Manchus revived a critical element of Chinese administration that had fallen into disuse, the State Examination System,[723] the system that guaranteed that China's bureaucrats would not be the random sons sired by nobles, but would be hired on the basis of merit and would be among the best-educated in the world—masters of literature, poetry, "music, archery and horsemanship, arithmetic, writing, and knowledge of the rituals and ceremonies."[724]

The nomadic armies of Islam would someday suture together an empire in which an ambitious traveler like the 14th-century master of curiosity Ibn Battuta could travel from Spain to China, could speak a universal language—Arabic—wherever he went, and could accept a position as a judge in any of the central cities he stopped in. No matter what continent that city was in. Why? Because every capital's ruling class used the language of the conquerors, Arabic, the protocols of the Arab peoples, and the codes of Islamic law, codes in which Ibn Battuta was an expert.[725]

All of these empire-builders and empire re-makers, these top predators in the human eco-system—the Indo-Europeans, the Vikings, the Mongols, the Manchus, and the Muslims—began as barbarians. Few of them started out literate. Few of them initially knew how to build a major city. But all idealized violence. All idealized killing.

And all put themselves in the saddle, raiding, breaking, then riding empires originally organized and infrastructured by others. So did another folk who made war with the gleam of blood lust in their eyes, a sedentary people who followed the top predator strategy to the nth degree—sewing together an empire that nurtured cultural diversity, one in which cities could tear down their defensive walls and open themselves to the world. That highly disciplined gang of gore-lovers, warriors who attacked with a disciplined rigor that the rest of Europe could not believe, was...the Romans.

But not all predators are alike. When it comes to strategies for grabbing the lands and goods of others, the Muslims would make all the top predators of history—all of the world's barbarian conquerors—look like amateurs. To repeat, they would seize a swatch of land 11 times the size of the conquests of Alexander the Great, five times the size of the Roman Empire, and seven times the size of the USA. And the Muslims would keep up these territorial conquests. As we'll soon see, they would pursue a path of unprecedented imperialism and colonialism for over 12 centuries.

Why was Islam able to pull off this radical increase in the magnitude of conquest? Because militant Islam would have a weapon that the Mongols, the Vikings, the Indo-Europeans, and even the pre-Christian Romans lacked—a worldview prefabricated to demand war, to win, to rake in the riches, to reorganize captured societies, and to install the earliest believers—usually Arabs—at the top, then to take a deep breath and go out to conquer more.

Even more important, militant Islam would have a belief system that, like the caste system of the Hindus,[726] would cement the captured people in their place. It would insert into its victims a picture of the invisible world that would make *voluntary* subservience, utter submission (a core meaning of the word "Islam"[727]), permanent. Muhammad Ali Al Hashmi in his book *The Ideal Muslimah*[728] gives a description of how complete and overwhelming this submission would be. Though Al Hashmi is describing the perfect faith of a woman, he is also presenting the stooped-and-chastened attitude toward fate that would be basic to all those whom Islam subjugates:

> One of the most prominent distinguishing features of the Muslim woman," writes Al Hashmi, "is her deep faith in Allah (SWT), and her sincere conviction that whatever happens in this universe, and whatever fate befalls human beings, only happens through the will and decree of Allah (SWT); whatever befalls a person could not have been avoided, and whatever does not happen to a person could not have been made to happen. A person has no choice in this life but to strive towards the right path and to do good deeds—acts of worship and other acts—by whatever means one can, putting all his trust in Allah (SWT), submitting to His will, and believing that he is always in need of Allah's (SWT) help and support.[729]

In other words, no matter how dire your situation in life, no matter how much you are humiliated and kept low, live with it. If you are a man and you want to take revenge for your fate, do a good deed: vent your hostilities on an unbeliever by "fighting in the way of Allah."[730] Do your best to pick an unbeliever whose earthly goods you can steal, whose wives you can expropriate, and whose lands you can force your victim to farm until harvest time comes and he is forced to split the fruit of his labor with you.

Muhammad insured subservience by using a conformity-enforcer and enemy-crumbler called terror. Terror, in fact, was a weapon Muhammad wielded with delight. He used the word over and over again:

I have been made victorious with terror (cast in the hearts of the enemy), and while I was sleeping, the keys of the treasures of the world were brought to me and put in my hand.[731]

I have been helped by terror (in the hearts of enemies): spoils [the plunder looted from enemies in raids or in war] have been made lawful to me: the earth has been made for me clean and a place of worship; I have been sent to all mankind and the line of prophets is closed with me.[732]

Soon shall We cast terror into the hearts of the unbelievers[733] ... Remember thy Lord inspired the angels (with the message): "I am with you: give firmness to the believers: I will instill terror into the hearts of the unbelievers."[734] ... Against them make ready your strength to the utmost of your power including steeds of war to strike terror into (the hearts of) the enemies of Allah.[735] ... ye are stronger (than they) because of the terror in their hearts (sent) by Allah.[736]

Muhammad knew the psychology of conquest. Unrelenting terror produces what seminal psychologist Martin Seligman calls "learned helplessness,"[737] a phenomenon so heavily researched that it's the subject of over 78,000 journal articles. Put an animal—a lab rat or a dog—in a cage with a floor that produces electrical shocks. Unpredictable tortures. Totally unjust and undeserved punishments. When the first shock hits, the dog will howl, jump, scramble, and claw, trying to find an escape. But deliver the shocks over and over again, without a predictable pattern, and some dogs will eventually lay down on the electrified floor and give up, passively taking the shock. Most astonishing, when a dog has reached this stage of utter submission, if you open the cage door, the poor creature will not even walk out.[738] It will continue absorbing new shocks. It won't register the existence of an easy escape through the open door. Look into the matter further, and you'll discover that the forlorn pup has had its will disabled by a chemical that the body produces when the situation seems hopeless: substance P.[739]

The bottom line: endless terror generates a physiological and emotional passivity that leaves an animal or a human too will-less to leave his torture chamber even when the exit is wide open.[740] Muhammad seems to have intuited this deep structure of your psychology and mine.

Muhammad was piecing together something remarkable, a superorganism. What's a superorganism? Your body is an organism. But it's also a massive collaborative effort. It's composed of a hundred trillion cells. Each of those cells is capable of living on its own. Yet your body survives thanks to the existence of a collective identity—a you. In 1911,[741] Harvard biologist William Morton Wheeler noticed that ant colonies pull off the same trick. From 20,000 to 36 million ants work together to create a collective identity, the identity of a community, a society, a colony, or a supercolony. Wheeler observed that the colony of individuals behaved as if it were a single organism. An organism like you and me. He called the result a "superorganism."[742]

Horrible as it may be, overwhelming fear can be a bonding mechanism, one of a growing superorganism's most potent forms of social glue. As we're about to see, it can make the loser assume a position as a voluntary lower class in the social system of the victor, an underdog trying to rise in the eyes of his overlord by following the overlord's ways. This explains why people abducted by force and mistreated by their prison-masters often go through "The Stockholm Syndrome."[743] They fall in love with their captors, and some become fervent converts to their captors' beliefs. Long-term terror triggers a physiological, emotional, and perceptual change in its victims. It reduces its targets from proud competitors for top status in the pecking order to obedient subjects grateful to simply be allowed to remain alive, despite their new status at the pecking order's bottom.

This neural[744] and emotional switching process helps explain why Germany and Japan, fascist nations that fought the European and American democracies tooth and nail in World War II, eventually rolled over like puppies, adopted the very forms of democratic government they'd been battling, and became America's closest allies.

Both countries were fire-bombed until their cities were ruins, their citizens' normal lives were utterly stripped away, and they were threatened with starvation and with the dread of planes approaching to drop yet another load of explosives.

You'd think that inhuman treatment of this kind would evoke a never-ending hatred of the victor. Instead, it triggers the response that brings peace to pecking orders,[3] the bowing and scraping that researchers of animal

---

3. Like early Islam's militants, the Iroquois Indians used the bonding power of terror...and worse. They marched enormous distances to make war on unsuspecting Native American villagers. Once they'd conquered a settlement, they took the inhabitants who remained alive as prisoners, tortured them until they broke them, then distributed them as slaves. The Iroquois approach showed the hunger of one superorganism to swallow another in a particularly graphic way. If the Iroquois warriors failed to crack the will of a captive and make him or her suitably subservient, they took another approach to digesting their victim. They ate him. Literally. (see: Daniel Richter, *The Ordeal of the Longhouse: The Peoples of the Iroquois League in the Era of European Colonization*. Chapel Hill, NC: University of North Carolina Press, 1992.)

and human behavior call "submission gestures."[745] It resets your mind and your body, flooding you with an internal cascade of chemical poisons and passivity inducers—substance P and glucocorticoids, your stress hormones.[746] And it triggers what psychoanalytic theorist Anna Freud, Sigmund Freud's youngest daughter, calls "identification with the oppressor."[7]

Since 624 A.D., militant Islam has used the Stockholm Effect, learned helplessness, and identification with the oppressor to cement its occupied territories in place as tissues in its growing superbeast.

*　*　*

Once terror has done its job, the militant Muslims of the last 14 centuries have rammed down the throats of those they've conquered a picture of the invisible world with some of the sharpest and most un-spit-outable meme-hooks humanity has ever seen. If you abandon Islam, the punishment is swift and brutal—death. A deep dive into the eternity where you will be roasted over a spit while you scream for mercy. Then, when your skin is finally burned to a crisp and falls off, Allah will give you a new skin so that you can be roasted and scream with pain all over again.[748]

"Merciful" Gods can be very unforgiving!

*　*　*

Studies of ecological systems show that when the top predator changes, the social system, the system of who preys on whom and how, shifts utterly.[749] For example, Charles C. Mann cites anthropologists and archaeologists who believe that when Native Americans entered the Americas, they created two new forms of ecosystem. They used fire to clear the land of central North America and gave birth to something brand new on this continent, something utterly man-made... prairies. And they used botanical artistry in South America to create another new kind of cradle for life—the rainforest.[750] The rainforest favored new plant species. And the prairie encouraged the spread of bison, elk, and mule deer.[751]

But a new top predator changes more than the food web. Among humans, the top predator changes the web that generates the collective intelligence. Barbarian conquerors—human top predators—can change the very nature of mass mind.

The Lunge For Global Conquest

> The aims of the life of Muhammad..., as the Last
> Messenger of God on this earth, were:
>
>> to destroy idolatry and polytheism;
>> to proclaim the absolute Oneness of the Creator;
>> to deliver the Creator's Message to mankind;
>> to complete the system of religion and law;
>> to purify the souls of men and women;
>> to eradicate injustice, iniquity and ignorance;
>> to establish a system of peace with justice;
>> to create an apparatus in the form of a political
>>   state for the realization of all the foregoing
>>   aims, and one which would also maintain the
>>   momentum of his work.
>
> Within the 23 years of his ministry as God's
> Messenger, Muhammad had achieved all these aims.
>
> —Sayed Ali Asgher Razwy[752]

THE HOLY BOOKS OF ISLAM, the Qur'an and the Hadith, are not the only religious founding volumes that revel in violence. Killing is at the core of the Jewish and Christian Old Testament. It is at the heart of the Hindu Vedas. And it is at the core of the founding books of Western civilization, *The Iliad* and *The Odyssey*. But modern Hindus, Christians, and Jews have rejected... or forgotten...the genocide and mass murder preached in their holy books. What we call fundamentalist Islam, militant Islam, Jihadism, extremist Islam, Islamism, or Islamofascism has not.

There's good reason. The meme-weave of Islam is unlike that stitched by the founder of any other major modern religion. Buddhism was a worldview laid out in 500 B.C. by a man who rejected war and who tried to relieve mankind of its suffering. Christianity was founded in roughly 30 A.D.[753] by a small-town savior who recommended turning the other cheek to violence. Both Christianity and Buddhism eventually went global. And both eventually inspired armed conflict. But neither Buddha nor Christ would have approved of the murderous deeds launched in their names.

In tune with the founder effect, both Christianity and Buddhism have ever so slowly inched back to activism on behalf of the goals of their founding fathers—peace. We'll see how this unlikely turn in ethics and morality has happened in a few chapters.

Meanwhile, Islam's founder, Muhammad, was, unlike Buddha and Jesus, a man who built holy bloodshed into his belief system. As Muhammad said about his addiction to warfare on behalf of a weave of memes, "By Allah, I will not cease to fight for the mission with which God has entrusted me until He makes me victorious or I perish."[754] When Muhammad used the word "fight" he was not talking about internal struggle or impassioned persuasion. He was talking about killing.

More important for you and me, Muhammad built a political system designed to go global, with an aspiring global government, a global law code, and a global military policy. That aim—global governance, global imperialism—was built into the roots of Muhammad's religion. And the 21st century is ripe for memes built on a global scale. How in the world did Muhammad pull this off?

* * *

I was sent with the sword.... My sustenance has been made below the shadow of my spear. Humiliation and abasement have been laid upon the one who opposes my command.
    —Muhammad[755]

Islam has enjoined Muslims to establish not only a society based on Islam but also expects Muslims to establish a government based on Islam. In fact, it has promised true believers to make them rulers on the earth.
    —Sarwat Saulat, a moderate Muslim biographer of Muhammad[756]

How did Islam go global? How did a picture of the invisible world conceived in an obscure corner of an equally obscure desert turn into a "complete system"[757] that aimed to girdle the planet with just one legal code, just one set of manners and morals, and just one god? By harnessing the founder effect, the top predator trick, and the primitive power of picking on the little guy. By molding a culture on the example of a prophet of conquest, a man who made religion, government, and war synonymous, a man who dared to dream outrageously big—Muhammad.

In 629 A.D., thanks to the lucrative victories over the Jews of the Banu Qaynuqa, over the Jews of the Banu Nadir, and over the Jews of the Banu Quraiza, the Muslims were wealthy[758]...wealthy enough to grow ambitious. And wealthy enough to make their superorganism and the memes that drove it voracious. As one of Muhammad's Islamic biographers puts it, after the "destruction of the [Jewish] Banu Qurayzah ...All Arab tribes admired Muslim power, dominion, and the new prestige of Muhammad as sovereign of Madinah." The biographer is no ordinary writer. He's Muhammad Haykal, a man we've referred to before. Haykal, who died in 1956, graduated from France's most prestigious university, the Sorbonne, then went on to become the Minister of Education for Egypt, the Minister of State for Egypt's Interior Ministry,[759] and the editor of the Egyptian newspaper *Al Siyasa*. His biography of Muhammad is endorsed by the Arab Republic of Egypt's Supreme Council of Islamic Affairs,[760] is published in English by Indonesia's Islamic Book Trust,[761] and is brought to you online by the Muslim Witness-Pioneer organization, dedicated "to spreading and establishing the message of Islam."[762] In other words, Haykal was a mainstream Egyptian Muslim whose words are still being actively spread today.

Haykal explains that after the beheading of the men of the Banu Quraiza, Muhammad was at a turning point...a very big one. Islam's next challenge was to fight its way up the pecking order of nations. "The Islamic message," Haykal says, "was not meant for Madinah alone, but for the whole of mankind. The Prophet and his companions still faced the task of preparing for the greater task ahead, namely bringing the word of God to the wide world...."[763]

Muhammad had nurtured global ambitions for a long time. In 627 A.D., when he was supervising the building of the ditch that saved Medina in the Battle of the Trench, one of his soldiers wore himself out attacking a rock that would not give in to his pick. The Prophet climbed down into the trench, took the man's iron tool by the handle, and hit the stone with three blows so hard that "lightning showed beneath the pick."[764] Then he explained to the amazed digger that each blow had a meaning. Said the Prophet, "The first means that God has opened up to me the Yaman; the second [blow means that God has opened to me] Syria and the West; and the third [blow means that God has opened to me] the East."[765] "Yaman," Yemen, was the South. It was the Arab link to the ocean trade with India, Indonesia, Malaysia, and China.[766] "The East" included India, the steppes and mountains of Central Asia, Southeast Asia, and the Asian island nations of the Pacific Rim. And "Syria and the West" referred to Iraq, Turkey...and Europe.

Just in case the planetary scope of his words wasn't clear, Muhammad declared that "Allah drew the ends of the world near one another for my sake and I have seen its eastern and western ends. And the dominion of my Ummah [body of followers] would reach those ends."[767] Added one of Muhammad's soldiers, "The Prophet used to promise us that we should eat the treasures of [the Persian emperor] Chosroes and Caesar [the Roman Emperor]."[768]

In other words, at the very least the Prophet guaranteed those who rallied to his cause the land and goods of the two massive empires that controlled the Middle East, parts of Asia, North Africa, and substantial slivers of Europe: the Persian Empire and the Roman/Byzantine Empire.

In 629 A.D., thanks to his easy wins over the Jews, Muhammad had more than treasures aplenty. He also had the confidence to make his first move toward establishing the continent-swallowing mega-empire he had promised his followers. Muhammad sent letters to half a dozen of the major world leaders of his day.[769] The list of these you-have-won-the-lottery recipients included six superpower sovereigns—the Persian Emperor Chosroes II, the Eastern Roman[4] emperor Hercules (Heracles), the Negus of Abyssinia, the governor of Egypt,[770] the Governor of Syria,[771] and the ruler of Bahrain.[772]

Says Muhammad Haykal, "Heraclius and Chosroes" alone "were at the time the chiefs of ...the greatest states of the age and the makers and arbiters of world policy and world destiny. ...No state or community could think of opposing them."[773] In other words, the Persian Empire and the Eastern Roman Empire were superpowers. Yet each letter was a carefully worded "invitation" to Islam.[774] As you may have guessed, Muhammad's "invitations" were actually military ultimatums in disguise.[775] Islamic sources are very insistent on "punishment for...denying the invitation to Islam."[776] In his letters, the Prophet demanded that the kings convert to the religion of Allah or suffer the consequences. Those consequences were what Ibn Ishaq calls the "onslaught" of "war."[777]

---

4. Remember, the Eastern Roman Empire's capital was Constantinople, otherwise known as Byzantium. But in the days of Muhammad, this wasn't regarded as a Byzantine Empire. It was seen as a new Rome even more Roman than the original. (See Edward Gibbon, *The Decline and Fall of the Roman Empire, Volume II: 395 A.D.–1185 A.D.* New York: The Modern Library, New York.)

By sending his letter to a head of state like the Byzantine Emperor Hercules, Muhammad demonstrated an audacity that Haykal calls "amazing."[7] And amazing it was. When Hercules was puzzled and asked where Muhammad's letter had come from, he was told that it was from a people too backward for Hercules to bother his head about: "from the Arabs, people of sheep and camels."[779] It had come from insignificant barbarians.

But never underrate barbarians.

Muhammad still ruled only one flyspeck, one unheard-of city—Medina, a town of a mere thousand souls lost in the vastness of the Arabian desert. He hadn't even conquered Mecca. Yet. Hercules, on the other hand, ruled one of the biggest empires of the day, an empire that held territory on three continents and that spanned so many cultures that it dizzies the imagination.[780] Yet Muhammad-the-insignificant told Hercules-the-mighty:

> "I invite you to Islam and if you become a Muslim you will be safe, and Allah will double your reward, and if you reject this invitation of Islam you will be committing a sin by misguiding your subjects."[781]

In other words, if you refuse to impose Islam on your citizens, you'll be hung out to dry on one of Islam's meme-hooks. You'll send all of those you rule to torture in an eternity whose endless centuries make our few fleeting years on this planet seem insignificant. What, according to the Qur'an, happens to you if you sin by dooming your subjects to the never-ending fire? Military defeat and an endless sizzle on the coals of the inferno. Says the Qur'an, "Say to those who reject Faith: 'Soon will ye be vanquished and gathered together to hell an evil bed indeed (to lie on)!'"[7]

The Qur'an adds that Allah gives his armies "permission...to annihilate [their] enemy."[783] "How many towns," says the Qur'an, "have We destroyed (for their sins)?"[784] Or, as the 13th-century Islamic scholar Imam Ibn Taymiyyah[785] would someday sum it up, "whoever has heard the summons of the Messenger of God...and has not responded to it, must be fought."[786]

What did this mean in reality for the lands of the six rulers who received Muhammad's invitations? A good deal more than any of them imagined. Writes Mohammad Haykal, "within barely thirty years of the time he sent those missions, the kingdoms of these kings were conquered by the Muslims."[787] And those kingdoms would simply be Allah's appetizers. The entrees would be yet to come. How in the world did such an outlandish reversal of world power, a total change in the pecking order of nations, occur?

How Much Earth Can You Eat in 100 Years?

> Any nonreligious [i.e. non-Islamic] power, whatever
> form or shape, is necessarily an atheistic power, the
> tool of Satan; it is part of our duty to stand in its path
> and to struggle against its effects. Such Satanic power
> can engender nothing but corruption on earth, the
> supreme evil which must be pitilessly fought and
> rooted out. To achieve that end, we have no recourse
> other than to overthrow all governments that do not
> rest on pure Islamic principles, and are thus corrupt
> and corrupting, and to tear down the traitorous, rotten,
> unjust, and tyrannical administrative systems that
> serve them.
>
> —Ayatollah Khomeini, the founding father of today's
> Islamic Republic of Iran[788]

AT THE HEIGHT OF THE COLD WAR, President Dwight D. Eisenhower said, "What makes the Soviet threat unique in history is its all-inclusiveness. Every human activity is pressed into service as a weapon of expansion. Trade, economic development, military power, arts, science, education, [and] the whole world of ideas."[789] Eisenhower was right about the potential power of what he described, a totalitarian superorganism, a massively conformity-enforced social beast battling for top predator status. But he was wrong when he said that this totalitarian social strategy was "unique in history." He overlooked the 14-century-long history of militant Islam.

By 629 A.D., when the battle of Khaibar was over, Muhammad had invented precisely what Eisenhower described…a new form of superorganism—a totalitarian military dictatorship with a full-time army, an army paid with taxes and loot sucked from the unbelievers. Muhammad had crafted a dictatorship with a meme-team that covered every aspect of life from the direction in which you urinate and your daily schedule to what you believe, one of the very few military dictatorships in history to come complete with a brand new picture of the invisible world. Muhammad's new squad of memes demanded perpetual war[790] and "dawa"—conversion by persistent persuasion. Muhammad's new worldview also said you won more prizes if you died "fighting in the way of Allah"[791] than if you remained alive.

Every new form of superorganism is a gamble, a guess on the best way to mine a niche in a rapidly evolving world. Muhammad's guess turned out to be one of the best in history.

*   *   *

You'll recall that Muhammad inflicted mass murder. He perpetrated what we would call war crimes—genocide or ethnic cleansing—on four groups of Jews: the Banu Qaynuqa, the Banu Nadir, the Banu Quraiza and the Jews of Khaibar. He used ethnic expulsion, genocide and torture for a reason. He brutalized the small fry to frighten the big fish into surrender. And his strategy worked. First three Jewish towns, Fadak, Wadi al Qura, and Tayma, gave up to the Muslim warriors with barely a struggle.[792] Then the leader of Yemen heard the news of Muhammad's "total destruction of Jewish power,"[793] converted to Islam, and brought Yemen into the Muslim fold.[794] A very big score.

Most important, in 630 A.D., the strategy of using attacks on Jews to "cast terror into the hearts of the unbelievers"[795] paid off big-time. It landed Muhammad the ultimate prize, the city he had grown up in. The city at the center of religious tourism. The city that had mounted three expeditions to annihilate him. The city he had fought at Badr, Uhud, and the Battle of the Trench. The city of his archenemies and former neighbors: Mecca! When Muhammad and his troops showed up outside of Mecca, the Meccans were well aware of the slaughter and devastation Muhammad had spread among Arabia's Jews. So they caved in without a fight,[796] preferring life as Muslims to death as indigenous idol worshippers, to death by "cutting heads to pieces."[797] Picking on the nerds had paid off.

The Meccans had an additional incentive to switch sides and go with Islam. Thanks to its lucrative victories over the Jews, the Muslim political, military, and religious system appeared to be the winning idea of the moment, the worldview whose military triumphs promised the biggest material and genetic rewards, the biggest sexual rewards, to those who would fight under its banner. And the Meccans liked to fight. To repeat what Maulana A.S. Muhammad Abdul Hai says, war and looting were the Meccans' "hobby."[798] Now that the Meccan military hobbyists were a part of the Muslim community, the spread of Islam and its memes—its overall approach to life—would speed up dramatically.

*   *   *

Would Muhammad be able to do with Mecca what he had done with Medina? Would he be able to stamp his own personality on the city's culture? The answer lies in yet another character trait that Muhammad—the key man in Islam's founder effect—would bequeath to his followers.

The Prophet had a problem with laughter. Satan laughed.[799] Muhammad's enemies laughed—usually when they were mocking him.[800] But Muhammad spoke sternly to his followers, damned them when they displeased him, and discouraged anything that looked like humor.[801] Said he,

> O followers of Muhammad! By Allah! If you knew that which I know you would laugh little and weep much.[802]

Muhammad had been the butt of many a joke in his first years preaching Islam. He may also have been given a rough time when he was a kid. After all, he was an orphan being raised by an uncle so lacking in wealth and power that he'd been forced to ask others to feed and house his two sons. So to Muhammad, there was nothing funny about humor. In fact, humor, he said, was a form of attack: "hostility" he proclaimed, "begins with joking."[803]

When Muhammad took Mecca in 630 A.D.,[804] one of the town's citizens had two slave girls, two "singing girls." Research has shown that adolescent girls often mount vicious pecking order attacks.[805] They don't plot violent wars of spears and swords, but prefer onslaughts of putdowns and of cutting words.[806] The hottest news topic in Mecca in 630 A.D. was the invasion and takeover pulled off by Muhammad, the man about to remake the town in his own image. So the two girls improvised songs on this headline topic, uplifting their voices in what early Islamic historian al-Tabari calls "satire about the Messenger of God."[807] Not a good idea.

Muhammad ordered that both girls be killed. When one ran for her life, a brave companion of Muhammad's took off after her with his war horse and trampled her to death. Just for good measure, Muhammad had the owner of the adolescent satirists executed, too.[808]

Humor—a device for airing society's problems in a new light, a device that often involves not-so-hidden criticism of manners, mores, and leaders—was something Islam ruled out of the picture.[809] In an act that impoverished his culture further, Muhammad also forbade the use of musical instruments.[810]

Another incident shows more of the totalitarian form of society Muhammad, with his intolerance and anger, was crafting.

Muhammad drove home his message of absolute obedience, death-sentence-enforced obedience, in Mecca by issuing a hit list of ten people in this, his old hometown, that he wanted rubbed out. One of the victims on the list—Abdallah bin Sa'd—had acted as a scribe for Muhammad, writing down many of the key passages of the Qur'an.[811] So what was the scribe's crime? Says one of Islam's most important historians, the tenth-century Persian al-Tabari, when Muhammad "was dictating 'Exalted in power, full of Wisdom,'"Abdullah would change the wording and "write it 'Oft-Forgiving, Most Merciful,' thus changing it."[812] Later on, when Muhammad preached, he'd use the words that Abdallah had written, not those Allah had originally "spoken" through Muhammad's mouth.[813] To Abdallah this seemed a suspicious way of handling the direct revelations of God. So he rejected Islam and went back to Mecca and to the beliefs of his forefathers.

Abdallah wasn't enthusiastic about being murdered for his quiet act of peaceful dissent. When he found that he was an assassination target, he fled to his foster brother for protection. His foster brother kept Abdallah hidden until "after the people of Mecca had become calm."[814] Then he took Abdallah to the spot where Muhammad was holding court in the newly conquered city and asked for mercy.

The foster brother pleaded for a pardon. Muhammad said nothing. The foster brother pleaded some more. Muhammad still sat in stony silence. So the foster brother pleaded the case all over again. Finally, Muhammad said a grudging yes, he'd let Abdallah live. When Abdallah and his relieved foster brother left the room and were out of earshot, Muhammad turned on "his companions who were around him" in one of his common moods—a fury. How had his stalwarts failed him? By not understanding what he really wanted. "By God, I kept silent so that one of you might go up to him and cut off his head!" said the Prophet angrily. Then "why didn't you give me a signal, Messenger of God?" asked one of Muhammad's lieutenants. The Prophet spat out a simple sentence, "A prophet does not kill by making signs."[815]

In other words, Muhammad wanted his companions to understand that in his presence they should cut down any dissenter immediately, no matter how much Muhammad pretended to be forgiving and beneficent. In Muhammad's presence the default mode was murder.

Thus was born the form of intolerant dictatorship, the violently meme-policed dictatorship, that today has made the Middle East one of the poorest regions in the world.[816] Thus was born one of the world's longest-lasting and widest-spread social and political structures, a political system that has survived nearly 1,400 years. How can we account for this contradiction—one of the world's most vigorously explosive meme teams, a collective personality with astonishing longevity, a culture that has taken more territory than any other in history, yet a culture that all too often withers its wealth production, squelches its potential sources of vitality, kills its critics, its protesters, its innovators, and its artists or terrifies them into silence? What's wrong with this picture? What hooks in Islam and what collective mind or muscles in the political and military system that Muhammad assembled and that his followers have done their best to replicate account for Islam's extraordinary success?

How To Be a Perfect Human

> "The Prophet [Muhammad] said, 'A single endeavor
> (of fighting) in Allah's Cause in the forenoon or in
> the afternoon is better than the world and whatever
> is in it.'"
>
> —Sahih Bukhari, Book #52, Hadith #50[817]

MUHAMMAD WAS A VIRTUOSO at doing something few men or women before or since have achieved—ratcheting the Founder Effect up to a level far higher than mere instinct, psychology, or biology alone have ever achieved. Muhammad's attempt to remain a shaper of men and women for the rest of time paid off. The generations of the faithful who came after his death labored with astonishing diligence to insure that every word, gesture, and quirk of their founder would remain at the core of the Muhammadan civilization.

Muhammad died in 632 A.D. After his death, the faithful assembled Muhammad's revelations from God in the Qur'an.[818] And they compiled eyewitness accounts of the Prophet's every gesture and word in a massive set of volumes called the Hadith.[819] For the next 14 centuries, Islamic judges and scholars would dictate every detail[820] of a pious Muslim's life based on the example Muhammad had left behind—the examples chronicled in the Qur'an and the Hadith.

What were the personality traits that Muhammad stamped permanently into his believers? To find out we have to answer a question posed by Azzam Publications, an online information site for militant Muslims that quietly shut itself down after 9/11.[821] Before the website disappeared, its creators, "your brothers at Azzam Publications," wrote that "There is no such thing as a 'moderate' or 'liberal' Muslim. If there was, in what category would be place[d] the Prophet Muhammad...? Would we say he is a moderate, a liberal, an extremist, a fanatic, [or] a terrorist?"[822]

The boys at Azzam then took a stab at an answer to their own question. Muhammad, they said, "certainly would not be a moderate or liberal since he ordered 600–700 Jewish males to be beheaded in Madinah.... He also fought in 27 battles for the sake of Allah. Are we now going to call him a terrorist as well?"[823]

Good question!

Muhammad left many personal examples and many meme-hooks. Among the most important was the obligation to kill unbelievers. Yes, I said kill. Killing for the sake of a simple goal: to expand the empire of Islam. Hard to believe, right? But according to one of modern Islam's most influential interpreters, Hassan Al-Banna, the founder of the Muslim Brotherhood, a group with enormous clout in the Middle East, in Europe,[824] and in America,[825] "All Muslims must make jihad. Jihad is an obligation from Allah on every Muslim and cannot be ignored nor evaded."[826] In Al-Banna's opinion, Allah demands that even the most frightened, "those who are scared to the utmost degree to plunge into battle and to face death" turn themselves around and "unflinchingly and bravely," see that they must "welcome death, and that if they die in jihad, they will receive the most magnificent recompense for their lives."[827] To prove that he is correctly channeling Muhammad—and the God who spoke through Muhammad—Al-Banna quotes Muhammad's words, "concerning warfare against the treacherous polytheists: 'Fight against them so that Allah will punish them by your hands and disgrace them and give you victory over them.'"[828]

But surely I'm taking statements out of context. Surely Muhammad did not enjoy killing and did not insist that all his male followers come to enjoy it, too. Oh, really? Here's Al-Banna quoting Muhammad again: "I wish I could be killed in the Way of Allah, then live again so that I may be killed again, then live again so that again I may be killed, then live again so that again I may be killed."[829] Judging from these words, Muhammad enjoyed war. And he was indicating that his male followers should learn to enjoy it, too.

But Muhammad only mentions being killed in these quotes, not killing. Surely he did not have killing in mind. Really? Says the Prophet in the Qur'an, "slay the pagans wherever ye find them and seize them beleaguer them and lie in wait for them in every stratagem (of war)."[830] The believers, Muhammad says, "fight in His [Allah's] cause and slay and are slain."[831]

How often should a good Muslim make war? Al-Banna quotes the work of an 18th-century Muslim scholar from Bengal,[832] "the author of the Majma', al-Anhar fi Sharh Multaqal-Abhar...'It is fard (obligatory) on us to fight with the enemies. The Imam must send a military expedition to the Dar-al-Harb [the lands of the unbelievers] every year at least once or twice.'"[833] To achieve paradise, every adult male must make jihad. Not spiritual jihad. The real deal, the jihad in which you kill non-believers. The jihad in which you enter the lands of the unbelievers and conquer those lands. You cannot simply sit home and let others do the fighting. Says the Qur'an, "those who strive and fight hath He distinguished above those who sit (at home) by a special re-ward."[834] Emphasized the holy book, "Warfare is ordained for you, though it is hateful unto you, but it may happen that ye hate a thing which is good for you."[835] No other founder of a modern worldview, a modern governmental system, a modern religion, or a modern civilization, has made killing obliga-tory. And conquest.

What's more, Muhammad put that killing in a broader framework, in a big picture. He said, "It is not for any prophet to have captives until he hath made slaughter in the land."[836] Another translation puts it even more chill-ingly: "It is not for a prophet to have captives [of war] until he inflicts a mas-sacre."[837] In other words, kill, kill, kill into you have driven the few remaining unbelievers into defecate-in-your-pants terror. Take advantage of learned helplessness, substance P, and the Stockholm Syndrome. Then, when the survivors prostrate themselves at your feet begging for you to spare their lives and offering any price, insist that they convert. Insist that they convert to Islam and willingly take up a position on the bottom of the pecking order, the bottom of society. Your society. The society that you, the jihadist, rule. Either add new peoples to the Ummah of Islam or eradicate them. As Hassan Al-Banna put it, "only Islam can save mankind from itself. And jihad on the individual and international scale will be a necessary part of this process of change."[838]

Is Islam a peaceful religion? Said Muhammad, "Let it be known that Paradise lies in the shadows of the swords."[839] This is not peace; it is the sys-tem of a top predator. It is perpetual war.

* * *

There are moderates in Islam. And there are reformers. We'll meet a few of them later. But no pollster has tried to ascertain how many moderate Muslims there are. Despite the lack of data, it's reasonable to believe that the modern-ist, pluralist, tolerant Muslims are in the hundreds of millions.

Yet holiness, righteousness, manners, and decency in extremist Islam and in most of mainstream[840] Muslim culture are based on the example set by Muhammad.[841] According to one of Muhammad's many Islamic biographers, "Sincerely tread the footsteps of Allah's final Messenger [Muhammad]... observe his glorious actions and attitudes, and most import-ant of all follow them, as the faithful among his companions did."[842] Another Islamic biographer titles his book, "The Last Prophet [Muhammad]: A Model

For All Time."[843] And today's Muslim biographers agree that Muhammad is not just a paragon whose actions Muslims should imitate. He is a model of virtue for you and me.[844]

Though Islamic literature occasionally refers to Muhammad as a "Prophet of Peace,"[845] he was anything but. Muhammad called himself by many names. One of those was "*nabiyyu 'l-malhamah*," "the Prophet of War."[846,847] Muhammad's followers have also praised him as "he who was sent with sword"[848] and "Muhammad the Conqueror"[849]—one of Osama bin Laden's phrases. "Your brothers at Azzam Publications" point out with pride that Muhammad was a man who used weapons and went into battle, a man who killed. And Muhammad was a military dictator, a totalitarian[850] who used executions and assassinations on a regular basis. Or, as the Ayatollah Khomeini put it,

> The leaders of our religion were all soldiers, commanders, and warriors. They put on military dress and went into battle in the wars that are described for us in our history; they killed, and they were killed. The Commander of the Faithful himself [Muhammad] (upon whom be peace) would place a helmet on his blessed head, don his coat of chain mail, and gird on a sword.[851]

In 624 A.D.,[852] Allah told Muhammad that he and his followers had permission to wage Jihad[853]—to Crusade, to make Holy War.[854] Muhammad said that terror, killing,[8] and trickery[856] would be Jihad's three basic tools.

Muhammad's ideas worked. Mightily. Says a biography of Muhammad from the Islamic Universal Sunnah Foundation in Pakistan, the Prophet started with an army of only four Muslims, but grew that force to an army of thirty thousand.[857] Explains the Foundation's biography, during Muhammad's eight years of "conquest" he, his "Islamic army," and his "undaunted soldiers of Islam...took control" of all "the vastness of the Arabian Peninsula" and forced Arabia's citizens "to convert to Islam or to accept the supremacy of the Muslims as their rulers."[858]

Muhammad's biographers are proud of the Prophet's role as what they call a "military leader."[859] The most telling mark of Muhammad's war-making and empire-founding prowess may be one simple statistic. According to Pakistan's Universal Sunnah Foundation, under Muhammad's generalship, "Islam spread on an average of 822 square kilometres per day."[860] That's over 317 square miles. Per day.

Or, as the fifth edition of ISIS' gorgeously art-directed magazine *Dābiq*, the November 21, 2014, issue, put the legacy that ISIS felt Muhammad had left to them: "The shade of this blessed [ISIS] flag will expand until it covers all eastern and western extents of the Earth, filling the world with the truth and justice of Islam."[861] Then *Dābiq* quotes a phrase from the Hadith that you've seen before, "Indeed, Allah gathered the Earth for me, and thus I saw its eastern and western extents, and indeed the reign of my Ummah will reach what was gathered for me from the Earth."[862]

As a leader of Hezbollah said as long ago as 1986, "Don't believe that we want an Islamic republic in Lebanon. ...What Hezbollah wants is a world Islamic republic."[863]

Thanks to Muhammad's example, Islam became and remains the most successful imperialist enterprise in the modern world. And it wants its stature as top player in the empire game back. It wants its prestige, its superiority, its ability to reprogram other societies, its ability to subjugate, and its sheer power. It wants to be top predator. It wants what we want. It wants the form of control—the form of cultural self-replication—we call saving the world.

* * *

When Muhammad died in 632 A.D., there was a squabble over who should take his place. Muhammad's best friend, Abu Bakr, won. He became the "caliph," the "successor" of Muhammad. And he took Muhammad's global ambitions seriously—very seriously indeed. For good reason. Without its Prophet, the Islamic community was in danger of falling apart. Battle is a bonding mechanism,[864] a way to give a superorganism the social glue it needs to survive. It's also a way to test your new social structure by gambling your males on growth. Abu Bakr apparently sensed the adhesive power of us versus them[865]—the cohesion you get when you pit our team against their team, our gang against their gang,[866] our good guys against their bad guys. And Abu Bakr sensed the extra boost you get in cohesion when your battle between groups spills blood.[867] After Muhammad's death in 632 A.D., says sociologist of Islam Reuben Levy, "war... was the normal state, ...peace ... was the period of the year when campaigning was not possible."[868]

The victories early Islam achieved were staggering. In 634 A.D., a mere two years after the Prophet breathed his last, the armies of Islam conquered Iraq.[869] In 637 A.D., five years after Muhammad's death, the Muslim forces did something impossible. They conquered a superpower. They toppled the emperor of Persia, sacked the Persian capital, Ctesiphon (the home base of Nestorian Christianity), and took over the massive Persian Empire. That same year, 637 A.D., the desert Arabs of Islam snatched the city most holy to Jews and Christians, Jerusalem. Muhammad's new meme-team—a worldview that idealized obedience, killing and expansionary conquest—was on a road test in the real world and was proving that it had remarkable horsepower!

In 640 A.D., eight years after Muhammad's demise, the Muslims went even more multi-continental. They conquered Syria outright and began their penetration of the Sudan in Africa. In roughly 642 A.D., the second Caliph, Omar, reportedly issued the following order to his governor in Syria—"Strike terror into wrongdoers and make heaps of mutilated limbs out of them."[870] This psyche-slamming strategy—Muhammad's strategy of terror—like the rest of militant Islam, worked.

In 642 A.D., a mere ten years after Muhammad's death, the Muslim armies conquered Egypt, began to take Afghanistan, and started sending delegations to China, winning Chinese converts, and building China's first mosque.[871] In 654 A.D., 22 years after Muhammad's departure unto paradise, a Muslim fleet of over two hundred ships clobbered a Byzantine navy of five hundred vessels in the Mediterranean, [872] demonstrating that a tribe of camel-herding desert traders and Sinbad-the-sailor type Indian Ocean seafarers could be deadly both on land and on sea. In 674 A.D., Islam established a colony in a place so far away that no previous Middle Eastern or European conqueror had even tried to add it to his package of real estate—the Pacific Rim island of Sumatra—five thousand miles east of Mecca.[873]

But this totally-against-the-odds conquest of an immense territory was just the beginning. From 642 to 705 A.D., Islam grabbed the entire Mediterranean coast of Africa—Libya, Tunisia, Morocco, and Algeria. In Africa, the wives of indigenous kings killed themselves so that they wouldn't become sex toys—slave girls—in the hands of the Muslim invaders. One of these queens, the Western African Sudanese ruler Dahia-Al Kahina, a Jew, either committed suicide or died in battle, depending on which account you read,[874] in 705 A.D. after leading her troops against the Arabs and driving the growing hordes of Allah north to Tripolitania.[875]

From 711 to 714 A.D., the Islamic governor of Iraq, al-Hajjaj bin Yousef, a man who called himself "The Bone Crusher," went on a campaign to expand the empire of Islam even further. He ordered his generals to conquer a breathtaking swath of territory—Central Asia's Turkestan[876] (including today's Chinese province of Xinjiang),[877] swatches of India, all of Spain, and to tighten control of North Africa. His orders for the treatment of unbelievers were simple: infidels should either be killed, imprisoned, or turned into second-class citizens, dhimmi.[878] And he had a reputation as one of the four men in early Islam to kill 100,000 people.[879] A positive reputation. Muhammad would have been proud.

The armies sent by "The Bone Crusher" into Europe were led by an ally newly won over to Islam, a newly converted Berber slave, Tarik ibn Ziyad.[880] Ziyad's troops crossed the Straits of Gibraltar, toppled the Christian King of Spain—the Visigoth Roderick—seized his entire kingdom, then advanced into southern France.[881]

In 712 A.D., a mere 80 years after the death of the one true Prophet, the Bone Crusher's Arab troops and their rapidly expanding cohort of foreign allies took Muhammad's example of nonstop military expansion even farther and conquered Sind in Western Pakistan. This was a perfect base for more attacks on an only partially conquered India.[882] And attack is exactly what the armies of Islam did. Said one Sufi Muslim, Amir Khusrau, "The whole country, by means of the sword of holy warriors, has become like a forest denuded of its thorns by fire. Had not the Law granted exemption from death by the payment of poll-tax the very name of Hind[us], root and branch, would have been extinguished."[883]

According to medieval historian K.S. Lal,[884] a total of 80 million Hindus died or were converted at the hands of Muslim invaders.[885] Then, as in most of their new territories, the Arabs capped their victories with colonialism.[886] Entire clans of Arabs left the Middle East and settled in the conquered swatches of India,[887] lording it over the natives, hoarding the wealth, wiping out indigenous cultures, and imposing Islamic law.

A hungry meme team was having a feast.

In 750 A.D., the Empire of Islam seized a broader swath of land and ocean than any previous empire had ever grabbed—broader than the empires of the Assyrians, the Persians, the Romans, or the Chinese. In fact, broader than all those empires combined. Islam penetrated further into the Pacific Rim by taking Indonesia's Aceh province and faced its first showdown with a Chinese army. The warriors of Islam defeated the unbeatable Chinese at the Battle of Talas in Kazakhstan,[888] and reportedly learned paper-making from their Chinese captives. Islam also seized the vital Asian Silk Road trading city of Samarkand...a town through which super-high-end Chinese goods flowed to Europe and to the Middle East.

Muhammad's totalitarian political meme and his picture of the invisible world worked military wonders. No empire in history had ever shown such astonishing multi-continental capabilities. In 750 A.D., 5,300 miles and a continent away from Aceh, Muslim Arabs turned the African area of Mombasa into an export center for three upscale luxury items from Africa's distant heartlands—ivory, gold, and black slaves. Eventually Islam's African empire would cover roughly six million square kilometers,[889] and the multi-continental Muslim trade in African slaves would uproot over 112 million blacks from their homes, would kill 84 million of them, and would put over 28 million blacks on sale in slave markets from one end of the empire of Islam to the other.[890] This outdid the Western slave trade's appalling 11 million black Africans displaced and a million killed by a staggering multiple of more than ten to one. At the same time, in 750 A.D., Muslim armies grabbed a legendary source of snow-white slaves, the Caucasus mountains.[891] The enslaved women of the Caucasus were so prized as trophies and sex toys in Muslim harems that they became known as "Circassian beauties."[892]

From the victim's point of view, the Islamic conquest was Armageddon, the end of the world, apocalypse now. Egypt was a thoroughly Christian land that gave birth to Christianity's monastic movement and to legendary Christian heroes of piety like St. Paul of Thebes. St. Paul of Thebes was credited as Christianity's first hermit. He lived in Egypt's southern mountains and ate only fruits and water.[893] But John the Bishop of the Egyptian island of Nikiou, says that when:

> The Muslims arrived in Nikiou. There was not one single soldier to resist them. They seized the town and slaughtered everyone they met in the street and in the churches—men, women and children, sparing nobody. Then they went to other places, [and] pillaged and killed all the inhabitants they found…. It is impossible to describe the horrors the Muslims committed.[894]

Muhammad's strategy of "casting terror"[895] into the hearts of those who refused to see the truth of Islam was demonstrating just how effective it could be. At the Armenian town of Dvin in 642 A.D., a mere ten years after Muhammad's death, Sepeos writes that a Muslim "army rushed in and butchered the inhabitants of the town by the sword…gorging itself on booty." Then, writes Sepeos, "After a few days' rest, the Ishmaelites [Arabs] went back whence they had come, dragging after them a host of captives, numbering thirty-five thousand."[896]

One Islamic source, Dr. A. Zahoor, claims that the reports of war crimes and atrocities in Islam's world-sweeping days of imperialism and colonialism radically misrepresent history. The armies of Islam, says Dr. Zahoor, showed such mercy, such concern for those they attacked, and such "lofty moral principles" that entire cities surrendered happily to the soldiers of Islamic justice.[897] That claim seems debatable.

Entire cities—like the 40,000-population Jewish metropolis of Caesarea whose "terrible scenes" John of Nikiou noted—disappeared entirely. Forty-one cities in just one small portion of the Jewish Holy Land, Sharon, were sand-blasted off the face of the Earth. Or, to put it in the more delicate words of the ninth-century Muslim historian Abu Al-Abbas Ahmad Bin Jab Al-Baladhuri,[8] after "the Arab conquest...all trace of them is lost."[899]

In Celicia, adds Michael the Syrian, "when [the head of the Islamic empire, the Caliph] Mu'awiyah arrived he ordered all the inhabitants to be put to the sword.... After gathering up all the wealth of the town, they set to torturing the leaders to make them show them things [treasures] that had been hidden." Thus did a new generation of Muslims follow their founder's example when he had ordered a captured Jewish leader tortured to discover where a conquered town's treasures were hidden. Then Mu'awiya's troops followed another of Muhammad's examples and "led everyone into slavery—men and women, boys and girls."[900]

The citizens of Egypt's most glorious city, Alexandria, were spared this slaughter. But they lived to regret it. Their Arab conquerors levied a tax that John of Nikiou says brought them "to the point of offering their children in exchange for the enormous sums that they had to pay each month."[901]

These taxes went to pay, feed, and equip the growing armies of Islam. The Caliph Omar,[9] the man who took over as second head of the Muslim community two years after Muhammad's death, said that once the infidels were defeated, those who were still alive should be left to till their expropriated farms[903] so that the ummah—the global body, the superorganism of Islam—could levy the taxes necessary "to pay the wages and food of the warriors..."[904] Why was this vital? Said Omar, it would give Islam's "troops...the necessary means to carry on the holy war [jihad]" without cease and to support the "soldiers and mercenaries" needed to make sure that "the infidels would [not] return to their former possessions."[905]

Conquered peoples were the fingers of the growing Muslim superorganism, and were put to work feeding its jaws and teeth. And those jaws and teeth were not just the tribal bands Muhammad had led. They were full-time armies dedicated to cleansing the world of idolatry, to eradicating indigenous legal, political, and religious systems, and to replacing false beliefs, false governments, and false laws with the God-given "complete system"[906]—the totalitarian system—of Islam.

A key Greek island symbolized the manner in which Islam cut out the heart of each local culture and planted the meme team of Islam in its place. That island was Rhodes—home to the ruins of one of the Seven Wonders of the Ancient World—a colossal 11-story-high, 936-year-old statue of the Greek God of the Sun, Helios, a monument that had once straddled Rhodes' harbor, with one enormous foot standing on one side of the inlet to the port and the other gigantic foot planted on the opposite bank. The armies of the One True faith "went to Rhodes, and devastated it." They sold the remains of the Colossus of Rhodes to a scrap merchant who carted the stone, iron, and bronze off to Turkey on nine hundred camels.[907] That's the top predator's secret strategy. Why make riches when you can take them? Why accept the memes of the natives when you can replace them? Or when you can keep them and use them to rule the peoples you have swallowed?

Equal tales of atrocity could be told about every major civilization on the planet, including the civilization of the West. In fact, they have been, by Western authors like Noam Chomsky[908] and Howard Zinn.[909] But European and American imperialism have come nowhere near Islam's achievement. Within 110 years of Muhammad's death, Islam, the first modern religion created by a holy-war-maker and political dictator with global ambitions, had taken a territory whose extent you know—the size of seven United States and of five Roman Empires. Yes, five Roman Empires!!!

What's more, Islam possessed an advantage that few other top predators had even imagined—a system that covered every aspect of life, one that came complete with a worldview, a governmental structure, a judicial system, laws, a military philosophy, and a routine of daily discipline—an all-encompassing meme team with which militant Islam could assert mind-control over its shattered victims.

The result—through violence, terror, trade, and persuasion, Islam opened the skulls of indigenous cultures and implanted its own memetic brain, doing this with far more permanence than any imperialist power had achieved before or since. As we've seen, the citizens of the lands subjugated by Muslim conquerors or converted by Muslim traders have remained faithful to the religion of their conquerors for as long as 1,300 years. That's what the founder effect can do when your founder is hell-bent on digesting every empire of his day, on giving each conquered empire a new soul, and on utterly changing its mass mind. That's what the founder effect can do when one of its primary tools is gut-wrenching terror.

* * *

Muhammad was driven by memes...a team of them that assembled themselves in his head in 22 years of inspiration, revelation, and thought.[910] Muhammad pulled together a superorganism. That superorganism entered the pecking order and pecked its way to the top. It proved itself in the real world. It showed an ability to grab the top predator slot in a way that no imperialist power before or since has demonstrated. Today Islam has been briefly pecked back toward the bottom. But Islam's memes are still trying to feed new peoples and new nations to the superorganism of Islam and to raise that superorganism ever higher in the pecking order. And militants like the members of ISIS, al Qaeda, and Boko Haram are laboring to return Islam to the stature it had for 1,200 years, as Planet Earth's top predator. What's more, they are working to complete the work that Muhammad himself laid out for them—or was it Allah: total domination of the Earth.

* * *

Meanwhile both the pecking order and its combatants are evolving. Evolving into new forms of group IQ, new forms of learning machines, new forms of mass mind. And preparing to fight with new weaponry. Weaponry that can eradicate our species. Nuclear, chemical, and biological weaponry.

The problem for you and me is that militant Islam's global jihad has never stopped. From the seventh century onward, Islam isolated, encircled, besieged, and terrified the West in ways that we moderns prefer to forget. John Esposito, professor of International Affairs and Islamic Studies at Georgetown University and director of the Prince Alwaleed Center for Muslim-Christian Understanding, like many other writers on the topic, justifies the ferocity of today's Islamic anti-Western sentiments by reminding us, "Many in the Arab and Muslim world view the history of Islam and of the Muslim world's dealings with the West as one of victimization and oppression at the hands of an expansive imperial power."[911] He is right about the modern Islamic perception. But he is wrong about the facts.

It was the *Islamic* empire that held the upper hand in the struggle between East and West for over 1,100 years. The Muslim conquest of the Middle

East in the seventh century A.D. gave Islam the land of the Jews and, more important geopolitically, the land of Christianity's birth. Islam became the permanent occupier of Christianity's motherland, the territory that gave birth to most of the Fathers of the Church, territory that included Galatia, Bithynia, Pontus and Cappadocia—where St. Paul established many of the first Christian churches. These are the cities to which St. Paul wrote the letters, the epistles, central to the New Testament.

Islamic Imperialists took Syria, whose capital, Damascus, was one of the earliest major Christian centers. Damascus, as you've glimpsed, was the city St. Paul set out for when he fell off his ass and was smacked by a vision of blinding light. Four hundred years later, Syria was the land of Christian ascetics like St. Simeon the Stylite, who lived on a 60-foot-high, custom-built masonry column in the desert for 36 years to demonstrate his dedication to Christ.[912] Four Christian basilicas were built around the pillar of St. Simeon when he died.[913] St. Simeon's act of sacred endurance took place in a Christian and Jewish land that has remained in Islamic hands for roughly 1,379 years.

Christianity counterattacked in the 12th century with the Crusades. The Crusades were imitations of an Islamic invention, Holy War, Jihad. They came only after Europe had been pounded and surrounded for 384 years by the forces of jihad. And they were a miserable failure.

The Crusaders' battles were over a postage-stamp-sized piece of territory, primarily the land where Christ had lived and preached—land Christ was able to reach on foot. The traditional Jewish land of Israel. And the Crusaders were initially greeted with enthusiasm by many of the region's Islamic rulers, who had divided the Middle East into tiny Muslim principalities, then gone to war with each other. To some of these petty sultans, princes, atabegs,[914] and emirs, the foreign invaders seemed like superb allies with whose help they could crush a rival or two.[915]

The knights of the cross—the Western Crusaders—were hideously barbaric and bloody. When they besieged Jerusalem in 1099, they promised safety to many of the city's communities if those communities would help them breach the city's walls. But once the Crusaders penetrated the city's defenses they broke their promises and killed every man, woman, and child they could find. One ancient historian[916] says that the blood became a flood that swelled up to the Christian warriors' ankles.[917]

But these European butchers did not retain their reconquered fiefdoms in the Christian and Jewish Holy Land long. They were expelled by 1187...

giving them a total stay of 88 years, a flea's sneeze compared to Islam's nearly 1,400-year grip on the indigenous lands of North Africa, the Middle East, Central Asia, and much of the Pacific Rim. Nonetheless, according to historian Amin Maalouf, the author of *The Crusades Through Arab Eyes*,[918] modern Arabs tend to see today's world events as a continuation of the Crusades. And so do many of us.

Frankly, we are blind to the blunt facts of history. We forget that for seven hundred years after the fall of the Crusader states, Islamic forces returned to the attack, crusading against and capturing Greece, parts of Italy, and chunks of Eastern Europe, raiding towns in Sicily, the Italian coasts, Cornwall, Ireland, England,[919] France, Brittany, Ile de Groix, the Biscay coast, Portugal, and Spain. We forget that in 1625 the naval forces of the Islamic Jihad established a base on the island of Lundy off the coast of England to support its raids on towns in Britain.[920] We forget that seaborne Muslim Crusaders took more than a million Europeans as slaves.[921] We forget that these Muslim Holy Sailors followed the principles of jihad established by Muhammad in his land-based military campaigns. The Islamic sea-warriors seized the citizens of entire villages as slaves and took the goods of these captives as loot, just as the Qur'an's chapter eight, "The Spoils of War, The Booty,"[922] says they should.

One night in 1631, for example, the Islamic raiders silently slid their warships onto the Irish beach near the town of Baltimore.[923] In the morning Baltimore was a ghost town. All the citizens had been taken captive or killed. Those allowed to live were destined for sale in the slave markets of cities like Algiers,[924] Damascus, Baghdad, and Mecca. And their homes were stripped of everything of value. This is the "booty" and the "loot" that the Qur'an and the biographies of Muhammad promise to the faithful. The "generosity"[925] of Allah.

Twelfth-century Islamic military tactician Abu Bakr of Tortosa[926] went through the Qur'an and the Hadith to derive Allah's own dictates for combat. He wrote, "In the battle he [a commander] must urge his men to victory, by ...promising those who are steadfast the rewards of Allah if they should reach the next world, and, if they remain alive in this world, tribute and an extra share of booty."[927] Towns like Baltimore provided that extra booty. And they provided this sanctified loot in the beginning of the modern era, 15 years after William Shakespeare had gone to his grave. Yes, after. No wonder Shakespeare wrote of Muslim warriors and of Islam's gargantuan navies in his play about a converted[928] Muslim general, *Othello*.[929]

There's much more that we forget. We forget that in the two centuries straddled by Shakespeare's life (1564–1616), the 1500s and 1600s, the

Muslims were advancing relentlessly on Europe. As historian Peter O'Brien writes, "In a series of Danubian campaigns the Turks first galloped into Belgrade (1521) and from there crossed the Hungarian plain—routing the [Hungarian] royal army at Mohacs in 1526 in a mere two hours." Then the Muslim Turks laid "siege to Vienna in 1529" and kept going, "swallow[ing] up all of St. Stephen's dominions, including [Hungary's capital] Buda in 1541, and beyond into southern Ukraine and Lithuania."[930] The result? As 17th-century English historian Richard Knolles wrote in his 1603 *Generall Historie of the Turkes*, the Muslim Turks were "the terror of Europe"[931] and "the greatest terror of the World."[932] Europe was seized by an overwhelming anxiety, a *Türkenfurcht*,[933] a "dread of the Turks,"[934] a fear so overpowering that Martin Luther wrote three entire works on the topic—a book *On War Against the Turk*, his Military Sermon[935] against the Turk, and an introduction to a 1543 translation of the Qur'an.[936] Some thought that all of Christendom was about to end at the hands of the Muhammadan invaders. One Venetian diplomat to the court of the Turkish Sultan feared that Christendom was facing "a great extermination."[937] Flemish diplomat Ogier Ghiselin de Busbecq, who acted as the Austrian King Ferdinand's ambassador to the court of the Caliph of Islam and Ottoman Sultan Suleiman the Magnificent in 1554 and 1556, put it differently. He called the upcoming Muslim Anschluss an "infinite destruction"[938] and "a devastation that passes all belief."[939] Here's how he put it:

> The Turkish armies are like mighty rivers swollen with rain, which, if they can trickle through at any point in the banks which restrain them, spread through the breach and cause infinite destruction. Even so, and with still more terrible results, the Turks, when once they have burst the barriers which restrain them, spread far and wide and cause a devastation which passes all belief.[940]

No wonder that in 1555, a French poet advised the Christian population to abandon Europe utterly and to try life all over again in the New World.[941] And when Halley's comet arrived in 1682, "countless Europeans" felt it was a divine sign that the extermination at the hands of the Muslims was nigh.[942]

We forget all of this. And we forget a good deal more. We forget that for 1,094 years—from 711 A.D.[943] to 1805 A.D.[944]—much of the Mediterranean was an "Islamic Lake,"[945] a private sea that Christians sailed at their peril. We forget that the forces of Islam gathered over three hundred warships and close to 30,000 fighters for just one epic Mediterranean battle against the combined navies of Christendom, 1571's Battle of Lepanto. It was one of the very few seaborne showdowns that the Muslims lost.[946] And we forget that a mere six months later, the followers of the one true prophet took their revenge and chased the Christian fleet back to its homeports.

We forget that Islam's naval guerrilla jihadists preyed on Mediterranean commercial shipping, capturing, enslaving, and chaining Europeans like Miguel Cervantes—the author of *Don Quixote*—to the oars of their galleys.[947] We forget why the Muslim "corsairs" could afford to pounce at will. The Empire of Islam "made the entire coast of the Mediterranean from the Straits of Gibraltar to Croatia and Slovenia—two thirds of its total shoreline—a nearly unbroken stretch of" Muslim "territory more than ten thousand miles long"[948] into a "Muslim lake."[949]

We forget that back on land Muhammad's militant followers were just as successful. We repress the brutal fact that until 1826 the rulers of the Islamic empire forced Christian parents in Albania, Serbia, Greece, and Hungary to give up their male children to Muslim overlords, slave masters who brought up these ten-year-olds on the Qur'an, killed the boys who would not accept Islam, then turned the remainder into crack Muslim soldiers known as Janissaries.[950]

We forget what Islamic historian Dr. Mohsin Farooqi makes plain when he reminds his fellow Muslims that from roughly 1530 to 1780, in his opinion, "Europe [was] under Muslim Rule"—the rule of what Farooqi calls with great pride a reign of "terror of Muslim invaders."[9]

And we forget that militant Islam's 1,200-year-long imperialist push landed it more of the world than Muhammad had ever heard of. Islam conquered Africa's Libya, Tunisia, Morocco, Algeria, Egypt, Sudan, Somalia,[952] Kenya, Zanzibar, northern Nigeria, Uganda, and Ghana. Islam swallowed all of Spain, took Eastern Europe's Bulgaria,[9] Albania, Serbia,[9] Macedonia,[9] Bosnia, and Herzegovina.[9] Muslim armies seized and held the birthplace of Zoroastrianism—Iran. And it wiped Iran's Zoroastianism out root and branch. As we've seen, militant Islam grabbed the birthplace of Hinduism and Buddhism, India. Militant Islam also bagged the South Caucasus,[9] Asia's Afghanistan, Pakistan, Dagestan, Turkmenistan, Tajikistan, Chechnya, Kyrgistan, and Uzbekistan. Militant Islam invaded China's Xinjiang Province and seduced or seized most of the 19,185 Pacific Rim islands of Indonesia, Malaysia, Sumatra, Aceh, Brunei, and parts of the Philippines.

Modern Western imperialism is a blip by comparison. Western civilization is extraordinary at expanding the powers of the individual with computers, smartphones, GPS, Google, YouTube, and Facebook. But outside of the Americas, it's been a failure as a top predator. Most of the heavy-handed European and American imperialism in the Middle East, the "oppression at the hands of an expansive imperial power"[958] that's so resented by today's Arabs began less than a century ago, after the First World War. Syria was only under Western control for 21 years, and Egypt for 77.[959] On the other side of the scales, southern Spain remained under the Muslim yoke over ten times as long, for 781 years. Greece—a Christian land that had been the home of Plato and Aristotle—was under Muslim dominion for 381 years. Jerusalem, the capital of the Jews and the major Christian site of pilgrimage, was under Muslim occupation for a staggering 1,241 years. More than a millennium. More important, St. Augustine's North African homeland, the Christian monastic movement's birthplace, Egypt, and the capital of Christian Eastern Orthodoxy, Constantinople, are still in Muslim hands today. They've been in Muslim hands for as much as 1,377 years.[960] That's imperialism.

Does that mean we should feel humiliated and itch for revenge? No. We have gotten past such things. But Islam has not. Like the Nuer, Islam uses an unquenchable sense of humiliation as an excuse for nonstop expansion.

Muhammad generated a radically new and ravenous social learning machine, a new group IQ. The achievements of the Prophet's militant followers showed that that a heavily weaponized collective intelligence—a totalitarian military dictatorship shored up by a religion and endowed by its founder with planet-spanning ambitions—could work wonders. It could create a superorganism that persists for 14 centuries in its global aspirations, a superorganism that fights for 14 centuries to "liberate" its fellow humans and to bring them the "truth" of the legal, political, military, and religious system dictated to Muhammad by God Himself.

Why was Islam so rip-roaringly successful? Because to Islam's militants, slaughter and pillage—earmarks of the top predator strategy—have often been a mark of holiness and virtue. They've been hallowed by the Founder Effect. They follow the examples set by Muhammad. They obey the Prophet's order to "instill terror into the hearts of the unbelievers."[961] And they carry out God's commandment to bring the one true belief to all the world, God's commandment to take control of all humanity and its property on behalf of a hungry meme.

* * *

The result has been the longest world war in history—a nearly 1,400-year-long planetary struggle that subsides for a century or two, then flares up again on a frontline 17,000 miles wide—from the Philippines, Thailand, Kashmir, India, China, Chechnya, Dagestan, Bosnia, and Kenya, to South Africa, Nigeria, the Sudan, Algeria, Israel, Paris, London, Madrid, Trinidad, Amsterdam, Washington, and New York.

Militant Muslims view the world very differently than you and I do. We divide the world into North and South, developed and developing, rich and poor. Long ago, medieval Muslim scholars also divided the world into two zones, Dar el Islam (the abode of Islam) and Dar el Harb (the abode of war).[962] The abode of Islam was the Arab homeland and the conquered territory whose spirit had been broken and whose inhabitants had submitted to life under the yoke of Islam. The abode of war was the land of the unbeliever, the land of those who had not yet been terrified, overwhelmed, beaten, and converted to utter submission, to the state described by the literal meaning of the Arabic word "Islam."

These two territorial spheres, explained the Muslim scholars, are in a state of perpetual war.[963] The very words "Dar al-Harb" mark the land of the unbeliever—your land and mine—as a battleground. They literally say that the territory of those of us who do not submit to Islam is the abode of bloodshed until the day of judgement.[964] A Muslim statesman is only allowed the temporary expedient of peace with us infidels if his forces are not yet strong enough to beat our pants off.[965]

If you and I refuse to believe that there is only one god, Allah, and that Muhammad is his prophet, we set ourselves up for preemptive war. Maulana A.S. Muhammad Abdul Hai was an internationally respected Qur'anic interpreter of the mid-20th century who traced his family's roots straight back to Muhammad's best friend and successor, caliph Abu Bakr.[966] Maulana is a title given only to a tiny elite of Islam's scholars and interpreters. Abdul Hai writes, "where ever a danger to Islam emerges, it should be curbed before it could galvanize itself into a big force against Islam. Islam is a system of life, a complete code of life and to safeguard it, it is not enough to defend [it] in case of an attack by the anti-Islamic forces. Rather, it is also essential to make efforts to undermine anti-Islamic systems, to establish Islam...to plunge into the arrays of [the] enemy to remove their threat. That is why the Holy Prophet... said, 'Now it will not be so that people attack us, rather we will come out to attack them.'"[967]

Preemptive war is a strategy that the United States employed in its second Iraq War. It's also a strategy the Spanish, the French, and the English used in conquering the New World and that the Dutch, the Portuguese, and the English used when they grabbed a slew of Pacific islands from their Islamic masters starting in roughly 1602.[968] It's a strategy the U.S. may someday employ again in response to Iran's nuclear threat. But it is not a strategy we invented. Militant Islam beat us Westerners to preemptive war by 876 years.

What's a Group IQ?

GROUPS HAVE A COLLECTIVE INTELLIGENCE—an intelligence in which individuals like you and me collaborate the way the trillion cells[969] of your brain and central nervous system collaborate to make the intelligence you call you. The clue to that intelligence comes from the world of chimpanzees and baboons.

Which have bigger brains, chimpanzees or baboons? If you guessed chimps, you're right. Chimpanzees are our closest relatives on the planet. They share between 98.3% and 99.5%[970] of our genes, depending on who's counting. They are way up there in animal brainpower. An average chimp's brain is twice as big as the brain of a baboon.[971]

Now for question number two. Which are smarter, chimpanzees or baboons? The answer is...baboons.[972] But how could that be? Chimps are brainier. Shouldn't they also be, well, umm, brainier? Brighter by far? If baboons are winners on IQ measures, doesn't that mean that intelligence is not just a matter of brain matter? The answer is yes, there's more to intellect than the number of neurons in your skull. So what's the extra ingredient you need to turn brains into smarts? The answer is a bit surprising. Nimble minds need more than just a lot of synapses between brain cells. They need the power of groups. They need a force that pulses from the web of connection between group members...from the sum that's bigger than its parts. They need what Gerardo Beni calls "swarm intelligence,"[973] what Pierre Levy calls "collective intelligence"[974] and what you and I can call "Group IQ."[975]

The ultimate test of intelligence is adaptability—how swiftly you can solve a complex problem, whether that problem is couched in words, in images, in crises, or in everyday life. The arena where intelligence is most important is not the classroom or the laboratory, it's the real world. When you measure adaptability by the ability to turn disasters into opportunities and wastelands into paradises, how do big-brained chimpanzees and small-brained baboons do? Or, to put it differently, how adaptable, clever, mentally agile, and able to solve real-world problems have chimpanzees and baboons proven to be?

You can tell by the number of appeals made on TV, radio, and print to save these primates' tails. Jane Goodall has toured the world since 1986[976] alerting us to a simple fact. The environment that allows chimps to live is rapidly disappearing. To save the chimps, we must save the environmental niche that gives them life. How many activists have you seen pleading to save the environment of baboons? None. Is there a reason? Yes. Baboons have been called "the rats of Africa."[977] No matter how badly you desecrate their environment, they find a way to take advantage of your outrage.[978] One baboon group, the Pumphouse Gang, was under study for years by primatologist Shirley Strum.[979] When Strum began her baboon-watching in 1972,[980] the Pumphouse Gang lived off the land in Kenya and ate a healthy, all-natural diet. They ate blossoms and fruits when those were in season. When there were no sweets and flowery treats, the baboons dug up roots and bulbs.

Then came disaster—the meddling of man. Farmers took over parts of the baboons' territory, plowed it, built houses, and put up electrified fences around their crops. Worse, the Kenyan military erected a base, put up homes for the officers' wives and kids, and trashed even more of the baboons' terri- tory by setting aside former baboon land for a giant garbage heap. If this had happened to a patch of forest inhabited by chimps, the chimpanzee tribes would have been devastated. But not the baboons.

At first, the Pumphouse Gang maintained its old lifestyle and continued grubbing in the earth for its food. Then came a new generation of adoles- cents. Each generation of adolescent baboons produces a few curious, uncon- ventional rebels. Normally a baboon troop splits up in small groups and goes off early in the day to find food. But one of the adolescent nonconformists of the Pump House Gang insisted on wandering by himself. His roaming took him to the military garbage dump. The baboon grasped a principle that chimps don't seem to get. One man's garbage is another primate's gold. One man's slush is another animal's snow cone.

The baboon rebel found a way through the military garbage heap's barbed wire fence, set foot in the trash heap, and tasted the throwaways. Pay dirt. He'd hit a concentrated source of nutrition. When they came back to their home base at the end of the day, the natural-living baboons, the ones who had stuck to their traditional organic food-gathering strategies, to their daily grind digging up tubers, came home dusty and bedraggled, worn out by their work. But the adolescent who invented garbage-raiding came back energetic, rested, strong, and glorious. As the weeks and months went by, he seemed to grow in health and vigor. Other young adolescent males became curious. Some followed the nonconformist on his daily stroll into the unknown. And, lo, they too discovered the garbage dump and found it good.

Eventually, the males who made the garbage dump their new food source began to sleep in their own group, apart from the organic, natural-living old-timers. As they grew in physical strength and robustness, these Young Turks challenged the old males to fights. The youngsters' food was superior and so was their physical might. They had a tendency to win their battles. Females attracted by this power wandered outside the ancestral troop and spent increasing amounts of time with the rebel males[981]—who continued to increase their supply of high-quality food by inventing ways to open the door latches of the houses of the officers' wives, and learned how to open kitchen cupboards and pantries, and who also invented ways to make their way through the electrified fences of farmers and gather armloads of corn. The health of the males and females in the garbage-picking group was so much better than that of the old troop that a female impregnated in the gang of garbage-pickers and farm-raiders was able to have a new infant every 12 months.[982] The females in the old, conservative, natural-diet group were stuck with a new infant only every 18 to 24 months.[983] The innovators were not only humiliating the all-organic conservatives in pitch battles, they were outbreeding them.

Why were the baboons so much smarter than chimpanzees? Why were they able to innovate and to surf the waves of change and the currents of the strange? Because they didn't just think as individuals, they thought as a group. Their individualistic, curious adolescents were antennae, probing the possibilities of the unknown. These explorers and innovators sometimes went off on their own while the main troop broke up into small groups to do their wandering. But at night the small groups and the individualists gathered in the shelter of cliffs and bluffs to sleep together in crowds of as many as two hundred[984] to seven hundred.[985] And in the morning, through body-language arguments between the males about where to go during the day, these groups and rebels shared information at the base of their sleeping cliffs. They compared notes.[986]

Chimps are not wanderers. They are stick-in-the-muds and stay-at-homes. They patrol their existing territory. And they live in groups of a mere 15 to 35. They don't get together in nightly multi-group conventions to compare notes.

The result? When the old environmental slot of chimps wears out or is wiped away, chimpanzees have no options, no fallback, or, more important, no fall-forward positions. Baboons have smaller brains. But they have smarter Group IQs. And they can turn any environmental challenge you toss their way from disaster into opportunity. Chimps cannot.

Here's one more guess about why the group IQ of baboons is higher than the group IQ of chimps. When one group of chimps separates and becomes two groups, those two groups eventually replace peaceful competition with war. And I mean a war in which the losing group is exterminated...in which its adult males are murdered down to the last one and in which only the most delicious females, the fertile ones, are kept alive. When baboon groups split up, the groups compete with a far less genocidal form of violence. They have fights, brawls, gang bangs, and bullying sessions. They use their might and hurt each other. But they don't wipe each other out. They don't kill each other. They don't pursue systematic genocide.

The result is that the alternative strategies pursued by each baboon group can live on in the baboon mass mind.

The bottom line? Baboons are on the increase in Africa. Chimps have relatively humongous brains, yet they are on the path to extinction. And that population increase or shrinkage is a direct measure of adaptability, a measure of intelligence, a numerical indicator of group IQ.

*   *   *

In reality, the 14-century-long struggle of Islam against the unbelievers, Islam's nearly 1,400-year-long war to take the world, is a battle of mass minds, of collective intelligences, of group IQs testing their powers against each other. One uses the strategies, structures, and beliefs dictated by Muhammad. The other uses a secular meme scheme fashioned a mere 250 years ago in the Age of Enlightenment, in the days of the American Revolution, and in a series of bloody idea-driven internal wars—Europe's revolutions of 1789, 1830, and 1848. How long will it take before this competition between Islam and Western enlightenment produces a clear winner? That we shall have to see.

The Power of Perseverance

> "The same God, who has already given thee so large a portion of the Roman empire, will not deny the remnant, and the capital [Constantinople]. His providence, and thy power, assure thy success; and myself, with the rest of thy faithful slaves, will sacrifice our lives and fortunes."
> —Amurath
> Vizier to the Ottoman Sultan Mehmed II[987]

> "Beware of the gold and silver of the Romans: in arms we are superior; and with the aid of God, and the prayers of the prophet, we shall speedily become masters of Constantinople."
> —Mehmed II's reply to the Vizier[988]

ONE LESSON THAT HISTORY is whispering to us involves the importance of multi-generational projects, projects designed to deliver their fruits in the time of our great-great-grandchildren and beyond.

This planet's competition between collective intelligences—its clash of civilizations—now poses a critical question. Can one collective brain outrun others when it is obsessed with quarterly profits, exit strategies, overnight wins, and instant gratification? Can it be more nimble than its rivals if it fails to focus on long-term goals, very long long-term goals?

Islam's meme has proven to be an utter failure at producing wealth for the majority of its citizens in the 20th and 21st centuries.[989] In fact, it's lowered the human development index scores in the Muslim nations below the scores of Mongolia, Kyrgyzstan, Viet Nam, Georgia, and Jamaica.[990] But Islam's focus is not short-term. Islam zeroes in on long-term goals and on multi-generational projects—primarily long-term military projects. And in those, it has had overwhelming success.

As one *Al Qaeda Manual* puts it, the warrior of Jihad "should be patient in performing the work, even if it lasts a long time."[991] ISIS' magazine adds these words from the Qur'an: "be patient. Allah is with the patient."[992] And patient the forces of Islam have been. After the right to Jihad was revealed to Muhammad in 624 A.D.,[993] one of the Hadith says, "The Prophet Muhammad was asked: 'What city will be conquered first, Constantinople or Romiyya [Rome]?' He answered: 'The city of Heracles [Hercules] will be conquered first' — that is, Constantinople."[994] For 776 years the Muslims tried to take Constantinople.[995] They began to strip the city of the bulk of its enormous empire within just five years of Muhammad's death—in 637 A.D.[996] And they methodically nibbled at what was left for centuries. But Constantinople—the city—held firm.

Why was taking this one city worth so much multi-generational effort? As you know, Constantinople was the New Rome,[9] the heir to the Empire of Rome itself. It was also the capital city of Eastern Christianity. Its emperor claimed to be in direct contact with God and to speak on God's behalf to the entire world. His only rival as the voice of Christianity was a Roman who seemed poverty-stricken by comparison—the Pope. Ever since its fall to the barbarian Visigoths nearly a thousand years earlier, the Pope's Rome had been half-deserted and had been stripping the marble from its ancient buildings and pavements to build new, far shabbier structures or to simply make lime.[9]

But Constantinople glittered with riches.[999] The clothes of its leading citizens were woven with threads of gold. The dishes on which those leading citizens served formal dinners were gold as well. The chamber in which the Emperor deigned to see delegations of high-level visitors from lands as distant as a newly established princedom of the Vikings, Russia, had walls of gold many stories high, walls studded with the golden heads of mechanical lions and birds, golden heads that roared and sang.

The aisles of Constantinople's churches were paved with silver.[1000] Constantinople's artisans filled the city with ivory carvings of biblical themes, from the story of Adam and Eve to the story of Joshua and the battle of Jericho. What's more, Constantinople was rich in export revenues. It had stolen the secret of silk-making from the Chinese, then had poured out silks of its own, exporting them at a mind-boggling price to kings, queens, and to the super-rich thousands of miles away. And Byzantine glass bottles and tiles were exquisite, world-famous,[1001] and fetched a pretty nummus (Byzantium's bronze penny) on the international luxury market.

But by 1453, the 817-year-long battle of Islam against Constantinople and its empire had finally stripped the city of almost all of its imperial territories and had cut off its supply of raw materials. What's more, for centuries

Constantinople's emperor and the Roman pope had squabbled over who carried the full weight and authority of the Roman Caesars and who was Christianity's authentic connection with heaven. In 1203, the Roman Christians—the Christian kings of Europe and their knights—had mounted a Crusade and, instead of attacking the Muslims, had attacked, raped, and sacked Constantinople.[1002] So the city was alienated from—and weakened by—what should have been its Christian allies.

As a result in 1453 Constantinople was down to a mere whisper of its original population[1003] and had only 7,000 soldiers, 2,000 of whom were foreign mercenaries. This was a pitiful number of fighters with which to defend the city's 42 miles of 36-foot-high inner and outer walls.

Allah had kept the forces of the jihad from capturing Constantinople ever since Muhammad had sent his letter inviting the Byzantine Emperor Hercules to capitulate to Islam in 629 A.D., 824 years earlier. Now Allah would teach his loyal followers how patience and belief pays off.

The Emperor of Constantinople shut down the city's small number of mosques and put pressure on the citizens who had converted from Christianity to Islam to return to the Christian fold. According to the Qur'an, this sort of "attack on Islam" is a legitimate cause for war.[1004] So the leader of the Islamic Empire of the day, the Ottoman Emperor Mehmed II, seized the opportunity. He and his father had already built permanent forts just outside the city to cut it off from aid and reinforcement. Then on April 2, 1453, Mehmed camped his forces—over 100,000 of them—outside of Constantinople. His troops trained the world's biggest cannon on the city—a 27-foot-long monster called "the Basilic"[1005] that fired a ball weighing more than four refrigerators—1,200 pounds. The giant cannon opened holes in the city's layers of walls, lanes wide enough for files of invaders to penetrate. But it took three hours to reload the Basilic. The citizens and threadbare troops of Constantinople scrambled to repair the breaches while the warriors of Islam labored to reload their superweapon.

Meanwhile, the warriors of Islam had dug tunnels designed to reach the walls of Byzantium, to undermine their foundations, and to cause them to collapse. The Byzantines told each other, "have patience till God shall have delivered the city from the great dragon who seeks to devour us."[1006] But they were praying to the wrong god. It was Allah who would deliver on his promises, not Jesus or Jehovah.

Fifty-four days after the siege of Constantinople began, on May 29, 1453, Mehmed ordered his troops to assault the pummeled and exhausted city.

Within hours, the Muslim troops had killed the Emperor of Constantinople as he led what was left of his forces. When Mehmed entered the city in a triumphal display, the few citizens who remained alive greeted him with flowers and hoped for the best. They got the worst. For seven hours Mehmed's troops looted and plundered.[1007]

What's more, the laws of Islam gave the victorious troops the right to seize Constantinople's remaining citizens—all of them—as "the property of the victor,"[1008] to be ransomed, enslaved, kept for sexual purposes, used for labor, or to be sold.

Allah had promised his believers Constantinople and Rome. And Allah had delivered on one of those promises. But as Sheikh Yousef Al-Qaradhawi, known as "one of the most influential clerics in Sunni Islam," said in 2002, "The other city, Romiyya, remains… This means that Islam will return to Europe as a conqueror and victor."[1009]

What sort of lesson in patience would Allah teach his global body of followers—his Ummah—before he would deliver on this second promise? What trials would the people of Islam have to undergo before Allah would give them the city of Rome...and its former Empire, Europe?

And what about the other portions of the planet that were still drowning in darkness and disbelief? As the Muslim website Islamic World says, "The Qur'an clearly and directly asks all human beings to surrender to God (Allah)."[1010] Then the website invites you to "see the audio & video streaming of A Worldwide Islamic State."

The patience that finally brought Constantinople to Islam is the mark of a superorganism that may have been slow to master modern industrial and scientific technology, but is a superorganism that doesn't see things in just the short term, a culture whose memes guarantee that it will stick to a project for centuries.

That's one mark of a group IQ.

The Struggle For Europe

"dear youth of Islam everywhere, ...dear knights of
Muhammad the Conqueror, ...let your supplies be
continuous so that you may... [continue] fighting
steadfastly the treacherous Romans ...."
—Osama bin Laden, 2004[1011]

There will not be any place left for the camp of kufr [for
unbelievers] to exist on the Earth, not even as humbled
dhimmi subjects [second-class citizens] living amongst
the Muslims.
—ISIS magazine *Dābiq*, issue 7, p. 65

DOES ISLAM REALLY STAND A CHANCE of finally achieving its ancient aim
of taking Europe? Could it ever possibly reach top predator status in England,
France, Germany and the rest of the European nations?

Memes, genes, and superorganisms use a host of strategies to expand
their sway. Some are conscious. Many more are unconscious. Among those
that straddle the line between consciousness and invisibility are reproductive strategies, strategies that show up in different cultural attitudes toward
sex, toward the role of women, and toward socially acceptable—or socially
required—family size.

Reproductive strategies came to the surface in 2004 when conservatives
in the U.S. looked at demographic figures and realized that they were winning the battle for the American mass mind in part by out-reproducing their
rivals, liberals.[1012]

Reproductive strategies reared their heads again in 2012, when writers at
New York Magazine and *Slate* spotlighted research by Belgian demographer
Ron Lesthaeghe. Lesthaeghe demonstrated that you could tell whether a
state in the USA would vote Republican or Democrat by looking at its family
size. Families with lots of children voted Republican. Families with fewer
children voted Democratic. Which meant that there was more to the battle
over issues like abortion, women's rights, and gay rights than met the eye.
Beneath the surface, Republicans and Democrats were fighting for different
reproductive strategies.[1013]

But the most telling war of reproductive strategies in the 21st century is the one between dar el Harb and dar el Islam[1014]—the home of War, your home and mine, and the home of Islam.

A dedicated Muslim, Ali Mazrui, director of the Institute of Global Cultural Studies, and writer and host of the nine-part PBS series *The Africans*,[1015] says that "When Islamic fundamentalism is combined with the zeal and dedication of jihad... the culture of procreation merges with the culture of combat." What does he mean? "Fundamentalist Muslim families...," Mazrui explains, "resort to having more and more children as a strategy for 'multiplying in the name of Allah.'"[1016] Then Mazrui gets down to brass tacks. "Procreation itself," he says in words we've heard from him before, "can be counted as a form of jihad."[1017]

That jihad—that war of the womb—gains from a simple rule: "If the father is Arab, the child is Arab, regardless of race or ethnic origins of the mother."[1018] And if the father is a Muslim, his child is a Muslim. Mazrui calls the resulting Islamic reproductive approach "competitive procreation."[1019]

Then Mazrui gives an example of how effective "competitive procreation" can be. "Islam originally arrived in Africa as a religion on the run," he reports. "The first Muslim refugees arrived in Ethiopia early in the seventh century A.D., fleeing from persecution in polytheistic Arabia." They were fleeing persecution in Mecca. On Muhammad's orders. Mazrui continues, "The refugees presumably decided that intermarrying with Ethiopians and having large families was a way to strengthen their kinship ties in the Horn of Africa, and to expand their local Muslim communities in exile."[1020] Thus, Mazrui says, began "Islam's culture of procreation."[1021]

Then things turned nasty. "The second significant arrival of Islam in Africa," he says, "occurred in Egypt in A.D. 639. This time the Arabs arrived as conquerors rather than as refugees. But how was the Egyptian population not only converted to another religion (Islamization), but also transformed into Arabs (Arabization) over the centuries? How was this Arabization accomplished in the rest of North Africa and in much of the Nile Valley as well?" Good questions. And Mazrui is kind enough to answer them. "Historically," he writes, "the culture of procreation among the conquering Arabs reinforced their jihad culture of combat. North Africa and much of the Nile Valley were Arabized as much by Arab intermarriage as by Arab conquests. The patrilineal system of the Arabs was part of their population policy, destined to transform a continent and affect the world. ...By the end of the twentieth century, half the population of Africa was professing Islam."[1022]

And, Mazrui implies, with patience the remaining half of Africa's population will someday be Muslim, too.

Just in case he hasn't gotten his message across, Mazrui repeats, "Preference for large families...was often deeply rooted in...the imperative of jihad."[1023] And that preference often continues, he says, "when the family is middle class."[1] Remember, Mazrui is a Muslim whose works often portray Islam as a victim of imperialism, not an aggressor.[1025] So he's skipped over the way that the "Islamizers" and "Arabizers" have used what the Qur'an calls "those whom thy right hand possesses"[1026] to increase the numbers of the faithful. He neglects rape, forced sex with slave girls, and forced sex with female prisoners. Mazrui also fails to explain what the modern Arab Muslims of the northern Sudan intend to do when, as he reports, they head south to the black portion of the country, Darfur—the land of Muslim raids and Muslim rape—saying, "I am going south—to bring into the world 40 more Arabs before I die!"[1027] Mazrui fails to tell us that these "40 more Arabs" will be produced by rape. Despite these omissions, Mazrui is telling you and me that one of militant Islam's goals is to win more of the world by out-reproducing us.

How does this apply to Europe? The fact is that Europe's Muslim population in 2004 was growing at three times the rate of the non-Muslim population.[1028] And from 2005 to 2010, the average non-Muslim European woman had 1.5 children. The average Muslim woman in Europe out-reproduced the average British woman by 67%. She had 2.2 children.[1029] That's according to a calm and measured source, the Pew Research Center. Others were less calm. Wrote Vincent Cooper in *The Commentator*, "Britain is in denial. If population trends continue, by the year 2050, Britain will be a majority Muslim nation."[1030] The usually staid *London Times* in a 1999 article was even more emphatic. It reported that the Muslim population of the UK "multiplied 10 times faster than the rest of society."[1031] For comparison, the *Times* added, "In the same period the number of Christians in the country fell by more than 2 million."[1032] Where did these numbers come from? Said the *Times*, from "research by the Office for National Statistics." You can't get much more authoritative than that. *The Commentator*'s Vincent Cooper blamed the native British fertility lag on what he called Europe's "death bed demography."[1033] What did he mean?

Says the Pew Research Center, "The number of Muslims in Europe has grown from 29.6 million in 1990 to 44.1 million in 2010. Europe's Muslim population is projected to exceed 58 million by 2030."[1034] 58 million, that's just a tad less than the entire population of Italy. This is where "death bed demography" comes in. Europe's indigenous population is in a nosedive.[1035] To keep a population even, you need a reproductive rate of 2.1 children per woman. Europe's reproductive rate is below two. In fact, it's way below two. It's 1.5.[1036]

The result has made headlines. Britain's *Telegraph* proclaims that "Europe is slowly dying."[1037] And *The Guardian* warns of a "population disaster" and a "perfect demographic storm.[1038]

Is this demographic shift an accident? Actually, it's an old biological pattern. One that modern militant Islam has turned from an instinctual response to an overt power ploy. It's the battle of opposing reproductive strategies that population biologists call "*r*" and "*K*."[1039] The *r* reproductive strategy involves having lots of kids and gambling their lives…often in anticipation of violence.[1040] The opposite of *r* is the *K* strategy.[1041] *K* relies on having just a few kids, investing in them heavily, and protecting them mightily. The *r* and *K* instincts appear in everything from "bacteria, flies, mice, weeds, and rabbits"[1042] to guppies,[1043] minnows,[1044] voles[1045]…and to human beings. In fact, these reproductive tactics sometimes shape the very foundations of human culture.

The battle in America between pro-abortion and anti-abortion forces, for example, is a battle between opposing reproductive strategies. More to the point are the reproductive strategies that may help militant Islam achieve its ancient goal of returning "to Europe as a conqueror and victor."[1046]

The Muslim population explosion is giving Islam's European community a "youth bulge,"[1047] a disproportionate number of young. A handful of the leaders of Europe's roughly 45 million Muslims[1048] very openly want to use these youths to pick up where the conquerors of Constantinople left off. London-based Sheikh Omar Bakri Mohamed made a promise before the British threw him out of their land: "We will remodel this country in an Islamic image. We will replace the Bible with the Qur'an."[1049] How did Bakri Mohamed intend to remodel England? You can find a hint in the title of four conferences he put together in 2003, conferences in London, Manchester, Birmingham and Leicester. The title of these gatherings: "The Magnificent 19." Who were the Magnificent 19? The "heroic" hijackers who had demolished New York's World Trade Center on 9/11.[1050] And you can find yet another hint of how Bakri Mohamed intends to "replace the Bible with the Qur'an" in the fact that half of the terrorist attacks on British soil from 2000 to 2015 were reportedly planned by Bakri Mohamed and his group, al-Muhajiroun. Bakri Muhammad was using one of Muhammad's favorite tools for conquest: terror. And another: competitive procreation.

Surely Bakri Mohamed's extremist form of Islam doesn't have a prayer of digesting Britain. Or does it? The British cleric is not just a crank caterwauling in the wilderness. Bakri Mohamed's organization al-Muhajiroun[1051] is an international organization. It reportedly has had, "no fewer than 30 offices across Britain, with branches in France and throughout the Middle East."[1052] The group also has had "offices across the developed world— in Kuwait, … South Africa, Lebanon, Bangladesh, Mauritius, Syria and Algeria."[1053]

What's more, Bakri Mohamed's Al-Muhajiroun has organized yearly British celebrations of the Islamic triumph of 9/11, and has put together a conference in London called "The Choice Is In Your Hands: Either You're With the Muslims or with the Infidels." Just in case Bakri Mohamed's calls for Jihad against unbelievers fail to wipe false beliefs like yours and mine off the face of Allah's Earth, the Sheikh is practicing the if-we-can't-beat-them-we'll-outpopulate-them reproductive strategy, the *r* strategy, the "culture of procreation [that] merges with combat."[1054] As of 2014, he had ten children.[1055]

No wonder a 1997 study of churchgoers in London predicted that Islam would become the number one religion in Britain by 2002, with more mosque-going believers than churchgoing Anglican Christian "idolaters."[1056] The prediction was too optimistic. Britain's *The Guardian* suspected that the number of Muslims regularly attending religious services in Britain had outpaced the number of Anglicans showing up in church by as early as 2001.[1057]

What's more, the young men and women of European Islam are increasingly shedding their identification with the West.[1058] Even if they were born in Europe…in fact, even if their parents were born in Europe, they are embracing a global Islamic identity. Take the case of Omar Abaaoud, who moved from Morocco to Belgium in 1975,[1059] started a clothing store in Brussels' Molenbeek district, did well, then opened a second store.[1060] Abaaoud sent his son, Abdelhamid, to an upscale school.[1061] He explains that "Our family owes everything to this country."[1062] Brussels treated Omar Abaaoud and his family well. Continues Abaaoud, "We had a wonderful life, yes, even a fantastic life here." How did this affect his son Abdelhamid? "Abdelhamid was not a difficult child and became a good businessman,"[1063] says his dad.

What Omar did not know is that his son was not popular. He was a bully who harassed both students and teachers and stole wallets.[1064] Says a classmate, "he was a little jerk."[1065] Eventually Abdelhamid went to jail for "petty crimes."[1066] Not because he was living under poverty and oppression. But because, wealthy as his middle-class family was, material advantages were not enough. In jail he apparently encountered something that offered to give his life meaning, something that offered to put him in touch with something bigger than himself—Islam. Jihadist Islam.[1067] Something that could turn his bullying into a blessed skill. Abdelhamid went to Syria to join ISIS,[1068] ran a recruitment network enticing other Muslim kids born in Europe to join the Islamic State's Syria-based jihad, and began to plan terrorist attacks on Europe itself. On November 13, 2015, he masterminded and participated in one of those attacks—an attack in which, according to ISIS, "eight brothers wrapped in explosive belts and armed with machine rifles"[1069] struck in six places at once: four bars and restaurants, a concert hall, and a national soccer stadium, a stadium in whose audience the prime minister of France sat. Those attacks would kill 129 people. All of these six targets were in what an ISIS statement of responsibility would call "the capital of prostitution and obscenity"—Paris.

The U.S. Department of State's Timothy Savage calls what Abdelhamid Abaaoud went through "re-Islamization"[1070] and reports that it is "significantly more pronounced among younger Muslims." One result: as early as 2004, when Abaaoud was 17, Europe's young, middle-class Muslims were reportedly more enthusiastic about signing on with radical and jihadist organizations than the youth in Islamic countries.[1071] Or so said Malcolm Turnbull, the future prime minister of Australia, who served as a director of the Australian Liberal Party's Menzies Research Centre.[1072] Claimed Turnbull in 2004, mosques in Hamburg, London, Marseilles, and even Montreal were bringing in more jihadist recruits "than any Saudi Madrassa."[1073]

Some of these recruits, in the words of Osama bin Laden,[1074] were "competing among themselves for fighting and killing you."[1075] Or, as ISIS' official spokesman, Shaykh Abu Muhammad al-'Adnani, says in the pages of the ISIS magazine *Dābiq*:

> If you can kill a kafir [unbelieving] American or European...then rely upon Allah, and kill them in any manner possible, regardless of the method. [1076]

The result? The killer of *Wall Street Journal* reporter and peace activist Daniel Pearl in Pakistan in 2002 was born and raised by a middle-class Muslim family in England.[1077] The bombers of four subways and buses in

London on July 7, 2005, were also kids from solid, middle-class English homes, Muslim-English homes.[1078] The attackers who killed 12 people in January 7, 2015, in the office of the weekly French satirical magazine *Charlie Hebdo*, were, says a headline in *The Guardian*, "born, raised and radicalised in Paris." Yes, not only born and raised in Paris, but radicalized there.[1079]

But more than procreative strategies are aiding the growth of militant Islam in Europe. It's that youth bulge thing. When we're in our teens and twenties, we have a powerful need for idealistic goals…goals in which we sacrifice ourselves for a higher purpose and for the poor and the oppressed. Goals in which we give up our lives for the good of the superorganism. Often those transcendent ideals contribute to the advancement of a multi-generational cause.

Peace is one good example of a multi-generational ideal in the West. We've dreamed of achieving peace since the prophet Isaiah imagined a day when the nations "shall beat their swords into plowshares, and their spears into pruning hooks"[1080] and since Jesus said, "blessed are the peacemakers: for they will be called children of God."[1081]

Those dreams have turned into Western movements for over a thousand years. The Middle Ages were violent, and not everyone was happy about it. Not everyone enjoyed the perpetual killings inflicted by rampaging knights. Mass demonstrations for peace erupted in Europe as early as the 900s A.D. And they coalesced in a "Peace of God" movement whose first declarations emerged from the Council of Toulouges-Roussillon in 1027[1082] and the Council of Limoges in 1031.[1083] The concluding document from the Council of Limoges showed that the public was fed up with the perpetual war made by men in armor. It called down God's anger "upon all knights, upon their arms and their horse."[1084] More than six hundred years later, the modern peace movements took hold. The Quakers adopted pacifism in 1652.[1085] In 1693, William Penn, the Quaker founder of Pennsylvania, suggested a "European League, or Confederacy" complete with a European Parliament. His goal was clear in the title of the document he wrote on the topic: "An Essay towards the Present and Future Peace of Europe by the Establishment of an European Dyet, Parliament, or Estates."[1086] Penn had written "an essay on peace."[1087]

Twenty years later in 1713, Charles-Irénée Castel de Saint-Pierre, the son of a Marquis, wrote *A Project to Render Perpetual Peace in Europe*—an entire book that proposed a European union, another book with peace as its goal. A farther 48 years down the line, in 1761, Jean Jacques Rousseau made a splash when he published a commentary on St. Pierre's *Project of Perpetual Peace*, an essay in which Rousseau backed St. Pierre's proposal of a multinational federation. And German super-philosopher Immanuel Kant took a crack at an international system to stop war in 1795 with his "Perpetual Peace: A Philosophical Sketch,"[1088] a work in which he laid out a series of steps that he felt would gradually allow Europe's states to coexist in peace.

Then the peace movement went from philosophy to activism. The first national American Peace Society was founded in 1828.[1089] And in 1848, the son of a Massachusetts pencil manufacturer,[1090] Henry David Thoreau, objected to an 1846 war between his home country, the USA, and Mexico. In protest against the war and against slavery, he stopped paying his taxes for what he recalled as "six or seven years."[1091] Since the loss to the state was only a penny and a half a year, the tax collector ignored the first few years of infringement.[1092] Then one day Thoreau says he was "going to the shoemaker's to get a shoe which was mended"[1093] in the town where he lived, Concord, Massachusetts. That's when Concord's sheriff, Sam Staples,[1094] nabbed him and hauled him off to jail.

Thoreau was hoping for a nice, long, publicizable martyrdom. He was hoping for what he called going to jail for "nothing but principle." But that's not how things worked out. To quote UCLA English professor Barbara Packer in her book *The Transcendentalists*, Sheriff

> Staples told an interviewer that he had just gotten home from locking up Thoreau with the rest of the inmates and had taken off his boots when word was brought to him that a veiled woman had appeared at the jail with 'Mr. Thoreau's tax' in an envelope. Unwilling to go to the trouble of unlocking the prisoners he had just locked up. Staples waited till morning to release Thoreau—who, he remembered, "was mad as a devil when I turned him loose."[1095]

Why was Thoreau angry? He was hoping for a jail term that would make headlines. He wanted to make a statement. And one night in jail wouldn't do it. So he was forced to make that statement in a lecture. A January 26, 1948, lecture to the Concord Lyceum on "The Rights and Duties of the Individual in Relation to the Government ('Resistance to Civil Government')." That lecture would prove to have more power than any jail sentence. Far more. Four years after Thoreau's death, the lecture would appear with a few changes in a multi-volume anthology of Thoreau's work put together by his sister, Sophia.[1096] The new version would carry an equally new title: *Civil Disobedience*.[1097] That essay would inspire the next 150 years of protests for peace. And, astonishingly, it would influence the nonviolent tactics of India's Mahatma Gandhi[1098] and civil rights movement leader Martin Luther King, Jr.[1099] In fact, Thoreau's *Civil Disobedience* would become vital to the civil rights revolution of the mid- to late 20th century.

Peace movements have been major components of Western civilization for over 1,100 years. And, believe it or not, they've worked. Partially. According to Stephen Pinker's *The Better Angels of Our Nature* and according to research cited in my book *The Lucifer Principle*, the rate of violence in the West is one-tenth what it was in 1650. One-tenth—a reduction of 90%. That's in spite of the 752,000[1100] deaths of America's Civil War and the 70 million deaths[1101] of Europe's two world wars. But there have been no comparable peace movements in Dar el Islam.

Militant Islam offers one of the highest ideals a meme can present—the mission of saving the world, of liberating you and me so we can embrace the truth, of giving those of us who live in the darkness of unbelief the only freedom and light that counts, the freedom to live under the God-given laws of Shariah and the "complete system of life" of Islam. That's a multi-generational project on a grand scale. But the means to that ideal, the tool for the liberation of humanity, is not peaceful protest. It is not civil disobedience. It is jihad. And jihad, as one young Egyptian told Britain's Grenada TV in 1987, "is a tree that feeds on blood and grows on severed limbs."[1102] What's more, Muhammad made something clear during his lifetime. He would tolerate no dissent. None. In fact, dissenters were to be killed. Quickly and brutally.

Tomorrow's Goal: Seizing the Empire of Rome

> We will conquer your Rome, break your crosses,
> and enslave your women...[and] will sell your sons
> as slaves at the slave market.
> —From ISIS' Magazine, *Dābiq*[1103]

THE JIHADISM FOUNDED on Muhammad's example has deep roots in Europe. Roots far more sturdy than you are supposed to know. In Holland, filmmaker Theo Van Gogh was murdered for offending Islam in 2004. More about that highly disturbing murder in a few minutes. When news of Van Gogh's assassination hit the headlines, *The London Telegraph* reports, "Lawyers, accountants, computer specialists, nurses, and businessmen" fled by the thousands, terrified that a jihad had erupted in their home country.[1104] Some Dutch were afraid that their growing Muslim population would someday obliterate the country's "polder"[1105] system—Holland's extraordinary mechanism for secularism, tolerance and pluralism. Meanwhile, a 2002 report from Holland's Internal Security Service revealed that "one-fifth of the 32 state-sponsored Muslim grade schools received financial support from fundamentalist Islamic organizations."[1106] That's not a high fraction. But then the Dutch television news program *Nova* reported that children in Holland's Islamic schools were taught "to battle people until they acknowledge that Allah is the only God."[1107] This helped generate a mass exodus.

Meanwhile, Germany was headquarters for a global network of radical Islamic organizations richly funded by Saudi Arabia,[1108] extremist organizations that have been entrenching themselves in the heart of Europe since the 1950s, when their leaders were expelled from countries like Egypt for their extremism. Under the cover of umbrella groups like the Saudi-funded Muslim World League[1109] and the Saudi-underwritten World Assembly of Muslim Youth,[1110] these groups have slowly made themselves the official spokespeople for Europe's mainstream Islamic community.

In fact, these groups have smothered, repressed, outmaneuvered, and outspent more moderate groups. Highly prominent extremist organizations like the Islamic Society of Germany, the Islamic Center of Geneva, the Islamic Center of Munich, and the Aachen Islamic Center[1111] met frequently with

Europe's cabinet ministers,[1112] politicians, and the press.[1113] When they spoke German, French, and English, they promoted the notion that Islam is a religion of peace. But when they spoke in Arabic and Turkish, they declared that "our youngsters... [will] go back to Islam and make jihad for the sake of Allah" and that their own role was to provide "a shield protecting our fellow citizens from assimilation into barbaric Europe."[1114]

That's little wonder when you realize that the Islamic Society of Germany was founded with the aid of ex-Nazis. Let me repeat that: ex-Nazis. The Society was a beachhead for the jihadist Muslim Brotherhood, has ties with al Qaeda, and runs "a network that now reaches around the world." So says "Stefan Meining. The historian and TV journalist working for southern Germany's regional Bayerischer Rundfunk network"[1115] whose archival research one of Germany's most highly respected magazines, *Der Spiegel*, regards as superb. Says *Der Spiegel*:

> Meining carefully traced how this community of ex-Nazis built a mosque in Munich after founding the Mosque Construction Commission in 1960. Today, the Mosque Construction Commission goes by the name of the Islamic Society of Germany (IGD) and has become Germany's most important Muslim organization, with longstanding close links to the Muslim Brotherhood, a radical fundamentalist group based in Egypt. Meining's research has revealed that two former prominent members of the IGD are also associated with al-Qaida. "If you want to understand the structure of political Islam, you have to look at what happened in Munich," Meining told the *Wall Street Journal*. "Munich is the origin of a network that now reaches around the world."[1116]

In many of Germany's Muslim schools, radical teachings were reportedly central to the curriculum.[1117] In fact, Germany was so much a home to its militant population that one of the key centers of Egypt's Muslim Brotherhood—the jihad-obsessed organization founded in 1928 by Hassan al-Banna[1118]—was in Munich and one of the chief headquarters of Syria's Muslim Brotherhood was not in Damascus or Cairo. It was in the German city of Aachen.[1119]

No wonder there were Muslim riots in the German city of Hamburg in 2013. Or, as the Gatestone Institute puts it,

In July [2013], Muslim mobs ushered in the beginning of Ramadan with three nights of rioting in Hamburg. The unrest began on the evening of July 12 when more than 150 Muslim youths attacked police and burned cars in Altona, the westernmost district of Hamburg. More than 100 riot police were deployed to restore order. An 11-minute video of the Hamburg unrest, with cries of "Allahu Akbar!" ("Allah is Greater!") can be viewed... on YouTube.[1120]

And no wonder the plans for 9/11 were laid out not in the Middle East, but in Germany. In Hamburg.[1121] Among Germany's extremist Muslims.

Then there was Belgium, home to Abdelhamid Abaaoud, the mastermind of the Paris Massacre. And home to 70 mosques and to three hundred Islamic centers. Not all Belgian Muslims were radicals. Far from it. As you know, Omar Abaaoud, Abdelhamid's father, was an assimilated Muslim grateful to the Western culture in which he prospered. But as early as 2002, the Intelligence Committee of the Belgian Parliament said that moderate Muslims were effectively gagged in cities like Brussels. According to an Intelligence Committee report, "the Saudi-backed Salafi movement has created a religious 'state' within Belgium. Activists operate their own 'Islamic police' to enforce Islamic rules...Group members are circulating videos of Osama bin Laden and have carried out paramilitary training and parachute jumps in the Ardennes."[1122] The Ardennes is the area of dense European forests through which the Germans invaded France in World War I and World War II.[1123] Its mere mention can make those who know their history nervous. No wonder that in 2002, the *Telegraph* of London concluded that Belgium is "a launch pad for terrorists."[1124] Yes, in 2002. Well over a decade ago.

Many American intellectuals said that rumors of these Muslim enclaves in Europe were mere racist propaganda. But these shariah zones are apparently real. They helped produce Abdelhamid Abaaoud.

And there's the United States, where "pro-Palestinian" groups have worked successfully to infiltrate movements like Black Lives Matter.[1125]

*   *   *

France may have given us a preview of European jihad as early as November 2005 thanks to an influx of North African Arab laborers and asylum-seekers who had large families, and whose children and grandchildren grew France's

Islamic population to five million by 2004.[1126] In three hundred[1127] suburbs, towns and cities including Paris, Dijon, Marseilles, Toulouse, Rouen, Bordeaux, Avignon, Nice, Cannes, Nantes, Lille Saint-Dizier,[1128] and Strasbourg, Islamic rioters—most of them Muslim youths born and raised in France—went on what the mayor of Acheres, one of the French suburbs under attack, called a "perfectly organized"[1129] series of urban guerrilla-style arson attacks, shooting buckshot at police and using cars and motorcycles to spread flames from the resorts of France's Mediterranean coast to the German border.

This was a high-tech uprising. Said Patrick Hamon, a spokesman for France's national police, "Youths are communicating by cell phones or e-mails. They organize themselves, arrange meetings, [and] some prepare the Molotov cocktails."[1130] The participants in this Muslim World-Wide-Webbed rebellion barbecued a total of over 9,071 French cars.[1131] They torched two French nursery schools in a single night,[1132] burned a youth center, a police station, a film studio, shops, and a factory, torched an entire parking lot of cars, threw firebombs into ambulances waiting for emergency patients, and spread gas in the interior of a bus full of passengers, then lit the match.

To top it off, the makers of this possible sneak peek at Jihad 3.0 went online, using Arab-language websites like tajdeed.net and alsaha.com[1133] to warn of more violence to come. Wrote one of the Internet warriors, who signed himself Rania, "Civil war is declared. There will no doubt be deaths. Unfortunately, we have to prepare." Said another Web warrior, "We are going to destroy everything. Rest in peace, guys."[1134]

There were "copycat riots" in Brussels, Berlin, and Rotterdam.[1135] And there were nearly simultaneous riots in Arhus, Denmark. Some say that these riots were not spontaneous imitations of France's Muslim upheaval.[1136] The outbursts were well-coordinated, and were fed instructions and encouragement by global jihadists half a planet away.

Meanwhile, the majority of Western news analysts said that the French disturbance had nothing to do with Islam and was by no means a Holy War. But according to reports from Paris, both tajdeed.net and alsaha.com called the mayhem in France "a new jihad."[1137] This jihadist call was echoed on the streets, where, according to *Chicago Tribune* foreign correspondent Tom Hundley, writing from Paris, the rioters "scuffled with police and set fire to cars while chanting, 'The holy war has begun.'"[1138] The strife went on for 21 days and nights.[1139]

Islamic spokesgroups, reporters, and mainstream Western politicians tried to explain away the violence as the product of the standard

Western litany of social sins—poverty, oppression, unemployment, and humiliation—all elements that undoubtedly came into play. The unemployment rate among France's Muslims was a staggering 30%.[1140] And the French Observatory Against Racism reported that it had sent 325 resumes to French employers, resumes with identical work experience and credentials, but with different names and places of origin. The result: the odds of getting a job if you had a name of North African origin were seriously stacked against you. Native Frenchmen or French women were five times as likely to be hired as you were.[1141]

What's more, there were strong voices of moderation in the French Islamic community. Reuters reported that "imams and mosque groups in the suburbs have called for calm"[1142] and described "the sight of imams and local Muslim leaders in the suburbs calming down angry teenagers who reject all other authority."[1143]

But not all this moderation was what it seemed. The Union of French Islamic Organizations issued a fatwa stating that the riots were in violation of Islam. Said the fatwa, "Aggression is forbidden by Islam according to the verse [Qur'an 2:190]: 'Begin not hostilities. Lo! Allah loveth not aggressors.'"[1144] This statement sounds peaceful. But it isn't. It's designed to mislead.

The quote that actually appears in the Qur'an's Chapter 2 verse 190 reads, "Fight in the cause of Allah those who fight you but do not transgress limits; for Allah loveth not transgressors."[1145] The next sentence in the Qur'an is telling. It reads, "And slay them wherever ye catch them and turn them out from where they have turned you out."[1146] This is not an order for peace. It is an instruction for battle. And the restraint it calls for isn't kindness toward the enemy. It's a warning not to disobey your military leaders. Not to break ranks and start the fight prematurely. It's a warning to remain strictly disciplined and strictly obedient. The Union of French Islamic Organizations' fatwa seemed to embody one of Muhammad's basic strategies in war—"guile,"[1147] dishonesty and surprise. As you know, Muhammad summed it up when he said "war is deceit."[1148] In other words, as Muhammad's first biographer, Ibn Ishaq spelled out in great detail, jihad is made by carefully using lies.[1149]

Intellectuals writing in Arabic agreed that the causes of the riots were joblessness and discrimination, not Islam. But these same intellectuals warned that the French riots could easily be repeated worldwide. Wrote an editorial writer in Iran's daily newspaper *Jomhouri-ye Eslami*, "Discrimination is also rising in England, Germany, America, Canada, and many other Western countries."[1150] What *Jomhouri-ye Eslami* called "this disease" of discrimination against Muslims was eroding "the patience of the people who had for years suffered from the racist discrimination." Discrimination and racism, added *Jomhouri-ye Eslami*, were turning a "quiet movement...to overt and violent rebellion."[1151] Al-Arabiya TV director Abd Al-Rahman al-Rashed warned that the violence "will recur in the future, even if it calms down for some time."[1152]

A C-SPAN panel discussion convened by the Islamic group CAIR—The Council on American-Islamic Relations, the Saudi-backed group that the United Arab Emirates would later designate "terrorist,"[1153] a group that enforces Western self-censorship—warned against Arab bashing. Like so many others, its panelists said that only one factor had triggered the European disturbances—discrimination. But halfway around the world an Indian expert on Islamic activism from the South Asia Analysis Group told a different story. He said the riots had started spontaneously, then had been prodded along by three international extremist groups:[1154] Hizb ut-Tahrir, which operates in 40 countries, Lashkar-e-Toiba, based in Pakistan, and Jamaat-ul-Fuqra,[1155] a New York- and Pakistan-based Jihadist group that gave the world the shoe bomber, Richard Reid, a middle-class kid born in London of a Jamaican father[1156] who walked into a passenger plane with his explosives hidden in the tongue, lining,[1157] and sole of his shoe.[1158]

In 2002, Reid boarded American Airlines flight 63 from Paris to Miami, waited until the plane was in flight, lit a match, bent over in his passenger seat, and was about to light a triacetone triperoxide fuse protruding from his shoe's tongue. A passenger screamed and the 6'4" Reid was wrestled to the floor by two flight attendants, doused with water passed cup by cup by passengers, and sedated by two doctors on the flight.[1159]

The South Asia Analysis Group expert who felt that far more than discrimination had triggered the French riots was B. Rahman, a former Indian cabinet member whom the American news service UPI calls "one of Delhi's top security advisers and commentators on Islamic affairs."[1160] The militant Islamic groups Hizb ut-Tahrir, Lashkar-e-Toiba, and Jamaat-ul-Fuqra, Rahman claimed, used their sleeper cells in France to pour oil on the flames. Meanwhile UPI added that the radical Algerian Salafist Group for Preaching and Combat (the GSP) claimed credit for the rampage. The long-range goal of the organizations that took the lead in prolonging the French riots, said Rahman is—surprise, surprise—world rule...a global caliphate.[1161]

In Washington, the right-wing Center for Immigration Studies set up a panel discussion between three experts during the last days of the French riots. Like Rahman, the panelists asserted that the extremist Muslim European agenda was even more ambitious than mere Holy War. The speakers, Mark Krikorian, executive director of the Center for Immigration Studies, Frank Gaffney, president of the Center for Security Policy, and Stephen Steinlight, Fellow at the Center for Immigration Studies, said those behind the riots were aiming for a short-term goal of "bantustans" in Europe: enclaves ruled by Islamic leaders and run according to Islamic holy law—shariah. In exchange for these Islamic micro-states on European soil, the Muslim leaders would keep the citizens in Islamic European communities from erupting in further violence.[1162] The riots were allegedly being used as part of a belief-driven protection racket. They were part of a new strategy to take territory. Slowly. Multi-generationally. Inch by inch and decade by decade. European territory.

Said Krikorian, Gaffney, and Steinlight, these Muslim micro-states would be stepping stones to a grander goal—once again, a global caliphate.[1163]

Is the notion of a global caliphate a Muslim-basher's fantasy? Is it an Islamophobic delusion conjured up by right-wing hate? When the French riots erupted, the publisher of a deeply Islamic, pro-Holy War website, *Jihad Unspun*, wrote bluntly that "global jihad is breaking out. .... How will we rebuild the Caliphate if we cannot work together? ... Brothers and sisters, the time is now for us to rise."[1164]

Does the notion of Islam's global rule, the notion of a worldwide caliphate, extend to America? Apparently the answer is yes. In 2006, two admitted Islamic "terrorists" appeared on the Philadelphia-based TV show *Your Morning on CN8* and gave a potent sense of the global unity of today's militant Islam.[1165] The first, Walid Shoebat, a Palestinian from a prominent family who had successfully bombed an Israeli bank, was asked why the privileged son of Arab aristocrats would turn to violence. Said Shoebat, "My grandfather was good friends with Mohammad Amin al-Husayni, the grand mufti of Jerusalem. He was called the Fuehrer of the Muslim world."

Why was the grand mufti called "the Fuehrer"? The grand mufti met with Adolf Hitler, corresponded with him frequently, lived for four years in Berlin as a guest of the Nazi government, was given seven luxurious Berlin residences, a chauffeured Mercedes, a weekly stipend of $10,000, and a lavish food allowance so he could woo other Muslim leaders to the Nazi cause.[1166] He was also named an honorary Aryan. Topping it all off, the mufti toured Germany's Oranienburg concentration camp, met with SS head Reichsführer Heinrich

Himmler, and helped the SS recruit between 24,000 and 27,000 Muslim Bosnians to the SS ranks.[1167] A key SS task was killing Jews.[1168] Most important, the grand mufti shared Hitler's vision of exterminating the Jews utterly, the vision of "killing Jews wherever Arabs found them."[1169] On top of all that, the mufti was a man who Palestinian founding father Yasser Arafat met when he was 17 and who Arafat "came to adore and emulate."[1170]

But back to Walid Shoebat on *CN8*. Shoebat explained, "It's not like you join a terror organization. People don't understand in the West. They think it's like the Unabomber. You know, 'What goes on in the mind of a terrorist.'" But, says Shoebat, in fact, "It's the collective incitement of millions of children. In school, in the social arena, in clubs, in the mosque, on the Temple Mount, in the streets, in the graffiti." In other words, jihad is taught in some Muslim schools as the norm.

The interviewer clearly did not believe what he heard. He did not believe that Holy War—that violence in the name of Islam—is taught in mainstream schools anywhere in the world. "Are you saying it's part of the culture?" he asked. "Are you saying it's part of the upbringing of the children of Palestine, the children of Iraq right now?" Shoebat answered, "Absolutely. Absolutely. When I was six years old, I go to school, just before the Six Day War, we sing 'Arabs are beloved, and Jews are dogs.' So you can see it's not just in the Palestinian area, it's in Jordan, it's in Lebanon, it's in Cairo, it's in Syria, it's all over."

But what was the connection between the culture of Palestine and the eight million strong[1171] Islamic community of the USA in 2006? The *CN8* interviewer turned from Shoebat to Ibrahim Abdullah, another admitted terrorist born and raised in Dearborn, Michigan, and asked if similar things are happening in the USA. Answered Abdullah, "Organizations who are funding terrorist organizations all over the country...usually... you'll find they start in Dearborn, Detroit, because that is the home base of many of these organizations. ...As far as cultivating the mentality of the children, that's absolutely truthful. [In Dearborn] It is just like it is in the West Bank. And not just the West Bank, throughout the Middle East, in the Muslim world as a whole."

The interviewer tried to make sure that he understood Abdallah correctly. "So what you're saying, then, Ibrahim," he asked, "is that right here, in our country, as we are speaking to viewers living here in the United States, you're saying that there are cells of terrorists, young men being cultivated right in our borders?" Abdallah answered, "Right. But what I'm trying to explain to you is that it's not an obscure thing that just started happening. This is part of the culture. You're born and raised with this hatred in your mind and in your heart. I mean for America and Israel. Primarily the Jew and Christian. And that is what the target is."[1172]

Which brings us to CAIR, the Council for American-Islamic Relations. CAIR presents itself as the leading voice of moderate Islam in America. CAIR has been brought in as a trusted ally by the FBI, the Justice Department, the Department of Homeland Security, the Department of Defense, and the Bush[1173] and Clinton White House.[1174] Whenever Islam is accused of harboring violence, spokesmen from CAIR pop up on as many television shows as they can reach, explaining that "Islam is a religion of peace." But that's not what CAIR says in private.

Omar Ahmad is CAIR's founding president. At a 1993 Hamas meeting in Philadelphia, a meeting that intelligence analyst Stephen Coughlin explains "led to the formation of CAIR," Ahmad said point blank, "you send two messages: one to the Americans and one to the Muslims."[1175] In other words, you dissimulate, you use guile, you employ deception, you lie. All tools that Muhammad felt were vital to war and to conquest. Ahmad reportedly admitted to an all-Muslim audience in California as early as 1998 that "Islam isn't in America to be equal to any other faith, but to become dominant. The Qur'an ... should be the highest authority in America, and Islam the only accepted religion on Earth."[1176] In other words, Shariah should replace the American constitution. A close CAIR ally,[1177] Abdul Rahman al-Amoudi, the founder of the American Muslim Council, added that "If we are outside this country, we can say, Oh, Allah, destroy America." Presumably al-Amoudi feels it's unwise to say such a thing on the *Today Show*. Nonetheless, al-Amoudi, the "destroy America" fan, was invited to events celebrating the opening of "the State Department's Office of International Religious Freedom in Washington"[1178] in 1998. Then, al-Amoudi suffered a small slip-up. In the words of Human Rights Watch, "In July 2004. a U.S. federal court sentenced Abdulrahman M. Alamoudi, a U.S. citizen and founder of the American Muslim Council, to 23 years in prison for illegal business dealings with Libya related to a plot to kill then-Saudi Crown Prince Abdullah."[1179]

Remember, on American TV, CAIR repeats a consistent mantra, "Islam is a religion of peace." But, again, that's not the way CAIR acts in private. In fact, CAIR has been named a "terrorist organization." It hasn't earned that label from a flaming right-wing Islamophobic gang. It's been dubbed "terrorist" "by the United Arab Emirates,"[1180] a nation whose officials can read what CAIR dignitaries say in their private language, Arabic. This may explain why, in a case against a George Mason University honors graduate, Sabri Benkahla, who went to Pakistan to join the Taliban, the U.S. government stated that "from its founding by Muslim Brotherhood leaders, CAIR conspired with other affiliates of the Muslim Brotherhood to support terrorists."[1181]

So CAIR was founded by "Muslim Brotherhood leaders." Hmmm. That's interesting. Dig a little deeper, and you discover that in its 1991 *Explanatory Memorandum On the General Strategic Goal for the Group In North America*, the Muslim Brotherhood laid out a simple goal:

> The Ikhwan [members of the Muslim Brotherhood] must under-stand that their work in America is a kind of grand Jihad in elimi-nating and destroying the Western civilization from within and "sabotaging" its miserable house by their hands and the hands of the believers so that it [Western civilization] is eliminated and God's religion is made victorious over all other religions.[1182]

Since Islam is a political and military structure disguised as a religion, that means the world will be ruled by just one leader, a caliph, using just one law code, shariah.

Which means that *Jihad Unspun*, the leader of CAIR, and many others were calling for a new form of global superorganism, one run by a meme that was built for worldwide rule by its founder 1,376 years earlier. As Osama bin Laden liked to say, this "clash is in fact a clash of civilizations,"[1] a world war that girdles the globe and that has a front line extending, according to Osama, to "Tajakestan, Burma, Kashmir, Assam [India], Philippines, Fatani [Thailand], Ogadin [in Africa], Somalia, Eritrea [in Northern Africa], Chechnya...Kashmir, Pakistan and everywhere."[1184] As the Muslim Brotherhood puts it in its plan for North America, this is a jihad to bring back what Muhammad established in Medina, "the most magnificent and fabulous civilization humanity knew."[1185] In this battle of memes and of su-perorganisms of global size, the Muslim mass mind's ability to think in multi-generational terms and its policy of "competitive reproduction"[1186] may give it an edge over the Western collective intelligence, a mass mind that is often blind to anything longer than a two-year plan.

In France, Belgium, and the United States, modernist, pluralist Western civilization and modernist, pluralist Muslims are pitted against a militant Muslim subculture and its political and military worldview, a worldview that's been on a winning streak far longer than the modern nations of the

United States, France, or Belgium[1187] have existed. The question is which world-view—the liberal or the jihadist—will win in the end.

* * *

If Indian security expert B. Rahman is wrong and there were no foreign agita-tors in the French riots of 2005, who were the "ringleaders" of the Paris riots? What mosques did they attend? What doctrines had they been taught?

Could a statement by one Islamic author, Dr. Ali Muhammad Naqvi, pro-vide a clue? "Islam," he says, "addresses all of mankind as a single unit. Its system is not for a nation, but for the whole human society. It is the duty of Muslims to fight unyieldingly against every other ideology and school in-cluding nationalism, communism and liberalism, politically and intellectu-ally and they should not rest until the school of God [Islam] comes to dominate over the personal, social, political, economic, intellectual and reli-gious life of man."[1188]

* * *

But the French riots were just a preview. Remember Abdelhamid Abaaoud, the son of a well-to-do owner of two clothing stores in Brussels who was radicalized in jail? How could a kid from an upscale European school become a jihadist radical in a Belgian prison? Belgium's Sudinfo.be reports that 45% of the "inmates in Belgian prisons are Muslim."[1189] And even the head of the Muslims of Belgium is concerned about radicalization campaigns in the pris-ons of Belgium. He "asks that the practice of religion be formalized" to prevent the radicals from aggressively spreading their views.[1190]

The head of the Muslims of Belgium expressed his concern about radi-calization in prison in 2013. Apparently, his concern was not enough. Muslim radicals are at work in jails all over the world. In a prison, the jihadist re-cruiters have a perfect environment—a hothouse for jihadist conversion. They have a population that enjoys violence, that breaks secular laws, and that has been humiliated by imprisonment. Society has told these inmates that they are the scum of the earth. Jihadist Islam tells these prisoners that they are the very opposite. If they convert to Islam, they can have authority over all of humanity. They can be heroes and aristocrats. How? By doing what they love. Violent deeds. Murder. Torture. And by taking advantage of Allah's generosity—looting the goods of those who do not believe. They are no longer thieves and murderers. They are knights destined for an express trip to paradise. All they have to do is kill and plunder under the auspices of Islam. And under the strict control of military leaders. Leaders disguised as ordinary citizens. The deal jihad offers is unbeatable. And the inmates have one more thing: plenty of spare time. Spare time in which to be indoctrinated in the basics of Islam.

The result is converts like Richard Reid, the shoe bomber, who converted to Islam in Britain's Blundeston prison, then became an aspiring suicide bomber.[1191]

How long have militant Muslims been recruiting potential jihadists in Western jails?

When he was 20 years old, Malcolm Little was jailed for breaking and entering and larceny. While he was in Boston's Charlestown State Prison, he was converted to Islam. Not by infiltrators of the prison, but by a persuasive relative's letters. Prison proved the perfect place to take a deep dive into a new religion, a privileged place in which to read. Said Little, "months passed without my even thinking about being imprisoned. In fact, up to then, I had never been so truly free in my life."[1192] Why? Malcolm was reading everything he could get his hands on about world history and philosophy. He was reading the preachings of Black Muslim leader Elijah Muhammad. And he was corresponding with the Black Muslim leader. But he pored through books, devouring them all night long by the tiny bit of light that slipped onto the floor of his cell. Then he hid the books when the guard made his rounds. Malcolm was in search of every shred of evidence he could find on "how the white man had brought upon the world's black, brown, red and yellow peoples every variety of the sufferings of exploitation."[1193] And he found it hidden in plain sight—in the books of historians like Will and Ariel Durant and H.G. Wells. With a little help from *Uncle Tom's Cabin* and the pamphlets of the Abolitionist Anti-Slavery Society of New England.[1194] When was Malcolm Little's prison conversion to Islam? Between 1946 and 1952. Over 60 years ago.

Malcolm Little then changed his name to Malcolm X and became a hero of the black community. Walk down the shopping street of a black neighborhood, and you are likely to see posters on sale of Malcolm X with what appears to be an M2 Carbine machine gun.[1195] That is not an image of peace.

In fact, Imam Benjamin Karim, who used to act as opening speaker for Malcolm X in front of packed congregations at Malcolm's mosque, his Temple Number 7 in Harlem, recalls the theology he would preach to the crowd:

I would talk a bit about the question: WHICH ONE WILL SURVIVE THE WAR OF ARMAGEDDON? Black people who are Christians are taught, and believe, that the war referred to is war between spiritual forces, between the concepts of good and evil. We taught that the war is one that will take place on this earth, a war between the oppressed and their oppressors—a race war. ...It will be a war in which there will be a winner, a war where one side will survive and the other perish. In this war, this final war, in the final phases of this final war, no prisoners will be taken.[1196]

Fortunately, the Islamic sect in which Malcolm X became a leader, the Nation of Islam, has never put its ideas of war into action. The only terrorism it's perpetrated was against fellow Nation of Islam members who strayed. And the most important figure who went off the track was Malcolm X. When the Nation of Islam's leader, Elijah Muhammad, saw Malcolm Little as a threat, he had Malcolm assassinated while the charismatic younger leader was giving a speech at Manhattan's Audubon Ballroom in 1965.[1197]

Like many Western Muslim groups, the Nation of Islam had a bone-deep Saudi connection. The movement's founder, Wallace D. Fard, according to the group's website and to numerous other sources, was "an Arab born in Mecca, Saudi Arabia in 1877."[1198] And the United Arab Emirates and Qatar contributed to the Nation of Islam's funding. But the most generous Middle Eastern funding source was Muammar Qaddafi's Libya, which gave the group three multimillion-dollar cash infusions.[1199] Why do you suspect that distant nations were funding a group in the USA?

Since Malcolm X's days in prison, the Muslim effort to gather converts in American prisons has become more sophisticated. And more focused. It's no longer the monopoly of a splinter movement like the Nation of Islam. As long ago as 2006, Donald Van Duyn, deputy assistant director of the Counterterrorism Division of the FBI, testified before the Senate Committee on Homeland Security that, "Prison radicalization primarily occurs through anti-U.S. sermons provided by contract, volunteer, or staff imams."[1200] You read that right. Our prison system is paying official imams to preach a form of Islam crackling with violence. And it is allowing radical preachers to come in as volunteers. In the name of freedom of religion. And what form of radical Islam are these radicals preaching? Says Van Duyn, either the Saudi-backed "Salafi form of Sunni Islam"[1201] or the "extremist view of Shia Islam similar to that of the government of Iran and Lebanese Hizballah."[1202] What do these two forms of radical Islam—the Saudi and the Iranian—have in common? Backing from big money. Middle Eastern money. And jihad. The focus on making the globe Islamic via violent war. Or, as Van Duyn puts it, "charismatic elements within prison have used the call of Global Jihad as a source of inspiration to recruit others for the purpose of conducting terrorist attacks in the United States."[1203] Adds the *Washington Times*, "U.S. officials have said several hundred Americans, many of whom converted to Islam in prison, traveled in the past several years to Yemen for terrorist training with al Qaeda in the Arabian Peninsula."[1204] In a report commissioned by the U.S. Department of Justice, Mark S. Hamm, a terrorism specialist at Indiana State University's Department of Criminology and Criminal Justice, says that "America's prisoners" are even singled out as "candidates for conversion" in "al-Qaeda training manuals."[1205]

What makes prison converts perfect for terrorism? And for jihad? Says Van Duyn, "Some radicalized Islamic inmates are current or former members of street or prison gangs, indicating an emerging 'crossover' trend from gang member to Islamist extremist."[1206] The discipline and violence of gang life are perfect training grounds for war, for jihad against the West.

Joy Brighton writes in *The Daily Caller*, "Our government has been contracting and paying Muslim Brotherhood front groups, such as GSISS (The Graduate School of Islamic and Social Sciences) and ISNA (Islamic Society of North America) to screen and assign Muslim prison chaplains for at least 8 years."[1207] As Brighton points out, Egypt and Saudi Arabia have outlawed the Muslim Brotherhood as a terrorist organization. But Muslim Brotherhood-affiliated imams are paid substantial sums to act as prison chaplains. Brighton gives examples that are scary:

> Chaplain Umar Abdul-Jalil — was hired at an annual salary of $76,602 even though he served 14 years for dealing drugs. In 2006, he was suspended for two weeks without pay after declaring that "the greatest terrorists in the world occupy the White House." He continues to oversee 40 prison chaplains.
>
> According to the *Wall Street Journal*, Wallace Gene Marks converted under Imam Umar while in prison for weapon possession. He was hired as one of the first paid Muslim chaplains in 1975 and has hired nearly 45 chaplains. [1208]

The extremist Imams know what they are doing. Writes Brighton:

> Imam Umar says that prison "is the perfect recruitment and train-
> ing grounds for radicalism and the Islamic religion" and that 9/11
> hijackers should be honored as martyrs. "Funded by the Saudi
> government he traveled often to Saudi Arabia and brought that
> country's harsh form of Islam to New York's expanding ranks of
> Muslim prisoners."[1209]

If Brighton is right, here are some of the results of this prison radicalization. In her words:

- In April 2010, Larry James murdered his mother, pregnant wife,
  7-month-old son, 3-year-old niece and 16-year-old niece for
  refusing to convert to Islam. James converted in 2007, while in
  a U.S. prison.
- Then two months ago [in 2014] Colleen Hufford, a 54-year-old
  grandmother and factory worker in Oklahoma, was beheaded
  with a produce knife by Alton Nolen who likely converted to
  Islam in a U.S. prison. Nolen is being charged with workplace
  violence.
- Last month NYPD officer Kenneth Healey, 25, was axed to death
  with a hatchet to the side of the head. He was not attacked by a
  "lone wolf," but by ex-con Zale Thompson. New York City Police
  Commissioner William Bratton has called it a terrorist attack,
  and the NYPD might want to look at Thompson's record in
  California where he did two brief terms in California prisons. [1210]

How are Muslim radicalizers doing in their recruitment efforts in
American jails? "The statistics are staggering," Brighton wrote in 2014, "and
woefully out of date. One out of three African-American inmates in U.S. prisons converts to Islam while incarcerated. This statistic is no longer limited to
African-Americans in prison. The *Huffington Post* reported an estimated
35,000–40,000 inmates convert to Islam each year, and that 15 percent of the
total U.S. prison population or 350,000 inmates are Muslim. This is more
than 18 times the national representation of Muslims in America, reported
to be 0.8 percent."[1211]

Brighton and Brown, the two authors quoted above, are suspect. They
are what the Organization of Islamic Nations call "Islamophobes." They

research and write about the dark side of Islam, the jihadist side. And the Islamophobia campaign brands people like them as "racists." But are they just ill-informed bigots? Or are they right? Only one thing will tell: their accuracy. If what they say is true, it is crucial to take them seriously.

One expert from inside the Muslim world, Saudi professor Nasser Bin Suleiman Al-Omar, the man behind the website www.almoslim.net, offers the following evaluation:

> America is collapsing from within...Islam is advancing according to a steady plan, to the point that tens of thousands of Muslims have joined the American army and Islam is the second largest religion in America. Today, America is defeated. I have no doubt, not even for a minute, that America is on its way to destruction.[1212]

America, says Al-Omar, will be conquered "from within."

*   *   *

I first became aware of the Muslim recruitment effort in 1981. In pursuit of the forces of history, the mass passions that make history, I jumped ship from 15 years in science and started a company in 1976 in an area I did not know—popular music. That company, The Howard Bloom Organization, Ltd., became the biggest PR firm in the music industry. Said Danny Goldberg, former president of Atlantic Records and Polygram Records, in his book *Stumbling Upon Genius*, "Howard Bloom did not regard public relations as an attempt to placate spoiled rock stars. He saw it as an applied science." Then, in 1988, I went back to my science full-time, having learned intense lessons in the shifts of mass moods and the workings of mass mind.

In 1981, Sylvia Robinson, founder of Sugar Hill Records and the producer of the first commercial rap record, "Rapper's Delight," came to my office on 55th Street off Lexington Avenue in Manhattan and asked if I'd help her publicize a group she had discovered in the South Bronx, Grandmaster Flash and the Furious Five. Sylvia wanted me to do more than help her publicize a band. She wanted me to help put that band's genre—rap—on the map. I was up for it. I loved helping emerging subcultures find their voice. But a few months later, a record company executive who was rapidly rising toward what would soon be record-company-president status took me aside in the hallway of his company of the moment, Chrysalis Records. "Look, Bloom," he said, "you've worked very hard to establish your credibility in the music industry. This music you're working with is shit. You know it's shit. I know it's shit. It's going to be over in six months. And when it is, it will explode and leave shit all over your face." That was a cue to work on rap even harder.

There was another figure who had spotted rap's potential and moved in early in the game. His name was Louis Farrakhan. Farrakhan had a terrific ear for talent. He would swoop in on a young, inexperienced rapper early in his or her career, when he or she was confused and in need of guidance. He would "educate" him or her. One of his most famous early converts was the critically admired band Public Enemy.[1213] What two books were the foundation of Farrakhan's "education"? A book that the Russian secret police, the Okhrana, had fabricated in 1905[1214] to take the heat off the tsar after that ruler had ignominiously lost a war with Japan. The falsified book claimed to be the meeting notes of a group of Jews who got together to plot world wars and global financial collapses. Its title: *The Protocols of the Elders of Zion*. Tellingly, Farrakhan's Nation of Islam was the distributor of the Protocols in the United States. The second book in Farrakhan's "education" was *The International Jew*, a vituperatively anti-Semitic book by Henry Ford.[1215] These were two of the books with which Adolph Hitler[1216] had justified the murder of six million Jews, the Holocaust. What movement did Louis Farrakhan lead? The Nation of Islam, the biggest Muslim group in America's black community.[1217] The group that had recruited Malcolm X.

Farrakhan was using Muhammad's strategy. Find converts among those on the bottom of the social ladder. Then give your recruits a feeling of power by pitting them against a nerd, an enemy too small to retaliate. Farrakhan's group of choice had been the folks the Qur'an called "apes and swine"—monkeys and pigs.[1218] The group whose members would be pointed out by the very stones behind which they were hiding, and even the stones would call for their death. The Jews. Precisely the group Muhammad had targeted. And Muhammad had made a wise choice. Nearly 1,400 years after his death, there were still Jews to target. And at a mere 16 million globally, they were far too small to pose a danger to Islam's 1.6 billion.

By the way, on a tour of rogue nations in 1996—a tour that would include Saddam Hussein's Iraq and Muammar Qaddafi's Libya—Farrakhan would show up in Iran in time to celebrate the 17th anniversary of Iran's Islamic Revolution. It was widely reported that Farrakhan would tell the Iranians exactly what they wanted to hear: "God will not give Japan and Europe the honor of bringing down the United States, this is an honor God will bestow upon Muslims."[1219] Farrakhan would later deny the quote.[1220]

But it was also reported that he said, "It is an act of mercy to white people that we end your world... We must end your world and bring in a new world."[1221] And "We are at war and we never stop fighting for justice. You must have force... don't drop your gun and don't forget to squeeze."[1222] But back to 1981.

After watching Farrakhan at work in the newly unfolding rap community, I discovered that Farrakhan was using the same techniques with which he fished for converts among rappers in another arena rich in potential converts: America's prisons.[1223]

Thirty-five years later, according to the blog *Prison Culture*, "A California law officer estimates that Muslims do 50% of their recruiting in prisons."[1224] The same thing happens in prisons in Europe.[1225] The result? Abdelhamid Abaaoud, the child of privilege born in Belgium, was radicalized in prison and became a recruiter for ISIS in Europe. He slipped back and forth between ISIS territory in Syria and Brussels. He took advantage of the tide of Syrian refugees[1226] inundating Europe to do it. He even recruited his 13-year-old brother, Younes.[1227] Then he was given a promotion and became an organizer. What did he organize? You already know the answer: the Paris massacres, the simultaneous attacks on six locations in Paris that killed 130 people and injured 368 on November 13, 2015. "The Blessed Paris Invasion on the French Crusaders."[1228]

* * *

To repeat, Western thinking says that terrorism is bred by poverty and the lack of jobs. Abdelhamid Abaaoud was not poor, underprivileged, or lacking a job. He was wealthy, comfortable, and had business opportunities. So why was he prey to radicalization? Like you and me, he apparently wanted to dedicate himself to something bigger than himself, to a project that would change and seemingly upgrade the world, a project that would lift all of humanity, a project that would give his life meaning in a grand scheme of things. A grand scheme that would put Abdelhamid Abaaoud and those with whom he labored on the top of the hierarchical ladder, on the top of the global pecking order. Islam provides that framework of meaning.

So does Western civilization, but we haven't learned to articulate the idealistic value of what we are achieving.

What are the positives we are missing? Every worldview that appeals to our idealism makes a promise: to lift the poor and the oppressed. And Western civilization, our civilization, does it best. In fact, Western civilization has delivered on its promises to the poor and the oppressed far more than any other civilization in history.

Here are some startling facts:

- If you'd been born in 1850, your expected lifespan would have been 37.5 years. If you'd been born in the West in 2000, your expected lifespan would have been 78.5 years. Chinese emperors were willing to spend almost all of their wealth to achieve an extra four years of life. But Western civilization has added another 40. Western civilization has more than doubled the human lifespan. No other civilization in the history of the world—not the Chinese, Egyptian, Muslim, or Russian Marxist—has ever pulled this off.
- If you'd been the poorest paid worker in London in 2012, a personal assistant, you would have earned what an entire tenement full of the poorest paid workers in London were paid in 1850. You would have earned what seven Irish dockworkers made.
- If you gave a bunch of average Western kids today a Stanford-Binet IQ test from 1916, today's kids would register as near-geniuses. They'd register an average IQ of roughly 135. That's an IQ jump of 35 points.
- If you'd been a member of an indigenous culture in the days of the Noble Savage, one of those tribes that "lives in peace and harmony with nature," your odds of dying a violent death at the hands of your fellow human beings would have been ten times what they are in the West today. Since 1650, Western civilization has upped the level of peace by a factor of ten.
- If you'd been born in 2000, you would have been four inches taller than if you'd been born in 1850.

If our great-great-grandparents could double our lifespans, we owe another doubling to our great-great-grandkids. If our great-great-grandparents could septuple our salaries, we owe another septupling to our great-great-grandkids. If our great-great-grandparents could add an extra 35 points to our IQ, we owe another 35 points to our great-great-grandkids. If our great-great-grandparents could up the level of peace by a factor of ten, we owe an equally radical upgrade in the level of peace to our great-great-grandkids. And if our great-great-grandparents could add four inches to our height, then we owe at least another four inches to our great-great-grandkids.

Many Muslim leaders would say that these are all material gifts. None of them are spiritual. Yes and no. The new human powers created by Western civilization have set the spirit of the average Westerner soaring in ways that were available to only the highest aristocrats of world history. And soaring in many ways that even those aristocrats could never conceive. But that's a subject that would take another book.

*   *   *

The kind of Islam that won over Abdelhamid Abaaoud boasts that its goal—a one-world globe ruled by strict Shariah—will provide "to the world the most magnificent and fabulous civilization humanity"[1229] has ever known. Meanwhile, we are top-heavy with self-criticism. And self-loathing. Frankly, we need self-criticism. But we need to be able to admire our positives as clearly as we see our negatives. Meanwhile, militant Islam has been using our self-loathing to disable us. Islam has been articulating its big picture framework of meaning since 629 A.D. And today, it is doing that articulating in Europe and the USA. Including in European and American prisons. Unfortunately, the jihadist framework of meaning demands killing. "Making great slaughter in the land."[1230] Your land and mine.

The Kill List

Are You a Blasphemer?

TODAY'S ISLAM FOLLOWS Muhammad's kill-the-opposition example. It is not kind to its dissenters and its critics. It is not forgiving of those who speak up for tolerance, pluralism, and human rights. It is not gentle to the sort of people from whom Muslim peace movements might spring. The reason? The founder effect.

In roughly 1971, a baby named Aasiya Noreen was born in Ittan Wali, a small village in the countryside 30 miles outside Pakistan's second largest city, Lahore. Aasiya would be commonly known as Asia Bibi. Declan Walsh of England's *The Guardian*—who was stationed in Pakistan when he reported in depth on the Asia Bibi story—calls Ittan Wali "a sleepy Punjab village."[1231] But Ittan Wali was not as sleepy as it seemed.

When Asia Bibi was a little less than 20 years old,[1232] she married a brick maker with three children, then had two children of her own. She was proud of her husband's work. She says, "His boss often used to say to his dozen workers: 'You are the pillars of the construction industry. By making bricks all day you're helping to build buildings and make Pakistan great!'" Asia spelled out the meaning she took from the boss' statement: "So Ashiq was doing work that was important for our country."[1233]

Asia, her husband, and their five children lived in a modest house with a blue iron gate[1234] on a corner in the village. But there was a problem. Asia Bibi and her husband were Christians.

Christians are Pakistan's biggest minority.[1235] Yet Christians are usually relegated to the dirtiest, most contemptible jobs—as cleaners and sweepers. Their neighbors call them "impure"[1236] and unclean. One of the most influential interpreters of Islam in the modern world, the founder of the Islamic Revolution in Iran, the Ayatollah Khomeini, gives an insight into the attitude of Pakistan's rural Muslims toward the Christians in their neighborhood when he says,

Every part of the body of a non-Muslim individual is impure, even the hair on his hand and his body hair, his nails, and all the secretions of his body. Any man or woman who denies the existence of God, or believes in His partners [the Christian Trinity], or else does not believe in His Prophet Muhammad, is impure (in the same way as are excrement, urine, dog, and wine).[1237]

Yes, you read that right. The Ayatollah said unbelievers are as impure as excrement and urine. Why does the message of an Iranian religious leader give insight on the attitudes of Pakistanis? Because both come from the same source—the founding documents of Islam. Both come from the life of Muhammad. Topping it all off, the word for unbelievers, kafir, carries an emotional charge similar to the forbidden English word "nigger."[1238] "Kafir," "impure" and its synonym "filthy" were words that Asia Bibi's Muslim neighbors would soon use against her.[1239] Big-time.

Roughly 40% of Pakistan's population is modernist, pluralist, tolerant, and in favor of human rights.[1240] But Pakistan's Muslim liberals would not be the cause of Asia Bibi's troubles. Her troubles would come from Pakistan's extremists. Extremists who constitute roughly the other 60% of Pakistan's population. Extremists like her neighbors.

Despite the fact that Ittan Wali was just 30 miles from a major city, *The Guardian* reports that two militant extremist groups were active in the region: Lashkar-e-Taiba—the militant group behind the November 26, 2008, Mumbai attacks that killed 164 people in India[1241]—and Sipah-e-Sahaba, a group *The Guardian* calls "vicious."

To get a sense of the sentiments of the extremists, it's wise to look at the treatment of blasphemy in Pakistan. Blasphemy is against the law. It is punished with a death sentence. But the death sentences meted out by Pakistan's courts are not what counts. The real danger of death comes from idealistic, pious, highly committed citizens. Citizens highly committed to Islam. We call these citizens extremists. But there's a more accurate way to look at it. These are citizens who take Muhammad's examples of virtue seriously. In 1997, when Asia Bibi was roughly 26 years old, a Pakistan High Court judge in the city of Lahore, Arif Iqbal Bhatti, acquitted three accused blasphemers, including two Christian men, Salamat and Rehmat Masih, of blasphemy. What did the judge's action in the spirit of the "all forgiving" Allah earn him? He was assassinated in 1998. In his chambers at the High Court.[1242] This took place only 30 miles away from Asia Bibi's home.

Being a Christian in Ittan Wali was as unsafe as being a High Court judge in Lahore. In August 1, 2009, 30 miles from Ittan Wali, Muslims would soon riot, roused by a rumor that Christians had torn out pages of a Qur'an and trampled on the scatter of paper at the end of a wedding. The followers of the one true prophet burned Christian homes and killed between seven and ten people. Says Minhas Hameed, about his 75-year-old father, "The first man who was shot on his forehead was my father. He died on the spot. They had clearly targeted him with a telescope."[1243] Adds Asia Bibi in a book she later wrote with a French journalist, Anne-Isabelle Tollet:[1244]

> We often used to hear about Christians being massacred by Muslims. How could we forget what happened in Gojra, fifty kilometres from Ittan Wali? Everyone was talking about this appalling event; even villagers who weren't Christians were shocked by it. Apparently, a crowd of angry Muslims went into the village of Korian and destroyed hundreds of houses belonging to Christian families, who were all living in the same neighbourhood. The furious Muslims said the Christians had profaned the holy Koran by tearing out pages and trampling on them as they left church after a wedding. Ashiq and I found this very hard to believe. It doesn't sound like the Christians here to provoke Islam, particularly after they'd just celebrated a wedding in the house of God. But the angry Muslims didn't stop there: the next day they were saying all over the district that Christians had insulted the Koran. So, to avenge themselves, hundreds and hundreds of furious Muslims—no one had ever seen rage like it... attacked the big Christian colony in Gojra. They sowed terror everywhere, smashing everything in their path with iron bars, including Protestant churches. On the local news they said the police did nothing to stop the murderers, not even when they started setting fires. Everything that would burn went up in smoke, and not just houses either. Ten Christians were burned alive in the flames, in their own homes, including three women and three children. They died so horribly. When we heard the story of this murderous insanity, I shook all over and grabbed Ashiq's arm. 'Do you think that could happen to us?' 'No, don't worry. You know people round here wouldn't hurt us,' he had said confidently.[1245]

Asia Bibi's husband, Ashiq, was wrong. Violence toward those who "insult" Islam or its Prophet is one of Islam's strongest meme-hooks. And its most violent.

On June 13, 2009, when Bibi was buying spices, the shopkeeper made a suggestion,

> 'Why don't you go falsa [berry]-picking tomorrow in that field just outside the village? You know the one: it belongs to the Nadeems, the rich family who live in Lahore. The pay is two hundred and fifty rupees.'[1246]

Falsa berries are small purple and black berries loaded with antioxidants. They are eaten with salt and black pepper, and taste like sherbet. They are also reputed to relieve thirst and to cool you down.[1247] So Bibi showed up the next day at the falsa berry field.

The date was June 14, 2009.[1248] When Asia reached the field, she says there were already 15 women there "bent double, their backs half hidden by the tall bushes."[1249] Those women were her neighbors. Muslim neighbors. For example, there was Musarat, the elderly village gossip, a seamstress who seldom came to the fields to earn money at the harvest. But Asia guesses times were bad for Musarat's family and she needed the cash.

Within seconds, a hard-faced female overseer came over to Asia, handed her a bowl, and said that if she filled it with berries, she would be paid 250 rupees. But there was a catch. Asia's bowl was much bigger than the bowls of the Muslim women.[1250] Bibi explains, "I looked at the huge bowl and thought I would never finish before sunset. Looking at the other women's bowls, I also realized mine was much bigger. They were reminding me that I'm a Christian. That kind of thing happens all the time. Christians often get paid less than Muslims for the same work. Luckily Ashiq didn't suffer that kind of thing."[1251]

Asia, a sweet woman with a big smile who looks younger than her years, had a few other problems. She had a long history with the women in the field. Those women had "urged" her over and over again to convert to Islam. But judging from what Asia says, these conversion efforts were not compassionate attempts at persuasion. They were more like put-downs by bullies. One of her neighbors, for example, yelled at her, "You should convert to Islam to redeem yourself for your filthy religion."[1252] But we'll get to that in a minute.

There was another difficulty that would come to haunt Asia Bibi. Asia had disagreed with one of the village elders, Chaudhry Muhammad Tufail. Reports Declan Walsh of Britain's *The Guardian*, who was stationed in Pakistan for nine years and researched Asia Bibi's dilemma in depth, "There was an argument over water, and she said that his buffalo were eating the fodder for her goats."[1253] That quarrel would later prove to be one cause of Asia's downfall.

But, as you can see, Asia Bibi's real stumbling block was simple. She was not a Muslim. She was a Christian. She was an unbeliever. She was a dhimmi.[1254] In the eyes of her Muslim neighbors, she was a second-class citizen,[1255] one who was lucky that Islam was generous enough to tolerate her existence.

Christianity made Asia Bibi, to repeat, "unclean,"[1256] something like an untouchable in India. The Muslim women of the village with whom she picked the fields were on her case constantly. Repeats Shehrbano Taseer, daughter of a man who will become crucial to this story in a minute—the governor of the Punjab province of Pakistan, Salmaan Taseer—"She said those women used to badger her to convert to Islam." Explained Taseer, "One day she just got fed up with it." What happened?

Back to the berry field. Recalls Asia,

> I look at my fellow pickers, heads and hands buried in the bushes or in their bowls. They look so busy with their work. Despite the heat they're still going at it with the same energy they had at the start. I pull up a bucketful of water and dip in the old metal cup resting on the side of the well. The cool water is all I can think of. I gulp it down and I feel better; I pull myself together. Then I start to hear muttering. I pay no attention and fill the cup again, this time holding it out to a woman next to me who looks like she's in pain. She smiles and reaches out ... At exactly that moment Musarat pokes her ferrety nose out from the bush, her eyes full of hate: 'Don't drink that water, it's haram.' [forbidden, taboo, polluted][1257] I jump out of my skin and tip the water out before the woman has had time to take it. Musarat addresses all the pickers, who have suddenly stopped work at the sound of the word 'haram.' 'Listen, all of you, this Christian has dirtied the water in the well by drinking from our cup and dipping it back in several times. Now the water is unclean and we can't drink it! Because of her!'[1258]
>
> It's so unfair that for once I decide to defend myself and stand up to the old witch. 'I think Jesus would see it differently from Muhammad.' Musarat is furious. 'How dare you think tor the Prophet, you filthy animal!' Three other women start shouting even louder.

'That's right, you're just a filthy Christian! You've contaminated our water and now you dare to speak for our Prophet! Stupid bitch, your Jesus didn't even have a proper father, he was a bastard, don't you know that? Muhammad had a proper father who acknowledged him, his name was Abdullah. Ever heard of Abdullah? Jesus was unclean, just like you.' I stand my ground. 'That's not true. Go and ask the village mullah.' Musarat comes over as though she's going to hit me and yells: 'You should convert to Islam to redeem yourself for your filthy religion.' I feel a pain deep inside. We Christians have always stayed silent: we've been taught since we were babies never to say anything, to keep quiet because we're a minority. But I'm stubborn too and now I want to react, I want to defend my faith. I don't want to let these women attack my religion in such an insulting way. I take a deep breath to fill my lungs with courage. 'I'm not going to convert. I believe in my religion and in Jesus Christ, who died on the cross for the sins of mankind. What did your Prophet Muhammad ever do to save mankind? And why should it be me that converts instead of you?'

That's when the hatred bursts out from all sides. All around me the women start screaming. 'How dare you say such a thing about our Prophet!'[1259]

Recalls Asia's 20-year-old neighbor Maafia, who was one of the women screaming, "She got very annoyed. But it was normal. We could not drink from that glass." And here's the kicker, the most crucial line: "She is Christian, we are Muslim, and there is a vast difference between the two. We are a superior religion."[1260] Got that? "A superior religion." Islam is dominant over all other religions. A fact the Qur'an stresses over and over again.[1261] In the words of the Qur'an, Islam is "over all religions."[1262] After a Muslim conquest, if you are of another faith and wish to remain alive, you must pay the tax for protection, the act that to many signals a simple fact—that you are now a subhuman in a society where only Muslims are full-fledged human beings.[1263] You are like the citizens of Khaibar, the few people who Muhammad allowed to remain alive. The surviving people of Khaibar were permitted to live on the condition that they paid 50% of what they produced to the Muslims. A tax of 50%. What would Grover Norquist, the foaming-at-the-mouth American anti-tax activist, say about that? And the survivors of Khaibar were allowed to live on the condition that they exist in perpetual humiliation. As the

Qur'an says, "humiliating is the punishment of those who reject Faith."[1264] This sort of humiliation appears in jihadist literature as a nonstop theme.[1265] It's the sort of humiliation you can see in a pronouncement whose details we'll briefly revisit in a minute, the Ayatollah Khomeini's strenuous statement that unbelievers are as unclean as excrement and urine.[1266] To some Muslim extremists, only Muslims have dignity. All others are dogs[1267] allowed to survive only by Muslim generosity. Where did these outrageous ideas come from? From Muhammad, who said in chapter nine, verse 28 of the Qur'an, "Truly the pagans are unclean."[1268]

When the Muslim women lashed Asia Bibi with cutting insults to her Christianity, Asia made another mistake. A mistake you've already seen. She said, "I believe in my religion and in Jesus Christ, who died on the cross for the sins of mankind. What did your Prophet Muhammad ever do to save mankind?"

The response? As Asia recalls it, the Muslim women screamed,

> 'How dare you say such a thing about our Prophet! You're nothing! You're just a piece of filth, you don't deserve to live! You're nothing and your children are the same! You'll pay dearly for what you've just said about our holy Prophet!'
> All this spite and loathing upsets me, but I come back at them.
> 'I didn't say anything bad, I just asked you a question.'
> One of them grabs my bowl and tips the berries into her own. Another one shoves me and Musarat spits in my face with all the scorn she can manage. A foot lashes out and they push me. I fall down. They laugh. "Bitch! Filthy whore! You've had it now."[1269]

And those were not idle words. The Muslim women wanted to show their power. They wanted revenge. They wanted punishment. So they went to the village mullah, 31-year-old Maulvi Muhammad Saalim, a bearded man who darkened his eyes with kohl. And they complained that Asia Bibi had insulted Muhammad. Saalim was a cleric who, in his sermons, railed for half an hour "against the evils of drinking, gambling, kite-flying, pigeon-racing, cards and, oddly enough, insurance. 'All of these are the work of the devil,' he says."[1270] In other words, Saalim was a puritan, a fundamentalist, and a severe one. But Saalim did not get this way on his own. He was the product of eight years in one of the Madrasas, the 35,000[1271] Pakistani religious schools that some have called "terrorist factories."[1272] The Madrasas are schools supported by Saudi Arabia to spread its own brand of jihadism, its own brand of Islamic extremism—the Wahhabi sect.[1273] And, like the Saudis, Saalim was passing his form of Islam along. He now had a Madrasa of his own and was teaching 150 pupils Deobandi Islam, an Islam related to the Saudi Wahhabi tradition.

For a clue to that tradition, ponder this: it's the severe jihadist Islam that gave us 9/11's 19[1274] suicide bombers. Yes, a tradition very similar to that of Osama bin Laden's is taught as a normal matter of fact in 35,000 Pakistani schools. And experts who have studied the matter say Osama-like Islam is taught even more enthusiastically in Pakistan's state schools.[1275] No wonder Maulvi says about Deobandi Islam "It is the way of God."[1276]

And there's a catch. If Islam is right and following Muhammad's example step by step and day by day is the true way to righteousness, then Deobandi and Wahhabi Islam are more the way of god than the modernist, pluralist, tolerant Islam of roughly 40% of Pakistan's population. No matter how much you and I would want it to be otherwise.

The village elder, Chaudhry Muhammad Tufail, the man with whom Asia had quarreled over buffalo, grass, goats, and water, the man "who controls land deeds and access to water" in Ittan Wali, backed the female field laborers' blasphemy charges. So did the imam of the local mosque, Qari Muhammad Salim. Which means that Asia Bibi had three influential figures on her case.

Says Britain's *Telegraph*, "The incident was forgotten until a few days later when Mrs Bibi said she was set upon by a mob."[1277] As for what the mob did to Bibi, here's how she describes it:

> At that moment, I was hit in the face. My nose is hurting. I am bleeding. I am half stunned. They pull me as though I were a stubborn donkey. I can do nothing other than suffer and pray that it stops. I look at the crowd, which seems to triumph at my feeble resistance. I stagger. The blows fall on to my legs, on to my back, behind my head... 'Do you want to convert, to belong to a religion worthy of the name?' 'No, please, I am a Christian. I beg you...' And with the same fury, they continue to beat me. One arm is really hurting. I think it may be broken. 'Death to the Christian!' the angry mob scream.[1278]

Says the *Telegraph*, "The police were called and took her to a police station for her own safety." But there was a catch. "The police were under pressure from this Muslim mob, including clerics, asking for Asia to be killed because she had spoken ill of the Prophet Muhammad."[1279] So after the police saved her life, they registered a blasphemy case against her."[1280] Which means that on June 19, 2009, Asia Bibi found herself in prison.[1281] Charged with a crime that's punishable by death.

When Asia Bibi got her day in court, things did not get better. Pakistan uses a modified Shariah law.[1282] And in Shariah law, the testimony of an unbeliever has only half the validity of a Muslim's.[1283] And a woman's testimony is half that of a man's.[1284] So Bibi's side of the story was automatically discounted.[1285] Heavily. In the words of the authors of *Persecuted: The Global Assault on Christians*, "she didn't stand a chance."[1286]

On November 2010, over a year and a half after Asia was locked up in prison, she received her sentence, a sentence pronounced by a Muslim judge in a Muslim court using Muslim law, a sentence decided in the court of the Muslim city of Sheikhupura. The judge was Muhammed Naveed Iqbal. His sentence? Death by hanging.[1287]

Asia Bibi describes the day of her sentencing like this: "I cried alone, putting my head in my hands. I can no longer bear the sight of people full of hatred, applauding the killing of a poor farm worker. I no longer see them, but I still hear them, the crowd who gave the judge a standing ovation, saying: 'Kill her, kill her! Allahu Akbar!' The court house is invaded by a euphoric horde who break down the doors, chanting: 'Vengeance for the holy prophet. Allah is great!' I was then thrown like an old rubbish sack into the van... I had lost all humanity in their eyes."[1288]

Asia Bibi's local Mullah, one of the three men who had formally accused her of blasphemy, Maulvi Muhammad Saalim, says he "wept for joy" at the death sentence. And he was not alone in his delight. The holy man says, "We had been worried the court would award a lesser sentence. So the entire village celebrated."[1289] The village celebrated in the spirit of Muhammad, who praised Allah for generously allowing Muslims to kill non-Muslims and to divvy up their goods among the faithful. The village celebrated in the spirit of what one early follower called the marvelousness[1290] of killing on behalf of Allah and his Prophet.

On November 20, 2010, a man of power would come to Asia Bibi's defense. Just the sort of man who could make Muslim peace movements possible. And it would be his undoing. He was the governor of the Punjab Province, the most populous and powerful[1291] province in Pakistan, Salmaan Taseer. How did Salmaan Taseer become interested in the Asia Bibi case? Through his 20-year-old daughter, Shehrbano Taseer. Remember, Pakistan's citizens are divided between extremists and liberals. Many of the liberals are modernist pluralists, people who believe in democracy and human rights. Taseer and his family were deep believers in the liberal philosophy. Shehrbano Taseer had apparently read local coverage of what was happening to Asia Bibi in Pakistan's liberal newspapers and had been tweeting about it. She felt it was an outrage. Then the governor took his family for a vacation to a winter residence that the government maintained on a hill above Islamabad. There was spare time. Family time. Shehrbano showed her tweets[1292] about Asia Bibi to her dad. She recalls, "He took the phone, read the tweets, and sat and thought about it for several hours. Then he said we should do something."[1293]

Taseer took advantage of his power and prestige to do more than just something. He did several things. He decried Pakistan's blasphemy law and its death sentence as a "black law."[1294] He talked to the President of Pakistan, Asif Ali Zardari, about a presidential pardon for Asia Bibi, and got Zardari to declare that he was "completely behind"[1295] the idea. But, most important, the governor went with his daughter and his wife, Aamna,[1296] to meet with Asia Bibi in prison. Topping it all off, on November 20, 2010, Taseer threw a press conference in the prison, included his wife and daughter, and had photos of himself and his family shot with Asia Bibi. The press conference made headlines.[1297]

Governor Taseer validated a person who was being treated as subhuman. He validated a fellow human who was being treated as a holy target. And the clergy did not like it. In fact, the clerics were furious. Yes, the official interpreters of Muhammad's legacy were outraged. So a mob gathered in front of Taseer's central Lahore residence and burned the governor in effigy. In a country where religiously motivated assassinations and suicide bombings are common, being burned in effigy is a far more disturbing statement than it is in the West.

Despite all the street chaos, Pakistan's President Ali Zardari was poised to grant Asia Bibi a pardon when, on November 24, 2010, "a nationally known mufti," Muneer Ur Rehman, said,[1298] "If the president pardons Asia Bibi, we will raise our voices across the country until he is forced to take his decision back."

And the Lahore High Court issued a "stay order," an order prohibiting a presidential pardon.[1299]

That's when the real executioners of Pakistan—the religious leaders, the street mobs, and the pious assassins—got their motors running. Pakistan is the land of street demonstrators calling for death. Specifically, the death of dissenters. Pakistan is the nation whose angry street mobs demanded the death of Salman Rushdie for his book *The Satanic Verses* in 1989. It is the nation whose angry street mobs called for the deaths of Danish cartoonists for insulting the prophet in 2005. Roughly 40% of the citizens of Pakistan want a civil society with dialogue and freedom of speech. But the other 60% wants the intolerance that Muhammad established as a standard in Medina and Mecca. Intolerance enforced by murder. And should you run afoul of that other 60% of Pakistan's citizens, should you run afoul of the mobs inspired by Muhammad's intolerance, may Allah have mercy upon you.

On December 3, 2010, reported *The Guardian*, "a radical cleric in Peshawar's oldest mosque offered a $500,000 rupee [$5,000] reward to anyone who killed Bibi."[1300]

Three days later, on December 6, 2010, the imam of the village mosque in Ittan Wali, Asia Bibi's hometown, Qari Muhammad Salim, one of the village threesome who had called for the blasphemy charge and who had stated that he had cried for joy when he learned that Bibi had been sentenced to death, answered a key question. What would happen if Asia Bibi were pardoned? "If the law punishes someone for blasphemy, and that person is pardoned, then we will also take the law in our hands,"[1301] said Salim. That's the voice of Pakistan's street executioners. And that's the voice of Muhammad, the man who made killing dissenters the default mode.

No wonder Asia Bibi's husband, Ashiq, said that if she were released, "No one will let her live. The mullahs are saying they will kill her when she comes out." Added Bibi, "After the newspaper reports, 10 million Pakistanis are ready to kill me by their own hands."[1302] *The American Thinker's* Carol Brown[1303] claims that a survey backs Bibi's estimate of the numbers crying for her death. Brown may get that idea from a statement made by Senator Rand Paul in 2013. Paul said, "Pew Research did a poll which indicated that 21 percent of Egyptians, 15 percent of Jordanians, and 13 percent of Pakistani Muslims find terrorism acceptable if not laudable. A minority? To be sure. But if you add up the numbers in just three countries, over 40 million Muslims sympathize with violence against Christians."[1304] Do the arithmetic on the Pew Survey that Paul is referring to, and you discover that his figures are right.

Meanwhile, Asia Bibi's husband and her five children were fugitives in their own country. To get an idea of what that's like, *The Guardian's* Declan Walsh dug into the plight of another family on the run from blasphemy charges. He writes, "At a Lahore safe house, a family described how the blasphemy law had ruined their lives. Yusuf Masih and his wife Suria have been on bail since last July, when a local mullah had them charged with blasphemy. Their crime was to have put scrap plastic sheeting on the roof of their outdoor toilet, to keep out the rain. Unknown to them, the sheet contained a religious verse. 'We had no idea,' says Masih, a stubble-chinned cook who cannot read or write. ...But like almost all blasphemy victims, there is no question of returning home." The pair are staying in houses of relatives and a Christian charity's safe house. Says Walsh, when they snuck back to their home "two weeks ago to collect a few belongings, they found the place ransacked. 'They took everything,' says Masih."[1305] But remember, taking everything from unbelievers over whom you've shown your authority, taking the booty, is not just legitimate in Muhammad's Islam. It is the "generosity" of God himself. The generosity of Allah to his faithful.

Western papers, trying to make excuses for the inexcusable, pointed out that despite the death penalty that Pakistani law imposes on those who commit blasphemy, no Pakistani blasphemy prisoner has ever been executed for the crime. But the real danger does not come from the courts, hideous as their decisions may be. It comes from the streets. It comes from private citizens. *The Guardian* reported early in 2016 that when it comes to blasphemy, "Up to 40 people have been killed by vigilantes, including policemen, according to human-rights workers."[1306] And alleged blasphemers have not just been killed by the pious in their homes or in the streets. They've been killed in prison by fellow inmates or by the prison guards.

On December 7, 2010, two very high-level Pakistani government officials went to bat for Asia Bibi. They pushed for a presidential pardon. One was Pakistan's Minority Affairs Minister Shahbaz Bhatti, the only Christian in the government.[1307] And the second was Salmaan Taseer, the governor of the Punjab province, the man we met a few pages ago. Says Bhatti, "I will go to every knock for justice on her behalf and I will take all steps for her protection."[1308] Taking every knock would turn out to have a higher price than Bhatti imagined.

A week later, the extremists mounted their answer to these two Muslim liberals. On December 14, 2010, in Rawalpindi, Mohammad Saleem of the Jamiat Ulema-e-Pakistan Party led a demonstration. The crowds chanted a simple message: "Hang her, hang her."[1309]

On December 30, 2010, two weeks after the "hang her" protest, Bhatti and Taseer pushed for a modification of the blasphemy laws. At first it looked like they had a chance. Then came more uproar on the streets.[1310] The

Pakistani government knuckled under to street pressure—to extremists—and announced that it would not tamper with the blasphemy laws.[1311] But that was not the end of the matter. Far from it.

The extremists had supporters high in the government. On roughly January 1, 2011, Rehman Malik, Pakistan's interior minister, announced that "he would personally shoot anyone found guilty of blasphemy."[1312] There were very few complaints against his stance. In fact, "personally shooting" those suspected of insufficient belief in the Prophet was about to go from rhetoric to reality.

On Tuesday, January 3, 2011, the real killings began. In Pakistan's capital, Islamabad, a city with a metropolitan population of two million, Salmaan Taseer, the governor of Punjab, the man who had gone way out on a limb for Asia Bibi, the man who had visited her in jail, and the man who had thrown a press conference with her, the man who had come to represent Pakistan's liberal, modernist, tolerant, pluralist community, was about to pay the price. Taseer was finishing a late lunch with a friend, Pakistan's powerful Minister of State for Labour and Manpower, Sheikh Waqas Akram.[1313] Taseer's meal was prawn masala and French onion soup.[1314] The location was a suave restaurant, one of Taseer's favorites, Table Talk, an eatery frequented by foreigners and prominent politicians. Table Talk was located in an elite, upscale shopping district, the Kohsar Market. A market not far from the house where Taseer was staying with a relative.[1315] When Taseer and Waqas were ready to leave, it was 4:15 p.m.[1316] Taseer was about to get into his chauffeured car,[1317] a small, sleek silver Honda.[1318] Taseer knew he was at risk from the extremists. But he had Pakistan's best security. The Punjab government had provided him with a team of a dozen bodyguards, including nine bodyguards[1319] from its Elite Force.[1320] That team included a 26-year-old who had begun as an ordinary policeman, had moved up through the ranks, and had trained hard to become a commando. His name was Malik Mumtaz Hussain Qadri, and he had escorted Taseer from the city of Rawalpindi to Islamabad that morning, a 33-minute ride. Qadri was armed for business. He was carrying a state-issued[1321] MP5 submachine gun,[1322] a gun that can spit out 30 bullets at a rate of 15 bullets per second. But instead of watching out for threats, Qadri turned toward the governor, shouted "Allah-o-Akbar,"[1323] and emptied his weapon. He pumped two magazines[1324] of ammunition into the man he'd been hired to protect. Which means he actually stopped to reload.[1325] And none of the other 11 bodyguards did a thing. When he was finished, Qadri threw his submachine gun to the ground and surrendered.

Here's how Qadri describes what he did. Bear with his broken English. It's worth it:

> The Governor with another after having lunch in a restaurant walked to his vehicle. In adjoining mosque I went for urinating in the washroom and for making ablution. When I came out with my gun, I came across Salman Taseer. Then I had the occasion to address him, "your honour being the Governor had remarked about blasphemy law as black law, if so it was unbecoming of you." Upon this he suddenly shouted and said, "Not only that it is black law, but also it is my shit." Being a Muslim I lost control and under grave and suddenly provocation, I pressed the trigger and he lay dead in front of me. I have no repentance and I did it for "Tahafuz-iNamoos-i-Rasool" [to preserve the honor of the prophet]. Salman offered me grave and sudden provocation. I was justified to kill him.[1326]

Later, in court, two eyewitnesses would deny that this exchange of words with Taseer, the exchange calling Pakistan's blasphemy law "shit," ever took place.[1327] And the court would conclude that it was a mere "story" and an "afterthought,"[1328] a fantasy conjured to boost Qadri's justification for the killing. But the killing itself was no fantasy.

Taseer was hit by 28 bullets[1329] "in the presence of a dozen police officials and several bystanders."[1330] And, to repeat, none of Taseer's other bodyguards did a thing to stop the killing.[1331] Says the BBC, "There has been speculation that other guards in the governor's security detail agreed with Qadri they would turn a blind eye to the attack."[1332] That is very conceivable. Meanwhile, Taseer was rushed to the Polyclinic Hospital.[1333] The 28 bullets from the bodyguard's gun had produced a total of 32 wounds.[1334] By the time the governor arrived at the hospital, he was dead.

When Mumtaz Qadri was arrested and sitting in the police station with his hands cuffed behind him, he sang poetry in praise of, guess who? Muhammad.[1335]

Why did Qadri murder the man he was assigned to protect? The answer was in the poetry he was singing in the police station. Says the BBC News, "Qadri claimed it was his religious duty to kill the governor over his support for liberal reforms to blasphemy law."[1336] In court, Qadri, with help from his attorneys, put it like this:

Salmaan Taseer...publically exposed himself as a sympathiser of condemned prisoner namely Mst. Aasia [Bibi], who was sentenced to death by a Court of law for use of derogatory remarks about the Holy Prophet Mohammad (Peace Be Upon Him).[1337]

But sympathy with an alleged blasphemer was not the end of Taseer's crimes in his killer's eyes. Taseer also

called Blasphemy Law as [a] "Black Law." To criticize such law and to challenge it as [if] it was [a] man-made law [is] tantamount to directly defiling the sacred name of the Holy Prophet Mohammad.[1338]

If you criticize a law that comes from the Qur'an and from the life of the Prophet Muhammad, you are criticizing God's own messenger to mankind. You are insulting God's communiqués. You are committing blasphemy. That was Qadri's argument. Added Qadri:

"I have not committed murder of an apostate like Suleman Taseer... contrary to dictums of the Holy Quran and Sunnah."[1339]

In other words, the killing was not murder. Why? Because it was demanded by Islam's holy books, the Qur'an and the Sunnah. And because Governor Salmaan Taseer was an apostate. He was a man who had once been a Muslim but had abandoned his religion. And killing apostates is required by the Qur'an. It is demanded by the examples of Muhammad's life. It is required by the examples laid out in the earliest records of the life the Prophet—the Sunnah. Let me repeat that. The Prophet's examples are holy. The stories you are reading about in this book are commandments. Absolute commandments. And those commandments include what the website of Atlanta's Masjid Abu Bakr Islamic Center calls Muhammad's "silent permissions."[1340] Like Muhammad's silence when he wanted to indicate that killing an apostate and a dissenter—his former scribe—was the default mode and needed no word from him.

One important thing to keep in mind. Thanks to Muhammad's example, 64 percent of Pakistanis support the death penalty for people who leave Islam. Sixty-four percent support the death penalty for apostates.[1341]

Qadri said he was merely being faithful to Muhammad's example. That is the essence of Muslim piety. And that's the power of one of the most significant founder effects in human history. A founder effect reaching out across a gulf of 1,379 years.

But there's more. Qadri said it was Governor Taseer who was breaking the law, not him. Explained Qadri's court statement, "Salman Taseer himself was responsible for commission of an offence...punishable to death." He was guilty for supporting Asia Bibi. But Qadri's statement gave lengthy evidence that Taseer was also killable for another offense: he had been born a Muslim, then had become an apostate, "an infidel."[1342] He drank scotch, married a Sikh woman, and ate pork.[1343] All offenses punishable by assassination. As if that weren't enough, said Qadri's statement, Taseer was "a bully of Americans," a puppet of the Americans, "So nature had to take its own course and justice was done. It is a lesson for all the apostates, as finally they have to meet the same fate."[1344] Stray from Islam and you can be killed by any pious Muslim at random. A very powerful meme-hook indeed. A very powerful conformity enforcer.

Later, Qadri's lawyers would argue in the Supreme Court that:

> being a devout Muslim the appellant was under a religious and moral, and hence legal, obligation to kill an apostate who had committed the offence of blasphemy.[1345]

In other words, "punishing a blasphemer was a religious duty enjoined on everyone."[1346] Argued the defense attorneys, "the guard had acted on his own interpretation of the blasphemy law and teachings of the Holy Quran after being influenced by speeches of a religious scholar."[1347] Or, as one court document put it, "the appellant had acted under the influence of some religious speakers on the basis of whose inciting, provocative and instigating speeches made in a religious meeting the appellant had made up his mind to kill Mr. Salman Taseer."[1348]

Significantly, no Pakistani paper dared name the religious scholar who had motivated Qadri. Not even the liberal papers. Not a single one.

In death, Taseer became even more a symbol of Pakistan's pluralist, modernist, tolerant community.[1349] And on January 5, 2011 thousands turned up for the governor's funeral in Lahore in spite of warnings by the Taliban and some clerics.[1350] Thousands showed their courage. And their commitment to pluralism, tolerance, and a civil society.

But that was nothing to the support that was about to emerge for Salmaan Taseer's killer. On January 5, 2011, two days after the assassination and the same day as Taseer's funeral, Taseer's murderer, Mumtaz Qadri, appeared in court in Lahore for the first time. Reported the Pakistani newspaper *Dawn*, by the time of his court appearance, Qadri had been elevated to the status of a hero. Explains both the *Pakistan Christian Post* and Canada's CBC, the "majority of Ulema (Islamic scholars) and Islamic groups praised the assassination.... A rowdy crowd slapped the accused on the back and kissed his cheek as he was escorted inside."[1351] But that's not all. "Lawyers showered the suspected killer...with rose petals when he arrived at court Wednesday and an influential Muslim scholars group praised the assassination."[1352] Yes, lawyers, educated men who should be committed to the rule of law, threw rose petals. To celebrate a killer.

When it comes to lawyers, says the *Guardian*, "Qadri also attracted some of the country's most senior lawyers to his defence team, including two former judges" and the former chief justice of the Lahore High Court.[1353] Representing Qadri in court was not only prestigious, it was a holy deed. What's more, reports the *Guardian*, "Public support for Qadri was so great that the army chief at the time of the murder, Gen Ashfaq Kayani, reportedly told western ambassadors he could not publicly condemn Qadri because too many of his soldiers sympathised with the killer."[1354]

When Qadri's first court appearance was over, on January 5, 2011, a photo in Pakistan's newspaper *Dawn* showed Qadri in the back of a police van being taken back to jail. His hands were cuffed behind him. But he was shouting Muslim slogans. Shouting Allah ahu Akhbar, shouting his dedication to a killer god and a killer prophet.[1355]

Muhammad would have been proud. Death is the default for one who criticizes Islam—that was the Prophet's message. And those who carry out assassinations are working, Muhammad said, on behalf of God. No wonder that "rowdy crowd" we saw a few paragraphs ago "slapped" Mumtaz Qadri "on the back and kissed his cheek as he was escorted inside."[1356] No wonder, "As he left the court, a crowd of about 200 sympathizers chanted 'death is acceptable for Muhammad's slave.'" And no wonder the suspect stood at the back door of an armored police van with a flower necklace given to him by an admirer around his neck and repeatedly yelled, "God is great."[1357]

Meanwhile, says Pakistan's *Dawn*, "more than 500 clerics and scholars from the group Jamaat Ahle Sunnat said no one should pray or express regret for the killing of the governor."[1358] This was a surprise. The Jamaat Ahle Sunnat and its form of Islam, Barelvi Islam, were considered moderate. Muslim but moderate. And Barelvi Islam was the majority Islam of Pakistan. Nonetheless, the five hundred clerics "issued a veiled threat to other opponents of the blasphemy laws. 'The supporter is as equally guilty as one who committed blasphemy,' the group warned in a statement, adding that politicians, the media and others should learn 'a lesson from the exemplary death.'"[1359] The death of Salmaan Taseer, said this mainstream, moderate, religious group, was "exemplary." In other words, others should follow the example of Mumtaz Qadri. The example of a killer. Which left a question: just how moderate is Pakistan's moderate Islam?

Acknowledged the *Guardian*, "In death Taseer has been deified as the fountainhead of liberal Pakistan."[1360] But which is stronger in Pakistan, liberalism or Muhammad's brand of intolerant and murderous Islam? That's a question that hung in the balance in 2011. It's a question that still hangs in the balance today. And that balance is crucial to the world.

*   *   *

Why is the attitude of street mobs, amateur killers, and religious leaders in Pakistan of global significance? Pakistan has between 120 and 130 nuclear warheads.[1361] And it has the cruise missiles and ballistic rockets to deliver those nukes to places as far away as India, China, and Israel.[1362] What's more, it has something we'll get back to a bit later, super stealth submarines with a range of 11,000 miles, submarines capable of reaching the coasts of the USA. Submarines able to carry cruise missiles with nuclear warheads. If the jihadists, the extremists, ever get their hands on those weapons, we will all be in trouble. Are there any indications that the extremists could take control of Pakistan and its weaponry? Take a look at a few more of the events that followed the death of Salmaan Taseer and judge for yourself.

On January 9, 2011, "50,000 protesters marched in the southern city of Karachi against the proposed reforms"[1363] to Pakistan's blasphemy laws. A few thousand very brave liberals had shown up for the funeral of Salmaan Taseer, the symbol of moderation. But roughly ten times as many showed up to celebrate holy murder.[1364] And once again, some of the moderates made you wonder how moderate they were. The rally supporting severe blasphemy laws, blasphemy laws with a death sentence, "was attended by all major Muslim groups and sects in the city, including moderates and conservatives." Most important, "Many of the demonstrators held banners in support of Qadri."[1365] Yes, many held banners supporting Governor Salmaan Taseer's killer.

What's more, "Posters for the rally singled out Sherry Rehman, a brave ruling party MP who shared Taseer's outspoken views, for criticism."[1366] As of

March 21, 2016, Rehman was still alive. But one preacher in the city had already dubbed her Wajib ul Qatal, "deserving of death."[1367] And in Pakistan, phrases like that from holy men are all too often followed by murder.

Then there was the plight of Asia Bibi. She was kept in solitary confinement, allegedly for her own protection. To keep her from being visited by any more supporters like Salmaan Taseer, a Pakistani court ruled that the only people who could visit her were her husband and her attorney. Meanwhile, she was under threat from other inmates and was beaten or bullied by prison guards. Her life was constantly at risk. As the Legal Aid Society of Karachi pointed out, "five persons accused of blasphemy had died in police custody in recent years."[1368]

But things were just as dangerous outside of prison, at least for those who dared cross the blasphemy-killing enthusiasts. Things were treacherous tor dissenters. In June, 2010, Minority Affairs Minister Shahbaz Bhatti said that he got his first death threats. "He was told that he would be beheaded if he attempted to change the blasphemy laws. In response, he told reporters that he was 'committed to the principle of justice for the people of Pakistan' and willing to die fighting for" Asia Bibi's release. To repeat, Bhatti was the only Christian member of Pakistan's cabinet. But that wasn't all. He had the audacity to be photographed with Asia Bibi's husband. He would pay dearly for these acts of courage. But not quite yet.

On January 2011, the *Guardian*'s Declan Walsh visited Asia Bibi's neighbor, 20-year-old Maafia Bibi. Maafia was a Muslim. What's more, she was one of the women who had argued with Bibi, then had complained to the town's imam and urged a sentence of blasphemy, a death sentence. Talking about Asia Bibi, Maafia became impatient. She asked Walsh, "Why hasn't she been killed yet? You journalists keep coming here asking questions but the issue is resolved. Why has she not been hanged?"[1369]

This is where Shahbaz Bhatti, the government minister who had said he was "willing to die fighting for" Asia Bibi's release from prison, comes in. Nine months after he received his first death threats, on March 2, 2011, Bhatti got his wish. He was shot dead by gunmen who ambushed his car near his residence in Islamabad.

And another four months down the line, on August 26, 2011, in Lahore, Governor Salmaan Taseer's 28-year-old son Shahbaz was driving his racy silver Mercedes Kompressor[1370] to work at First Capital Group, one of the companies founded by his father.[1371] Shahbaz was stopped by a Prado jeep and a motorcycle, was kidnapped, bundled into the jeep and taken to captivity in Afghanistan.[1372] The abduction was the work of Pakistan's Taliban.[1373] One of the conditions for Shahbaz's release was the release of his dad's killer, the new folk hero, Mumtaz Qadri.[1374] A slew of Pakistani newspapers reported that Taseer was released after a year and a half in captivity on February 16, 2013. Those reports, said Taseer's family, were false. Shahbaz was not released until March 8, 2016, after five years in captivity.[1375]

Despite tumultuous activity on behalf of the guard who had killed Punjab's governor, on October 1, 2011, the Pakistani courts gave Mumtaz Qadri—the guard who killed the governor—the sentence of death.[1376] It took courage to issue such a verdict. It took guts to go against the opinion of the religious street mobs. Remember, those feverish crowds included both extremist and moderate Muslims. But the courage of the court would not be rewarded. Far from it. The judge who delivered the sentence had to flee Pakistan.[1377]

Meanwhile, what was happening with Asia Bibi, the accidental catalyst for these religious killings? A few months later, author Raymond Ibrahim reported that "she still languishes in jail, sick and isolated, and regularly beaten by both prison guards and Muslim inmates." Ibrahim explained, "In late 2011 it was reported that the female prison officer assigned to provide security for Asia beat her, 'because of the Muslim officer's anti-Christian bias while other staff members deployed for her security looked on in silence.'"[1378]

In the West, petitions were circulated on Asia Bibi's behalf. One attracted close to 700,000[1379] signatures from one hundred countries. But those were petitions from kafirs, from despised unbelievers. They were petitions from Christian activists. And another kafir, Pope Benedict XVI, publicly called for the charges against Asia Bibi to be dismissed. But remember, unbelievers are as impure as excrement and urine. And that includes the Pope.

Adds Wikipedia, "Ooberfuse, a Christian pop band based in the United Kingdom collaborated with the British Pakistani Christian Association, and released a song titled 'Free Asia Bibi' with a music video that included 'a disturbing visual portrayal of the squalid prison conditions where Bibi is being held.'"[1380]

Most important, French journalist Anne Isabelle Tollet set up a complex communication system with Asia. The writer passed notes to Asia Bibi's husband. The husband passed the notes to Asia, who answered the questions they contained and sent her replies back to Tollet via her husband. The result was an autobiography called *Blasphemy: A Memoir: Sentenced to Death over a Cup of Water*. And a Polish team made an 84-minute documentary, *Freedom For Asia Bibi*,[1381] based on the book.

Did any of this outcry help? Apparently not. Muhammad's imprint, his founder effect, held too strong a grip over Pakistan's street mobs and Pakistan's religious leaders. Including Pakistan's so-called moderate religious leaders. Muhammad's example worked as effectively and as pitilessly as the Prophet would have wished.

But the death of one governor and of one government minister was not the end of things. In April of 2014, an attorney named Rashid Rehman was handling "a blasphemy case of a professor in Multan."[1382] Yes, another blasphemy case. And Rehman was willing to get involved despite the danger associated with blasphemy cases. But, says a fellow lawyer, Rehman "was threatened by some goons belonging with a religious party in the court room and in the presence of a judge, but no action was taken."[1383] Threatened in the presence of a judge. In a court room. And the judge didn't dare reprimand those making the threats. Very common in Pakistan. Disturbingly common.

Who was Rashid Rehman? He was a human rights lawyer with superb credentials and a track record of activism. In fact, he was a coordinator for the Human Rights Commission of Pakistan.[1384] But let's be clear about how militant Islam regards human rights. Human rights are made by man. And that's a problem. Why? Only God has a right to issue laws. Only Allah can issue pronouncements about the entitlements and obligations of his "slaves," people like you and me. To issue man-made laws is an affront to Allah. It is at the least Jahiliyya, the state of evil, ignorance, and idol worship that existed before Muhammad showed up to replace the darkness with light in the seventh century. And at worst, human rights, in the words of ISIS and Boko Haram, are a false religion.[1385] Human rights are idolatry. Human rights are a form of blasphemy. And by now, you know the punishment for blasphemy. In May 2014, Rashid got his comeuppance for "defending a university lecturer accused of blasphemy." "Armed gunmen stormed the chamber of Rashid Rehman and started indiscriminate firing on Wednesday evening, injuring Rehman and two of his associates present there," senior police official Zulfiqar Ali told AFP.[1386] Actually, Rehman was more than injured. He was dead.

Then in May 2014, Asia Bibi's "appeal hearing was delayed for the fifth time."[1387] By now she'd been in jail for five years.

How was the man who had killed Asia Bibi's biggest defender, the man who had gunned down Punjab governor Salmaan Taseer, doing? Was he being beaten by prison guards? Was he living in fear that another prisoner or a prison guard would end his life? Far from it. Very far. The Pakistani newspaper *Dawn* said he had become "the prison king."[1388] On November 1, 2014, *Dawn* offered this report:

> from inside Adiala prison, Mumtaz Qadri continues to dole out death sentences, of which he is still sole judge and jury. So complete appears his control, so unquestioned his elevation to punisher rather than punished that it seems he can use the prison guards to carry out the punishments he decides must be doled out. As an internal investigation revealed this week, Mohammad Yousuf, a guard who had been deployed to watch over Qadri, became the latest tool with which this prison king wielded his wrath. In this case, it took just two weeks to wash over any qualms Yousuf may have had. At the end of two weeks, Yousuf, a guard, and a member of the Elite Force walked into the barracks where blasphemy convict Mohammad Asghar and blasphemy accused Pastor Zafar Bhatti were being housed. They were his appointed targets. Once inside, Yousuf shot Asghar, a 70-year-old man with paranoid schizophrenia. Frail and in ill health, Asghar was the perfect victim, easily vanquished. It was Asghar's insanity that had landed him in prison; his senseless ramblings collected and provided as proof of blasphemy. In a country without empathy, there is no room for insanity."[1389]

Asghar, the alleged blasphemer, lived. But the incident was an example of Qadri's power. It was an example of the stature he'd acquired by killing. Killing in the name of Muhammad. It was an example of what one of Muhammad's early followers called the "marvelousness"[1390] of Islam, the marvelousness that comes from an obedient Muslim's willingness to kill, his willingness to murder in order to keep fellow believers in line.

Britain's *The Guardian* was amazed by Qadri's treatment. It added that "Qadri enjoys special prison perks and has recorded best-selling albums of devotional songs."[1391] From jail. But that was just the tip of the iceberg. Qadri was a street hero. A legend in his own time. Two religious groups offered $100,000 for the weapon Qadri had used to murder Taseer.[1392] In the spirit of the collection of 11 swords of Muhammad and the single sword of his son-in-law Ali on display in Turkey's Topkapi Museum and in Cairo's Hussain mosque.[1393] What's more, a mosque had been named after Qadri[1394] and hundreds more lawyers and judges had come to his defense.[1395] *The Diplomat* says Qadri had become a national symbol, a folk hero, the "emblem of resistance with respect to any reform to Pakistan's blasphemy law."[1396] And that blasphemy law, says *The Diplomat*, "has become a veritable guillotine for religious minorities."[1397] More accurately, a hangman's noose. A fact that religious mobs loved.

Complained Salmaan Taseer's daughter about her father's killer, "He is treated like a king in prison. Women bring him their children for him to teach."[1398] But that was just one point of view. Zahid ur Rashidi, a religious scholar and supporter of Qadri, said the government should immediately release 'our national hero' and introduce strict religious law. Shariah. Why? "Because the legal system is un-Islamic, young people become desperate and take the law into their own hands,"[1399] the holy scholar explained. In other words, this religious authority wanted more of what we'd call Islamic extremism, not less. No wonder one modernist, pluralist Pakistani lawyer said, "We are all afraid."[1400]

While Mumtaz Qadri, the killer, was being celebrated, the opposite was happening to Asia Bibi. On October 16, 2014, her latest appeal was dismissed by Lahore's High Court. What's worse, the court "upheld her death sentence."

And, as if to remind all Pakistanis that those who don't toe Muhammad's line were treading dangerous ground, Pakistan's *Dawn* newspaper reported, "In November 2014, a Christian couple who worked at a brick kiln in Kot Radha Kishan (Kasur), were killed brutally by being burnt to death in the kiln fire, ostensibly over blasphemy."[1401] What a surprise!

Ten months later, on July 22, 2015, the Supreme Court of Pakistan suspended Asia Bibi's death sentence.[1402] Not permanently. Just for the duration of the appeals process. Just long enough for the court to finish weighing her fate. But Asia Bibi was on death row. And she was still there was as of March, 2016.[1403]

As I'm writing this manuscript, Asia Bibi has experienced seven years of solitary confinement on death row interrupted by beatings. *The Guardian* reports: "These cases often go on for a decade."[1404] And angry crowds numbering in the thousands are camped out in Islamabad demanding that she be executed now, immediately.[1405]

But, remember, the hangman's noose of the state is not Asia Bibi's gravest threat. The local mullah who slapped the original blasphemy sentence on Asia Bibi says that if the court system ever lets her out of jail, a private citizen will take over the religious responsibility of killing her. He tells the *Guardian*,

"A passionate Muslim would reach her and kill her." "Would he do the job himself?" asks the *Guardian*'s Declan Walsh. "There are good Muslims everywhere," he responds with a shrug. "Anything can happen." The implication? Good Muslims are killers. They have to be. At least those Muslims who follow Muhammad's commandments. Remember what Muhammad said when he declared that the world will no more care about the mother of five whom one of his followers executed, a dissenting poetess, than it will care about two goats butting heads together in the scrubland? Death for dissenters is the default mode.

*　*　*

On September 3, 2015, three judges of Pakistan's Supreme Court took their lives in their hands and stood up for moderation, tolerance, and pluralism. They heard Mumtaz Qadri's appeal of his death sentence. Qadri's appeal would not solely focus on Qadri's act of murder. The three Supreme Court judges would also try to determine whether Governor Salmaan Taseer was what Qadri claimed, a blasphemer.[1406] In addition, the judges in Qadri's case would try to rule on whether private citizens had the right to act as judge and executioner toward those who had been accused of blasphemy. In other words, the appeal of Qadri would put two other suspects on trial: the rule of Constitutional law, and the man who had been killed, Governor Salmaan Taseer.[1407]

Qadri's defense lawyers repeated an argument they'd used many times: that Punjab's governor, Salmaan Taseer, had been an apostate and had committed blasphemy. They argued that it is the right and obligation of every believing Muslim to kill apostates and blasphemers. And they demonstrated unequivocally that Mumtaz Qadri had God and His one true Prophet on his side. The mountain of sacred literature they brought to bear was overwhelming. Sacred literature proving that killing an apostate or a blasphemer is what Muhammad himself demanded. The killer's defenders cited 18 verses in the Qur'an and 30 passages from the Hadith,[1408]

Then there was a reference "to two decisions rendered by Caliphs Umar and Ali (May Allah Almighty be pleased with them)" and "opinions recorded by some renowned scholars of Islam in respect of liability of a person who has committed blasphemy." All that plus "opinions of some religious scholars justifying extrajudicial killing of an apostate and also of his supporters." Yes, religious sources calling for the killing of even an apostate's "supporters."

Supporters who provided the kind of aid and comfort that Governor Taseer had provided to Asia Bibi.

The judges stood up against all of this and upheld Qadri's death sentence. Even though doing such a thing had been fatal to many jurists and attorneys before them. What motivated them? They cited Qur'anic verses demanding that a Muslim check and double-check the facts before acting on a serious accusation against another Muslim. They added that "in a democratic society citizens have a right to contend, debate or maintain that a law has not been correctly framed by the State." The way Salmaan Taseer had demanded changes to Pakistan's blasphemy laws. The judges affirmed that citizens have a right to demand that any "law promulgated by the State ought to contain adequate safeguards against its misapplication or misuse by motivated persons." And the judges pointed out that because of the sloppiness and severity of Pakistan's blasphemy laws, they were most frequently used in personal quarrels to "settle scores."[1409] These would be ordinary statements in any other society. But they are extraordinary acts of courage in today's Pakistan.

And the three judges added one more thing: they said that if we accept the argument that a person driven by religious motivations has a right to take the law into his own hands, "then a door shall become open for religious vigilantism which may deal a mortal blow to the rule of law in this country where divergent religious interpretations abound and tolerance stands depleted to an alarming level."[1410] Allowing a lone wolf like Mumtaz Qadri to be judge, jury and executioner could kill the rule of law in Pakistan.

Despite all the pressure, all the threats, and all the bloodshed, three judges were willing to stand up for another side of Muhammad. Said the judges, "If our religion of Islam comes down heavily upon commission of blasphemy then Islam is also very tough against those who level false allegations of a crime." In fact, the judges referred on page two of their verdict to these words of the Prophet: "If a profligate [person] should bring you some news, verify it, lest you should visit [harm] on some people out of ignorance, and then become regretful for what you have done."[1411]

Three judges were willing to stand up for a side of Muhammad we haven't examined in this book, the side of Muhammad that stood for a level of civility. At least within a society that has completely surrendered to Islam. But that side of Muhammad's legacy is seen too little in Pakistan. It is seen too little in one of Islam's biggest, most militarily powerful, and most influential nations. It is seen too seldom in Islam's first-ever nuclear weaponized nation.

Has Pakistan become more liberal, tolerant, and modern since Asia Bibi was sent to jail? Or since Salmaan Taseer was assassinated? Said the Pakistani paper *Dawn* in November 1, 2014, "According to the Center for Research and Strategic Studies in Islamabad, blasphemy cases are on the rise with vigilante mobs and armed assailants all meting out death sentences on the streets of Pakistan."[1412] Blasphemy cases are increasing. *Dawn* said of blasphemy, it was "an allegation whose very mention is in Pakistan, a death sentence."[1413] And, added *Dawn*, "Mumtaz Qadri, the prison king, the arbiter of death sentences rules inside prison, but beyond the walls of Adiala is another prison, equally repressive, equally unable to deliver freedom or justice, ruled also by prison kings."[1414]

Said the BBC in 2015, "Since 1990, at least 65 people have been killed in cases linked to blasphemy, according to data collected by Reuters news agency."[1415] In another article, the BBC called the street killers who enforce orders they believe come directly from Muhammad "lynch mobs."[1416]

But that just scratches the surface. Pakistan's Supreme Court quotes the following figures, from a Karachi Legal Aid Society Judicial Training Toolkit:

> The known blasphemy cases in Pakistan show that from 1953 to July 2012, there were 434 offenders of blasphemy laws in Pakistan.... Since 1990, 52 people have been extra-judicially murdered, for being implicated in blasphemy charges. ...During 2013, 34 new cases were registered under the blasphemy laws. While at least one death sentence for blasphemy was overturned during the year, at least another 17 people were awaiting execution for blasphemy and at least 20 others were serving life sentences.

According to the Pakistani *Daily Times*, ChristiansinPakistan.com and the *Vatican News*, in 2014, the number of blasphemy cases went up to 1,400.[1417] In other words, the number of blasphemy cases set new records. The figure came from a Pakistan Institute of Labour Education and Research (PILER) seminar in Pakistan's biggest city, Karachi, on "Human Rights, Religious Freedom, Social Inclusion & Political Participation of Minority."[1418] In a sense, it was a miracle that this seminar was able to take place. It was a testament to the courage of Pakistan's moderate, pluralist, tolerant Muslims. Why? Because the worst punishment does not come from the courts. Says ChristiansinPakistan.com, "blasphemy accusations are followed by mobs attacking the family and houses of the accused." Needless to say, "Nisar Shar, who is a spokesman for the lawyers association in Karachi, said, 'Even for lawyers it has become dangerous to do their job and defend a defendant accused of blasphemy.'"[1419]

No kidding.

Remember, the Supreme Court that heard Mumtaz Qadri's appeal from a death sentence added something crucial: "The majority of blasphemy cases are based on false accusations." They are brought, says the Court, to "settle scores."[1420] Reformers wanted to change the law so it couldn't be used to settle grudges. But those reformers were stopped in their tracks. Often stopped dead.

Kumar Malani, a member of Pakistan's parliament, speaks for hundreds of thousands of Pakistanis when he says, "the time is right to profess for the human rights. We should not be segregating ourselves into the Muslims and non-Muslims."[1421] However, Malani may be taking his life in his hands when he makes that statement.

*   *   *

Anti-blasphemy laws are not unique to Pakistan. They exist in 14 other Islamic nations.[1422] And as we'll see in a few snips, they may soon spread to your land or mine. But first, back to the founder effect.

A Pakistani female lawyer and former judge, Majid Razvi, says the problem starts in grammar school: "If we analyze our school syllabus we would find that gradually hatred is incorporated."[1423] Who is the ultimate cheerleader stoking this hatred and violence? Not some wild-eyed imam. The prophet Muhammad.

And what does this intolerance toward non-Muslims or those who stray from the one true faith produce? A meme-hook with a power to punish, a meme-hook that metes out death.

*   *   *

One indication that Pakistan has a hope of justice, a hope of the escape from "we-value-death-more-than-you-value-life" extremism: on February 29, 2016, Mumtaz Qadri, the murderer of Punjab's liberal governor, was hung by the neck until he was dead in the prison he had ruled like a king—Rawalpindi's Adiala Jail. The verdict of three judges who saw the brighter side of Muhammad was vindicated. Alas, in a grisly way.

But Pakistan's extremism also showed its head. Reported Pakistan's *Dawn*, "protests...erupted in Hyderabad, Rawalpindi, Karachi and Lahore after the announcement [of the hanging] by leaders of the movement to free

Mumtaz Qadri." What's more, "security" was "beefed up in the whole country as protests are growing violent."[1424] Protestors—as many as 8,000 of them in Karachi alone—pelted cars with stones and "broke window panes."[1425] In Rawalpindi, the city where Qadri was hanged, bus service was suspended and, said *Pakistan Today*, "schools and shops were forcefully shut across the city."[1426] Two days later, when Qadri was buried, as many as 100,000 mourners[1427] showed up. It was one of the three biggest funeral crowds in Pakistan's history. These tens of thousands were peaceful, but the words they chanted were not: "The punishment for a blasphemer is beheading," and "Qadri, your blood will bring the revolution."[1428] Typical of the split that afflicts Pakistan like an open wound—the conflict between its extremists and its modernists. A lethal conflict.

As Salmaan Taseer's son, Aatish Taseer, wrote in *The New York Times*: "I wondered, what happens when an ideology of hate is no longer just coming from the mouths of Saudi-funded clerics but has infected the body of the people? What do you do when the madness is not confined to radical mosques and madrasas, but is abroad among a population of nearly 200 million?"[1429] Two hundred million with nuclear weapons. As Aatish put it, this form of militant Islam, "is not, as some like to claim, medieval. It's not even traditional. It is modern in the most basic sense: It is utterly new."[1430] Aatish points out something crucial, the future of "the 100,000 people who came to grieve for Mumtaz Qadri...reminds us that their existence is tied up with our own."[1431] The future of the blasphemy killers may well determine our future. Yours and mine.

What impact did Mumtaz Qadri's execution have on Asia Bibi? Did she gain greater freedom? Far from it. "A statement issued from Islamabad's Lal Masjid," Pakistan's famous Red Mosque, "called on the government to execute 'the blasphemer Asia Bibi as soon as possible and not bow to international pressure.'"[1432]

Did all of this turmoil really come from just one cup of water and from the kind of comment that you and I make on Facebook when discussing religion every day? No. It came from what Islamic scholars call a total system of life. It came from a unified judicial, governmental, military, liturgical, and theological system. It came from a system that springs from the living example of just one man. It came from a system based on the stories of his deeds. And it came from his words. It came from the legacy of the prophet Muhammad. In other words, it came from one of history's most astonishing examples of the founder effect.

Who is Gagging Islam's Liberals?

> Re: the term "moderate Islam"—"These descriptions are very ugly, it is offensive and an insult to our religion. There is no moderate or immoderate Islam. Islam is Islam and that's it."
>
> —Turkish Prime Minister Recep Tayyip Erdogan[1433]

> "We cannot accept insults to Islam under the guise of freedom of thought."
>
> —Turkish Prime Minister Recep Tayyip Erdogan[1434]

IT'S LITTLE WONDER, then, that until the Egyptian Movement for Change's Kefaya (Enough) street demonstrations in 14 Egyptian cities from 2004 to 2006,[1435] Iran's Green Movement of 2009,[1436] and the Arab Spring of 2011,[1437] Islam had never developed an equivalent to the West's protest, free speech, peace, and human rights movements. Islam had never developed a permanent protest industry. And Islam had seldom, if ever, fought for the rights of others to lead their own way of life. The pluralist, tolerant, modern Muslims who rose up in the Arab Spring helped topple tyrants. But they were crushed by new tyrannies—the military dictatorship in Egypt, the violent crackdown in Iran,[1438] the civil war in Syria, and the treacherous chaos in Libya.

The fact is that there are many Muslims who long for pluralism, tolerance, and democracy. But too many are kept silent by the threat of punishment from those who control the public spaces of Islam. Islam's "liberals" are silenced by Holy War enthusiasts, by militant nationalists, and by clerics. They are silenced by those who follow in the footsteps of Muhammad. By those who, like Muhammad, believe that the punishment for dissent against Islam is death.

* * *

In Bangladesh, Mohammad Mahbubul Alam is the editor of the *Daily Al Ihsan*, a self-styled "international Islamic magazine" that on its front page calls for curses and punishment against "those people who reject faith," including "the Jews and the polytheists" and "Christians of all nations."[1439] Doesn't sound very pluralist or tolerant, does it? On March 31, 2013,[1440] Alam led a delegation of religious leaders that met with "a committee of the Prime Minister's Office."[1441] The purpose of Alam and his delegation? To present a list of 84 "secular" bloggers and to demand that the Bangladesh government prosecute them.

You have to understand something about the word "secular." To most Westerners, that's a positive term. But, if you want to live, do not use it in Pakistan[1442] or Bangladesh. In the South Asian Muslim world, the word "secular" means atheist. And atheists are to be killed.

The government ignored the religious leaders' punishment request. So Pakistan's pious took over. From 2013 to 2016, twenty[1443] of the 84 secular bloggers were assassinated in Bangladesh, including Niloy Neel, whose home was invaded in 2015 by six men with machetes pretending that they wanted to rent a flat. Four of the armed men isolated Neel's wife in one room while the other two took Neel to his bedroom and hacked him to pieces. What was his crime? According to police, he and the nineteen other secularists "wrote against Islam and mocked Prophet Muhammad."[1444] In other words, Neel's atheism, secularism, and advocacy of human rights were anti-Islamic. In the words of Imran H. Sarkar, head of the Bangladesh Blogger and Activist Network, Neel "was the voice against fundamentalism and extremism and was even a voice for minority rights—especially women's rights and the rights of indigenous people."[1445] And Neel was just one of the 84 secular bloggers on the hit list—some of whom were hacked apart with knives and meat cleavers[1446] on the streets in front of horrified pedestrians.[1447]

Meanwhile, in Saudi Arabia in 2015, Ashraf Fayadh, a poet and leader of Saudi Arabia's budding art scene who had curated an exhibit at the Venice Biennale, was sentenced to death "for renouncing Islam."[1448] So, like the poets who fled from Muhammad's murderous meme-policing in 624 A.D., Islamic "liberals" have been muzzled for nearly 1,400 years.

In the battle between memes within the Islamic community, liberalism has always lost.

* * *

In the 11th, 12th, and 13th centuries, a form of Islam flourished in Baghdad, India, and central Asia that opened the door to an alternative, non-militant Islam. It was Sufism, a mystic interpretation of Islam that held on to the notion of jihad as warfare, but that emphasized spiritual jihad,[1449] a journey through the inner world.[1450] In Baghdad 'Abd al-Qadir al-Jilani focused on the quest for ecstatic emotions, on summoning those emotions by reciting poetry that praised Muhammad at the top of your lungs, and on practicing kindness and charity.[1451] In India, Chistiya Sufism[1452] also deemphasized wars of conquest and focused on music, poetry, and the care of the poor.[1453] Two hundred years later, the appeal of Chistiya Sufism would help take Islam from a religion that only .2% of Indians believed in to one that was followed by 3.2 million Indians.[1454] And many of these Indians were won over by the honey of the Sufi nonviolent form of Islam, not by the vinegar of Islamic terror.[1455]

Then came the Muslim Indian Emperor Akbar's[1456] attempt to introduce pluralism to Islam in 1582. Akbar promoted tolerance toward Hindus, Jains,[1057] Zoroastrians,[1058] Buddhists, and Christians. His pluralist form of Islam was called *Din-i Ilahi*.[1459] Akbar also promoted *sulh-i kull*, "universal peace."[1460] But he didn't get very far. Akbar's movement never attracted "more than 19 adherents."[1461] Yes, that's right, 19! What's more, orthodox Muslims opposed his policies as heresy and crushed them when Akbar died in 1605.[1462]

And Sufism was not always as peaceful as it's made out to be in the West. In the 1670s, the Moroccan Sufi Lyusi[1463] laced into his local sultan, Ismail, demanding that he rule justly. In the process, he called on the Sultan to wage war in a holy cause as Islam said he should...killing as an "obligation to God and his people."[1464] In the 19th and early 20th centuries, some Sufi leaders went from merely insisting on war to organizing armies and leading them in attacks against European occupying forces and against old-line Muslim ruling families.[1465] Their justification? They were following the example of combat set by Muhammad. Then came Saudi Arabia's Wahhabis and Salafists, passionate Holy Warriors and missionaries who fanned out around the globe and who condemned the Sufis utterly, labeled them un-Islamic, and outlawed Sufism in one Islamic country after another.[1466] They, too, were inspired by the standard of intolerance set by Muhammad.

Still, this wasn't the end of Islamic liberalism. In 1876, a reform-oriented cleric in what remained of the Ottoman Empire issued a fatwa—a religious decree—deposing the ruler of worldwide Islam, the Caliph. A new caliph took the old one's place, a new Sultan who introduced a constitution with a parliament and with guarantees of religious liberty and freedom of speech.[1467] This move helped pave the way for today's Islamic-but-secular Turkey. But outside of Turkey, liberal Islam had almost no influence. And in today's Turkey, the nation's leader, Recep Tayyip Erdogan, has thrown the secularists out of power, is slowly closing in on the liberals, and is aiming for an "Islamist" state. A state more in keeping with Muhammad's grim examples.

Though movements toward Islamic liberalism kept popping up in the early 20th century, they were too weak to reach the mainstream. From 1919 to 1924 in India, the Khilafat Movement[1468] supported the idea that Islam should be one global, unified empire ruled by the Ottoman Caliph in Constantinople—the city that Muslims had violently pried from the hands of Christians in 1453 and had renamed Istanbul.[1469] As dangerous as a faction dedicated to a global empire may seem, the Khalifat Movement[1470] produced some welcome surprises. The leaders of the movement allied with Mahatma Gandhi's drive for Indian independence from the British.[1471] And some of the Khalifat movement's leaders[1472] may have been Muslim pluralists and modernists, early Muslim "liberals."

Among them was Abul Kalam Azad.[1473] Born in Mecca and raised in India, Azad had cultural pluralism in his blood. He was the son of an Arab mother and of an Indian Muslim Sufi of Afghan origins. In 1920, Azad took big chances, bucked the traditionalists, and promoted the concept of Tajdid—of Islamic innovation—instead of traditional Taqliq.[1474] Taqliq was Islam's way of hyper-activating the Founder Effect. It demanded rigid conformity to Islam's seventh-century ways, including conformity to Muhammad's bloody policies. Azad wanted Taqliq to go. In his books, Azad reportedly called for an Indian state based on separation of mosque and state, plus a secular, democratic, pluralist government within whose rule all religions and all cultures might coexist.[1475]

Alas, I suspect that very few Muslims today have heard of Azad. Instead, today's Muslims have been force-fed the philosophies of men like Muhammad ibn Abd al-Wahhab al-Tamimi[1476]—founder of Wahhabism, the jihadist religion taught in Saudi-sponsored schools in nearly every major Western and Eastern city in the world.[1477] The Saudi government has allegedly spent an astonishing $100 billion[1478] to build mosques, establish Muslim community centers, endow chairs at elite American universities, provide "teacher training,"[1479] and supply textbooks from Tokyo,[1480] Buenos Aires, São Paulo, and Brasilia to Los Angeles, Chicago,[1481] Detroit,[1482] and the Virginia suburbs of Washington, DC.[1483] The goal? To promote Wahhab's version of Islam. A jihadist version. Today's Muslims have also been swayed by the thoughts of men like Sayyed Qutub, the fundamentalist thinker whose writings inspired Osama bin Laden to declare war—worldwide jihad—

on America in his August 23, 1996 "Declaration Of War Against The Americans."[1484]

And hundreds of millions of today's Muslims have been weaned on the attitudes of Hasan al-Banna,[1485] founder of the Muslim Brotherhood—one of Islam's most successful movements in the early 21st century. The Muslim Brotherhood's motto reads, "Allah is our objective. The Prophet is our leader. The Qur'an is our law. Jihad is our way. Dying in the way of Allah is our highest hope."[1486] All these men—Muhammad ibn Abd al-Wahhab al-Tamimi, Sayyed Qutub, and Hasan al-Banna—were militants dead serious about converting or killing unbelievers like you and me.

Those who espouse Islamic liberalism often risk their lives. Let's go back to Salman Rushdie, an Islamic novelist born in Bombay who worked as a journalist in Pakistan then became discontented and moved to England.[1487] Rushdie was put under a death sentence for his novel *The Satanic Verses*. Pakistani street mobs rioted over the novel's alleged insults to Islam in 1989. Five of the rioters were shot by police. And it appears that none of the rioters had actually read the book. When the Ayatollah Khomeini, leader of the Islamic Revolution in Iran, saw the coverage of the riots on television, he issued a fatwa—a religious edict—calling for Rushdie's death and for the deaths of others involved with Rushdie's book.[1488] Said the Ayatollah, "I call on all zealous Muslims to execute them quickly, wherever they find them." The Ayatollah gave extra oomph to his edict by putting a price of three million dollars on Rushdie's head. Then an Iranian Islamic organization upped the ante by another $2.8 million.[1489] Rushdie took these threats seriously. He remained in hiding from 1989 to 1998.[1490]

The fatwa against Rushdie terrified publishers and editors in the West, making them extremely leery of publishing books like the one you're reading now. Fifteen hundred American bookstores took *The Satanic Verses* off their shelves.[1491] Why? Khomeini's fatwa extended not only to Rushdie, but to "all involved in its [*The Satanic Verses*] publication who were aware of its content." These words were backed by action. Bookstores in Berkeley, California; York, England; and London's West End were bombed.[1492] Other bombs were found outside of bookstores in England's Guilford, Nottingham, and Peterborough.[1493]

This was a battle of memes, a bloody one. *The Satanic Verses'* Japanese translator was stabbed to death. The book's Italian translator was knifed, but lived. Its Norwegian publisher was shot but managed to cling to life. And in Sivas, Turkey, demonstrators denounced the Muslim who had translated *The*

Satanic Verses into Turkish. These street mobs did more than chant for the translator's death. They set a local hotel on fire, killing 37 hotel guests.[1494]

But Rushdie was not the only author to be targeted for "un-Islamic" views. There was Taslima Nasrin,[1495] an Islamic novelist from Bangladesh. Her newspaper articles and her book *Shame* made the mistake of protesting against the Islamic treatment of women and minorities. That was more than the street rioters and amateur assassins of extremist Islam could take. In 1994, there were riots in the central roadways of Bangladesh over Nasrin's un-Islamic freedom of speech. The government of Bangladesh decreed that her writings were riddled with "anti-Islam sentiments and statements that could destroy the religious harmony of Bangladesh."[1496] So Nasrin was forced to go into hiding in Sweden.[1497] At least she wasn't killed like the poetess Asma, the mother of five about whom Muhammad said, "Who will rid me of Marwan's daughter?"[1498]

Then there was the case of Naguib Mahfouz, an Egyptian novelist who won the Nobel Prize for Literature in 1988. You'd think that the Arab-speaking world would be proud of this honor, even though it came from the barbaric and pagan West. But you'd be wrong. Mahfouz's novels were banned in many Islamic countries because the author had once made the un-Islamic move of supporting the 1978 Camp David peace treaty between Egypt and Israel. But that's not all. An influential extremist interpreter of Islam, Omar Abdul-Rahman (the man who inspired the 1993 bombing of five basement floors of New York's World Trade Center),[1499] told a journalist that Mahfouz's work had helped lay the base for Salman Rushdie's heresy. That did it. In 1994 Mahfouz was stabbed in the neck with a kitchen knife[1500] in front of his house in Cairo. He lived, but the 82-year-old author was forced to surround himself with bodyguards for the rest of his life.[1501]

These are just the tips of the iceberg—the merest hints of the way in which today's militant Islamic community follows Muhammad's example of rigid meme-policing and terrifies would-be liberals into silence. African journalist Isioma Daniel[1502] was forced to flee her homeland, Nigeria, when she wrote a column about violent Islamic protests against the 2002 Miss World Pageant, a pageant scheduled to take place in Nigeria's capital, Abuja.[1503] Referring to Muhammad's sexual appetites, appetites Allah himself sanctioned in the Qur'an,[1504] Daniel said: "The Muslims thought it was immoral to bring 92 women to Nigeria and ask them to revel in vanity. What would Muhammad think? In all honesty, he would probably have chosen a wife from one of them." These words were probably true. As you've seen. But they triggered three days of riots that claimed the lives of more than 220 people. A government official in the Nigerian state of Zamfara issued a fatwa declaring: "Like Salman Rushdie, the blood of Isioma Daniel can be shed. It is binding on all Muslims, wherever they are, to consider the killing of the writer as a religious duty." Daniel was forced to go into hiding in the U.S. And her homeland, Nigeria, is not even a Muslim nation. Only 50% of its citizens followed the religion of Muhammad at the time.[1505]

There are many other examples of this sort. Turkey's Islamist/feminist writer Konca Kuris was kidnapped, tortured, and killed by the militant, Iranian-backed movement Hezbollah in the Turkish town of Konya in 1998. Turkish secularist and newspaper columnist Ahmet Taner Kislali died when a bomb went off beneath the hood of his car the following year. Then there's the punishment of Iranian history professor Hashem Aghajari, who told a Tehran audience in 2002 not to consider the words of extremist religious leaders as sacred and not to follow militant Islam "like monkeys." Aghajari was sentenced to death for "apostasy"—for abandoning Islam. In a second trial, Aghajari was once again given the death sentence. A third trial finally concluded that Aghajari, had, indeed, "insulted sacred Islamic tenets," but gave him a lighter sentence—three years in prison.[1506]

Despite these threats, there are figures like Munawar Anees, a Nobel Peace Prize nominee, former Advisor to the Deputy Prime Minister of Malaysia,[5] and founder of two of the leading journals of Islamic studies in the Islamic world.[6] Dr. Anees—who has been tortured in a Malaysian prison—ends his letters with these words: "I have sworn upon the altar of God eternal hostility against every form of tyranny over the mind of man." Anees makes it clear in his signature file that this statement comes from a founder-effect generator named Thomas Jefferson.

And there's Kamal Nawash, founder of the Free Muslim Coalition Against Terrorism in Washington, DC.[1507] Nawash runs one of a handful of Islamic anti-extremist groups, groups whose leaders erect websites but usually hide in anonymity and seldom reveal their names. Nawash is one of the few who dares to disclose his identity and to make his statements in public.

---

5. The former prime minister Dr. Anees served was Anwar Ibrahim—who was groomed as the successor to Malaysia's "duly-elected" prime minister—the country's actual dictator Mahathir Muhammad. In 1998, *Newsweek* Magazine named Anwar Ibrahim "The Asian of the Year." And in 1999, when Ibrahim emerged as Mahathir Muhammad's chief critic, he was jailed on what most believe were trumped up charges of sexual misbehavior. (See the chapter on Anwar Ibrahim in: John L. Esposito, John Obert Voll, *Makers of Contemporary Islam*. New York: Oxford University Press, 2001: pp. 177–198.)

6. *Periodica Islamica* and *The International Journal of Islamic and Arabic Studies.*

And there's a new crop of Muslim reformers taking advantage of their freedom of speech in America and the West.

Among them are "reformers" who may not be what they claim. A good example is Muhammad Tahir-ul-Qadri (not to be confused with Mumtaz Qadri, the assassin of Punjab's governor). Qadri is a Pakistani Qur'anic scholar and politician. He claims to be something that Muhammad predicted, the one man who "at the beginning of every Islamic century" revives the pure and holy teachings of the Prophet, and does it for the entire Umma,[1508] for the worldwide community of Islam. In other words, Qadri boldly claims a unique religious authority.

In 1981, at the beginning of a Muslim century, Qadri founded Minhaj-ul-Quran—The Path of the Qur'an—in Lahore. In its English-language materials, Minhaj-ul-Quran says that it is dedicated to "abridging the communication gap between different communities and religions and...promoting peace by educating young minds about classical Islamic sciences." Today Minhaj-ul-Quran claims that it is "working in over 100 countries around the globe."[1509]

In May of 1989, Qadri also founded a Pakistani political party, Pakistan Awami Tehreek, the Pakistan People's Movement. The party says that it is committed to "fighting hard to serve the people of Pakistan in the way a true democratic government" should. It promises to cut red tape, maximize Pakistan's resources, minimize the nation's debt, set private industry free to compete, and to work for "equality, inclusiveness, putting people first" thus providing "basic facilities of life and equal job opportunities."[1510] From 1990 to 2004, Qadri held an elected seat in Pakistan's National Assembly, Pakistan's lower house of parliament. Then he resigned in protest against Pakistani president Pervez Musharraf's dual position as head of government and head of the army.

Most important, on March 2, 2010, as the Pakistani newspaper *Dawn* explains it, "Qadri issued a historic 600-page-long religious decree or fatwa on suicide bombings citing references from the holy Quran, Hadiths and texts from various Islamic scholars. His fatwa aimed to highlight the importance of peace in Islam and the fact that suicide bombings are strictly prohibited in the religion." Qadri's fatwa claimed that Islam is a religion of peace. But did it preach peace to Muslims? Or did it simply attempt to make Islam seem peaceful to Westerners? Was it an act of "guile" and "deceit"?

Qadri had moved to Canada in 2005, five years before he issued his fatwa, and it was while he was in Canada that he wrote the Fatwa on Terrorism

& Suicide Bombings. Then Qadri introduced his document in a series of mass events. Not mass events in Cairo, Baghdad, Damascus, or Islamabad, but mass events in London. The Fatwa on Terrorism & Suicide Bombings was unveiled at a press conference in Westminster's Central Hall in London. Then came:

- A peace camp. Its location? Once again, England.
- A Peace for Humanity Conference. Location? London.
- An Interfaith Collective Peace Prayer. At the London Peace for Humanity Conference.
- A European launch of the peace fatwa…in Denmark.
- A "Seminar Delegitimizing the Al Qaeda Narrative." Where? Not in one of al Qaeda's strongholds in Pakistan, Qadri's home country. In Oslo, Norway.
- A speech at the U.S. Institute of Peace…in Washington, DC.
- And on June 15, 2015, an Islamic Curriculum for Peace and Counter Terrorism. But, alas, this, too, was launched in England.[1511]

Qadri received huge press attention for his efforts. He was invited to talk up his fatwa at the 2011 World Economic Forum in Davos, Switzerland. And his fatwa landed in the hands of Pope Benedict XVI. To his credit, Qadri's fatwa was also endorsed by Egypt's Al-Azhar University, one of the most respected centers of theological opinion in the Islamic world. The problem is that most of this attention was in the West. It's the Islamic world where a fatwa calling for peace and banning suicide bombing needs to wield influence. In the West, it simply helps pull the wool over the eyes of those who want to believe that Islam is harmless, those who want to ignore the murderous deeds of Muhammad.

One of Qadri's websites says something admirable:

Dr Tahir-ul-Qadri said that the Holy Prophet (peace be upon him) stated that a time would come when the youth and immature people with imperfect knowledge will spread chaos by using his 'Sunna' and Islam. They would spill blood of innocent people and talk about establishing the dominance of truth but they would have nothing to do with Islam or his 'Sunna.' He (PBUH) ordained to the faithful to crush such elements with full might.[1512]

In other words, explains Qadri, Muhammad said that ISIS, al Qaeda, and Boko Haram should be crushed. But is Qadri saying this to his fellow Muslims? Or is this a PR effort to throw you and me off the track?

On yet another webpage, Qadri reveals motives that may not be as pluralistic and tolerant as his words aimed at Westerners make them out to be. He says that his purpose in founding Minhaj-ul-Quran is "the revival of Islam."[1513] That would be great if Qadri is promoting a truly peaceful form of Islam. However Minhaj, says Qadri, is dedicated to "the Da'wa work…to communicate its [Islam's] message effectively across the five continents of the world." Da'wa means missionary work—trying to convert the rest of us to Islam—inviting us to Islam. But remember the consequences of not accepting that invitation: death.[1514]

Minhaj is also dedicated to "the spread of Islamic teachings and safeguarding the faith of youth." That means not letting the young escape Islam. On top of that, Minhaj is committed to an "all-embracing and all-encompassing struggle" and to the principle of "universalism." There is a word for this sort of struggle in Islam: jihad. And "universalism" tends to mean not a tolerant acceptance of all humanity, but the global spread of what Qadri calls "the supreme banner of Mercy of the Prophet Muhammad." Is this the banner of Mercy that was raised over mass murders like that in Khaibar?

What's more, as one of the most severe but best informed critics of Islam, Robert Spencer, points out,[1515] Qadri's fatwa against suicide bombing and terrorism never, in its more than five hundred pages, tries to give a peaceful interpretation—or any interpretation—of the five verses of the Qur'an that say "slay them wherever you catch them." Slay whom? Those who turn away from Islam. And unbelievers like you and me.

*　*　*

Then there are the genuine moderates and liberals.

Qadri says that Islam is a religion of peace.[1516] One Muslim reformer who in her youth was dedicated to jihad disagrees strongly with Qadri. She says point-blank that "Islam is not a religion of peace."[1517] That reformer is Ayaan Hirsi Ali. Ayaan Hirsi Ali grew up in Somalia in a strict Muslim family. Her mother used almost every household prop including the kitchen's cooking fire to put a fear of Islam's hell into the emotional core of her children. When she was a teenager, Hirsi Ali discovered the philosophy of the Muslim Brotherhood, a group that says jihad is one of the first principles of Islam.

She became a jihad enthusiast. "As a sixteen- and seventeen-year-old girl in Kenya," she says, "I believed in jihad." Jihad looked to her like a way to escape her family, have personal freedom, and dedicate herself to a higher purpose. She recalls:

> For me, jihad was something to aspire to beyond chores for my mother and grandmother and my dreaded math class. The ideal of holy war encouraged me to get out of the house and engage in charitable work for others. It gave me a focus for my inner struggle; now I could struggle to be a better Muslim. Every prayer, every veil, every fast, every acknowledgment of Allah signaled that I was a better person or at least on the path to becoming one. I had value, and if the hardships of life in the Old Racecourse Road section of Nairobi felt overwhelming, it was only temporary. I would be rewarded in the afterlife.[1518]

Then Hirsi Ali's notions of jihad morphed. She explains:

> That's how jihad is generally first presented to most young Muslims—as a manifestation of the inner struggle to be a good Muslim. It's a spiritual struggle, a path toward the light. But then things change. Gradually, jihad ceases to be simply an inner struggle; it becomes an outward one, a holy war in the name of Islam by an army of glorious "brothers."[1519]

Eventually, Ali Hirsi's father arranged a marriage for her. To a Muslim member of her clan in Canada. A man who she says "spoke in half-learned Somali and half-learned English"[1520] and who "wanted six sons."[1521] Ali Hirsi was not enthusiastic about this choice. Her flight to Canada had a stopover in Dusseldorf, Germany. Ali Hirsi left the plane and never got back on again. Instead, she took refuge in Europe, eventually ending up in Amsterdam. The culture she was exposed to there was utterly alien to her. She saw people who would have been left to misery in Somalia, but in Holland were taken care of by the welfare system of the state. She saw life defined by individual achievement, not by killing on behalf of the tribe or the faith. She reveals that she was "stunned by the near-total absence of violence. I never saw Dutch people engaging in physical confrontations. There were no threats or fear. If two or three people were killed, it was considered a crisis of the social order and spoken about as such. Two or three violent deaths in my Somali homeland were considered completely ordinary and unremarkable."[1522] Slowly the appeal of this new way of life won her over. She put herself through college and grad school and got a master's degree in political science from the University of Leiden. And she won a seat in the Dutch House of Representatives.

But Hirsi Ali was appalled at the way women are treated in the Islamic world—from the honor killings of teenage girls who have "stained the family honor" to the beatings of wives, beatings for which instructions are given by religious scholars in books and on television.[1523] So she wrote a film about this institutionalized abuse—*Submission*. The filmmaker who turned Hirsi's words into visuals was Theo Van Gogh, the great-grandson of Vincent Van Gogh's brother. Hirsi Ali's film was shown on Dutch public TV and became an Internet sensation, drawing more than three-quarters of a million views.

But the project was Van Gogh's undoing. Islam's killers of dissent took offense. So one day as Theo Van Gogh was bicycling through Amsterdam's streets he was assaulted. By whom? By a Muslim born in Holland, a Muslim who lived off the welfare of the Dutch state. The attacker emptied a handgun into Van Gogh, slashed at him with a large knife, plunged the knife into Van Gogh's chest until it reached his backbone, then used a smaller knife to pin a manifesto to Van Gogh's body. Here's how Ayaan Hirsi Ali describes it in her book *Heretic: Why Islam Needs a Reformation Now*:

> my collaborator on a short documentary film, Theo van Gogh, had been murdered in the street in Amsterdam by a young man of Moroccan parentage named Muhammad Bouyeri. First he shot Theo eight times with a handgun. Then he shot him again as Theo, still clinging to life, pleaded for mercy. Then he cut his throat and attempted to decapitate him with a large knife. Finally, using a smaller knife, he stuck a long note to Theo's body.

What did that note say? Says Hirsi Ali, it

> was structured in the style of a fatwa, or religious verdict. It began, "In the name of Allah—the Beneficent—the Merciful" and included, along with numerous quotations from the Qur'an, an explicit threat on my life: ...'Mrs. Hirshi [sic] Ali and the rest of you extremist unbelievers. Islam has withstood many enemies and persecutions throughout History. . . . AYAAN HIRSI ALI YOU WILL SELF-DESTRUCT ON ISLAM!' On and on it went in the same ranting

vein. "Islam will be victorious through the blood of the martyrs. They will spread its light in every dark corner of this earth and it will drive evil with the sword if necessary back into its dark hole.... There will be no mercy shown to the purveyors of injustice."[1524]

Injustice, in Muhammad's dark form of Islam, is any form of government that does not use the laws of Shariah. It's any society in which Muslims are not dominant. It's any society in which unbelievers are not second-class citizens humiliated by paying a protection tax. In other words, there will be injustice until the day Islam rules the entire population of the globe. Just as Muhammad said it would in 629 A.D., the year he wrote his letters to the emperors.

The note from the killer of Theo Van Gogh said that Islam "will drive evil with the sword if necessary back into its dark hole." What is evil? I am for writing this book. You are for reading it. And you and I are evil because we have not submitted our souls, our minds, and our bodies to the One True Prophet and his message. You and I will be evil until we become Muslims.

* * *

Holland's intellectuals subtly support Amsterdam's Muslim killers. And they do it in the name of freedom and tolerance. They cover for the extremists, denying the jihadists' existence in their midst and attacking anyone who delivers a message critical of Islam's murderous side. So Hirsi Ali fled to the United States and now splits her time between New York and London.

There are other genuine Muslim reformers, people like Asra Nomani, whom we'll meet in a minute, and Wafa Sultan. Here's the list that Ayaan Ali Hirsi gives in her book *Heretic*:

> There is a growing number of ordinary Muslim citizens in the West who are currently braving death threats and even official punishment in dissenting from Islamic orthodoxy and calling for the reform of Islam. These individuals are not clergymen but "ordinary" Muslims, generally educated, well read, and preoccupied with the crisis of Islam. Among them are Maajid Nawaz (UK), Samia Labidi (France), Afshin Ellian (Netherlands), Ehsan Jami (Netherlands), Naser Khader (Denmark), Seyran Ateş (Germany), Yunis Qandil (Germany), Bassam Tibi (Germany), Raheel Raza (Canada), Zuhdi Jasser (U.S.), Saleem Ahmed (U.S.), Nonie Darwish (U.S.), Wafa

Sultan (U.S.), Saleem Ahmed (U.S.), Ibn Warraq (U.S.), Asra Nomani (U.S.), and Irshad Manji (U.S.).

Almost all of these are calling for a Muslim reformation. They want Islam to discard the brutality and perpetual war demanded by Muhammad. They call for the sort of revolution in Islam that Martin Luther pulled off in Christianity in 1517 when he nailed his 95 theses to the door of the Castle Church in Wittenberg, Germany. Luther took God out of the hands of the Catholic Church's vast hierarchy of popes, bishops, and priests, and made divinity available to anyone who could read. When it comes to a Muslim parallel to Lutheranism, that's what Ayaan Ali Hirsi is all about. Says she:

> My argument is for nothing less than a Muslim Reformation. Without fundamental alterations to some of Islam's core concepts, I believe, we shall not solve the burning and increasingly global problem of political violence carried out in the name of religion.[1525]

But Islam's modernist revolutionaries do not call for their reformation in Pakistan, Saudi Arabia, Egypt, Malaysia, or Indonesia. They do not talk about a modernist, pluralist reform in any of the world's 57 self-declared Islamic States. Calls of this kind could lose them their lives. Instead, the reformers live in the West. And here—especially in the United States—the orders that demand that the faithful hack them apart with knives or machetes or shoot them for their "blasphemies" are ignored. The reformers are attacked by other and far less lethal means. But those other means have clout.

Weaponizing a Word: Islamophobia

Islam is a religion but it is also a political doctrine, and you will not be able to name the threat precisely unless you understand exactly what Islam is, ...[it is] the antithesis of the idea of America...[and] American political theory and practice.

Political correctness is literally eroding our systems from within and killing it. Radical Islamists are, obviously, exploiting that. They have defined us as the enemy and we haven't defined them as the enemy. They are exploiting our weaknesses and political correctness is our weakness.[1526]

—Ayaan Ali Hirsi

The Ikhwan [members of the Muslim Brotherhood] must understand that their work in America is a kind of grand Jihad in eliminating and destroying the Western civilization from within and "sabotaging" its miserable house by their hands and the hands of the believers so that it is eliminated and God's religion is made victorious over all other religions.[1527]

—The Muslim Brotherhood, An Explanatory
Memorandum On the General Strategic Goal
for the Group In North America

HOW DO YOU GET LOVERS of free speech to become their own censors? How do you get those committed to tolerance to become intolerant? Of each other? How do you get them to muzzle free speech in the name of, guess what? Free speech! Sounds impossible, right?

Wrong. In 1998, the Organization of Islamic Cooperation began a push for a United Nations resolution "combating defamation of religions."[1528] The OIC includes all 57 Islamic nations and claims to be "the collective voice of the Muslim world."[1529] Defamation is a term with a noble history in the West. It was used from 1913 onward by Jews to counter anti-Semitism. Those Jews founded the Anti-Defamation League of the B'nai B'rith[1530] in response to the

Marietta, Georgia, lynching of a Jewish mechanical engineer and pencil factory superintendent, Leo Frank.[1531] The Anti-Defamation League did its best to counter the anti-Semitism of World War I in America, then the anti-Semitism that would lead to the Holocaust.[1532] Meanwhile, prominent Muslims like the Mufti of Jerusalem, the Muslim Brotherhood's founder Hassan al-Banna, and Iraqi Prime Minister Rashid Ali al-Gaylani sided with the Nazis, met with Hitler and his top lieutenants, were funded by the Nazis, lived for years in Berlin, and enthusiastically supported the fuehrer's drive to exterminate the Jews.[1533]

By making off with the word "defamation," the Muslim nations were deliberately using a term with emotional resonance. A term that would mean little in a nation like Pakistan, where the defamation of non-Muslim religions is applauded. But a term with meaning to Americans and Europeans. "Defamation" wouldn't catch fire. But another word would.

Seven years after its push to muzzle "defamation," in December, 2005, the Organization of Islamic Cooperation held what it called The Third Extraordinary Session of the Islamic Summit in Mecca, Muhammad's old power center. That's when the representatives came up with their magic word. Islamophobia. But where did that geopolitical sledgehammer of a term come from?

The word Islamophobia got its start in France from 1902 to 1925, when it cropped up six times in articles or books.[1534] The best-known mention is in a 1925 book[1535] written by the highly respected French painter Étienne Dinet and by the 48-year-old[1536] Algerian he had hired years earlier to act as a guide to Islam's legends, culture, and spirituality. Dinet apparently used his guide, Sliman ben Ibrahim, to gain access to many a private moment in Algeria. The results were paintings of semi-nude teenage Muslim girls bathing, wrestling, and tree climbing. Plus an occasional threesome of Muslim warriors. The pictures won awards. Many of them. Together Dinet and ben Ibrahim created eight illustrated books on the exotica of Algeria's Islamic world, books designed to reach a French audience.[1537] Sliman ben Ibrahim, the guide, became one of Dinet's closest friends. And ben Ibrahim was apparently highly persuasive. So was the sight of the teenage girls Islam offered as wives. In roughly 1908, Dinet, the painter, who had split his time between France and Algeria for close to ten years, converted to Islam, wrote a passionate biography of the Prophet,[1538] and upped his time living in Algeria to three-quarters of the year.[1539] Dinet's 1925 book with Ibrahim, The Orient as Seen From the Occident, had what one reviewer called "the zeal of a convert."[1540] It attacked

Western scholars who dared to write skeptical biographies of Muhammad, claiming that Islamophobia could lead Western thinkers into "aberration."[1541] Why? Because according to another Dinet and ben Ibrahim book, their 1918 biography *The Life of Mohammad: The Prophet of Allah*,[1542] Muhammad was "the superman who came into the world at Makkah [Mecca]" and must be taken seriously as "our Lord Mohammad, the Prince of Prophets."[1543]

Dinet could afford his embrace of Islam. Militant Islam's threat to the West seemed to be at an end. Islam was on its heels. Turkey, the heir to the caliphate, had been the sick man of Europe for 156 years.[1544] What's more, the Turks had fought on the losing side in the recently concluded First World War. The caliphate was at an end. Why? The Turkish empire was being dismembered. And Muslim soldiers from Algeria had laid aside jihad and had fought on the French side in World War I. They had fought under the banner of Western secular Christendom. The threat of Christendom's extermination, the Türkenfurcht,[1545] the "dread of the Turks," that motivated Martin Luther to write three books and that drove one French poet to advise that the Christian population flee from Europe and try life all over again in the New World[1546] was over. Seemingly for good.

But who had a better handle on Islam's resilience, its adaptability, its patience and stubbornness, and its militants' commitment to jihad, the few folks who still feared militant Islam or those like Dinet who decried an "acces de délire islamaphobe,"[1547] an attack of Islamophobic delirium? Who were closer to delirium, those who thought there was no further danger from militant Islam or those who were a bit more concerned? If you'd told someone in 1925 about the events of the World Trade Center, Paris, and Brussels, your listener would have accused you of intolerant, alarmist delusions. But those "delusions" would prove to be real. All too real.

The word Islamophobia demonstrated its true powers when it transited from French to English. The man who forged that transition was a brilliant intellectual publicist, one who did his absolute best to mislead the West about militant Islam: Edward Said. In 1993, Edward Said took to the pages of what may be the most influential publication among the intellectual elite, the *New York Times Sunday Magazine*. Said's message? The threat of Islam was "phony."[1548] Utterly false. A fabrication. Eight years later came 9/11. But we are getting ahead of ourselves.

In 1985, Edward Said used the term Islamophobia in an article that appeared in the journal *Race & Class*[1549] and reappeared in at least three other books and publications.[1550] Professor Said deliberately surfed the waves of Western tolerance when he said that Islamophobia was akin to anti-Semitism. Or, as Said put it, Islamophobia "stemmed from the same source, has been nourished at the same stream as anti-Semitism." What's more, to understand Islamophobia, all we have to do is understand "the cultural mechanisms of anti-Semitism."[1551] Oh, and one more thing: we have to hate Israel. In other words, we have to ignore Islam's nearly 1,400-year history of murderous anti-Semitism. But that's not all. Professor Said also wanted us to overlook Islam's 1,100-year history of imperial conquest and the modern Islamic militants' goal of "liberating" the entire world. And we complied. We covered our eyes. With our help, Edward Said was able to make the world's 1.6 billion Muslims—with their 57 nations, their territory seven times the size of the United States, and their oil wealth—appear to be a tiny, picked-upon minority. He was able to portray a giant as a nerd. He got us to shut our eyes, to paraphrase the Muslim Brotherhood's "Strategic Goal," by our own hands.

Quite an accomplishment. And it worked.

Said had clout. In 1996, the UK's Runnymede Trust, "an independent charity concerned with research and social policy surrounding race and ethnicity,"[1552] picked up the word Islamophobia and ran with it. The Runnymede Trust established a Commission on British Muslims and Islamophobia. Then it produced "a consultation paper," a paper aimed at the British government on "Islamophobia its features and dangers."[1553] And in 1997, The Runnymede Trust issued a full-scale report, *Islamophobia: A Challenge for Us All.* Why the use of the new word? Said the Runnymede Trust, "anti-Muslim prejudice has grown so considerably and so rapidly in recent years that a new item in the vocabulary is needed so that it can be identified and acted against."[1554] The Runnymede Trust report was, according to Chris Allen, who is considered one of the leading scholars[1555] on the topic, "a hugely influential document, shaping and influencing much of the writing and thought about Islamophobia that has since emerged."[1556] In fact, the report "was launched at the House of Commons by" Britain's "Home Secretary, Jack Straw MP."[1557] In other words, it was treated as if it were an official British government document. But that was just the beginning. The Runnymede Trust continued to release reports on Islamophobia, reports with heft.

So much heft that the United Nations got into the game. On December 7, 2004, just three years after 9/11, the UN threw a "Seminar on Confronting Islamophobia," a seminar at such an august level that it was addressed by a superstar of international affairs, the Secretary General of the UN, Kofi Annan, who declared, "When a new word enters the language, it is often the result of a scientific advance or a diverting fad. But when the world is compelled to coin a new term to take account of increasingly widespread bigotry, that is a sad and troubling development."[1558] Yes, the head of the United Nations declared that fear of Islam was a form of "bigotry." It was an irrational and unacceptable prejudice with no truth behind it.

So by the time the Organization for Islamic Cooperation seized on the word "Islamophobia," it had already been weaponized. In the December, 2005, Extraordinary Session of the Organization of Islamic Cooperation in Mecca, the organization's Islamic Summit, the OIC issued a ten-year plan against "Islamophobia." The 57 nations of the OIC called for the United Nations and all the nations of the West to pass laws banning this mysterious new offense, Islamophobia. In fact, the OIC called for "deterrent punishment,"[1559] punishment so severe that it would stop Islamophobes before they dared open their mouths. And the OIC set up an "observatory of the Organization of Islamic Cooperation...to monitor all forms of Islamophobia, issue an annual report thereon, and ensure cooperation with the relevant Governmental and Non-Governmental Organizations (NGOs) in order to counter Islamophobia."[1560]

Islamophobia was, guess what? A new term for blasphemy—a term specifically aimed at the blasphemy of Westerners. The representatives of 57 Islamic governments were trying to do to you and me what they had done to Asia Bibi and Salmaan Taseer. They were trying to shut us up.

Surely such an absurd plan would never work. Or would it? The OIC had muscle. And it had money to achieve its goals. Its budget was $17.5 million a year, funded by countries including Saudi Arabia, Kuwait,[1561] and Iran.[1562] In other words, it had access to vast amounts of oil money. But that was just a hint of its power. When it embarked on a campaign, the OIC could count on support from the public relations and lobbying apparatuses of 57 nations, many of whose budgets are fattened by petro-dollars. What's more, the OIC bills itself as "the second-largest intergovernmental organization after the United Nations."[1563] In fact, it is the United Nations' biggest voting bloc, with the ability to turn its whims into official UN policy. And, as writer Mark Durie points out, the OIC is the only multi-governmental body dedicated to advancing a religion.[1564] Or should we say a political and military system disguised as a religion? A totalitarian system.

In 2005, roughly a hundred Muslims a day were being killed in Islamic countries. They were being slaughtered by Muslim extremists, jihadists, in suicide bombings and assaults by gunmen. But the OIC was focused on something it deemed more urgent. It was determined to shut down "insults to Islam."[1565] The organization targeted truthful headlines covering events like the *Charlie Hebdo* massacre that killed 12 in Paris, the Paris attacks a year later that killed 130, the attacks in Brussels, and the almost daily violent atrocities in the Islamic world.

Complained the OIC in its eighth annual report on Islamophobia, "Many prominent speakers on the issue excuse other works of violence, such as those committed by the White Supremacists, Fundamentalist Christians, etc. as the work of 'a few crazy people,' while the violence of Muslim groups was classified by the media as 'dangerous terrorist attacks.' By always casting violence by radical Muslims, in this light, Islamophobia is being cultured in Western minds." The OIC report went on to say that "with ongoing turmoil in the Middle East and the expansion of the jihadist group ISIS, the Islamic faith had increasingly fallen victim to this sort of public prejudice."[1566]

Hmmm, so reports of the massacres perpetrated by ISIS, al Qaeda, and Boko Haram are mere prejudice. Interesting.

Here are two examples of the sort of Islamophobia that the OIC wanted Western nations to stop with "deterrent punishment." As reported in the OIC's eighth report on Islamophobia in 2015:

> Bill Maher, an American comedian while the host of a popular TV program in the U.S., was spouted [sic] in his viral debate in October 2014 with Ben Affleck saying that 'Islam is the mother lode of bad ideas.'[1567]
>
> President Miloš Zeman of the Czech Republic...stated without any doubt in May 2014 that Islamic ideology, rather than individual groups of religious fundamentalists, was behind violent actions similar to the gun attack at the Jewish Museum in Brussels that killed four people. As widely aired by media in that week, two Israeli tourists and a member of the museum staff were killed by an unknown shooter on 24 May 2014 and another staff member died of his injuries on the following day. Zeman's speech sharply condemning the hideous attack, post [sic] on his official website on 27 May 2014, inter alia, stating: "I will not be calmed down by statements that it is only small marginal groups. I believe, on the contrary, this xenophobia and this racism or anti-Semitism stem

from the very nature of the ideology on which these fanatical groups rely." He even said that one of the sacred texts of Islam called for the killing of Jews, so that the President was intentionally trying to link the Islamic ideology with violence.[1568]

Do you see any problems here? Like the attempt to muzzle legitimate criticism of Islam? The attempt to stop the sort of debate with which Martin Luther and Voltaire brought us the Reformation and the Age of Enlightenment? The failure to attempt to stop those who use Islam to justify violence: ISIS, Boko Haram, and al Qaeda? The failure to stand in the way of that violence and to eradicate the terrorists?

Not to mention, outright misrepresentation. OK, let's use the real word: outright lies. Or, as deliberate lying to deceive an enemy is known in Shiite Islam, taqiyya.[1569] Take the OIC complaint that the president of the Czech Republic "said that one of the sacred texts of Islam called for the killing of Jews." The OIC report implies that Zeman's statement about the killing of Jews in the sacred texts of Islam is false. But the sacred texts of Islam *do* call for the killing of Jews. Many times. Remember this quote from the Hadith, one of the most profoundly sacred texts in all of Islam:

> The Hour [the day of judgement] will not take place until the Muslims fight the Jews and the Muslims kill them, and the tree will say: "Oh, Muslim, servant of God, there is a Jew behind me, kill him!"[1570]

The result of pressure from the OIC was a 2011 UN resolution "against intolerance towards all religions." But numerous UN representatives recognized that this was really a resolution against intolerance directed at only one religion: Islam. Meanwhile, the OIC lobbied countries in Europe, South America, and North America to pass laws outlawing insults to religion.

And the OIC campaign worked. It didn't change laws. But something equally important happened. Western intellectuals began to police the critics of Islam. They became internal enforcers of censorship. Why? Why did those who should be the greatest defenders of freedom of speech turn against their own freedom? Because of Western guilt. Guilt over slavery. Guilt over racism against blacks. Guilt over imperialism. Guilt over colonialism. The OIC and its 57 member nations played on that guilt like Mozart playing a piano. The Islam Lobby—the combined PR[1571] and lobbying organizations of 57 Muslim countries—aided by the pressure groups they support, groups like CAIR and the American-Arab Anti-Discrimination Committee, turned us Westerners into our own thought police.

And the OIC did more. It recruited international power players into what the publication *The American Muslim* calls a full-time Islamophobia industry. It pulled in organizations from Britain's Commission for Racial Equality and the Council of Europe to UNESCO and the European Union Agency for Fundamental Rights. In 1995, Jordan's Prince Hassan lectured the UN General Assembly on Islamophobia. In 2011, the ACLU put out a report, *Nothing to Fear: Debunking the Mythical "Sharia Threat."* The Islamophobia industry established its own peer-reviewed journal, *Islamophobia Studies Journal*, and arranged to have it published by Berkeley University's Center for Race and Gender. An *Islamophobia Studies Yearbook*—a peer-reviewed publication—has been put out annually in German and English since 2010. Its goal is to establish courses preaching that Islamophobia is an illness in universities worldwide. To insure that this happens, even on the elementary school level, the Office for Democratic Institutions and Human Rights in Warsaw, Poland, puts out a guidebook called *Guidelines for Educators on Countering Intolerance and Discrimination against Muslims: Addressing Islamophobia through Education.* The Office for Democratic Institutions and Human Rights has had annual roundtables on the topic since 2011. One of those roundtables was hosted in Strasbourg by the Council of Europe. And the *Guidelines for Educators* is published jointly by the Council of Europe and UNESCO.

Meanwhile, in 2010, CAIR, the Council for American Islamic Relations, formed a full-time Islamophobia department that puts out an annual Islamophobia report. Has the Islamophobia Industry accomplished anything? On August 30, 2010, *Time Magazine* did a cover story on Islamophobia. And, brags *The American Muslim*, *The Nation* ran a series on the subject.[1572]

You can see the real intent of the OIC's anti-Islamophobia campaign in its impact on the people that the Muslim community needs the most—its reformers, its liberals, and its moderates. Two of those moderates are Ayaan Hirsi Ali and Asra Nomani. Hirsi Ali, in her 2015 book *Heretic: Why Islam Needs a Reformation Now*,[1573] calls for an Islam that erases violence from its ideology and ends the notion that Islam is forever dominant and must struggle until it brings its "light"—and intolerance—to all of mankind. She calls for an Islam that allows its adherents to participate in a secularized, globalized, modern world. And she calls for an Islam that honors freedom of speech. Her calls for a liberal Islam do not make her popular among the Islamophobia-hunters.

In September of 2013, Hirsi Ali got a phone call from the president of Brandeis University explaining that the institution wanted to honor her with an honorary degree in social justice.[1574] Hirsi Ali had more than earned that degree. As you know, she had come from a primitive Somali family, become a teen enthusiast for jihad, then struggled on behalf of the freedom of 800 million Muslims—the Muslim community's women—and on behalf of freedom of thought for Muslims male and female alike. That took courage. Six months later, the president of Brandeis called with bad news. The university was revoking its invitation. Why? The Council for American Islamic Relations. The Council for American Islamic Relations is an "American" pressure group affiliated with the jihadist Muslim Brotherhood,[1575] funded by Saudi Arabia[1576] and "blacklisted as a terrorist organization by the United Arab Emirates."[1577] CAIR, which also tried to end my publishing career in 1998, had circulated a petition on Change.org accusing Ali of "extreme Islamophobia." Hirsi Ali had also been attacked in letters from 87 Brandeis faculty members. Their complaint?

> I was guilty of suggesting, says Hirsi, that "violence toward girls and women is particular to Islam or the Two-Third World, thereby obscuring such violence in our midst among non-Muslims, including on our own campus [and] ... the hard work on the ground by committed Muslim feminist and other progressive Muslim activists and scholars, who find support for gender and other equality within the Muslim tradition and are effective at achieving it."[1578]

It takes powerfully deficient or powerfully manipulated intellect to say such things. Hirsi Ali was one of the most prominent Muslim "feminist and... progressive Muslim activists" on the planet. And date rape on the Brandeis campus, reprehensible as it is, is nothing compared to stabbing, stoning, or beating your daughters and sisters to death in "honor killings," an all too common practice in the Muslim world. Date rape on American campuses does not justify the beating of women that is recommended[1579] in Shariah law.[1580]

But the Islamophobia campaign had over-ridden common sense. Not to mention truth. Or, as Ali Hirsi put it:

> You who call yourselves liberals must understand that it is your way of life that is under threat. Withdraw my right to speak freely, and you jeopardize your own in the future.[1581]

But Hirsi Ali was not the only Muslim reformer to be attacked by this Westernized blasphemy hunt, this Islamophobia campaign. Asra Nomani is a distinguished female Muslim journalist born in Bombay and raised in West Virginia who worked for Reuters, then was a staff reporter at the *Wall Street Journal* for 11 years. In 2002 a fellow *Wall Street Journal* reporter and close friend, Daniel Pearl, was beheaded by extremists after being kidnapped from Nomani's house in Karachi, Pakistan, where he was living. Nomani started "the Pearl Project, a faculty-student investigation into the murder of *Wall Street Journal* reporter Daniel Pearl,"[1582] despite the fact that Pearl was Jewish, and that the Qur'an says that Allah transformed the Jews into "apes and swine."[1583] Nomani was tolerance incarnate.

In 2003 Nomani challenged the rules that make women shuffle into a mosque through a back door and pray separately from the men. For her effrontery, she was "put on trial at her mosque to be banished."[1584] She responded in the spirit of Martin Luther with "99 Precepts for Opening Hearts, Minds and Doors in the Muslim World."[1585]

In 2005, Nomani wrote a book, *Standing Alone: An American Woman's Struggle for the Soul of Islam*. In it, she describes fighting "the sexism and intolerance in her local mosque" and battling "for the rights of modern Muslim women who are tired of standing alone against the repressive rules and regulations imposed by reactionary fundamentalists."[1586]

In April, 2015, Nomani was invited to speak at Duke University. She wanted "to argue for a progressive, feminist interpretation of Islam."[1587] Then she was hit by the Organization of Islamic Cooperation's Islamophobia hunters. Says she, "the Duke University Center Activities and Events had cancelled my talk after the president of the Duke chapter of the Muslim Students Association sent an email to Muslim students about my 'views' and me, alleging that I have a nefarious 'alliance' with 'Islamophobic speakers' and noting that a Duke professor of Islam, Omid Safi, had 'condemned' me."[1588] Shades of Asia Bibi!

The Duke Muslim Students Association is a member of the national Muslim Students Association, an umbrella organization widely acknowledged to be a front group for the radical Muslim Brotherhood.[1589] Yes, the same Muslim Brotherhood whose head was elected president of Egypt in

2012 and whose motto says, "Allah is our goal, the Prophet is our leader, the Quran is our constitution, Jihad is our way, and death for Allah [martyrdom] is our most exalted wish."[1590] The same Muslim Brotherhood that British Prime Minister David Cameron, after an in-depth government study, called "opaque...secretive," and "counter to British values of democracy, the rule of law, individual liberty, equality and the mutual respect and tolerance."[1591] The Muslim Students Association was set up with money from the Saudis and is one of a phalanx of groups that Saudi Arabia implanted in the West in the 1960s to challenge "'liberal' and 'Westernized'"[1592] Islam and to spread the Saudis' jihadist form of Islam. Many of these groups, says the Center for Security Policy, have been "tightly controlled and financed by the Saudi government and the Wahhabi clergy."[1] The Muslim Students Association has been on the front lines of the OIC's war to stamp out Islamophobia.[1594] And the Duke University branch of the Muslim Students Association used our Western sensitivities about tolerance to level intolerance in Nomani's direction.

When Nomani asked for the "evidence" against her, her invitation to Duke was reinstated. But her talk had been so sullied with accusations of thought crime that only nine people showed up to hear her.

What do Asra Nomani and Ayaan Ali Hirsi have in common? Both of them are calling for a Muslim reformation. They are calling for an overt repudiation by Muslims of Muhammad's murderous side. They are calling for a pluralist, tolerant, free-speech Islam that can exist at peace with the West. And Muslim pressure groups are shutting them out of the very places that are supposed to be the ultimate bastions of debate and self-criticism, universities. These Muslim reformers are being denied their freedom of speech by pressure groups like the Muslim Students Association, organizations that are underwritten by a nation that disseminates one of the most backward-looking forms of Islam on the planet—Saudi Arabia.[1595]

The Islamophobia campaign is an attempt to expand the sort of blasphemy hunting that has put Asia Bibi on death row, that killed Punjab's governor, Salmaan Taseer, and that put garlands of flowers around the neck of Taseer's killer. It is an effort to export that murderous intolerance from Asia and the Middle East to the West—to America and Europe. And it is succeeding. Muslim liberals are being trashed by non-Muslim liberals. Islam's potential reformers are being battered by those who don't realize that the Muslim nations' invention of Islamophobia is a free-speech muzzler. Muslim liberals are assaulted by those who don't realize that Islamophobia hunters damage the Muslim community and give extremists the upper hand. Muslim moderates are assaulted by the intellectual elite and by universities for "insulting the prophet" and "insulting Islam." But Muslim liberals and reformers are not assaulted physically, the way they would be in Saudi Arabia, Bangladesh, or Pakistan. They are not murdered. At least not yet.

Which leaves you and me with an obligation: to defend modernist, pluralist, tolerant Muslims and, yes, Islam's reformers, for all we're worth. They are the hope for a more peaceful world.

*　*　*

There is a trick to the word Islamophobia. A phobia is a mental illness. It's an irrational fear like the fear of spiders (arachnophobia), the fear of snakes (ophidiophobia), the fear of open or public spaces (agoraphobia), or the fear of tiny rooms (claustrophobia). It is a delusion, a phantasm, a mirage. A phobia is a disease you go to a psychotherapist to cure. What's more, the word deliberately plays on Western concerns about racism and anti-Semitism. It plays on our intolerance of intolerance.

But is fear of militant Islam irrational? Is it a delusion and a disease? Were the 2001 attacks on the World Trade Center, the 2005 suicide bombings on London's buses and subways, the 2015 assault on France's Charlie Hebdo, the 2015 six simultaneous attacks on Paris, and the 2016 attacks in Brussels fantasy? Was the war between Islam and the West from 711 A.D. to 1862[1596] a dream? Were events like the 773-year-long takeover of Spain, the attempt to conquer France in 732 A.D., and the sieges of Vienna in 1529 and 1683 phantasms, ghosts, nasty nightmares cooked up by insidious folks who wanted to pick on poor, innocent Islam? Or were these assaults on the West real?

Are al Qaeda, the Islamic State, and Boko Haram real? Or are they, too, racist, xenophobic fantasies? And is there racism and xenophobia in the world of militant Islam? Is there hatred for you and me? Is there, in fact, hatred of everything we stand for—hatred of tolerance, hatred of pluralism, hatred of freedom of speech, and hatred of democracy? Or are these clever fabrications that rabid right-wingers are trying to foist off on you and me to cover for their own nefarious deeds?

Do militant Muslims have a phobia of their own? An irrational hatred of the West? An irrational hatred, in fact, of all non-believers, whether those unbelievers are in the United States, England, France, or China and Thailand? Are beheadings, kidnappings, and mass murders in the Philippines, Kenya, and Nigeria clever hoaxes, insane delusions, or are they a matter of fact? Who has the real phobias, the real irrational hatreds, the activists of ISIS, al Qaeda, and Boko Haram, or you and me?

And one more point. When an irrational fear has a history of motivating conquests, massive, history-changing conquests, is it really irrational? Or is it a turbocharger for a superorganism hungry to increase its sway? Is it a tool of power? A cutting edge with which to change the very face of reality? Is militant Islam's xenophobia a blade in a killing machine? And if it is, why are there no complaints about it? No protests, no words to make it seem diseased, no protesters, no conferences, no attempts to stigmatize kafirophobia. Why no effort by the West to decry the crowds who call for killing in Tehran or Lahore? Does this silence make our intellectual elite accomplices in the mass murders of New York, Paris, and Brussels? And in mass murders yet to come?

*   *   *

Munawar Anees, Kamal Nawash, Ayaan Ali Hirsi, and Asra Nomani are exceptions. Hopeful exceptions. Necessary exceptions. For nearly 1,400 years, the militant form of Islam practiced by Muhammad himself has hijacked Muslim culture and has frightened its liberals into silence. But calling this a hijacking is a bit like saying that Thomas Jefferson and George Washington hijacked American culture. Thomas Jefferson and George Washington are the marrow, meat, and core of American culture. And Muhammad is the marrow, meat, and core of Islam. Mainstream Islam.

Sometimes, a founder IS a culture. It's the founder effect.

Who Is the Real Killer?

"Europe [the West] is nothing but a collection of unjust dictatorships; all of humanity must strike these troublemakers with an iron hand if it wishes to regain its tranquility. If Islamic civilization had governed the West, we would no longer have to put up with these barbaric goings-on unworthy even of wild animals."

—Ayatollah Ruhollah Khomeini, founder of the Iranian Islamic Revolution[1597]

To instill terror into the hearts of the enemy is essential in the ultimate analysis to dislocate his faith. An invincible faith is immune to terror. A weak faith offers inroads to terror. … Terror cannot be struck into the hearts of an army by merely cutting its lines of communication or depriving it of its routes to withdraw. It is basically related to the strength or weakness of the human soul. It can be instilled only if the opponent's faith is destroyed.[1598]

—Brigadier S.K. Malik, in his *Qur'anic Concept of War*

MUSLIM CRITICS POINT TO THE WEST'S bloody track record and tell us that we are the real villains on this planet, not poor, helpless, subjugated, oppressed Muslims. And in part they are right. Our two World Wars in the 20th century killed a combined total of roughly 70 million human beings.[1599] Our two great social experiments—the Marxist-Leninist transformation of Russia, and the Marxist Revolution of Mao Zedong in China, a revolution based on the philosophy of a German Westerner, Karl Marx—killed another 80 million. With our atomic bombs, we Westerners wiped out two Japanese cities in less time than it takes to read this page. Even our conventional weapons in World War II produced firestorms that sucked the oxygen out of the lungs of innocent civilians miles from the center of impact and roasted them alive as they suffocated and died.

What's more, we warred to influence the lives of others in Korea, Viet Nam, and in Algeria, where the French fought from 1954 to 1962 to quash a local War of Independence that cost between 350,000 and 1.5 million lives.[1600] And we invaded Afghanistan and Iraq, killing uncountable numbers of civilians and destabilizing the Middle East.

Like nearly every human tribe that's ever existed, we have been violent, destructive, and greedy for land, wealth, prestige, and power. We have been barbarians.

But, as you've seen, the West has developed something that Islam never achieved—an internal self-correction[1601] mechanism, a protest industry.[1602] In the mid-1780s, the West began a mass movement to stop one of its own nightmarish crimes against humanity…slavery.[1603] A mere 20 years later, the anti-slavery movement began to achieve its purpose. The British Parliament passed the Abolition of the Slave Trade Act on March 25, 1807.[1604] Then, in the 1890s, the West developed a highly organized anti-Imperialist movement,[1605] a movement that eventually forced the nations of Europe to abandon almost all of the foreign lands they had taken.

The West did all of this, in part, because of the Founder Effect. One of its most influential founders, Jesus, preached that the meek shall inherit the earth. Islam uses the Founder Effect to imprison itself. It dictates that there is just one prophet,[1606] and his name is Muhammad. There is just one pattern of personality that all must follow, Muhammad's pattern. In the West we allow ourselves many founders, many role models. One of the most vividly remembered prophets in our pantheon of founding figures was not a warrior and a political leader like Muhammad. He was a man who believed profoundly in ministering to the poor, in turning the other cheek, and in rendering to Caesar what was Caesar's. He believed in separation of church and state. Above all else, he believed in compassion. "Blessed are the merciful, for they shall receive mercy,"[1607] he said. The most savage things he ever did were to send a herd of pigs over a cliff and to curse a fig tree.

The example of that founder, Jesus, stood behind the activists who kicked off the anti-slavery movement in the 18th century, the anti-war movement in the mid-19th century,[1608] the anti-Imperialist movement in the late 19th century, and the human rights movement that began with these shocking words in 1776: "all men are created equal."[1609]

Paul Kengor, a political scientist and historian of the role of religion in the White House, claims that Jesus was a vivid figure in the imaginations of all 43 American presidents from George Washington to George W. Bush.[1610] Jesus was also alive in the mind of Barack Obama.[1611] He was alive in these presidents' guiding ideas and he was alive in their worldviews, in their weave of memes. No matter what crimes these men may have committed against humanity, Jesus was somewhere in their minds saying "no."

It is not easy for me to admit this. I'm a Jew and an atheist. Jesus was, to me, just another nice Jewish kid—not a man in whose name my ancestors or yours should have been killed. But the fact is that in his name you and I have gained many of our freedoms. That's the founder effect.

Ironically, once the West got a conscience, it used its troops to protect Arabs and Islam. In World War I, Lawrence of Arabia helped create the modern sense of Arab identity and solidarity. He united the bickering Arab tribes of the Hijaz, the stretch of sand, stone, and mountains in which Muhammad had lived, so they could fight another group of Muslims who held them in an iron grip—the inheritors of the Ottoman Empire, the folks we call "the Turks."

In 1992[1612], the West mobilized its armies to defend European Muslims who were attacking and were under attack from genocidal neighbors. Bosnia had a Muslim president, Alija Izetbegović.[1613] Yes, a Muslim president. Izetbegović had published a Manifesto in 1970 declaring that, "there can be neither peace nor coexistence between the Islamic faith and non-Islamic social and political institutions" and that "the Islamic movement must and can, take over political power as soon as it is morally and numerically so strong that it can not only destroy the existing non-Islamic power, but also to build up a new Islamic one."[1614] Sound familiar? The Serbians living in Bosnia accurately sensed that this was a declaration of war. A declaration of jihad. We ignored Izetbegović's writings and supported him. We supported a Muslim community led by a man with extremist tendencies.

Meanwhile foreign mujahideen—what Osama bin Laden called "knights" of jihad—trickled into the Balkan areas of the former nation of Yugoslavia in June 1992 to fight the local unbelievers.[1615] These holy warriors were largely Arab veterans of the 1979–1989 war that drove the infidel Soviets out of Afghanistan—the war that brought us al Qaeda and Osama bin Laden. And these holy soldiers were reportedly provided with sophisticated weapons and financing by Iran, Syria, Turkey, Egypt, and Saudi Arabia.[1]

The use of the "terror" that Muhammad had made central to the militant Muslim meme soon reared its head. The Balkan Mujahideen revived an old technique, one straight out of the playbook of Muhammad—beheading. Beheading local Christians then displaying their heads on poles. Sympathetic Muslims around the world purchased videotapes and DVDs of these beheadings and were filled with pride by the sight. But you and I were not supposed to know about these tapes.

Slobodan Milosevic, the *Christian* Serbian leader in the Bosnian neighborhood, built a legitimate complaint over Muslim violence into an excuse for ethnic cleansing and mass murder. His forces attacked Muslim civilians, brutally raped the women and young girls, rounded up the men of fighting age, packed them in trucks, forced them to dig mass graves, then executed them with a bullet to the back of the head, and expelled the women, the children, and the old from the cities and towns in which they and their ancestors had lived for generations.[1617] Teams of memes were duking it out with a vengeance. But when the tide of battle turned dramatically against the Muslims and when over a million Islamic civilians[1618] of the former Yugoslavia had been burned out of—or in—their homes, a United Nations force composed primarily of Americans, British, and Russians came to the Muslims' defense.[1619] The West committed the lives of over 39,000 soldiers—39,000 young Western men and women[1620]—for over ten years at a cost of more than six billion dollars[1621] to end the atrocities perpetrated against Bosnia's Muslims.

What is the difference, then, between Americans and militant Muslims? Why do I claim that they, not we, are the barbarians? It's a question of degree. When Syria's president from 1971 to 2000, Hafez al-Assad, seized power, he ran into violent resistance from Islamic fundamentalists—members of the Muslim Brotherhood. To overcome this opposition, Assad embarked on a mass extermination of over 20,000 fundamentalists in the town of Hama.[1622] Then in 2000, his son, Bashar al-Assad, a man trained as an ophthalmologist in Britain,[1623] took over the family business: running Syria. In 1979 and 1980, Bashar's father had allied with the Iranians and the Russians. The Saudis—who are Sunnis—were afraid that the Shiite Iranians would topple them from power and exterminate or subjugate all of the world's Sunni Muslims. So the Saudis took advantage of the Arab Spring in 2011 to try to roll back Iran's power. To do it, the Saudis tried to use the Arab Spring's street demonstrators to topple Bashar Assad and end his Iranian embrace. Thanks to the Saudis and the Iranians, what began as an Arab Spring in Damascus turned into a proxy war. We know it better as something that it's not—the Syrian Civil War. In reality, it was a sock puppet war between Saudi Arabia and Iran. The Saudis supported the "opposition." And the Iranians supported Bashar al-Assad. With help from the Russians. Lots of help.

Meanwhile, Bashar al-Assad applied the lessons he learned from his dad to hold onto power. One of those lessons: when in doubt, exterminate. The battle over who will rule Damascus killed over 470,000 Syrians[1624] and left more than 11 million[1625] homeless. No American president since the end of the Civil War in 1865 has exterminated his political opponents to secure his position in office.

But mass killing to settle internal domestic matters is not limited to Syria. When Jordan's moderate King Hussein was hosting a mass of Palestinian refugees in his country in the 1960s, he ran into trouble. In 1968 and 1969 the Palestinians kicked off over five hundred violent "incidents," attacking Jordanians, holding them up at gunpoint, kidnapping them, and reportedly killing Jordanian soldiers by hammering nine-inch nails into their heads.[1626] Then the Palestinians went a step farther and tried to assassinate their host, King Hussein, and seize control of Jordan's government. There was a logic to this. Jordan was a new name for 77% of Britain's Palestinian Mandate.[1627] It could be legitimately interpreted as Palestinian land. Hussein solved his problem in 1970 with a military attack on the Palestinians that drove them out of the country...and that killed over 10,000 in the process.[1628] This murderous chain of events, known as "Black September," was started by a highly regarded Muslim politician, Yasser Arafat,[1629] the Palestinian leader who would go on to win a Nobel Peace Prize.[1630]

A Palestinian group called Black September would get its revenge on Jordan by penetrating the 1972 Summer Olympics in Munich, Germany, and killing one German policeman and 11 Olympic athletes.[1631] Israeli athletes. Following the ancient Islamic practice of picking on the nerd.

Nineteenth-century American leaders like Abraham Lincoln and Benjamin Harrison[1632] handled similar problems by doing what Assad and Hussein did—exterminating Native American tribes or mounting internal wars against dissidents like the Mormons[1633] and the Southern Confederates. But it's been over 110 years since an American head of state has followed the example of Assad or King Hussein and killed tens of thousands to solve an internal conflict.

Muslim citizens of the Middle East are frequently encouraged by their leaders to take to the streets and to chant for the death of Americans, Israelis, and Jews. American students at military academies like West Point are also encouraged to shout "Kill! Kill! Kill!"[1634]—a chilling thought. But average civilians like you and me do not take to the streets screaming for the murder of others. Nor would we tolerate it if an organization arose that made such chants fashionable in our country.

But our human rights and the civic habits that support them have been around for a mere 225 years. Militant Islam has been around over six times as long. That's a difference of over a thousand years! And the worldwide superorganism of Islam—its empire—has covered more territory than any other empire in history, has held that territory for over 1,300 years, and has hooked itself into the minds of its conquered peoples with a permanence that our ideals have never achieved—despite the worldwide stretch of CNN, MTV, Google, Facebook, Twitter, and Instagram.

One result? Muhammad's jihadism and totalitarianism are not relics of an antique belief smoothed and gentled by time. The death sentence for leaving Islam is as vigorously alive today as it was in Muhammad's day. No other modern religion dares impose a death sentence for apostasy—for changing your mind and for leaving your old faith behind. But the death sentence for expressing dissent is alive and well in many of the world's 57 Islamic nations. It's not just alive and kicking in Pakistan. Hossein Soodmand was a veteran of the Iranian military who converted to Christianity while he was still in uniform and went to work at the Anglican Christian Hospital in Isfahan.[1635] Yes, a Christian hospital. Soodmand was born into a Muslim family. But he converted to Christianity. That's apostasy. What's worse, when he left Isfahan, he ran a basement church in Mashhad. Soodmand was arrested in April 1990, was repeatedly urged to give up his Christianity and return to Islam, but refused. He was hung on December 3, 1990.[1636]

Look, Islam also has its positives, its memetic seducers. Explains Muhammad Haykal, a member of Islam's overclass, its Arab conquering race, "Muhammad, the pure Arab and pure Semite, was calling men to the monotheistic truth with strong and emphatic words which penetrate to the nethermost depths of consciousness. His revelation overwhelmed and intoxicated the soul. It caused man to transcend himself."[1637] What's more, says Haykal, "(t)he system of principles Islam elaborated came nearer than any other to enable man to attain perfection and to realize the absolute, or the highest ideals in time-space."[1638] And Haykal adds there's yet another memetic lure that draws men and women to Islam. "Muhammad," says Haykal, "achieved...political and worldly power."[1639] And so do those who follow in his footsteps, his followers.

Meme-hooks like these have kept conquered societies in the Islamic fold, bowing five times a day to Mecca, far longer than any peoples conquered by the Romans ever bowed to pagan Rome.

In August 2, 2006, Pulitzer Prize-winning Harvard historian Caroline Elkins[1640] appeared on the *Charlie Rose Show*. Rose billed Elkins as the world's leading historian of imperialism. But this prize-winning historian made a very strange statement. She proclaimed bluntly that no empire in history had ever won the hearts and minds of the people it conquered. She was wrong. Islam won the hearts and minds of its victims so completely that conquered peoples from Algeria to Indonesia[1641]—a stretch of 14,265 miles—still embrace the Middle Eastern belief system that was beaten into their ancestors with terror or that seduced their forefathers and foremothers with the possibility of winning Islam's rewards. Algeria, Indonesia, and 55 nations in between were once conquered peoples or peoples committed to religions like Buddhism and Christianity, yet today they are passionately Muslim.

And Islam still itches to expand.

Said a thoroughly modern, Westernized Cairo constitutional lawyer, Dr. A.K. Aboulmagd[1642] in the 1980s, "I even venture sometimes to say that Islam was not meant to serve the early days of Islam, when life was primitive and when social institutions were still stable and working. It was...meant to be put in a freezer and to be taken out when it will be really needed. And I believe that the time has come. ...The mission of Islam lies not in the past, but in the future."[1643] His view is widespread in the Muslim world.

In other words, a good-hearted, modern, liberal Muslim wearing a Western suit and tie is telling us that the time for the Islamic meme to expand its empire is now. What does that mean for you and me?

The 21st-Century Jihad

"It is our duty to globalize the world around Islam."[1644]
— Saleh Al-Munajjd on Saudi Arabia's Al-Majd TV[1645]

"Western civilization's credibility as the one capable of leading the world to happiness and man to stability— is shaken... Only one nation is capable of resuscitating global civilization, and that is the nation [of Islam]... While the false cultures sink in the swamp... The Islamic message... is to save the human race."
— Sheikh Abd Al-Rahman Al-Sudayyis, Imam of the Al-Haraam mosque in Mecca

"History is not a spectator sport."
— Robert Zubrin

WHEN EVERY CHICKEN KNOWS HER PLACE in the pecking order and puts up with her rank, no matter how lowly, there is farmyard peace. But when a new chicken is tossed into the barnyard and pecking-order positions are up for grabs, all hell breaks loose. There's a brawl. The same thing happens when the geopolitical environment changes. Power vacuums open. Pecking order positions are up for grabs. Among humans, this often leads to conflict...or to outright war.

A radically new geopolitical environment has appeared in the 21st century—a globalized environment, an environment radically transformed by computers, by smart phones, by the Internet, by upgrades in freight transportation, and by the emergence of something we'll get into in a few minutes—mega-markets and mega-organisms, superorganisms whose cells are smaller superorganisms.

Five pecking-order players, five mega-sized superorganisms, are trying to grab top spot in this digitally and demographically upscaled new land of risk and opportunity, in this barnyard shaken by new possibilities. The competitors for lead position at the trough are Europe, the United States, militant

Islam, India, and China. Which one stands the best chance of coming out on top? Which will be most blessed by the rule of the learning machine: to he who hath it shall be given; from he who hath not even what he hath shall be taken away?

China's economy is growing faster than any in the history of mankind. China is the only nation ever to have almost a four-trillion-dollar trade surplus.[1646] And China adds the equivalent of the gross domestic product of one of the world's most successful nations, South Korea, to its GDP every year. That's the productivity of ten South Koreas added to the Chinese economy every decade. The rules of the learning machine often favor economic leaders. "He who gets, gets more," say social learning machine rules, and, "nodes the system finds useful gain strength, influence, and allies." All this may soon put China at the head of the flock.

On the other hand, the economies of most of the world's 57 Islamic nations are doing very poorly,[1647] especially the Muslim economies in the Middle East. Only oil bolsters the wealth of Islam's petrocrats—a fact that's true for half-Muslim Nigeria, for fully Muslim Malaysia, for Muslim Saudi Arabia, and for Muslim Iran. So Islam's future prospects look poor. After all, learning machine rules say that, "He who loses is left out. Nodes that prove useless grow weak, become isolated, or die."

But Islam has two advantages in the global shoving match for top position. Advantage number one: Islam has a stratagem that's been vital to its meme team ever since Muhammad issued his "invitations to the kings"—his ultimatums to the emperors of his day. That trick is Islam's emphasis on the word "one": one God, one prophet, and, most important, one government, one law code, and one unified military system. Yes, one government, one *global* government. That global government is the longed-for caliphate. And it comes along at a time when many Westerners long for a one-world government.

What's a caliphate? It's a central government ruled by one man and one man only—a Commander of the Faithful who runs the sort of kill-the-opposition regime that Muhammad established in Medina and Mecca. The caliphate is not just a militant Muslim fantasy. It existed for 1,292 years, moving from Damascus to Baghdad to Egypt to Spain,[1648] and finally to Istanbul, the captured Christian city of Constantinople.[1649] The caliphs lived in opulence, had enormous harems,[1650] and had the last word on the life or death of every citizen, on the life and death of what some caliphs called every "slave," of their empire. But the empire of Islam was so immense that the caliphs were seldom able to govern it all. The caliphs also couldn't stop the Muslim world's internal battles, battles between leaders, tribes, sects, dynasties, and clans for pecking-order supremacy.

Now with modern technology, Islam's dream of ruling the world from one central city may finally be achievable. It may stand a chance of becoming reality. Islam is the only superorganism with a meme team—a worldview and a "total system of life"—that was built for global rule by its founder.

Islam's second advantage is another direct gift from Muhammad: the eagerness of its militants to solve political disputes with violence. Violence is a potent force multiplier, especially in a world peppered with democratic societies. Hitler never got more than 37.3 percent[1651] of the vote in Germany. Nearly 63 percent of Germans voted against him. Why did the fuehrer with the Charlie Chaplin mustache come out on top? Brute force. Violence. Hitler's brown shirts[1652] and stormtroopers beat people in the streets, broke into their homes, dragged them to "torture cellars,"[1653] and were more than willing to kill.[1654]

When Japan's militant right-wingers wanted to take over their country in 1936, they simply murdered four of the duly elected heads of Japan's democratic government, tried to assassinate the prime minister but accidentally killed his brother instead,[1655] and were able to make policy for the next nine years. No campaigning and electioneering necessary. Violence is a force multiplier.

But Islam takes political violence a step beyond that of the Japanese militarists and Adolph Hitler. The chant among young Muslim jihadists is this: "We love death more than you love life."[1656] Why? Because those who die killing unbelievers have an express ticket to fame, sex, and paradise. The result: suicide bombers. A weapon Jihadists brag that unbelievers simply cannot equal.[1657]

What do these Muslim advantages amount to? To cite Cairo constitutional lawyer Dr. A.K. Aboulmagd[1658] once again: "I even venture sometimes to say that Islam was not meant to serve the early days of Islam.... It was...meant to be put in a freezer and to be taken out when it will be really needed. And I believe that the time has come." One of the bloodiest barnyard battles of the 21st century is a contest to see whether Dr. Aboulmagd is right.

* * *

Meanwhile the very nature of the barnyard has changed. Thanks to globalization, we are undergoing an evolutionary quantum leap. The hunger of meme-teams and the gluttony of superorganisms is shifting from the massive multi-continentalism of Islam's first 1,238 years and of Britain's 19th-century Victorian empire. It is switching to worldview-driven ambitions aimed at domination of the planet. Sometimes better known as "liberation" of the planet.

The West often denies that it wants dominance, yet it coheres around a set of values—of memes, of ideas—that it sees as necessary imperatives for all of the humans on this globe. These include democracy, freedom of speech, gender equality, multicultural tolerance, and human rights...*our* kind of human rights. We Westerners have attempted to spread these memes—these values—through the International Court of Justice, through UN Peacekeepers, and through Non-Governmental Organizations, organizations out to heal the wounds of an injured world.

And we've attempted to spread our worldview through one of our most heavily disguised forms of cultural imperialism—our idealism—our planet-girdling anti-globalist, anti-capitalist, Occupy Wall Street movements. Our Greenpeace, Doctors Without Borders, and Amnesty International style movements. Movements that use smartphones, iPads, wireless connectivity, and laptops to weave formerly isolated peoples into a seven-continent struggle for social justice and for eco-consciousness, a struggle for a global Gaian paradise conceived and led by Westerners.

Even our conservatives are trying to spread their free-market philosophy globally via organizations like the Economic Freedom Network[1659] and the Ayn Rand Institute's Ayn Rand Institute Europe.[1660]

Then there's Roman Catholicism, Mormonism, Pentecostalism, Anglicanism, and Evangelical Christianity, five other carriers of Western values. All are spreading explosively[1661] in lands as far apart as South America, Africa, and Asia, including Russia[1662] and China.[1663]

These culture-crusades hint at our hunger for global unity. More hints that some of us hunger for new forms of global integration come from the birth of supranational organizations like the European Union, NAFTA,[1664] CAFTA,[1665] ASEAN (The Association of Southeast Asian Nations),[1666] APEC (Asia-Pacific Economic Cooperation),[1667] the World Muslim Congress,[1668] the Organization of Islamic Cooperation,[1669] the World Bank, the International Monetary Fund, and the Asian Infrastructure Investment Bank.[1670] China and 14 other Asian nations have created an integrated Asian free-trade zone that boasts 1.7 billion customers, and claims to be the biggest free trade zone in the world.[1671]

What's more, China is building "the largest economic development scheme on the face of the earth"[1672]—a New Silk Road. A new Silk Road that would make the geopolitical quilts of all previous transnational amalgamations look like mere Kleenexes. The New Silk Road will be an 8,077-mile transport belt from China to Europe with Russia and central Asia on its path. It will involve rebuilding ports in foreign countries, installing high-speed rail, laying new pipelines, and constructing new roadways. It is destined to cover "dozens of countries with a total population of over" three billion people.[1673] The Chinese have announced that they will put $46 billion into just one small part of the New Silk Road, the route between China and Pakistan. And China will "inject $62 billion of its foreign exchange reserves into the three state-owned policy banks that will finance expansion of the new Silk Road."[1674] The New Silk Road's rail line for cargo started operation on November 18, 2014, when a train carrying a thousand tons of consumer goods left the city of Yiwu to Madrid 8,077 miles away. Yiwu is one of the biggest wholesale centers for consumer goods on Earth. The journey took 21 days. When high-speed rail is completed, the trip will take two days.[1675]

The Chinese have high hopes for the peace-making power of their New Silk Road. Reports Helen Wang in *Forbes*, "Economic development, as strategists in Beijing argue, will remove the appeal of radical Islam in China and Pakistan, Afghanistan and central Asia."[1676] That seems highly unlikely. But it's a nice wish. There's another Chinese wish behind the New Silk Road: to eclipse the United States in global power.

Then there's what China has been up to in the Western Hemisphere. China's quietly moved to spread its influence in a way that defies its old rules of empire. Those ancient ways of doing things involved expanding by conquering the nations conveniently located on the Chinese borders. When it came to distant foreigners, the Chinese emperors didn't leave their palaces.[1677] They required the pitiful barbarians to send emissaries who arrived in the Chinese court bowing, scraping, and bearing gifts.[1678]

But in 2001 Chinese president Jiang Zemin did something utterly unprecedented—something utterly un-Chinese. He left Beijing and went on an international tour, visiting six Latin American nations, signing cooperation agreements, and calling "on China and Latin America" to work toward building what he called "a new international order," an order designed "as a counterbalance to what it [China] views as overwhelming American hegemony."[1679]

Three years later, in November, 2004, Chinese President Hu Jintao followed up Jian Zemin's performance by flying to Brazil, Argentina, Chile, and Cuba and signing a total of 39 strategic partnership and bilateral cooperation agreements.[1680]

Then China got even more cheeky. It convinced the European Union to enter a strategic partnership that would include "cooperation in banking and international finance, energy and raw materials, anti-terror and nuclear nonproliferation, [and] technology transfer."[1681] By 2016, the EU website on the Strategic Partnership explained that "the 1985 EU-China trade and cooperation agreement has grown to include foreign affairs, security matters and international challenges such as climate change and global economy governance."[1682] The website explained that "The EU is... China's biggest trading partner." And the Strategic Partnership issued an EU-China 2020 Strategic Agenda for Cooperation. That 2020 Strategic Agenda revealed that "creation of the EU-China Comprehensive Strategic Partnership in 2003 has deepened and broadened cooperation in a wide range of areas, and the EU and China have become highly interdependent as a result."[1683]

China appeared to be quietly positioning itself for the day when Islam and the United States would bleed each other into exhaustion, allowing the growing Chinese megapower to step in and become the new hegemon, the new alpha superorganism in the global pecking order, the master of the "New International Order"[1684] that Jiang Zemin spoke of, the keeper of a new planetary peace.

Whether China succeeds in its ambition to make this the Chinese Century or not, one thing is certain. We are witnessing the emergence of a new form of memetic struggle—a struggle between superorganisms more massive than any social structures the human race has ever seen. Perhaps we should call these new politico-cultural blocs mega-organisms. Why? The populations of Islam, China, and India are *each* bigger than the entire human population on this planet in 1850. In that peak year of the Industrial Revolution, there were 1.2 billion[1685] *Homo sapiens* spreading their genes and their ideas, and working hard to make riches from the minerals, plants, and animals on this globe. In 2012, the number of Muslims alone trumped that figure dramatically. It was, as we've seen before, 1.6 billion.[1686] In 2013, the number of Chinese was also bigger than the entire population of humans on this planet in 1850. It was 1.357 billion.[1687] And the number of Westerners was a paltry 760 million.[1688] But even that was more than the total human population of the planet in 1700.[1689]

When there are shakeups in a barnyard pecking order, that's when upstarts can step in and take over. And takeover is jihadism's goal. Global takeover. That's been the goal for nearly 1,400 years.

*   *   *

Militant Islam's response to the shift from superpowers to megapowers has been what we call "terrorism." That word radically underrates the militants' true aim—a thrust for a revival of the pecking order supremacy that Islam held from roughly 637[7] A.D. to 1827[8]—a renewal of the global battle between Dar el Harb and Dar el Islam. As one highly influential handbook for jihad—*The Management of Savagery* by Abu Bakr Naji—puts it, it's time to build a "bridge to the Islamic state which has been awaited since the fall of the caliphate" by running non-believers through "the stage of 'the power of vexation and exhaustion,' then the stage of 'the administration of savagery,' then the stage of 'the power of establishment—establishing the state.'"[1690] Establishing the caliphate.

Attacks on civilians in Paris and Brussels are manifestations of "the stage of 'the power of vexation and exhaustion'" and "the stage of 'the administration of savagery.'"

Thanks to the Internet, the electronically augmented jihad went global as early as August 23, 1996, when Osama bin Laden's "First Bayan (Statement)," his "Declaration of War Against the Americans," was spread by the World Wide Web. In the next decade, the dot.com Jihad murdered victims and terrorized non-believers in India, Kashmir, the Philippines, Thailand, South Africa, Bosnia, Chechnya, Moscow, China, Kenya, the Sudan, Somalia, Nigeria, New York, Washington, Paris, Madrid, London, Brussels, and even in the Caribbean nation of Trinidad and Tobago, where the nation's militant Muslims, led by the group Jama'at al Muslimeen, attempted a violent takeover of the government as long ago as 1990.[1691] Western newspapers shut their eyes and pretended that this worldwide Holy War was merely a series of local "separatist" incidents. It was not.

---

7. When the Muslim armies defeated the Sassanian Persians, sacked their capital Ctesiphon—the home base of Nestorian Christianity—and conquered most of Iraq.

8. When the English, French, and Russians allied and destroyed the Ottoman-Egyptian fleet.

The Ayatollah Khomeini, whose words are revered in Iran as the founding principles of today's Iranian Islamic Republic, let you and me know that we are the intended victims of global jihad when he said something that bears repeating:

> "Muslims have no alternative... to an armed holy war against profane governments. ...Holy war means the conquest of all non-Muslim territories. ...It will ...be the duty of every able-bodied adult male to volunteer for this war of conquest, the final aim of which is to put Qur'anic law in power from one end of the earth to the other. ...all other wars of conquest... are unjust and tyrannical and disregard the moral and civilizing principles of Islam."[1692]

Just in case you and I thought that we weren't targets of this "war of conquest," Khomeini told us exactly where we stood in his world and in the world of the Iranian Republic he founded: "The leaders of the USSR and of England and the president of the United States," he said, "are ...infidels..." OK, so our leaders were on the Ayatollah's hit list. But surely those of us who demonstrate for peace and human rights will be spared. Or will we? Remember, the Ayatollah insists, "Every part of the body of a non-Muslim individual is impure, even the hair on his head and his body hair, his nails, and all the secretions of his body. Any man or woman who denies the existence of God, or believes in His partners [Jesus Christ, the Holy Ghost, and the Virgin Mary], or else does not believe in His Prophet Muhammad, is impure (in the same way as are excrement, urine, dog, and wine)[sic]." Impure—that was a death sentence for Asia Bibi. But when it comes to you and me, that isn't too bad. Is it?

Here's the Ayatollah's kicker: "Islam does not allow peace between... a Muslim and an infidel."[1693] The Ayatollah explains that Islam has been forced to "obliterate many tribes"[1694] to defend the purity of Islam. Yes, he said "obliterate." As in mass murder and genocide. Others put it differently. They call for "The Annihilation of the Infidels."[1695] In fact, "annihilation of the infidels" is a phrase that's repeated many a time by modern militant Muslim leaders. Why? Because it's in the Qur'an.[1696] Because it comes from Muhammad's extermination of the males of the Jewish Banu Quraiza in 627 A.D. Writes Seif Al-Din Al-Ansari, a militant writer for the online Islamic magazine *Al-Ansar*, "The Annihilation of the Infidels is a Divine Decree."[1697] Period!

The battle between meme teams and the superorganisms they assemble is serious stuff. It puts you and me in the cross-hairs. And it's evolving. Its nature is changing day by day.

*   *   *

Jihadism's grab for the gold ring, the global gold ring, in this rapidly shifting game is driven by Muhammad, his words, his life, and the example he set in 65 military campaigns. It is driven by his lessons about how to conquer using "guile" and "terror." And it is driven by Muhammad's demand that Islam conquer the world.

Is Militant Islam Real?

FROM 1992 TO 2001, Abul Aziz Said,[1698] John L. Esposito,[1699] Edward Said,[1700] and Phebe Marr,[1701] all recognized experts, delivered what sounded like a perfectly reasonable message. Extremist Islam does not pose a threat to the West. Then came a series of attacks in New York, London, Madrid, Paris, and Brussels hinting that the claims of the experts were radically off base. Attacks that killed 3,389.[1702]

Yet the claim that an Islamic enemy is an artificial creation, the product of a scare campaign mounted by the right wing, continues to pop up over and over again. Why?

Because the right-wingers do, in fact, often benefit from the threat posed by militant Islam...no matter how real that threat. Companies in the Bush family's clique—corporations like the mega-oil-services-and-construction corporation Halliburton[1703] and like the mega-engineering firm Bechtel[1704] —made [1705] a jaw-dropping $42.3 billion[1706] from just the War in Iraq. Add in the dollars from America's war in Afghanistan and from the 1990–1991 Gulf War, and you are talking money. You can frost that greenback-cake with the fact that American president George W. Bush used the public's highly emotional reaction to 9/11 to boost his approval ratings.

But why is the threat of jihadism real? Not because of American right-wingers. Because of Muhammad. Because of his deliberate legacy. Because of his social engineering. Masterful social engineering. Some of the best social engineering in history. And some of the most enduring. But social engineering based on a love of murder, a hatred of dissent, and a brilliant but savage use of terror.

*   *   *

There's another factor at work beneath the surface—racism. Racism that's the very opposite of the "prejudice" that the Organization of Islamic Cooperation and its Islamophobia hunters are determined to stamp out.

The "Islamic-threats-are-phony" arguments are driven by a need that rats, dogs, and humans share, the need for an illusion of control. Let's go back to the poor lab rats and dogs who were tortured by experimental psychologists to give us insight into our emotions. And let's dive into evidence from the phenomenon that its discoverers call "learned helplessness." In 1968, Rockefeller University's Jay Weiss hooked the tails of 192 rats to a live electric wire. He gave some of the rodents a control switch, but left the others to simply grin and bear the pain. When a jolt of electricity struck, the unsuspecting rodents would at first scurry and jump to find a quick way out. The luckier of the beasts would soon discover their control buttons. When the current sizzled their sterns, they would lunge for the switch and turn it off, rescuing both themselves and their switchless fellow sufferers. Remember, both the rats with control and those without it were hooked to the same live wire. Both were jolted with shocks at the very same time. And both were saved when the rat with the switch cut the juice. Yet some of the rats whose frantic searches resulted in no discovery of a means of control would eventually give up their struggle, lie down on the cage floor, and accept their shocks with an air of resignation. Even worse, the rats without the control levers would end up physical wrecks—scrawny, unkempt, and ulcerated—while those who could slam the current off stayed reasonably plump and fit. All this despite the fact that each and every rat received exactly the same surge of current for exactly the same amount of time and at exactly the same instant. But here's the bottom line: Rats with a control button stayed relatively active. Their health held up. So did their ability to perceive.[1707] Whether we are rats, dogs, or human beings, we all need a sense of control.

The Islamic apologists promote the view that no one would dislike us if we simply rid ourselves of right-wing scaremongers and stopped occupying Islamic lands. And the folks on the far *right* are just as convinced that things would go much better for America if we could only rid ourselves of liberals, the politically correct, and the "left-leaning media." Not to mention homosexual plotters, abortion supporters, promoters of evolution, and godless secularists. Then there are the 9/11 conspiracy theorists, who want us to sic our dogs on rogue CIA agents and the Mossad. And there are the folks who believe that ISIS was created by the very same villains—the CIA and the Mossad. Both the right and the left push the notion that we can solve our problems and eliminate all threats by purging ourselves of despicable internal cancers. Both the right and the left promote the illusion that we have a button at our fingertips with which we can turn off our punishment. Both the left and right use the primitive and profoundly foul instinct that hits seven rats on a hot plate. An instinct to solve the problem of the moment by picking on someone weak and beating the bejeezus out of him. Someone in our own community.

Charlie Wilson's War, the book that George Crile of *60 Minutes* wrote after his dinner with me in 1988, says that we created al Qaeda. Yes, our politicians and our CIA, Crile implies, made al Qaeda the way that Jehovah made man out of mud. And he's partly right. But only partly. To repeat, he neglects Islam's nearly 1,400-year tradition of multi-continental jihad. He neglects 1,388 years of jihadism against the West. And against the rest. The rest of the world. He neglects jihadism's nearly 1,400-year-long war against us unbelievers. And he neglects the way in which Muhammad laid jihad as a cornerstone in the architecture of worldwide Islam. He overlooks the fact that, in the words of Usaama bin Abdullah al Khayyat, imam of the Sacred Mosque in Mecca, "The Prophet ...exerted maximum effort to instill...the concept of Jihaad deep into the hearts of his companions and his followers who were to come after him."[1708]

Why do persistent claims that our enemies are within reveal a peculiar form of racism? Because these beliefs assume that only we omnipotent Westerners can do evil deeds. Worse, these beliefs assume that those outside of our own society are primitive pygmies, too weak to endanger us, too weak to make...and to change... history. This is racism in reverse! And it's wrong. Profoundly wrong.

Militant Islam has been making history for close to 1,400 years. It has been girdling the globe and imposing its rule for six times as long as the United States has existed. And it wants to fulfill a mission—to rule the Earth. All of it. Where did militant Islam get that mission? From Muhammad. Now how we confront Muhammad's legacy is up to you and me.

* * *

On April 16, 2015, in the Pakistani city of Lahore, a woman was driving her car to work. She was Debra Lobo, a 55-year-old American who had married a Christian professional from Pakistan in 1998 and had moved to Karachi, where she was "vice principal for student's affairs at Karachi Medical and

Dental College and a professor of community medicine."[1709] On Shaheed-e-Millat road—a four-lane boulevard bulging with ultra-modern architecture and named for one of Pakistan's founding fathers[1710]—a motorbike pulled alongside her. On it were two men. One aimed a gun at Lobo and fired. Lobo was hit by bullets. One tore through one of Lobo's cheeks and exited out the other. The second bullet hit her arm. She was rushed to Aga Khan Hospital. And she lived. But something crucial came from this failed assassination. It was the printed flyer the gunmen left behind. The flyer was from a Pakistani branch of ISIS, the Islamic State, a state that's working hard to be a worldwide caliphate, a one-world government. Here's a part of the flyer's text:[1711]

> "We Will Burn America"
> O Crusaders! We are the Lions of Daulah
> Al-Islamiyyah, the Falcons of our Caliph.
> Today we killed this Kansas lady 'Lobo.'
> We shall lie in wait until we ambush you and kill
> you wherever you may be until we confine and
> besiege you in America and then God willing,

WE Will BURN AMERICAN!

Who do you suspect inspired these words, the CIA? Or Muhammad?

Some enemies are false. They don't exist. Some enemies are real. Which is militant Islam?

What Jihadists Want From You

ON MAY 12, 2004, Osama Bin Laden, a leader whose words are still held in high regard,[1712] explained what he and other leaders like him want from you and me. In a message to the worldwide community of Islam he wrote, "The main confrontation," is "a religious and doctrinal one, not an economic or military one." "The clash," he said, "is in fact a clash of civilizations"[1713]—a clash of ideas, a clash of views of the world. In other speeches, Bin Laden said that only one form of government is permissible in this world—government based on the laws that God himself gave to Muhammad in the seventh century, shariah, strict Qur'anic law. Any other form of government, he said with emphasis, is "horrific."[1714]

For those of us who still didn't get it, Osama spelled out our democracy's most appalling sin. "Rather than ruling by the Shariah of Allah in its Constitution and Laws, [you] choose to invent your own laws as you will and desire."[1715] Continued an outraged Osama, you refuse to "accept Islam to be the source of all legislation."[1] In other words, instead of ruling by a religious code of law—by the only religious code of law given to humans by God himself—you and I dare elect parliaments and congresses to do something Satanic: to flick a finger in the face of God and to write man-made laws. Said Osama, this is why "Democracy [is] the faith of the ignorant" and secular "freedom" is a Satanic "lie."[1]

"Why are we fighting and opposing you?" asked Osama. "What are we calling you to, and what do we want from you? The first thing that we are calling you to is Islam. The religion of the Unification of God; of freedom from associating partners with Him [Islamic code for Christianity], and rejection of this; of complete love of Him, the Exalted;" Then Osama commanded us to "the discarding of all the opinions, orders, theories and religions which contradict with the religion He sent down to His Prophet Muhammad."[1718]

In other words, Osama called for a worldwide end to Christianity, Buddhism, Judaism, yoga, New Age beliefs, Marxism, secularism, humanism, atheism, Darwinism, constitutions, and separation of church and state.

It should have come as no surprise, then, that on October 17, 2004, in London, three highly articulate, intelligent, British-born Muslims were part of a London street mob that shouted, "Make way for Islam, we want Islam."[1719] A CNN cameraman asked these gentlemen what their beef was. The middle-class, Western-dressed British Muslims answered that their version of Islam "is not just a hatred for America. It is a hatred for the whole of Western philosophy and Western civilization, freedom, democracy, human rights, international law, all of these fake concepts that have been passed to us and behind that we have been oppressed. It is a hatred of all of this."[1720]

In other words, extremist Islam is a hatred of everything that you and I believe in. But it is more than mere animosity. It is a manifestation of a multi-generational enterprise to wipe things like democracy and human rights off the face of the Earth.

To drive home that point, on November 2, 2004, in Amsterdam, the 26-year-old Dutch Moroccan Muslim who butchered filmmaker Theo Van Gogh while he was bicycling[1721] left a message pinned to van Gogh's body with a knife. You recall that the young "knight"[1722] of jihad imitated the killers of Ka'b the poet. He slashed Van Gogh's throat, tried to decapitate him, repeatedly stabbed Van Gogh's body, then drove a knife to the hilt into the corpse's chest. Finally, he used a smaller knife to hold up a five-page "open letter" that predicted the downfall of the "infidel enemies of Islam" and that stated, "I know definitely that you, Oh America, will go down. I know definitely that you, Oh Europe, will go down. I know definitely that you, Oh Netherlands, will go down."[1723] How very Muhammad.

But we Westerners weren't the only ones on the receiving end of modern Islam's lunge to have it all, to take this globe for Muhammad. From January 2004 to July 2005 in southern Thailand, an ongoing jihad killed 860 Thais in 18 months. As you've seen, vendors at Thailand's mosques sold CDs of beheadings with titles like "Jihad in Chechnya 2000." Buddhist monks were slashed to death and Buddhist temples bombed. Grocers were threatened for selling pork. Twenty-five teachers were killed for teaching the "idol worship" of Buddhism and the godlessness of modern secularism instead of the one and only truth that children need in life—Islam. In the spirit of Muhammad's treatment of many of his victims, the severed heads of the Buddhists were left in prominent places as a warning to unbelievers.[1724]

At the same time, on January 3, 2004, in Kashmir—a territory wedged between Muslim Pakistan and Hindu India—two mujahideen—makers of jihad—attacked a crowded railway station and killed four security men, then were mowed down by counter-fire.[1725] The attackers' goal was to liberate Kashmir from the "pagans," "polytheists," and "idol-worshippers" of Hindu and Buddhist India and to put Kashmir under Islamic rule. As of March 31, 2016, CNN calculated that the modern jihad over Kashmir had killed 47,000 people.[1726] But way back in 2004, AP had a higher figure. It estimated the death toll at 65,000.[1727] In fact, the toll was far higher. CNN and AP overlooked a key fact: that Islam's war to take over this region of the world had been going on for 1,375 years.

Roughly three weeks later, on February 27, 2004, a bomb on a SuperFerry[1728] near Manila in the Philippines killed 116 people. The Philippine jihadist group Abu Sayyaf claimed the credit.[1729]

Then, on March 11, 2004, 13 bombs on commuter trains in Spain were triggered to explode simultaneously at the height of Madrid's rush hour. Ten went off, killing 191 people and wounding 1,460.[1730] Al Qaeda in Europe claimed responsibility. Said al Qaeda's taped statement, "You love life and we love death, which gives you an example of what the prophet Muhammad said...the blood will flow more and more, and these attacks will seem very small."[1731] The founder effect was still very much alive in the modern world.

And the use of Muhammad's techniques of surprise, ambush, and terror worked.[9] They achieved something we thought only we imperialist Americans could pull off—regime change. The bombings convinced voters in the Spanish elections that took place three days after the attack to toss out their conservative government and to vote in socialists who promised to give the Muslims more of what they demanded.

In 2011[1732] ISIS picked up where Osama bin Laden left off. And, like the British Muslims in the streets of London, ISIS targeted a key set of Satanic horrors: democracy, human rights, freedom, nationalism, and minority rights.[1733]

---

9. In 1127 A.D. the Spanish-born traveler and scholar Abu Bakr Muhammad ibn al-Walid al-Tartushi, Abu Bakr of Tortosa, went through the holy books of Islam and the books of fiqh, the collected rulings of Islamic scholars, to derive God's own laws for warfare, the stratagems used by Allah's one true prophet, Muhammad. He came to the conclusion, "As to those whom it is lawful to slay, the fiqh declares that a Muslim in war may slay any unbeliever (idolater) whether combatant or not" and "...war means deception... the most effective stratagem in war is the ambush. Not too many men must be employed in it; one good one being better than ten thousand others...in surprise lies destructive effect." Reuben Levy, *The Social Structure of Islam: Being the Second Edition of the Sociology of Islam*. Cambridge, England: Cambridge University Press, 1957. p. 456.

The casualties in the worldwide rash of operations like this, military assaults from Moscow to Malaysia, were less than the combined total of deaths in America's wars in Viet Nam and Iraq. But that will not always be the case. On August 18, 2004, Iranian Revolutionary Guards intelligence theoretician Hassan Abbassi reportedly taped a speech discussing an Iranian "strategy drawn up for the destruction of Anglo-Saxon civilization." He explained, "There are 29 sensitive sites in the U.S. and in the West. We have already spied on these sites and we know how we are going to attack them."[1734]

This claim sounds ridiculous. But on September 9, 2004, Iran launched a missile with a range of 1,200 miles—meaning this weapon could reach the more than 150,000 U.S. troops stationed in the Middle East at the time.[1735] It could also reach Russia, Turkey, Saudi Arabia, India, and Israel, a country Iran's leaders have repeatedly said must be "wiped off the face of the map."[1736]

Meanwhile, as long ago as 2004, the world suspected that Iran was developing nuclear warheads for these missiles.

To drive home the seriousness of its military threat, Iran ran a highly publicized series of war exercises in April 2005. It named the exercises for the world's first jihadist, "The Holy Prophet." The Iranians showed off five new varieties of allegedly homegrown and home-built highly sophisticated missiles.[1737] And on April 12, 2006, Iran's president, Mahmoud Ahmadinejad, went on national television to make what was calculated to be a stunning statement: "I formally declare that Iran has joined the club of nuclear countries."[1738]

This wasn't as surprising as it seemed. In 1998, Pakistan, one of the two most populous Islamic nations in the world,[1739] tested what the country's Prime Minister Zulfikar Ali Bhutto proudly called "The Islamic Bomb,"[1740] Islam's first nuclear weapon. Metallurgical engineer Dr. A.Q. Khan,[1741] the "Father of the Islamic Bomb" became a national hero, and helped his country stockpile an arsenal of small, powerful nuclear warheads. Way back in 1987, Iran was the first customer[1742]—and thus a key financier—for Dr. Khan's nuclear warhead business.[1743] As early as 1987,[1744] Khan was selling Iran centrifuge parts and plans[1745] and what *The Washington Post*'s Dafna Linzer calls "a starter kit for uranium enrichment...[and] the makings of a nuclear weapons program."[1746] Then, on February 4, 2004, the Pakistani government gave in to American pressure and put Dr. Khan under house arrest.[1747] An initial spate of information indicated that Khan had been selling atomic-bomb-making equipment along with Chinese plans for sophisticated, compact nuclear warheads to North Korea and Libya. Some reports also claimed that Khan had close ties to the early 21st century's most prominent leader of Jihad, Osama bin Laden.[1748]

On December 24, 2004, American intelligence officials were shocked to discover that Dr. Khan's Islamic nuclear network went much farther than they thought. In fact, it had "tendrils...in more than 30 countries" including Afghanistan, Egypt, Iran, Ivory Coast, Kazakhstan, Kenya, Mali, Mauritania, Morocco, Niger, Nigeria, North Korea, Saudi Arabia, Senegal, Sudan, Syria, Tunisia, and the United Arab Emirates.[1749] Intelligence officials wondered, "what other countries, or nonstate groups, beyond Libya, Iran and North Korea, received what one Bush administration official called Dr. Khan's 'nuclear starter kit.'"[1750] Khan's package deal for his "starter kit" worked like this: buy a hundred million dollars' worth of nuclear equipment and Khan threw in the plans for a thoroughly tested, ultra-compact, Chinese-designed, missile-ready nuclear warhead for free. The suspected list of customers included Syria, Egypt, Saudi Arabia, Sudan, Malaysia, Indonesia, Algeria, Kuwait, Myanmar, and Abu Dhabi.

Western stories about A.Q. Khan failed to reveal something even more ominous. In 2002, Pakistan had two[1751] superstealth[1752] Agosta 90B attack submarines[1753] built with technology purchased from France's Direction de Construction Naval International—an arm of the French Navy responsible for developing and manufacturing all of France's next-technology ships.[1754] In 2005, using the French technology, the Pakistanis completed the construction of a third Agosta 90B superstealth sub in their Karachi Naval Shipyard.[1755] Each of these subs carries 16 cruise missiles,[1756] missiles that can be equipped with nuclear warheads.[1757] More important, the range of these submarines is 11,000 miles.[1758] In other words, these subs can easily reach England, France, and the United States. And their missiles are capable of targeting roughly 35% of the American population.[1759] According to the U.S. Navy, the ships are nearly undetectable using current sonar.[1760]

What's more, in 2015 Pakistan concluded a deal with the Chinese to buy eight Chinese S-20 stealth subs.[1761] Again, the Pakistanis wanted more than just the vessels. They wanted the know-how to make the subs on their own. So the deal required the Chinese to establish a training facility in Karachi, to build four of the subs in Chinese shipyards, and to teach the Pakistanis how to build four subs in Karachi. Each of these S-20 submarines can launch 18 nuclear-tipped Babur missiles with a range of 435 miles. And each sub has a range of 9,206 miles, not quite enough to reach New York or the coasts of

Maryland near Washington, but easily able to reach the coasts closest to London, Paris, and to Islam's long-lusted-for prize in Europe, Rome.

Because of possible support for extremists like ISIS' Abu Bakr al-Baghdadi in the Pakistani military,[1762] because of over 20 years[1763] of intense support for terrorist groups in the powerful Pakistani Inter-Services Intelligence agency,[1764] and because of support for militants in the Pakistani population[1765]—because of the sort of sentiments that made the killer of Punjab's governor a national hero—there is a significant risk that the subs may someday fall into militant hands.[1766] Jihadist hands.

Topping it all, in 2015 Pakistan revealed that it was developing "tiny" nuclear devices. These were designed to nuke Indian troops in battle. They were tactical weapons. But imagine how handy they would be for terrorists. One result: Georgetown University's C. Christine Fair, a leading expert on the Pakistani military, reported that Pakistan has "the fastest growing nuclear arsenal" in the world and estimated that "within the next five to ten years, it is likely to double that of India, and exceed those of France, the United Kingdom, and China."[1767] In fact, Pakistan in 2015 had four plutonium production reactors and was cranking out new nuclear weapons at the rate of 20 per year.[1768]

But these are not the only ways in which jihadist, militant Islam, Muhammad's own form of Islam, was arming for new forms of battle in the age of mega-organisms. Between 1982 and 2006, Iran supplied its Lebanese surrogate, Hezbollah, with over 20,000[1769] rockets, rockets intended to help Hezbollah[1770] achieve the prime goal of Hezbollah's founding document—the "obliteration" of Israel.[1771] Today that number of rockets tops 100,000.[1772] These were rockets that Hezbollah could test by launching them at Israeli towns like Tsfat and Tiberias and cities like Haifa and Nazareth[1773] so that their shortcomings could be analyzed and their technology upgraded.[1774] They were also rockets that Hezbollah could use to follow Muhammad's founding pattern—do something grisly to the little guys, something so grisly that it terrorizes the big guys into surrender. The little guys Allah himself had picked as Islam's permanent scapegoats, as its easy targets, as its nerds, were, of course, the Jews.

Meanwhile the Muslim world's publicists, PR and lobbying firms,[1775] and propaganda specialists were softening up the West for the extermination of Israel by demonizing the Jewish nation in the Western press. How? Iran's proxy in Lebanon, Hezbollah, built weapons bunkers[1776] close to towns and near a UN outpost,[1777] built a command bunker and above-ground compound in a heavily populated suburban Beirut neighborhood,[1778] positioned its artillery pieces between apartment buildings,[1779] and prepared to fire its rockets from what the Australian *Sunday Mail* called "high density residential areas"[1780]—including the balconies of high-rise apartment buildings in Beirut's eastern suburbs. Then it started a war, forcing the Jews to aim their weapons at civilians. Next Hezbollah operatives set up checkpoints, stopped journalists, seized all film and footage of Hezbollah's war-making,[1781] and made up for it by giving reporters and camera crews guided tours of the hospitals where wounded children lay dying. Though the wounds these children endured were the result of a deliberate Hezbollah strategy, Hezbollah's attempt to portray the Israelis as child-killers in the Lebanon War of 2006 succeeded. A nation that kills seven-year-olds deserves annihilation, doesn't it?

The strategy worked. In fact, it worked so well that another Iranian ally, Hamas, adopted it in 2014 when it used rocket attacks on civilian targets in Israel to start a war in Gaza. Four thousand rocket attacks. Because Hamas placed its weapons next to, on top of, and on the balconies of schools, hospitals, and homes, Israel's counterattack killed 2,142 civilians. And that was the plan. Create headlines demonizing Israel. Use civilians as human shields so that Israel's defensive strikes could be portrayed as the deliberate murder of women and children.[1782]

And on March 9, 2016, after signing a deal with America promising not to develop nuclear weapons, Iran broke a prohibition placed upon it by a United Nations resolution, Resolution 2231, and launched two 1,200-mile-range sophisticated, high-accuracy missiles capable of carrying nuclear warheads. The hulls of the rockets were decorated with these words painted in Farsi and Hebrew: "Israel must be wiped off the Earth."[1783] The quote was taken from the revered founder of Iran's Islamic Revolution: the Ayatollah Khomeini.

The inscription was designed to flaunt Iran's commitment to the extermination of what it calls "the Zionist entity." For the most part, the Western press, attempting not to wound Islamic sensibilities, failed to report the missile's official—and genocidal—graffiti. The Organization of Islamic Cooperation's Islamophobia campaign worked wonders.

Those who see a mass murder about to happen and fail to try to stop it are accomplices. What does that make the Western press?

* * *

Muhammad's strategy for taking Mecca peacefully was to attack the Jewish Banu Quraiza and the Jewish city of Khaibar, using gruesome victories over the Hebrews to terrify the Meccans into surrendering without a fight. If Iran or its puppet, Hezbollah, nuke Israel, which big guys might they terrify into surrender? What nations might cave in to what Islamic scholar and TV personality Ali Mazrui calls "Islamization"[1784]? My guess is that the surrender-target is the remaining slice of "Rome"[1785] and "the West"[1786] that Allah promised to Muhammad—all of Europe.

*   *   *

Look, those who want to "annihilate" us are not madmen. They're rational and they're something more—they're idealists. Militant Islam is out to save you and me. If we are tricked into following false laws, believing in false gods, and sticking to what Osama bin Laden called false "opinions, orders [and] theories,"[1] if we follow the "scientific method"[1788] that ISIS despises, we will go to an unspeakably painful hell. Our earthly life is but a brief interlude, a brief test, an entrance exam, an SAT, to see if we can follow God's path. But the real prize—admission to hell or heaven—is forever. Militant Islam wants to save you so you can spend the time that really matters, the time that lasts the longest, the time from your death to the Day of Judgement, in the luxurious upper rooms of paradise. Only if your eyes are opened to the example of Muhammad, only if you are persuaded to drop all other "opinions, orders, theories"[1789] and religions, only if you live under God's own legal code, Shariah,[1790] can Islam save you.

What happens if you stubbornly refuse Islam? What happens if you cannot be won over to the light? You must be wiped out. Why? To keep you from corrupting the minds of others and dragging them down to hell with you.

Could Islam's superstealth subs and nuclear missiles someday give substance to the words of a Saudi al Qaeda leader, Louis Attiya Allah, in January 2004? Said Attiya Allah, the next attack against America "will be a surprising blow, that is, one that is completely unexpected. They cannot conceive or imagine the way in which it will be carried out... It is a great blow. That is, the losses that will be caused to America and the Western world in its wake will be very great. Due to its magnitude, the blow will change the international balances of powers..."[1791] And could the Pakistani stealth submarines and Pakistani nuclear weapons someday give reality to a statement reported by the Associated Press in May 2004 that "An al-Qaida leader has said 4 million Americans will have to be killed 'as a prerequisite to any Islamic victory.'"[1792]

Could a hungry militant Islamic superorganism really use nuclear weapons to expand, to achieve "victory" over what Osama bin Laden called "the worst civilization witnessed by the history of mankind"[1793]—our civilization? Surely the jihadis would be deterred by the fact that any nuclear attack on America could bring a retaliatory attack that could erase cities like Tehran or Karachi from the face of the map. No problem, say some Muslims. "Allah will know his own."[1] In other words, death-by-nuke would do the citizens of Tehran and Karachi a favor. It would give every believing Muslim in Tehran or Karachi an express trip to paradise.[1795]

A 21st-century jihadist we've already met, Seif Al-Din Al-Ansari, writing in al Qaeda's online magazine *Al-Ansar*, declared in 2002, "The elements of the collapse of Western civilization are proliferating...In spite of all the characteristics of power at their command, these infidel states are no more than a handful of creatures on the speck of dust called Planet Earth....Allah told us of the certainty of the annihilation of the infidels...by means of the Muslim group, which would, in accordance with the Islamic commandment...torture them...The question now on the agenda is, how is the torture Allah wants done at our hands to be carried out?"[1796] The answer to that question may be easy now that Allah has given Islam's warriors what the Qur'an calls "the fire whose fuel is Men and Stones"[1797]... the fire of nuclear weaponry.[1798]

*   *   *

When Iranian President Mahmoud Ahmadinejad threw a press conference over a decade ago, in September 2006, to report on his visit to Senegal, Cuba, Venezuela, and the United Nations, he said, "And God willing, with the force of God behind it, we shall soon experience a world without the United States and Zionism."[1799] He'd also made the same word-for-word statement the previous year.[1800] It is very unlikely that Ahmadinejad was proposing a thought experiment. He was proposing a reality that Iran and its fellow Muslim states would be able to achieve with their coming weaponry. And with the existing 120 Islamic nuclear bombs of Pakistan.[1801] Bombs that could easily fall into the hands of ISIS.

*   *   *

It all goes back to the Nuer and their insatiable appetite for land. An appetite fueled by a worldview of humiliation. Raymond Kelly,[1802] the specialist in the Dinka and the Nuer, is on to something basic. To produce a perpetually hungry culture, a killer culture, make sure your people have a source of humiliation that won't quit until they own everything in sight.

Militant Islam demands that Muslims be on top. It demands that Muslims allow others to live only if they take a role as second-class citizens in a purely Muslim state and pay the jizya, a tax designed to shame. It demands that Islam rule every inch of land on God's own speck of dust—the planet Earth. Anything less is humiliation. Humiliation of the Muslims. So Muslims in the West can never be happy. At least not according to the standards of the Hadith and the Qur'an. Not according to the standards of al Qaeda, Boko Haram, the Iranian Islamic Revolution, and the Islamic State. That is, good Muslims cannot be happy until Shariah rules every land. And that includes your land and mine.

Muslims are obligated to raid the lands of the infidels,
occupy them, and exchange their system of governance
for an Islamic system, barring any practice that
contradicts Shari'a from being publicly voiced among
the people, as was the case in the dawn of Islam. ...
They say that our Shari'a does not impose our particular
beliefs upon others; this is a false assertion. For it
is, in fact, part of our religion to impose our particular
beliefs upon others. ... Thus whoever refuses the
principle of terror against the enemy also refuses the
commandment of Allah the Exalted, the Most High,
and His Shari'a
                —Osama bin Laden[1803]

PUT YOURSELF IN THE MIND of the Caliph of the Islamic State, Abu Bakr al-Baghdadi, for a minute. You are the Khalifah, the global ruler, of an Islamic State promised by God to Muhammad 1387 years ago.[1804] You are not a sadist. You do not enjoy killing. But you have a job, one of the most important jobs on the planet—saving humanity.

You know with absolute certainty that God has made this planet. God has made punishment, forgiveness, charity, and weapons. And God has made you and me. God has also told us the one true way to follow his will, the one true way to avoid roasting in hell.

What's more, God has done his utmost to communicate his commands to those of us He has made. He has sent between 25 and 240 thousand prophets,[1805] each delivering His truths. Those truths are not limited to mere religion. They include, as you know, what many Muslim scholars refer to as "a complete system of life"[1806]—a system of government, a system of laws, a system of manners, a system of worship, and even a system of military practice.[1807]

Each prophet was given this total system, this Holy bundle of instructions on how to conduct a good life. Some of those prophets were listened to. Many were not. Among those who got the ear of mankind were Abraham, Moses, and Jesus.[1] To each, God delivered the same message—the message you can find word-for-word today in Islam's holy book, the Qur'an. Then what happened? According to mainstream Islam, the Jews took the word of God and perverted it. Generation after generation, they adapted Moses' holy orders to fit the needs of their time. Each adaptation, each adjustment, and each new update twisted the original truth and turned it into a lie. Those lies are what the Jews call their Torah, the Old Testament of the Bible.

The same thing happened with Jesus. According to Islam, God gave Jesus the complete truth—the truth of Islam. The word-for-word truth that's in the Qur'an. Then Jesus' followers mangled Jesus' message, perverted it, and turned it from a truth to a savage distortion, a distortion that has led hundreds of millions to the fires of eternal torment—to the fires of hell.

Despite mankind's pigheadedness, God the all-merciful gave it one last shot. He sent one final messenger to humanity—Muhammad, a man of absolute honesty. Muhammad delivered God's code of life—his religion, his governmental system, his laws, his court system, his manners, and his military orders. And for the first time, a people did not screw up God's message. For the first time a people realized that to remain true to your creator, you have to reject the lies of "modern," secular thought. You have to shun the temptation to twist the truth to fit the present. You have to look back, straight back to the life of Muhammad.

Which people finally managed this act of supreme fidelity, this act of total obedience and commitment? The Muslims. First the Arabs, a uniquely noble race.[1809] Then all those who said yes to the truth that "There is no god but Allah and Muhammad is His Prophet."[1810] Only the Muslims accepted the form of utter submission to Allah's will known in God's own language, Arabic, as "Islam."

Remember, you are Abu Bakr al-Baghdadi. You are in the 21st century. It's 1,394 years after Muhammad established his—and God's—rule in the tiny desert town of Medina. Nearly 80 percent of your fellow 21st-century humans are literally on the path to hell. They are misled by lies like democracy, freedom, human rights, separation of mosque and state, Christianity, Darwinism, and Buddhism. They live in the shackles of a tyranny they do not see.

God gave us his own laws from 622 to 632 A.D. Yet over five billion humans suffer under the oppression of profane governments like those in the United States, Canada, Mexico, Brazil, Argentina, England, France, Germany, Nigeria, Kenya, South Africa, India, Thailand, and China. The leaders of this huge slice of humanity believe that man can write his own constitutions, that groups of men and women gathered in Congresses and Parliaments can write laws, and that God's slaves[1811]—his creations—have "rights" that defy God's will. Because of these false notions, over five billion of your fellow humans will suffer an eternity in an afterlife so painful that they'll be roasted over a spit, screaming while their skin is burned inch by inch. Then, when the ash of their crisped and blackened dermal tissue falls off, they'll be given a new skin so they can feel the same pain all over again.[1812]

You are Abu Bakr al-Baghdadi. You are the first real caliph since "the crusader powers" used the Sykes-Picot agreement to "ruthlessly" cut asunder the lands of Islam in 1916.[1813] You want to liberate all of mankind. What would you do? Would you sit by idly while five billion of your fellow humans live in darkness and are condemned to an eternity of torture? Or would you bring them the light? Would you open their eyes to truth? Would you liberate them so they can enter paradise? And would you perform this liberation even if it meant the deaths of hundreds of thousands? If you had nuclear weapons, would you bring truth to the misguided even if it meant the deaths of millions? As an idealist out to save man and womankind, as an upholder of truth and justice, would you look back to what you know is the single template of righteousness, the single guide to God's wishes, the life of Muhammad, before you decide?

To understand men like Abu Bakr al-Baghdadi and his subordinate, Boko Haram's leader Abubakar Shekau, to understand the heads of groups like Hezbollah and Hamas, to understand the militant Muslims making headlines today and who will make headlines tomorrow, you have to understand the key to their way of thinking. Like them, you have to understand the life of Muhammad. You have to understand the Muhammad Code.

Epilogue: Why Did We Attack Iraq?

MUHAMMAD SAID THAT WAR is guile and deception.[1814] But that was nearly 1,400 years ago. Just how far will guile and deception take you in the modern world? Can they be used to puppeteer a superpower?

Or, to put it differently, have you ever wondered why the United States attacked Iraq in March, 2003? You know the emotional catalyst: we had been deeply stung by the destruction of the World Trade Center on September 11, 2001. But the 19 airplane hijackers who had rammed planes into the tallest building in America and into the Pentagon had not been from Iraq, most of them had come from Saudi Arabia. And the group they were a part of, al Qaeda, was based in Afghanistan, not Iraq. What's more, that group, al Qaeda, loathed and despised Iraq's dictator, Saddam Hussein. They wanted to behead him, not collaborate with him. Yet we invaded Iraq. A country that had nothing to do with 9/11. And we got bogged down in one of the longest wars[1815] in our history, an eight-year-and-nine-months battle.[1816] Twice as long as the Civil War or World War I. Why? The answer just may be Muhammad's legacy of guile and deception. Oh, and one more key ingredient: Iran.

We were told that we had evidence that Iraq had weapons of mass destruction. Chemical, biological, and nuclear weapons. Years later we learned that no such weapons existed. And many Americans concluded that president George W. Bush had lied. The skeptics were certain that no proof of weapons of mass destruction had existed. Bush and his team had made them up. Why? A war in Iraq was a good way to shovel money to Bush family friends who popped up a few pages ago, friends like the nice folks at Bechtel[1817] and Halliburton.[1818] A war in Iraq was a good way to up Bush's approval ratings. A war in Iraq was an excuse to pass the Patriot Act, an "anti-terrorism" law that undermined America's human rights.[1819] And a war in Iraq was revenge for Iraq's insistence on humiliating the Bush family. A mosaic covered the floor of the entrance to the 18-story,[1820] elite Al-Rashid

Hotel[1821] in Baghdad. That mosaic bore a portrait of guess who? George H.W. Bush, George W. Bush's father. And in the Islamic world, stepping on someone is an ultimate insult.

What gave us the impression that there were weapons of mass destruction in Iraq? Did we have evidence, or was George Bush so intent on attacking Iraq that he was willing to twist fragile threads of fantasy into false tales of hard proof? The answer is that we *did* have hard proof. The problem is that we didn't realize who it was coming from...and why.

The tale of that proof of weapons of mass destruction begins in 1979, when a flea-sized enemy hit us where it hurt. The student mobs of the Islamic Iranian Revolution of 1979 stormed our embassy in Tehran, took its 60 inhabitants hostage, and made them the subject of obsessive daily headlines in the United States for 444 days.[1822]

With this move, Iran achieved its first victory, a victory that we didn't see. Iran influenced an American regime change. We had a president, Jimmy Carter, who declared "the moral equivalent of war," a crash program to achieve energy independence from foreign and especially from Middle Eastern oil. Some of us have learned in the decades since then how vitally we needed that alternative energy initiative and how deeply we suffered for its abandonment. In the 1980s, we led the world in renewable energy technology. Today the leaders are the Chinese.[1823] Yet we voted Carter out of office and brought in Ronald Reagan, who immediately stripped our alternative energy programs down to a near-death, skeletal state and left us vulnerable to manipulation by oil powers for a quarter of a century. We voted in Ronald Reagan in part because Jimmy Carter could not get our hostages out of guess what country? Iran.

The Iranians deliberately withheld the release of our hostages until Jimmy Carter left office and sent those hostages back to us "15 minutes after Ronald Reagan took the oath of office,"[1824] thus putting a strange seal of approval on the new Republican president. Later the Iranians would humiliate Reagan by killing 299 American and French servicemen in the Beirut Barracks Bombing.[1825] Our response? We pulled our troops out of Lebanon.[1826] Then the Reagan administration broke the law[1827] and sold some of our most advanced weapons—508 TOW anti-tank missiles and 500 HAWK surface-to-air missiles[1828]—to Iran in exchange for help in sneaking money to Nicaragua's contras.[1829]

The ability of Iran's new militant rulers to influence political decisions on a continent far, far away—North America—should have served as a warning. It didn't. We shut our eyes to a simple fact. The Iranian Revolution's goals were not merely local, they were global.

The George Washington and Thomas Jefferson of the Islamic Revolution was, as you know, the Ayatollah Ruhollah Musawi Khomeini. Here's how Khomeini outlined his vision of Iran's future:

> We will export our revolution throughout the world...until the calls 'there is no god but God and Muhammad is the messenger of God' are echoed all over the world.[1830]

This principle was so fundamental to the new Iran that it was built into the Iranian Constitution of 1979.[1831] As the Preamble to the Iranian Constitution put it, "The Assembly of Experts...fram[ed] the Constitution...with the hope that this century will witness the establishment of a universal holy government and the downfall of all others."[1832] And the Islamic Revolution's "armed forces...will have as their mission sacred battle in the name of god for the extension of divine sovereignty of god in the world."[1833] You read that right: the "extension of divine sovereignty of god in the world." The entire world.

But one step at a time. The first "profane government" whose "downfall" the Iranians wanted to achieve was right next door in Iraq. It was the secular government of Saddam Hussein. So Iran worked hard to light the coals of revolution under Saddam's feet. It called on Iraq's Shiites and Kurds to overthrow the Iraqi dictator. It gave money to the Shiite anti-Saddam underground. And in one month alone, April, 1980, Iran managed to assassinate 20 officials of Saddam's government.[1834] The Iranians imagined that these moves would topple Saddam from power in a matter of weeks. But Saddam's downfall stubbornly refused to arrive.

Believe it or not, Saddam Hussein tried to avoid war. Among other things, he extended an invitation to Iran's premier to visit Baghdad. But his attempts to befriend Iran failed. Finally, on September 22, 1980, Saddam counterattacked. Back here in America, we welcomed the resulting war against a nation that had humiliated us—Iran. So we used one of our most popular and most absurdly ineffectual strategies, embargoes and sanctions, to make sure that the Iran-Iraq War would bleed Iran dry.[1835] After all, Iran's weapons were American. They were the tanks,[1836] the F-4s, the F-5s, and the F-14[1837] fighter jets that we had sold to our former client in Iran, the man who ruled Iran from 1941 to 1979,[1838] Shah Mohammad Reza Pahlavi. Without spare parts and ammunition, we were sure the Iranian military would fall apart. Yet Iran's collapse stubbornly refused to materialize. Why?

Civilizations that turn catastrophe into opportunity are those that thrive. And Iran turned catastrophe into the start of something radically new—a homegrown armaments industry.[1839] An industry underwritten by the profits of Iran's energy industry. Iran's Revolution and the Iran-Iraq War that followed more than doubled the price Iran could charge per barrel for its oil.[1840] So despite our economic sanctions,[1841] Iran had money. And with that money it was able to buy training and technology. Advanced weapons technology. Weapons technology from the Russians. Weapons technology from the Chinese. Even weapons technology from the North Koreans[1842] and the Ukrainians,[1843] who built many of the Soviet Unions' most sophisticated weapons.[1844] But Iran never wanted to be dependent on a foreign power like America again. It used the technologies it acquired to build its own engineering and manufacturing expertise and to start its own thoroughly modern heavy weapons industry.

What's more, Iran found more opportunity in catastrophe. It had eight years in which to learn the strengths and weaknesses of imported weapons in the finest laboratory of all—battle. It had eight years of war with Saddam Hussein in which to get the hands-on experience it would later use when it developed and manufactured its own tanks,[1845] its own fighter jets,[1846] and yet another weapon—its own missiles.[1847] Including its own nuclear-capable missiles.

Iran was convinced that its Revolution was an expression of the will of God Himself. With Allah on the Iranian side, toppling Saddam Hussein should have been a snap. But it was not. The Iran-Iraq War cost $1.9 trillion,[1848] a million lives,[1849] eight years, and ended in a bitter stalemate with Saddam still in power.

Most nations hit with losses like these would go home and lick their wounds. But Iran had a mission: "to strengthen the struggle for the victory of the oppressed and dispossessed people throughout the world," to "pave the way for …a unique and just universal community,"[1850] to put "Qur'anic law in power from one end of the earth to the other," and to make Iran what its former President Mahmoud Ahmadinejad called "an invincible world power." How do you get back on the track of invincibility when you've been stopped dead in your footsteps by a failure to take even the country next door? You consult the example of Muhammad.

One man who literally examined every record of Muhammad's life was Abu Bakr of Tortosa, a 12th-century scholar who went through Islam's holy books, the Qur'an, the Hadith, the Sunnah, and the Fiqh, to find the

Prophet's own strategies for war. "War means deception,"[1851] he concluded, paraphrasing Muhammad himself. "Surprise," he said, is the ultimate weapon.[1852] And "ambush" is the ultimate ploy.[1853] Ambush is, indeed, what Iran would set up for us.

If London's *The Guardian*[1854] and the *Columbia Journalism Review*[1855] have got it right, and I believe they have, when toppling Saddam with open war turned out to be impossible, the Iranians found a far cheaper way to oust the Iraqi dictator from power—a less expensive method with many an extra advantage.[1856]

A 1972 American television advertisement for a grotesquely wholesome cereal—Quaker Oats Life—gets across the essence of the Iranian brainstorm. It was an ad so popular that it ran for 12 years and inspired years of spin-offs. In it, a four-year-old, a five-year-old, and a three-and-a-half-year-old[1857] sit around a breakfast table with bowls of the suspicious-looking whole-grain cereal in front of them. A cereal so healthy that its manufacturer swears it helps "promote healthy hearts."[1858] The two older brothers debate about who should taste the cereal first. Neither of them is enthusiastic about the prospect. Then it hits them. The three-and-a-half-year-old is too naïve to understand the danger to his taste buds. The two shout their solution in unison, "Let's get Mikey." Meaning, "Let's let Mikey do it."

And who could Mikey be? Who might be naïve enough to knock Saddam Hussein out of power and hand over Iraq ever so slowly to Iran? How about George W. Bush and his sidekick, Vice President Dick Cheney?

But how do you, the head of Iranian intelligence, reach Bush and Cheney? How do you play perceptual jiu-jitsu on the American White House? You feed the ambition of a man named Ahmad Chalabi.

Ahmad Chalabi was a native Iraqi who had left Baghdad with his when he was 12 years old and had entered MIT when he was a me Chalabi had gotten his Ph.D. in math from the University of Chicag birthplace of the neoconservative movement, and had made fri important fellow students, future luminaries like Richard Perl Wolfowitz,[1861] men who would have a powerful say on foreign George W. Bush. In fact, Wolfowitz would go on to head the Wor would resign in an ethics scandal.[1862]

After graduating from the University of Chicago, Cha papers on math and taught at the American Universi Lebanon.[1863] But Chalabi was from a Shi'ite family with e nance and politics. CNN reports that his father "was one men and a president of the Iraqi Senate before the family went into exile in the 1950s."[1864] What's more, *The Wall Street Journal* explains that his "uncle started the Rafidain Bank of Baghdad, once the largest bank in the Middle East."[1865] So it was not surprising when Chalabi left academia to found the Petra Bank in Jordan. What <u>was</u> surprising is that Chalabi left Jordan abruptly when his bank couldn't come up with the cash to meet a new law on reserve requirements. In fact, it was claimed that Chalabi "fled" Jordan and was "convicted in absentia on 31 charges of embezzlement, theft, misuse of depositor funds and currency speculation, and sentenced by a Jordanian court to 22 years in jail."[1866] All this was overlooked when Chalabi went to Washington. After all, he was Western-educated, intelligent, charismatic,[1867] and had friends in high places. What's more, he was expert at cultivating people in power. For example, Chalabi made his first contact with the CIA in 1992, and spent the next ten years developing more relationships in Washington.

Iran has what *Asharq Alawsat*—one of the world's most influential international Arabic daily newspapers—calls a "large machine of deception and confusion."[1868] In roughly 1997,[1869] nine years after the Iran-Iraq War, Chalabi got what he apparently considered hot information on Iraq's weapons programs. It came from experts Chalabi thought could see through the walls of Iraq's secret operations as if they were made of glass—high sources in Iranian intelligence—sources that included the head of Iran's intelligence agency himself.[1870] Scott Ritter, a high-profile weapons inspector whose territory was Iraq, says that, "When I met [Mr. Chalabi] in December 1997 he said he had tremendous connections with Iranian intelligence. He said that some of his best intelligence came from the Iranians and offered to set up a meeting for me with the head of Iranian intelligence."[1871] Iraq, according to the Iranians, had weapons of mass destruction. And these sizzling Iranian tip-offs about Iraq's weapons of mass destruction came complete with eyewitnesses: three defectors who could verify the tales. So Chalabi spilled his weapons of mass destruction information to every[1872] powerful person on his list—to CIA director James Woolsey, to members of Congress, to figures in the Pentagon, and to his high-placed Washington neoconservative University of Chicago friends and their acquaintances, notably Richard Perle, Paul Wolfowitz[1873] and Douglas Feith.[1874] The CIA and the INR, The U.S. Department of State Bureau of Intelligence and Research, weighed Chalabi's information,[1875] then decided it was useless. But that was not the end of the matter. Far from it.

Chalabi's information worked its way to the White House, where it was vigorously championed by the office of Vice President Dick Cheney and showed up on the desk of President George W. Bush. Super investigative journalist Seymour Hersh explains that

> Chalabi's defector reports were now flowing from the Pentagon directly to the Vice President's office, and then on to the President, with little prior evaluation by intelligence professionals. When INR analysts did get a look at the reports, they were troubled by what they found. "They'd pick apart a report and find out that the source had been wrong before, or had no access to the information provided," Greg Thielmann told me. "There was considerable skepticism throughout the intelligence community about the reliability of Chalabi's sources, but the defector reports were coming all the time. Knock one down and another comes along. Meanwhile, the garbage was being shoved straight to the President."[1876]

While he had the White House chewing on his information, Chalabi also worked the real levers of public perception, the gatekeepers of the media, taking his scoops to the folks at *60 Minutes, "The New York Times, The Washington Post, The Wall Street Journal, The New Yorker, Vanity Fair, Time, Newsweek, The Atlantic Monthly* ... *USA Today*, the *New York Daily News*, UPI, and Fox News."[1877] Chalabi's hope was that the United States would help[1878] him topple Saddam Hussein and would make him, Ahmad Chalabi, the new Iraqi ruler, the "George Washington of Iraq."[1879]

The White House took the weapons-of-mass-destruction bait. The result was our ruinous 2003 War in Iraq. A war in which we did exactly what Iran needed. We toppled Saddam Hussein. And we became mired, bogged down, unable to get out. At a high price. We went from a balanced budget[1880] from 1998 to 2001 to a 10.15 trillion dollar debt by the year 2011.[1881] The biggest debt in the world's history.

What's worse, we made Iraq vulnerable to a "democratic" takeover by the only Iraqi political party Saddam could not wipe out—Iraq's Shiite mosque network, a network that had hosted the Iranian Revolution's leader, Ayatollah Khomeini, in its headquarters city,[1882] Najaf, from 1964 to 1978,[1883] a network that sent the bulk of its religious taxes to Iran[1884] and a network that was conveniently run by an Iranian.[1885] What's more, as you'll see in a minute, Iran controlled not just one army in Iraq but two. Without realizing it, we were turning Iraq into an Iranian province.

But Iran still needed more out of us. And Iran got it.

In 2008, when America had been bogged down in Iraq for five painful years and when America's treasury was drained, Iran revealed the next move in its perceptual game, the next move in its 28-year-long war to take over Iraq. That move? Make what looks like ...peace! Here's how the deception worked. In 2008, Brigadier General Qassem Soleimani was head of the Iranian Islamic Revolutionary Guards' foreign operations unit, the Quds Force.[1886] He had been its head since 1998[1887] and was still in charge in 2016. The Quds Force[1888] was in charge of Iran's covert[1889] and terrorist[1890] operations. What's more, Soleimani's Quds Force controlled at least five proxy armies. These Iranian proxy armies were Hamas[1891] in Gaza, Hezbollah in Lebanon, the Houthis[1892] in Yemen, and at least two armies in Iraq—Muqtada El-Sadr's Mehdi Army[1893] and the Badr Organization. El Sadr's Mehdi Army[1894] was roughly 60,000 members in size and was the source of much of the Iraqi violence against civilians that sickened Americans from 2003 to 2008.[1895] And the Badr Organization was a group of Iraqis who had fought side by side with the Iranians against Saddam Hussein in the Iran-Iraq War of 1980–1988.[1896] Yes, Iraqis who had fought with the Iranians. The result? The Badr Organization was an Iranian fifth column. And in 2003, the members of the Badr Organization had joined the Iraqi army, the Iraqi security force and the Iraqi security ministry. They infiltrated the country's key tools of control. Which meant that while wearing their military and police uniforms, these Iranian proxies were accused of assassinating Sunni Muslims, looting citizens, and imposing Shariah law in Iraq's south, where they virtually ran the Iraqi government's security operations. It was even said that the Badr Organization's men in the Iraqi Army and in the Iraqi police force attempted to impose traditional clothing rules on women and threatened them with rape or death if they went to university.[1897] Meanwhile America, anxious to escape its Iraqi trap, planned to hand over control to the very groups that the Badr Organization had infiltrated—the police and the army. Was the Badr Organization really obedient to Iran?[1898] On the surface, it was hard to say. And that's apparently how Iran wanted it.

The head of the Iranian Quds Force, Brigadier General Soleimani, said that Iraq, Lebanon and Gaza were in his "portfolio."[1899] And in 2008, the groups in Soleimani's portfolio brought in big dividends. Hezbollah, one of the groups in Soleimani's charge, started a ten-day civil war in Lebanon in the spring of 2008 and managed to oust Lebanon's president and replace him with a candidate they found more amenable to their interests.

Hezbollah also landed itself a seat in the Lebanese cabinet and veto power[1900] over Lebanon's government. So Lebanon was slowly coming under Iran's control. Hamas, another armed group in Soleimani's portfolio, took over Gaza in an armed coup in June 2007 and by 2008 controlled Gaza with an iron fist. Chalk up another win for Brigadier General Soleimani and the Iranians. But Iraq continued to elude Iranian control despite the turmoil that the Iranians had fomented by arming and training the Mehdi Army, by backing the Badr Brigade, and, if American intelligence was right, even by arming and training Shiite insurgents.[1901]

The turmoil in Iraq wore us Americans down. Thanks to the Mehdi Army, the insurgents, and to our attempts to pacify Iraq, as many as 152[1902] innocent Iraqi civilians died a day in car bombings, walk-in suicide bombings, and even donkey cart bombings.[1903] And thanks to improvised explosive devices, roadside bombs and shaped charges—explosives cleverly designed to pierce the weak points of tanks or armored personnel carriers—we lost a slow and painful trickle of American soldiers every week. Where did these sophisticated shaped charges come from? And where did Iraqi insurgents learn to make their own? It appears that the Iraqi fighters were taken for training to... Iran.[1904]

American TV networks gave intense daily coverage to the continuing war in Iraq from 2003 to roughly 2006. In those years, Iraq dominated the headlines. But in 2008 the grimness was more than we could take. America's TV news producers responded by dramatically decreasing their Iraqi coverage, pulling their correspondents out of Iraq, and making it difficult even for the few correspondents left in Baghdad to get their stories on air. Why? The American public wanted out. How was Iran playing that public sentiment? How was it using America's war weariness? By promising us what we yearned for: peace.[1905]

Iran capitalized on our exhaustion by mounting, of all things, another deception—a move of war disguised as a peace blitz. Iran appears to have instructed its closest ally, Syria, to make peace gestures toward an enemy both Syria and Iran hated with all their souls, Israel. Syria complied by entering not-so-secret negotiations with Israel mediated by the Turks.[1906] Meanwhile Iran told Hamas to do something previously impossible in Gaza—to agree to a truce with the Israelis.[1907] Hamas had bucked, struggled, and kicked against truces in the past.[1908] After all, its charter document, the Hamas Covenant,[1909] commits it to the utter annihilation of Israel. Here's how the Hamas Charter puts it:

The Islamic Resistance Movement aspires to the realisation of Allah's promise, no matter how long that should take. The Prophet, Allah bless him and grant him salvation, has said:

"The Day of Judgement will not come about until Muslims fight the Jews (killing the Jews), when the Jew will hide behind stones and trees. The stones and trees will say O Muslims, O Abdulla, there is a Jew behind me, come and kill him. Only the Gharkad tree (evidently a certain kind of tree) would not do that because it is one of the trees of the Jews." (related by al-Bukhari and Muslim).[1910]

Sound familiar?

But this time, Hamas miraculously obeyed. This was a powerful testament to Iran's power over its proxies. Then Iran instructed another group that had previously been allergic to nonviolence, Hezbollah, to stop all military menacing in Lebanon. Hezbollah went remarkably quiet.[1911] But that was just the beginning.

On roughly April 4, 2008, Iran's Brigadier General Soleimani had a secret meeting with Iraqi president Jalil Talabani in which Soleimani made some amazing promises.[1912] Instead of calling the current Iraqi government an illegitimate American puppet, Soleimani said the opposite, that Iraq's current government was thoroughly legitimate. In fact, Soleimani promised to support the Iraqi government for all he was worth. Resistance to the government of Iraq had traditionally come from Muqtada al-Sadr's Mehdi Army, which had thrown an uprising in Iraq's capital, Baghdad, as recently as March, 2008.[1913] Soleimani promised that from now on when the Iraqi Army marched into a town, the Mehdi Army would lay down its arms. A promise that seemed virtually impossible.

Soleimani also listed a set of Iranian goals that coincided precisely with America's Iraq War objectives and asked Talabani to tell America that he was willing to discuss these shared objectives at any time and any place. How very gentlemanly.

When the meeting was over, Soleimani delivered. Muqtada el-Sadr—the head of the Mehdi Army—disappeared from Iraq altogether. He was ordered back to Iran for "religious training." The sub-leaders of the Mehdi Army's militias were also ordered to come to Iran where they could be controlled. Then came Iran's orders to feign peace. The first time the Iraqi army had marched into Basra in March 2008,[1914] it had been chased out of town by heavily armed Iranian proxy armies. But after Soleimani gave his word, everything changed. Now when the Iraqi Army marched into Basra, Mosul, Amara and the Sadr City section of Baghdad in March 2008, the local militias did precisely what Soleimani had promised—they laid down their arms. They did not, however, give up their arms.[1915] They were still equipped to fight another day. But that fact didn't seem to register with Iraq's officials. The Iraqi leadership was exultant. They felt they were now capable of controlling their own country. And that they no longer needed America's troops. A delusion that was very welcome guess where? In Washington, where the Barack Obama administration had just taken control of the White House. An administration that had campaigned on the promise to get us out of Iraq.

Astonishingly, Iran showed even more support for the Iraqi government installed by the hated "occupation forces," the Americans. How? In June 2008, at the height of Iran's covert peace offensive, Tehran hosted an official visit to Tehran from Iraqi Prime Minister Nouri al-Maliki, a man who was no stranger to Iran. Al-Maliki had spent eight years in Iran as an exile.[1916] It appears that Al Maliki was from the very beginning an Iranian pawn. He was Iran's man at the top of the Iraqi government. So it should not have come as a surprise when Al-Maliki and his Iranian hosts signed a security pact. A very strange security pact. One that was not "binding for both sides."[1917] But a pact that, like all the other Iranian moves of Iran's 2008 peace offensive, gave the impression of stability... and peace.

What did this peace blitz achieve for the Iranians? America was anxious to get out of Iraq. In the Congressional elections of 2006 the Democrats had campaigned—and won—on the promise that America would withdraw from Iraq. In 2008, Barack Obama, as you've seen, had also made withdrawing American forces a key promise of his presidential campaign. And George W. Bush's stated objectives in Iraq had also been a stable democratic government...and peace.[1918] This is precisely what Soleimani and Iran delivered. The appearance of peace, stability, and democracy. The more peace and democracy, the sooner we Americans could declare victory and go home.

But once we left, guess who was poised to take over? Guess who was poised to work the levers of power, sliding into the control seat slowly and silently after Western headlines swiveled from Iraq to the next hot spot?

* * *

Why did the two top Americans in Iraq call this "a brilliant tactical game"?[1919] Why did the Saudis claim that this was a ploy designed to allow Iran to encircle the Arab world? Why did *Asharq Al-Awsat*, one of the most influential international Arab newspapers of all, say that the real occupier of Iraq was not the United States? The "actual occupier in Iraq" was Iran?[1920] And how did this advance a grander goal, toppling what Osama bin Laden used to call "the worst civilization witnessed by the history of mankind"[1921] and what the Ayatollah Khomeini, whose words are worth repeating, called "nothing but a collection of unjust dictatorships...troublemakers [responsible for] barbaric goings-on unworthy even of wild animals."[1922] Osama and the Ayatollah meant the civilization of freedom of speech, pluralism, and secularism... your civilization and mine.

* * *

Or as Iranian President Mahmoud Ahmadinejad put it,

> The great powers...kill the peoples in Palestine, Iraq, Afghanistan, and Lebanon, and turn them into refugees... They operate all the terrorist groups in Iraq and Palestine....They fill all their warehouses with atomic, biological, and chemical weapons. ...they cause the greatest damage to natural resources ...The powers are willing to destroy the planet several times over, in order to line the pockets of the world's capitalists, parties, and great powers....they have failed in the proper management of the world....
>
> Today, the Iranian people is recognized as a model for all the peoples of the world. ...the world is left with only one light, one banner, and one people, which has preserved the hope in the hearts of all the peoples. This is the great and courageous people of Iran.... the Iranian people—because of its past culture, its past civilization, its intelligent youth, its human and material potential—has the capacity to quickly become an invincible global power. This will happen as soon as it achieves advanced technologies.[1923]

Could Ahmadinejad have been referring to the nuclear technologies that Iran has been working on since its deal with Pakistani nuclear weapons developer A.Q. Khan in 1987?[1924] The nuclear technologies that the JCPOA, a nuclear arms agreement Iran signed in 2015 with the United States and five other great powers,[1925] guaranteed to leave almost entirely in place? The agreement that says that Iran will continue "its own long-term enrichment and enrichment R&D plan"[1926] without outside interference. In fact, with outside technical "assistance"?[1927] The agreement that, according to the Head of the Atomic Energy Organization of Iran (AIOLI) Ali-Akbar Salehi, one of the deal's negotiators, has a simple bottom line: "our enrichment activity was recognized by the international community."[1928]

*   *   *

Who left the goal that drove Mahmoud Ahmadinejad, Osama bin Laden, and the Ayatollah Khomeini? Who left the imperatives that drive ISIS, al Qaeda, and Boko Haram? Who left the legacy of toppling all governments that are "unjust" and "tyrannical" because they are not run by the laws of Shariah and because they are not governed by Muslims? Who left the commandment that all the world, from Paraguay to Pennsylvania and from Budapest to Beijing must become Muslim? Who wrote the letters to the emperors in 629 A.D.? Who left the ideas that led to the biggest empire in the history of the world—an empire 11 times the size of the conquests of Alexander the Great, five times the size of the Roman Empire, and seven times the size of the United States? Who told suicide bombers that they would go straight to the seventh level of heaven and be greeted by virgins "so beautiful, pure and transparent (that) the marrow of the bones of their legs will be seen through the bones and the flesh"?[1929] Who put sex in paradise? And who made war—and killing—an obligation of very able-bodied male until the Day of Judgement?[1930] The only true prophet to mankind. The only man whose every move was a communiqué from the creator of the universe, a directive from the God who made this planet from a clod of mud and who made you and me from clots of blood. That one true prophet was, you guessed it, Muhammad.

And Muhammad's example—a legacy preserved in the Qur'an, the Hadith, the biographies of ibn Ishaq, and al-Tabari, not to mention in the hearts of passionate jihadis from one end of this Earth to the other—is the Muhammad Code.

Endnotes

1. Paradigm Shift, Part II, *Dābiq*, November 18, 2015, issue 12, p. 49.

2. AP, May 25, 2004. NBCNews.com. "Report: Al-Qaida has 18,000 ready to strike. Think tank says network boosted by U.S. conflict in Iraq," updated 5/25/2004 8:48:07 a.m. ET. www.nbcnews.com/id/5057703/ns/us_news-security/t/report-al-qaida-has-ready-strike/#.VoDTXvkrJ5Q 12-28-2015

3. Franz-Stefan Gady, "Will Pakistan Soon Have the World's Third-Largest Nuclear Arsenal? Just how many nuclearweapons does Pakistan have?" *The Diplomat*, August 31, 2015, thediplomat.com/2015/08/will-pakistan-soon-have-the-worldsthird-largest-nuclear-arsenal/

4. Department of the Navy, Why the United States Needs SURTASS LFA, SURTASS LFA EIS, www.surtass-lfa-eis.com/WhyNeed/index.htm

5. Amnesty International, "Nigeria: Abducted women and girls forced to join Boko Haram attacks," April 15, 2015, www.amnesty.org/en/latest/news/2015/04/nigeria-abducted-women-andgirls-forced-to-join-boko-haram-attacks/
Amnesty International, "Nigeria: 'Our Job Is To Shoot, Slaughter And Kill'—Boko Haram's Reign Of Terror In North East Nigeria," Index number: AFR 44/1360/2015, April 14, 2015, www.amnesty.org/en/documents/afr44/1360/2015/en/

6. A Selection Of Military Operations By The Islamic State, *Dābiq*, Issue 12, November 18, 2015, p. 26.

7. 'Ali Akbar Ghifari, *Beacons of Light*, translated and annotated by Dr. Mahmoud M. Ayoub, originally published in 1399, Beirut, Lebanon: 1979. Reprinted online by the Aalulbayt Global Information Center "to spread the Shi'ite culture through the WEB and create a kind of strong relation between the theological class and the public, [Aalulbayt Global Information Center] is being managed under the supervision of the office of His Eminence, Grand Ayatollah Sistani (may Allah protect him)." www.al-shia.com/html/eng/books/becons-of-light/03.htm See also: "The Prophet (peace and blessings be upon him) also said, 'I am the Prophet of mercy and I am the Prophet of war.' Dr. Ahmad Abu Al-Wafa, Professor of the International Law at the Faculty of Law, Cairo University. "Killing Wounded Enemy Soldiers." Fatwa Bank. IslamOnline 64.233.187.104/search?q=cache:yL84yM3tRoAJ:www.islamonline.net/fatwa/english/FatwaDisplay.asp%3FhFatwaID%3D103297+%22the+prophet+of+war%22&hl=en&client=googlet And see "The Prophet of War" in Osama bin Laden, Complete Text Of Sheikh Osama Bin Laden's Latest Message To Ummah, May 12, 2004, retrieved from the World Wide Web May 14, 2004, www.jihadunspun.net/intheatre_internal.php?article=572&list=/home.php&

8. Complete Text of Sheikh Osama Bin Laden's Latest Message to Ummah, May 12, 2004, p. 4. thesis.haverford.edu/dspace/bitstream/handle/10066/5111/OBL20030506.pdf

9. Muhammad P.B.U.H. As Religious, Political And Military Leader, Universal Sunnah Foundation, Lahore, Pakistan, www.usf.edu.pk/wyw-40.html

10. Rukmini Callimachi, "ISIS Enshrines a Theology of Rape," *New York Times*, August 13, 2015, www.nytimes.com/2015/08/14/world/middleeast/isis-enshrines-a-theology-of-rape.html?_r=0 12-31-2015

11. Rukmini Callimachi, "ISIS Enshrines a Theology of Rape," *New York Times*, August 13, 2015, www.nytimes.com/2015/08/14/world/middleeast/isis-enshrines-a-theology-of-rape.html?_r=0 12-31-2015

12. *Dābiq*, October 11, 2014, fourth issue.

13. William McCants, "The Believer: How an Introvert with a Passion for Religion and Soccer Became Abu Bakr Al-Baghdadi, Leader of the Islamic State," Brookings Institute, September 1, 2015, aa61a0da3a709a1480b1-9c0895f07c3474f663 6f95b6bf3db172.r70.cf1.rackcdn.com/content/research/essays/2015/thebeliever.html

14. William McCants, "The Believer: How an Introvert with a Passion for Religion and Soccer Became Abu Bakr Al-Baghdadi, Leader of the Islamic State," Brookings Institute, September 1, 2015, aa61a0da3a709a1480b1-9c0895f07c3474f663 6f95b6bf3db172.r70.cf1.rackcdn.com/content/research/essays/2015/thebeliever.html

15. William McCants, "Don't (Completely) Blame America for Baghdadi," *Lawfare*, September 13, 2015, www.lawfareblog.com/dont-completely-blame-america-baghdadi

16. John K. Cooley, *Unholy Wars: Afghanistan, America and International Terrorism*, London: Pluto Press, 1999. Ahmed Rashid, "A fateful alliance," *Far Eastern Economic Review*; Hong Kong; Sept. 30, 1999; Volume: 162 Issue: 39, pp. 58-59, proquest.umi.com/pqdweb?TS=990068093&RQT=309&CC=1&Dt-p=1&Did=000000045247460&Mtd=1&Fmt=4, downloaded May 16, 2001. Charles Allen, *God's Terrorists: The Wahhabi Cult and the Hidden Roots of Modern Jihad*, Boston: Da Capo Press, 2006, p. 272.

17. William McCants, "The Believer: How an Introvert with a Passion for Religion and Soccer Became Abu Bakr Al-Baghdadi, Leader of the Islamic State," Brookings Institute, September 1, 2015, aa61a0da3a709a1480b1-9c0895f07c3474f663 6f95b6bf3db172.r70.cf1.rackcdn.com/content/research/essays/2015/thebeliever.html

18. Patrick Haenni, Sami Amghar, "The Myth of Muslim Conquest" *CounterPunch*, January 13, 2010, http://www.counterpunch.org/2010/01/13/the-myth-of-muslim-conquest/

19. Sawsan Ramahi, "The Muslim Brotherhood and Salafist Jihad (ISIS): different ideologies, different methodologies," *Middle East Monitor*, September 29, 2014, www.middleeastmonitor.com/20140929-the-muslim-brotherhood-and-salafist-jihad-isis-different-ideologies-different-methodologies/

20. William McCants, "The Believer: How an Introvert with a Passion for Religion and Soccer Became Abu Bakr Al-Baghdadi, Leader of the Islamic State," Brookings Institute, September 1, 2015, aa61a0da3a709a1480b1-9c0895f07c3474f663 6f95b6bf3db172.r70.cf1.rackcdn.com/content/research/essays/2015/thebeliever.html

21. Judit Neurink, "Isis leader Abu Bakr al-Baghdadi repeatedly raped US hostage Kayla Mueller and turned Yazidi girls into personal sex slaves— Systematic rape has become an increasingly powerful recruiting tool for Isis," *The Independent*, Friday 14 August 2015, www.independent.co.uk/news/world/middle-east/isis-leader-abu-bakr-al-baghdadiexposed-as-serial-rapist-of-hostages-who-madewomen-his-personal-10456237.html 12-31-2015

22. Atika Shubert and Bharati Naik, Bryony Jones, "Convert or die: ISIS chief's former slave says he beat her, raped U.S. hostage," CNN, September 11, 2015, www.cnn.com/2015/09/09/middleeast/al-baghdadi-isis-slave/

23. Atika Shubert and Bharati Naik, Bryony Jones, "Convert or die: ISIS chief's former slave says he beat her, raped U.S. hostage," CNN, September 11, 2015, www.cnn.com/2015/09/09/middleeast/al-baghdadi-isis-slave/

24. Atika Shubert and Bharati Naik, Bryony Jones, "Convert or die: ISIS chief's former slave says he beat her, raped U.S. hostage," CNN, September 11, 2015, www.cnn.com/2015/09/09/middleeast/al-baghdadi-isis-slave/

25. PulseVideoStar, "Watch Horrible Video—Islamic State Beheads US Journalist James Foley," YouTube, August 21, 2014, www.youtube.com/watch?v=XiibqwTF4y0

26. Atika Shubert and Bharati Naik, Bryony Jones, "Convert or die: ISIS chief's former slave says he beat her, raped U.S. hostage," CNN, September 11, 2015, www.cnn.com/2015/09/09/middleeast/al-baghdadi-isis-slave/

27. Atika Shubert and Bharati Naik, Bryony Jones, "Convert or die: ISIS chief's former slave says he beat her, raped U.S. hostage," CNN, September 11, 2015, www.cnn.com/2015/09/09/middleeast/al-baghdadi-isis-slave/

28. Atika Shubert and Bharati Naik, Bryony Jones, "Convert or die: ISIS chief's former slave says he beat her, raped U.S. hostage," CNN, September 11, 2015, www.cnn.com/2015/09/09/middleeast/al-baghdadi-isis-slave/

29. Owen Holdaway, John Hall, "U.S. hostage Kayla Mueller had her fingernails pulled out before being repeatedly raped by ISIS leader: Yazidi sex slave reveals torment of aid worker's harrowing final months as the secret wife of al-Baghdadi," MailOnline, *Daily Mail*, September 9, 2015, February 4, 2016, www.dailymail.co.uk/news/article-3227607/U-S-hostage-Kayla-Muellerfingernails-pulled-repeatedly-raped-ISIS-leader-Yazidi-sex-slave-reveals-torment-aid-worker-sharrowing-final-months-forced-secret-wife-Al-Baghdadi.html #ixzz43hbX3YlJ

30. Atika Shubert and Bharati Naik, Bryony Jones, "Convert or die: ISIS chief's former slave says he beat her, raped U.S. hostage," CNN, September 11, 2015, www.cnn.com/2015/09/09/middleeast/al-baghdadi-isis-slave/

31. Atika Shubert and Bharati Naik, Bryony Jones, "Convert or die: ISIS chief's former slave says he beat her, raped U.S. hostage," CNN, September 11, 2015, www.cnn.com/2015/09/09/middleeast/al-baghdadi-isis-slave/

32. Atika Shubert and Bharati Naik, Bryony Jones, "Convert or die: ISIS chief's former slave says he beat her, raped U.S. hostage," CNN, September 11, 2015, www.cnn.com/2015/09/09/middleeast/al-baghdadi-isis-slave/

33. Atika Shubert and Bharati Naik, Bryony Jones, "Convert or die: ISIS chief's former slave says he beat her, raped U.S. hostage," CNN, September 11, 2015, www.cnn.com/2015/09/09/middleeast/al-baghdadi-isis-slave/

34. Atika Shubert and Bharati Naik, Bryony Jones, "Convert or die: ISIS chief's former slave says he beat her, raped U.S. hostage," CNN, September 11, 2015, www.cnn.com/2015/09/09/middleeast/al-baghdadi-isis-slave/

35. Atika Shubert and Bharati Naik, Bryony Jones, "Convert or die: ISIS chief's former slave says he beat her, raped U.S. hostage," CNN, September 11, 2015, www.cnn.com/2015/09/09/middleeast/al-baghdadi-isis-slave/

36. Atika Shubert and Bharati Naik, Bryony Jones. "Convert or die: ISIS chief's former slave says he beat her, raped U.S. hostage," CNN, September 11, 2015, www.cnn.com/2015/09/09/middleeast/al-baghdadi-isis-slave/

37. Atika Shubert and Bharati Naik, Bryony Jones, "Convert or die: ISIS chief's former slave says he beat her, raped U.S. hostage," CNN, September 11, 2015, www.cnn.com/2015/09/09/middleeast/al-baghdadi-isis-slave/

38. The Research and Fatwa Department of the Islamic State, "Questions and Answers on Taking Captives and Slaves," in MEMRI, Islamic State (ISIS) Releases Pamphlet On Female Slaves, Middle East Media Research Institute, December 4, 2014, www.memrijttm.org/islamic-state-isis-releases-pamphlet-on-female-slaves.html

39. Atika Shubert and Bharati Naik, Bryony Jones, "Convert or die: ISIS chief's former slave says he beat her, raped U.S. hostage," CNN, September 11, 2015, www.cnn.com/2015/09/09/middleeast/al-baghdadi-isis-slave/

40. Atika Shubert and Bharati Naik, Bryony Jones, "Convert or die: ISIS chief's former slave says he beat her, raped U.S. hostage," CNN, September 11, 2015, www.cnn.com/2015/09/09/middleeast/al-baghdadi-isis-slave/

41. Judit Neurink, "Isis leader Abu Bakr al-Baghdadi repeatedly raped US hostage Kayla Mueller and turned Yazidi girls into personal sex slaves—Systematic rape has become an increasingly powerful recruiting tool for Isis," The Independent, Friday 14 August 2015, www.independent.co.uk/news/world/middle-east/isis-leader-abu-bakr-al-baghdadiexposed-as-serial-rapist-of-hostages-who-madewomen-his-personal-10456237.html 12-31-2015

42. Judit Neurink, "Isis leader Abu Bakr al-Baghdadi repeatedly raped US hostage Kayla Mueller and turned Yazidi girls into personal sex slaves—Systematic rape has become an increasingly powerful recruiting tool for Isis," The Independent, Friday 14 August 2015, www.independent.co.uk/news/world/middle-east/isis-leader-abu-bakr-al-baghdadiexposed-as-serial-rapist-of-hostages-who-madewomen-his-personal-10456237.html 12-31-2015

43. AcT Now Darfur Wikispaces, what are the differences between the various cultures and ethnic groups? Tangient LLC, actnowdarfur.wikispaces.com/what+are+the+differences+between+the+various+cultures+and+ethnic+groups%3F

44. Ali A. Mazrui, "Islamic Doctrine and the Politics of Induced Fertility Change: An African Perspective," Population and Development Review, Vol. 20, Supplement: The New Politics of Population: Conflict and Consensus in Family Planning, 1994, pp. 128.

45. Meghan Keneally, "Kayla Mueller: ISIS Hostage Had Spent Her Life Working for Others, Parents Say," ABC News, February 10, 2015, abcnews.go.com/International/kayla-mueller-isis-hostage-spent-life-working-parents/story?id=28863017 8-23-2016

46. Owen Holdaway, John Hall, "U.S. hostage Kayla Mueller had her fingernails pulled out before being repeatedly raped by ISIS leader: Yazidi sex slave reveals torment of aid worker's harrowing final months as the secret wife of al-Baghdadi," Daily Mail, UK, February 4, 2016, www.dailymail.co.uk/news/article-3227607/U-S-hostage-Kayla-Mueller-fingernails-pulled-repeatedly-raped-ISIS-leader-Yazidi-sex-slave-reveals-torment-aid-worker-s-harrowing-final-months-forced-secret-wife-Al-Baghdadi.html#ixzz4lCgxjfny

47. Sara Aridi, "Why Kayla Mueller, raped repeatedly by ISIS leader,refused to escape. A teenage girl, who had also been held and raped by the ISIS leader, revealed the conditions of Kayla Mueller's captivity to US officials," Christian Science Monitor, August 15, 2015, www.csmonitor.com/World/2015/0815/Why-Kayla-Mueller-raped-repeatedly-by-ISISleader-refused-to-escape 8-15-2015

48. The Verse of the Sword, Chapter 9, verse 5, the Mohsin Khan translation. Quranic Arabic Corpus, corpus.quran.com/translation.jsp?chapter=9&verse=5 1-3-2016

49. Rebekah L. Sanders, "Mueller boyfriend: How I fled ISIL, tried to save Kayla," The Arizona Republic, February 18, 2015, in USA Today, www.usatoday.com/story/news/nation/2015/02/18/alkhani-interview-mueller/23601191/

50. Owen Holdaway, John Hall, "U.S. hostage Kayla Mueller had her fingernails pulled out before being repeatedly raped by ISIS leader: Yazidi sex slave reveals torment of aid worker's harrowing final months as the secret wife of al-Baghdadi," *Daily Mail*, UK, February 4, 2016, www.dailymail.co.uk/news/article-3227607/U-S-hostage-Kayla-Mueller-fingernails-pulled-repeatedly-raped-ISIS-leader-Yazidi-sex-slave-reveals-torment-aid-worker-s-harrowing-final-months-forced-secret-wife-Al-Baghdadi.html#ixzz4ICgxjfny

51. Islamicworld, Definition of Khalifah/Caliph, islamicworld.net/khalifah/definition.htm, 1-3-2016

52. Muhammad H. Haykal, *The Life of Muhammad*. Translated by Isma'il Raji al-Faruqi. Kuala Lumpur, Malaysia: Islamic Book Trust, 2002, p. 400.

53. Atika Shubert, Bharati Naik, Bryony Jones, "Convert or die: ISIS chief's former slave says he beat her, raped U.S. hostage," CNN, September 11, 2015, www.cnn.com/2015/09/09/middleeast/al-baghdadi-isis-slave/

54. Atika Shubert, Bharati Naik, Bryony Jones, "Convert or die: ISIS chief's former slave says he beat her, raped U.S. hostage," CNN, September 11, 2015, www.cnn.com/2015/09/09/middleeast/al-baghdadi-isis-slave/

55. Atika Shubert, Bharati Naik, Bryony Jones, "Convert or die: ISIS chief's former slave says he beat her, raped U.S. hostage," CNN, September 11, 2015, www.cnn.com/2015/09/09/middleeast/al-baghdadi-isis-slave/

56. Atika Shubert, Bharati Naik, Bryony Jones, "Convert or die: ISIS chief's former slave says he beat her, raped U.S. hostage," CNN, September 11, 2015, www.cnn.com/2015/09/09/middleeast/al-baghdadi-isis-slave/

57. David S. Cohen, Remarks of Under Secretary for Terrorism and Financial Intelligence David S. Cohen at The Carnegie Endowment For International Peace, "Attacking ISIL's Financial Foundation," U.S. Department of the Treasury, October 23, 2014, www.treasury.gov/press-center/press-releases/Pages/jl2672.aspx 1-28-2016

58. Kathy Gilsinan, "How Is ISIS Still Making Money?", *The Atlantic*, November 21, 2015, www.theatlantic.com/international/archive/2015/11/how-is-isis-still-making-money/416745/, 1-28-2016

59. Judit Neurink, "Isis leader Abu Bakr al-Baghdadi repeatedly raped US hostage Kayla Mueller and turned Yazidi girls into personal sex slaves— Systematic rape has become an increasingly powerful recruiting tool for Isis," *The Independent*, Friday 14 August 2015, www.independent.co.uk/news/world/middle-east/isis-leader-abu-bakral-baghdadiexposed-as-serial-rapist-of-hostageswho-madewomen-his-personal-10456237.html

60. Judit Neurink, "Isis leader Abu Bakr al-Baghdadi repeatedly raped US hostage Kayla Mueller and turned Yazidi girls into personal sex slaves— Systematic rape has become an increasingly powerful recruiting tool for Isis," *The Independent*, Friday 14 August 2015, www.independent.co.uk/news/world/middle-east/isis-leader-abu-bakr-al-baghdadiexposed-as-serial-rapist-of-hostages-who-madewomen-his-personal-10456237.html

61. Judit Neurink, "Isis leader Abu Bakr al-Baghdadi repeatedly raped US hostage Kayla Mueller and turned Yazidi girls into personal sex slaves— Systematic rape has become an increasingly powerful recruiting tool for Isis," *The Independent*, Friday 14 August 2015, www.independent.co.uk/news/world/middle-east/isis-leader-abu-bakr-al-baghdadiexposed-as-serial-rapist-of-hostages-who-madewomen-his-personal-10456237.html

62. Atika Shubert, Bharati Naik, Bryony Jones, "Convert or die: ISIS chief's former slave says he beat her, raped U.S. hostage," CNN, September 11, 2015, www.cnn.com/2015/09/09/middleeast/al-baghdadi-isis-slave/

63. Judit Neurink, "Isis leader Abu Bakr al-Baghdadi repeatedly raped US hostage Kayla Mueller and turned Yazidi girls into personal sex slaves— Systematic rape has become an increasingly powerful recruiting tool for Isis," *The Independent*, Friday 14 August 2015, www.independent.co.uk/news/world/middle-east/isis-leader-abu-bakr-al-baghdadiexposed-as-serial-rapist-of-hostages-who-madewomen-his-personal-10456237.html 12-31-2016

64. James Gordon Meek, "ISIS Leader Abu Bakr Al-Baghdadi Sexually Abused American Hostage Kayla Mueller, Officials Say," ABC News, Aug 14, 2015, abcnews.go.com/International/isis-leader-abu-bakr-al-baghdadi-sexually-abused/story?id=33085923 8-23-2016

65. Rory Carroll, "Kayla Mueller's boyfriend reveals new details of trip that ended in Isis ambush," *The Guardian*, February 19, 2015, www.theguardian.com/world/2015/feb/19/kayla-mueller-boyfriend-new-details-isis-kidnapping-aleppo 1-28-2016

66. Atika Shubert, Bharati Naik, Bryony Jones, "Convert or die: ISIS chief's former slave says he beat her, raped U.S. hostage," CNN, September 11, 2015, www.cnn.com/2015/09/09/middleeast/al-baghdadi-isis-slave/

67. Owen Holdaway, John Hall, "U.S. hostage Kayla Mueller had her fingernails pulled out before being repeatedly raped by ISIS leader: Yazidi sex slave reveals torment of aid worker's harrowing final months as the secret wife of al-Baghdadi," MailOnline, *Daily Mail*, September 9, 2015, February 4, 2016, www.dailymail.co.uk/news/article-3227607/U-S-hostage-Kayla-Muellerfingernails-pulled-repeatedly-raped-ISIS-leader-Yazidi-sex-slave-reveals-torment-aid-worker-sharrowing-final-months-forced-secret-wife-Al-Baghdadi.html#ixzz43hbX3YIJ

68. Rukmini Callimachi, "ISIS Enshrines a Theology of Rape," *New York Times*, August 13, 2015, www.nytimes.com/2015/08/14/world/middleeast/isis-enshrines-a-theology-of-rape.html?_r=0 12-31-2015

69. Rukmini Callimachi, "ISIS Enshrines a Theology of Rape," *New York Times*, August 13, 2015, www.nytimes.com/2015/08/14/world/middleeast/isis-enshrines-a-theology-of-rape.html?_r=0 12-31-2015

70. Rukmini Callimachi, "ISIS Enshrines a Theology of Rape," *New York Times*, August 13, 2015, www.nytimes.com/2015/08/14/world/middleeast/isis-enshrines-a-theology-of-rape.html?_r=0 12-31-2015

71. Rukmini Callimachi, "ISIS Enshrines a Theology of Rape," *New York Times*, August 13, 2015, www.nytimes.com/2015/08/14/world/middleeast/isis-enshrines-a-theology-of-rape.html?_r=0 12-31-2015

72. Rukmini Callimachi, "ISIS Enshrines a Theology of Rape," *New York Times*, August 13, 2015, www.nytimes.com/2015/08/14/world/middleeast/isis-enshrines-a-theology-of-rape.html?_r=0 12-31-2015

73. Rukmini Callimachi, "ISIS Enshrines a Theology of Rape," *New York Times*, August 13, 2015, www.nytimes.com/2015/08/14/world/middleeast/isis-enshrines-a-theology-of-rape.html?_r=0 12-31-2015

74. Atika Shubert, Bharati Naik, Bryony Jones, "Convert or die: ISIS chief's former slave says he beat her, raped U.S. hostage," CNN, September 11, 2015, www.cnn.com/2015/09/09/middleeast/al-baghdadi-isis-slave/

75. Atika Shubert, Bharati Naik, Bryony Jones, "Convert or die: ISIS chief's former slave says he beat her, raped U.S. hostage," CNN, September 11, 2015, www.cnn.com/2015/09/09/middleeast/al-baghdadi-isis-slave/

76. Atika Shubert, Bharati Naik, Bryony Jones, "Convert or die: ISIS chief's former slave says he beat her, raped U.S. hostage," CNN, September 11, 2015, www.cnn.com/2015/09/09/middleeast/al-baghdadi-isis-slave/

77. Owen Holdaway, John Hall, "U.S. hostage Kayla Mueller had her fingernails pulled out before being repeatedly raped by ISIS leader: Yazidi sex slave reveals torment of aid worker's harrowing final months as the secret wife of al-Baghdadi," *Daily Mail*, UK, February 4, 2016, www.dailymail.co.uk/news/article-3227607/U-S-hostage-Kayla-Mueller-fingernails-pulled-repeatedly-raped-ISIS-leader-Yazidi-sex-slave-reveals-torment-aid-worker-s-harrowing-final-months-forced-secret-wife-Al-Baghdadi.html#ixzz4ICgxjfny

78. Atika Shubert, Bharati Naik, Bryony Jones, "Convert or die: ISIS chief's former slave says he beat her, raped U.S. hostage," CNN, September 11, 2015, www.cnn.com/2015/09/09/middleeast/al-baghdadi-isis-slave/

79. Atika Shubert, Bharati Naik, Bryony Jones, "Convert or die: ISIS chief's former slave says he beat her, raped U.S. hostage," CNN, September 11, 2015, www.cnn.com/2015/09/09/middleeast/al-baghdadi-isis-slave/

80. Atika Shubert, Bharati Naik, Bryony Jones, "Convert or die: ISIS chief's former slave says he beat her, raped U.S. hostage," CNN, September 11, 2015, www.cnn.com/2015/09/09/middleeast/al-baghdadi-isis-slave/

81. Owen Holdaway, John Hall, "U.S. hostage Kayla Mueller had her fingernails pulled out before being repeatedly raped by ISIS leader: Yazidi sex slave reveals torment of aid worker's harrowing final months as the secret wife of al-Baghdadi," *Daily Mail*, UK, February 4, 2016, www.dailymail.co.uk/news/article-3227607/U-S-hostage-Kayla-Mueller-fingernails-pulled-repeatedly-raped-ISIS-leader-Yazidi-sex-slave-reveals-torment-aid-worker-s-harrowing-final-months-forced-secret-wife-Al-Baghdadi.html#ixzz4ICgxjfny

82. Owen Holdaway, John Hall, "U.S. hostage Kayla Mueller had her fingernails pulled out before being repeatedly raped by ISIS leader: Yazidi sex slave reveals torment of aid worker's harrowing final months as the secret wife of al-Baghdadi," *Daily Mail*, UK, February 4, 2016, www.dailymail.co.uk/news/article-3227607/U-S-hostage-Kayla-Mueller-fingernails-pulled-repeatedly-raped-ISIS-leader-Yazidi-sex-slave-reveals-torment-aid-worker-s-harrowing-final-months-forced-secret-wife-Al-Baghdadi.html#ixzz4ICgxjfny

83. Owen Holdaway, John Hall, "U.S. hostage Kayla Mueller had her fingernails pulled out before being repeatedly raped by ISIS leader: Yazidi sex slave reveals torment of aid worker's harrowing final months as the secret wife of al-Baghdadi," *Daily Mail*, UK, February 4, 2016, www.dailymail.co.uk/news/article-3227607/U-S-hostage-Kayla-Mueller-fingernails-pulled-repeatedly-raped-ISIS-leader-Yazidi-sex-slave-reveals-torment-aid-worker-s-harrowing-final-months-forced-secret-wife-Al-Baghdadi.html#ixzz4ICgxjfny

84. Judit Neurink, "Isis leader Abu Bakr al-Baghdadi repeatedly raped US hostage Kayla Mueller and turned Yazidi girls into personal sex slaves—Systematic rape has become an increasingly powerful recruiting tool for ISIS," The Independent, Friday 14 August 2015, www.independent.co.uk/news/world/middle-east/isis-leader-abu-bakr-al-baghdadiexposed-as-serial-rapist-of-hostages-who-madewomen-his-personal-10456237.html 12-31-2015

85. Judit Neurink, "Isis leader Abu Bakr al-Baghdadi repeatedly raped US hostage Kayla Mueller and turned Yazidi girls into personal sex slaves—Systematic rape has become an increasingly powerful recruiting tool for ISIS," The Independent, Friday 14 August 2015, www.independent.co.uk/news/world/middle-east/isis-leader-abu-bakr-al-baghdadiexposed-as-serial-rapist-of-hostages-who-madewomen-his-personal-10456237.html 12-31-2015

86. Judit Neurink, "Isis leader Abu Bakr al-Baghdadi repeatedly raped US hostage Kayla Mueller and turned Yazidi girls into personal sex slaves—Systematic rape has become an increasingly powerful recruiting tool for ISIS," The Independent, Friday 14 August 2015, www.independent.co.uk/news/world/middle-east/isis-leader-abu-bakr-al-baghdadiexposed-as-serial-rapist-of-hostages-who-madewomen-his-personal-10456237.html 12-31-2015

87. Rukmini Callimachi, "ISIS Enshrines a Theology of Rape," New York Times, August 13, 2015, www.nytimes.com/2015/08/14/world/middleeast/isis-enshrines-a-theology-of-rape.html?_r=0 12-31-2015

88. Rukmini Callimachi, "ISIS Enshrines a Theology of Rape," New York Times, August 13, 2015, www.nytimes.com/2015/08/14/world/middleeast/isis-enshrines-a-theology-of-rape.html?_r=0 12-31-2015

89. Rukmini Callimachi, "ISIS Enshrines a Theology of Rape," New York Times, August 13, 2015, www.nytimes.com/2015/08/14/world/middleeast/isis-enshrines-a-theology-of-rape.html?_r=0 12-31-2015

90. Rukmini Callimachi, "ISIS Enshrines a Theology of Rape," New York Times, August 13, 2015, www.nytimes.com/2015/08/14/world/middleeast/isis-enshrines-a-theology-of-rape.html?_r=0 12-31-2015

91. Said Barack Obama, "They try to portray themselves as religious leaders, holy warriors. They are not religious leaders, they are terrorists. We are not at war with Islam. We are at war with people who have perverted Islam." Mary Alice Salinas, Luis Ramirez. "Obama: 'Ugly Lie' That West Is at War With Islam," Voice of America, February 19, 2015 www.voanews.com/content/president-obama-to-conclude-anti-extremist-summit/2650187.html

92. Umm Samayyah al-Muhajirah, "Slave Girls or Prostitutes?" Dābiq, Issue 9, May 21, 2015, p. 46.

93. The Sword of Islam, David Darlow, producer/director, Brian Park and Fiona Moffitt, research, Rod Caird, executive producer, Granada TV, Manchester, England, 1987. This extraordinary documentary, one of the few to probe the hostile world of Islamic fundamentalism in the 1980s, was the result of an 18-month investigation in Beirut, Cairo and Iran.

94. Kevin Baron, "Obama: ISIS Losing Territory, Influence As American Troops Push South in Syria," Defense One, December 14, 2015, www.govexec.com%2Fdefense%2F2015%2F12%2Fobama-isis-losing-territory-influence-american-troops-push-south-syria%2F124473%2F

95. Dābiq, issue 12, p. 25.

96. Dābiq, issue 12, p. 41.

97. Dābiq, issue 12, p. 3.

98. n.a. "Baqiyah (It Will Remain)," Dābiq, Issue 12, November 18, 2015, p. 18.

99. n.a. "A Selection of Military Operations By The Islamic State," Dābiq, Issue 12, November 18, 2015, p. 25.

100. Barbara Starr, Catherine Shoichet, "Russian plane crash: U.S. intel suggests ISIS bomb brought down jet," CNN, Wed November 4, 2015, www.cnn.com/2015/11/04/africa/russian-plane-crash-egypt-sinai/

101. Jason Draper, "Schweppes Gold," Thirsty Dudes, January 17, 2012, www.thirstydudes.com/review/schweppes-gold-2065

102. Islamic State, "Urgent: Statement about the Blessed Paris Invasion on the French Crusaders," retrieved from the World Wide Web November 14, 2015, townhall.com/tipsheet/katiepavlich/2015/11/14/isis-claims-responsibility-for-paris-terror-attackn2080755

103. Islamic State, "Urgent: Statement about the Blessed Paris Invasion on the French Crusaders," townhall.com/tipsheet/katiepavlich/2015/11/14/isis-claims-responsibility-for-paris-terror-at-tackn2080755 downloaded November 14, 2015.

104. Islamic State, "Urgent: Statement about the Blessed Paris Invasion on the French Crusaders," townhall.com/tipsheet/katiepavlich/2015/11/14/isis-claims-responsibility-for-paris-terror-at-tackn2080755 downloaded November 14, 2015.

105. Islamic State, "Urgent: Statement about the Blessed Paris Invasion on the French Crusaders," townhall.com/tipsheet/katiepavlich/2015/11/14/isis-claims-responsibility-for-paris-terror-at-tackn2080755 downloaded November 14, 2015

106. Islamic State, "Urgent: Statement about the Blessed Paris Invasion on the French Crusaders," townhall.com/tipsheet/katiepavlich/2015/11/14/isis-claims-responsibility-for-paris-terror-at-tackn2080755 downloaded November 14, 2015.

107. Osama bin Laden. Complete Text Of Sheikh Osama Bin Laden's Latest Message To Ummah May 12, 2004. Jihad Unspun. Retrieved from the World Wide Web May 14, 2004 www.jihadunspun.net/intheatre_internal.php?article=572&list=/home.php&

108. *Dābiq*, issue 12, p. 25.

109. Islamic State, "Urgent: Statement about the Blessed Paris Invasion on the French Crusaders," townhall.com/tipsheet/katiepavlich/2015/11/14/isis-claims-responsibility-for-paris-terror-at-tackn2080755 downloaded November 14, 2015.

110. Islamic State, "Urgent: Statement about the Blessed Paris Invasion on the French Crusaders," townhall.com/tipsheet/katiepavlich/2015/11/14/isis-claims-responsibility-for-paris-terror-at-tackn2080755 downloaded November 14, 2015.

111. San Bernardino Shooting Suspects Id'd; 1 Born In Chicago, ABC7 Chicago, December 04, 2015, abc7chicago.com/news/san-bernardino-shooting-suspects-idd;-1-born-in-chicago/1107868/

112. Christopher Goffard, "They met online, built a life in San Bernardino—and silently planned a massacre—Syed Rizwan Farook wanted a wife 'who takes her religion very seriously.' He found Tashfeen Malik online. They seemed the answer to each other's longings. What ignited their rage?" *LA Times*, December. 5, 2015, graphics.latimes.com/san-bernardino-syed-farook-tashfeen-malik/

113. Christopher Goffard, "They met online, built a life in San Bernardino—and silently planned a massacre," *LA Times*, December. 5, 2015, graphics.latimes.com/san-bernardino-syed-farook-tashfeen-malik/

114. Polly Mosendz, "FBI: San Bernardino Shooters Were Radicalized," *Newsweek*, December 7, 2015, www.newsweek.com/fbi-san-bernardino-shooters-were-radicalized-402178

115. Geneva Sands, Jack Date, "Everything We Know About the Weapons Used in the San Bernardino Massacre," ABC News, Dec 4, 2015, abcnews.go.com/US/weapons-san-bernardino-massacre/story?id=35584257

116. Meghan Keneally, "San Bernardino Shooters Had More Than 6,000 Rounds of Ammo, Police Say," ABC News, December 3, 2015, abcnews.go.com/US/san-bernardino-shooters-arsenal-detailed-injury-count-increases/story?id=35551325

117. Geneva Sands, Jack Date, "Everything We Know About the Weapons Used in the San Bernardino Massacre," ABC News, Dec 4, 2015, abcnews.go.com/US/weapons-san-bernardino-massacre/story?id=35584257

118. Pamela Engel, "Here's the ISIS message the female San Bernardino shooter posted on Facebook during the attack," *Business Insider*, December 17, 2015, www.businessinsider.com/isis-message-tashfeen-malik-posted-on-facebook-during-attack-2015-12

119. Dionne Searcey, Marc Santoranov, "Boko Haram Ranked Ahead of ISIS for Deadliest Terror Group," *New York Times*, November 18, 2015, www.nytimes.com/2015/11/19/world/africa/boko-haram-ranked-ahead-of-isis-for-deadliest-terror-group.html

120. Edward Delman, "The World's Deadliest Terrorist Organization—It's not ISIS," *The Atlantic*, November 18, 2015, www.theatlantic.com/international/archive/2015/11/isis-boko-haram-terrorism/416673/

121. Mark Anderson, "Terrorist killings up by 80% in 2014, fuelling flow of refugees, report says," *The Guardian*, UK, November 17, 2015, www.theguardian.com/global-development/2015/nov/17/terrorist-killings-up-by-80-per-cent-2014-fuelling-flow-refugees-global-terrorism-index

122. The Institute for Economics and Peace, 2015 Global Terrorism Index, The Institute for Economics and Peace, economicsandpeace.org/wp-content/uploads/2015/11/Global-Terrorism-Index-2015.pdf

123. Rose Troup Buchanan, "Isis overtaken by Boko Haram as world's deadliest terror organisation," *The Independent*, UK, 17 November 2015, www.independent.co.uk/news/world/africa/boko-haram-overtakes-isis-as-worlds-deadliest-terror-organisation-a6737761.html

124. iCasualties, Iraq, Operation Iraqi Freedom lists 4,815 Americans killed. iCasualties, Iraq, Operation Iraqi Freedom, icasualties.org/ downloaded from the World Wide Web 1-4-2016

125. *Dābiq*, Issue 12, p. 25.

126. Paradigm Shift, Part II, *Dābiq*, November 18, 2015, issue 12, p. 49.

127. *Dābiq*, Issue 12, p. 38.

128. *Dābiq*, Issue 12, p. 3.

129. *Dābiq*, Issue 12, p. 47.

130. *Dābiq*, Issue 12, p. 18.

131. Says one British Muslim protestor to CNN, "It is not just a hatred for America [that we are expressing]. It is a hatred for the whole of Western philosophy and Western civilization. Freedom, democracy, human rights, international law, all of these fake concepts that have been passed to us.... It is a hatred for all of this." Battle for Iraq's Destiny, CNN, August 16, 2004, edition.cnn.com/TRANSCRIPTS/0408/16/i_ins.00.html, 12-28-2015

132. *Dābiq*, Issue 12, p. 52.

133. *Dābiq*, Issue 12, p. 39.

134. *Dābiq*, Issue 12, p. 52.

135. Abu Jafar Muhammad ibn Jarir ibn Yazid ibn Kathir al-Tabari, *The History of al-Tabari: English translation of 'at Tareekh al-Tabari*," trans. M.V. McDonald, Albany: State University of New York Press, Volume VII, p. 97.

136. Sahih Bukhari. Book 52, Hadith 176–177. Translated by M. Muhsin Khan. SearchTruth.com. "Search Truth is a non-profit organization aimed at utilizing the latest technologies available in order to spread the Word of Allah and the Sunnah of the Holy Prophet (pbuh) to as large an audience as possible." www.searchtruth.com/searchHadith. php?keyword=There+is+a+Jew+hiding+behind+ me&translator=1&search=1&book=&start= 0&records_display=10&search_word=exact

137. Rendel Harris, "Hadrian's Decree of Expulsion of the Jews from Jerusalem," *The Harvard Theological Review*, Vol. 19, No. 2 (Apr., 1926), pp. 199–206, links.jstor.org/sici?sici=0017-8160 (192604)19%3A2%3C199%3C199%3AHDOEOT%3E2.0. CO%3B2-R. Wikipedia, "Jewish Diaspora." en.wikipedia.org/wiki/Jewish_diaspora#Roman_ destruction_of_Judea.

138. James Maxwell Miller, *A History of Ancient Israel and Judah*. Louisville, KY: Westminster John Knox Press, 1986, p. 318. Gregorio F. Zaide, *World History*. Quezon City, Philippines: Rex Bookstore, Inc., 1965, p. 61.

139. David Eggenberger, *An Encyclopedia of Battles: Accounts of Over 1,560 Battles from 1479 B.C. to the Present*. North Chelmsford, MA: Courier Corporation, 2012, p. 210.

140. Flavius Josephus, *The Jewish War of Flavius Josephus: A New Translation*, Volume II, trans. Robert Traill. London: Houlston and Stoneman, 1851, p. cixxi.

141. James J. Bloom, *The Jewish Revolts Against Rome, A.D. 66-135: A Military Analysis*. Jefferson, North Carolina: McFarland, 2010, p. 204. en.wikipedia.org/ wiki/Jewish_diaspora 1-4-2016

142. Raymond P. Scheindlin, *A Short History of the Jewish People: From Legendary Times to Modern Statehood*. Oxford: Oxford University Press, 1998, p. 51.

143. Raymond P. Scheindlin, *A Short History of the Jewish People: From Legendary Times to Modern Statehood*. Oxford UK: Oxford University Press, 1998, p. 54. "Palestine." (2007). In *Encyclopædia Britannica*. Retrieved January 5, 2007, from Encyclopædia Britannica Online, www.britannica.com/eb/article-45049. Richard S. Hess, "Early Israel in Canaan—A Survey of Recent Evidence and Interpretations," reprinted with permission from *Palestinian Exploration Quarterly* 125 (1993), pp. 125–42, individual.utoronto.ca/mfkolarcik/jesuit/ richardhess.htm

144. Thomas C. Oden, *Early Libyan Christianity: Uncovering a North African Tradition*. Westmont, Illinois: InterVarsity Press, 2011, p. 214.

145. Jane S. Gerber, *Jews of Spain: A History of the Sephardic Experience*. New York: Simon and Schuster, 1994, p. 2. Wikipedia, "History of the Jews in Spain—Early History," en.wikipedia.org/wiki/ History_of_the_Jews_in_Spain#Early_history_. 28before_300.29 1-4-2016

146. Esther Benbassa, *The Jews of France: A History from Antiquity to the Present*. Princeton: Princeton University Press, 2001, p. 3. Wikipedia, "History of the Jews in France—Roman-Gallic Epoch," en.wikipedia.org/wiki/ History_of_the_Jews_in_France#Roman-Gallic_ epoch 1-4-2016

147. "Palestine," *Encyclopædia Britannica*. 2007. Encyclopædia Britannica Online. 5 Jan. 2007 www.britannica.com/eb/article-45061.

148. Abu Al-Abbas Ahmad Bin Jab Al-Baladhuri. *The Origins of the Islamic State* (Kitab Futuh al-Buldan), translated by Philip Khuri Hitti, originally published 1816. New York: Cosimo Classics, 2011.

149. Abu Al-Abbas Ahmad Bin Jab Al-Baladhuri, *The Origins of the Islamic State* (Kitab Futuh al-Buldan).

150. Michael Neumann, author of "The Case Against Israel," claims that the practice of reciting, "Next year in Jerusalem" is a medieval invention. However he cites no evidence or sources. Michael Neumann, "Ethnic Nationalism Versus Common Sense: Response to a Zionist Book Review," *Swans Commentary*, April 24, 2006, www.swans.com/library/art12/mneu02.html

151. Mitchell Bard, "Pre-State Israel: Jewish Claim To The Land Of Israel," The Jewish Virtual Library, www.jewishvirtuallibrary.org/jsource/History/ The_Jewish_Claim_To_The_Land_Of_Israel.html 1-29-2016

152. Moshe Gil, *A History of Palestine, 634–1099*. Cambridge, UK: Cambridge University Press, p. 59.

153. The actual figure for the relationship between the territory of Israel and the expanse of New York State is .15682318415. In other words, Israel is just a tad more than one-sixth the size of New York State. Here is the raw information: 8,550 square miles=Israel; 54,520 square miles=New York State.

154. Arab lands in Arabia alone are spread over 1,184,000 square miles. (Martin Gilbert, *The Routledge Atlas of Arab-Israeli Conflict*. London: Routledge, 1974, p. 7.) But the Arab lands reach far beyond the Arabian Peninsula. They include, for example, most of North Africa. Rachel Neuwirth claims that the total territory held by Arabs is five million square miles. (Rachel Neuwirth, "A better framework for peace," *American Thinker*, July 15, 2004, www.americanthinker.com/2004/07/a_ better_framework_for_peace_1.html) There are 640 acres per mile. So the total number of acres held by Arab nations is far greater than the 757,760,000 acres held by Arabs in Arabia, and may be as high as 3.2 billion acres if Neuwirth is correct.

155. UNESCO, *A History of Land Use in Arid Regions*, 1953.

156. O.J.R. Howarth, *The Geographical Journal*, 1893, London: Royal Geographical Society, p. 299. "Nabataean." *Encyclopædia Britannica*. 2007. Encyclopædia Britannica Online. 6 Jan. 2007 www.britannica.com/eb/article-9054597.

157. In 1962, when I was doing this research, the Arab League consisted of Egypt, Syria, Lebanon, Iraq, Transjordan (now Jordan), Saudi Arabia, Yemen, Libya, Sudan, Tunisia, Morocco, Kuwait, and Algeria. These nations would later be joined by Bahrain, Oman, Qatar, and the United Arab Emirates (1971); Mauritania (1973); Somalia (1974); the Palestine Liberation Organization (PLO; 1976); Djibouti (1977); and the Comoros (1993). "Arab League." *Encyclopædia Britannica*. 2007, Encyclopædia Britannica Online. 6 Jan. 2007, www.britannica.com/eb/article-9008144.

158. Qur'an, 2:65, 5:60, and 7:166, The Holy Qur'an. Translation by Abdullah Yusufali. Complete online text. Retrieved March 20, 2005, from the World Wide Web www.wam.umd.edu/~stwright/rel/islam/, and The Noble Qur'an, quran.com/search?q=apes "The Jews, who are the nation of pigs and monkeys, are nothing but a source of evil, corruption, tribulation and war. ...Our war against them is continuous." Abdul-Azeez Al-Qaari, *The Menace of the Jews*, Translated by Hazem Ragab, Mecca: Alminbar.com—Alminbar.com - the Orator's garden and the Muslim's provision. Here you will find a variety of material to help you prepare for your sermons. Retrieved January 6, 2007, from the World Wide Web www.alminbar.com/khutbaheng/819.htm

159. As of 1998, there were 14.2 million Jews on this planet. (Religion Statistics: Jews by country. NationMaster.com, www.nationmaster.com/graph-t/rel_jew-religion-jews.) Cairo's metropolitan population, on the other hand, was more than 15.2 million. ("Cairo," NationMaster.com, www.nationmaster.com/encyclopedia/Cairo)

160. Wikipedia, "List of Largest Cities in the Organization of Islamic Cooperation," en.wikipedia.org/wiki/List_of_largest_cities_in_Organisation_of_Islamic_Cooperation_member_countries

161. Reuh Alleah Khumaynei (Ayatollah Khomeini), *Sayings of the Ayatollah Khomeini: Political, Philosophical, Social, and Religious*. New York: Bantam Books, 1980, p. 28.

162. The conventional translation of this policy advice from the Qur'an is, "tumult and oppression are worse than slaughter." The Holy Qur'an. chapter 2, verse 191. Translation by Abdullah Yusufali. Complete online text. Retrieved November 19, 2001, from the World Wide Web, www.wam.umd.edu/~stwright/rel/islam/

163. Qur'an, chapter 2,verse 24. Translation by Abdullah Yusufali.

164. Reuh Alleah Khumaynei (Ayatollah Khomeini), *Sayings of the Ayatollah Khomeini: Political, Philosophical, Social, and Religious*. New York: Bantam Books, 1980, p. 4.

165. "Imam Khomeini set 'roadmap' for justice, progress: Leader," *Tehran Times*, Saturday, June 6, 2015, www.tehrantimes.com/Index_view.asp?code=247152 12-28-2015 "Rahbar's address at Imam Khomeini's anniversary," June 2015, *Crescent International*, Newsmagazine of the [Iranian] Islamic Movement, www.crescent-online.net/2015/06/rahbars-address-at-imam-khomeinis-anniversary-crescent-onlinenet-4995-articles.html Imam Khomeini Airport, Imam Khomeini Relief Committee. "Nigeria's leader of the Islamic Movement of Nigeria, Ibrahim Zakzaky, inspired by Khomein," www.thedailybeast.com/articles/2015/12/23/nigeria-s-khomeini-spreading-iran-s-revolution-to-africa.html I said, 'Dad! Everyone in kindergarten is Muslim — they know about Imam Khomeini but they call him Santa!' Zahra Noorbakhsh, comedian www.npr.org/2015/12/23/460726559/what-american-muslims-do-on-christmas-new-traditions-emerge. The fighting between political elites "is attributed to sectarianism." "widespread violence among the parliamentary and political elites...One ought to recall what happened on Aug. 26, 2013, when Mulla [Sunni] and Kadhim al-Sayadi [Shiite] got into a fistfight because of a photograph of [the late] Ayatollah Ruhollah Khomeini, Read more: www.al-monitor.com/pulse/originals/2015/12/iraq-violence-politicians-assassination-insults.html#ixzz3vf2jw71x Iranian President Hassan Rouhani delivers a speech under portraits of Iran's supreme leader, Ayatollah Ali Khamenei (L) and Iran's founder of the Islamic Republic, Ayatollah Ruhollah Khomeini (R), on the eve of the 25th anniversary of the Islamic revolutionary leader Ayatollah Ruhollah Khomeini's death, at his mausoleum in a suburb of Tehran on 3 June, 2014 - See more at: www.middleeasteye.net/columns/us-hawks-give-iran-hardliners-ammunition-against-rouhani-1924888937#sthash.E3t4m7Lj.dpuf www.reuters.com/news/picture/conglomerate-controlled-by-irans-supreme?articleId=USKCN0RF0E920151021&slideId=1079462798 www.tehrantimes.com/Index_view.asp?code=247152 www.middleeasteye.net/columns/us-hawks-give-iran-hardliners-ammunition-against-rouhani-1924888937 www.al-monitor.com/pulse/originals/2015/12/iraq-violence-politicians-assassination-insults.html# www.tehrantimes.com/Index_view.asp?code=3448

166. U.S. Department of the Treasury, Joint Plan of Action (JPOA) Archive and Joint Comprehensive Plan of Action (JCPOA) Archive, www.treasury.gov/resource-center/sanctions/Programs/Pages/jpoa_archive.aspx U.S. Department of State, Joint Comprehensive Plan of Action, www.state.gov/e/eb/tfs/spi/iran/jcpoa/

167. Islamic Republic News Agency (IRNA), "Summary of provisions of CJPOA (3)— Summary of provisions of Comprehensive Joint Plan of Action," *IRNA*, Tehran, July 14, 2015, www.irna.ir/en/News/81683548/

168. The Middle East Media Research Institute, Special Dispatch Series — No. 785, Al-Zarqawi's Message to the Fighters of Jihad in Iraq on September 11, 2004, No. 785. September 15, 2004. www.memri.org/bin/latestnews.cgi?ID=SD78504

169. "World Trade Center," *Encyclopædia Britannica* 2005 Deluxe Edition CD.

170. The author of this Amazon.com review signed himself as "Nassir Isaf, Bainbridge Island, WA."

171. Abu Abdullah Usama bin Laden, Declaration Of War Against The Americans Occupying The Land Of The Two Holy Places: A Message from Usama bin Mohammed bin Laden unto his Muslim Brethren all over the world generally, and in the Arab Peninsula specifically. August 26, 1996. Retrieved from the World Wide Web May 05, 2004 www.intellnet.org/documents/300/080/382.htm

172. Osama bin Laden, Complete Text Of Sheikh Osama Bin Laden's Latest Message To Ummah May 12, 2004. Jihad Unspun. Retrieved from the World Wide Web May 14, 2004: www.jihadunspun.net/intheatre_internal.php?article=572&list=/home.php&

173. Thomas Carlyle, *On Heroes, Hero-Worship, and the Heroic in History*. Originally published 1841. Berkeley: University of California Press, 1993.

174. Sydney Smith, *The Works of the Rev. Sydney Smith*. London: Longman, Brown, Green, and Longmans, 1846, p. 102.

175. Sarah E. Mendelson and Theodore P. Gerber, "Failing the Stalin Test," From *Foreign Affairs*, January/February 2006 www.foreignaffairs.org/20060101facomment85101/sarah-e-mendelson-theodore-p-gerber/failing-the-stalin-test.html

176. Benedict says that a culture picks out a personality type, a set of "the intentions it [a culture] selects and makes its own." She says, "The cultural pattern of any civilization makes use of a certain segment of the great arc of potential human purposes and motivations. ... ...The great arc along which all possible human behaviors are distributed is far too immense and too full of contradictions for any one culture to utilize" Ruth Benedict, *Patterns of Culture*. New York: New American Library, 1950. Originally published 1934, p. 219. See also p. 234.

177. Ruth Benedict, *Patterns of Culture*, p. 130.

178. Ruth Benedict, *Patterns of Culture*, p. 130.

179. Ruth Benedict, *Patterns of Culture*, p. 227.

180. Hilary Lapsley, *Margaret Mead and Ruth Benedict: The Kinship of Women*. Amherst, MA: University of Massachusetts Press, 1999.

181. Benedict derived much of her information from her close friend—and possible lover—Margaret Mead, who saw similar contrasts between the New Guinean tribes the Arapesh and the Mundugumor. See: Margaret Mead, *The Mountain Arapesh*. New Brunswick, NJ: Transaction Publishers, 2002. Originally published 1938. See also: Library of Congress. Commemoration of the 100th anniversary of Margaret Mead's birth. Margaret Mead: *Human Nature and the Power of Culture. Sex and Temperament*. February 15, 2006, "Mead...found among the Arapesh a temperament for both males and females that was gentle, responsive, and cooperative. Among the Mundugumor (now Biwat), both males and females were violent and aggressive, seeking power and position." www.loc.gov/exhibits/mead/field-sepik.html. Jan E. Stets and Peter J. Burke, "Femininity/Masculinity." In Edgar F. Borgatta and Rhonda J.V. Montgomery (eds.). *Encyclopedia of Sociology*, Revised Edition. New York: Macmillan, 2000. pp. 997–1005. wat1203.ucr.edu/papers/00b.pdf.

182. Ruth Benedict, *Patterns of Culture*. Originally published 1934. New York: New American Library, 1950.

183. Benedict cites a Kwakiutl youth who says, "I will not block the road my father laid out for me. I will not break the law my chief laid down for me." Ruth Benedict, *Patterns of Culture*, p. 185. Benedict calls this "time-binding." She also takes note of a culture as a superorganism...referring to Alfred Kroeber's concept of culture as "superorganic." (Ruth Benedict, *Patterns of Culture*, p. 213.) She writes, "It is obvious that the sum of all the individuals in Zuni make up a culture beyond and above what those individuals have willed and created. The group is fed by tradition; it is 'time-binding.' It is quite justifiable to call it an organic whole." (Ruth Benedict, *Patterns of Culture*, p. 214.) Benedict also says, "A culture, like an individual, is a more or less consistent pattern of action. ...The whole... is not merely the sum of all its parts, but the result of a unique arrangement and interrelation of the parts that has brought about a new entity." (Ruth Benedict, *Patterns of Culture*, p. 42.)

184. For examples, see passages like the following: "Then to sum up, my dear Clinias, I said, the truth is that in all those things which we said at first were good, the question is not how they are in themselves naturally good, but this is the point, it seems. If ignorance leads them, they are greater evils than their opposites, inasmuch as they are more able to serve the leader which is evil; but if intelligence leads, and wisdom, they are greater goods, while in themselves neither kind is worth anything at all." (Plato, *The Collected Dialogues of Plato, Including the Letters*. Edited by Huntington Cairns and Edith Hamilton. New York: Pantheon Books, 1961, p. 395.) In other words, if a leader is intelligent and wise, the society he leads will be good. If a leader is ignorant, the society he leads will be evil. See also the interpretation of Plato's Republic by Reader in Philosophy at Scotland's University of St. Andrews. Leslie Stevenson, *Seven Theories of Human Nature*. New York: Oxford University Press, 1988, p. 32. Stevenson refers to Plato's Republic, lines 543–576.

185. Munemi Yamada, "A case of acculturation in a subhuman society of Japanese monkeys," *Primates*, Volume 1, Issue 1, Mar 1957, Pages 30–46, DOI 10.1007/BF01667197, URL dx.doi.org/10.1007/ BF01667197. John E. Frisch, "Individual Behavior and Intertroop Variability in Japanese Macaques." In Phyllis C. Jay, ed., *Primates: Studies in Adaptation and Variability*. New York: Holt, Rinehart and Winston, 1968, p. 246.

186. John E. Frisch, "Individual Behavior and Intertroop Variability in Japanese Macaques." In Phyllis C. Jay, ed., *Primates: Studies in Adaptation and Variability*. New York: Holt, Rinehart and Winston, 1968, p. 246.

187. John E. Frisch, "Individual Behavior and Intertroop Variability in Japanese Macaques." In Phyllis C. Jay, ed., *Primates: Studies in Adaptation and Variability*. New York: Holt, Rinehart and Winston, 1968, p. 246.

188. John E. Frisch, "Individual Behavior and Intertroop Variability in Japanese Macaques." In Phyllis C. Jay, ed., *Primates: Studies in Adaptation and Variability*. New York: Holt, Rinehart and Winston, 1968, p. 247.

189. John E. Frisch, "Individual Behavior and Intertroop Variability in Japanese Macaques." In Phyllis C. Jay, ed., *Primates: Studies in Adaptation and Variability*. New York: Holt, Rinehart and Winston, 1968, p. 247. To see the impact of leaders on a human society, take a look at this quote on the Vikings: "among the Viking peoples, perhaps to a larger degree than in any other society of their time, the history of the three great nations tends to be a mere record of the policies and achievements of their great men." Thomas Downing Kendrick. *A History of the Vikings*. New York: Charles Scribner's Sons, 1930, reprinted by New York: Dover Press, 2004, p. 117.

190. Mayr, E. *Animal Species and Evolution*. Harvard University Press, Cambridge, Massachusetts, 1963. Wikipedia. "The Founder Effect." en.wikipedia.org/ wiki/Founder_effect

191. Martin, Eden R.; Speer, Marcy C. "Founder Effect." 3 July 2006. www.bookrags.com/sciences/ genetics/founder-effect-gen-02.html

192. "Founders usually have a major impact on how the group defines and solves its external problem of surviving and growing, and how it will internally organize itself and integrate its own efforts. Because they had the original idea, founders will typically have their own notion, based on their own cultural history and personality, of how to get the idea fulfilled. Founders not only have a high level of self-confidence and determination, but typically they also have strong assumptions about the nature of human nature and relationships, how truth is arrived at, and how to manage time and space. Since they started the group, they tend to impose their assumptions on the group and to cling to them until such time as they become unworkable or the group fails and breaks up. As new members and leaders come into the group, the founder's assumptions and beliefs will gradually be modified, but they will always have the biggest impact on what will ultimately be the group's culture." p. 15. Edgar H. Schein, "The Role of the Founder in the Creation of Organizational Culture," pp. 14–25. In edited by Peter J. Frost, Larry F. Moore, Meryl Reis Louis, Craig C. Lundberg, Joanne Martin, *Reframing Organizational Culture*. Thousand Oaks, CA: Sage Publications: 1991, p. 15. Edgar H. Schein, a professor at MIT's Sloan School of Management and an expert in organizational culture. "Founders and subsequent leaders continue to influence and maintain organizational culture." p. 18 in a subsection called "Effect Mediated by Founders or Leaders" "When the founder of an organization decides who to bring in as initial key players in the organization and how to structure the organization, ...they hire people who share their own values, and they create organizational structures that reflect those values. Schneider's Attraction-Selection-Attrition (ASA) model states this explicitly, and argues that an eventual outcome of this process... is increased homogeneity within organizations on a variety of dimensions, including personality and values and cultural perceptions." p. 78 "It is also well established that organizational founders and leaders affect their organizations' structures and cultures." p. 79

Handbook of Global Leadership: The Globe Study of 62 Societies by Robert J. House, Paul J. Hanges, Mansour Javidan, Peter W. Dorfman. Thousand Oaks, CA: Sage Publications, 2004 "Culture, Leadership, and Organizations reports the results of a ten-year research program, the Global Leadership and Organizational Behavior Effectiveness research program (GLOBE)", carried out by "a team of 170 scholars" "to study societal culture, organizational culture, and attributes of effective leadership in 62 cultures" "A key outcome of ASA processes [attraction-selection-attrition] is a continual narrowing...by self-selection. ...this homogenization process can produce sufficient similarity...that the organization can be thought of as having a 'modal personality type'." Lawrence R. James, Michelle D. Mazerolle, *Personality in Work Organizations*. Thousand Oaks, CA: Sage Publications, 2002, p. 59. "In India, Negandhi reported that the owners and founding families' authority and influence on the running of the firm is much higher that what was prevalent in firms operating in western countries. Conformity pressures such as coercive persuasion exercised by powerful people can serve to exert a great deal of social influence as young managers seek inclusion to the power circle." Herbert J. (EDT) Davis, S.R. (EDT) Chatterjee, Mark (EDT) Heuer, *Management in India: Trends and Transition*. Thousand Oaks, CA: Sage Publications, 2006, p. 136. "The Norwegian version of sustainable development dates back to the first settlers who came by boat to the territory around 10,000 years ago. ...Puritan values were welcomed in Norway because they complied with the values of prudence and resource consciousness that dates back to the first settlers." Anne Kristine Haugestad, Research Fellow Department of Sociology and Political Science Norwegian University of Science and Technology. Presentation at "Citizenship & the Environment," an ESRC Seminar Series, Seminar 2, "Environmental Citizenship in Practice (I)", 29–30 April, 2004, The Open University, Milton Keynes.

193. Shaka Zulu's approximate birth date. See Wikipedia, "Shaka." en.wikipedia.org/wiki/Shaka#Early_years

194. Donald R. Morris, *The Washing of the Spears: A History of the Rise of the Zulu Nation under Shaka and Its Fall in the Zulu War of 1879*. New York: Simon and Schuster, 1986. Angus McBride, *Zulu War*. Oxford: Osprey Publishing, 1976, p. 4.

195. Robert B. Edgerton, *Africa's Armies: A History from 1791 to the Present*. Boulder, CO: Westview Press: 2002, p. 10.

196. Murray Davies, *Commanding Change: War Winning Military Strategies for Organizational Change*. Westport, CT: Praeger Publishers, 2001, p. 40.

197. Donald R. Morris, *The Washing of the Spears: A History of the Rise of the Zulu Nation under Shaka and Its Fall in the Zulu War of 1879*. New York: Simon and Schuster, 1986, pp. 44–45.

198. Leonard L. Thompson, *A History of South Africa*: Third Edition. New Haven, CT: Yale University Press, 2000, pp. 81–83.

199. Donald R. Morris, *The Washing of the Spears: A History of the Rise of the Zulu Nation under Shaka and Its Fall in the Zulu War of 1879*. New York: Simon and Schuster, 1986, p. 52.

200. Donald R. Morris, *The Washing of the Spears: A History of the Rise of the Zulu Nation under Shaka and Its Fall in the Zulu War of 1879*. New York: Simon and Schuster, 1986, pp. 51-52.

201. Donald R. Morris, *The Washing of the Spears: A History of the Rise of the Zulu Nation under Shaka and Its Fall in the Zulu War of 1879*. New York: Simon and Schuster, 1986, p. 52.

202. Donald R. Morris, *The Washing of the Spears: A History of the Rise of the Zulu Nation under Shaka and Its Fall in the Zulu War of 1879*. New York: Simon and Schuster, 1986, p. 52.

203. Donald R. Morris, *The Washing of the Spears: A History of the Rise of the Zulu Nation under Shaka and Its Fall in the Zulu War of 1879*. New York: Simon and Schuster, 1986, p. 53.

204. Donald R. Morris, *The Washing of the Spears: A History of the Rise of the Zulu Nation under Shaka and Its Fall in the Zulu War of 1879*. New York: Simon and Schuster, 1986: p. 53.

205. Donald R. Morris, *The Washing of the Spears: A History of the Rise of the Zulu Nation under Shaka and Its Fall in the Zulu War of 1879*. New York: Simon and Schuster, 1986, p. 53.

206. Donald R. Morris, *The Washing of the Spears: A History of the Rise of the Zulu Nation under Shaka and Its Fall in the Zulu War of 1879*. New York: Simon and Schuster, 1986, p. 53.

207. Donald R. Morris, *The Washing of the Spears: A History of the Rise of the Zulu Nation under Shaka and Its Fall in the Zulu War of 1879*. New York: Simon and Schuster, 1986, p. 67.

208. Byung-joon Ahn, "The Man Who Would Be Kim." *Foreign Affairs*, November/December 1994.

209. Raymond Case Kelly, *The Nuer Conquest: The Structure and Development of an Expansionist System*. Ann Arbor, MI: University of Michigan Press, 1985.

210. Elliott Sober and David Sloan Wilson, *Unto Others: The evolution and psychology of unselfish behavior*. Cambridge, MA: Harvard University Press, 1998. David Sloan Wilson, *Darwin's Cathedral: Evolution, Religion, and the Nature of Society*. Chicago: University of Chicago Press, 2002. Frederick Crews, E.O. Wilson, Jonathan Gottschall, and David Sloan Wilson, *The Literary Animal: Evolution and the Nature of Narrative (Rethinking Theory)*. Evanston, IL: Northwestern University Press, 2005.

211. David Sloan Wilson. D.S. Wilson on Palmer et al. Personal communication. December 7, 1998.

212. Raymond C. Kelly, *The Nuer Conquest: The Structure and Development of an Expansionist System*. Ann Arbor, MI. University of Michigan Press, 1985: p. 236–238.

213. "The maximal level of cattle per capital holdings that could be achieved was not sufficient to satisfy Nuer pastoral aspirations. ...There is, in short, no evidence that the analytically identifiable ensemble of interrelationships characteristic of the Nuer sociocultural system manifests internal regulatory properties conducive to the cessation of territorial expansion." Raymond C. Kelly, *The Nuer Conquest: The Structure and Development of an Expansionist System*. Ann Arbor, MI. University of Michigan Press, 1985, p. 236.

214. Raymond C. Kelly, *The Nuer Conquest: The Structure and Development of an Expansionist System*. Ann Arbor, MI. University of Michigan Press, 1985: p. 53.

215. Richard Dawkins, *The Selfish Gene*. New York: Oxford University Press, 1976.

216. Camilo Mora, Derek P. Tittensor, Sina Adl, Alastair G.B. Simpson, Boris Worm, "How Many Species Are There on Earth and in the Ocean?" *PLoS Biology*, 2011; 9 (8): e1001127 DOI: 10.1371/journal.pbio.1001127. Census of Marine Life. "How many species on Earth? About 8.7 million, new estimate says." ScienceDaily. *ScienceDaily*, 24 August 2011. www.sciencedaily.com/releases/2011/08/110823180459.htm.

217. Camilo Mora, Derek P. Tittensor, Sina Adl, Alastair G.B. Simpson, Boris Worm, "How Many Species Are There on Earth and in the Ocean?" *PLoS Biology*, 2011; 9 (8): e1001127 DOI: 10.1371/journal.pbio.1001127 , journals.plos.org/plosbiology/article?id=10.1371/journal.pbio.1001127 3-16-2016

218. United States Census Bureau, U.S. and World Population Clock, www.census.gov/popclock/ 1-5-2016

219. Maulana A.S. Muhammad Abdul Hai (Rah.), *Holy Life of Hazrat Muhammad (Hayyat-E-Tayyaba)*. Delhi, India: Islami Academy, 1984. www.al-islamforall.org/litre/Englitre/Hmohd.htm

220. F.E. Peters puts The Year of the Elephant at 552 A.D. (F.E. Peters, *Muhammad and the Origins of Islam*. Albany: State University of New York Press, 1994: p. 95). Wikipedia puts the date 18 years later, at 570 A.D. (Wikipedia, "Year of the Elephant." en.wikipedia.org/wiki/Year_of_the_Elephant.

221. Wikipedia, "Ethiopia." en.wikipedia.org/wiki/Ethiopia

222. Since the reign of Ezana of Axum. See Wikipedia, "Ezana." en.wikipedia.org/wiki/Ezana.

223. Richard Pankhurst, "History of Trade between Ethiopia, Arabia, and the Horn of Africa." *Addis Tribune*, Addis Adaba, Ethiopia. www.addistribune.com/Archives/2002/07/26-07-02/History.htm

224. Wikipedia, "Abraha." en.wikipedia.org/wiki/Abraha

225. John M. Kistler, *War Elephants*. Lincoln, NE: University of Nebraska Press, 2007, p. 177. The Holy Qur'an, 105:1. Translation by Abdullah Yusufali. Complete online text. Retrieved January 5, 2016, from the World Wide Web www.wam.umd.edu/~stwright/rel/islam/

226. Abu al-Walid Muhammad al-Azraqi. Akhbar Makka, ed. F. Wüstenfeld. *Die Chroniken der Stadt Mekka*, vol. 1. Leipzig, 1858; rp. Khayats, 1964. Quoted in F.E. Peters, *Muhammad and the Origins of Islam*. Albany: State University of New York Press, 1994, pp. 93-94.

227. Ibn Ishaq, *Sirat Rasoul Allah: The earliest biography of Muhammad*, by ibn Ishaq. An abridged version Edited by Michael Edwardes. Retrieved June 7, 2006, from the World Wide Web www.faithfreedom.org/Articles/sira/02.htm

228. Ibn Ishaq, *The Life of Muhammad—Apostle of Allah*. Edited by Michael Edwardes. London: The Folio Society, 1964, p. 27. Ibn Ishaq, *Sirat Rasoul Allah: The earliest biography of Muhammad*, by ibn Ishaq. An abridged version Edited by Michael Edwardes. Retrieved June 7, 2006, from the World Wide Web www.faithfreedom.org/Articles/sira/02.htm "twice a year during the sacred months, pilgrims were drawn to Holy Mecca on pilgrimage, and their fee of homage was the provisions, on which the Quraysh and the other Meccans lived. Trade enters nowhere into this equation, particularly not the long-distance trade read by some of the comentators into verse 2 of Sura 106. Trade may have been a background issue, however...some of Muhammad's audience appears to have opposed it, or such seems to be the sense of verse 198 in Sura 2, "It is no fault for you to aspire to the Lord's bounty," immediately preceded and followed by detailed prescriptions regarding pilgrimage "in the well-known months."...the "Lord's bounty" was reaped by interested parties: namely, the holy-day fairs (mawasim). ...Peoples who, by reason of danger or distance, did not normally associate came together in and around Mecca under the protection of the truce of God to worship and, it seems clear, to trade. Al Azraqi's is the most detailed sketch of the market fairs: "And the Hajj was in the month of Dhu al-Hijja. People went out with their goods and they ended up in Ukaz on the day of the new moon of Dhu al-Qa'da. They stayed there twenty nights during which they set up in the Ukaz their market of all colors and goods in small houses. The leaders and foremen of each tribe oversaw the selling and buying among the tribes where they congregated in the middle of the market. After twenty days they leave for Majanna, and they spend ten days in its market, and when they see the new moon of Dhu al-Hijja they leave for Dhu al-Majaz, where they spend eight days and nights in its markets. They leave Dhu al-Majaz on the 'day of tawarih,' so called because they depart from Du al-Majaz for Urfa after they have taken water (for their camels) from Dhu al-Majaz. They do this because there is no drinking water in Urfa, nor in Muzdalifa. The 'day of tawarih' was the last day of their markets...." a practice that did not extend, as we shall see, to Mecca. Therefore the wealth of the pre-Islamic Quraysh had nothing to do, as it certainly did in the Islamic era, with trading with pilgrims at Mecca during the Hajj season. If Meccans traded, it was elsewhere. ...the Quraysh's own status as a holy tribe, a condition

formally institutionalized not long before Muhammad's birth by the confederation known as the Hums." [hb, p. 94] Francis E. Peters, *Muhammad and the Origins of Islam*. Albany: State University of New York Press, 1994 books.google.com/books?vid=ISBN0791418758&id= 0OrCo4VyvGkC&pg=PA94&lpg=PA95&printsec= 8&dq=%22the+hums%22&sig=KjYej_Z3ELj0-eyMlz_ 6dMS0SDQ

"Some decades earlier the Quraysh had begun to establish the of [sic] 'The Hums,' which imposed acceptance of Quraysh priority over the other Arab tribes. 'We are the sons of Abraham, men of honour, governors of the house of Allah, inhabitants of Mecca. No Arab has such virtue as we, nor such dignity as we. No man of the Quraysh should honour territory which is secular in the way he honours that which is sacred. For if he does so the Arabs will slight his honour, and will say of the Quraysh, "They have honoured that which is profane [outside the sacred limits] in the same way as that which is sacred [within the sanctuary of the holy territory of Mecca]." Accordingly the Quraysh abandoned certain holy ordinances of pilgrimage enjoined by the religion of Abraham, saying: 'We are the inhabitants of the sacred city of Mecca and it is not proper for us to leave it and honour another place as we honour Mecca. We are the Hums, the people of the sacred place.' But they imposed the ordinances on all other Arabs born either without or within the limits of Mecca.

They next invented new observances for themselves. They announced that it was not proper for the Hums to prepare eqth [milk dried and reduced to powder], to melt fat, or to enter a camel-hair tent whilst they were in a state of purity and sanctity [performing the ceremonies of the pilgrimage]. They added even to these rules, saying that persons who had come from outside the sacred city ought not to eat food they had brought in with them, whether they came as pilgrims or visitors. The pilgrims' first circuit of the Kab a should be made in dress provided by the Hums, or, if such could not be procured, in no dress at all; but rich men or women unwilling to do either could walk around the temple in the garments in which they had arrived, provided they afterwards threw them away and neither touched them any more nor allowed anyone else to touch them. The Arabs were induced to agree to this and made the circuit of the Kaba, the men naked, and the women clad only in an open cassock.
Ibn Ishaq from www.faithfreedom.org/Articles/ sira/02.htm

229. These practices began not long before or after the Year of the Elephant, 552 A.D. Francis E. Peters, *Muhammad and the Origins of Islam*. Albany: State University of New York Press, 1994, p. 95.

230. n.a. *The Life of The Last Prophet: Prophet Muhammad*. www.thewaytotruth.org/ catindex7.html

231. The fact that the Prophet was born on a Monday comes to us courtesy of Muhammad's first biographer, Ibn Ishaq, who wrote an extensive history of the Prophet's life in approximately 760 A.D. Ibn Ishaq lived in Medina and pulled together traditional tales of the Prophet's life and conquests, then settled in Baghdad, where he was underwritten by the Caliph Mansur as he wrote his masterwork, *Sirat Rasoul Allah*. Ibn Ishaq,*The Life of Muhammad—Apostle of Allah*. Edited by Michael Edwardes. London: The Folio Society, 1964, p. 17.

232. This biography of Muhammad is compiled from the following sources: Muhammad H. Haykal, *The Life of Muhammad*. Translated by Isma'il Raji al-Faruqi. Kuala Lumpur, Malaysia: Islamic Book Trust, 2002. Maulana A.S. Muhammad Abdul Hai (Rah.), *Holy Life of Hazrat Muhammad (Hayyat-E-Tayyaba)*. Delhi, India: Islami Academy, 1984.
www.al-islamforall.org/litre/Englitre/Hmohd.htm
n.a. Prophet Muhammad — A brief biography. Islamic Occasions—Truth, Wisdom, and Justice. Website designed by Akramulla Syed. Last Updated: 01 September 2004,
www.ezsoftech.com/islamic/infallible1a.asp#01
Ahmad Ibn Yahya Al-Baladhuri, *The Origins of the Islamic State (Futuhul Buldan)*. (Written in approximately 880 A.D.).
al-islam1.org/encyclopedia/chapter4/8.html.
Shaykh Safi ur-Rahmaan Mubarakfoori, *Seerah of the Final Messenger of Allaah: The Sealed Nectar (Ar-Raheeq al-Makhtoom)*. According to one online Islamic bookstore, this biography of the Prophet was "awarded First prize by the Muslim world league at world-wide competition on the biography of the Prophet held at Makkah." The bookstore, Islamic Goods Direct [www.islamicgoodsdirect.co.uk/product_info.php/products_id/1750], does not give the date of the award. Retrieved August 30, 2005, from the World Wide Web www.witness-pioneer.org/vil/Books/SM_tsn/
Hazrat Moulana Sayyed Abul Hassan Ali Nadwi (R.A.), *The Seerah of Muhammad (Sallallahu Laiyhi Wassallam): (The Last Prophet: A Model For All Time)*. Al-Islaah Publications. Retrieved August 31, 2005, From the World Wide Web: Alislaah3.Tripod.Com/
Sayed Ali Asgher Razwy, *A Restatement of the History of Islam and Muslims—CE 570 to 661.* Published by: World Federation of KSI Muslim Communities. United Kingdom. Reproduced with permission by the Ahlul Bayt Digital Islamic Library Project Ahlul Bayt Digital Islamic Library Project. al-islam.org/restatement/29.htm
Maulana A.S. Muhammad Abdul Hai, *Holy Life of Hazrat Muhammad (Hayyat-E-Tayyaba)*. Al-Islam Society. ("Al-Islam propagation society is a Non-profit socio-educational organization founded with the objective of facilitating the spread of accurate and authentic knowledge about Islam among the different nations of the world. Our aim is to work for proper understanding of Islam by all and to work to strengthen the moral and social fabric of the peoples of the world. We envisage a universal society which is bound by mutual understanding and brotherhood and which is honoured by the presence of Islam.")
Al-Islamforall.org.

www.al-islamforall.org/litre/Englitre/Hmohd.htm.
Compiled from the publications of Said Nursi and Fethullah Gulen, *Islam by Questions: Answers to selected questions about Islam*. 2000.
www.islamanswers.net/moreAbout/Uhud.htm
Sahih Bukhari. Translator: M. Muhsin Khan. MSA-USC Hadith Database. USC-MSA Compendium of Muslim Texts. University of Southern California.
www.usc.edu/dept/MSA/fundamentals/hadithsunnah/bukhari/
Shaykh Safi ur-Rahmân Mubarakpûri, *Ar-Rahîq al-Makhtûm (The Sealed Nectar)* — a comprehensive biography of Muhammad. www.quraan.com/index.aspx?tabindex=4&tabid=11&bid=7
Seerah of the Final Messenger of Allaah: "The Story of the Prisoners of the Battle of Badr." Shaykh Safi ur-Rahmaan Mubarakfoori from Ar-Raheeq al-Makhtoom.
Retrieved July 16, 2005, from the World Wide Web www.sunnahonline.com/ilm/seerah/0005.htm
n.a. *A Brief Biography of the Life of the Holy Prophet Habibullah (beloved) (pbuh) Holy Wars*. Islamiccoccasions.com—Truth Wisdom & Justice. www.ezsoftech.com/islamic/infallible1e.asp
Universal Sunnah Foundation, Pakistan. *The Prophet Muhammad: Biography of the Holy Prophet*. In Islamic Paths. www.islamic-paths.org/Home/English/Muhammad/Book/Biography/Chapter_33.htm or www.usf.edu.pk/ *Sahih Bukhari* translated by M. Muhsin Khan. in SearchTruth.com. Retrieved February 15, 2006, from the World Wide Web SearchTruth.com. "Search Truth is a non-profit organization aimed at utilizing the latest technologies available in order to spread the Word of Allah and the Sunnah of the Holy Prophet (pbuh) to as large an audience as possible." Retrieved February 15, 2006, from the World Wide Web www.searchtruth.com
Sahih Muslim, The Book of Faith (Kitab Al-Iman)' of Sahih Muslim. Translated by Abdul Hamid Siddiqui. In SearchTruth.com.
www.searchtruth.com/hadith_books.php
Sarwat Saulat, *The Life of The Prophet*. Islamic Publications Ltd., Lahore, Pakistan, 1983. William H. McNeill and Marilyn Robinson Waldman, *The Islamic World*. University of Chicago Press, Chicago, 1983. H.G. Wells, *The Outline of History*. Macmillan, New York, 1926. J.M. Roberts, *The Pelican History of the World*. Penguin Books, Harmondsworth, Middlesex, England, 1980. Edward Gibbon, *The Decline and Fall of the Roman Empire*. Penguin Classics, New York, 1985.
233. Marion Kaplan, "Who Were The Ancient Arab Sea Traders?" Copyright 2002 CanBooks nabataea.net/who1.html

234. One eager Christian, Jay Smith, even turns to sources like "the Doctrina Iacobi, the earliest testimony of Muhammad and of his 'movement' available to us outside Islamic tradition; a Greek anti-Jewish tract which was written in Palestine between 634 and 640 A.D. (Brock 1982:9; Crone-Cook 1977:3)", "an Armenian chronicle from around 660 A.D., which is ascribed by some to Bishop Sebeos (Sebeos 1904:94-96; Crone-Cook 1977:6)", and "the Continuatio Byzantia Arabica, which is a source dating from early in the reign of the caliph Hisham, who ruled between 724–743 A.D." to prove that either Mecca didn't exist at all, that Mecca was not located on a spot that could have possibly given it the least importance in trade, and that even if Mecca did exist, it was an unknown— and anonymous—backwater. Jay Smith, "The Bible and The Qur'an: An Historical Comparison." The Muslim-Christian Debate Website. ©1997 Hyde Park Christian Fellowship. debate.org.uk/topics/history/ bib-qur/qurdoc.htm

235. en.wikipedia.org/wiki/Arabian_sea

236. Marion Kaplan, "Who Were The Ancient Arab Sea Traders?" Copyright 2002 CanBooks nabataea.net/who1.html

237. Marion Kaplan, "The History and Construction of The Dhow." Copyright 2002 Canbooks nabataea. net/ships.html

238. Martin Gray, "Mecca, Places of Peace and Power," sacredsites.com/middle_east/ saudi_arabia/mecca.html 9-30-2016

239. Ibn Ishaq, *Sirat Rasul Allah: The earliest biography of Muhammad*, An Abridged Version archive.org/details/Sirat-lifeOfMuhammad By-ibnIshaq 1-6-2016, p. 60. Ira M. Lapidus, *A History of Islamic Societies*. Cambridge: Cambridge University Press, 2002, p. 14.

240. "The History of Kaaba." Hajj (Pilgrimage) web site. Submission.org--Your Best Source for Islam (Submission) on the Internet. www.submission.org/hajj/kaaba.html

241. Khalid Mecci, "Leaf from the Prophet's Life: War and Peace." Children's Corner. *Islamic Voice*, Vol. 12-07, No. 139, July 1998. Retrieved June 7, 2006, from the World Wide Web www.islamicvoice.com/july.98/child.htm

242. Sarwat Saulat, *The Life of The Prophet*. Islamic Publications Ltd., Lahore, Pakistan, 1983.

243. Sarwat Saulat, *The Life of The Prophet*. Islamic Publications Ltd., Lahore, Pakistan, 1983, p. 8.

244. Maulana A.S. Muhammad Abdul Hai (Rah.), *Holy Life of Hazrat Muhammad (Hayyat-E-Tayyaba)*. Delhi, India: Islami Academy, 1984. www.al-islamforall.org/litre/Englitre/Hmohd.htm. Medina was called Yathrib at the time. After Muhammad arrived, the town was renamed Medina al-Nabi, the city of the Prophet. For simplicity, I've followed the Muslim practice and have used the name Medina throughout this book. James Stuart Olson, Lee Brigance, Nicholas Charles Pappas, *An Ethnohistorical Dictionary of the Russian and Soviet Empire*. Westport, Connecticut:

Greenwood Publishing Group, 1994, p. 759. David Levinson, *Religion: A Cross-cultural Encyclopedia*. Santa Barbara, CA: ABC-CLIO, 1996, p. 91.

245. Bernard Lewis, *The Arabs in History*. New York: Oxford University Press, 2002, p. 40.

246. Bihar Anjuman, "Biography of Prophet Mohammad (PBUH) ....A Quiz to refresh your memory," www.biharanjuman.org/ prophet-biography-quiz.htm 3-17-2016

247. As we'll see later in this book, Muhammad said that humor was a form of attack. "Hostility," he proclaimed, "begins with joking." "The Prophet, sallallahu alayhe wa sallam. Abu Hurairah said that the prophet, sallallahu alayhe wa sallam, was told, "O Prophet of Allah, you are joking with us." He said, "I only say what is true." (Tirmithi) Another hadith relates that the prophet, sallallahu alayhe wa sallam, would nickname Zeinab bint Um Salama by repeatedly calling her 'O Zuweinab.'Other Ahadith relate that the Prophet, sallallahu alayhe wa sallam, would play and joke with small children. Thus we see that joking is a Sunnah. Sufyan bin Uyayna was asked, "Is joking prohibited?" He replied, "It is a Sunnah, but the point is that it must be done appropriately." Many of the scholars agree that. Omar (Radhiallahu anhu) said, "I admire the man who is like a child with his family (playful), and once he leaves them, he is more serious." Thabit ibn Ubaid said, "Zayd ibn Thabit was one of the most humorous men in his home. Outside of his home, he was as serious as any man." It is also related that ibn Abbas asked some of his guests to have light and humorous conversation so that they would have a good time and not feel bored. Rabi'a said, "Virtue is made of six parts, three while in town (at the place of your home) and three while on a journey. The first three are reciting the Qur'an, frequently being at the mosque, and spreading the way of Allah to other lands. The three parts while traveling are spending, showing virtuous behaviour and joking in what Allah has permitted." Ibn Abbas said, "Joking appropriately is permissible, for the Prophet, sallallahu alayhe wa sallam, joked but he only said what was true." Al Khalil bin Ahmad al Fraheedi said, "People would feel imprisoned if they did not joke." Prohibition of joking: On the other hand, some of the scholars have prohibited joking and they are supported by some Ahaddeth. It is related that the Prophet, sallallahu alayhe wa sallam, said, "Everything has a beginning and hostility begins with joking." Ja'far ibn Muhammad said, "Beware of joking for it causes embarrass- ment." Ibrahim al-Nakh'i said, "Joking shows foolishness and arrogance." Imam ibn Abdul Bar said, "Some of the scholars denounced joking for what it causes of offences, spite and malice between people."" Islam and the sense of humor By Soumy Ana: Jumad al-Awwal 1423 — July– August 2002. "Taqwa Palace, Palace of Faith." Ummah.com—The Muslim Directory Online. www.ummah.com/islam/taqwapalace/humour.pdf

248. Sarwat Saulat, *The Life of The Prophet*, Islamic Publications Ltd., Lahore, Pakistan, 1983, pp. 9–10.

249. "Muhammad." *Encyclopædia Britannica*, from Encyclopædia Britannica Deluxe Edition 2005 CD. Copyright © 1994–2004 Encyclopædia Britannica, Inc. May 30, 2004.

250. Ibn Ishaq, *Sirat Rasoul Allah, An abridged version*, archive.org/details/Sirat-lifeOfMuhammad By-ibnIshaq 1-6-2016, p. 10.

251. Muhammad H. Haykal, *The Life of Muhammad (Allah's peace and blessing be upon him)*. By Muhammad Husayn Haykal, translated by Isma'il Razi A. al-Faruqi. Retrieved June 7, 2006, from the World Wide Web www.witness-pioneer.org/vil/ Books/MH_LM/Muhammad_From_Birth_to_ Marriage.htm. Hāshim, Banu (Quraysh clan) and Muhammad. *Encyclopædia Britannica*, from Encyclopædia Britannica Deluxe Edition 2005 CD. Copyright © 1994–2004 Encyclopædia Britannica, Inc. May 30, 2004.

252. Sarwat Saulat, *The Life of The Prophet*. Islamic Publications Ltd., Lahore, Pakistan, 1983: pp. 8–9.

253. Ibn Ishaq, *Sirat Rasoul Allah*, An abridged version, p. 22, archive.org/details/Sirat-lifeOf MuhammadBy-ibnIshaq "Most of the Meccan people did trade for a living. Abu Talib also dealt with trade for a while. However, he no longer had the financial strength to trade due to having too many members in his family, tribal wars, and outbreaks of famine and drought. For this reason, he was unable to attain another opportunity in joining a caravan after the previous journey he made to Syria with our Holy Prophet (PBUH). He was making a living by doing some jobs in Mecca." The Prophet goes to Damascus for the second time, The Prophet Muhammad (PBUH)—The Pride of the Universe, www.resulullah.org/en/ prophet-goes-damascus-second-time

254. "Key Figures in Muhammad's Life." The Islam Project. www.theislamproject.org/muhammad/ muhammad_08_KeyFiguresinMuhammadsLife.htm Fethullah Gülen. "The Prophet's Life Before His Prophethood." In Prophet Muhammad: Aspects of His Life- 1. From Fethullah Gulen: A Life Dedicated to Humanity and Peace. Tuesday, 18 September 2001 en.fgulen.com/content/view/913/2/

255. Maulana A.S. Muhammad Abdul Hai (Rah.), *Holy Life of Hazrat Muhammad (Hayyat-E-Tayyaba)*. Delhi, India: Islami Academy, 1984. www.al-islamforall.org/litre/Englitre/Hmohd.htm

256. "Khālid ibn al-Walid." *Encyclopædia Britannica*, from Encyclopædia Britannica Deluxe Edition 2005 CD. Copyright © 1994–2004 Encyclopædia Britannica, Inc. May 30, 2004.

257. Ibn Ishaq, *Sirat Rasoul Allah: The earliest biography of Muhammad*, by ibn Ishaq. An abridged version Edited by Michael Edwardes. www.faithfreedom.org/Articles/sira/01.htm. Maulana A.S. Muhammad Abdul Hai (Rah.), *Holy Life of Hazrat Muhammad (Hayyat-E-Tayyaba)*. Delhi, India: Islami Academy, 1984. Retrieved June 7, 2006, from the World Wide Web www.al-islamforall.org/litre/Englitre/Hmohd.htm

258. Muhammad H. Haykal, *The Life of Muhammad (Allah's peace and blessing be upon him)*. by Muhammad Husayn Haykal, translated by Isma'il Razi A. al-Faruqi. www.witness-pioneer.org/vil/ Books/MH_LM/Muhammad_From_Birth_to_ Marriage.htm

259. Wikipedia, "Bilad al-Sham." en.wikipedia.org/ wiki/Bilad_al-Sham

260. "The Prophet goes to Damascus for the second time," The Prophet Muhammad (PBUH)—The Pride of the Universe, www.resulullah.org/en/ prophet-goes-damascus-second-time

261. Ross Burns, *Damascus: A History*. London: Routledge, 2007, p. 97.

262. Ross Burns, *Damascus: A History*. London: Routledge, 2007, p. 79.

263. Nancy Khalek, *Damascus After the Muslim Conquest: Text and Image in Early Islam*. New York: Oxford University Press, 2011, pp. 3–4, 49.

264. Muhammad H. Haykal, *The Life of Muhammad (Allah's peace and blessing be upon him)*. by Muhammad Husayn Haykal, translated by Isma'il Razi A. al-Faruqi. www.witness-pioneer.org/vil/ Books/MH_LM/Muhammad_From_Birth_to_ Marriage.htm. Sayed Ali Asgher Razwy, *A Restatement of the History of Islam and Muslims— CE 570 to 661*. Published by: World Federation of KSI Muslim Communities. United Kingdom. Reproduced with permission by the Ahlul Bayt Digital Islamic Library Project Ahlul Bayt Digital Islamic Library Project www.al-islam.org/restatement/5.htm

265. Ibn Ishaq, *Sirat Rasoul Allah: The earliest biography of Muhammad*, by ibn Ishaq. An abridged version Edited by Michael Edwardes. Retrieved June 7, 2006, from the World Wide Web www.faithfreedom.org/Articles/sira/01.htm. Muhammad H. Haykal, *The Life of Muhammad (Allah's peace and blessing be upon him)* by Muhammad Husayn Haykal, translated by Isma'il Razi A. al-Faruqi. www.witness-pioneer.org/vil/ Books/MH_LM/Muhammad_From_Birth_to_ Marriage.htm

266. Ibn Ishaq, *Sirat Rasoul Allah: The earliest biography of Muhammad*, by ibn Ishaq. An abridged version Edited by Michael Edwardes. Retrieved June 7, 2006, from the World Wide Web www.faithfreedom.org/Articles/sira/01.htm

267. Dr. A. Zahoor and Dr. Z. Haq, *Biography of Prophet Muhammad*. Books and E-Books on Muslim History and Civilization. Copyright 1990, 1997, 1998 Retrieved January 3, 2005, from the World Wide Web www.cyberistan.org/islamic/muhammad.html

268. Khadija's business abilities, from Tamam Kahn, *Untold: A History of the Wives of the Prophet Muhammad*. Monkfish Book Publishing (April 2, 2013), n.p.

269. Mulla Muhammad Baqir, Behaar al-Anwaar, vol. 16 p. 22, Serat Online, www.seratonline.com/6664/the-mother-of-believers-hazrat-khadijah-s-a/

270. Says one of Muhammad's biographers, Sarwat Saulat, the "merchandise of Khadija alone was equal to those of the collected merchandise of the rest of the Quraish." Sarwat Saulat, *The Life of The Prophet*, p. 10.

271. N.a. "Biographical Sketch of Muhammad's Life," The Islam Project, www.islamproject.org/muhammad/muhammad_05_BioSketchof Muhammad.htmWikipedia. 1-5-2016

272. Ibn Ishaq, *Sirat Rasoul Allah: The earliest biography of Muhammad*, by ibn Ishaq. An abridged version Edited by Michael Edwardes. Retrieved June 7, 2006, from the World Wide Web www.faithfreedom.org/Articles/sira/02.htm Muhammad H. Haykal, *The Life of Muhammad (Allah's peace and blessing be upon him)*. by Muhammad Husayn Haykal, translated by Isma'il Razi A. al-Faruqi. Retrieved June 7, 2006, from the World Wide Web www.witness-pioneer.org/vil/Books/MH_LM/Muhammad_From_Birth_to_Marriage.htm

273. Sarwat Saulat, *The Life of The Prophet*, Islamic Publications Ltd., Lahore, Pakistan, 1983, pp. 10, 123

274. Sarwat Saulat, *The Life of The Prophet*, Islamic Publications Ltd., Lahore, Pakistan, 1983, p. 11.

275. Sarwat Saulat, *The Life of The Prophet*, Islamic Publications Ltd., Lahore, Pakistan, 1983, p. 11.

276. Sarwat Saulat, *The Life of The Prophet*, Islamic Publications Ltd., Lahore, Pakistan, 1983, pp. 10, 123

277. *The Life of Mohammed*, Translated from the Arabic of Abdulfeda, Abu-'l-Fidā Ismā'īl Ibn-'Alī, trans. William Murray, London: Elgin, 1830, p. 208.

278. Ibn Ishaq, *Sirat Rasoul Allah: The earliest biography of Muhammad*, by ibn Ishaq. An abridged version Edited by Michael Edwardes. Retrieved June 7, 2006, from the World Wide Web www.faithfreedom.org/Articles/sira/02.htm

279. Ibn Ishaq, *Sirat Rasoul Allah: The earliest biography of Muhammad*, by ibn Ishaq. An abridged version Edited by Michael Edwardes. Retrieved June 7, 2006, from the World Wide Web www.faithfreedom.org/Articles/sira/02.htm. Sarwat Saulat, *The Life of The Prophet*. Islamic Publications Ltd., Lahore, Pakistan, 1983, pp. 12–13.

280. A. Guillaume, *The Life of Muhammad: A Translation of Ibn Ishaq's Sirat Rasul Allah*. New York: Oxford University Press, 1955, eighteenth printing, 2004, pp. 105–106.

281. Sarwat Saulat, *The Life of The Prophet*. Islamic Publications Ltd., Lahore, Pakistan, 1983, p. 14.

282. "Muhammad was unlettered." The Prophet Muhammad's Life Prior To His Messengership Promised His Prophethood. *The Life of The Last Prophet: Prophet Muhammad*. Last Updated on August 05, 2000 The Way to Truth—Discover Islam. www.thewaytotruth.org/prophetmuhammad/prior.html

283. Ibn Ishaq, *Sirat Rasoul Allah: The earliest biography of Muhammad*, by ibn Ishaq. An abridged version Edited by Michael Edwardes. Retrieved June 7, 2006, from the World Wide Web www.faithfreedom.org/Articles/sira/03.htm. Sarwat Saulat, *The Life of The Prophet*. Islamic Publications Ltd., Lahore, Pakistan, 1983, p. 15.

284. Ibn Ishaq, *Sirat Rasoul Allah: The earliest biography of Muhammad*, by ibn Ishaq. An abridged version Edited by Michael Edwardes. Retrieved June 7, 2006 from the World Wide Web www.faithfreedom.org/Articles/sira/03.htm

285. Sarwat Saulat, *The Life of The Prophet*. Islamic Publications Ltd., Lahore, Pakistan, 1983, p. 15.

286. Sarwat Saulat, *The Life of The Prophet*. Islamic Publications Ltd., Lahore, Pakistan, 1983, p. 15.

287. A. Guillaume, *The Life of Muhammad: A Translation of Ibn Ishaq's Sirat Rasul Allah*. New York: Oxford University Press, 1955, eighteenth printing, 2004, p. 106.

288. A. Guillaume, *The Life of Muhammad: A Translation of Ibn Ishaq's Sirat Rasul Allah*. New York: Oxford University Press, 1955, eighteenth printing, 2004, p. 106.

289. Ibn Ishaq, *Sirat Rasoul Allah: The earliest biography of Muhammad*, by ibn Ishaq. An abridged version Edited by Michael Edwardes. Retrieved June 7, 2006, from the World Wide Web www.faithfreedom.org/Articles/sira/03.htm

290. A. Guillaume, *The Life of Muhammad: A Translation of Ibn Ishaq's Sirat Rasul Allah*. New York: Oxford University Press, 1955, eighteenth printing, 2004, p. 106.

291. Ibn Ishaq, *Sirat Rasoul Allah: The earliest biography of Muhammad*, by ibn Ishaq. An abridged version Edited by Michael Edwardes. Retrieved June 7, 2006, from the World Wide Web www.faithfreedom.org/Articles/sira/03.htm

292. A. Guillaume, *The Life of Muhammad: A Translation of Ibn Ishaq's Sirat Rasul Allah*. New York: Oxford University Press, 1955, eighteenth printing, 2004, p. 107.

293. Ibn Ishaq, *Sirat Rasoul Allah: The earliest biography of Muhammad*, by ibn Ishaq. An abridged version Edited by Michael Edwardes. Retrieved June 7, 2006, from the World Wide Web www.faithfreedom.org/Articles/sira/03.htm

294. Ibn Ishaq, Sirat Rasoul Allah, An abridged version, p. 22, archive.org/details/Sirat-lifeOfMuhammadBy-ibnIshaq

295. Ibn Ishaq, *Sirat Rasoul Allah: The earliest biography of Muhammad*, by ibn Ishaq. An abridged version Edited by Michael Edwardes. Retrieved June 7, 2006, from the World Wide Web www.faithfreedom.org/Articles/sira/03.htm

296. Sarwat Saulat, *The Life of The Prophet*. Islamic Publications Ltd., Lahore, Pakistan, 1983, p. 17.

297. Ibn Ishaq, *Sirat Rasoul Allah: The earliest biography of Muhammad*, by ibn Ishaq. An abridged version Edited by Michael Edwardes. Retrieved June 7, 2006 from the World Wide Web www.faithfreedom.org/Articles/sira/03.htm

298. Sarwat Saulat, *The Life of The Prophet*. Islamic Publications Ltd., Lahore, Pakistan, 1983, p. 16.

299. Muhyadheen Muhammad, Irumbuzhi, *Soul of the Qur'an*, Volume 1. Kerala, India: Straightpath Quran Education, p. 52.

300. Ibn Ishaq, *Sirat Rasoul Allah: The earliest biography of Muhammad*, by ibn Ishaq. An abridged version Edited by Michael Edwardes. Retrieved June 7, 2006 from the World Wide Web www.faithfreedom.org/Articles/sira/03.htm

301. Ibn Ishaq, *The Life of Muhammad—Apostle of Allah*. Edited by Michael Edwardes. London: The Folio Society, 1964, p. 41. Ibn Ishaq, *Sirat Rasoul Allah: The earliest biography of Muhammad*, by ibn Ishaq. An abridged version Edited by Michael Edwardes. Retrieved June 7, 2006 from the World Wide Web www.faithfreedom.org/Articles/sira/03.htm

302. Sahih Muslim, v3, pp. 79–80. Adapted from: Mohammad Jawad Chirri,Brother of Muhammad (pbuh&hf). Translated and quoted in: "How is This Possible?" A Shi'ite Encyclopedia. www.al-islam.org/encyclopedia/chapter3/8.html

303. Sahih Muslim, v3, pp. 79–80. Adapted from: Mohamad Jawad Chirri, Brother of Muhammad (pbuh&hf). Translated and quoted in: "How is This Possible?" A Shi'ite Encyclopedia.www.al-islam.org/encyclopedia/chapter3/8.html

304. Muhammad's exact words were: "O children of Ka'ab Ibn Lu'ay, save yourselves from Hell. O children of Murrah lbn Ka'ab, save yourselves from Hell. O children of Hashim save yourselves from Hell. O Fatimah, save yourself from Hell. For I do not possess any protection for you from God, except that you have relations to me which I would like to observe." Sahih Muslim, v3, pp. 79–80. Adapted from: Mohamad Jawad Chirri, Brother of Muhammad (pbuh&hf). Translated and quoted in: "How is This Possible?" A Shi'ite Encyclopedia. www.al-islam.org/encyclopedia/chapter3/8.html

305. F.E. Peters, *Muhammad and the Origins of Islam*. Albany: State University of New York Press, 1994, p. 96. The Holy Qur'an. Chapter 1, verse 1. Translation by Abdullah Yusufali. Retrieved January 5, 2007, from the World Wide Web www.wam.umd.edu/~stwright/rel/islam/

306. Sarwat Saulat, *The Life of The Prophet*. Islamic Publications Ltd., Lahore, Pakistan, 1983, p. 19.

307. Sarwat Saulat, *The Life of The Prophet*. Islamic Publications Ltd., Lahore, Pakistan, 1983, p. 19.

308. Sarwat Saulat, *The Life of The Prophet*. Islamic Publications Ltd., Lahore, Pakistan, 1983, p. 19.

309. Sarwat Saulat, *The Life of The Prophet*. Islamic Publications Ltd., Lahore, Pakistan, 1983, p. 20.

310. Ibn Ishaq, *Sirat Rasoul Allah: The earliest biography of Muhammad*, by ibn Ishaq. An abridged version Edited by Michael Edwardes. Retrieved June 7, 2006, from the World Wide Web www.faithfreedom.org/Articles/sira/03.htm. Ibn Ishaq, *Sirat Rasoul Allah: The earliest biography of Muhammad*, by ibn Ishaq. An abridged version Edited by Michael Edwardes. Retrieved June 7, 2006, from the World Wide Web www.faithfreedom.org/Articles/sira/03.htm

311. Ibn Ishaq, *The Life of Muhammad—Apostle of Allah*. Edited by Michael Edwardes. London: The Folio Society, 1964, p. 41.

312. Ibn Ishaq, *The Life of Muhammad—Apostle of Allah*. Edited by Michael Edwardes. London: The Folio Society, 1964, p. 41.

313. Ibn Ishaq, *The Life of Muhammad—Apostle of Allah*. Edited by Michael Edwardes. London: The Folio Society, 1964, p. 42.

314. Ibn Ishaq, *The Life of Muhammad—Apostle of Allah*. Edited by Michael Edwardes. London: The Folio Society, 1964, pp. 42-47.

315. Sarwat Saulat, *The Life of The Prophet*, Islamic Publications Ltd., Lahore, Pakistan, 1983, p. 21.

316. Ibn Ishaq, *The Life of Muhammad—Apostle of Allah*. Edited by Michael Edwardes. London: The Folio Society, 1964, p. 48.

317. A.H. Sheriff, A.S. Alloo, "Bilal the Great African Muslim," Bilal Muslim Mission of Kenya, www.al-islam.org/bilal-s-bedtime-stories-a-h-sheriff-a-s-alloo/bilal-great-african-muslim 1-5-2016

318. Sarwat Saulat, *The Life of The Prophet*. Islamic Publications Ltd., Lahore, Pakistan, 1983, p. 21.

319. Sarwat Saulat, *The Life of The Prophet*. Islamic Publications Ltd., Lahore, Pakistan, 1983, p. 21.

320. Ibn Ishaq, *The Life of Muhammad—Apostle of Allah*. Edited by Michael Edwardes. London: The Folio Society, 1964, pp. 47–48.

321. Sarwat Saulat, *The Life of The Prophet*. Islamic Publications Ltd., Lahore, Pakistan, 1983, p. 21.

322. Ibn Ishaq, *The Life of Muhammad—Apostle of Allah*. Edited by Michael Edwardes. London: The Folio Society, 1964, p. 48.

323. Sarwat Saulat, *The Life of The Prophet*. Islamic Publications Ltd., Lahore, Pakistan, 1983, p. 22.

324. Ibn Ishaq, *The Life of Muhammad—Apostle of Allah*. Edited by Michael Edwardes. London: The Folio Society, 1964, p. 48. Sarwat Saulat, *The Life of The Prophet*. Islamic Publications Ltd., Lahore, Pakistan, 1983, p. 123.

325. Ibn Ishaq, *The Life of Muhammad—Apostle of Allah*. Edited by Michael Edwardes. London: The Folio Society, 1964, p. 49. Sarwat Saulat, *The Life of The Prophet*, Islamic Publications Ltd., Lahore, Pakistan, 1983, p. 123.

326. Muhammad H. Haykal, *The Life of Muhammad (Allah's peace and blessing be upon him)* by Muhammad Husayn Haykal, translated by Isma'il Razi A. al-Faruqi. www.witness-pioneer.org/vil/Books/MH_LM/malevolent_conduct_of_quraysh.htm

327. Ibn Ishaq, *The Life of Muhammad—Apostle of Allah*. Edited by Michael Edwardes. London: The Folio Society, 1964, p. 50.

328. Ibn Ishaq, *The Life of Muhammad—Apostle of Allah*. Edited by Michael Edwardes. London: The Folio Society, 1964, pp. 41–42.

329. Sarwat Saulat, *The Life of The Prophet*. Islamic Publications Ltd., Lahore, Pakistan, 1983, p. 123.

330. Ibn Ishaq, *Sirat Rasoul Allah, An abridged version*, p. 30, archive.org/details/Sirat-lifeOfMuhammad By-ibnIshaq 1-6-2016

331. Ibn Ishaq, *Sirat Rasoul Allah, An abridged version*, p. 30, archive.org/details/Sirat-lifeOfMuhammad By-ibnIshaq 1-6-2016

332. Ibn Ishaq, *Sirat Rasoul Allah: The earliest biography of Muhammad*, by ibn Ishaq. An abridged version Edited by Michael Edwardes. Retrieved June 7, 2006, from the World Wide Web www.faithfreedom.org/Articles/sira/03.htm

333. Ibn Ishaq, *Sirat Rasoul Allah: The earliest biography of Muhammad*, by ibn Ishaq. An abridged version Edited by Michael Edwardes. Retrieved June 7, 2006, from the World Wide Web www.faithfreedom.org/Articles/sira/03.htm

334. Sarwat Saulat, *The Life of The Prophet*. Islamic Publications Ltd., Lahore, Pakistan, 1983, p. 8.

335. Ibn Ishaq, *The Life of Muhammad: A Translation of Ibn Ishaq's Sirat Rasul Allah*. An abridged version, p. 43, Archive.org, archive.org/stream/Sirat-lifeOfMuhammad By-ibnIshaq/SiratIbnIahaqInEnglish#page/n1/mode/2up 1-6-2016

336. Sarwat Saulat, *The Life of The Prophet*. Islamic Publications Ltd., Lahore, Pakistan, 1983, p. 11.

337. Sir John Bagot Glubb, "Medina—History." *Encyclopædia Britannica*. 2007. Encyclopædia Britannica Online. www.britannica.com/eb/article-37817.

338. Khilafah.com, "Who were the Ansar?" Published on 11th January 2011. www.khilafah.com/who-were-the-ansar/ 1-6-2016

339. "They had only gone out making for the caravan [to raid it] because they wanted booty," says Ishaq of "the army...with the apostle" on one of his early raids. Ibn Ishaq, *The Life of Muhammad: A Translation of Ibn Ishaq's Sirat Rasul Allah*. Trans A. Guillaume, New York: Oxford University Press, 1955, eighteenth printing, 2004, p. 321. "The Spoils of War surah was handed down because we quarreled about the booty. So Allah took it away from us and gave it to His Apostle. When He did, we learned to fear Allah and obey his Messenger.... For in truth, our army had gone out with the Prophet seeking the caravan because we wanted its booty." Muhammad ibn Ishaq, *Sirat Rasul Allah (The Life of the Apostle of God)*. Quoted in Islam Exposed. HinduUnity.org: Promoting & Supporting the Ideals of the Bajrang Dal: V.H.P., Youth Wing Bharat. www.hinduunity.org/ po81.ezboard.com/fhinduunityislamexposedarchivesonly.showMessage?topicID=221.topic Supported by A. Guillaume, *The Life of Muhammad: A Translation of Ibn Ishaq's Sirat Rasul Allah*. New York: Oxford University Press, 1955, eighteenth printing, 2004, pp. 321–327. Also Craig Winn, www.prophetofdoom.net/ "Hardly two years had passed in Madinah and the migrants had left all their belongings in Makkah and were empty-handed." Maulana A.S. Muhammad Abdul Hai (Rah.), *Holy Life of Hazrat Muhammad (Hayyat-E-Tayyaba)*. Delhi, India: Islami Academy, 1984. www.al-islamforall.org/litre/Englitre/Hmohd.htm

340. "even if they [the Meccan army coming to the caravan's defense] just extricate their caravan forcefully, the Muslims will lose their credibility and in future, it would be very easy for nearby tribes to dwarf Muslims and put them in tight corner, acting on Quraysh's directions." *Holy Life of Hazrat Muhammad (Hayyat-E-Tayyaba)*. Delhi, India: Islami Academy, 1984. www.al-islamforall.org/litre/Englitre/Hmohd.htm

341. Once again, "They had only gone out making for the caravan because they wanted booty." A. Guillaume, *The Life of Muhammad: A Translation of Ibn Ishaq's Sirat Rasul Allah.* New York: Oxford University Press, 1955, p. 321. For a typical example of the importance of plunder to the early Muslims and the guiltless ease with which they seized it, take a look at the following from Ibn Ishaq: "Abul-As [Muhammad's son-in-law, who refused to convert to Islam]...went to Syria trading with his own money and that of the Quraysh [the Meccans] which they entrusted to him, for he was a trustworthy man. Having completed his business, he was on his way home when one of the apostle's raiding parties fell in with him and took all he had...The raiders went off with their plunder...." A. Guillaume, *The Life of Muhammad: A Translation of Ibn Ishaq's Sirat Rasul Allah.* New York: Oxford University Press, 1955, eighteenth printing, 2004: 316. For an equally intense account, one that reveals the use of arrows, lances, and stones as weapons and the emphasis on gathering weapons, war animals, and clothing as booty, try this passage from the Hadith of Sahih Muslim. It tells the tale of how a simple horse-tender left his job and family and became wealthy and semi-famous as a full-time soldier fighting for Muhammad and Allah: "I was a dependant [sic] of Talha b. Ubaidullah. I watered his horse, rubbed its back. I served Talha (doing odd jobs for him) and partook from his food. I had left my family and my property as an emigrant in the cause of Allah and His Messenger (may peace be upon him). When we and the people of Mecca had concluded a peace treaty and the people of one side began to mix with those of the other, I came to a tree, swept away its thorns and lay down (for rest) at its base; (while I lay there), four of the polytheists from the Meccans came to me and began to talk ill of the Messenger of Allah (may peace be upon him). I got enraged with them and moved to another tree. They hung their weapons (to the branches of the tree) and lay down (for rest). (While they lay there), somebody from the lower part of the valley cried out: Run up, O Muhajirs! Ibn Zunaim has been murdered. I drew my sword and attacked these four while they were asleep. I seized their arms and collected them up in my hand, and said: By the Being Who has conferred honour upon Muhammad, none of you shall raise his head, else I will smite his face. (Then) I came driving them along to the Holy Prophet (may peace be upon him). (At the same time). my uncle Amir came (to him) with a man from" Abalat called Mikraz. Amir was dragging him on a horse with a thick covering on its back along with seventy polytheists. The Messenger of Allah (may peace be upon him) cast a glance at them and said: Let them go (so that) they may prove guilty of breach of trust more than once (before we take action against them). So the Messenger of Allah (may peace be upon him) forgave them. On this occasion, God revealed the Qur'anic verse:" It is He Who restrained their hands from you and your hands from them in the valley of Mecca after He had granted you a victory over them"

(xlviii. 24). Then we moved returning to Medina, and halted at a place where there was a mountain between us and Banu Lihyan who were polytheists. The Messenger of Allah (may peace be upon him) asked God's forgiveness for one who ascended the mountain at night to act as a scout for the Messenger of Allah (may peace be upon him) and his Companions. I ascended (that mountain) twice or thrice that night. (At last) we reached Medina. The Messenger of Allah (may peace be upon him) sent his camels with his slave, Rabah, and I was with him. I (also) went to the pasture with the horse of Talha along with the camels. When the day dawned, Abd al-Rahman al-Fazari made a raid and drove away all the camels of the Messenger of Allah (may peace be upon him), and killed the man who looked after them. I said: Rabah, ride this horse, take it to Talha b. 'Ubaidullah and Inform the Messenger of Allah (may peace be upon him) that the polytheists have made away with his camels. Then I stood upon a hillock and turning my face to Medina, shouted thrice: Come to our help I Then I set out in pursuit of the raiders, shooting at them with arrows and chanting a (self-eulogatory) verse in the Iambic metre: I am the son of al-Akwa' And today is the day of defeat for the mean. I would overtake a man from them, shoot at him an arrow which, piercing through the saddle, would reach his shoulder. and I would say: Take it, chanting at the same time the verse And I am the son of al-Akwa' And today is the day of defeat for the mean. By God, I continued shooting at them and hamstringing their animals. Whenever a horseman turned upon me, I would come to a tree and (hid myself) sitting at its base. Then I would shoot at him and hamstring his horse. (At last) they entered a narrow mountain gorge. I ascended that mountain and held them at bay throwing stones at them. I continued to chase them in this way until I got all the camels of the Messenger of Allah (may peace be upon him) released and no camel was left with them. They left me; then I followed them shooting at them (continually) until they dropped more than thirty mantles and thirty lances, lightening their burden. On everything they dropped, I put a mark with the help of (a piece of) stone so that the Messenger of Allah (may peace be upon him) and his Companions might recognise them (that it was booty left by the enemy). (They went on) until They came to a narrow valley when so and so, son of Badr al-Fazari joined them. They (now) sat down to take their breakfast and I sat on the top of a tapering rock. Al-Fazari said: Who is that fellow I am seeing? They said: This fellow has harassed us. By God, he has not left us since dusk and has been (continually) shooting at us until he has snatched everything from our hands. He said: Four of you should make a dash at him (and kill him). (Accordingly), four of them ascended the mountain coming towards me. When it became possible for me to talk to them, I said: Do you recognise me? They said: No. Who are thou? I said: I am Salama, son of al-Akwa'. By the Being Who has honoured the countenance of Muhammad (may peace be upon him) I can kill any of you I like but none of you will be able to kill me. One of them said: I think (he is right). So they returned. I did not move from my place until I saw the horsemen of the Messenger of Allah (may peace be upon him), who came riding through the trees. Lo! the foremost among them was Akhram al-Asadi. Behind him was Abu Qatada al-Ansari and behind him was al-Miqdad b. al-Aswad al-Kindi. I caught hold of the rein of Akhram's horse (Seeing this). they (the raiders) fled. I said (to Akhram): Akhram, guard yourself against them until Allah's Messenger (may peace be upon him) and his Companions join you. He said:) Salama, if you believe In Allah and the Day of Judgment and (if) you know that Paradise is a reality and Hell is a reality, you should not stand between me and martyrdom. so I let him go. Akhram and Abd al-Rahman (Fazari) met in combat. Akhram hamstrung Abd al-Rahman's horse and the latter struck him with his lance and killed him. Abd al-Rabman turned about riding Akhram's horse. Abu Qatada, a horse-man of the Messenger of Allah (may peace be upon him), met 'Abd al-Rahman (in combat), smote him with his lance and killed him. By the Being Who honoured the countenance of Muhammad (may peace be upon him), I followed them running on my feet (so fast) that I couldn't see behind me the Companions of Muhammad (may peace be upon him), nor any dust raised by their horses. (I followed them) until before sunset they reached a valley which had a spring of water, which was called Dhu Qarad, so that they could have a drink, for they were thirsty. They saw me running towards them. I turned them out of the valley before they could drink a drop of its water. They left the valley and ran down a slope. I ran (behind them), overtook a man from them, shot him with an arrow through the shoulder blade and said: Take this. I am the son of al-Akwa'; and today is the day of annihilation for the people who are mean. The fellow (who was wounded) said: May his mother weep over him! Are you the Akwa' who has been chasing us since morning? I said: Yes, O enemy of thyself, the same Akwa'. They left two horses dead tired on the hillock and I came dragging them along to the Messenger of Allah (may peace be upon him). I met 'Amir who had with him a container having milk diluted with water and a container having water. I performed ablution with the water and drank the milk. Then I came to the Messenger of Allah (may peace be upon him) while he was at (the spring of) water from which I had driven them away. The Messenger of Allah (may peace be upon him) had captured those camels and everything else I had captured and all the lances and mantles I had snatched from the polytheists and Bilal had slaughtered a she-camel from the camels I had seized from the people, and was roasting its liver and hump for the Messenger of Allah (may peace be upon him). I said: Messenger of Allah, let me select from our people one hundred men and I will follow the marauders and I will finish them all so that nobody is left to convey the news (of their

destruction to their people). (At these words of mine), the Messenger of Allah (may peace be upon him) laughed so much that his molar teeth could be seen in the light of the fire, and he said: Salama, do you think you can do this? I said: Yes, by the Being Who has honoured you. He said: Now they have reached the land of Ghatafan where they are being feted. (At this time) a man from the Ghatafan came along and said: So and so slaughtered a camel for them. When they were exposing its skin, they saw dust (being raised far off). They said: They (Akwa' and his companions) have come. So. they went away fleeing. When it was morning, the Messenger of Allah (may peace be upon him) said: Our best horseman today is Abu Qatada and our best footman today is Salama. Then he gave me two shares of the booty—the share meant for the horseman and the share meant for the footman, and combined both of them for me. Intending to return to Medina, he made me mount behind him on his she-camel named al-Adba'. While we were travelling, a man from the Ansar who could not be beaten in a race said: Is there anyone who could compete (with me) in race to Medina? Is there any competitor? He continued repeating this. When I heard his talk, I said: Don't you show consideration to a dignified person and don't you have awe for a noble man? He said: No, unless he be the Messenger of Allah (may peace be upon him). I said: Messenger of Allah, may my father and mother be thy ransom, let me get down so that I may beat this man (in the race). He said: It you wish, (you may). I said (to the man): I am coming to thee, I then turned my feet. sprang up and tan [sic] and gasped (for a while) when one or two elevated places were left and again followed his heel and again gasped (for a while) when one or two elevated places were left and again dashed until I joined him and gave a blow between his shoulders. I said: You have been overtaken, by God. He said: I think so." Sahih Muslim, Book #019, Hadith #4450. *The Book of Faith (Kitab Al-Iman)' of Sahih Muslim.* SearchTruth.com. www.searchtruth.com/searchHadith.php?keyword= Khaibar+booty&translator=2&search= 1&book=&start=0&records_display=10&search_ word=all

342. Ibn Ishaq, *Sirat Rasoul Allah: The earliest biography of Muhammad,* An Abridged Version, archive.org/details/Sirat-lifeOfMuhammad By-ibnIshaq p. 61.

343. Ira M. Lapidus, *A History of Islamic Societies.* Cambridge: Cambridge University Press, 2002, p. 14.

344. Quoted in Hafiz Abdul Salam Bin Mohammad, *Jihad In The Present Time*. Jamatdawa.org. Retrieved December 29, 2002, from the World Wide Web www.jamatdawa.org/english/faq/index.htm Here's another translation of the quote: "Jihad (holy fighting in Allah's Cause) is ordained for you (Muslims) though you dislike it, and it may be that you dislike a thing which is good for you and that you like a thing which is bad for you. Allah knows but you do not know." (سورة البقرة , Al-Baqara, Chapter #2, Verse #216) Qur'an, Mohsin Khan translation. SearchTruth.com. www.searchtruth.com/search.php?keyword=though+you+dislike+it&chapter=&translator=5&search=1&start=0&records_display=10&search_word=exact.

345. Ruhollah Khomeini, *Islam and Revolution: Writings and Declarations of Imam Khomeini*, trans. Hamid Algar. Berkeley: Mizan Press, 1981, p. 35.

346. A. Guillaume, *The Life of Muhammad: A Translation of Ibn Ishaq's Sirat Rasul Allah*. New York: Oxford University Press, 1955, eighteenth printing, 2004, p. 381.

347. *Shahih Bukhari*, Volume 3, Book 50, Number 891. www.usc.edu/dept/MSA/fundamentals/hadithsunnah/bukhari/050.sbt.html#003.050.891.

348. Brannon Wheeler, "Swords of the Prophet Muhammad." Visiting Distinguished Professor of History and Politics United States Naval Academy. www.usna.edu/Users/humss/bwheeler/swords/faqar.html. Brannon Wheeler, "Index of the Swords of the Prophet Muhammad." U.S. Naval Academy. www.usna.edu/Users/humss/bwheeler/swords/index_of_swords.html Deobandimuslim. Swords of Holy Prophet (Pbuh). Posting on Alhuda International. www.alhudapk.com/forum/forum_posts.asp?TID=980

349. Ibn Ishaq, *Sirat Rasoul Allah, An abridged version*, p. 40, archive.org/details/Sirat-lifeOfMuhammadBy-ibnIshaq 1-6-2016

350. 22: 39, The Holy Qur'an. Translation by Abdullah Yusufali. Complete online text. Retrieved January 29, 2016, from the World Wide Web www.wam.umd.edu/~stwright/rel/islam/

351. Hazrat Moulana Sayyed Abul Hasan Ali Nadwi (R.A.), *The Seerah of Muhammad (Sallallahu Laiyhi Wassallam): (The Last Prophet: A Model For All Time)*. Al-Islaah Publications. Retrieved August 31, 2005, From the World Wide Web: alislaah3.tripod.com/alislaah/id7.html

352. al-Tabari refers to the "wealth," the "money and merchandise" that the Meccans were carrying as easy loot, "(easy) booty." Though there were 70 Meccan horsemen accompanying the caravan, to the Muslims this was a paltry number, says al-Tabari, who describes how the Muslims waxed enthusiastic when they heard of "the fewness of their [the Meccans'] numbers." Al-Tabari also implies that the Muslims' greed was piqued because they realized that the horsemen were not wearing their armor and carrying the heavy weapons of war. Al-Tabari quotes the Qur'an's comment on this raid: "And ye longed that other than the armed one might be yours." al-Tabari, *The History of al-Tabari* English translation of "at Tareekh al-Tabari." *Volume VII: The Foundation of the Community*. Translated by M.V. McDonald. Albany: State University of New York Press, 1987, p. 29.

353. "They said that when the apostle heard about the Abu Safyan coming from Syria, he summoned the Muslims and said, 'This is the Quraysh caravan containing their property. Go out to attack it, perhaps God will give it as prey.'" A. Guillaume, *The Life of Muhammad: A Translation of Ibn Ishaq's Sirat Rasul Allah*. New York: Oxford University Press, 1955, p. 289.

354. n.a. "Holy Wars." Islamicoccasions.com—Truth Wisdom & Justice. ezsoftech.com/islamic/badr.asp

355. Sarwat Saulat, *The Life of The Prophet*. Islamic Publications Ltd., Lahore, Pakistan, 1983.

356. Maulana A.S. Muhammad Abdul Hai (Rah.), *Holy Life of Hazrat Muhammad (Hayyat-E-Tayyaba)*. Delhi, India: Islami Academy, 1984. www.al-islamforall.org/litre/Englitre/Hmohd.htm

357. Al-Bukhari Volume 5, Book 59, Number 289. In Muhammad Saed Abdul-Rahman, *Military Expeditions led by the Prophet (pbuh) (Al-Maghaazi)*. wahabs.com/hadith/hadith_e/Military%20Expeditions%20led%20by%20the%20Prophet%20(pbuh)%20(Al-Maghaazi).htm. Sahih Muslim Book 19 Number 4360. www.usc.edu/dept/MSA/fundamentals/hadithsunnah/muslim/019.smt.html#019.4360

358. Hazrat Moulana Sayyed Abul Hassan Ali Nadwi (R.A.), *The Seerah of Muhammad (Sallallahu Laiyhi Wassallam): (The Last Prophet: A Model For All Time)*. Al-Islaah Publications. Retrieved August 31, 2005, From the World Wide Web: alislaah3.tripod.com/alislaah/id7.html

359. Al-Tabari's full name is a bit too much to burden you with. It's Abu Ja'far Muhammad ibn Jarir ibn Yazid ibn Kathir al-Tabari. See Wikipedia, "Muhammad ibn Jarir al-Tabari." en.wikipedia.org/wiki/Muhammad_ibn_Jarir_al-Tabari

360. "the Messenger of God killed many polytheists of Quraysh at Badr." al-Tabari, *The History of al-Tabari* English translation of "at Tareekh al-Tabari." *Volume VII: The Foundation of the Community*. Translated by M.V. McDonald. Albany: State University of New York Press, 1987, p. 85.

361. Maulana A.S. Muhammad Abdul Hai (Rah.), *Holy Life of Hazrat Muhammad* (*Hayyat-E-Tayyaba*). Delhi, India: Islami Academy, 1984. www.al-islamforall.org/litre/Englitre/Hmohd.htm

362. At the Battle of the Trench, a small group of Meccan horsemen, Meccan "knights," manage to gallop over a weak spot in the defensive ditch. The leader of this group dares the Muslims to send him one warrior to determine by single combat which side has won. Ali goes out to take up the challenge... but the Meccan hero is his uncle. The uncle begs Ali to go back and explains that he does not want to kill his own nephew. Too bad, says Ali, "But I want to kill you." The Meccan, disabled by wounds he sustained years earlier at the Battle of Badr, strikes a mighty blow that slices through Ali's shield and gives Ali a mild blow to the head. Unfortunately, this turns out to be a bad move. The Meccan's sword is now stuck in Ali's shield. So Ali swings his sword at his uncle's neck, slices an artery, sees his uncle fall to the ground and die, then lets out a mighty cry of "Allah Akhbar." When Ali returns from the battle "smiling with joy," the first question one of the Muslim lieutenants of Muhammad asks him is "if he had stripped him of his armour." Ali replies that

"I forebore to take his garments
Though had I been vanquished he would have taken mine."

In other words, you normally stripped a man you'd killed of his armor, his weapons, and even his clothes.
A. Guillaume, *The Life of Muhammad: A Translation of Ibn Ishaq's Sirat Rasul Allah*. New York: Oxford University Press, 1955, eighteenth printing, 2004, pp. 455–456.
In the same battle, one of the Meccan knights manages to storm the trench, but is stoned to death. Writes Ibn Ishaq, "The Muslims got possession of his body," stripped it of everything of value, "and asked the apostle to let them sell his effects." Muhammad's reply, in essence, was: I don't care. Do whatever you like. A. Guillaume, *The Life of Muhammad: A Translation of Ibn Ishaq's Sirat Rasul Allah*. New York: Oxford University Press, 1955, eighteenth printing, 2004, p. 456. For more examples of how bodies were stripped for their plunder, see A. Guillaume, *The Life of Muhammad: A Translation of Ibn Ishaq's Sirat Rasul Allah*. New York: Oxford University Press, 1955, eighteenth printing, 2004, pp. 571–572.

363. A. Guillaume, *The Life of Muhammad: A Translation of Ibn Ishaq's Sirat Rasul Allah*. New York: Oxford University Press, 1955, eighteenth printing, 2004, p. 571.

364. al-Tabari, *The History of al-Tabari*. English translation of "at Tareekh al-Tabari." *Volume VII, The Foundation of the Community*. Trans. M.V. McDonald. Albany: State University of New York Press, 1987, p. 85.

365. A magic sword that later became important to the legend of Ali—the companion of the prophet around whom the Shiite sect formed. Dhū al-faqār. (2005). *Encyclopædia Britannica*. Retrieved December 29, 2005, from Encyclopædia Britannica Premium Service www.britannica.com/eb/article-9030236. "Dhu al-Faqar is the name of this sword, taken as booty by the prophet Muhammad at the Battle of Badr." Brannon Wheeler, "Swords of the Prophet Muhammad." Visiting Distinguished Professor of History and Politics United States Naval Academy. www.usna.edu/Users/humss/bwheeler/swords/faqar.html Deobandimuslim. Swords Of Holy Prophet (Pbuh). Posting on Alhuda International. www.alhudapk.com/forum/forum_posts.asp?TID=980

366. "From the Queen of Saba to a Modern State: 3,000 years of civilization in southern Arabia." YemenWeb.com. Founder: Sharaf Mutaher Alkibsi. Retrieved September 15, 2002. 4/29/01 www.yemenweb.com/info/_disc/0000002b.htm

367. "From the Queen of Saba to a Modern State: 3,000 years of civilization in southern Arabia." YemenWeb.com. Founder: Sharaf Mutaher Alkibsi. Retrieved September 15, 2002. 4/29/01 www.yemenweb.com/info/_disc/0000002b.htm

368. "The apostle ordered that the dead should be thrown into a pit. ...As they threw them into the pit the apostle stood and said, 'Oh people of the pit, have you found that what God threatened is true?'" A. Guillaume, *The Life of Muhammad: A Translation of Ibn Ishaq's Sirat Rasul Allah*. New York: Oxford University Press, 1955, eighteenth printing, 2004, pp. 305, 319. *Sahih Bukhari. Volume 5, Book 58, Number 193*. www.usc.edu/dept/MSA/fundamentals/hadithsunnah/bukhari/sbtintro.html

369. Ibn Ishaq, *Sirat Rasoul Allah: The earliest biography of Muhammad*, by ibn Ishaq. An abridged version Edited by Michael Edwardes. Retrieved June 7, 2006, from the World Wide Web www.faithfreedom.org/Articles/sira/13.htm

370. "The Battle of Badr." Al-Islam.org. www.al-islam.org/history/history/badr.html

371. al-Tabari, *The History of al-Tabari*: English translation of "at Tareekh al-Tabari." Albany: State University of New York Press: Book VII, p. 66.

372. al-Tabari, *The History of al-Tabari*: English translation of "at Tareekh al-Tabari." Albany: State University of New York Press: Book VII, p. 66. See also A. Guillaume, *The Life of Muhammad: A Translation of Ibn Ishaq's Sirat Rasul Allah*. New York: Oxford University Press, 1955, eighteenth printing, 2004, p. 308.

373. Hazrat Moulana Sayyed Abul Hassan Ali Nadwi (R.A.), *The Seerah of Muhammad (Sallallahu Laiyhi Wassallam): (The Last Prophet: A Model For All Time)*. Al-Islaah Publications. Retrieved August 31, 2005, from the World Wide Web alislaah3.tripod.com/alislaah/id7.html

374. Maulana A.S. Muhammad Abdul Hai (Rah.), *Holy Life of Hazrat Muhammad (Hayyat-E-Tayyaba)*. Delhi, India: Islami Academy, 1984. www.al-islamforall. org/litre/Englitre/Hmohd.htm

375. "Badr was the site of one of the Arab fairs where they used to hold a market every year," says Ibn Ishaq, Muhammad's first Islamic biographer. This explains the presence of the well—the pit into which Muhammad had the bodies of his enemies thrown. A. Guillaume, *The Life of Muhammad: A Translation of Ibn Ishaq's Sirat Rasul Allah*. New York: Oxford University Press, 1955, eighteenth printing, 2004, p. 296.

376. "Battle of Badr was an important one from the point of its consequences and impacts. In fact, it was the first instalment [sic] of punishment for atheists, from Allah, for denying the invitation to Islam. This battle made it clear as to who deserved the survival more? Islam or heathenism (certainly Islam) and how the things will take shape in future." Maulana A.S. Muhammad Abdul Hai (Rah.), *Holy Life of Hazrat Muhammad (Hayyat-E-Tayyaba)*. Delhi, India: Islami Academy, 1984. www.al-islamforall.org/litre/Englitre/Hmohd.htm

377. Shaykh Safi ur-Rahmaan Mubarakfoori, "Seerah of the Final Messenger of Allaah: The Story of the Prisoners of the Battle of Badr From Ar-Raheeq al-Makhtoom," www.sunnahonline.com/ilm/ seerah/0005.htm Retrieved July 16, 2005, from the World Wide Web. In one of the Hadith, the phrase used is "It is not befitting for a prophet that he should take prisoners until the force of the disbelievers has been crushed..." Shahih Muslim. Book 019, Number 4360. www.usc.edu/dept/MSA/fundamentals/ hadithsunnah/muslim/019.smt.html#019.4360 Yet another translation is "It is not fitting for an apostle that he should have prisoners of war until he hath thoroughly subdued the land." The Holy Qur'an. Translation by Abdullah Yusufali. Complete online text. www.wam.umd.edu/~stwright/rel/ islam/. Then there's Ibn Ishaq's version, "God said, 'It is not for any prophet,' i.e. before thee, 'to take prisoners' from his enemies 'until he has made slaughter in the earth,' i.e. slaughtered his enemies until he drives them from the land.'" A. Guillaume, *The Life of Muhammad: A Translation of Ibn Ishaq's Sirat Rasul Allah*. New York: Oxford University Press, 1955, pp. 326–327. See also: Qur'an (8 : 67) cited in Allama Shibli Nu'mani, Sirat-un-Nabi, The Battle of Badr, retrieved September 14, 2004, from the World Wide Web www.geocities.com/badr_313/battle.htm "This work is an extract of the Second Volume of English Translation of Sirat-un-Nabi originally written in Urdu by the late 'Allama Shibli Nu'mani, a well-known Muslim historian who requires no commendation. His famous work Sirat-un-Nabi also hardly stands in need of any introduction. The book Sirut-un-Nabi is translated by Mr. Budayuni who has the full command of both the languages, Urdu as well as English."

378. *Sahih Bukhari*, Book #52, Hadith #46. Sahih Bukhari translated by M. Muhsin Khan, in SearchTruth.com. www.searchtruth.com/searchHadith.php? keyword=rewards+booty&translator= 1&search=1&book=&start=0&records_ display=10&search_word=all

379. Imam Ibn Taymiyyah, "The Religious and Moral Doctrine On Jihad." From "al-Siyaasa al-shar`iyya fee islaah al-raa`ee wa al-raa`iyya" (Governance according to God's Law in reforming both the ruler and his flock). Retrieved November 19, 2001, from the World Wide Web www.islaam.com/ilm/ibnta. htm. Or as one modern Islamic writer, Maulana A.S. Muhammad Abdul, puts it, "Jihad (holy war) is the touchstone in Islamic movement." Maulana A.S. Muhammad Abdul Hai (Rah.), *Holy Life of Hazrat Muhammad (Hayyat-E-Tayyaba)*. Delhi, India: Islami Academy, 1984. www.al-islamforall.org/litre/ Englitre/Hmohd.htm

380. Edgar H. Schein, "The Role of the Founder in the Creation of Organizational Culture." pp. 14–25. In edited by Peter J. Frost, Larry F. Moore, Meryl Reis Louis, Craig C. Lundberg, Joanne Martin, *Reframing Organizational Culture*. Thousand Oaks, CA: Sage Publications: 1991, p. 15.

381. Dr. Rafat Amari, "Ramadan And Its Roots," Religion Research Institute, religionresearchinstitute.org/ramadan/roots.htm 1-29-2016

382. Sahih al-Bukhari, Book of Merits of the Helpers in Madinah (Ansaar), 63: 42, sunnah.com/bukhari/63/113 1-30-2016

383. Sahih al-Bukhari, Book of Merits of the Helpers in Madinah (Ansaar), 63: 42, sunnah.com/bukhari/63/113 1-30-2016

384. Sahih al-Bukhari, Book of Merits of the Helpers in Madinah (Ansaar), 63: 42, sunnah.com/bukhari/63/113 1-30-2016

385. Sahih al-Bukhari, Book of Merits of the Helpers in Madinah (Ansaar), 63: 42, sunnah.com/bukhari/63/113 1-30-2016

386. Sahih al-Bukhari, Book of Merits of the Helpers in Madinah (Ansaar), 63: 42, sunnah.com/bukhari/63/113 1-30-2016

387. Sahih al-Bukhari, Book of Merits of the Helpers in Madinah (Ansaar), 63: 42, sunnah.com/bukhari/63/113 1-30-2016

388. Daniel M.T. Fessler, Colin Holbrook, "Marching into battle: synchronized walking diminishes the conceptualized formidability of an antagonist in men." Biology Letters of the Royal Society, Published 27 August 2014. DOI: 10.1098/rsbl.2014.0592.

389. William H. McNeill, Keeping Together in Time: Dance and Drill in Human History. Cambridge, MA: 1995.

390. Wikipedia, "Muslim Prayer: Prayer in congregation." en.wikipedia.org/wiki/Muslim_prayer#Prayer_in_congregation

391. "Islam is an Arabic word the root of which is Silm and Salam. It means among others: peace, greeting, salutation, obedience, loyalty, allegiance, and submission to the will of the Creator of the Universe." University of Southern California, USC-MSA Compendium of Muslim Texts. Islamic Glossary. Muslim Student Association. www.usc.edu/dept/MSA/reference/glossary/term.ISLAM.html

392. Wikipedia, "Qibla." en.wikipedia.org/wiki/Qibla

393. "One Direction, One people, One God, in The Religion of Islam," www.islamreligion.com www.islamreligion.com/articles/3203/one-direction-one-people-one-god/ For pictures of the movements of prayer in Islam, see "How to Pray in Islam," www.wikihow.com/Pray-in-Islam 1-30-2016

394. Wikipedia, "Muslim Prayer: Prayer in congregation." en.wikipedia.org/wiki/Muslim_prayer#Prayer_in_congregation

395. Al Tabari, The History of Al-Tabari: The Conquest of Arabia: The Riddah Wars A.D. 632–633/A.H. 11, Fred McGraw Donner trans., Albany: State University of New York Press, 1993, p. 11.

396. "Jamaat ul-Fuqra," South Asia Intelligence Review. www.satp.org/satporgtp/countries/pakistan/terroristoutfits/jamaat-ul-fuqra.htm

397. "Jemaah Islamiyah," Council on Foreign Relations. October 3, 2005. www.cfr.org/publication/8948/

398. Valerius Geist and the members of the International Paleopsychology Project. 1997–2001.

399. Mary Douglas. Natural Symbols: Explorations in Cosmology. New York: Pantheon Books, 1982.

400. al-Tabari, The History of al-Tabari English translation of "at Tareekh al-Tabari." Volume VII: The Foundation of the Community. Translated by M.V. McDonald. Albany: State University of New York Press, 1987, p. 94.

401. A. Guillaume, The Life of Muhammad: A Translation of Ibn Ishaq's Sirat Rasul Allah. New York: Oxford University Press, 1955, p. 364.

402. A. Guillaume, The Life of Muhammad: A Translation of Ibn Ishaq's Sirat Rasul Allah. New York: Oxford University Press, 1955, p. 365.

403. Muhammad H. Haykal, The Life of Muhammad. Translated by Isma'il Raji al-Faruqi. Islamic Book Trust, Kuala Lumpur, Malaysia 2002, pp. 243–244.

404. A. Guillaume, The Life of Muhammad: A Translation of Ibn Ishaq's Sirat Rasul Allah. New York: Oxford University Press, 1955, eighteenth printing, 2004, p. 365.

405. A. Guillaume, The Life of Muhammad: A Translation of Ibn Ishaq's Sirat Rasul Allah. New York: Oxford University Press, 1955, eighteenth printing, 2004, p. 365.

406. A. Guillaume, The Life of Muhammad: A Translation of Ibn Ishaq's Sirat Rasul Allah. New York: Oxford University Press, 1955, eighteenth printing, 2004, p. 365.

407. Sahih Bukhari. Book #59, Hadith #369. Sahih Bukhari translated by M. Muhsin Khan. in SearchTruth.com. SearchTruth.com. Search Truth is a non-profit organization aimed at utilizing the latest technologies available in order to spread the Word of Allah and the Sunnah of the Holy Prophet (pbuh) to as large an audience as possible. www.searchtruth.com/searchHadith.php?keyword=ashraf&translator=1&search=1&book=&start=0&records_display=10&search_word=all. For other versions of the story of the assassination of Ka'b, see Bukhari (Book #45, Hadith #687), (Book #52, Hadith #270)(Book #52, Hadith #271)(Book #59, Hadith #369) Sahih Bukhari translated by M. Muhsin Khan. in SearchTruth.com. www.searchtruth.com/searchHadith.php?keyword=ashraf&translator=1&search=1&book=&start=0&records_display=10&search_word=all. For a version of this bloody, anti-Semitic tale told to European Muslim children, see: The Stories of the Prophets, Narrated by Al-Imam Ibn Kathir (194 - 256) A.H. PROPHET MUHAMMAD (peace be upon him) Part 3. Islam Channel, London—Kids Section. www.islamchannel.tv/kidsSection/ProphetStories/prophetMuhammad3.htm

408. Muhammad's precise words, according to his first biographer, Ibn Ishaq, were these: "Who will rid me of Ibnu'l-Ashraf [the poet Ka'b]?" A. Guillaume, *The Life of Muhammad: A Translation of Ibn Ishaq's Sirat Rasul Allah*. New York: Oxford University Press, 1955, eighteenth printing, 2004, p. 367.

409. "Ka'b said. 'They are none but my brother Muhammad bin Maslama and my foster brother Abu Naila.'" Bukhari (Book #59, Hadith #369) *Sahih Bukhari* translated by M. Muhsin Khan. SearchTruth.com. www.searchtruth.com/ searchHadith.php?keyword=ashraf&translator= 1&search=1&book=&start=0&records_display=10&search_word=all. A. Guillaume, *The Life of Muhammad: A Translation of Ibn Ishaq's Sirat Rasul Allah*. New York: Oxford University Press, 1955, eighteenth printing, 2004, p. 367.

410. "Ka'b said. 'They are none but my brother Muhammad bin Maslama and my foster brother Abu Naila.'" Bukhari (Book #59, Hadith #369) *Sahih Bukhari* translated by M. Muhsin Khan. SearchTruth.com. www.searchtruth.com/ searchHadith.php?keyword=ashraf&translator= 1&search=1&book=&start=0&records_display=10&search_word=all. A. Guillaume, *The Life of Muhammad: A Translation of Ibn Ishaq's Sirat Rasul Allah*. New York: Oxford University Press, 1955, eighteenth printing, 2004, p. 367.

411. al-Tabari, *The History of al-Tabari*. English translation of "at Tareekh al-Tabari." *Volume VII, The Foundation of the Community*. Trans. M.V. McDonald. Albany: State University of New York Press, 1987: p. 95. See also: A. Guillaume, *The Life of Muhammad: A Translation of Ibn Ishaq's Sirat Rasul Allah*. New York: Oxford University Press, 1955, eighteenth printing, 2004, p. 367.

412. al-Tabari, *The History of al-Tabari*. English translation of "at Tareekh al-Tabari." *Volume VII, The Foundation of the Community*. Trans. M.V. McDonald. Albany: State University of New York Press, 1987: p. 95. See also: A. Guillaume, *The Life of Muhammad: A Translation of Ibn Ishaq's Sirat Rasul Allah*. New York: Oxford University Press, 1955, eighteenth printing, 2004, p. 367. al-Tabari, *The History of al-Tabari*. English translation of "at Tareekh al-Tabari." Volume VII. Albany: State University of New York Press, p. 95.

413. "Invitation to Islam, Issue 5, October 1998." thetruereligion.org, Your authentic guide to Islamic belief, culture and civilization. thetruereligion.org/modules/wfsection/article. php?articleid=63

414. A. Guillaume, *The Life of Muhammad: A Translation of Ibn Ishaq's Sirat Rasul Allah*. New York: Oxford University Press, 1955, eighteenth printing, 2004, p. 368. al-Tabari, *The History of al-Tabari*. English translation of "at Tareekh al-Tabari." *Volume VII, The Foundation of the Community*. Trans. M.V. McDonald. Albany: State University of New York Press, 1987, pp. 96–97.

415. A. Guillaume, *The Life of Muhammad: A Translation of Ibn Ishaq's Sirat Rasul Allah*. New York: Oxford University Press, 1955, eighteenth printing, 2004, p. 368. See also: al-Tabari, *The History of al-Tabari*. English translation of "at Tareekh al-Tabari." *Volume VII, The Foundation of the Community*. Trans. M.V. McDonald. Albany: State University of New York Press, 1987, p. 97.

416. Bukhari (Book #59, Hadith #369) *Sahih Bukhari* translated by M. Muhsin Khan. SearchTruth.com. Search Truth is a non-profit organization aimed at utilizing the latest technologies available in order to spread the Word of Allah and the Sunnah of the Holy Prophet (pbuh) to as large an audience as possible. Retrieved February 15, 2006, from the World Wide Web www.searchtruth.com/searchHadith.php?keyword=ashraf&translator=1&search= 1&book=&start=0&records_display=10&search_word=all

417. Bukhari (Book #59, Hadith #369) *Sahih Bukhari* translated by M. Muhsin Khan. SearchTruth.com. Search Truth is a non-profit organization aimed at utilizing the latest technologies available in order to spread the Word of Allah and the Sunnah of the Holy Prophet (pbuh) to as large an audience as possible. Retrieved February 15, 2006, from the World Wide Web www.searchtruth.com/searchHadith.php? keyword=ashraf&translator=1&search= 1&book=&start=0&records_display=10&search_word=all

418. Bukhari (Book #59, Hadith #369) *Sahih Bukhari* translated by M. Muhsin Khan. SearchTruth.com. Search Truth is a non-profit organization aimed at utilizing the latest technologies available in order to spread the Word of Allah and the Sunnah of the Holy Prophet (pbuh) to as large an audience as possible. Retrieved February 15, 2006, from the World Wide Web www.searchtruth.com/searchHadithphp?keyword= ashraf&translator=1&search=1&book=&start= 0&records_display=10&search_word=all

419. A. Guillaume, *The Life of Muhammad: A Translation of Ibn Ishaq's Sirat Rasul Allah*. New York: Oxford University Press, 1955, eighteenth printing, 2004, p. 368.

420. A. Guillaume, *The Life of Muhammad: A Translation of Ibn Ishaq's Sirat Rasul Allah*. New York: Oxford University Press, 1955, eighteenth printing, 2004, p. 368.

421. A. Guillaume, *The Life of Muhammad: A Translation of Ibn Ishaq's Sirat Rasul Allah*. New York: Oxford University Press, 1955, eighteenth printing, 2004, p. 369.

422. A. Guillaume, *The Life of Muhammad: A Translation of Ibn Ishaq's Sirat Rasul Allah*. New York: Oxford University Press, 1955, eighteenth printing, 2004, p. 369.

423. A. Guillaume, *The Life of Muhammad: A Translation of Ibn Ishaq's Sirat Rasul Allah*. New York: Oxford University Press, 1955, eighteenth printing, 2004, p. 672.

424. A. Guillaume, *The Life of Muhammad: A Translation of Ibn Ishaq's Sirat Rasul Allah*. New York: Oxford University Press, 1955, eighteenth printing, 2004, p. 673.

425. A. Guillaume, *The Life of Muhammad: A Translation of Ibn Ishaq's Sirat Rasul Allah*. New York: Oxford University Press, 1955, eighteenth printing, 2004, p. 672.

426. A. Guillaume, *The Life of Muhammad: A Translation of Ibn Ishaq's Sirat Rasul Allah*. New York: Oxford University Press, 1955, eighteenth printing, 2004, p. 674.

427. A. Guillaume, *The Life of Muhammad: A Translation of Ibn Ishaq's Sirat Rasul Allah*. New York: Oxford University Press, 1955, eighteenth printing, 2004, p. 672.

428. Random House Webster's Unabridged Dictionary. V3.0. Random House, Inc. 1999.

429. A. Guillaume, *The Life of Muhammad: A Translation of Ibn Ishaq's Sirat Rasul Allah*. New York: Oxford University Press, 1955 , eighteenth printing, 2004, p. 674.

430. A UNIVERSAL PROCALAMIATON [sic] TO ALL THE PEOPLE OF ISLAM. Published by the National Society of Defense The Seat of the Caliphate 1333 (1915 A.D.) Printed in the Muta'at al Hairayet. b5d0811d8c45c6669a3c-15ea537f15ed4efe57ad2 b340d89534a.r42.cf1.rackcdn.com/OTTOMAN%20 WWI%20FATAWA%20for%20Jihad%20-%20A%20 UNIVERSAL%20PROCALAMIATON.pdf

431. al-Tabari, *History of al-Tabari Vol. 7, The: The Foundation of the Community: Muhammad At Al-Madina a.d. 622-626/Hijrah-4 A.H.* trans. M.V. McDonald, Albany: SUNY Press, 2015, pp. 100–101.

432. A leader of a wealthy sheep-herding tribe in the Hijaz whom al-Tabari calls "Abu Rafi the Jew." This assassination occurs at the usual hour—night— after Abu Rafi entertains guests for dinner, then goes upstairs to sleep with his family. The tale is rich in details and in the use of the weapons Muhammad encouraged in war: lies and deception. The story also includes the usual "then I hit him [with my sword] and covered him with wounds, but could not kill him, so I thrust the point of my sword into his stomach until it came out through his back. At that I knew I had killed him." al-Tabari, *The History of al-Tabari* English translation of "at Tareekh al-Tabari." *Volume VII: The Foundation of the Community*. Translated by M.V. McDonald. Albany: State University of New York Press, 1987, pp. 99–101.

433. al-Tabari, *History of al-Tabari Vol. 7, The Foundation of the Community: Muhammad At Al-Madina A.D. 622-626/Hijrah-4 A.H.* trans. M.V. McDonald, Albany: SUNY Press, 2015, pp. 100–101.

434. quoted in The Murder of Abu 'Afak. From *The Kitab Al Tabaqat Al Kabir (Book of the Major Classes)*, Volume 2, By Ibn Sa'd, (2), page 32. answering-islam.org.uk/Muhammad/Enemies/ abuafak.html

435. Muhammad H. Haykal, *The Life of Muhammad*. Translated by Isma'il Raji al-Faruqi. Islamic Book Trust, Kuala Lumpur, Malaysia 2002, p. 243.

436. *Kitab al Tabaqat al Kabir (The book of The Major Classes)*, Volume 2, by Ibn Sa'd, (2), page 32: Retrieved February 18, 2006, from the World Wide Web. "Abu 'Afak." en.wikipedia.org/wiki/Abu_%27Afak

437. A. Guillaume, *The Life of Muhammad: A Translation of Ibn Ishaq's Sirat Rasul Allah*. New York: Oxford University Press, 1955, eighteenth printing, 2004, p. 675.

438. Actually, "a Hanif": HANEEF. people who during the time of Jahiliyyah rejected the idolatry in their society. These people were in search for the true religion of Prophet Abraham. University of Southern California. USC-MSA Compendium of Muslim Texts. Islamic Glossary. www.usc.edu/dept/MSA/reference/glossary/term. HANIF.html

439. A. Guillaume, *The Life of Muhammad: A Translation of Ibn Ishaq's Sirat Rasul Allah*. New York: Oxford University Press, 1955, eighteenth printing, 2004, p. 675.

440. A. Guillaume, *The Life of Muhammad: A Translation of Ibn Ishaq's Sirat Rasul Allah*. New York: Oxford University Press, 1955, eighteenth printing, 2004, pp. 675–676.

441. A. Guillaume, *The Life of Muhammad: A Translation of Ibn Ishaq's Sirat Rasul Allah*. New York: Oxford University Press, 1955, eighteenth printing, 2004, pp. 675–676.

442. A. Guillaume, *The Life of Muhammad: A Translation of Ibn Ishaq's Sirat Rasul Allah*. New York: Oxford University Press, 1955, eighteenth printing, 2004, pp. 675–676.

443. A. Guillaume, *The Life of Muhammad: A Translation of Ibn Ishaq's Sirat Rasul Allah*. New York: Oxford University Press, 1955, eighteenth printing, 2004, p. 676.

444. From Ibn Sa'd's *Kitab al-Tabaqat al-Kabir*, translated by S. Moinul Haq, volume 2, page 31. Quoted in "Asma bint Marwan," en.wikipedia.org/ wiki/Asma_bint_Marwan. Confirmed in Muhammad H. Haykal, *The Life of Muhammad*. Translated by Isma'il Raji al-Faruqi. Islamic Book Trust, Kuala Lumpur, Malaysia 2002, p. 243.

445. A. Guillaume, *The Life of Muhammad: A Translation of Ibn Ishaq's Sirat Rasul Allah*. New York: Oxford University Press, 1955, eighteenth printing, 2004, p. 676.

446. A. Guillaume, *The Life of Muhammad: A Translation of Ibn Ishaq's Sirat Rasul Allah*. New York: Oxford University Press, 1955, eighteenth printing, 2004, p. 676.

447. A. Guillaume, *The Life of Muhammad: A Translation of Ibn Ishaq's Sirat Rasul Allah*. New York: Oxford University Press, 1955, eighteenth printing, 2004, p. 676.

448. A. Guillaume, *The Life of Muhammad: A Translation of Ibn Ishaq's Sirat Rasul Allah*. New York: Oxford University Press, 1955, eighteenth printing, 2004, p. 676.

449. A. Guillaume, *The Life of Muhammad: A Translation of Ibn Ishaq's Sirat Rasul Allah*. New York: Oxford University Press, 1955, eighteenth printing, 2004, p. 676.

450. 'Abdul-'Azeez Al-Qaari. Translated by Hazem Ragab. "The Menace of the Jews." Mecca. Alminbar. com — the Orator's garden and the Muslim's provision. Here you will find a variety of material to help you prepare for your sermons. Retrieved January 6, 2007, from the World Wide Web www.alminbar.com/khutbaheng/819.htm

451. Daniel G. Freedman, *Human Sociobiology; a holistic approach*, pp. 46, 169–70. By the way, *female* campers also sorted themselves out in a hierarchy. But the process by which they arrived at their social arrangement was a bit different than that of the boys. It involved *more* vicious backbiting and less physical forms of cruelty. Yet the cruelty was so potent that at one time or another it reduced the camp counselors to tears. Said one of these counselors, "Now I know why no one studies junior high school girls! They are so cruel and horrible that no one can stand them." (Freedman, p. 47–9.)

452. According to David W. McMillan, scapegoating defines group boundaries. David W. McMillan, "Sense of Community," Journal of Community Psychology, 24.4 (1996): pp. 315–325, see p. 317.

453. Research on how frustration and/or pain lead to aggression kicked off in 1939 with Dollard, Miller, and Doob's frustration aggression hypothesis. Dollard, J., Doob, L.W., Miller, N., Mower, O.H., & Sears, R.R., *Frustration and Aggression*. New Haven, CT: Yale University Press, 1939. See also: Russell A. Dewey, "Psychology: An Introduction," Aggression, Psych Web, 2007-2014, www.intropsych.com/ch15_social/aggression.html

454. R.F. Ulrich and N.H. Azrin, "Reflexive Fighting In Response to Aversive Stimulation," *Journal of the Experimental Analysis of Behavior*, October, 1962, pp. 511–520, especially p. 516.

455. Frans de Waal, *Our Inner Ape: A Leading Primatologist Explains Why We Are Who We Are*. Penguin, 2006 pp. 157–158, 168.

456. Frans de Waal, *Our Inner Ape: A Leading Primatologist Explains Why We Are Who We Are*. Penguin, 2006, pp. 157–158, 168.

457. Muhammad was dead serious about wiping out all religions that disagreed with his. When he was still living in Mecca, the Meccans grew fearful of his growing strength and offered him a deal. "That he will leave us alone and we will leave him alone, that he will leave us to practice our religion and we shall leave him to practice his." Muhammad turned this offer down cold and countered it with a blunt demand: "that you witness with me that there is no God but God and repudiate all that you worship besides Him." Muhammad H. Haykal, *The Life of Muhammad*. Translated by Isma'il Raji al-Faruqi. Islamic Book Trust, Kuala Lumpur, Malaysia 2002: p. 135.

458. A. Guillaume, *The Life of Muhammad: A Translation of Ibn Ishaq's Sirat Rasul Allah*. New York: Oxford University Press, 1955, eighteenth printing, 2004, p. 368. al-Tabari, *The History of al-Tabari*: English translation of "at Tareekh al-Tabari." Albany: State University of New York Press: Volume 7, p. 97.

459. Muhammad H. Haykal, *The Life of Muhammad*. Translated by Isma'il Raji al-Faruqi. Islamic Book Trust, Kuala Lumpur, Malaysia 2002, p. 249.

460. al-Tabari, *The History of al-Tabari*: English translation of "at Tareekh al-Tabari." Albany: State University of New York Press. Volume VII, p. 97.

461. A. Guillaume, *The Life of Muhammad: A Translation of Ibn Ishaq's Sirat Rasul Allah*. New York: Oxford University Press, 1955, eighteenth printing, 2004, p. 369. See also al-Tabari, *The History of al-Tabari*: English translation of "at Tareekh al-Tabari." Albany: State University of New York Press. Volume VII, p. 97.

462. "Though Muslims came back victorious from Badr...their financial condition was very weak." Maulana A.S. Muhammad Abdul Hai (Rah.), *Holy Life of Hazrat Muhammad (Hayyat-E-Tayyaba)*. www.al-islamforall.org/litre/Englitre/Hmohd.htm

463. "I got a she-camel in my share of the war booty on the day (of the battle) of Badr, and the Prophet had given me a she-camel from the Khumus. When I intended to marry Fatima, the daughter of Allah's Apostle, I had an appointment with a goldsmith from the tribe of Bani Qainuqa' to go with me." Translation of Sahih Bukhari, Book 53: Volume 4, Book 53, Number 324: USC-MSA Compendium of Muslim Texts www.usc.edu/dept/MSA/fundamentals/hadithsunnah/bukhari/053.sbt.html

464. A. Guillaume, *The Life of Muhammad: A Translation of Ibn Ishaq's Sirat Rasul Allah*. New York: Oxford University Press, 1955, eighteenth printing, 2004, p. 363. Muhammad Haykal tries to give more solid justifications for Muhammad's war against the Banu Qaynuqa. The Jews, he said, played a trick on a desert woman when she came to them to remodel her jewelry. The Jews pinned the trailing edge of her robe to the wall. When she stood up and began to walk, her robe unraveled and left her naked. The Jews laughed, says Haykal, and the woman cried. "Seeing what happened, a Muslim passerby jumped upon the shopkeeper and killed him on the spot." When the Jews killed the Muslim, Muhammad showed up on the scene threatening to trounce the Jews the way he'd beaten the Meccans at the Battle of Badr, the Jews shouted their own words at Muhammad, "O Muhammad," they said, "Do not fall under the illusion that you are invincible." Says Haykal, "After this little option was left to the Muslims but to fight the Jews." Muhammad H. Haykal, *The Life of Muhammad*. Translated by Isma'il Raji al-Faruqi. Islamic Book Trust, Kuala Lumpur, Malaysia 2002, p. 245.

465. A. Guillaume, *The Life of Muhammad: A Translation of Ibn Ishaq's Sirat Rasul Allah*. New York: Oxford University Press, 1955, eighteenth printing, 2004, p. 363.

466. A. Guillaume, *The Life of Muhammad: A Translation of Ibn Ishaq's Sirat Rasul Allah*. New York: Oxford University Press, 1955, eighteenth printing, 2004, p. 363.

467. A. Guillaume, *The Life of Muhammad: A Translation of Ibn Ishaq's Sirat Rasul Allah*. New York: Oxford University Press, 1955, eighteenth printing, 2004, p. 363. Muhammad was given a convenient excuse for warfare now and in the future by the angel Gabriel, who appeared to Muhammad after the Jews had refused to switch religions. Said Allah through Gabriel, "If thou [even] fearest treachery from any folk, then throw back to them their treaty fairly." In other words, if you have the slightest suspicion that others may oppose you in word or deed, it's legitimate to break any treaty you have with them...and to attack them. "The messenger of God said, 'I fear the Qaynuqa.'" And that was it. Says al-Tabari, "It was on the basis of this verse," on the basis of this conversation with Gabriel, "that the Messenger of God advanced on" the Banu Qaynuqa. al-Tabari, *The History of al-Tabari*, English translation of "at Tareekh al-Tabari." *Volume VII: The Foundation of the Community*. Translated by M.V. McDonald. Albany: State University of New York Press, 1987, p. 86.

468. Muhammad H. Haykal, *The Life of Muhammad*, translated by Isma'il Raji al-Faruqi, Kuala Lumpur, Malaysia: Islamic Book Trust, 2002, p. 245.

469. A. Guillaume, *The Life of Muhammad: A Translation of Ibn Ishaq's Sirat Rasul Allah*. New York: Oxford University Press, 1955, eighteenth printing, 2004, p. 363.

470. al-Tabari, *The History of al-Tabari*, English translation of "at Tareekh al-Tabari." *Volume VII: The Foundation of the Community*, Translated by M.V. McDonald. Albany: State University of New York Press, 1987, p. 86.

471. Muhammad H. Haykal, *The Life of Muhammad*, translated by Isma'il Raji al-Faruqi, Kuala Lumpur, Malaysia: Islamic Book Trust, 2002, p. 245.

472. A. Guillaume, *The Life of Muhammad: A Translation of Ibn Ishaq's Sirat Rasul Allah*. New York: Oxford University Press, 1955, eighteenth printing, 2004, p. 363.

473. A. Guillaume, *The Life of Muhammad: A Translation of Ibn Ishaq's Sirat Rasul Allah*. New York: Oxford University Press, 1955, eighteenth printing, 2004, p. 363. Haykal says Muhammad was grabbed by the edge of his shield. But Ishaq is a primary source. Haykal's biography, thick as it is—over 600 pages long—does not give the origin of its facts. Muhammad H. Haykal, *The Life of Muhammad*, translated by Isma'il Raji al-Faruqi, Kuala Lumpur, Malaysia: Islamic Book Trust, 2002, p. 245.

474. "Mawali." www.princeton.edu/~batke/itl/denise/mawali.htm. University of Southern California. USC-MSA Compendium of Muslim Texts. Islamic Glossary. www.usc.edu/dept/MSA/reference/glossary/term.MAWLAYA.html.

475. al-Tabari, *The History of al-Tabari*. English translation of "at Tareekh al-Tabari." *Volume VII, The Foundation of the Community*. Trans. M.V. McDonald. Albany: State University of New York Press, 1987: p. 86. Here's the version in Guillaume's Ishaq: "By God, I am a man who fears that circumstances may change." A. Guillaume, *The Life of Muhammad: A Translation of Ibn Ishaq's Sirat Rasul Allah*. New York: Oxford University Press, 1955, eighteenth printing, 2004, p. 363. And the version from Haykal: "By God, I will never agree to such a judgement, for I fear the turns of fortune." Muhammad H. Haykal, *The Life of Muhammad*. Translated by Isma'il Raji al-Faruqi. Islamic Book Trust, Kuala Lumpur, Malaysia 2002: p. 363.

476. A. Guillaume, *The Life of Muhammad: A Translation of Ibn Ishaq's Sirat Rasul Allah*. New York: Oxford University Press, 1955, eighteenth printing, 2004, p. 363.

477. al-Tabari, *The History of al-Tabari*: English translation of "at Tareekh al-Tabari." Albany: State University of New York Press. Book VII, p. 86.

478. Myriad Islamic books give this title, "The Prophet of Mercy," to Muhammad. For one example, see: Osman Nuri Topbas, *Muhammad: The Prophet of Mercy: Scenes from His Life*. Turkey: Erkan Publications. N.d. See also: "Abu Musa Ash'ari reported that Allah's Messenger (may peace be upon him) mentioned many names of his and said: I am Muhammad, Ahmad, Muqaffi (the last in succession), Hashir, the Prophet of repentance, and the prophet of mercy." *Sahih Muslim*, Book #030, Hadith #5813. Sahih Muslim. *The Book of Faith (Kitab Al-Iman)' of Sahih Muslim*. Translated by Abdul Hamid Siddiqui. In SearchTruth.com. www.searchtruth.com/searchHadith.php? keyword=prophet+of+mercy&translator= 2&search=1&book=&start=0&records_ display=10&search_word=exact

479. al-Tabari, *The History of al-Tabari*: English translation of "at Tareekh al-Tabari." Albany: State University of New York Press. Volume VII, p. 87.

480. al-Tabari, *The History of al-Tabari*. English translation of "at Tareekh al-Tabari." *Volume VII, The Foundation of the Community*. Trans. M.V. McDonald. Albany: State University of New York Press, 1987: p. 87.

481. al-Tabari, *The History of al-Tabari*. English translation of "at Tareekh al-Tabari." *Volume VII, The Foundation of the Community*. Trans. M.V. McDonald. Albany: State University of New York Press, 1987: p. 87.

482. Qur'an. book 59, verse 2. Mohsin Khan translation. SearchTruth.com, as of 2016, SearchTruth.com identified itself as "a non-profit website aimed at utilizing the latest technologies to develop the Islamic Softwares." www.searchtruth.com/chapter_display.php? chapter=59&translator=5&mac=. Also Qur'an Book 59, Verses 2–7. The Holy Qur'an. Translation by Abdullah Yusufali. Complete online text. www.wam.umd.edu/~stwright/rel/islam/

483. Section 59, Verses 1-6. The Holy Qur'an. Translation by Abdullah Yusufali. Complete online text. www.wam.umd.edu/~stwright/rel/islam/.

484. The Holy Qur'an. Chapter 59 verse 4. Translation by Abdullah Yusufali. Complete online text. www.wam.umd.edu/~stwright/rel/islam/

485. A. Guillaume, *The Life of Muhammad: A Translation of Ibn Ishaq's Sirat Rasul Allah*. New York: Oxford University Press, 1955: pp. 385–386.

486. Ruhollah Khomeini, *Islam and Revolution: Writings and Declarations of Imam Khomeini*. Hamid Algar trans. Berkeley, California: Mizan Press, 1981, pp. 35, 219. Khomeini's view of Christ may become a little clearer if you realize that standard Islamic doctrine asserts the Old and New Testament are insidious corruptions of God's word, and that these perversions were later "corrected" by the Qur'an.

487. "The Moral System of Islam," III&E Brochure Series; No. 6 (published by The Institute of Islamic Information and Education (III&E)). USC-MSA Compendium of Muslim Texts. www.usc.edu/dept/ MSA/humanrelations/moralsystem.html Reprinted with the permission of World Assembly of Muslim Youth (WAMY), P.O. Box 10845, Riyadh 11443, Saudi Arabia.

488. Sahih Bukhari translated by M. Muhsin Khan. in SearchTruth.com. "Search Truth is a non-profit organization aimed at utilizing the latest technologies available in order to spread the Word of Allah and the Sunnah of the Holy Prophet (pbuh) to as large an audience as possible." Retrieved February 15, 2006, from the World Wide Web SearchTruth.com. www.searchtruth.com/ searchHadith.php?keyword=anger&translator= 1&search=1&book=&start=0&records_display= 50&search_word=all

489. *Sahih Bukhari* translated by M. Muhsin Khan. in SearchTruth.com. Retrieved February 15, 2006, from the World Wide Web SearchTruth.com. www.searchtruth.com/ searchHadith.php?keyword=fear&translator= 1&search=1&book=&start=0&records_display= 50&search_word=all

490. *Sahih Bukhari* translated by M. Muhsin Khan. in SearchTruth.com. Retrieved February 15, 2006, from the World Wide Web SearchTruth.com. www.searchtruth.com/ searchHadithphp?keyword=punish&translator= 1&search=1&book=&start=0&records_display= 50&search_word=all

491. *Sahih Bukhari* translated by M. Muhsin Khan. in SearchTruth.com. Retrieved February 15, 2006, from the World Wide Web SearchTruth.com. www.searchtruth.com/ searchHadithphp?keyword=obey&translator= 1&search=1&book=&start=0&records_display= 50&search_word=all

492. *Sahih Bukhari* translated by M. Muhsin Khan. in SearchTruth.com. Retrieved February 15, 2006, from the World Wide Web SearchTruth.com. www.searchtruth.com/ searchHadithphp?keyword=fight&translator= 1&search=1&book=&start=0&records_display= 50&search_word=all

493. Sarwat Saulat, *The Life of the Prophet*. Islamic Publications Ltd., Lahore, Pakistan, 1983.

494. Hazrat Moulana Sayyed Abul Hassan Ali Nadwi (R.A.), *The Seerah of Muhammad (Sallallahu Laiyhi Wassallam): (The Last Prophet: A Model For All Time)*. Al-Islaah Publications. Retrieved August 31, 2005, From the World Wide Web: alislaah3.tripod.com/ alislaah/id8.html

495. A. Guillaume, *The Life of Muhammad: A Translation of Ibn Ishaq's Sirat Rasul Allah*. New York: Oxford University Press, 1955, eighteenth printing, 2004, p. 519.

496. Hazrat Moulana Sayyed Abul Hassan Ali Nadwi (R.A.), *The Seerah of Muhammad (Sallallahu Laiyhi Wassallam): (The Last Prophet: A Model For All Time)*. Al-Islaah Publications. Retrieved August 31, 2005, From the World Wide Web: alislaah3.tripod.com/alislaah/id8.html. A. Guillaume, *The Life of Muhammad: A Translation of Ibn Ishaq's Sirat Rasul Allah*. New York: Oxford University Press, 1955, eighteenth printing, 2004, p. 372.

497. Hazrat Moulana Sayyed Abul Hassan Ali Nadwi (R.A.), *The Seerah of Muhammad (Sallallahu Laiyhi Wassallam): (The Last Prophet: A Model For All Time)*. Al-Islaah Publications. Retrieved August 31, 2005, From the World Wide Web: alislaah3.tripod.com/alislaah/id8.html

498. "March and take booty." Qur'an, chapter 48, verse 15. "All the booty that ye may acquire (in war)." Qur'an, chapter 8, verse 41. "Allah (on the other hand) will swiftly reward those who [who stand firm in war]."

499. *Sahih Muslim*. Book 001, Number 0209. www.usc.edu/dept/MSA/fundamentals/hadithsunnah/muslim/001.smt.html#001.0209. "Huyayy, the enemy of Allah, was brought out. He was wearing a rose-colored suit of clothes that he had torn all over with fingertip-sized holes so that it would not be taken as booty." al-Tabari, *The History of al-Tabari* ("Tarikh al-rusul wa'l muluk"), *Volume VIII, The Victory of Islam*. Trans. Michael Fishbein. Albany: State University of New York Press, 1997, p. 35. "He is in the (Hell) Fire. The people then went to look at him and found in his place, a cloak he had stolen from the war booty." Sahih Bukhari, Book #52, Hadith #308. *Sahih Bukhari* translated by M. Muhsin Khan. in SearchTruth.com. Retrieved February 15, 2006, from the World Wide Web SearchTruth.com. www.searchtruth.com/searchHadith.php?keyword=cloak+stolen+booty&translator=1&search=1&book=&start=0&records_display=10&search_word=all

500. A. Guillaume, *The Life of Muhammad: A Translation of Ibn Ishaq's Sirat Rasul Allah*. New York: Oxford University Press, 1955, eighteenth printing, 2004, p. 379.

501. Sarwat Saulat, *The Life of the Prophet*. Islamic Publications Ltd., Lahore, Pakistan, 1983, p. 124.

502. "The apostle made for a rock on the mountain to climb it. He had become heavy by reason of his age, and moreover he had put on two coats of mail, so when he tried to get up he could not do so. Talha b. 'Ubaydullah squatted beneath him and lifted him up until he settled comfortably upon it [on the rock]." A. Guillaume, *The Life of Muhammad: A Translation of Ibn Ishaq's Sirat Rasul Allah*. New York: Oxford University Press, 1955, eighteenth printing, 2004, p. 383.

503. A. Guillaume, *The Life of Muhammad: A Translation of Ibn Ishaq's Sirat Rasul Allah*. New York: Oxford University Press, 1955 eighteenth printing, 2004, p. 381.

504. Muhammad H. Haykal, *The Life of Muhammad*. Translated by Isma'il Raji al-Faruqi. Islamic Book Trust, Kuala Lumpur, Malaysia 2002, p. 267. A. Guillaume, *The Life of Muhammad: A Translation of Ibn Ishaq's Sirat Rasul Allah*. New York: Oxford University Press, 1955, eighteenth printing, 2004, p. 380.

505. Hazrat Moulana Sayyed Abul Hassan Ali Nadwi (R.A.), *The Seerah of Muhammad (Sallallahu Laiyhi Wassallam): (The Last Prophet: A Model For All Time)*. Al-Islaah Publications. Retrieved August 31, 2005, From the World Wide Web: alislaah3.Tripod.Com/Alislaah/. A. Guillaume, *The Life of Muhammad: A Translation of Ibn Ishaq's Sirat Rasul Allah*. New York: Oxford University Press, 1955, eighteenth printing, 2004, p. 381.

506. A. Guillaume, *The Life of Muhammad: A Translation of Ibn Ishaq's Sirat Rasul Allah*. New York: Oxford University Press, 1955, eighteenth printing, 2004, p. 380.

507. A. Guillaume, *The Life of Muhammad: A Translation of Ibn Ishaq's Sirat Rasul Allah*. New York: Oxford University Press, 1955, p. 381.

508. Hazrat Moulana Sayyed Abul Hassan Ali Nadwi (R.A.), *The Seerah of Muhammad (Sallallahu Laiyhi Wassallam): (The Last Prophet: A Model For All Time)*. Al-Islaah Publications. Retrieved August 31, 2005, From The World Wide Web: alislaah3.tripod.com/alislaah/id8.html. A. Guillaume, *The Life of Muhammad: A Translation of Ibn Ishaq's Sirat Rasul Allah*. New York: Oxford University Press, 1955, p. 382. Sarwat Saulat says that this is the only man Muhammad ever killed in war. Al-Tabari disagrees. He writes, "the Messenger of God killed many polytheists of Quraysh at Badr." al-Tabari, *The History of al-Tabari*, English translation of "at Tareekh al-Tabari." *Volume VII: The Foundation of the Community*. Translated by M.V. McDonald. Albany: State University of New York Press, 1987, p. 85. Sarwat Saulat, *The Life of the Prophet*, Islamic Publications Ltd., Lahore, Pakistan, 1983, p. 114.

509. A. Guillaume, *The Life of Muhammad: A Translation of Ibn Ishaq's Sirat Rasul Allah*. New York: Oxford University Press, 1955, pp. 385-386.

510. George Sale, *The Koran: Commonly Called the Alcoran of Mohammed*: Translated Into English Immediately from the original Arabic. London: T. Malden, 1801, pp. 32, 344, 663.

511. Sayed Ali Asgher Razwy, *A Restatement of the History of Islam and Muslims—CE 570 to 661*. Battle of the Trench. Published by: World Federation of KSI Muslim Communities. United Kingdom. Reproduced with permission by the Ahlul Bayt Digital Islamic Library Project Ahlul al-islam.org/restatement/26.htm

512. Hazrat Moulana Sayyed Abul Hassan Ali Nadwi (R.A.), *The Seerah of Muhammad (Sallallahu Laiyhi Wassallam): (The Last Prophet: A Model For All Time)*. Al-Islaah Publications. Retrieved August 31, 2005 From the World Wide Web: alislaah3.tripod.com/alislaah/id8.html. A. Guillaume, *The Life of Muhammad: A Translation of Ibn Ishaq's Sirat Rasul Allah*. New York: Oxford University Press, 1955: pp. 385–386.

513. Hazrat Moulana Sayyed Abul Hassan Ali Nadwi (R.A.), *The Seerah of Muhammad (Sallallahu Laiyhi Wassallam): (The Last Prophet: A Model For All Time)*. Al-Islaah Publications. alislaah3.tripod.com/alislaah/id8.html

514. Ibn Ishaq, *Sirat Rasul Allah: The earliest biography of Muhammad, An Abridged Version* archive.org/details/Sirat-lifeOfMuhammad By-ibnIshaq 1-6-2016, p. 71.

515. Qur'an. chapter 3, verse 13. The Holy Qur'an. Translation by Abdullah Yusufali. Complete online text. www.wam.umd.edu/~stwright/rel/islam/

516. "Then He said to His prophet to make the believers wish to fight and desire battle: 'And do not think that those who were killed for God's sake are dead, nay they are alive with their Lord being nourished, glad with the bounty that God has brought them and rejoicing.... I have brought them to life again and they are with Me being nourished in the rest and bounty of the Garden, rejoicing in the bounty that God has brought them for their striving on His account, and happy...God having removed from them fear and sorrow." A. Guillaume, *The Life of Muhammad: A Translation of Ibn Ishaq's Sirat Rasul Allah*. New York: Oxford University Press, 1955, eighteenth printing, 2004, p. 399. "It has been reported on the authority of Jabir that a man said: Messenger of Allah, where shall I be if I am killed? He replied: In Paradise. The man threw away the dates he had in his hand and fought until he was killed" (i.e. he did not wait until he could finish the dates). In the version of the tradition narrated by Suwaid we have the words: "A man said to the Holy Prophet (may peace be upon him). on the day of Uhud...." *Sahih Muslim*. Book 020, Number 4678, *Sahih Muslim*. Book 14, Number 2514. www.usc.edu/dept/MSA/fundamentals/hadithsunnah/muslim/020.smt.html#020.4678 . "The pulpits of gold are kept there for the Prophets (SAW)s and chairs made of pearl are arranged for the martyrs and the maidens with big lustrous eyes will get down from their upstairs rooms. ...the maidens with big lustrous eyes ascend to the upstairs rooms. Which are made of green emerald and red ruby. 110 Hadith Qudsi Chapter No: 1, ahadith.co.uk/searchresults.php?page=3&q=ascended&rows=10 Web's Largest Hadith Library (Insha' Allah) As Salamu Alaykum. This is the most comprehensive hadith library, which puts the most renowned hadith collections at the tip of your fingers. Currently there is just over 10000 ahadith. 'When your brethren were killed as martyrs in the battle of Uhud, Allah put their souls into some green birds which arrived at the rivers of Paradise, ate from its fruits and took shelter beside lanterns, made of gold, and suspended in the shade of the divine Throne. When they enjoyed eating, drinking and sleeping, they said: 'Who will convey to our brethren on earth that; (we are alive in Paradise where we are provided with sustenance, so that they would neither renounce fighting in the way of Allah nor retreat at the time of war).' Allah, the Glorified, said: 'I shall inform them of you.'" Chapter no: 1, 110 Ahadith Quds, Hadith no. 34, Narrated/Authority of Ibn Abbas, mobile.ahadith.co.uk/chapter.php?page=4&cid=144 www.iad.org Steven Stalinsky. Special Report — No. 23 November 26, 2003 No. 23 The 'Islamic Affairs Department' of the Saudi Embassy in Washington, D.C. www.memri.org/bin/latestnews.cgi?ID=SR2303

517. "Narrated Abdullah ibn Abbas: "The Prophet (peace_be_upon_him) said: When your brethren were smitten at the battle of Uhud, Allah put their spirits in the crops of green birds which go down to the rivers of Paradise, eat its fruit and nestle in lamps of gold in the shade of the Throne. Then when they experienced the sweetness of their food, drink and rest, they asked: Who will tell our brethren about us that we are alive in Paradise provided with provision, in order that they might not be disinterested in jihad and recoil in war? Allah Most High said: I shall tell them about you; so Allah sent down; "And do not consider those who have been killed in Allah's path." till the end of the verse." Sunan Abu-Dawud Book 14, Number 2515. www.usc.edu/dept/MSA/fundamentals/hadithsunnah/abudawud/014.sat.html#014.2514 Sunan Abu-Dawud Book 14, Number 2515.

518. Steven Stalinsky. Special Report — No. 23 November 26, 2003 No. 23 The 'Islamic Affairs Department' of the Saudi Embassy in Washington, D.C. www.memri.org/bin/latestnews.cgi?ID=SR2303

519. Sahih Muslim. Book 040, Number 6795: www.usc.edu/dept/MSA/fundamentals/hadithsunnah/muslim/040.smt.html#040.6795

520. Wikipedia, "Houri," en.wikipedia.org/wiki/Houri#cite_note-Bukhari_476-15 1-13-2016. Wikipedia's wrap-up of descriptive phrases from the original sources is terrific.

521. Sahih al-Bukhari, 4:54:476

522. Quran 78:33

523. Quran 56:22–23, Quran 37:48, Quran 52:20.

524. Quran 56:22–23

525. Quran, 38:52, see the full list of accepted translations in "AYAT Sad 38:52," Qur'an Index, Islam Awakened, islamawakened.com/quran/38/52/

526. "The Hoor Al Ayn Of Jannah Paradise," Islam The True Religion Of One God, July 15, 2011, islamreligion1.wordpress.com/2011/07/15/the-hoor-al-ayn-of-jannah-paradise/

527. Abu `Isa Muhammad ibn `Isa at-Tirmidhi, Sunan al-Tirmidhi, hadith: 5638

528. Sahih Bukhari, Volume 4, Book 54, Number 476: www.usc.edu/dept/MSA/fundamentals/hadithsunnah/bukhari/054.sbt.html#004.054.476

529. Usaamah Khayyaat, The Virtues of Martyrdom. Trans. Hazem Ragab. Retrieved August 31, 2005, from the World Wide Web: www.alminbar.com/khutbaheng/1478.htm.

530. According to Hasan al-Banna, founder of the Muslim Brotherhood, this quote is reported in three of the Hadith: Al Bukhari, Muslim and Abu Dawud. Imam Hasan al-Banna, "Kitab ul Jihad" in Sayyid Qutb, Milestones, Ibn Taymiyyah, Abu Muhammad Maqdisi, Abdullah Azzam, Books by Ibn Taymiyyah Maqdisi and Abdullah Azzam, edited by A.B. al-Mehri, publisher Moscow: Рипол Классик Ripol Classic Publishing House, no date, p. 226. However the phrase is often translated "Paradise is under the shades of swords." Sahih Bukhari Chapter No: 54.

531. al-Tabari, The History of al-Tabari. English translation of "at Tareekh al-Tabari." Volume VII. Albany: State University of New York Press, p. 156. The Nadir are also referred to in some accounts as the Nuzair. Munawar Anees, personal correspondence, September 2, 2005.

532. al-Tabari, The History of al-Tabari. English translation of "at Tareekh al-Tabari." Volume VII, The Foundation of the Community. Trans. M.V. McDonald. Albany: State University of New York Press, 1987: p. 159.

533. A. Guillaume, The Life of Muhammad: A Translation of Ibn Ishaq's Sirat Rasul Allah. New York: Oxford University Press, 1955, eighteenth printing, 2004, p. 437.

534. A. Guillaume, The Life of Muhammad: A Translation of Ibn Ishaq's Sirat Rasul Allah. New York: Oxford University Press, 1955, eighteenth printing, 2004, p. 437.

535. Qur'an chapter 59, verses 5–6. The Holy Qur'an. Translation by Abdullah Yusufali. Complete online text. www.wam.umd.edu/~stwright/rel/islam/

536. al-Tabari, The History of al-Tabari: English translation of "at Tareekh al-Tabari." Albany: State University of New York Press. Book VII, p. 159.

537. J.C. Parikh, B. Pratap. "An evolutionary model of a neural network." Journal of Theoretical Biology, May 7, 1984: 31-8; J.J. Hopfield. "Neural networks and physical systems with emergent collective computational abilities." Proceedings of the National Academy of Sciences of the United States of America, April 1982: 2554-8. Howard Bloom, Global Brain: The Evolution of Mass Mind from the Big Bang to the 21st Century. New York: John Wiley & Sons, 2000.

538. Mark 4:25

539. Michael R.A. Chance, ed., assisted by Donald R. Omark. Social Fabrics of the Mind. Sussex, UK: Psychology Press, 1988; M.R.A. Chance. and R. Larson, editors. The Structure of Social Attention. New York: Wiley, 1976; M.R.A. Chance and C. Jolly. Social Groups of Monkeys, Apes, and Men. New York: Dutton, 1970; Michael Chance. "Attention Structure as the Basis of Primate Rank Orders." J.R.A.I. 2(4), 1967: 503–518; Michael Chance. "Attention Structure as the Basis of Primate Rank Orders". Man 2: 503–518 (n.d.); J. Itani. "Social structures of African great apes." Journal of Reproduction and Fertility, Supplement 28, 1980: 33–41; G.R. Emory. "Comparison of spatial and orientational relationships as manifestations of divergent modes of social organization in captive groups of Mandrillus sphinx and Theropithecus gelada." Folia Primatologica, 24:4, 1975: 293–314; Lionel Tiger and Robin Fox. The Imperial Animal: 39–40. For a brief roundup of information on attention structures, see: Daniel G. Freedman, Human Sociobiology: A Holistic Approach: pp. 36–39.

540. A. Guillaume, The Life of Muhammad: A Translation of Ibn Ishaq's Sirat Rasul Allah. New York: Oxford University Press, 1955, eighteenth printing, 2004, p. 437.

541. A. Guillaume, *The Life of Muhammad: A Translation of Ibn Ishaq's Sirat Rasul Allah*. New York: Oxford University Press, 1955, eighteenth printing, 2004, p. 437.

542. al-Tabari, *The History of al-Tabari*. English translation of "at Tareekh al-Tabari." *Volume VII: The Foundation of the Community*. Translated by M.V. McDonald. Albany: State University of New York Press, 1987, p. 159.

543. A. Guillaume, *The Life of Muhammad: A Translation of Ibn Ishaq's Sirat Rasul Allah*. New York: Oxford University Press, 1955, eighteenth printing, 2004, p. 437.

544. A. Guillaume, *The Life of Muhammad: A Translation of Ibn Ishaq's Sirat Rasul Allah*. New York: Oxford University Press, 1955, eighteenth printing, 2004, p. 438.

545. A. Guillaume, *The Life of Muhammad: A Translation of Ibn Ishaq's Sirat Rasul Allah*. New York: Oxford University Press, 1955, eighteenth printing, 2004, p. 438.

546. Ahmad Ibn Yahya Al-Baladhuri, *The Origins of the Islamic State* (*Futuhul Buldan*). (Written in approximately 880 A.D.) al-islam1.org/encyclopedia/chapter4/8.html.

547. Ahmad Ibn Yahya Al-Baladhuri, *The Origins of the Islamic State* (*Futuhul Buldan*). (Written in approximately 880 A.D.) al-islam1.org/encyclopedia/chapter4/8.html.

548. A. Guillaume, *The Life of Muhammad: A Translation of Ibn Ishaq's Sirat Rasul Allah*. New York: Oxford University Press, 1955, eighteenth printing, 2004, pp. 438–439.

549. A. Guillaume, *The Life of Muhammad: A Translation of Ibn Ishaq's Sirat Rasul Allah*. New York: Oxford University Press, 1955, eighteenth printing, 2004, p. 441.

550. A. Guillaume, *The Life of Muhammad: A Translation of Ibn Ishaq's Sirat Rasul Allah*. New York: Oxford University Press, 1955, eighteenth printing, 2004, pp. 438–439.

551. Qur'an— chapter 4: verse 94. The Holy Qur'an. Translation by Abdullah Yusufali. Complete online text. www.wam.umd.edu/~stwright/rel/islam/

552. Alan Booth, Greg Shelley, Allan Mazur, Gerry Tharp, Roger Kittok, "Testosterone, and winning and losing in human competition," *Hormones and Behavior*, Volume 23, Issue 4, December 1989, pp. 556–571, www.sciencedirect.com/science/article/pii/0018506X89900421 3-17-2016. Allen Mazur, Theodore A Lamb, "Testosterone, status, and mood in human males," *Hormones and Behavior*, Volume 14, Issue 3, September 1980, pp. 236–246, www.sciencedirect.com/science/article/pii/0018506X8090032X 3-17-2016

553. A. Guillaume, *The Life of Muhammad: A Translation of Ibn Ishaq's Sirat Rasul Allah*. New York: Oxford University Press, 1955, eighteenth printing, 2004, p. 437.

554. Reuh Alleah Khumaynei (Ayatollah Khomeini), *Sayings of the Ayatollah Khomeini: Political, Philosophical, Social, and Religious*. New York: Bantam Books, 1980, p. 28.

555. Even Muhammad Haykal, an extremely anti-Jewish biographer of Muhammad, admits that the Jews had ample reason to resent Muhammad. Referring to the Persian and the Eastern Roman rulers, he says "It would have been relatively easy for either emperor to remind the Jews of the fate of their co-religionists, the Banu Qurayzah, Banu al Nadir, and Banu Qaynuqa, who had previously been expelled from their dwellings after blockade, fighting, and war." Muhammad H. Haykal, *The Life Of Muhammad*. Translated by Isma'il Raji al-Faruqi. Islamic Book Trust, Kuala Lumpur, Malaysia 2002: p. 366.

556. Maulana A.S. Muhammad Abdul Hai uses the alternative name—the Banu Nuzair. Verification that these two names are synonymous comes from Dr. Munawar Anees, A Nobel Peace Prize Nominee, Former Education Minister of Malaysia, Founding Editor of Periodica Islamica, Founding Editor of the International Journal of Islamic and Arabic Studies, member of the Royal Academy of Jordan for Islamic Civilization Research, member of the UNESCO Group of Intellectuals of the World. Munawar Anees, personal communications, October 2005.

557. Maulana A.S. Muhammad Abdul Hai (Rah.), *Holy Life of Hazrat Muhammad* (*Hayyat-E-Tayyaba*). Delhi, India: Islami Academy, 1984. www.al-islamforall.org/litre/Englitre/Hmohd.htm. See an even more detailed account in: Shaykh Safi ur-Rahmaan Mubarakfoori, *Seerah of the Final Messenger of Allaah: The Sealed Nectar* (*Ar-Raheeq al-Makhtoom*). According to one online Islamic bookstore, this biography of the Prophet was "awarded First prize by the Muslim world league at world-wide competition on the biography of the Prophet held at Makkah." The bookstore Islamic Goods Direct [www.islamicgoodsdirect.co.uk/product_info.php/products_id/1750] does not give the date of the award. Retrieved August 30, 2005, from the World Wide Web www.witness-pioneer.org/vil/Books/SM_tsn/ch4s9.html. And see: Hazrat Moulana Sayyed Abul Hassan Ali Nadwi (R.A.), *The Seerah of Muhammad (Sallallahu Laiyhi Wassallam): (The Last Prophet: A Model For All Time)*. Al-Islaah Publications. Retrieved August 31, 2005, From the World Wide Web: alislaah3.tripod.com/alislaah/id9.html .

558. Hazrat Moulana Sayyed Abul Hassan Ali Nadwi (R.A.), *The Seerah of Muhammad (Sallallahu Laiyhi Wassallam): (The Last Prophet: A Model For All Time)*. Al-Islaah Publications. Retrieved August 31, 2005, From the World Wide Web: alislaah3.tripod.com/alislaah/id9.html

559. A. Guillaume, *The Life of Muhammad: A Translation of Ibn Ishaq's Sirat Rasul Allah*. New York: Oxford University Press, 1955, eighteenth printing, 2004, p. 453.

560. A. Guillaume, *The Life of Muhammad: A Translation of Ibn Ishaq's Sirat Rasul Allah*. New York: Oxford University Press, 1955, eighteenth printing, 2004, p. 450.

561. A. Guillaume, *The Life of Muhammad: A Translation of Ibn Ishaq's Sirat Rasul Allah*. New York: Oxford University Press, 1955, eighteenth printing, 2004, p. 452. For the reference to the implements with which the Muslims dug their trench as made of iron, see al-Tabari, *The History of al-Tabari* ("Tarikh al-rusul wa'l muluk"), *Volume VIII, The Victory of Islam*. Trans. Michael Fishbein. Albany: State University of New York Press, 1997, p. 11.

562. Hazrat Moulana Sayyed Abul Hassan Ali Nadwi (R.A.), *The Seerah of Muhammad (Sallallahu Laiyhi Wassallam): (The Last Prophet: A Model For All Time)*. Al-Islaah Publications. Retrieved August 31, 2005, from the World Wide Web: alislaah3.tripod.com/alislaah/id9.html .

563. Abdul Wahid Hamid, *Companions of the Prophet, Volume 2*. London: Muslim Education and Literary Services, 1985. p. 187.

564. Hazrat Moulana Sayyed Abul Hassan Ali Nadwi (R.A.), *The Seerah of Muhammad (Sallallahu Laiyhi Wassallam): (The Last Prophet: A Model For All Time)*. Al-Islaah Publications. Retrieved August 31, 2005, from the World Wide Web: alislaah3.tripod.com/alislaah/id9.html .

565. A. Guillaume, *The Life of Muhammad: A Translation of Ibn Ishaq's Sirat Rasul Allah*. New York: Oxford University Press, 1955, eighteenth printing, 2004, p. 452.

566. For the presence of the Jewish soldiers, see: A. Guillaume, *The Life of Muhammad: A Translation of Ibn Ishaq's Sirat Rasul Allah*. New York: Oxford University Press, 1955, eighteenth printing, 2004: p. 458.

567. al-Tabari, *The History of al-Tabari* ("Tarikh al-rusul wa'l muluk"), *Volume VIII, The Victory of Islam*. Trans. Michael Fishbein. Albany: State University of New York Press, 1997, p. 40.

568. A. Guillaume, *The Life of Muhammad: A Translation of Ibn Ishaq's Sirat Rasul Allah*. New York: Oxford University Press, 1955, eighteenth printing, 2004, p. 454.

569. A. Guillaume, *The Life of Muhammad: A Translation of Ibn Ishaq's Sirat Rasul Allah*. New York: Oxford University Press, 1955, eighteenth printing, 2004, pp. 459–460. See also Maulana A.S. Muhammad Abdul Hai (Rah.), *Holy Life of Hazrat Muhammad (Hayyat-E-Tayyaba)*. Delhi, India: Islami Academy, 1984. www.al-islamforall.org/litre/Englitre/Hmohd.htm.

570. Maulana A.S. Muhammad Abdul Hai (Rah.), *Holy Life of Hazrat Muhammad (Hayyat-E-Tayyaba)*. Delhi, India: Islami Academy, 1984. www.al-islamforall.org/litre/Englitre/Hmohd.htm

571. Qur'an, chapter 33, verse 9.

572. A. Guillaume, *The Life of Muhammad: A Translation of Ibn Ishaq's Sirat Rasul Allah*. New York: Oxford University Press, 1955, eighteenth printing, 2004, pp. 459–460.

573. A. Guillaume, *The Life of Muhammad: A Translation of Ibn Ishaq's Sirat Rasul Allah*. New York: Oxford University Press, 1955, eighteenth printing, 2004, p. 460.

574. Also known as "the Battle of Ahzaab" and "the Battle of the Confederates."

575. al-Tabari, *The History of al-Tabari* ("Tarikh al-rusul wa'l muluk"), *Volume VIII, The Victory of Islam*. Trans. Michael Fishbein. Albany: State University of New York Press, 1997, p. 40.

576. A. Guillaume, *The Life of Muhammad: A Translation of Ibn Ishaq's Sirat Rasul Allah*. New York: Oxford University Press, 1955, eighteenth printing, 2004, pp. 458–460, 469.

577. Qur'an. book 4, verse 95. The Holy Qur'an. Translation by Abdullah Yusufali. Complete online text. Retrieved November 19, 2001, from the World Wide Web www.wam.umd.edu/~stwright/rel/islam/

578. Qur'an. Chapter 3, verse 144. The Holy Qur'an. Translation by Abdullah Yusufali. Complete online text. Retrieved November 19, 2001, from the World Wide Web www.wam.umd.edu/~stwright/rel/islam/

579. Qur'an, Chapter 5, verses 57-63. The Holy Qur'an. Translation by Abdullah Yusufali. Complete online text. www.wam.umd.edu/~stwright/rel/islam/

580. *Sahih Bukhari*, Book 52, Hadith 176-177. Translated by M. Muhsin Khan. SearchTruth.com. www.searchtruth.com/searchHadith.php?keyword=There+is+a+Jew+hiding+behind+me&translator=1&search=1&book=&start=0&records_display=10&search_word=exact

581. Tabari gives the story a bit differently: "The Messenger of God... laid down his arms—that is, when he had come back from[the Battle of] the Trench—and the Muslims, too, laid down their arms. Then Gabriel came to him and said: "Have you laid down your arms? By God, the angels have not yet laid down their arms! Go out to them, and fight them!" al-Tabari, *The History of al-Tabari* ("Tarikh al-rusul wa'l muluk"), *Volume VIII, The Victory of Islam*. Trans. Michael Fishbein. Albany: State University of New York Press, 1997, p. 29.

582. *Sahih Bukhari*, Book #52, Hadith #68. Sahih Bukhari translated by M. Muhsin Khan. in SearchTruth.com. www.searchtruth.com/search Hadith.php?keyword=bath+gabriel&translator=1&search=1&book=&start=0&records_display=10&search_word=all. See also: Seerah of the Final Messenger of Allaah: The Story of the Prisoners of the Battle of Badr. Shaykh Safi ur-Rahmaan Mubarakfoori From Ar-Raheeq al-Makhtoom. Retrieved July 16, 2005, from the World Wide Web www.sunnahonline.com/ilm/seerah/0005.htm

583. To use a phrase from an Al-Qaida [sic] Statement On The Khobar Operation May 29, 2004. "Al-Qaida Organization of the Arab Gulf" Al-Qaida Statement On The Khobar Operation May 29, 2004. Jihad Unspun. www.strategic-road.com/confid/archiv/special310504_18.htm.

584. Saifur Rahman al-Mubarakpuri Jamia Salafia, Detailed Biography Of Our Noble Prophet Muhammad. "Ar-Raheeq Al-Maktoom" Memoirs of the Noble Prophet. Allaahuakbar.net. www.allaahuakbar.net/muhammad/invading_banu_quraiza.htm

585. A. Guillaume, The Life of Muhammad: A Translation of Ibn Ishaq's Sirat Rasul Allah. New York: Oxford University Press, 1955, eighteenth printing, 2004, p. 461. al-Tabari, The History of al-Tabari ('Tarikh al-rusul wa'l muluk"), Volume VIII, The Victory of Islam. Trans. Michael Fishbein. Albany: State University of New York Press, 1997, p. 28.

586. "When the Prophet returned from the Trench, laid down his arms and took a bath, Gabriel came to him covered in dust. 'Why have you laid down your sword? We angels have not set them down yet. It's time to go out against them.' The Prophet said, 'Where to go?' Gabriel said, 'This way,' pointing towards the Qurayza. So the Prophet went out to besiege them." Book #59, Hadith #443 see also Book #52, Hadith #68, Book #59, Hadith #448 Sahih Bukhari translated by M. Muhsin Khan. in SearchTruth.com. Retrieved February 15, 2006, from the World Wide Web. SearchTruth.com. www.searchtruth.com/searchHadith.php?keyword=trench+bath&translator=1&search=1&book=&start=0&records_display=10&search_word=all

587. "The Jews were divided into three major tribes according to their trades. These were tribes of goldsmiths, tillers and those involved in tanning." Universal Sunnah Foundation. Pakistan. The Prophet Muhammad: Biography of the Holy Prophet. In Islamic Paths. www.islamic-paths.org/Home/English/Muhammad/Book/Biography/Chapter_27.htm

588. A sample: "Narrated Anas: As if I am just now looking at the dust rising in the street of Banu Ghanm (in Medina) because of the marching of Gabriel's regiment when Allah's Apostle set out to Banu Quraiza (to attack them)." Sahih Bukhari, Book #59, Hadith #444. Sahih Bukhari translated by M. Muhsin Khan. in SearchTruth.com. Retrieved February 15, 2006, from the World Wide Web: www.searchtruth.com/searchHadith.php?keyword=gabriel+dust&translator=1&search=1&book=&start=0&records_display=10&search_word=all

589. A. Guillaume, The Life of Muhammad: A Translation of Ibn Ishaq's Sirat Rasul Allah. New York: Oxford University Press, 1955, eighteenth printing, 2004, p. 461.

590. A. Guillaume, The Life of Muhammad: A Translation of Ibn Ishaq's Sirat Rasul Allah. New York: Oxford University Press, 1955, eighteenth printing, 2004, p. 461. See also al-Tabari, The History of al-Tabari ('Tarikh al-rusul wa'l muluk"), Volume VIII, The Victory of Islam. Trans. Michael Fishbein. Albany: State University of New York Press, 1997, p. 29.

591. A sample: "Narrated Anas: As if I am just now looking at the dust rising in the street of Banu Ghanm (in Medina) because of the marching of Gabriel's regiment when Allah's Apostle set out to Banu Quraiza (to attack them)." Sahih Bukhari, Book #59, Hadith #444. Sahih Bukhari translated by M. Muhsin Khan. in SearchTruth.com. Retrieved February 15, 2006, from the World Wide Web: www.searchtruth.com/searchHadith.php?keyword=gabriel+dust&translator=1&search=&start=0&records_display=10&search_word=all

592. al-Tabari, The History of al-Tabari ('Tarikh al-rusul wa'l muluk"), Volume VIII, The Victory of Islam. Trans. Michael Fishbein. Albany: State University of New York Press, 1997, p. 28.

593. A. Guillaume, The Life of Muhammad: A Translation of Ibn Ishaq's Sirat Rasul Allah. New York: Oxford University Press, 1955, eighteenth printing, 2004, p. 461. See also al-Tabari, The History of al-Tabari ('Tarikh al-rusul wa'l muluk"), Volume VIII, The Victory of Islam. Trans. Michael Fishbein. Albany: State University of New York Press, 1997, p. 28.

594. al-Tabari, The History of al-Tabari ('Tarikh al-rusul wa'l muluk"), Volume VIII, The Victory of Islam. Trans. Michael Fishbein. Albany: State University of New York Press, 1997, p. 29. Saifur Rahman al-Mubarakpuri Jamia Salafia. Ar-Raheeq Al-Maktoom: Memoirs of the Noble Prophet. In the name of Alaah, Most Gracious, Most Merciful Allaahuakbar.net. ...An Invitation to Discover True Islaam. www.allaahuakbar.net/muhammad/invading_banu_quraiza.htm

595. A. Guillaume, The Life of Muhammad: A Translation of Ibn Ishaq's Sirat Rasul Allah. New York: Oxford University Press, 1955, eighteenth printing, 2004, p. 461.

596. al-Tabari, The History of al-Tabari: English translation of "at Tareekh al-Tabari." Albany: State University of New York Press: Volume VIII, p. 30. A. Guillaume, The Life of Muhammad: A Translation of Ibn Ishaq's Sirat Rasul Allah. New York: Oxford University Press, 1955, eighteenth printing, 2004: p. 462.

597. al-Tabari, The History of al-Tabari: English translation of "at Tareekh al-Tabari." Albany: State University of New York Press: Volume VIII, p. 33. A. Guillaume, The Life of Muhammad: A Translation of Ibn Ishaq's Sirat Rasul Allah. New York: Oxford University Press, 1955, eighteenth printing, 2004: p. 462.

598. al-Tabari, *The History of al-Tabari*: English translation of "at Tareekh al-Tabari": Volume VIII, Albany: State University of New York Press, p. 33. A. Guillaume, *The Life of Muhammad: A Translation of Ibn Ishaq's Sirat Rasul Allah*. New York: Oxford University Press, 1955, eighteenth printing, 2004: p. 462.

599. Hazrat Moulana Sayyed Abul Hassan Ali Nadwi (R.A.). *The Seerah of Muhammad (Sallallahu Laiyhi Wassallam): (The Last Prophet: A Model For All Time)*. Al-Islaah Publications. Retrieved September 6, 2005, From the World Wide Web alislaah3.tripod.com/alislaah/id11.html

600. Universal Sunnah Foundation, *The Prophet Muhammad Biography of the Holy Prophet,* Chapter 33: Battle of Khaibar, retrieved June 18, 2005, from the World Wide Web www.islamic-paths.org/Home/English/Muhammad/Book/Biography/Chapter_36.htm

601. Muhammad H. Haykal, *The Life of Muhammad*. Translated by Isma'il Raji al-Faruqi. Islamic Book Trust, Kuala Lumpur, Malaysia 2002, p. 311.

602. A. Guillaume, *The Life of Muhammad: A Translation of Ibn Ishaq's Sirat Rasul Allah*. New York: Oxford University Press, 1955, eighteenth printing, 2004, p. 464. Derafsh Kaviyani, "Massacre of Bani Quraiza." Retrieved September 14, 2004, from the World Wide Web www.derafsh-kaviyani.com/english/quraiza.html Copyright @1998 — @2004

603. A. Guillaume, *The Life of Muhammad: A Translation of Ibn Ishaq's Sirat Rasul Allah*. New York: Oxford University Press, 1955, eighteenth printing, 2004, p. 464. See also al-Tabari, *The History of al-Tabari*: English translation of "at Tareekh al-Tabari." Volume VIII, Albany: State University of New York Press, pp. 35, 40–41.

604. al-Tabari, *The History of al-Tabari ('Tarikh al-rusul wa'l muluk"), Volume VIII, The Victory of Islam*. Trans. Michael Fishbein. Albany: State University of New York Press, 1997, pp. 40–41.

605. A. Guillaume, *The Life of Muhammad: A Translation of Ibn Ishaq's Sirat Rasul Allah*. New York: Oxford University Press, 1955, eighteenth printing, 2004, pp. 464–465. See al-Tabari, *The History of al-Tabari ('Tarikh al-rusul wa'l muluk"), Volume VIII, The Victory of Islam*. Trans. Michael Fishbein. Albany: State University of New York Press, 1997, p. 36.

606. A. Guillaume, *The Life of Muhammad: A Translation of Ibn Ishaq's Sirat Rasul Allah*. New York: Oxford University Press, 1955, eighteenth printing, 2004, p. 465.

607. al-Tabari, *The History of al-Tabari ('Tarikh al-rusul wa'l muluk"), Volume VIII, The Victory of Islam*. Trans. Michael Fishbein. Albany: State University of New York Press, 1997, p. 38. A. Guillaume, *The Life of Muhammad: A Translation of Ibn Ishaq's Sirat Rasul Allah*. New York: Oxford University Press, 1955, eighteenth printing, 2004, p. 466.

608. A. Guillaume, *The Life of Muhammad: A Translation of Ibn Ishaq's Sirat Rasul Allah*. New York: Oxford University Press, 1955, eighteenth printing, 2004, p. 473.

609. A. Guillaume, *The Life of Muhammad: A Translation of Ibn Ishaq's Sirat Rasul Allah*. New York: Oxford University Press, 1955, eighteenth printing, 2004, p. 466.

610. Qur'an—chapter 4: verse 94. The Holy Qur'an. Translation by Abdullah Yusufali. Complete online text. www.wam.umd.edu/~stwright/rel/islam/

611. A. Guillaume, *The Life of Muhammad: A Translation of Ibn Ishaq's Sirat Rasul Allah*. New York: Oxford University Press, 1955, eighteenth printing, 2004, p. 471.

612. Muhammad H. Haykal, *The Life of Muhammad*. Translated by Isma'il Raji al-Faruqi. Islamic Book Trust, Kuala Lumpur, Malaysia 2002, p. 316.

613. al-Tabari, *The History of al-Tabari ('Tarikh al-rusul wa'l muluk"), Volume VIII, The Victory of Islam*. Trans. Michael Fishbein. Albany: State University of New York Press, 1997, p. 39.

614. "The phrase 'and those (slaves) whom your right hand possesses — whom Allaah has given to you' [al-Ahzaab 33:50] means, it is permissible for you take concubines from among those whom you seized as war booty. He [Muhammad] took possession of Safiyyah and Juwayriyah and he freed them and married them; he took possession of Rayhaanah bint Sham'oon al-Nadariyyah and Maariyah al-Qibtiyyah, the mother of his son Ibraaheem (peace be upon them both), and they were among his concubines, may Allaah be pleased with them both.' Tafsir Ibn Kathir, 3/500." Jurisprudence and Islamic Rulings > Transactions > Slavery > Question #10382: Ruling on having intercourse with a slave woman when one has a wife. Islam Q&A. Retrieved March 1, 2006, from the World Wide Web 63.175.194.25/index.php?ln=eng&QR=10382. See also: futureislam.wordpress.com/2011/08/19/ruling-on-having-intercourse-with-a-slave-woman-when-one-has-a-wife/

615. Narrated Jabir bin 'Abdullah: When I got married, Allah's Apostle said to me, "What type of lady have you married?" I replied, "I have married a matron." He said, "Why, don't you have a liking for the virgins and for fondling them?" Jabir also said: Allah's Apostle said, "Why didn't you marry a young girl so that you might play with her and she with you?' Sahih Bukhari translated by M. Muhsin Khan. Book #62, Hadith #17. www.searchtruth.com/searchHadith.php?keyword=play+with+her&translator=1&search=1&book=&start=0&records_display=10&search_word=exact

616. This advice from Muhammad on the sexual pleasures of virgins and young girls is repeated six times in the Hadith of Bukhari. Sahih Bukhari translated by M. Muhsin Khan. Book #34, Hadith #310; Book #62, Hadith #16; Book #62, Hadith #174; Book #64, Hadith #280; and Book #75, Hadith #396. SearchTruth.com. www.searchtruth.com/searchHadith.php?keyword=play+with+her&translator=1&search=1&book=&start=0&records_display=10&search_word=exact

617. Qur'an. chapter 33, verse 50. The Holy Qur'an. Translation by Abdullah Yusufali. Complete online text. www.wam.umd.edu/~stwright/rel/islam/

618. "What is meant by 'or (slaves) that your right hands possess' is slave women whom you own. ...' And those who guard their chastity (i.e. private parts from illegal sexual acts). Except from their wives or the (women slaves) whom their right hands possess for (then) they are not blameworthy.'...
"Islam allows a man to have intercourse with his slave woman... Our Prophet (peace and blessings of Allaah be upon him) also did that, as did the Sahaabah, the righteous and the scholars. ...it is not permissible for anyone to regard it as haraam or to forbid it. Whoever regards that as haraam is a sinner who is going against the consensus of the scholars.
Jurisprudence and Islamic Rulings > Transactions > Slavery > Question #10382: Ruling on having intercourse with a slave woman when one has a wife. Islam Q&A. Retrieved March 1, 2006, from the World Wide Web 63.175.194.25/index.php?ln=eng&QR=10382. See also: Qur'an Chapter 23, verses 5 and 6. The Holy Qur'an. Translation by Abdullah Yusufali. Complete online text. www.wam.umd.edu/~stwright/rel/islam/. See also Sahih Bukhari translated by M. Muhsin Khan. in SearchTruth.com. Book #89, Hadith #321. www.searchtruth.com/searchHadith.php?keyword=right%20hand&book=&translator=1&search=1&search_word=exact&start=30&records_display=10

619. Ali Mazrui, an Islamic academic, discusses sex and what he calls Islam's "culture of procreation... as a strategy for 'multiplying in the name of Allah.' Procreation itself," he says, "can be counted as a form of jihad. The Muslim ummah (global community of Muslims) is allowed to expand by divine intervention and biological impregnation." Ali A. Mazrui, "Islamic Doctrine and the Politics of Induced Fertility Change: An African Perspective." Population and Development Review, Vol. 20, Supplement: The New Politics of Population: Conflict and Consensus in Family Planning, (1994), pp. 131–132.
"because the Qur'an sanctioned the institution of slavery, no human law could abolish it. Also, slaves often converted to Islam, so ending the slave trade would restrict the spread of the faith." Patricia Risso, Merchants and Faith: Muslim Commerce and Culture in the Indian Ocean. Boulder, CO: Westview Press. 1995. Page Number: 94.

620. Ali A. Mazrui, "Islamic Doctrine and the Politics of Induced Fertility Change: An African Perspective." Population and Development Review, Vol. 20, Supplement: The New Politics of Population: Conflict and Consensus in Family Planning, (1994), pp. 131–132.

621. Ali A. Mazrui, "Islamic Doctrine and the Politics of Induced Fertility Change: An African Perspective." Population and Development Review, Vol. 20, Supplement: The New Politics of Population: Conflict and Consensus in Family Planning, (1994), pp. 131–132.

622. "When the events of Badr were over, God revealed al-Anfal (Surah 8) [Chapter 8 of the Qur'an, whose title means 'Spoils Of War, Booty'] in its entirety." al-Tabari, The History of al-Tabari: English translation of "at Tareekh al-Tabari." Albany: State University of New York Press. Tabari: Volume VII, p. 80. For the translation of the chapter title "al-Anfal" as "Spoils of War," see University of Southern California. USC-MSA Compendium of Muslim Texts. Translations of the Qur'an, Chapter 8. www.usc.edu/dept/MSA/quran/008.qmt.html.

623. About the division of the captured goods and families of the Banu Quraiza, Ibn Ishaq says, "The apostle... made known on that day the shares of horse and men.... According to its precedent and what the apostle did the divisions were made...." A. Guillaume, The Life of Muhammad: A Translation of Ibn Ishaq's Sirat Rasul Allah. New York: Oxford University Press, 1955, eighteenth printing, 2004: p. 466.

624. Qur'an—chapter 4: verse 94. The Holy Qur'an. Translation by Abdullah Yusufali. Complete online text. www.wam.umd.edu/~stwright/rel/islam/

625. Qur'an—chapter 5, verse 54. The Holy Qur'an. Translation by Abdullah Yusufali. Complete online text. www.wam.umd.edu/~stwright/rel/islam/ downloaded 1998.

626. "He will have seventy two Women of Paradise; And, he will be allowed to intercede for seventy of his family members (who would have otherwise gone to hell). (Tirmidhi & Ibn Maajah)" Usaamah Khayyaat, "The Virtues of Martyrdom." Trans. Hazem Ragab. Retrieved August 31, 2005, from the World Wide Web: www.alminbar.com/khutbaheng/1478.htm.

627. Sahih Bukhari, Volume 4, Book 54, Number 476. Translator: M. Muhsin Khan. MSA-USC Hadith Database. USC-MSA Compendium of Muslim Texts. University of Southern California. www.usc.edu/dept/MSA/fundamentals/hadithsunnah/bukhari/054.sbt.html#004.054.476

628. Life For A Forest, "The Yanomami Tribe" lifeforaforest.com/2015/08/31/the-yanomami-tribe/ 1-16-2016

629. Napoleon Chagnon, "Life Histories, Blood Revenge, and Warfare in a Tribal Population," Science, February, 1988, pp. 988–989. Helena Valero, Yanomama: The Narrative of a White Girl Kidnapped by Amazonian Indians, as told to Ettore Biocca, Dennis Rhodes, trans. New York: E.P. Dutton, 1970.

630. Merril D. Smith, *Encyclopedia of Rape*. Westport, Connecticut: Greenwood Publishing Group, 2004, p. 196.

631. A Graduate-Scholar Of The University, *A Literal Translation Of The First Three Books Of Prendeville's Livy*, Dublin: John Cumming, 1830, p. 11.

632. A Graduate-Scholar Of The University, *A Literal Translation Of The First Three Books Of Prendeville's Livy*, Dublin: John Cumming, 1830, p. 12.

633. Christian Roy, *Traditional Festivals: A Multicultural Encyclopedia*, Volume 2, Santa Barbara, CA: ABC-Clio, p. 173.

634. Plutarch called the event "the rape of the Sabine women." *Plutarch's Lives — Vol I. —* Translated from the Greek, with Notes and a Life of Plutarch by Aubrey Stewart, M.A., and the Late George Long, M.A. Worcestershire, UK: Read Books Ltd, 2015. See also Livy's passing mention of the "wrongs" that had been done to "the Sabine women." A Graduate-Scholar Of The University, *A Literal Translation Of The First Three Books Of Prendeville's Livy*, Dublin: John Cumming, 1830. p. 17.

635. Ibn Ishaq, *Sirat Rasoul Allah: The earliest biography of Muhammad*, by ibn Ishaq. An abridged version Edited by Michael Edwardes. Retrieved November 15, 2013, from the World Wide Web www.faithfreedom.org/Articles/sira/02.htm

636. "The Barrier" is the translation of the word Hijaz. Robert Alexander Harper, Aswin Subanthore, Charles F. Gritzner, Saudi Arabia, New York: Infobase Publishing, 2007, p. 24.

637. Maulana A.S. Muhammad Abdul Hai (Rah.), *Holy Life Of Hazrat Muhammad (Hayyat-E-Tayyaba)*. Delhi, India: Islami Academy, 1984. Retrieved November 15, 2013, from the World Wide Web www.al-islamforall.org/litre/Englitre/Hmohd.htm says 200 miles. Hazrat Moulana Sayyed Abul Hassan Ali Nadwi (R.A.), *The Seerah Of Muhammad (Sallallahu Laiyhi Wassallam)*: (*The Last Prophet: A Model For All Time*). Al-Islaah Publications. Retrieved November 15, 2013, From the World Wide Web: alislaah3.Tripod.Com/ says 70 miles. And the editor of the VIIIth volume of al-Tabari says the distance is 95 miles. al-Tabari, *The History of al-Tabari* ("Tarikh al-rusul wa'l muluk"), *Volume VIII, The Victory of Islam*. Trans. Michael Fishbein. Albany: State University of New York Press, 1997, p. 140.

638. Shaykh Safi ur-Rahmaan Mubarakfoori, *Seerah of the Final Messenger of Allaah: The Sealed Nectar (Ar-Raheeq al-Makhtoom)*. Retrieved November 15, 2013, from the World Wide Web www.witness-pioneer.org/vil/Books/MH_LM/ campaign_of_khaybar_and_missions_to_kings.htm

639. Universal Sunnah Foundation, Pakistan. *The Prophet Muhammad: Biography of the Holy Prophet*. In Islamic Paths. Retrieved November 15, 2013, from the World Wide Web www.islamic-paths.org/Home/English/Muhammad/ Book/Biography/Chapter_33.htm

640. Akram Diya al-Umari, excerpted from *Madinan Society At the Time of the Prophet*, International Islamic Publishing House & IIIT, 1991. In Bismika Allahuma. Retrieved November 15, 2013, from the World Wide Web www.bismikaallahuma.org/index.php/articles/ the-conquest-of-khaybar-and-of-the-remaining-jewish-strongholds-in-al-hijaz

641. Shaykh Safi ur-Rahmaan Mubarakfoori, *Seerah of the Final Messenger of Allaah: The Sealed Nectar (Ar-Raheeq al-Makhtoom)*. According to one online Islamic bookstore, this biography of the Prophet was "awarded First prize by the Muslim world league at world-wide competition on the biography of the Prophet held at Makkah." The bookstore, Islamic Goods Direct, [www.islamicgoodsdirect. co.uk/product_info.php/products_id/1750], does not give the date of the award. Retrieved November 15, 2013, from the World Wide Web www.witness-pioneer.org/vil/Books/MH_LM/ campaign_of_khaybar_and_missions_to_kings.htm

642. A. Guillaume, *The Life of Muhammad: A Translation of Ibn Ishaq's Sirat Rasul Allah*. New York: Oxford University Press, 1955, eighteenth printing, 2004, p. 519.

643. "Hejaz." (2006). *Encyclopædia Britannica*. Retrieved March 4, 2006, from Encyclopædia Britannica Premium Service www.britannica.com/ eb/article-9039858

644. *Sahih Bukhari*. Translator: M. Muhsin Khan. Volume 1, Book 8, Number 367. Retrieved November 15, 2013, from the World Wide Web www.usc.edu/ dept/MSA/fundamentals/hadithsunnah/ bukhari/008.sbt.html#001.008.367 Sahih Bukhari. Translator: M. Muhsin Khan. Volume 1, Book 8, Number 367. Retrieved November 15, 2013, from the World Wide Web www.usc.edu/dept/MSA/ fundamentals/hadithsunnah/bukhari/008.sbt. html#001.008.367

645. A. Guillaume, *The Life of Muhammad: A Translation of Ibn Ishaq's Sirat Rasul Allah*. New York: Oxford University Press, 1955, eighteenth printing, 2004, p. 511.

646. A. Guillaume, *The Life of Muhammad: A Translation of Ibn Ishaq's Sirat Rasul Allah*. New York: Oxford University Press, 1955, eighteenth printing, 2004, p. 511.

647. *Sahih Bukhari*. Translator: M. Muhsin Khan. Volume 1, Book 8, Number 367. Retrieved November 15, 2013, from the World Wide Web www.usc.edu/ dept/MSA/fundamentals/hadithsunnah/ bukhari/008.sbt.html#001.008.367

648. A. Guillaume, *The Life of Muhammad: A Translation of Ibn Ishaq's Sirat Rasul Allah*. New York: Oxford University Press, 1955, eighteenth printing, 2004, p. 511.

649. *Sahih Bukhari*. Translator: M. Muhsin Khan. Volume 1, Book 8, Number 367. Retrieved November 15, 2013, from the World Wide Web www.usc.edu/ dept/MSA/fundamentals/hadithsunnah/ bukhari/008.sbt.html#001.008.367

650. Maulana A.S. Muhammad Abdul Hai (Rah.), *Holy Life of Hazrat Muhammad (Hayyat-E-Tayyaba).* Delhi, India: Islami Academy, 1984. Retrieved November 15, 2013, from the World Wide Web www.al-islamforall.org/litre/Englitre/Hmohd.htm

651. A. Guillaume, *The Life of Muhammad: A Translation of Ibn Ishaq's Sirat Rasul Allah.* New York: Oxford University Press, 1955, eighteenth printing, 2004, p. 469.

652. A. Guillaume, *The Life of Muhammad: A Translation of Ibn Ishaq's Sirat Rasul Allah.* New York: Oxford University Press, 1955, eighteenth printing, 2004, p. 469.

653. al-Tabari, *The History of al-Tabari* ("Tarikh al-rusul wa'l muluk"), Volume VIII, *The Victory of Islam.* Trans. Michael Fishbein. Albany: State University of New York Press, 1997, p. 178.

654. al-Tabari, The History of al-Tabari ("Tarikh al-rusul wa'l muluk"), Volume VIII, The Victory of Islam. Trans. Michael Fishbein. Albany: State University of New York Press, 1997, p. 121.

655. al-Tabari, *The History of al-Tabari* ("Tarikh al-rusul wa'l muluk"), Volume VIII, *The Victory of Islam.* Trans. Michael Fishbein. Albany: State University of New York Press, 1997, p. 121.

656. al-Tabari, *The History of al-Tabari* ("Tarikh al-rusul wa'l muluk"), Volume VIII, *The Victory of Islam.* Trans. Michael Fishbein. Albany: State University of New York Press, 1997, p. 121.

657. al-Tabari, *The History of al-Tabari* ("Tarikh al-rusul wa'l muluk"), Volume VIII, *The Victory of Islam.* Trans. Michael Fishbein. Albany: State University of New York Press, 1997, p. 123.

658. A. Guillaume, *The Life of Muhammad: A Translation of Ibn Ishaq's Sirat Rasul Allah.* New York: Oxford University Press, 1955, eighteenth printing, 2004, p. 513.

659. A. Guillaume, *The Life of Muhammad: A Translation of Ibn Ishaq's Sirat Rasul Allah.* New York: Oxford University Press, 1955, eighteenth printing, 2004, p. 515. Al-Tabari has a different version of this torture: "Al-Zubayr kept twirling his firestick in his breast until Kinanah almost expired; then the Messenger of God gave him to Muhammad b. Maslamah, who beheaded him to avenge his brother Mahmud b. Maslamah." al-Tabari, *The History of al-Tabari* ("Tarikh al-rusul wa'l muluk"), Volume VIII, *The Victory of Islam.* Trans. Michael Fishbein. Albany: State University of New York Press, 1997, p. 122.

660. A. Guillaume, *The Life of Muhammad: A Translation of Ibn Ishaq's Sirat Rasul Allah.* New York: Oxford University Press, 1955, eighteenth printing, 2004, p. 515.

661. The exact number of Prophets Allah sent is not certain, but the Quran is quite clear that there were "messengers whom We have mentioned to you before, and messengers whom We have not mentioned to you" (Al-Nisa, 4:164). "It is obligatory, however, to believe in the 25 prophets mentioned by name in the Quran: Adam, Idris, Nuh (Noah), Hud (sent to the 'Aad people), Salih (sent to the Thamud), Ibrahim (Abraham), Lut (Lot), Isma'eel (Ishmael), Is-haq (Isaac), Ya'qub (Jacob) also known as Isra'eel (Israel), Yusuf (Joseph), Ayyub (Job), Shu'ayb (sent to Madyan), Musa (Moses), Harun (Aaron), Dhul-Kifl (Ezekiel), Dawud (David), Sulayman (Solomon), Al-Yasa', Ilyas (Elias), Yunus (Jonah), Zakariyya (Zacharias), Yahya (John), Isa (Jesus) and Muhammad (peace and blessings be upon them all)." Abu al-Hassan, "Prophets and messengers of Allah." *Gulf Times,* Doha, Qatar. August 11, 2006. www.gulf-times.com/site/topics/article.asp?cu_no=2&item_no=101919&version=1&template_id=47&parent_id=27

662. "Islam has very specific and detailed rules, easily referenced in the Quran and the hadith, for maintaining cleanliness including wudu, ablution before prayer; ghusl, bath after sexual intercourse and before prayer; trimming body hair from underarms and intimate areas; and proper washing, with water, after defecation." Naser I. Faruqui, "Islam and water management: Overview and Principles": International Development Research Center. Retrieved November 15, 2013, from the World Wide Web www.idrc.ca/en/ev-93948-201-1-DO_TOPIC.html Brannon M. Wheeler, *Applying the Canon in Islam: The Authorization and Maintenance of Interpretive Reasoning in Hanafi Scholarship*. Albany: State University of New York, 1996, pp. 53–54, 258.
On Urinating and Defecating
It is required that everyone, when urinating or defecating, hide his sexual parts from all pubescent persons, even his sister or his mother, as well as from any feebleminded person or children too young to understand. But husband and wife are not required to hide from each other. It is not indispensable to hide one's genitals with anything in particular; one's hand is enough. When defecating or urinating, one must squat in such a way as neither to face Mecca nor turn one's back upon it. It is not sufficient to turn one's sex organ away, while oneself facing or turning one's back on Mecca; and one's privates must never be exposed either facing Mecca or facing directly away from Mecca. Urinating and defecating are forbidden in four places: blind alleys, except with the permission of those living along them; the property of a person who has not given permission to do so; places of worship, such as a certain medersas [Arabic schools]; graves of believers, unless one does so as an insult to them. In three cases, it is absolutely necessary to purify one's anus with water: when the excrement has been expelled with other impurities, such as blood, for example; when some impure thing has grazed the anus; when the anal opening has been soiled more than usual.
Apart from these three cases, one may either wash one's anus with water or wipe it with some fabric or a stone. *THE LITTLE GREEN BOOK Selected Fatawah And Sayings of The Ayatollah Mosavi Khomeini* — translated into English by Harold Salemson — with a special introduction by Clive Irving Bantam Books, 1985 / ISBN: 0553140329, archive.org/stream/TheLittleGreenBook--AyatollahKhomeini/The%20Little%20Green%20Book%20%E2%80%94%20Ayatollah%20Khomeini_djvu.txt
663. CKN Nigeria, Full English Transcript Of Boko Haram Leader Abubakar Shekau's Latest Video, CKN Nigeria, May 7, 2014, www.cknnigeria.com/2014/05/full-english-transcript-of-boko-haram.html downloaded from the World Wide Web May 11, 2015.

664. CKN Nigeria, Full English Transcript Of Boko Haram Leader Abubakar Shekau's Latest Video, CKN NIGERIA, May 07, 2014, www.cknnigeria.com/2014/05/full-english-transcript-of-boko-haram.html downloaded from the World Wide Web 5-11-2015.
665. CKN Nigeria, Full English Transcript Of Boko Haram Leader Abubakar Shekau's Latest Video, CKN NIGERIA, May 07, 2014, www.cknnigeria.com/2014/05/full-english-transcript-of-boko-haram.html downloaded from the World Wide Web 5-11-2015
666. Maulana A.S. Muhammad Abdul Hai (Rah.), *Holy Life of Hazrat Muhammad (Hayyat-E-Tayyaba)*. Delhi, India: Islami Academy, 1984. Retrieved November 15, 2013, from the World Wide Web www.al-islamforall.org/litre/Englitre/Hmohd.htm A. Guillaume, *The Life of Muhammad: A Translation of Ibn Ishaq's Sirat Rasul Allah*. New York: Oxford University Press, 1955, eighteenth printing, 2004: p. 515.
667. When Muhammad Haykal explains why Muhammad allowed the Jews to stay on their land instead of ethnically cleansing them—expelling them as he'd done with the Banu Nadir and the Banu Qaynuqa—he says, "Khaybar had large areas of orchards and groves of date trees whose maintenance needed an experienced labor force. ... The Prophet...needed his army for the purpose of war and could not afford to demobilize his army for the sake of agriculture." Muhammad H. Haykal, *The Life of Muhammad*. Translated by Isma'il Raji al-Faruqi. Islamic Book Trust, Kuala Lumpur, Malaysia, 2002, p. 371.
668. Julius Caesar, *The Conquest of Gaul*. Translated by S.A. Handford. Harmondsworth, Middlesex, England: Penguin Books, 1982.
669. Quran—chapter 4: verse 94. The Holy Quran. Translation by Abdullah Yusufali. Complete online text. Retrieved November 15, 2013, from the World Wide Web www.wam.umd.edu/~stwright/rel/islam/
670. A. Guillaume, *The Life of Muhammad: A Translation of Ibn Ishaq's Sirat Rasul Allah*. New York: Oxford University Press, 1955, eighteenth printing, 2004, pp. 521–523.
671. A. Guillaume, *The Life of Muhammad: A Translation of Ibn Ishaq's Sirat Rasul Allah*. New York: Oxford University Press, 1955, eighteenth printing, 2004, p. 512.
672. *Sahih Bukhari*, Book #78, Hadith #698. Sahih Bukhari translated by M. Muhsin Khan. in SearchTruth.com. Retrieved November 15, 2013, from the World Wide Web www.searchtruth.com/searchHadith.php?keyword=Khaibar%20booty&book=&translator=1&search=1&search_word=all&start=10&records_display=10
673. A. Guillaume, *The Life of Muhammad: A Translation of Ibn Ishaq's Sirat Rasul Allah*. New York: Oxford University Press, 1955, eighteenth printing, 2004, p. 512.

674. A. Guillaume, *The Life of Muhammad: A Translation of Ibn Ishaq's Sirat Rasul Allah*. New York: Oxford University Press, 1955, eighteenth printing, 2004, p. 521.

675. A. Guillaume, *The Life of Muhammad: A Translation of Ibn Ishaq's Sirat Rasul Allah*. New York: Oxford University Press, 1955, eighteenth printing, 2004, p. 522.

676. A. Guillaume, *The Life of Muhammad: A Translation of Ibn Ishaq's Sirat Rasul Allah*. New York: Oxford University Press, 1955, eighteenth printing, 2004, p. 523.

677. A. Guillaume, *The Life of Muhammad: A Translation of Ibn Ishaq's Sirat Rasul Allah*. New York: Oxford University Press, 1955, eighteenth printing, 2004, p. 523.

678. Richard Dawkins, *The Selfish Gene*. New York: Oxford University Press, 1976.

679. A. Guillaume, *The Life of Muhammad: A Translation of Ibn Ishaq's Sirat Rasul Allah*. New York: Oxford University Press, 1955, eighteenth printing, 2004, p. 511.

680. A. Guillaume, *The Life of Muhammad: A Translation of Ibn Ishaq's Sirat Rasul Allah*. New York: Oxford University Press, 1955, eighteenth printing, 2004, p. 512.

681. A. Guillaume, *The Life of Muhammad: A Translation of Ibn Ishaq's Sirat Rasul Allah*. New York: Oxford University Press, 1955, eighteenth printing, 2004, p. 512.

682. A. Guillaume, *The Life of Muhammad: A Translation of Ibn Ishaq's Sirat Rasul Allah*. New York: Oxford University Press, 1955, eighteenth printing, 2004, p. 512.

683. A. Guillaume, *The Life of Muhammad, A Translation of Ibn Ishaq's Sirat Rasul Allah*. New York: Oxford University Press, 1955, eighteenth printing, 2004, p. 519.

684. *Sahih Bukhari*. Translator: M. Muhsin Khan. Volume 1, Book 8, Number 367. Retrieved November 15, 2013, from the World Wide Web www.usc.edu/dept/MSA/fundamentals/hadithsunnah/bukhari/008.sbt.html#001.008.367

685. A. Guillaume, *The Life of Muhammad: A Translation of Ibn Ishaq's Sirat Rasul Allah*. New York: Oxford University Press, 1955, eighteenth printing, 2004, p. 511. For another account of the "marriage" to Safiya, see Bukhari, Volume 3, Book 34, Number 437. www.usc.edu/org/cmje/religious-texts/hadith/bukhari/034-sbt.php#003.034.432 1-18-2016

686. A. Guillaume, *The Life of Muhammad: A Translation of Ibn Ishaq's Sirat Rasul Allah*. New York: Oxford University Press, 1955, eighteenth printing, 2004, pp. 514–515.

687. A. Guillaume, *The Life of Muhammad: A Translation of Ibn Ishaq's Sirat Rasul Allah*. New York: Oxford University Press, 1955, eighteenth printing, 2004, pp. 514–515.

688. A. Guillaume, *The Life of Muhammad: A Translation of Ibn Ishaq's Sirat Rasul Allah*. New York: Oxford University Press, 1955, eighteenth printing, 2004, pp. 514–515.

689. Sahih Al-Bukhari صحيح البخاري translation Book #34, Hadith #437 www.searchtruth.com/searchHadith.php?keyword=safiya&book=&translator=1&search=1&search_word=all&start=10&records_display=10

690. Wikipedia estimates her age at seventeen. "Safiyya bint Huyayy," Wikipedia, en.wikipedia.org/wiki/Safiyya_bint_Huyayy 1-30-2016

691. Muhammad H. Haykal, *The Life of Muhammad*. Translated by Isma'il Raji al-Faruqi. Islamic Book Trust, Kuala Lumpur, Malaysia, 2002, p. 128.

692. A. Guillaume, *The Life of Muhammad: A Translation of Ibn Ishaq's Sirat Rasul Allah*. New York: Oxford University Press, 1955, eighteenth printing, 2004, p. 517.

693. A. Guillaume, *The Life of Muhammad: A Translation of Ibn Ishaq's Sirat Rasul Allah*. New York: Oxford University Press, 1955, eighteenth printing, 2004, p. 517.

694. Bukhari, Book of Qualities of the Ansar, chapter: 'The Holy Prophet's marriage with Aisha, and his coming to Madina and the consummation of marriage with her.' Muhsin Khan, trans. Volume 5, Book 58, Number 234 and 236. Zahid Aziz, "Age of Aisha [ra] at time of marriage," The Lahore Ahmadiyya Movement, presenting Islam as peaceful, tolerant, rational, inspiring, www.muslim.org/islam/aisha-age.htm#_ftn3 1-18-2016

695. CKN Nigeria, Full English Transcript Of Boko Haram Leader Abubakar Shekau's Latest Video, CKN NIGERIA, May 07, 2014, www.cknnigeria.com/2014/05/full-english-transcript-of-boko-haram.html downloaded from the World Wide Web 5-11-2015

696. CKN Nigeria, Full English Transcript Of Boko Haram Leader Abubakar Shekau's Latest Video, CKN NIGERIA, May 07, 2014, www.cknnigeria.com/2014/05/full-english-transcript-of-boko-haram.html downloaded from the World Wide Web 5-11-2015

697. Muhammad H. Haykal, *The Life of Muhammad*. Translated by Isma'il Raji al-Faruqi. Islamic Book Trust, Kuala Lumpur, Malaysia, 2002, p. 373.

698. Ven. Bhikkhu Bodhi, "War and Peace: A Buddhist Perspective," Inquiring Mind, Spring 2014, www.inquiringmind.com/Articles/WarAndPeace.html, 1-19-2016

699. Said Jesus in the Sermon on the Mount, "Blessed are the peacemakers: for they shall be called the children of God." Matthew 5:9.

700. The word "conquer" appears 16 times and the word "conquest" 79 times in just one of the Hadith, that of Sahih Bukhari. (Sahih Bukhari, Translator: M. Muhsin Khan. MSA-USC Hadith Database. USC-MSA Compendium of Muslim Texts. University of Southern California. Retrieved November 15, 2013, from the World Wide Web www.usc.edu/cgi-bin/msasearch) Muhammad was driven by what we call "imperialism" and "colonialism." Here's a sample that shows these two drives at work in his vocabulary and his visions: Narrated Abu Zuhair:
I heard Allah's Apostle saying, "Yemen will be conquered and some people will migrate (from Medina) and will urge their families, and those who will obey them to migrate (to Yemen) although Medina will be better for them; if they but knew. Sham will also be conquered and some people will migrate (from Medina) and will urge their families and those who will obey them, to migrate (to Sham) although Medina will be better for them; if they but knew. 'Iraq will be conquered and some people will migrate (from Medina) and will urge their families and those who will obey them to migrate (to 'Iraq) although Medina will be better for them; if they but knew." Translation of Sahih Bukhari, Volume 3, Book 30, Number 99 Retrieved November 15, 2013, from the World Wide Web www.usc.edu/dept/MSA/fundamentals/hadithsunnah/bukhari/030.sbt.html#003.030.095

701. Bible (King James Version) Library Of The Future (R) 4th Edition Ver. 5.0 Irvine, CA: World Library, Inc., 1996. CD-ROM.

702. "In 1922, Haykal became editor of al-Siyasa, the voice of the Liberal Constitutionalist Party" Dr. Edmond Melhem. Sa'adeh on Hussein Haykal. home.iprimus.com.au/fidamelhem/SSNP/Sa%C2%B4adeh%20on%20Hussein%20Haykal.htm

703. Muhammad H. Haykal, The Life of Muhammad. Translated by Isma'il Raji al-Faruqi. Islamic Book Trust, Kuala Lumpur, Malaysia, 2002, p. 373.

704. "Predators at the top of the food chain are said to exercise a major controlling influence over the larger ecosystem, a special status indicated by a variety of terms, including 'top predator,' 'top carnivore,' 'summit predator,' and 'keystone predator'" (Terborgh 1988; Mills et al. 1993: 220). "A top predator is an animal at the apex of the food chain that connects all organisms in an ecosystem... Top predators perform several functions that are essential to the maintenance of natural systems as we currently enjoy them. Top predators stimulate evolutionary adaptations in prey species, influence to varying degrees the composition and structure of ecosystems, support an interconnected chain of other species and signal the integrity of ecosystems. (Curlee and Clark 1995: 19)
John Knight. Waiting for Wolves in Japan: An Anthropological Study of People-Wildlife Relations. Oxford, England: Oxford University Press, 2003.

705. The 4.1 billion-year-old date for life was established 39 years after Dawkins published The Selfish Gene. See Elizabeth A. Bella, Patrick Boehnkea, T. Mark Harrisona, and Wendy L. Maob, "Potentially biogenic carbon preserved in a 4.1 billion-year-old zircon," Proceedings of the National Academy of Sciences, November 24, 2015, vol. 112 no. 47, pp. 14518–14521.

706. Wikipedia, "Saliva." en.wikipedia.org/wiki/Saliva

707. Wikipedia, "Ruminant." en.wikipedia.org/wiki/Ruminant
Wikipedia, "Cud." en.wikipedia.org/wiki/Cud

708. A. Guillaume, The Life of Muhammad: A Translation of Ibn Ishaq's Sirat Rasul Allah. New York: Oxford University Press, 1955, eighteenth printing, 2004, p. 461.

709. A. Guillaume, The Life of Muhammad: A Translation of Ibn Ishaq's Sirat Rasul Allah. New York: Oxford University Press, 1955, eighteenth printing, 2004, p. 462. See also: al-Tabari, The History of al-Tabari ('Tarikh al-rusul wa'l muluk"), Volume VIII, The Victory of Islam. Trans. Michael Fishbein. Albany: State University of New York Press, 1997, p. 30.

710. A. Guillaume, The Life of Muhammad: A Translation of Ibn Ishaq's Sirat Rasul Allah. New York: Oxford University Press, 1955, eighteenth printing, 2004, p. 462. See also: al-Tabari, The History of al-Tabari ('Tarikh al-rusul wa'l muluk"), Volume VIII, The Victory of Islam. Trans. Michael Fishbein. Albany: State University of New York Press, 1997, p. 30.

711. A. Guillaume, The Life of Muhammad: A Translation of Ibn Ishaq's Sirat Rasul Allah. New York: Oxford University Press, 1955, eighteenth printing, 2004, pp. 461–462. See also: al-Tabari, The History of al-Tabari ('Tarikh al-rusul wa'l muluk"), Volume VIII, The Victory of Islam. Trans. Michael Fishbein. Albany: State University of New York Press, 1997, p. 30.

712. al-Tabari, The History of al-Tabari: English translation of "at Tareekh al-Tabari": Volume VIII, Albany: State University of New York Press, p. 30. A. Guillaume, The Life of Muhammad: A Translation of Ibn Ishaq's Sirat Rasul Allah. New York: Oxford University Press, 1955, eighteenth printing, 2004: p. 462.

713. al-Tabari, The History of al-Tabari: English translation of "at Tareekh al-Tabari": Volume VIII, Albany: State University of New York Press, p. 30. A. Guillaume, The Life of Muhammad: A Translation of Ibn Ishaq's Sirat Rasul Allah. New York: Oxford University Press, 1955, eighteenth printing, 2004: p. 462.

714. "Valhalla." Encyclopædia Britannica. 2006. Encyclopædia Britannica Online. 12 Oct. 2006 www.britannica.com/eb/article-9074709

715. Aleksander Pluskowski, The Archaeology of the Prussian Crusade: Holy War and Colonisation. London: Routledge, 2013.

716. This is an inference derived, in part, from Pausanias' account of the Ionian capture of Miletus in roughly 1,150 B.C., when the Ionian civilization was heavily Indo-European in character: But now when the Ionians conquered the old inhabitants of Miletus, they slew all the males except those that ran away from the captured city, and married their wives and daughters. Pausanias, *Pausanias' Description of Greece, Volume 2*, trans. Arthur Richard Shilleto, London: George Bell and sons, 1886, p. 4. Herodotus gives a similar account of the Ionian capture of Miletus (Herodotus, *The History of Herodotus. In Library of the Future, 4th Edition*, Ver. 5.0. Irvine, CA: World Library, Inc., 1996. CD-ROM.) The view I'm presenting is my own, but it is supported in its general outline by Robert Drews in his *Coming of the Greeks: Indo-European Conquests in the Aegean and the Near East*. For more, see Howard Bloom, *Global Brain: The Evolution of Mass Mind From the Big Bang to the 21st Century*, New York: Wiley, 2000. Goddess scholars like Marija Gimbutas believe rape culture entered Greek mythology with the Indo-Europeans. Marija Gimbutas, Miriam Robbins Dexter, *The Living Goddesses*. Berkeley, CA: University of California Press, 2001, pp. 154, 164. Thanks to the Indo-Europeans, say scholars like Gimbutas, the Greek gods amuse themselves with rape. From Zeus' rape of Europa, his rape of Leda, and the rape of his future wife Hera, to his failed attempt to rape Aphrodite, and his chase of the Titan goddess Asteria across the sky (she escaped rape by flying from the heavens as a quail and taking on the form of an island—Delos). Also take a look at the following hints from Indo-European languages: "tame, break.' Cf. Alb. dhente 'sheep; sheep and goats.' Also related to this root is Hitt. damas 'crush, rape' (especially of women); cf. Hom. Gk. damnemi 'marry, rape,' admes 'untamed; unmarried girl.' That the word had both meanings 'tame' and 'rape' may point to a symbolic connection between the taming of animals and the cohabitation ritual, as reflected in the Hittite laws discussed above and in Proto-Indo-European sacrifice rituals like the Ashvamedha." Thomas V. Gamkrelidze, Vjacheslav V. Ivanov, *Indo-European and the Indo-Europeans: A Reconstruction and Historical Analysis of a Proto-Language and Proto-Culture*. Walter de Gruyter, Jan. 1, 1995 p. 404. For the Ionian rape of the city of Miletus, see also: Robert Bittlestone, James Diggle, John Underhill, *Odysseus Unbound: The Search for Homer's Ithaca*, Cambridge: Cambridge University Press, Sept. 19, 2005, p. 342.

717. *A History of the Vikings*. New York: Charles Scribner's Sons, 1930, reprinted by New York: Dover Press, 2004, p. 119.

718. Thomas S. Noonan, "European Russia, c. 500–c. 1050." In *The New Cambridge Medieval History*, edited by Timothy Reuter. Cambridge, UK: Cambridge University Press, 1999, p. 508. en.wikipedia.org/wiki/Varangians en.wikipedia.org/wiki/Rurik en.wikipedia.org/wiki/Kievan_Rus%27 en.wikipedia.org/wiki/Rus%27_%28people%29

719. DK Publishing, *The Illustrated Encyclopedia of Warfare*. Penguin, Apr 16, 2012, p. 384.

720. Daniel J. Boorstin, *The Discoverers: A History of Man's Search To Know His World And Himself*. New York: Vintage Books, 1985.

721. Wikipedia, "Qing Dynasty." en.wikipedia.org/wiki/Qing_Dynasty

722. Wikipedia, "Taiwan." en.wikipedia.org/wiki/Taiwan

723. Wikipedia, "Imperial Examination." en.wikipedia.org/wiki/Imperial_examination

724. Wikipedia, "Imperial Examination." en.wikipedia.org/wiki/Imperial_examination

725. Ross E. Dunn, *The Adventures of Ibn Battuta: A Muslim Traveler of the Fourteenth Century*. Berkeley, CA: University of California Press, 1986.

726. Romila Thapar, *A History of India, Volume One*. Penguin Books, Harmondsworth, Middlesex, England, 1966 (1985 edition), pp. 29–35. D.D. Kosambi, *Ancient India: A History of Its Culture and Civilization*. Pantheon Books (A Division of Random House), New York, 1965, pp. 72–83. Patricia Bahree, *The Hindu World*. Silver Burdett Company, Morristown, NJ, 1985, p. 10. Chester G. Starr, *A History of the Ancient World*. Oxford University Press, New York, 1974, p. 166.

727. "Islam is an Arabic word the root of which is Silm and Salam. It means among others: peace, greeting, salutation, obedience, loyalty, allegiance, and submission to the will of the Creator of the Universe." University of Southern California. USC-MSA Compendium of Muslim Texts. Islamic Glossary. Muslim Student Association. www.usc.edu/dept/MSA/reference/glossary/term.ISLAM.html

728. Dr. Muhammad Ali Hashimi, *The Ideal Muslimah: The True Islamic Personality of the Muslim Woman as Defined in the Qur'an and the Sunnah*. Translated by Nasiruddin Al-Khattab, Saudi Arabia: International Islamic Publishing House, 1998. www.usc.edu/dept/MSA/humanrelations/womeninislam/idealmuslimah/

729. Dr. Muhammad Ali Al-Hashimi. Hajar, Um Isma'il, *The Ideal Muslimah: The True Islamic Personality of the Muslim Woman as Defined in the Qur'an and Sunnah*. Translated by Nasiruddin Al-Khattab. Published by International Islamic Publishing House. USC-MSA Compendium of Muslim Texts. University of Southern California. www.usc.edu/dept/MSA/humanrelations/womeninislam/idealmuslimah/ Also available at members.tripod.com/oum_abdulaziz/famous13.htm

730. The Holy Qur'an. Translation by Abdullah Yusufali. Complete online text. www.wam.umd.edu/~stwright/rel/islam/ downloaded 1998.

731. *Sahih Bukhari* translated by M. Muhsin Khan. (Book #52, Hadith #220) in SearchTruth.com. www.searchtruth.com/searchHadith.php?keyword=terror&translator=1&search=1&book=&start=0&records_display=10&search_word=all

732. Muhammad is quoted in the Hadith as saying one variation after another of these key lines. See: Sahih Muslim translated by Abdul Hamid Siddiqui. Book #004, Hadith #1062; Book #004, Hadith #1063; Book #004, Hadith #1066; Book #004, Hadith #1067. In SearchTruth.com. www.searchtruth.com/searchHadith.php?keyword=terror&translator=2&search=1&book=&start=0&records_display=10&search_word=all

733. The Holy Qur'an. Book 3, verse 151. Translation by Abdullah Yusufali. Complete online text. www.wam.umd.edu/~stwright/rel/islam/

734. The Holy Qur'an. Book 8, verse 12. Translation by Abdullah Yusufali. Complete online text. www.wam.umd.edu/~stwright/rel/islam/

735. The Holy Qur'an. Book 8, Verses 59-60. Translation by Abdullah Yusufali. Complete online text. www.wam.umd.edu/~stwright/rel/islam/

736. The Holy Qur'an. Chapter 59 verse 13. Translation by Abdullah Yusufali. Complete online text. www.wam.umd.edu/~stwright/rel/islam/

737. William R. Miller, Robert A. Rosellini and Martin E.P. Seligman, "Learned Helplessness and Depression," in Jack D. Maser and Martin E.P. Seligman, *Psychopathology: Experimental Models.* M.E. Seligman. "Learned Helplessness." *Annual Review of Medicine*, 23 1972: 407–412. W.R. Miller, M.E. Seligman. "Depression and learned helplessness in man." *Journal of Abnormal Psychology*, June 1975: 228–38; M.E. Seligman, G. Beagley. "Learned helplessness in the rat." *Journal of Comparative Psychology*, February 1975: 534–41.

738. Martin E.P. Seligman, Steven F. Maier, James H. Geer, "Alleviation Of Learned Helplessness In The Dog," *Journal of Abnormal Psychology* 1068, Vol. 73, No. 3, 256–262.

739. McElroy J.F., Weidemann K.A., Zeller K.L., et al. "Acute efficacy of the substance P (NK1) antagonist L-733,060 in rat learned helplessness, a chronic animal model of depression." Soc Neurosci Abs 1999; 25:31.15. Michael E. Thase, "Molecules That Mediate Mood," *The New England Journal of Medicine* (December 6, 2007), pp. 2400–2402.

740. William R. Miller, Robert A. Rosellini and Martin E.P. Seligman, "Learned Helplessness and Depression," in Jack D. Maser and Martin E.P. Seligman, *Psychopathology: Experimental Models.*

741. Jürgen Tautz, *The Buzz about Bees: Biology of a Superorganism*. Berlin: Springer, 2008, p. 3.

742. William Morton Wheeler, "The Termitodoxa, Or Biology And Society," *The Scientific Monthly*, February, 1920.

743. Pamela J. Baldwin, David J. Cooke, Jacqueline Howison, *Psychology in Prisons*. London: Routledge, 1990, pp. 119–120. *Donald W. Shriver Jr. An Ethic for Enemies: Forgiveness in Politics*, New York: Oxford University Press, 1995, p. 178. Peter Dzendrowskyj, Geoff Shaw, Lucy Johnston, Effects of nursing industrial action on relatives of Intensive Care Unit patients: a 16-month follow-up, *The New Zealand Medical Journal*, Vol 117, No 1205, November 5 2004, pp. 10–11, www.nzma.org.nz/journal/117-1205/1150/

744. Marcia Barinaga. "Neurobiology: Social status sculpts activity of crayfish neurons." *Science*, 19 January 1996: 290–291.

745. Eugene Rosa and Allan Mazur, "Incipient Status in Small Groups." *Social Forces*, Vol. 58. No. 1. September 1979, p. 34. Ana Pérez, Joaquim J. Veà, Functional Implications of Allogrooming in Cercocebus torquatus, *International Journal of Primatology*, April 2000, Volume 21, Issue 2, pp. 255–267.

746. Robert M. Sapolsky, "Lessons of the Serengeti: Why Some of Us Are More Susceptible to Stress," *The Sciences*, May/June, 1988, p. 42. B. Moghaddam, M.L. Bolinao, B. Stein-Behrens, R. Sapolsky, "Glucocorticoids mediate the stress-induced extracellular accumulation of glutamate." *Brain Research*, August 1994: 251-4. Robert M. Sapolsky, "Stress, Social Status, and Reproductive Physiology in Free-Living Baboons." In *Psychobiology of Reproductive Behavior: An Evolutionary Perspective*, edited by David Crews. Englewood Cliffs, NJ: Prentice Hall, 1987. Robert M. Sapolsky, "Stress in the Wild." *Scientific American.* January 1990: 116–123. Robert M. Sapolsky, *Why Zebras Don't Get Ulcers: An Updated Guide to Stress, Stress-Related Diseases, and Coping.* New York: W.H. Freeman & Co., 1998. David Berreby, *Us and Them: Understanding Your Tribal Mind.* New York: Little, Brown and Company, 2005.

747. Anna Freud, *The Ego and Mechanisms of Defense*. New York: International Universities Press, 1946.

748. "Those who reject Our Signs We shall soon cast into the fire: as often as their skins are roasted through We shall change them for fresh skins that they may taste the penalty: for Allah is Exalted in Power Wise." Holy Qur'an. AnNisaa, 56. www.wam.umd.edu/~stwright/rel/islam/Quran/4.html. English translations of the Qu'ran are available online from many Islamic sources, though these sources tend to appear and disappear rapidly. As of June 7, 2005, 625 online sources—primarily Islamic sources—included this quote. For one example, see: The Holy Qur'an. Translation by Abdullah Yusufali. Complete online text. www.wam.umd.edu/~stwright/rel/islam/

749. D.K. Letourneau, L.A. Dyer. "Density Patterns of Piper Ant-Plants and Associated Arthropods: Top-Predator Trophic Cascades in a Terrestrial System." *Biotropica*, Vol. 30, No. 2 (June 1998) , pp. 162–169. links.jstor.org/sici?sici=0006-3606%28199806%2930%3A2%3C162%3ADPOPAA%3E2.0.CO%3B2-M&size=LARGE. Guy Woodward and Alan G. Hildrew, "Invasion of a stream food web by a new top predator." *Journal of Animal Ecology*, Volume 70 Issue 2 Page 273 March 2001 www.blackwell-synergy.com/links/doi/10.1046/j.1365-2656.2001.00497.x David M. Post, M. Elizabeth Conners, Debra S. Goldberg, "Prey Preference by a Top Predator and the Stability of Linked Food Chains," *Ecology*, Vol. 81, No. 1 (Jan. 2000), pp. 8–14. links.jstor.org/sici?sici=0012-9658%28200001%2981%3A1%3C8%3APPBATP%3E2.0.CO%3B2-F&size=LARGE

750. "the Amazon rain forest may be largely a human artifact. ... In a widely cited article from 1989, William Balée, the Tulane anthropologist, cautiously estimated that about 12 percent of the nonflooded Amazon forest was of anthropogenic origin—directly or indirectly created by human beings. In some circles this is now seen as a conservative position. 'I basically think it's all human-created,' Clement told me in Brazil. He argues that Indians changed the assortment and density of species throughout the region. So does Clark Erickson, the University of Pennsylvania archaeologist, who told me in Bolivia that the lowland tropical forests of South America are among the finest works of art on the planet. 'Some of my colleagues would say that's pretty radical,' he said, smiling mischievously. According to Peter Stahl, an anthropologist at the State University of New York at Binghamton, 'lots' of botanists believe that 'what the eco-imagery would like to picture as a pristine, untouched Urwelt [primeval world] in fact has been managed by people for millennia.' The phrase 'built environment,' Erickson says, 'applies to most, if not all, Neotropical landscapes.'... Millennia of exuberant burning shaped the plains into vast buffalo farms. When Indian societies disintegrated, forest invaded savannah in Wisconsin, Illinois, Kansas, Nebraska, and the Texas Hill Country. Is it possible that the Indians changed the Americas more than the invading Europeans did? 'The answer is probably yes for most regions for the next 250 years or so' after Columbus, William Denevan wrote.... A keystone species, according to the Harvard biologist Edward O. Wilson, is a species "that affects the survival and abundance of many other species." Keystone species have a disproportionate impact on their ecosystems. Removing them, Wilson adds, 'results in a relatively significant shift in the composition of the [ecological] community.' ... When disease swept Indians from the land, ...After disease killed off the Indians, Kay believes, buffalo vastly extended their range. Their numbers more than sextupled. The same occurred with elk and mule deer." Charles C. Mann, "1491." *The Atlantic Monthly*, March 2002. Retrieved From the World Wide Web November 19, 2002 www.theatlantic.com/issues/2002/03/mann.htm

751. Charles C. Mann, *1491: New Revelations of the Americas Before Columbus*. New York: Knopf, 2005.

752. Sayyid Ali Ashgar Razwy, "The Death of Muhammad, the Messenger of God," in A Restatement of the History of Islam and Muslims, The Ahlul Bayt Digital Islamic Library Project, World Federation of Khoja Shia Ithna-Asheri Muslim Communities, United Kingdom, www.al-islam.org/restatement-history-islam-and-muslims-sayyid-ali-ashgar-razwydeath-muhammad-messenger-god

753. en.wikipedia.org/wiki/Jesus#Chronology

754. A. Guillaume, *The Life of Muhammad: A Translation of Ibn Ishaq's Sirat Rasul Allah*. New York: Oxford University Press, 1955, eighteenth printing, 2004, p. 500.

755. A quote from the hadith cited in: Mansour Abdul Hakeem. "Hadith: The Sword and the Spear." Nida'ul Islam. www.islam.org.au/articles/33/english/hadith(e).pdf

756. Sarwat Saulat, *The Life of The Prophet*. Islamic Publications Ltd., Lahore, Pakistan, 1983, p. 102.

757. Maulana A.S. Muhammad Abdul Hai (Rah.), *Holy Life of Hazrat Muhammad* (*Hayyat-E-Tayyaba*). Delhi, India: Islami Academy, 1984. www.al-islamforall.org/litre/Englitre/Hmohd.htm

758. "After the forced evacuation of Banu al-Nadir from Madinah and the events of the 'second Badr,' the campaigns of the Ghatafan and Dawmat al-Jandal…the Muslims…state of privation and need was largely ameliorated." Muhammad H. Haykal, *The Life of Muhammad*. Translated by Isma'il Raji al-Faruqi. Islamic Book Trust, Kuala Lumpur, Malaysia 2002, p. 299. Then the Battle of the Trench "with its resultant destruction of the Banu Qurayzah enabled the Muslims to establish themselves as Madinah's absolute masters. …All Arab tribes admired Muslim power, dominion, and the new prestige of Muhammad as sovereign of Madinah. The Islamic message, however, was not meant for Madinah alone, but for the whole of mankind. The Prophet and his companions still faced the task of preparing for the greater task ahead, namely bringing the word of God to the wide world…." Muhammad H. Haykal, *The Life of Muhammad*. Translated by Isma'il Raji al-Faruqi. Islamic Book Trust, Kuala Lumpur, Malaysia, 2002, p. 316.

759. Wikipedia, "Muhammad Husayn Haykal."en.wikipedia.org/wiki/Muhammad_Husayn_Haykal

760. see Supreme Council for Islamic Affairs, www.islamic-council.com/index.html.

761. "Islamic Book Trust Kuala Lumpur was established in 1991 with the objective of promoting Islamic books and literature." Islamic Book Trust Online Bookstore. www.ibtbooks.com/about_us.php

762. For more on the Witness-Pioneer, see www.witness-pioneer.org/. Muhammad Husayn Haykal, *The Life of Muhammad*. Translated by Isma'il Razi A. al-Faruqi. Published online by The Witness Pioneer, an organization "striving towards spreading and establishing the message of Islam…." www.witness-pioneer.org/vil/Books/MH_LM/default.htm

763. Muhammad H. Haykal, *The Life of Muhammad*. Translated by Isma'il Raji al-Faruqi. Islamic Book Trust, Kuala Lumpur, Malaysia, 2002, p. 316.

764. A. Guillaume, *The Life of Muhammad: A Translation of Ibn Ishaq's Sirat Rasul Allah*. New York: Oxford University Press, 1955, eighteenth printing, 2004, p. 452. For an even more vivid account of this incident, see: al-Tabari, *The History of al-Tabari* (*'Tarikh al-rusul wa'l muluk"*), Volume VIII, *The Victory of Islam*. Trans. Michael Fishbein. Albany: State University of New York Press, 1997, pp. 11–12.

765. A. Guillaume, *The Life of Muhammad: A Translation of Ibn Ishaq's Sirat Rasul Allah*. New York: Oxford University Press, 1955, eighteenth printing, 2004, p. 452.

766. Anthony Reid, *Southeast Asia in the Early Modern Era: Trade, Power, and Belief*. Cornell University Press, 1993, p. 162. Angela Schottenhammer, *The East Asian Mediterranean: Maritime Crossroads of Culture, Commerce and Human Migration*. Otto Harrassowitz Verlag, 2008, pp. 77, 92.

767. This quote is frequently used in Internet communications between modern Muslims. On March 7, 2006, this text appeared on 185 spots on the Internet in English and an uncountable number of sites in Arabic. It was particularly popular in postings on grassroots Muslim websites like myiwc.com, the Islamic Web-Community, american_muslims@yahoogroups.com, and khalifa.com (a group that calls for a one-world global caliphate). The quote's source is *Sahih Muslim*, The Book of Faith (Kitab Al-Iman)' of Sahih Muslim. Translated by Abdul Hamid Siddiqui. Book #041, Hadith #6904. In SearchTruth.com. www.searchtruth.com/searchHadith.php?keyword=the+ends+of+the+world+together+for+my+sake.&translator=2&search=1&book=&start=0&records_display=10&search_word=all
The full quote: "Thauban reported that Allah's Messenger (may peace be upon him) said: Allah drew the ends of the world near one another for my sake. And I have seen its eastern and western ends. And the dominion of my Ummah would reach those ends which have been drawn near me and I have been granted the red and the white treasure and I begged my Lord for my Ummah that it should not be destroyed because of famine, nor be dominated by an enemy who is not amongst them to take their lives and destroy them root and branch, and my Lord said: Muhammad, whenever I make a decision, there is none to change it. Well, I grant you for your Ummah that it would not be destroyed by famine and it would not be dominated by an enemy who would not be amongst it and would take their lives and destroy them root and branch even if all the people from the different parts of the world join hands together (for this purpose), but it would be from amongst them, viz. your Ummah, that some people would kill the others or imprison the others."

768. A. Guillaume, *The Life of Muhammad: A Translation of Ibn Ishaq's Sirat Rasul Allah*. New York: Oxford University Press, 1955, eighteenth printing, 2004, p. 452.

769. Sarwat Saulat, *The Life of The Prophet*. Islamic Publications Ltd., Lahore, Pakistan, 1983. A. Guillaume, *The Life of Muhammad: A Translation of Ibn Ishaq's Sirat Rasul Allah*. New York: Oxford University Press, 1955, eighteenth printing, 2004: p. 653. Muhammad H. Haykal, *The Life of Muhammad*. Translated by Isma'il Raji al-Faruqi. Islamic Book Trust, Kuala Lumpur, Malaysia, 2002, pp. 360–361. Hazrat Moulana Sayyed Abul Hassan Ali Nadwi (R.A.), *The Seerah of Muhammad (Sallallahu Laiyhi Wassallam): (The Last Prophet: A Model For All Time)*. Al-Islaah Publications. Retrieved August 31, 2005, From the World Wide Web: alislaah3.tripod.com/alislaah/id12.html.

770. The governor of Egypt was named Muqawqis. Hazrat Moulana Sayyed Abul Hassan Ali Nadwi (R.A.), *The Seerah of Muhammad (Sallallahu Laiyhi Wassallam): (The Last Prophet: A Model For All Time)*. Al-Islaah Publications. Retrieved August 31, 2005, from the World Wide Web: alislaah3.tripod.com/alislaah/id12.html.

771. The Governor of Syria was Harith Gassani.

772. The ruler of Bahrain was al-Mundhir bin Sawa.

773. Muhammad H. Haykal, *The Life Of Muhammad*. Translated by Isma'il Raji al-Faruqi. Islamic Book Trust, Kuala Lumpur, Malaysia, 2002, p. 363.

774. Sarwat Saulat's *The Life of The Prophet*. p. 223. Hazrat Moulana Sayyed Abul Hassan Ali Nadwi (R.A.), *The Seerah of Muhammad (Sallallahu Laiyhi Wassallam): (The Last Prophet: A Model For All Time)*. Al-Islaah Publications. Retrieved August 31, 2005, From the World Wide Web: alislaah3.tripod.com/alislaah/id12.html. Sarwat Saulat's *The Life of The Prophet*, p. 223. Muhammed H. Haykal (2002). *The Life of Muhammad*. Translated from the eighth edition by Isma'il Raji al-Faruqi. Kuala Lumpur: Islamic Book Trust. pp: 374–379. Dr. A. Zahoor and Dr. Z. Haq. "Prophet Muhammad's Letters To Kings (628 Ce)" Copyright © 1990, 1997. www.cyberistan.org/islamic/letters.html "Restatement Of History Of Islam: The Conquest of Khyber." Ahlul Bayt Digital Islamic Library Project material selected from our Library that is particularly appropriate for those who are new to Islam. Al-Islam.org. al-islam.org/ restatement/29.htm

775. Ibn Ishaq shows that he sees Muhammad's letters as ultimatums backed by force when he reports that Hercules, the head of the Eastern Roman Empire, "gathered the Romans [the Christians of the Eastern Roman Empire's lands in the Middle East] together" and explained that he wanted to give in to Muhammad's demand and "follow him [Muhammad] that it may be well with us in this world and the next." The Romans were outraged. They saw this shift of religion as more than just a matter of belief. They saw it as an Arab bid to subjugate them. According to Ibn Ishaq, "They said, 'Are we to be under the hands of the Arabs when we are a people with a greater kingdom, a larger population, and a finer country?" Then comes the kicker, the line that indicates that Ibn Ishaq views the "invitations" as military threats. Hercules says to his people, "Come and I will pay him [Muhammad] the poll-tax every year and avert his onslaught and get rest from the war by the money I pay him." A. Guillaume, *The Life of Muhammad: A Translation of Ibn Ishaq's Sirat Rasul Allah*. New York: Oxford University Press, 1955, eighteenth printing, 2004, pp. 656–657.

776. Maulana A.S. Muhammad Abdul Hai, *Holy Life of Hazrat Muhammad (Hayyat-E-Tayyaba)*. Al-Islam Society. (Al-Islam propagation society is a Non-profit socio-educational organization founded with the objective of facilitating the spread of accurate and authentic knowledge about Islam among the different nations of the world. Our aim is to work for proper understanding of Islam by all and to work to strengthen the moral and social fabric of the peoples of the world. We envisage a universal society which is bound by mutual understanding and brotherhood and which is honoured by the presence of Islam.") Al-Islamforall.org. www.al-islamforall.org/litre/Englitre/Hmohd.htm.

777. A. Guillaume, *The Life of Muhammad: A Translation of Ibn Ishaq's Sirat Rasul Allah*. New York: Oxford University Press, 1955, eighteenth printing, 2004, p. 657.

778. Muhammad H. Haykal, *The Life of Muhammad*. Translated by Isma'il Raji al-Faruqi. Islamic Book Trust, Kuala Lumpur, Malaysia, 2002, p. 365.

779. A. Guillaume, *The Life of Muhammad: A Translation of Ibn Ishaq's Sirat Rasul Allah*. New York: Oxford University Press, 1955, eighteenth printing, 2004, p. 654.

780. Map of the Byzantine Empire around 550. en.wikipedia.org/wiki/Image:Byzantium550.png.

781. Dr. A. Zahoor and Dr. Z. Haq. "Prophet Muhammad's Letters To Kings (628 Ce)" Copyright © 1990, 1997. www.cyberistan.org/islamic/letters.html. See also A. Guillaume, *The Life of Muhammad: A Translation of Ibn Ishaq's Sirat Rasul Allah*. New York: Oxford University Press, 1955, eighteenth printing, 2004, p. 655. Muhammad H. Haykal, *The Life of Muhammad*. Translated by Isma'il Raji al-Faruqi. Islamic Book Trust, Kuala Lumpur, Malaysia, 2002: p. 364.

782. Quran Chapter 3, verse 12. The Holy Qur'an. Translation by Abdullah Yusufali. Complete online text. www.wam.umd.edu/~stwright/rel/islam/

783. Quran Chapter 3, verse 152. The Holy Qur'an. Translation by Abdullah Yusufali. Complete online text. www.wam.umd.edu/~stwright/rel/islam/

784. Quran Chapter 7, verse 4. The Holy Qur'an. Translation by Abdullah Yusufali. Complete online text. www.wam.umd.edu/~stwright/rel/islam/

785. Aisha Bint Muhammad, "Ibn Taymiyyah." Jannah.org. www.jannah.org/articles/taymiyyah.html

786. Imam Ibn Taymiyyah, "The Religious and Moral Doctrine on Jihad." From "al-Siyaasa al-shar`iyya fee islaah al-raa`ee wa al-raa`iyya" (Governance according to God's Law in reforming both the ruler and his flock). www.islaam.com/ilm/ibnta.htm.

787. Muhammad H. Haykal, The Life of Muhammad. Translated by Isma'il Raji al-Faruqi. Islamic Book Trust, Kuala Lumpur, Malaysia, 2002, p. 365.

788. Ayatollah Khomeini, Sayings of the Ayatollah Khomeini. New York: Bantam Books, 1980, pp. 5–6. Yvette Hovsepian-Bearce, The Political Ideology of Ayatollah Khamenei: Out of the Mouth of the Supreme Leader of Iran, Routledge, 2015, p. 309.

789. President Dwight D. Eisenhower's Annual Message To The Congress On The State Of The Union, 1958. C-Span.org. www.c-span.org/executive/transcript.asp?cat=current_event&code=bush_admin&year=1958

790. Abbas J. Ali and Robert Camp, "The Middle East Conflict: Perpetual Jihad." Public Administration and Management: An Interactive Journal. 9 (1), 2004: pp. 46–69. Suhas Majumdar, Jihad: The Islamic Doctrine of Perpetual War. New Delhi. Voice of Dharma Books. 1994. www.bharatvani.org/books/jihad/ Robert Spencer and David Pryce-Jones, Islam Unveiled: Disturbing Facts About the World's Fastest Growing Faith. New York: Encounter Books, 2002. Zaid Shakir: "Jihad is Not Perpetual Warfare," Seasons. Autumn-Winter 2003–4.

791. The Holy Qur'an. Translation by Abdullah Yusufali. Complete online text. www.wam.umd.edu/~stwright/rel/islam/ downloaded 1998.

792. Muhammad H. Haykal, The Life of Muhammad. Translated by Isma'il Raji al-Faruqi. Islamic Book Trust, Kuala Lumpur, Malaysia 2002, pp. 371–372.

793. Muhammad H. Haykal, The Life of Muhammad. Translated by Isma'il Raji al-Faruqi. Islamic Book Trust, Kuala Lumpur, Malaysia 2002: p 376.

794. Muhammad H. Haykal, The Life of Muhammad. Translated by Isma'il Raji al-Faruqi. Islamic Book Trust, Kuala Lumpur, Malaysia 2002, p. 376.

795. Quran, chapter 3, verse 151.

796. "When Muhammad had finished with the decapitation of the Jews of the Bani Quraiza, he said about the people of Mecca, 'Now we shall attack them'—meaning Quraysh [the Meccans]—'and they will not attack us'—and thus it was, until God granted His Messenger the conquest of Mecca. In other words, thanks to the massacre of the Jews and the fear it spread, townsmen like the Meccans now gave in to the Muslims without resistance." al-Tabari, The History of al-Tabari ('Tarikh al-rusul wa'l muluk"), Volume VIII, The Victory of Islam. Trans. Michael Fishbein. Albany: State University of New York Press, 1997, p. 40.

797. A. Guillaume, The Life of Muhammad: A Translation of Ibn Ishaq's Sirat Rasul Allah. New York: Oxford University Press, 1955, eighteenth printing, 2004, p. 469. Abu Sufyan, leader of the Meccans, came to Muhammad in a desperate effort to save his own life and to make peace. Muhammad's men literally terrified Abu Sufyan into converting to Islam by continually threatening to cut off his head. One of many statements made to Abu Sufyan while he stood in front of Muhammad was this blunt threat from a Muslim trooper, al-Abbas: "Recite the testimony of truth before, by God, your head is cut off." The "testimony of truth" is the key statement that makes you a Muslim — "There is no God but Allah; Muhammad is the messenger of Allah." (al-Tabari, The History of al-Tabari ('Tarikh al-rusul wa'l muluk"), Volume VIII, The Victory of Islam. Trans. Michael Fishbein. Albany: State University of New York Press, 1997, p. 173).

798. Maulana A.S. Muhammad Abdul Hai (Rah.), Holy Life Of Hazrat Muhammad (Hayyat-E-Tayyaba). Delhi, India: Islami Academy, 1984. Retrieved November 15, 2013, from the World Wide Web www.al-islamforall.org/litre/Englitre/Hmohd.htm

799. The Prophet said, "Yawning is from Satan and if anyone of you yawns, he should check his yawning as much as possible, for if anyone of you (during the act of yawning) should say: 'Ha,' Satan will laugh at him." Sahih Bukhari. Volume 4, Book 54, Number 509. Translator: M. Muhsin Khan. MSA-USC Hadith Database. USC-MSA Compendium of Muslim Texts. University of Southern California. www.usc.edu/dept/MSA/fundamentals/hadithsunnah/bukhari/054.sbt.html#004.054.509

800. "Narrated 'Abdullah bin Mas'ud: Once the Prophet was offering prayers at the Ka'ba. Abu Jahl was sitting with some of his companions. One of them said to the others, 'Who amongst you will bring the abdominal contents (intestines, etc.) of a camel of Bani so and so and put it on the back of Muhammad, when he prostrates?' The most unfortunate of them got up and brought it. He waited till the Prophet prostrated and then placed it on his back between his shoulders. I was watching but could not do any thing. I wish I had some people with me to hold out against them. They started laughing and falling on one another. Allah's Apostle was in prostration and he did not lift his head up till Fatima (Prophet's daughter) came and threw that (camel's abdominal contents) away from his back. He raised his head and said thrice, 'O Allah! Punish Quraish.' [the tribe whose members were mocking him]" *Sahih Bukhari* Book #4, Hadith #241. Sahih Bukhari translated by M. Muhsin Khan. in SearchTruth.com. www.searchtruth.com/searchHadith.php?keyword= camel+laugh&translator=1&search=1&book= &start=0&records_display=10&search_word=all

801. From a bit of correspondence with a Muslim friend in Pakistan whose name, for his safety, I can't give:

Howard Bloom: Do you know that virtually only people who laugh in the Hadith are Satan and Muhammad's enemies in Mecca?

My Pakistani informant: "THAT hit me like a ton of bricks. It rings so true today even." April 21, 2006.

802. "O followers of Muhammad! By Allah! If you knew that which I know you would laugh little and weep much." *Sahih Bukhari.* Volume 2, Book 18, Number 154. Translator: M. Muhsin Khan. MSA-USC Hadith Database. USC-MSA Compendium of Muslim Texts. University of Southern California. www.usc.edu/dept/MSA/fundamentals/ hadithsunnah/bukhari/018.sbt.html#002.018.154

803. "The Prophet, sallallahu alayhe wa sallam. Abu Hurairah said that the prophet, sallallahu alayhe wa sallam, was told, "O Prophet of Allah, you are joking with us." He said, "I only say what is true." (Tirmithi) Another hadith relates that the prophet, sallallahu alayhe wa sallam, would nickname Zeinab bint Um Salama by repeatedly calling her 'O Zuweinab.'

Other Ahadith relate that the Prophet, sallallahu alayhe wa sallam, would play and joke with small children. Thus we see that joking is a Sunnah. Sufyan bin Uyayna was asked, " Is joking prohibited?" He replied, "It is a Sunnah, but the point is that it must be done appropriately." Many of the scholars agree with that. Omar (Radhiallahu anhu) said, "I admire the man who is like a child with his family (playful), and once he leaves them, he is more serious." Thabit ibn Ubaid said, "Zayd ibn Thabit was one of the most humorous men in his home. Outside of his home, hewas as serious as any man." It is also related that ibn Abbas asked some of his guests to have light and humorous conversation so that they would have a good time and not feel bored. Rabi'a said, "Virtue is made of six parts, three while in town (at the place of your home) and three while on a journey. The first three are reciting the Qur'an, frequently being at the mosque, and spreading the way of Allah to other lands.

The three parts while traveling are spending, showing virtuous behaviour and joking in what Allah has permitted." Ibn Abbas said, "Joking appropriately is permissible, for the Prophet, sallallahu alayhe wa sallam, joked but he only said what was true." Al Khalil bin Ahmad al Farahidi said, "People would feel imprisoned if they did not joke." Prohibition of joking:

On the other hand, some of the scholars have prohibited joking and they are supported by some Ahaddeth. It is related that the Prophet, sallallahu alayhe wa sallam, said, "Everything has a beginning and hostility begins with joking." Ja'far ibn Muhammad said, "Beware of joking for it causes embarrassment." Ibrahim al-Nakh'i said, "Joking shows foolishness and arrogance." Imam ibn Abdul Bar said, "Some of the scholars denounced joking for what it causes of offences, spite and malice between people."Islam and the sense of humor By Soumy Ana: Jumad al-Awwal 1423 — July–August 2002. Taqwa Palace, Palace of Faith. Ummah.com—The Muslim Directory Online. www.ummah.com/islam/taqwapalace/humour.pdf

804. Sarwat Saulat, *The Life of The Prophet,* Islamic Publications Ltd., Lahore, Pakistan, 1983, p. 125.

805. Ritch Savin Williams, *Adolescence: An Ethological Perspective.* New York: Springer Science & Business Media, 2012. Daniel G. Freedman. *Human Sociobiology: A Holistic Approach.* New York: Free Press, 1979, p. 49.

806. Psychologist Ritch Savin-Williams and his teams of grad students would discover the hierarchical cruelty of adolescent girls in research on all-girl summer camps in the early 1980s. Roberta L. Paikoff, Ritch C. Savin-Williams. "An exploratory study of dominance interactions among adolescent females at a summer camp." *Journal of Youth & Adolescence*, October 1983: 419–433.

807. al-Tabari, *The History of al-Tabari*: English translation of "at Tareekh al-Tabari." Albany: State University of New York Press: Book VIII, p. 179.

808. al-Tabari, *The History of al-Tabari ('Tarikh al-rusul wa'l muluk"), Volume VIII, The Victory of Islam.* Trans. Michael Fishbein. Albany: State University of New York Press, 1997.

809. Here's a typical pronouncement from Muhammad on two subjects, women and laughter: "The Prophet then mentioned about the women (in his sermon). "It is not wise for anyone of you to lash his wife like a slave, for he might sleep with her the same evening." Then he advised them not to laugh when somebody breaks wind and said, "Why should anybody laugh at what he himself does?" *Sahih Bukhari*, Volume 6, Book 60, Number 466. MSA-USC Hadith Database. USC-MSA Compendium of Muslim Texts. University of Southern California. www.usc.edu/dept/MSA/fundamentals/hadithsunnah/bukhari/060.sbt.html#006.060.466

810. Narrated Abu 'Amir or Abu Malik Al-Ash'ari: that he heard the Prophet saying, "From among my followers there will be some people who will consider illegal sexual intercourse, the wearing of silk, the drinking of alcoholic drinks and the use of musical instruments, as lawful. And there will be some people who will stay near the side of a mountain and in the evening their shepherd will come to them with their sheep and ask them for something, but they will say to him, 'Return to us tomorrow.' Allah will destroy them during the night and will let the mountain fall on them, and He will transform the rest of them into monkeys and pigs and they will remain so till the Day of Resurrection." *Sahih Bukhari* Book #69, Hadith #494v. Translated by M. Muhsin Khan in SearchTruth.com. "Search Truth is a non-profit organization aimed at utilizing the latest technologies available in order to spread the Word of Allah and the Sunnah of the Holy Prophet (pbuh) to as large an audience as possible." www.searchtruth.com/searchHadith.php?keyword=pigs+monkeys&translator=1&search=1&book=&start=0&records_display=10&search_word=all

811. A. Guillaume, *The Life of Muhammad: A Translation of Ibn Ishaq's Sirat Rasul Allah.* New York: Oxford University Press, 1955, eighteenth printing, 2004, p. 550.

812. Al-Tabari. Quoted in Sam Shamoun. "Response to Zakir Naik's Claims for the Quran 3." answering-islam.org.uk/Responses/Naik/quranclaims3.htm

813. Al-Tabari. Quoted in Sam Shamoun. "Response to Zakir Naik's Claims for the Quran 3." answering-islam.org.uk/Responses/Naik/quranclaims3.htm

814. al-Tabari, *The History of al-Tabari*: English translation of "at Tareekh al-Tabari." Albany: State University of New York Press: Book VIII, p. 179. See also A. Guillaume, *The Life of Muhammad: A Translation of Ibn Ishaq's Sirat Rasul Allah.* New York: Oxford University Press, 1955, eighteenth printing, 2004: 550.

815. al-Tabari, *The History of al-Tabari*: English translation of "at Tareekh al-Tabari." Albany: State University of New York Press: Book VIII, p. 179. See also A. Guillaume, *The Life of Muhammad: A Translation of Ibn Ishaq's Sirat Rasul Allah.* New York: Oxford University Press, 1955, eighteenth printing, 2004: 550.

816. United Nations Development Programme and Arab Fund for Economic and Social Development. "Arab Human Development Report 2002: Creating Opportunities for Future Generations." New York: The Regional Bureau for Arab States, United Nations Development Programme, 2002.

817. *Sahih Bukhari*, Book #52, Hadith #50. www.searchtruth.com/searchHadith.php?keyword=world&book=&translator=1&search=1&search_word=all&start=30&records_display=10

818. Wikipedia. "Origin and Development of the Qur'an." en.wikipedia.org/wiki/Qur%27an#Origin_and_development_of_the_Qur.27an.
For modern Muslim debates over the nature and purpose of the Qur'an see: Y.Y. Haddad, *Contemporary Islam and the Challenge of History.* Albany: State University of New York Press, 1982.

819. In fact, the Hadith may have been gathered from eyewitness accounts of Muhammad's life committed to paper or to oral tradition over one hundred years after Muhammad's death. See: Eerik Dickinson, *The Development of Early Sunnite Hadith Criticism: The Taqdima of Ibn Abi Hatim al-Razi.* Leiden, Netherlands: Koninklijke Brill: 2001, pp. vii–ix. "Muslim historians say that it was the caliph Uthman (the third caliph, or successor of Muhammad, who had formerly been Muhammad's secretary), who first urged Muslims both to write down the Qur'an in a fixed form, and to write down the hadith." Wikipedia, "Hadith." en.wikipedia.org/wiki/Hadith. Wikipedia, "History of Hadith." en.wikipedia.org/wiki/History_of_Hadith

820. for example, a Muslim cannot perform a prayer—one of the five communal prayers required per day—after "Defecation, urination, or passing gas." B. Aisha Lemu, *Islamic aqidah and fiqh: A Textbook of Islamic Belief and Jurisprudence*. Skokie, IL: IQRA' International Education Foundation. p. 62. Islam has commandments about things as simple as defecation and urination, commandments based on the words and life of Muhammad. "But, Abdullah [b. 'Umar'] said: when I was on the roof of our house when I saw the prophet defecating while sitting on two clay bricks facing Jerusalem." Brannon M. Wheeler, *Applying Canon in Islam: The Authorization and Maintenance of Interpretive Reasoning in Hanafi Scholarship*. Albany: State University of New York, 1996, p. 54. "Khadduri, in a footnote to his translation of this section, notes that Abu Da'ud [1:12] cites a report that Ibn 'Umar was seen urinating in the desert, sheltered by his camel, facing Makkah. Ibn 'Umar reports that the prophet allowed urination facing Makkah as long as there was a barrier between the person urinating and Makkah." The same rule applied to defecation. Brannon M. Wheeler, *Applying Canon in Islam: The Authorization and Maintenance of Interpretive Reasoning in Hanafi Scholarship*. Albany: State University of New York, 1996, pp. 53–54, 258. Yasin Dutton, *Origins of Islamic Law: The Qur'an, the Muwatta' and the Madinan Amal*. London: Curzon Press, 1999, p. 235.

821. According to one source, Globalterroralert.com, Azzam Publications was "widely considered to be the premiere English-language mouthpiece for Al-Qaida." Evan Kohlmann. Dossier: Azzam Publications UK (Azzam.com, Qoqaz.net) and Mazen Mokhtar. Globalterroralert.com. www.globalterroralert.com/azzam-mokhtar.pdf

822. Azzam Publications, "Farewell Message from Azzam Publications." November 20, 2001 IslamicAwakening.com—"Site dedicated to the blessed global Islamic Awakening." Retrieved from the World Wide Web May 05, 2004 www.as-sahwah.com/viewarticle.php?articleID=756

823. Azzam Publications, "Farewell Message from Azzam Publications." November 20, 2001 IslamicAwakening.com—"Site dedicated to the blessed global Islamic Awakening" Retrieved from the World Wide Web May 05, 2004 www.as-sahwah.com/viewarticle.php?articleID=756 Here's the full quote: "There is no such thing as a 'moderate' or 'liberal' Muslim. If there was, in what category would we place the Prophet Muhammad (SAWS)? Would we say he is a moderate, a liberal, an extremist, a fanatic, a terrorist, a fundamentalist? He certainly would not be a moderate or liberal since he ordered 600–700 Jewish males to be beheaded in Madinah after the Jewish tribe of Banu Qurayzah betrayed the Muslims and stabbed them in the back. He also fought in 27 battles for the sake of Allah. Are we now going to call him a terrorist as well? We ask Allah to give victory to those fighting for His Sake in the four corners of the Earth, to destroy their enemies and the hypocrites and to enable the Muslim Ummah to produce millions of martyrs as the price for victory in this Life and achieving Allah's Pleasure in the Next. Your brothers at Azzam Publications" 20 November 2001 IslamicAwakening.Com and ilaljibal.com, Farewell Message from Azzam Publications, ilaljibal.wordpress.com/2009/04/14/farewell-message/

824. The Muslim Brotherhood's Conquest of Europe by Lorenzo Vidino. *Middle East Quarterly*. Winter 2005, pp. 25–34, www.meforum.org/687/the-muslim-brotherhoods-conquest-of-europe 3-18-2016

825. Muslim Brotherhood, The Muslim Brotherhood's Strategic Plan For America—Court Document, 1991, Clarion Project, www.clarionproject.org/Muslim_Brotherhood_Explanatory_Memorandum 3-18-2016

826. Imam Shaheed Hasan Al-Banna Jihad — Hasan Al-Banna Online Library, Copyright © 1997 Prelude Ltd, www.qoqaz.net, downloaded 2008, and Official Website of Khalifah Institute, Malaysia, Islamic-World.net, www.islamic-world.net/book/jihad_preface.htm, 3-18-2016

827. Imam Shaheed Hasan Al-Banna Jihad — Hasan Al-Banna Online Library, Copyright © 1997 Prelude Ltd, www.qoqaz.net, downloaded 2008, and Official Website of Khalifah Institute, Malaysia, Islamic-World.net, www.islamic-world.net/book/jihad_preface.htm, 3-18-2016

828. Imam Shaheed Hasan Al-Banna Jihad — Hasan Al-Banna Online Library, Copyright © 1997 Prelude Ltd, www.qoqaz.net, downloaded 2008, and Official Website of Khalifah Institute, Malaysia, Islamic-World.net, www.islamic-world.net/book/jihad_preface.htm, 3-18-2016

829. From the Hadith of Al Bukhari and Muslim. Quoted in Imam Shaheed Hasan Al-Banna Jihad — Hasan Al-Banna Online Library, Copyright © 1997 Prelude Ltd, www.qoqaz.net, downloaded 2008, and Official Website of Khalifah Institute, Malaysia, Islamic-World.net, www.islamic-world.net/book/jihad_preface.htm 3-18-2016.

830. The Holy Qur'an. Translation by Abdullah Yusufali. Complete online text. Retrieved March 20, 2005, from the World Wide Web www.wam.umd.edu/~stwright/rel/islam/ chapter 9. At Tauba; verse 5.

831. The Holy Qur'an. Translation by Abdullah Yusufali. Complete online text. Retrieved March 20, 2005, from the World Wide Web www.wam.umd.edu/~stwright/rel/islam/ chapter 9, verse 111.

832. G.P. Tate, *The Kingdom of Afghanistan: A Historical Sketch*. Asian Educational Services, 1911, p. 41.

833. Imam Shaheed Hasan Al-Banna Jihad — Hasan Al-Banna Online Library, Copyright © 1997 Prelude Ltd, www.qoqaz.net, downloaded 2008, and Official Website of Khalifah Institute, Malaysia, Islamic-World.net, www.islamic-world.net/book/jihad_preface.htm 3-18-2016.

834. Qur'an. Chapter 3, verse 144. The Holy Qur'an. Translation by Abdullah Yusufali. Complete online text. Retrieved November 19, 2001, from the World Wide Web www.wam.umd.edu/~stwright/rel/islam/

835. Qur'an, 2:216 trans. M.M. Pickthall, www.islamawakened.com/quran/2/216/ 3-18-2016

836. Qur'an, 8:67, trans. M.M. Pickthall, corpus.quran.com/translation.jsp?chapter= 8&verse=67 3-18-2016

837. Qur'an, 8:67, trans. M.M. Pickthall, corpus.quran.com/translation.jsp?chapter= 8&verse=67 3-18-2016.

838. Imam Shaheed Hasan Al-Banna Jihad — Hasan Al-Banna Online Library, Copyright © 1997 Prelude Ltd, www.qoqaz.net, downloaded 2008, and Official Website of Khalifah Institute, Malaysia, Islamic-World.net, www.islamic-world.net/book/jihad_preface.htm 3-18-2016.

839. Quoted from the hadith of Al Bukhari, Muslim and Abu Dawud. In Imam Hasan al-Banna, *Kitab ul Jihad*, in Ibn Taymiyyah, Islamic Books by Ibn Taymiyyah Maqdisi and Abdullah Azzam, Moscow: Рипол Классик, Ripol Classic Publishing House: p. 226.

840. Here's what one mainstream, high-profile Islamic website says about following Muhammad's example:
We are commanded by God to follow the example of Muhammad (peace and blessings be upon him): You have a good example in God's Messenger for whoever looks unto God and the Last Day, and remembers God oft. (Al-Ahzab 33: 21)
God's Messenger is our leader. As we stand in prayer according to the way he prayed, we must also follow him in every walk of our life. Those who followed him in the first Islamic century were the real representatives of the true Islamic life. Concerning this period, God's Messenger told us that Muslim armies would arrive at the gates of cities, where they would be asked, "Did anyone among you see the Prophet?" The answer would be affirmative, and, therefore, they would be granted victory. Those who succeeded them would also perform jihad and they would be asked, "Are there any people among you who saw those who had seen the Prophet?" They would reply, "Yes," and the cities would be conquered by them. There would finally come the third generation, who would be asked, "Did anybody among you see those who had seen the followers of the Prophet's Companions?" When this question, too, received an affirmative answer, the conquest would also be bestowed upon them (Al-Bukhari and Muslim).
Again, in another narration by Al-Bukhari and Muslim, God's Messenger says concerning those three succeeding generations:
"The best of you are those who live in my period, then those who succeed them, and then those who follow them."
Those three generations strictly followed in the Prophet's footsteps and, accordingly, were granted great victories… (Fethullah Gulen, "The Prophets Were Examples." IslamOnline. August 3, 2005. www.islamonline.net/English/In_Depth/ mohamed/1424/kharitah/article32.shtml) IslamOnline, the source of this quote, is a mainstream, heavy-traffic Muslim website founded in 1997 by Sheikh Yusuf al-Qaradawi. What's mainstream and what is not in modern Islam is debatable. Qaradawi has been banned from the United States as a risk. (Owen Bowcott and Faisal al Yafai, "Scholar with a streetwise touch defies expectations and stereotypes." London, England: *Guardian Unlimited*. July 9, 2004. www.guardian.co.uk/religion/ Story/0,2763,1257458,00.html)
He has been called a hatemonger for his anti-Semitic statements. (Anti-Defamation League, "Sheik Yusuf al-Qaradawi: Theologian of Terror" August 1, 2005. www.adl.org/main_Arab_World/ al_Qaradawi_report_20041110.htm)

But the fact is that Qaradawi is a mainstream media personality in the Islamic world. He appears weekly on al Jazeera television, Islam's flagship satellite TV station. His show is in one of the most-watched categories of media in the Muslim world...shows that take questions from callers, then answer them by going back through the Qur'an, the Hadith, the Sunnah, and the Fiqh to give the closest approximation possible to the answer Muhammad would have given or to the example in Muhammad's own life that the caller should emulate. Al-Qaradawi's program is called *ash-Shariah wal-Hayat* (Islamic Law and Life). In the words of Wikipedia, "Among Muslims, Qaradawi is considered a mainstream moderate conservative offering balanced opinions." (Wikipedia, "Yusuf al-Qaradawi." en.wikipedia.org/wiki/Yusuf_al-Qaradawi.) More important, the Islamic website Positive Images says that Qaradawi is perceived by many as the symbol of thought-provoking, forward-thinking and moderate Islamic scholarship, and has gained a reputation as a messenger promoting dialogue within the Muslim community and with other faiths (Positive Images, Has Sheikh Yusuf al-Qaradawi Been Wronged?" www.positive-images.org.uk/articles/qaradawi.html)
To get your own sense of Qaradawi and of what is or is not mainstream in modern Islam, see: Yusuf al-Qaradawi. Al-Qaradawi full transcript, BBC News, July 8, 2004. news.bbc.co.uk/2/hi/programmes/newsnight/3875119.stm

841. Said Muhammad, "I have bequeathed to you that which will always be a guide to you, if you will take hold of it; the Book of God and the practices of my life." This saying and its implications have been critical in the development of Islam. (Muhammad Heikal, *The Return of the Ayatollah*, p. 80)

842. The author is referring to the following lines in the Qur'an: "Certainly you have in the Messenger of Allah an excellent exemplar for him who hopes in Allah and the latter day and remembers Allah much." (Holy Qur'an 33: 21)
n.a. *Prophet Muhammad—A brief biography*. Islamic Occasions—Truth, Wisdom, and Justice. Website designed by Akramulla Syed
Last Updated: 01 September 2004.
www.ezsoftech.com/islamic/infallible1a.asp#01.
"Our society could never be an Islamic one unless we sincerely tread the footsteps of Allah's final Messenger to mankind, heed his sayings, observe his glorious actions and attitudes, and most important of all follow them, as the faithful among his companions did." In short, Allah the most Glorious enjoins upon us to take the Prophet's behavior as an example, because he guides us to virtue and righteousness:
"Certainly you have in the Messenger of Allah an excellent exemplar for him who hopes in Allah and the latter day and remembers Allah much." Holy Qur'an (33: 21)
No author, *Prophet Muhammad — A brief biography*, www.ezsoftech.com/islamic/infallible1e.asp Islamic Occasions Network 21 October 2004.
This unsigned biography of Muhammad is widely available for Muslims online. It's also been published in book form via the self-publisher Lulu.

843. Hazrat Moulana Sayyed Abul Hassan Ali Nadwi (R.A.), *The Seerah of Muhammad (Sallallahu Laiyhi Wassallam): (The Last Prophet: A Model For All Time)*. Al-Islaah Publications. Retrieved August 31, 2005, from the World Wide Web: alislaah3.Tripod.Com/

844. The author is referring to the following lines in the Qur'an: "Certainly you have in the Messenger of Allah an excellent exemplar for him who hopes in Allah and the latter day and remembers Allah much." (Holy Qur'an 33: 21)
n.a. *Prophet Muhammad — A brief biography*. Islamic Occasions—Truth, Wisdom, and Justice. Website designed by Akramulla Syed Last Updated: 01 September 2004.
www.ezsoftech.com/islamic/infallible1a.asp#01

845. See books like: Saniyasnain Khan, *Prophet of Peace: Prophet Muhammad for Little Hearts*. New Delhi: Goodword Books, 2004. Qutubuddin Aziz, *The Prophet of Peace and Humanity*. North Haledon, NJ: Islamic Publications International, 1986.

846. "Others of the Prophet's names and epithets are reported in the hadith. Thus Muhammad ibn Isma'il al-Bukhari reported on the authority of Jubayr ibn Mut'im that he heard the Apostle of Allah say: "I have many names: I am Muhammad, I am Ahmad. I am al-mahi (the effacer), for through me Allah shall efface rejection of faith. I am al-hashir (the gatherer), for all men shall be gathered at my heels (on the last day). I am al-'aqib (the last to follow), after whom there shall be no other (prophet)." In another tradition: "I am the effacer" is taken to mean, he through whom the sins of those who follow him shall be effaced. In yet another tradition he is called al-muqaffi (that is he who followed all other prophets), nabiyyu 't-tawbah (the prophet of penitence), nabiyyu 'l-malhamah (the prophet of war), al-khatim (the seal), al-ghayth (the succorer), and al-mutawakkil (he who trusts in Allah)." 'Ali Akbar Ghifari. Originally published in 1399. Beirut, Lebanon: *Beacons of Light*, 1979 translated and annotated by Dr. Mahmoud M. Ayoub www.al-shia.com/html/eng/books/becons-of-light/03.htm.
See also: "The Prophet (peace and blessings be upon him) also said, 'I am the Prophet of mercy and I am the Prophet of war.'
Dr. Ahmad Abu Al-Wafa, Professor of the International Law at the Faculty of Law, Cairo University. "Killing Wounded Enemy Soldiers." Fatwa Bank. IslamOnline 64.233.187.104/search?q=cache:yL84yM3tRoAJ:www.islamonline.net/fatwa/english/FatwaDisplay.asp%3FhFatwaID%3D103297+%22the+prophet+of+war%22&hl=en&client=googlet.
And see "The Prophet of War" in Osama bin Laden, "Complete Text Of Sheikh Osama Bin Laden's Latest Message To Ummah May 12, 2004"
Retrieved from the World Wide Web May 14, 2004 www.jihadunspun.net/intheatre_internal.php?article=572&list=/home.php&
847. Osama bin Laden, "Complete Text Of Sheikh Osama Bin Laden's Latest Message To Ummah May 12, 2004." Retrieved from the World Wide Web May 14, 2004 www.jihadunspun.net/intheatre_internal.php?article=572&list=/home.php&
For another translation of at Tabarsi's *Beacons of Light*, see Abu Ali al Fadl ibn al Hasan ibn al Fadl at Tabarsi, *Beacons of Light: Muhammad, the Prophet, and Fatimah, the Radiant*. A Partial translation of I'lamu 'l Wara bi Alami 'l-Huda. Originally written 1076 A.D.–1154 A.D. Translated by Dr. Mahmoud Ayoub and Dr. Lynda Clarke. Tehran, Iran: World Organization For Islamic Services, 1986. Reproduced with permission by the Ahlul Bayt Digital Islamic Library Project. al-islam.org/beacons/3.htm

848. Al-Qaida Organization of the Arab Gulf. Transcript: Al-Qaida Statement On The Khobar Operation May 29, 2004. Retrieved June 11, 2004, from the World Wide Web: www.jihadunspun.net/
849. Osama bin Laden, "Complete Text Of Sheikh Osama Bin Laden's Latest Message To Ummah May 12, 2004." Retrieved from the World Wide Web May 14, 2004 www.jihadunspun.net/intheatre_internal.php?article=572&list=/home.php&
850. "After having overcome fascism, Nazism, and Stalinism, the world now faces a new totalitarian global threat: Islamism. We, writers, journalists, intellectuals, call for resistance to religious totalitarianism and for the promotion of freedom, equal opportunity and secular values for all." Ayaan Hirsi Ali, Chahla Chafiq, Caroline Fourest, Bernard-Henri Lévy, Irshad Manji, Mehdi Mozaffari, Maryam Namazie, Taslima Nasreen, Salman Rushdie, Antoine Sfeir, Philippe Val, Ibn Warraq. "MANIFESTO: Together facing the new totalitarianism." 1 March 2006. Judeoscope. www.judeoscope.ca/article.php3?id_article=0297
851. Ruhollah Khomeini, *Islam and Revolution: Writings and Declarations of Imam Khomeini*, trans. Hamid Algar. Berkeley, California: Mizan Press, 1981. p. 35.
852. Sarwat Saulat, *The Life of The Prophet*. Islamic Publications Ltd., Lahore, Pakistan, 1983.
853. Jihad implied global conquest from the very moment it was first revealed by Allah to Muhammad. One verse of Muhammad's revelation about Jihad says, "Fight against them until there be no more temptation...until the religion be Allah's, that is, until Allah alone shall be worshipped and none else besides him." Ibn Ishaq, *The Life of Muhammad: Apostle of Allah*. Michael Edwardes, ed. London: The Folio Society, 1964, p. 66. See also: Rudolph Peters, *Jihad in Mediaeval and Modern Islam*: The Chapter on Jihad from Averroes' Legal Handbook "Bidåayat Al-mudjtahid' and the Treatise 'Koran and Fighting' by the Late Shaykh-al-Azhar, Maòhmåud Shaltåut, Leiden: Brill, 1977, p. 42.

854. Sarwat Saulat, *The Life of The Prophet*. Islamic Publications Ltd., Lahore, Pakistan, 1983. Ibn Ishaq, *The Life of Muhammad: Apostle of Allah*. Michael Edwardes, ed. London: The Folio Society, 1964: p. 65.

855. Quoted in Hafiz Abdul Salam Bin Mohammad, "Jihad In The Present Time." Jamatdawa.org. Retrieved December 29, 2002, from the World Wide Web www.jamatdawa.org/english/faq/index.htm Here's another translation of the quote: "Jihad (holy fighting in Allahs Cause) is ordained for you (Muslims) though you dislike it, and it may be that you dislike a thing which is good for you and that you like a thing which is bad for you. Allah knows but you do not know." (سورة البقرة , Al-Baqara, Chapter #2, Verse #216) Qur'an, Mohsin Khan translation. SearchTruth. com. www.searchtruth.com/search.php?keyword= though+you+dislike+it&chapter=&translator= 5&search=1&start=0&records_display= 10&search_word=exact

856. This blunt quote from Muhammad, "War is deceit," comes to us from Muhammad's first and most important biographer, Ibn Ishaq: A. Guillaume, *The Life of Muhammad: A Translation of Ibn Ishaq's Sirat Rasul Allah*. New York: Oxford University Press, 1955, eighteenth printing, 2004, p. 458.

857. "The first battle of Islam was fought by four Muslims at Nakhla. In the battle of Badr the Muslims were only 313 in number. In the Battle of Uhud the Muslims landed with an army of seven hundred soldiers, but in the Battle of Tabuk, they stepped in the battle field with an army of thirty thousand." Universal Sunnah Foundation. Pakistan. *The Prophet Muhammad: Biography of the Holy Prophet*. In Islamic Paths. www.islamic-paths.org/ Home/English/Muhammad/Book/Biography/ Chapter_40.htm

858. Universal Sunnah Foundation, *The Prophet Muhammad: Biography of the Holy Prophet*. Chapter 40: "Muhammad P.B.U.H. as Religious, Political and Military Leader." www.islamic-paths.org/Home/English/Muhammad/ Book/Biography/Chapter_40.htm

859. Universal Sunnah Foundation. *The Prophet Muhammad: Biography of the Holy Prophet*. Chapter 40: "Muhammad P.B.U.H. as Religious, Political and Military Leader." www.islamic-paths.org/Home/English/Muhammad/ Book/Biography/Chapter_40.htm

860. Universal Sunnah Foundation. *The Prophet Muhammad: Biography of the Holy Prophet*. Chapter 40: "Muhammad P.B.U.H. as Religious, Political and Military Leader." www.islamic-paths.org/Home/English/Muhammad/ Book/Biography/Chapter_40.htm

861. Forward, *Dābiq*, Issue 5, p. 3. "Terror group says it will expand its rule over Islam's holy places in Saudi Arabia, as well as Jerusalem and Rome." *Jerusalem Post*, www.jpost.com/Middle-East/ ISIS-says-its-flag-will-wave-over-Jerusalem-even-if- the-Jews-dont-like-it-382907, downloaded 9-2-2015

862. Forward, *Dābiq*, Issue 5, p. 3.

863. *The Sword of Islam*. David Darlow, producer/ director, Brian Park and Fiona Moffitt, research, Rod Caird, executive producer, Granada TV, Manchester, England, 1987.

864. Glen H. Elder, Elizabeth C. Clipp, "Wartime Losses and Social Bonding: Influences Across 40 Years in Men's Lives," *Psychiatry*, Vol. 51, Issue 2, May 1988, pp. 177–198. Lionel Tiger, *Men in Groups*. Piscataway, NJ: Transaction Publishers, 1971, pp. 131, 172, 177, 210. Anthony Stevens, *Roots of War and Terror*, New York, Bloomsbury Publishing, 2005, p. 46. Helen S. Bateup, Alan Booth, Elizabeth A. Shirtcliff, Douglas A. Granger, "Testosterone, cortisol, and women's competition," *Human Behavior*, May 2002, Volume 23, Issue 3, pp. 181–192. Christian P. Potholm, *War Wisdom: A Cross-Cultural Sampling*. Lanham, MD: UPA, 2015, pp. 47, 50–51. Theodore D. Kemper, *Status, Power and Ritual Interaction: A Relational Reading of Durkheim, Goffman and Collins*. Farnham, UK: Ashgate Publishing, Ltd., Jan. 28, 2013, p. 176.

865. For a summary of social psychological research on the ease with which humans fall into us vs. them patterns, see Bertram H. Raven and Jeffrey Z. Rubin, *Social Psychology*, pp. 639–650.

866. Edward Sagarin, Robert J. Kelly, "Collective and Formal Promotion of Deviance," in M. Michael Rosenberg, Robert A. Stebbins and Allan Turowetz, ed., *The Sociology of Deviance*. New York: St. Martin's Press, 1982, p. 214. Howard Bloom, *The Lucifer Principle: A Scientific Expedition into the Forces of History*. New York: Atlantic Monthly Press, 1995.

867. Christian P. Potholm, *War Wisdom: A Cross-Cultural Sampling*. Lanham, MD: UPA, 2015, pp. 47, 50–51.

868. Reuben Levy, *The Social Structure of Islam: Being the Second Edition of the Sociology of Islam*. Cambridge, UK: Cambridge University Press, 1957, p. 422.

869. "In 600 Iraq was a province of the Persian Sasanian empire, to which it had belonged for three centuries. It was probably the most populous and wealthy area in the Middle East, and the intensive irrigation agriculture of the lower Tigris and Euphrates rivers and of tributary streams such as the Diyala and Karun formed the main resource base of the Sasanian monarchy. ...The first conflict between local Bedouin tribes and Sasanian forces seems to have been in 634, when the Arabs were defeated at the Battle of the Bridge. There a force of some 5,000 Muslims under Abu 'Ubayd al-Thaqafi was routed of the Persians. In 637 a much larger Muslim force under Sa'd ibn Abi Waqqas defeated the main Persian army at the Battle of Al-Qadisiyyah and moved on to sack Ctesiphon. By the end of the following year (638), the Muslims had conquered almost all of Iraq, and the last Sasanian king, Yazdegerd III, had fled to Iran, where he was killed in 651." *Encyclopædia Britannica*, "Iraq," retrieved December 28, 2004, from Encyclopædia Britannica Premium Service. www.britannica.com/eb/article?tocId=22883

870. Reuben Levy, *The Social Structure of Islam: Being the Second Edition of the Sociology of Islam*. Cambridge, UK: Cambridge University Press, 1957, p. 276. Andrew G. Bostom, "The Legacy of Jihad in Palestine," FrontPageMagazine.com, December 7, 2004. www.frontpagemag.com/Articles/ReadArticle. asp?ID=16235 The essential pattern of the jihad is captured in the following quote from the Islamic expert Bat Ye'or: "In the History of al-Tabari (Ta'rikh al-rusul wa'l-muluk), *(The History of al-Tabari (Ta'rikh al rusul wa'l-muluk)*, ed. by Ehsan Yarshater, vol. 12, transl. and ann. by Yohanan Friedmann, State University of New York Press, 1992) in the volume describing the conquest of Iraq by the Arab-Muslim armies, we read the recommendation given by Umar b. al-Khattab to the commander of the troops he sent to al-Basrah (636 c.e.). Umar said: "Summon the people to God; those who respond to your call, accept it from them, (This is to say, accept their conversion as genuine and refrain from fighting them) but those who refuse must pay the poll tax out of humiliation and lowliness. (Qur'an 9:29) If they refuse this, it is the sword without leniency." Bat Ye'or, "The Ideology of Jihad, Dhimmitude and Human Rights." Lecture given November 12, 2002 at Georgetown University. In *The Hoya*: Georgetown University's Newspaper of Record. Retrieved March 16, 2006, from the World Wide Web www.thehoya.com/viewpoint/111202/view_bat.cfm

871. Yusuf Abdul Rahman, "Islam and Muslims In China." 1997. Retrieved from the World Wide Web March 03, 2004, www.islamawareness.net/Asia/China/

872. Mario Apostolov, *The Christian-Muslim Frontier: A Zone of Contact, Conflict, or Cooperation*. New York: Routledge, 2004, p. 27; Reuben Lev, *The Social Structure of Islam: Being the Second Edition of the Sociology of Islam*. Cambridge, UK: Cambridge University Press, p. 452.

873. n.a. "Islam In Our Near North." Learning Islam. Islam Australia Network. October 13, 2007. islam.ii.net/channel/near_north.html

874. Patricia Ann Lynch, Jeremy Roberts, *African Mythology, A to Z*. New York: Infobase Publishing, 2010. Renée Levine Melammed, "His/Her Story: A Jewish warrior queen," *Jerusalem Post*, 08/05/2011, www.jpost.com/Magazine/Judaism/HisHer-Story-A-Jewish-warrior-queen 1-31-2016

875. www.swagga.com/queen.htm
Dahia-Al Kahina, Queen Kahina. She fought against the Arab incursion in North Africa where under her leadership Africans fought back fiercely and drove the Arab army northward into Tripolitania. Queen Kahina was of the Hebrew faith and she never abandoned her religion. Her opposition to the Arab incursion was purely nationalistic, since she favored neither Christians nor Muslims. Her death in 705 A.D. by Hassen-ben-Numam ended one of the most violent attempts to save Africa for the Africans. She prevented Islam's southward spread into the Western Sudan. After her death the Arabs began to change their strategy in advancing their faith and their power in Africa. The resistance to the southward spread of Islam was so great in some areas that some of the wives of African kings committed suicide to avoid falling into the hands of the Berbers and Arabs who showed no mercy to the people who would not be converted to Islam.

876. John S. Bowman, editor, *Columbia Chronologies of Asian History and Culture.* New York: Columbia University Press, 2000, p. 569. "Al-Walid." en.wikipedia.org/wiki/Al-Walid

877. en.wikipedia.org/wiki/Qutaibah_bin_Muslim

878. Said Hajjaj in a letter sent to Muhammad bin Qasim, one of his generals: "My ruling is given: Kill anyone belonging to the ahl-i-harb [combatants]; arrest their sons and daughters for hostages and imprison them. Whoever does not fight against us... grant them aman [safety] and settle their tribute [amwal] as dhimmah [protected person]." Derryl N. Maclean, *Religion and Society in Arab Sind*, Brill Academic Publishers, 1989 p. 37.

879. Al-Hajjaj Bin Yousef
Sourced from World Heritage Encyclopedia self. gutenberg.org/articles/al-hajjaj_bin_yousef

880. Jamil Ahmad, "Tariq Bin Ziyad." *Renaissance: A Monthly Islamic Journal*. An Affiliate of Al-Mawrid Institute of Islamic Studies. Lahore, Pakistan. www.renaissance.com.pk/marletf95.html. Ivan Van Sertima, editor, "The Golden Age of the Moor" (*Journal of African Civilizations*, Vol. 11, Fall 1991). New Brunswick, NJ: Transaction Press, 1991, p. 54.

881. David Nicolle, illustrated by Angus McBride, *Armies of the Muslim Conquest*. London: Osprey Publishing, 1993. p. 4.

882. John S. Bowman, *Columbia Chronologies of Asian History and Culture*. New York: Columbia University Press, 2000, p. 334.

883. Professor K.S. Lal, Voice of Dharma, New Delhi. voi.org/books/tfst/chii23.htm. See also K.S. Lal, *Muslim Slave System in Medieval India*. Voice of Dharma. Aditya Prakashan, New Delhi. www.voi.org/books/mssmi/, www.voi.org/books/mssmi/ch3.htm. In reading Indian sources on Islam, keep in mind that many Hindu Indians hate Muslims for the 1,300-year-long Islamic history of military assault, rape, pillage, conquest in their country, and ongoing war in their country. So Indian scholars tend to emphasize the darkest side of Islam. But the bias goes two ways. Many Muslims consider Hindu India one of the Great Satans. So statements from Indians tend to be radically anti-Islamic. And statements from Muslims about Indian Hindus and Buddhists are often vitriolic, militant, and wrathful.

884. John S. Bowman, *Columbia Chronologies of Asian History and Culture*. New York: Columbia University Press, 2000, p. 263.

885. "The historian Will Durant wrote in *The Story of Civilization* (1972) that the Muslim conquest of India was 'probably the bloodiest story in history.' The exact number of people killed during the invasions will never be known. Estimates are based upon the Muslim chronicles and demographic calculations. Prof. K.S. Lal estimated in his book *The Growth of Muslim Population in India* that between the years 1000 C.E. and 1500 C.E. the population of Hindus decreased by eighty million." en.wikipedia.org/wiki/Islamic_invasion_of_India

886. Prof. Yusuf Al-Qaradawi claims that the Islamic meme motivated its Arab followers to leave the desert for the cities...the cities others had established...and to stay there. According to Al-Qaradawi, Muhammad himself—in the Hadith—cursed Bedouins who grew homesick in the cities they'd conquered and wanted to return to their desert homes. Colonialism was a holy obligation. Prof. Yusuf Al-Qaradawi, *The Sunnah: A Source of Civilization*. Translated by El-Falah. Prophetmuhammadforall.org. www.prophetmuhammadforall.org/webfiles/downloads/english/sunnah.pdf

887. I.M. Lewis, *A Modern History of Somalia: Nation and State in the Horn of Africa*. Boulder, CO: Westview Press, 1988, p. 25.

888. Wikipedia, "Battle of Talas."
en.wikipedia.org/wiki/Battle_of_Talas
www.thenagain.info/WebChron/China/Talas.html
Battle of Talas River 751. For much of the early 700s,
the Chinese Empire, under the T'ang dynasty, was
successful in its foreign affairs. They recovered
crucial lands they had previously lost and stabilized
the Tibetan frontier. They secured trade routes
through central Asia and contained threats from the
Khitan and Hsi peoples. In the late 740s, Chinese
troops claimed lordship over Kabul and Kashmir of
India. But their string of victorious campaigns could
not last forever, as China discovered at Talas River
in 751. Islam's widespread emergence coupled with
China's over-expansion, led to the Battle at Talas
River, the only battle between Arab Muslim forces
and the army of the Chinese Empire. The Chinese
troops were led by Kao Hsien-chih, who had been
successful in battles in Gilgit and in the Farghana
region. But his success did not carry over, as the
Muslim armies were victorious. The Muslims chose
not to pursue the Chinese into central Asia. While
the battle in itself was of minor importance, its
ramifications on the future were very significant.
The Arabs were put in a position to extend their
Islamic influence throughout central Asia and its
silk routes. The T'ang (in China) lost a good amount
of power and their westward advance was halted.
Muslim shipping in the Indian Ocean improved,
which restricted the ocean's contacts with Hindu
and Buddhist areas. The Muslims were never able to
take control of the Himalayan northern borderlands.
Paper manufacturing, an unexpected byproduct
from the Battle of Talas, was first spread to
Samarkand and Baghdad, then from there carried
to Damascus, Cairo, and Morocco, and finally
entered Europe through Italy and Spain. This
diffusion originated when Chinese prisoners who
knew how to make paper, an art discovered in
China at least 650 years earlier, were taken by the
Arabs at the Talas River. But most importantly, the
Battle of Talas led to the An Lushan revolt, which
broke out in 755. This rebellion paralyzed China
for years and weakened the Tang dynasty until it
collapsed a century and a half later. Sources:
Twitchett, Denis, *The Cambridge History of China*
(Cambridge University, Cambridge, 1979). McNeil,
William, *The Rise of the West* (University of Chicago,
Chicago, 1963). Kennedy, Hugh, *The Prophet and the
Age of the Caliphates* (Longman, London, 1986).
Garraty, John A. and Peter Gay, *The Columbia History
of the World* (Harper and Row; New York, 1972).
Edited by: Frederick Skoglund Researched by: Joel
Card Written by: Kim Wentzler December 15, 1998
Text copyright 1996–9 by David W. Koeller.
dkoeller@northpark.edu. All rights reserved.

889. Just one Islamic-ruled slave-trading territory in
Africa, the Empire of Zanzibar, covered two million
square kilometers. It was said that "when the
flute plays in Zanzibar, all Africa dances."
All About Zanzibar. "Slaves & Ivory."
www.allaboutzanzibar.com/indepth/history/
id-01-01-34-slaves.htm

890. "The Scourge of Slavery," *Christian Action
Magazine*. Christian Action for Reformation and
Revival. South Africa.
www.christianaction.org.za/articles_ca/
2004-4-TheScourgeofSlavery.htm.
Remember this as you read these figures. "Some
historians argue that abolitionists inflated the
numbers of slaves in their reports in order to
heighten indignation and gain support for their
cause. Numbers are also a problem because of
high mortality rates, especially in transport."
(Patricia Risso, *Merchants and Faith: Muslim
Commerce and Culture in the Indian Ocean*. Boulder,
CO: Westview Press, 1995, p. 92.) But also keep in
mind that if the statistics are even twice as large as
the reality, the number of African lives affected by
the Islamic slave trade still boggles the imagination.

891. www.witness-pioneer.org/vil/Books/SH_CA/
chapter_1.htm
(The Witness Pioneer (WP) is spreading and
establishing the message of Islam...) "Early History
of Spread of Islam in (former) Soviet Union"
[Bennigsen. A. Islam in *The Soviet Union*, Pall Mall
Press, London]. Last modified: September 16, 2002
"Golden Horde." *Encyclopædia Britannica*. 2005.
Encyclopædia Britannica Premium Service.
2 Jan. 2005
www.britannica.com/eb/article?tocId=9037242
www.britannica.com/eb/article?tocId=9057862&
query=%22%C3%96z%20Beg%20%22&ct=eb
"Öz Beg." *Encyclopædia Britannica*. 2005.
Encyclopædia Britannica Premium Service.
4 Jan. 2005
www.britannica.com/eb/article?tocId=9057862.

892. Wikipedia, "Circassian beauties." Retrieved
1/4/2005, from the World Wide Web
en.wikipedia.org/wiki/Circassian_beauties

893. Wikipedia. "Paul the First Hermit,"
en.wikipedia.org/wiki/Paul_the_First_Hermit
Retrieved January 4, 2005, from the World Wide Web

894. *Chronique de Jean, évêque de Nikiou*, translated
from the Ethiopian with notes by Hermann
Zotenberg, Paris: Impr. Nationale, 1879, pp.
243–244. Translated in Philip K. Hitti (1996),
The Arabs: A Short History. Washington, DC:
Regnery Publishing: 93.

895. Section 59, Verses 1–6. The Holy Qur'an.
Translation by Abdullah Yusufali. Complete online
text. www.wam.umd.edu/~stwright/rel/islam/.

896. "Sepeos," excerpted in Bat Ye'or, *The Decline
of Eastern Christianity under Islam: From Jihad to
Dhimmitude: 7th — 20th Century*. Madison, NJ:
Fairleigh Dickinson University Press/Associated
University Presses (1996): 228.

897. Dr. A. Zahoor, "Islamic Civilization: Morality
in War" www.cyberistan.org/islamic/sibai6.html

898. Abu Al-Abbas Ahmad Bin Jab Al-Baladhuri,
*The Origins of the Islamic State (Kitab Futuh
al-Buldan)* by Abu Al-Abbas Ahmad Bin Jab
Al-Baladhuri, Philip K. Hitti, trans., Piscataway, NJ:
Gorgias Press LLC, 2002.

899. Andrew G. Bostom, "The Legacy of Jihad in Palestine." FrontPageMagazine.com, December 7, 2004. www.frontpagemag.com/Articles/ReadArticle.asp?ID=16235

900. "Michael the Syrian." Excerpted in Bat Ye'or, *The Decline of Eastern Christianity under Islam*, Madison, NJ: Fairleigh Dickinson University Press, 1996, pp. 442, 431.

901. *Chronique de Jean, évêque de Nikiou*, translated from the Ethiopian with notes by Hermann Zotenberg, Paris: Impr. Nationale, 1879, p. 261. Translated in Philip K. Hitti (1996) *The Arabs: A Short History*. Washington, DC: Regnery Publishing, p. 93.

902. en.wikipedia.org/wiki/Umar_ibn_al-Khattab Retrieved January 3, 2005, from the World Wide Web

903. "The native infidel population had to recognize Islamic ownership of their land, submit to Islamic law, and accept payment of the poll tax (jizya)." Andrew G. Bostom, "The Legacy of Jihad in Palestine." FrontPageMagazine.com, December 7, 2004. www.frontpagemag.com/Articles/ReadArticle.asp?ID=16235

904. "Umar b. al-Khattab (634–644) replies to the Muslims who demand the sharing-out of the lands of Iraq and Syria(-Palestine) among the conquerors. Quoted in Ye'or, Bat, *The Dhimmi: Jews and Christians under Islam* (Rutherford, NJ: Fairleigh Dickenson University Press, London and Toronto: Associated University Presses, 1985), p. 165.

905. "Umar b. al-Khattab (634–644) replies to the Muslims who demand the sharing-out of the lands of Iraq and Syria(-Palestine) among the conquerors. Quoted in Ye'or, Bat, *The Dhimmi: Jews and Christians under Islam* (Rutherford, NJ: Fairleigh Dickenson University Press, London and Toronto. Associated University Presses, 1985), p. 165.

906. "The Moral System of Islam," III&E Brochure Series; No. 6 (published by The Institute of Islamic Information and Education (III&E)). USC-MSA Compendium of Muslim Texts. Retrieved January 4, 2005, from the World Wide Web www.usc.edu/dept/MSA/humanrelations/moralsystem.html Reprinted with the permission of World Assembly of Muslim Youth (WAMY), P.O. Box 10845, Riyadh 11443, Saudi Arabia.

907. Wikipedia, "Colossus of Rhodes," en.wikipedia.org/wiki/Colossus_of_rhodes#Construction_and_fate

908. Noam Chomsky, *Hegemony or Survival: America's Quest for Global Dominance (The American Empire Project)*. New York: Owl Books, 2004.

909. Howard Zinn, *People's History of the United States: 1492 to Present (P.S.)*. New York: Harper Perennial Modern Classics, 2005.

910. Sarwat Saulat, *The Life of The Prophet*. Islamic Publications Ltd., Lahore, Pakistan, 1983.

911. John L. Esposito, *The Islamic Threat: myth or reality*, New York: Oxford University Press, 1992: p. 171.

912. Peter Brown, *The Body and Society: Men, Women, and Sexual Renunciation in Early Christianity*. Columbia University Press, New York, 1988. Rev. Robert F. McNamara. St. Simeon Stylite. "Saints Alive." St. Thomas the Apostle Roman Catholic Church, Rochester, NY, March 11, 2005. Retrieved January 5, 2006, from the World Wide Web www.stthomasirondequoit.com/SaintsAlive/id747.htm

913. Wikipedia, "Simeon Stylites," en.wikipedia.org/wiki/Simeon_Stylites

914. Jean Richard, *The Crusades, c. 1071–c. 1291*, translated by Jean Birrell. Cambridge, UK: Cambridge University Press, 1999, pp. 146–148.

915. "Al-Makrisi: Account of the Crusade of St. Louis." Medieval Sourcebook. Fordham University. www.fordham.edu/halsall/source/makrisi.html Marshall W. Baldwin, ed., *A History of the Crusades: The First Hundred Years*. University of Pennsylvania Press, Philadelphia, Pennsylvania, 1955. Ernle Bradford, *The Sword and the Scimitar: The Saga of the Crusades*. New York: G.P. Putnam's Sons, New York, 1974. Amin Maalouf, *The Crusades Through Arab Eyes*. New York: Schocken, 1989.

916. Rosalind Hill, ed., *Gesta Francorum et Aliorum Hierosolimitanoru: The Deeds of the Franks and other Pilgrims to Jerusalem*. London: Thomas Nelson and Sons, Ltd., 1962.

917. Aziz Atiya, *Crusade, Commerce and Culture*. Indiana University Press, Bloomington, Indiana, 1962. Marshall W. Baldwin, ed., *A History of the Crusades: The First Hundred Years*. Philadelphia: University of Pennsylvania Press, 1955. Ernle Bradford, *The Sword and the Scimitar: The Saga of the Crusades*. New York: G.P. Putnam's Sons, 1974. Frederic Duncalf, "The First Crusade: Clermont to Constantinople," in *A History of the Crusades: The First Hundred Years*, Marshall W. Baldwin, ed. Philadelphia: University of Pennsylvania Press, 1955.

918. Amin Maalouf, *The Crusades Through Arab Eyes*. New York: Schocken, 1989.

919. N.I. Matar, "The Renegade In English Seventeenth-Century Imagination," *Studies in English Literature, 1500–1900*. Vol. 33, issue 3, Restoration and Eighteenth Century (Summer, 1993), p. 489. Alan Trevarthan, "Spanish Raid 4 & Barbary pirates," *Cornish-L Archives*, May 1, 2001, archiver.rootsweb.ancestry.com/th/read/CORNISH/2001-05/0988752812

920. Giles Milton, *White Gold: The Extraordinary Story of Thomas Pellow and North Africa's One Million European Slaves*. Hodder & Stoughton Ltd. 2004, p. 13.

921. "The earliest geographic treatise composed in Arabic was that of Ibn Khurdadhbih, chief intelligence officer for the Caliphate in Media [in Northwestern Iran]. Writing around the middle of the ninth century, Ibn Khurdadhbih describes the commodities imported into Islam from the Mediterranean region. They include Slavic, Romi, Frankish, and Lombard slaves; Spanish and Romi maidens, beaver pelts, furs, storax, mastic and coral." A footnote reads: "by 'Frankish' the Arabic authors meant West European, and by 'Roman' they meant Greek, Roman, or simply Christian." Alauddin Samarrai, *Medieval Commerce and Diplomacy: Islam and Europe, A.D. 850–1300*, Saint Cloud, MN: St. Cloud State University, p. 3. Giles Milton, *White Gold: The Extraordinary Story of Thomas Pellow and North Africa's One Million European Slaves*. London: Hodder & Stoughton Ltd. 2004, p. 271. Robert C. Davis, *Christian Slaves, Muslim Masters: White Slavery in the Mediterranean, the Barbary Coast and Italy, 1500–1800 (Early Modern History)*. Houndmills, Basingstoke, Hampshire, UK: Palgrave MacMillan, 2004. "When Europeans Were Slaves: Research Suggests White Slavery Was Much More Common Than Previously Believed," Ohio State University News. March 8, 2004, researchnews.osu.edu/archive/whtslav.htm
Rory Carroll, "New book reopens old arguments about slave raids on Europe," *The Guardian*. March 11, 2004, www.guardian.co.uk/uk_news/story/0,3604,1166720,00.html

922. "When the events of Badr were over, God revealed al-Anfal (Surah 8) [Chapter 8 of the Qur'an, whose title means 'Spoils Of War, Booty'] in its entirety." al-Tabari, *The History of al-Tabari*: English translation of "at Tareekh al-Tabari." Albany: State University of New York Press, Volume VII, p. 80. For the translation of the chapter title "al-Anfal" as "Spoils of War," see University of Southern California. USC-MSA Compendium of Muslim Texts. Translations of the Qur'an, Chapter 8. www.usc.edu/dept/MSA/quran/008.qmt.html.

923. Rory Carroll, "New book reopens old arguments about slave raids on Europe," *The Guardian*. March 11, 2004. www.guardian.co.uk/uk_news/story/0,3604,1166720,00.html. Peter Hammond. "The Scourge of Slavery," *Christian Action Magazine*, vol. 4, 2004, www.christianaction.org.za/articles_ca/2004-4-TheScourgeofSlavery.htm.
Cindy Vallar, "Captives of the Barbary States." www.cindyvallar.com/BCcaptives.html

924. According to Barbary Pirate buff Cindy Vallar, 83 of the captives were taken to the port of Algiers. Cindy Vallar, "Captives of the Barbary States." www.cindyvallar.com/BCcaptives.html

925. A. Guillaume, *The Life of Muhammad: A Translation of Ibn Ishaq's Sirat Rasul Allah*. New York: Oxford University Press, 1955, eighteenth printing, 2004, p. 465.

926. Yassine Essid, *A Critique of the Origins of Islamic Economic Thought*. Leiden: Brill Academic Publishers, 1995, pp. 32–33.

927. Khalid M. Baheyeldin, "Abu Bakr Muhammad ibn al-Walid al-Tartushi." In "The Baheyeldin Dynasty." 2002. baheyeldin.com/history/abu-bakr-muhammad-ibn-al-walid-al-tartushi.html
Reuben Levy, *The Social Structure of Islam: Being the Second Edition of the Sociology of Islam* (Cambridge, England: Cambridge University Press, 1957), pp. 434, 456, *Questia*, 25 Nov. 2005, www.questia.com/PM.qst?a=o&d=10599969

928. Jonathan Bate: "Othello and the Other: Turning Turk: The subtleties of Shakespeare's treatment of Islam," in Renässansen Mellan Medeltid Och Modernitet, 2001, www2.idehist.uu.se/distans/ilmh/Ren/ 2-1-2016

929. Shakespeare identified Othello in the title of his play as *Othello, The Moor of Venice*. "Moor" is a term that means a Muslim from North Africa. ("Moor," *Oxford English Dictionary* (unabridged). Oxford: Oxford University Press, 2002. "Moor," Random House *Webster's Unabridged Dictionary*. V3.0. New York: Random House, 1998. Wikipedia, "Moors," en.wikipedia.org/wiki/Moors. However Thomas R. Arp and Greg Johnson point out that Iago refers to Othello's baptism and to a discussion with Desdemona, the heroine, in which "he clearly alludes to their shared belief in Christian salvation." See Thomas R. Arp, Greg Johnson, *Perrine's Literature: Structure, Sound, and Sense*. Boston: Thomson Higher Education, 2006, p. 56.

930. Peter O'Brien, *European Perceptions of Islam and America from Saladin to George W. Bush*. New York: Palgrave Macmillan, Dec. 23, 2008, pp. 75–76.

931. Peter O'Brien, *European Perceptions of Islam and America from Saladin to George W. Bush*. London: Palgrave Macmillan, Dec. 23, 2008, pp. 75–76.

932. Richard Knolles, *The general historie of the Turkes*. London: Adam Islip, 1603.

933. Felix Konrad, "From the 'Turkish Menace' to Exoticism and Orientalism: Islam as Antithesis of Europe (1453–1914)," EGO, European History Online, 2011-03-14, ieg-ego.eu/en/threads/models-and-stereotypes/from-the-turkish-menace-to-orientalism/felix-konrad-from-the-turkish-menace-to-exoticism-and-orientalism-1453-1914#TheImageof IslamintheEraoftheTurkishMenace 2-1-2016.
Nina Berman, *German Literature on the Middle East: Discourses and Practices, 1000–1989*, University of Michigan Press, 2011, p. 71.

934. William Roscoe, *The Life of Lorenzo de Medici*, Volume I, Basil: J.J. Tourneisen, 1799, p. 23. Captain James Edward Alexander, Travels to the seat of war in the East, through Russia and the Crimea, in 1829: with sketches of the imperial fleet and army, personal adventures, and characteristic anecdotes, Volume 2, London: Henry Colburn and Richard Bentley, 1830, p. 46.

935. Nicholas D. Proksch, "Luther's Eschatology And The Turks, Bethany Lutheran Theological Seminary, 2010 International Congress On Medieval Studies," Kalamazoo, MI, web.augsburg.edu/~mcguire/ Proksch_Luther_Turks.pdf, 2-1-2016

936. Sarah Henrich and James L. Boyce, "Martin Luther—Translations of Two Prefaces on Islam: Preface to the Libellus de ritu et moribus Turcorum (1530), and Preface to Bibliander Edition of the Qur'an (1543)", *Word & World* Volume XVI, Number 2, Spring 1996, pp. 250–251.

937. Peter O'Brien, *European Perceptions of Islam and America from Saladin to George W. Bush*. New York: Palgrave Macmillan, Dec. 23, 2008, pp. 75–76. Also quoted in M.S. Anderson, *The Origins of the Modern European State System, 1494–1618*. London: Routledge, 2014, p. 221.

938. M.S. Anderson, *The Origins of the Modern European State System, 1494–1618*. London: Routledge, 2014, p. 221.

939. Ogier Ghiselin de Busbecq, *The Turkish Letters of Ogier Ghiselin de Busbecq*, trans. Edward Seymour Forster. Baton Rouge, LA: LSU Press, 2005, p. 15.

940. Ogier Ghiselin de Busbecq, *The Turkish Letters of Ogier Ghiselin de Busbecq*, trans. Edward Seymour Forster. Baton Rouge, LA: LSU Press, 2005, p. 15.

941. Peter O'Brien, *European Perceptions of Islam and America from Saladin to George W. Bush*. New York: Palgrave Macmillan, Dec. 23, 2008, pp. 75–76.

942. Peter O'Brien, *European Perceptions of Islam and America from Saladin to George W. Bush*. New York: Palgrave Macmillan, Dec. 23, 2008, pp. 75–76.

943. Tom Scott, *Regional Identity and Economic Change: The Upper Rhine, 1450–1600* (Oxford: Oxford University, 1997) p. 5, Questia, 25 Nov. 2005, www.questia.com/PM.qst?a=o&d=49490796 Jason Goodwin, *Lords of the Horizons: A History of the Ottoman Empire*. New York: Picador, 2003. "the Moorish invasion of Spain in A.D. 711, which destroyed the Visigothic Empire, and this reshuffled the power alignments of all of western Europe. It also made the Mediterranean for a time an Islamic lake" www.biblebelievers.org.au/sephard.htm Quoted from Cushman Cunningham, *The Secret Empire*. Delhi: Leela Publishing, 2001, pp. 447–465.

944. "5/9/1795. Repeat this date after me. ...the Mediterranean Sea was an Islamic lake." Sheikh Hilaly Sermon at Sidon Mosque 13.02.04. This translation comes from the Australian Embassy in Beirut and was obtained by the ABC (Australian Broadcasting Company). www.abc.net.au/religion/ stories/s1058934.htm The Mediterranean ceased to be an Islamic Lake in June of 1805, when the American marines stormed "the shores of Tripoli" and forced the basha who harbored the Islamic navy, the "Barbary Corsairs," into signing a peace treaty—The Treaty of Tripoli, June 3, 1805. en.wikipedia.org/wiki/Tripoli#Tripolitan_War "Treaty of Peace, Amity, and Commerce Between the President and Citizens of the United States of America, and the Basha, Bey, and Subjects of Tripoli, in Bombay, Concluded June 4, 1805; Ratified by the Senate April 12, 1806," Treaties and Conventions Concluded between the United States of America and Other Powers, Since July 4, 1776, published by the Department of State, 1889, page 1084. In Jim Allison, ed. *The Constitutional Principle*, "Treaty of Tripoli, 1796, 1806." July 15, 1998. members.tripod.com/~candst/tripoli1.htm

945. The term "Islamic Lake" is used in book after book after book. For an example, see Carlos Fuentes, *The Buried Mirror: Reflections on Spain and the New World*, New York: Mariner Books, 1999, p. 85: "Mare Nostrum, the Mediterranean, had been [by 1492] to all effects and purposes an Islamic Lake for nearly eight hundred years...But soon the rise of a new Muslim power, the Ottoman Empire, once more threatened the Mediterranean." Dr. Mohsin Farooqui, an Islamic writer, puts it differently. In his view, the Muslim Turks "were masters of Mediterranean Sea." Dr. Mohsin Farooqi, "Europe Under Muslim Rule." Retrieved From the Worldwide Web November 07, 2002. www.jamatdawa.org/english/articles/history/ europe_under_islam_iv.htm See also: Jul 30, 2004 at 1:10am From: "Europe under Muslim rule Part I," Islamic Discussion Board, islamicrevival.proboards.com/ thread/453/europe-muslim-rule

946. Wikipedia, "Battle of Lepanto 1571." en.wikipedia.org/wiki/Battle_of_Lepanto_ %281571%29

947. Rudolph Schevill, *Cervantes*. New York: F. Ungar Publishing Company, 1966.

948. Wikipedia, "Battle of Lepanto 1571." en.wikipedia.org/wiki/ Battle_of_Lepanto_%281571%29

949. David Rollason, *Early Medieval Europe 300–1050: The Birth of Western Society*. Abingdon, Oxon, UK: Routledge, 2014, pp. 147, 173. Gene William Heck, *Charlemagne, Muhammad, and the Arab Roots of Capitalism*, Berlin: Walter de Gruyter, 2006.

950. Wikipedia, "Janissary," en.wikipedia.org/wiki/Janissary. Wikipedia, "Devşirme," en.wikipedia.org/wiki/Devshirmeh

951. Dr. Mohsin Farooqi, "Europe Under Muslim Rule." Retrieved from the World Wide Web November 07, 2002. www.jamatdawa.org/english/articles/history/europe_under_islam_iv.htm

952. I.M. Lewis, *A Modern History of Somalia: Nation and State in the Horn of Africa*. London: Longman Group, 1980.

953. Wikipedia, "Bulgaria," en.wikipedia.org/wiki/Bulgaria

954. Wikipedia, "Serbian Empire," en.wikipedia.org/wiki/Serbian_Empire. See also TheOttomans.org, "History, 1800–1900," www.theottomans.org/english/history/history1800_3.as Wikipedia, "Serbia—Turkish Conquest," en.wikipedia.org/wiki/Serbia#Turkish_conquest

955. Wikipedia, "Republic of Macedonia," en.wikipedia.org/wiki/Republic_of_Macedonia

956. The Balkan states formerly known as Yugoslavia were a battleground for Christianity and Islam for centuries. Serbia, Macedonia and Bosnia and Herzegovina fell to the Muslim Ottomans in the 14th and 15th centuries. Montenegro never succumbed to the Ottomans. Slovenia sought protection from the Muslim Ottomans by tucking itself into the Habsburg Empire, and Croatia was the scene of struggle between the Ottomans and the Christian Habsburgs. The Habsburgs finally prevailed.

957. John S. Bowman, editor, *Columbia Chronologies of Asian History and Culture*. New York: Columbia University Press, 2000, pp. 569–571.

958. John L. Esposito, *The Islamic Threat: Myth or Reality*. New York: Oxford University Press, 1992: p. 171.

959. British control over Egypt lasted 74 years, from 1882 to 1956. French control—under Napoleon—only lasted three years, from 1798 to 1801. "The French Invasion and Occupation, 1798-1801," Country Studies, countrystudies.us/egypt/20.htm 2-1-2016.

960. 1,377 years is the length of time Islam has held Egypt, which was taken by Muslim forces in 640 A.D.

961. Chapter 8. verse 12. The Holy Qur'an. Translation by Abdullah Yusufali.

962. Ali A. Mazrui held the following titles: Director, Institute of Global Cultural Studies, and Albert Schweitzer Professor in the Humanities, State University of New York at Binghamton, New York, USA; Albert Luthuli, Professor-at-Large, University of Jos, Jos, Nigeria; Andrew D. White, Professor-at-Large Emeritus and Senior Scholar in Africana Studies, Cornell University; and Chancellor, Jomo Kenyatta University of Agriculture and Technology, Juju, Kenya. See Ali A. Mazrui, "Pax Islamica: Muslim Values Between War And Peace." Lecture given at the American University School of Public Service, Washington, DC, November 12, 2003. www.swahilionline.com/features/articles/mazrui/mazrui10.htm

963. Basil Davidson, *Africa In History*. London: Weidenfeld and Nicolson, 1968, p. 219.

964. Wikipedia, "Dar al-Harb." en.wikipedia.org/wiki/Dar_al-Harb

965. See the interpretation of the Qur'an called Quran Tafsir Ibn Kathir: "(So do not lose heart) meaning, do not be weak concerning the enemies. (وَتَدْعُواْ إِلَى السَّلْمِ) (and beg for peace) meaning, compromise, peace, and ending the fighting between you and the disbelievers while you are in a position of power, both in great numbers and preparations. Thus, Allah says, (فَلاَ تَهِنُواْ وَتَدْعُواْ إِلَى السَّلْمِ وَأَنتُمُ الأَعْلَوْنَ) (So do not lose heart and beg for peace while you are superior) meaning, in the condition of your superiority over your enemy. If, on the other hand, the disbelievers are considered more powerful and numerous than the Muslims, then the Imam (general commander) may decide to hold a treaty if he judges that it entails a benefit for the Muslims. This is like what Allah's Messenger did when the disbelievers obstructed him from entering Makkah and offered him treaty in which all fighting would stop between them for ten years. Consequently, he agreed to that. Nullifying the Disbelievers' Deeds and the Command to chase Them," Quran Tafsir Ibn Kathir, www.qtafsir.com/index.php?option=com_content&task=view&id=2024&Itemid=103 2-1-2016. See also: David Robinson, *Muslim Societies in African History*. Cambridge, England: Cambridge University Press, 2004, p. 18. D.S. Roberts, *Islam: A Concise Introduction*. New York: Harper & Row, 1982, pp. 42–43. The interpretation cited as nearly universal by Roberts is probably derived from verses 191–193 of the Qur'anic chapter Al-Baqara, whose passages say, "slay them wherever ye catch them and turn them out from where they have turned you out; for tumult and oppression are worse than slaughter; ... Such is the reward of those who suppress faith. ...And fight them on until there is no more tumult or oppression and there prevail justice and faith in Allah." "Justice," in the eyes of many ancient and modern Muslims, means the imposition of Qur'anic law. "Faith" is understood to be faith in Islam. Hence the passage, in the eyes of many, instructs the pious to use slaughter to impose Qur'anic law and Islam, since slaughter is preferable to the continuance of non-Islamic codes and beliefs ("tumult and oppression").

966. Wikipedia, "Abdul Hai Arifi," en.wikipedia.org/wiki/Abdul_Hai_Arifi 2-1-2016

967. Maulana A.S. Muhammad Abdul Hai (Rah.), *Holy Life of Hazrat Muhammad (Hayyat-E-Tayyaba)*. Delhi, India: Islami Academy, 1984. www.al-islamforall.org/litre/Englitre/Hmohd.htm

968. 1602 is the date of establishment of the Dutch East India Company. See Wikipedia, "Dutch East Indian Company." en.wikipedia.org/wiki/Dutch_East_India_Company

969. Stephen L. Macknik, neuroscientist, SUNY Downstate, Professor and Empire Innovation Scholar, columnist for *Scientific American*, personal communication. The usual figure for the number of neurons in the brain is 100 billion, but that only counts the neurons of the cortex. See also: Maksim Stamenov, Vittorio Gallese, *Mirror Neurons and the Evolution of Brain and Language*. Amsterdam: John Benjamins Publishing, p. 70.

970. Jeremy Taylor, "Not a Chimp: The hunt to find the genes that make us human," OUP Oxford, UK: Oxford University Press, 2010.

971. David R. Begun, *The Real Planet of the Apes: A New Story of Human Origins*. Princeton, NJ: Princeton University Press, 2015, p. 170.

972. K.R.L. Hall, "Experiment and Quantification in the Study of Baboon Behavior in its Natural Habitat." In *Primates: Studies in Adaptation and Variability*, edited by Phyllis C. Jay. New York: Holt, Rinehart and Winston, 1968, pp. 120–130.

973. Gerardo Beni and Susan Hackwood, "The Maximum Entropy Principle and Sensing in Swarm Intelligence," in *Toward a Practice of Autonomous Systems: Proceedings of the First European Conference on Artificial Life*, Francisco J. Francesco Varela, Paul Bourgine, eds., Cambridge, MA: MIT Press, 1992, p. 153.

974. Pierre Lévy, *Collective Intelligence: Mankind's Emerging World in Cyberspace*. New York: Plenum Trade, 1997

975. Howard Bloom, *Global Brain: The Evolution of Mass Mind From the Big Bang to the 21st Century*. New York: John Wiley, 2000.

976. Jeanette Winter, *The Watcher: Jane Goodall's Life with the Chimps*. New York: Random House, 2011

977. "If you want to visit Lake Nakuru, you'd better get going," posted by egcolli, blog, "What Happens in Africa," whathappensinafrica.wordpress.com/2012/03/

978. Richard D. Estes, Daniel Otte (Illustrator), Kathryn Fuller, *The Safari Companion: A Guide to Watching African Mammals*. Post Mills, VT: Chelsea Green, 1993; Spook Skelton, *Spook's Photography Page*. "Savanna Baboon—Papio cynocephalus." sailfish.exis.net/~spook/babtxt.html February 1999.

979. Shirley C. Strum, *Almost Human: A Journey Into the World of Baboons*. New York: Random House, 1987: pp. 203–285.

980. University of Chicago, promotional text, *Almost Human: A Journey Into the World of Baboons*, Shirley C. Strum, press.uchicago.edu/ucp/books/book/chicago/A/bo3636173.html

981. Shirley C. Strum, *Almost Human: A Journey into the World of Baboons*: p. 177.

982. Shirley C. Strum, *Almost Human: A Journey into the World of Baboons*, p. 183.

983. Shirley C. Strum, *Almost Human: A Journey into the World of Baboons*, p. 183.

984. Hans Kummer, *In Quest of the Sacred Baboon: a Scientist's Journey*. Princeton: Princeton University Press, 1995. Sara J. Shettleworth, *Cognition, Evolution, and Behavior*. New York: Oxford University Press, 1998, p. 427.

985. Hans Kummer, Fred Kurt, "Social Units of a Free-Living Population of Hamadryas Baboons" in *Human Adaptation: The Biosocial Background*. Yehudi A. Cohen, ed. Chicago: Aldine Transaction, 2010, p. 131.

986. Stuart Altmann. "Baboon behavior." Wild Discovery *Wired*, October 12, 1998, eagle.online.discovery.com/cgibin/conversations_view/dir/Wild%20Discovery%20Wired/Baboons2/ Baboon%20behavior. A. Stolba, "Entscheidungsfindung in Verbanden von Papio hamadryas," Ph.D. Dissertation, Universitat Zurich, Zurich, 1979; H. Kummer, *Weise Affen am Roten Meer: Das sociale Leben der Wustenpaviane*, Munich, Germany, 1992; Jan A.R.A.M. van Hooff, "Understanding Chimpanzee Understanding," in *Chimpanzee Cultures*, ed. Richard W. Wrangham, W.C. McGrew, Frans B.M. de Waal, and Paul G. Heltne with assistance from Linda A. Marquardt. Cambridge, MA: Harvard University Press, 1994, pp. 279, 267–284. Christopher Boehm. "Four Mechanical Routes to Altruism." March, 1996, unpublished manuscript, p. 23. See also: Christopher Boehm. "Rational Preselection from Hamadryas to *Homo sapiens*: The Place of Decisions in Adaptive Process." *American Anthropologist*, June 1978, pp. 265–296; Hans Kummer, *Primate Societies: Group Techniques of Ecological Adaptation*. Chicago: Aldine Press, 1971.

987. Edward Gibbon, *The Decline and Fall of The Roman Empire*. www.ccel.org/g/gibbon/decline/volume2/chap68.htm#Assault

988. Edward Gibbon, *The Decline and Fall of The Roman Empire*. www.ccel.org/g/gibbon/decline/volume2/chap68.htm#Assault

989. United Nations Development Programme—Arab Fund for Economic and Social Development. Arab Human Development Report 2002: Creating Opportunities for Future Generations. Dr. Farrukh Saleem, "What went wrong?" Capital Suggestion. *The News International*, Pakistan. www.jang.com.pk/thenews/nov2005-daily/08-11-2005/oped/o6.htm . This article can also be found at: www.ummah.com/forum/archive/index.php/t-71358.html?s=160cc15ec49512993526b2071845322b

990. Countries Compared by Economy > Human Development Index. International Statistics at NationMaster.com, from the Human Development Report 2006, United Nations Development Programme. Aggregates compiled by NationMaster. Retrieved from www.nationmaster.com/country-info/stats/Economy/Human-Development-Index 2-1-2016

991. Al Qaeda Manual. *Second Lesson Necessary Qualifications And Characteristics For The Organization's Members.* www.disastercenter.com/terror/Al_Qaeda_Manual_SECOND_LESSON.htm Also available on this website: The Al Qaeda Manual, cryptome.org/alq-terr-man.htm For more from the al Qaeda training manual, see United States Department of Justice, Al Qaeda Training Manual, www.au.af.mil/au/awc/awcgate/terrorism/alqaida_manual/

992. *Dābiq*, issue 12, November 18, 2015. The passage quoted from the Qur'an is from 8:46.

993. Sarwat Saulat, *The Life of The Prophet*. Islamic Publications Ltd., Lahore, Pakistan, 1983.

994. "Yousef Al-Qaradhawi and Other Sheikhs Herald the Coming Conquest of Rome." December 6, 2002 No. 447. Retrieved June 22, 2005, from the World Wide Web: www.memri.de/uebersetzungen_analysen/themen/islamistische_ideologie/isl_rom_18_12_02.pdf

995. The first Muslim siege of Constantinople took place in 677 A.D. Islamic World. Khilafah al-'Alam al-Islami, *The Umayyad Khilafah.* islamic-world.net/islamic-state/umayyads.htm Retrieved July 7, 2005, from the World Wide Web

996. David Nicolle, *Yarmuk AD 636: The Muslim Conquest of Syria*. Oxford: Osprey Publishing, 1994.

997. Edward Gibbon, *The Decline and Fall of the Roman Empire, Volume III*. New York: The Modern Library, nd.

998. Daniel J. Boorstin, *The Discoverers: A History of Man's Search to Know His World and Himself*. New York: Vintage Books, 1985.

999. Metropolitan Museum, "Byzantium: Materials and Techniques," Retrieved July 7, 2005, from the World Wide Web www.metmuseum.org/explore/Byzantium/materials.html Glasstopia. "Glass is… History of Glass." Tama University, Tokyo, Japan. Retrieved July 10, 2005, from the World Wide Web www.glasstopia.com/e_site/glassis/history/w_history/originofglass/originofglass.html

1000. Metropolitan Museum, *Byzantium: Materials and Techniques*. Retrieved July 7, 2005, from the World Wide Web www.metmuseum.org/explore/Byzantium/materials.html

1001. Glasstopia. "Glass is… History of Glass." Tama University, Tokyo, Japan. Retrieved July 10, 2005, from the World Wide Web www.glasstopia.com/e_site/glassis/history/w_history/originofglass/originofglass.html .

1002. Ernle Bradford, *The Sword and the Scimitar: The Saga of the Crusades*. G.P. Putnam's Sons, New York, 1974.

1003. Edward Gibbon, *The Decline and Fall of The Roman Empire*. Retrieved July 9, 2005, from the World Wide Web www.ccel.org/g/gibbon/decline/volume2/chap68.htm#Assault

1004. Qur'an, verses 22:39, Chapter 41, and Qur'aan, 2:190]]

1005. Wikipedia, "Basilic." en.wikipedia.org/wiki/Basilic

1006. Edward Gibbon (nd), *The Decline and Fall of the Roman Empire, Volume III*. New York: The Modern Library. Edward Gibbon, *The Decline and Fall of The Roman Empire*. Retrieved July 9, 2005, from the World Wide Web www.ccel.org/g/gibbon/decline/volume2/chap68.htm#Assault *The Decline and Fall of The Roman Empire* by Edward Gibbon — In The East, Chapter LXVIII.

1007. "From the first hour (73) of the memorable twenty-ninth of May, disorder and rapine prevailed in Constantinople till the eighth hour of the same day." Edward Gibbon, *The Decline and Fall of The Roman Empire*.

1008. Arvind Ghosh, "Qur'an And The Kafir: All That An Infidel Needs To Know About The Qur'an But Is Embarrassed To Ask." islamreview.org/Qur'anKafir/chapter13.html Retrieved July 9, 2005, from the World Wide Web

1009. "Yousef Al-Qaradhawi and Other Sheikhs Herald the Coming Conquest of Rome," The Middle East Research Institute. Special Dispatch Series — No. 447. December 6, 2002. Retrieved July 9, 2005, from the World Wide Web www.memri.org/bin/articles.cgi?Area=sd&ID=SP44702

1010. Islamic World. Official Website of the Khilafah Institute. Khilafah al-'Alam al-Islami. islamic-world.net/islamic-state/ Retrieved July 9, 2005, from the World Wide Web

1011. Osama bin Laden, "Complete Text Of Sheikh Osama Bin Laden's Latest Message To Ummah May 12, 2004." Jihad Unspun. Retrieved from the World Wide Web May 14, 2004, www.jihadunspun.net/intheatre_internal.php?article=572&list=/home.php&

1012. Steve Sailer, "Baby Gap: How birthrates color the electoral map." *The American Conservative*, December 20, 2004. Retrieved July 9, 2005, from the World Wide Web www.amconmag.com/2004_12_06/cover.html. See also: Robin D. Perrin, "American Religion in the Post-Aquarian Age: Values and Demographic Factors in Church Growth and Decline," *Journal for the Scientific Study of Religion*, Vol. 28, No. 1 (Mar., 1989), pp. 75–89 doi:10.2307/1387253.

1013. Ron Lesthaeghe, Lisa Neidert, "U.S. Presidential Elections and the Spatial Pattern of the American 'Second Demographic Transition,'" Second Demographic Transition Project, University of Michigan, sdt.psc.isr.umich.edu/pubs/online/SDT-US-Vote2008_RL_ND.pdf 2-2-2016. Lauren Sandler, "Tell Me a State's Fertility Rate, and I'll Tell You How It Voted," *New York Magazine*'s The Cut, November 19, 2012, nymag.com/thecut/2012/11/states-conservative-as-their-women-are-fertile.html# 2-2-2016. Amanda Marcotte, "What Happens If Liberals Start Having More Babies?" *Slate* blogs, November 20, 2012, www.slate.com/blogs/xx_factor/2012/11/20/fertility_rates_and_the_election_what_happens_if_liberals_start_having_more.html 2-2-2016

1014. Ali A. Mazrui, "Pax Islamica: Muslim values between war and peace." Lecture given at the American University School of Public Service, Washington, DC, November 12, 2003. www.swahilionline.com/features/articles/mazrui/mazrui10.htm

1015. *The Africans*, with Ali Mazrui (PBS 1986). For more on Mazrui and his television series see: Richard Zoglin, "One Man's View of a Continent: The Africans, PBS," *Time Magazine*, Oct. 13, 1986. Retrieved July 9, 2005, from the World Wide Web www.time.com/time/magazine/article/0,9171,962528,00.html

1016. Ali A. Mazrui, "Islamic Doctrine and the Politics of Induced Fertility Change: An African Perspective," *Population and Development Review*, Vol. 20, Supplement: The New Politics of Population: Conflict and Consensus in Family Planning (1994), pp. 131-132.

1017. Ali A. Mazrui, "Islamic Doctrine and the Politics of Induced Fertility Change: An African Perspective," *Population and Development Review*, Vol. 20, Supplement: The New Politics of Population: Conflict and Consensus in Family Planning (1994), pp. 131-132.

1018. Ali A. Mazrui, "Islamic Doctrine and the Politics of Induced Fertility Change: An African Perspective," *Population and Development Review*, Vol. 20, Supplement: The New Politics of Population: Conflict and Consensus in Family Planning (1994), p. 122.

1019. Ali A. Mazrui, "Islamic Doctrine and the Politics of Induced Fertility Change: An African Perspective," *Population and Development Review*, Vol. 20, Supplement: The New Politics of Population: Conflict and Consensus in Family Planning (1994), p. 125.

1020. Ali A. Mazrui, "Islamic Doctrine and the Politics of Induced Fertility Change: An African Perspective," *Population and Development Review*, Vol. 20, Supplement: The New Politics of Population: Conflict and Consensus in Family Planning (1994), p. 131.

1021. Ali A. Mazrui, "Islamic Doctrine and the Politics of Induced Fertility Change: An African Perspective." *Population and Development Review*, Vol. 20, Supplement: The New Politics of Population: Conflict and Consensus in Family Planning (1994), p. 131.

1022. Ali A. Mazrui, "Islamic Doctrine and the Politics of Induced Fertility Change: An African Perspective." *Population and Development Review*, Vol. 20, Supplement: The New Politics of Population: Conflict and Consensus in Family Planning (1994), p. 132.

1023. Ali A. Mazrui, "Islamic Doctrine and the Politics of Induced Fertility Change: An African Perspective." *Population and Development Review*, Vol. 20, Supplement: The New Politics of Population: Conflict and Consensus in Family Planning, (1994), p. 125.

1024. Ali A. Mazrui, "Islamic Doctrine and the Politics of Induced Fertility Change: An African Perspective." *Population and Development Review*, Vol. 20, Supplement: The New Politics of Population: Conflict and Consensus in Family Planning, (1994), p. 132.

1025. Ali AlAmin Mazrui, *Africa Since 1935*. Berkeley, CA: University of California Press, 1993, p. 59.

1026. Qur'an. chapter 33, verse 50. The Holy Qur'an. Translation by Abdullah Yusufali. Complete online text. www.wam.umd.edu/~stwright/rel/islam/ Retrieved July 9, 2005, from the World Wide Web

1027. Ali A. Mazrui, "Islamic Doctrine and the Politics of Induced Fertility Change: An African Perspective." *Population and Development Review*, Vol. 20, Supplement: The New Politics of Population: Conflict and Consensus in Family Planning, (1994), p. 128.

1028. Timothy M. Savage, "Europe and Islam: Crescent Waxing, Cultures Clashing." *The Washington Quarterly*, Summer 2004, 27:3, pp. 25–50. © 2004 by The Center for Strategic and International Studies and the Massachusetts Institute of Technology

1029. "Based on an analysis of current trends in the 25 European countries for which data are available, Muslim women today will have an average of 2.2 children each, compared with an estimated average of 1.5 children each for non-Muslim women in Europe." Pew Research Center, Religion and Public Life, The Future Of The Global Muslim Population: Region: Europe, Pew Research Center, January 27, 2011, www.pewforum.org/2011/01/27/future-of-the-global-muslim-population-regional-europe/ "FactCheck: will Britain have a Muslim majority by 2050?", Factcheck, Channel4 TV, Britain, June 14, 2013, blogs.channel4.com/factcheck/factcheck-will-britain-have-a-muslim-majorityby-2050/13690

1030. Vincent Cooper, "The Islamic future of Britain," *The Commentator*, June 13, 2013, www.thecommentator.com/article/3770/the_islamic_future_of_britain 2-2-2016

1031. Richard Kerbaj, "Muslim population 'rising 10 times faster than rest of society,'" *The Times*, January 30, 2009, www.thetimes.co.uk/tto/news/uk/article1937685.ece

1032. Richard Kerbaj, "Muslim population 'rising 10 times faster than rest of society,'" *The Times*, January 30, 2009, www.thetimes.co.uk/tto/news/uk/article1937685.ece 2-2-2016

1033. Vincent Cooper, "The Islamic future of Britain," *The Commentator*, June 13, 2013, www.thecommentator.com/article/3770/the_islamic_future_of_britain 2-2-2016

1034. "The Future of the Global Muslim Population, Region: Europe," Pew Research Center, January 27, 2011, www.pewforum.org/2011/01/27/future-of-the-global-muslim-population-regional-europe/ 2-2-2016

1035. The Pew Forum on Religion & Public Life, "An Uncertain Road: Muslims and the Future of Europe." www.pewforum.org/2005/10/19/an-uncertain-road-muslims-and-the-future-of-europe/

1036. Pew Research Center, "The Future of the Global Muslim Population: Projections for 2010-2030," January 2011, p. 131 www.pewforum.org/files/2011/01/FutureGlobalMuslimPopulation-WebPDF-Feb10.pdf 2-3-2016. "Fertility rates for Muslims and non-Muslims," blogs.channel4.com/factcheck/wp-content/uploads/sites/9/2013/06/14_pew.jpg 2-3-2016

1037. Raziye Akkoc, "How Europe is slowly dying despite an increasing world population, Europe needs many more babies to avert a population disaster," *The Telegraph*, February 16, 2015, www.telegraph.co.uk/news/worldnews/11414064/How-Europe-is-slowly-dying-despite-an-increasing-world-population.html 2-3-2016

1038. Ashifa Kassam, Rosie Scammell, Kate Connolly, Richard Orange, Kim Willsher, Rebecca Ratcliffe, "Europe needs many more babies to avert a population disaster," *The Guardian*, August 22, 2015, www.theguardian.com/world/2015/aug/23/baby-crisis-europe-brink-depopulation-disaster 2-3-2016

1039. Agner Fog, "Cultural r/k Selection. Journal of Memetics — Evolutionary Models of Information Transmission," 1997. cfpm.org/jom-emit/1997/vol1/fog_a.html J.D. Nichols, W. Conley, B. Batt, A.R. Tipton, "Temporally Dynamic Reproductive Strategies and the Concept of R- and K-Selection," *American Naturalist*, Vol. 110, No. 976 (Nov.–Dec. 1976), pp. 995–1005. Lloyd Demetrius, "Reproductive Strategies and Natural Selection," *American Naturalist*, Vol. 109, No. 967 (May–June 1975), pp. 243–249.

1040. Frequently that violence is imposed on the animals that use the r strategy, not generated by those animals. Some animals—guppies for example—switch into the r mode when they're being rapaciously attacked by a predator. D.N. Reznick, J. Endler. "The impact of predation on life history evolution in Trinidadian guppies (*Poecilia reticulata*)." *Evolution*, 36, 1982, pp. 160–177.

1041. Edward O. Wilson, *Sociobiology: The Abridged Edition*. Cambridge, Massachusetts : The Belknap Press of Harvard University, 1980.

1042. Francis Heylighen and Jan L. Bernheim, From Quantity to Quality of Life: r-K selection and human development Principia Cybernetica Web. pcp.vub.ac.be/Papers/r-KselectionQOL.pdf

1043. D.N. Reznick, J. Endler. "The impact of predation on life history evolution in Trinidadian guppies (*Poecilia reticulata*)." *Evolution*, 36, 1982: pp. 160–177. D.N. Reznick, H. Bryga, J.A. Endler. "Experimentally induced life-history evolution in a natural population." *Nature*, 346, July 26, 1990, pp. 357–359. D.N. Reznick, F.H. Shaw, F.H. Rodd, Ruth G. Shaw, "Evaluation of the Rate of Evolution in Natural Populations of Guppies (*Poecilia reticulata*)." *Science*, 275, March 28, 1997, pp. 1934–1937.

1044. R.H.K. Mann. "The growth and reproductive strategy of the gudgeon, *Gobio gobio* (L.), in two hard-water rivers in southern England." *Journal of Fish Biology* Volume 17, Issue 2: Page 163 — August 1980 doi:10.1111/j.1095-8649.1980.tb02750.x

1045. Edward O. Wilson, *Sociobiology: The Abridged Edition*, The Belknap Press of Harvard University, Cambridge, Massachusetts, 1980.

1046. "Yousef Al-Qaradhawi and Other Sheikhs Herald the Coming Conquest of Rome." The Middle East Research Institute. Special Dispatch Series — No. 447. December 6, 2002. www.memri.org/bin/articles.cgi?Area=sd&ID=SP44702

1047. "A waxing crescent: Islam is growing. But ageing and slowing. That will change the world," *The Economist*, Jan 27th 2011, www.economist.com/node/18008022 2-3-2016

1048. "The Future Of The Global Muslim Population, Region: Europe," Pew Research Center, January 27, 2011, www.pewforum.org/2011/01/27/future-of-the-global-muslim-population-regional-europe/ 2-2-2016. Jocelyn Cesari, "European Islam: A Profile." In Shireen T. Hunter, ed., *Islam in Europe and in the United States, A Comparative Perspective*, Center for Strategic and International Studies, Washington, DC, 2002, pp. 11-15. euro-islam.info/PDFs/CSCI_Book.pdf 2-2-2016

1049. Paul Harris, Burhan Wazir, Jason Burke, "'We will replace the Bible with the Qur'an.'" London: *The Observer*, November 4, 2001. observer.guardian.co.uk/islam/story/0,,587375,00.html

1050. Sean O'Neill, "Rallies will highlight 'Magnificent 19' of Sept 11," *The Telegraph*, September 10, 2003, www.telegraph.co.uk/news/uknews/1441070/Rallies-will-highlight-Magnificent-19-of-Sept-11.html

1051. "On October 13, 2004 the disbandment of Al Muhajiroun was announced. However, it is believed that The Saviour Sect is to all intents and purposes Al Muhajiroun operating under a new name." Wikipedia, "Al-Muhajiroun—Disbandment." en.wikipedia.org/wiki/Al-Muhajiroun#Disbandment

1052. Arutz Sheva—IsraelNationalNews.com British Muslim Leader Justifies Chechen School Attack, www.israelnationalnews.com/news.php3?id=68558

1053. observer.guardian.co.uk/islam/story/0,1442,587375,00.html
'We will replace the Bible with the Koran in Britain,' Islam and the West: *Observer* special Paul Harris and Burhan Wazir in London, Jason Burke in Peshawar, Sunday November 4, 2001 *The Observer*.

1054. Ali A. Mazrui, "Islamic Doctrine and the Politics of Induced Fertility Change: An African Perspective." *Population and Development Review*, Vol. 20, Supplement: The New Politics of Population: Conflict and Consensus in Family Planning, (1994), p. 125.

1055. Stephanie Linning and Martin Jay, "New wife of preacher of hate Omar Bakri Muhammad applies for UK asylum for herself and their two children — where he already has wife and eight children," *Daily Mail*, July 10, 2014, www.dailymail.co.uk/news/article-2687895/Lebanese-wife-Omar-Bakri-left-wife-seven-children-Britain-applies-UK-asylum-two-children.html#ixzz3z9c0Ek00 2-3-2016.
Burhan Wazir, Jason Burke, Paul Harris, 'We will replace the Bible with the Koran in Britain,' Islam and the West: Observer special, *The Observer*, Sunday November 4, 2001, observer.guardian.co.uk/islam/story/0,1442,587375,00.html

1056. "Study says practicing Muslims will outnumber practicing Christians in Britain soon," Nando.net, from Agence France Presse, London, May 10, 1997, 7:31 p.m. EDT.

1057. Stephen Bates, "Decline in churchgoing hits CoE hardest." *The Guardian*. April 14, 2001. www.guardian.co.uk/uk_news/story/0,3604,473089,00.html

1058. United Nations Population Fund, "New Demographic Regime: Population Challenges and Policy Responses." Geneva, Switzerland: United Nations Publication, 2005, p. 16. Timothy M. Savage, "Europe and Islam: Crescent Waxing, Cultures Clashing." *The Washington Quarterly*, Summer 2004, 27:3 pp. 25–50. © 2004 by The Center for Strategic and International Studies and the Massachusetts Institute of Technology.

1059. David A. Graham, "The Mysterious Life and Death of Abdelhamid Abaaoud," *The Atlantic*, November 19, 2015, www.theatlantic.com/international/archive/2015/11/who-was-abdelhamid-abaaoud-isis-paris/416739/ 2-3-2016

1060. Svati Kirsten Narula, Adam Pasick, "Abdelhamid Abaaoud, the alleged Paris attack mastermind, recruited his 13-year-old brother to ISIL," *Quartz*, November 16, 2015, qz.com/551228/abdelhamid-abaaoud-the-alleged-paris-attack-mastermind-recruited-his-13-year-old-brother-to-isil/ 2-3-2016

1061. Associated Press, "Alleged Paris mastermind transformed in prison, father says," CBS News, November 18, 2015, www.cbsnews.com/news/who-is-isis-paris-attacks-mastermind-abdelhamid-abaaoud/ 2-3-2016

1062. Agence France Press, "What we know about Paris terror 'mastermind,'" *The Local France*, November 16, 2015, www.thelocal.fr/20151116/what-we-know-about-paris-attacks-mastermind 2-3-2016

1063. Agence France Press, "What we know about Paris terror 'mastermind,'" *The Local France*, November 16, 2015, www.thelocal.fr/20151116/what-we-know-about-paris-attacks-mastermind 2-3-2016

1064. Jacquelin Magnay, "Paris attacks: Hunt turns towards 'The Executioner,'" *The Australian*, November 21, 2015, www.theaustralian.com.au/in-depth/paris-terror-attacks/paris-attacks-hunt-turns-towards-the-executioner/story-fnyenp03-1227617497154 2-3-2016

1065. Jacquelin Magnay, "Paris attacks: Hunt turns towards 'The Executioner,'" *The Australian*, November 21, 2015, www.theaustralian.com.au/in-depth/paris-terror-attacks/paris-attacks-hunt-turns-towards-the-executioner/story-fnyenp03-1227617497154 2-3-2016

1066. Jacquelin Magnay, "Paris attacks: Hunt turns towards 'The Executioner,'" *The Australian*, November 21, 2015, www.theaustralian.com.au/in-depth/paris-terror-attacks/paris-attacks-hunt-turns-towards-the-executioner/story-fnyenp03-1227617497154 2-3-2016.
AP, "Alleged Paris mastermind transformed in prison, father says," CBS News, November 18, 2015, www.cbsnews.com/news/who-is-isis-paris-at-tacks-mastermind-abdelhamid-abaaoud/ 2-3-2016

1067. AP, "Alleged Paris mastermind transformed in prison, father says,"" CBS News, November 18, 2015, www.cbsnews.com/news/who-is-isis-paris-attacks-mastermind-abdelhamid-abaaoud/ 2-3-2016

1068. Agence France Press, "What we know about Paris terror 'mastermind,'" *The Local France*, November 16, 2015, www.thelocal.fr/20151116/what-we-know-about-paris-attacks-mastermind 2-3-2016

1069. Islamic State, France, "Urgent: Statement about the Blessed Paris Invasion on the French Crusaders," Townhall.com, townhall.com/tipsheet/katiepavlich/2015/11/14/isis-claims-responsibility-for-paris-terror-attack-n2080755 2-3-2016

1070. Timothy M. Savage, "Europe and Islam: Crescent Waxing, Cultures Clashing," *The Washington Quarterly*, Summer 2004, 27:3 pp. 25–50. © 2004 by The Center for Strategic and International Studies and the Massachusetts Institute of Technology.

1071. Malcolm Turnbull, "Demographic Change and International Affairs," Monday, December 13, 2004 Address by Malcolm Turnbull MP to the NSW Branch Australian Institute of International Affairs

1072. Wikipedia, "Malcolm Turnbull," en.wikipedia.org/wiki/Malcolm_Turnbull

1073. Malcolm Turnbull, "Demographic Change and International Affairs," Monday, December 13, 2004 Address by Malcolm Turnbull MP to the NSW Branch Australian Institute of International Affairs.

1074. Bin Laden's exact words were: "These youths love death as you loves [sic] life." Osama bin Laden, "Complete Text Of Sheikh Osama Bin Laden's Latest Message To Ummah May 12, 2004." Jihad Unspun. 2004, www.jihadunspun.net/intheatre_internal.php?article=572&list=/home.php& Retrieved July 9, 2005, from the World Wide Web

1075. bin Laden, "Complete Text Of Sheikh Osama Bin Laden's Latest Message To Ummah May 12, 2004." Jihad Unspun. Retrieved from the World Wide Web May 14, 2004 www.jihadunspun.net/intheatre_internal.php?article=572&list=/home.php&

1076. *Dābiq*, issue 12, p. 40.

1077. Pervez Musharraf, Book Extract: "How We Found Pearl buried in ten pieces." London: *Times Online*. September 26, 2006. www.timesonline.co.uk/article/0,,3-2374550,00.html

1078. "One suspected bomber was born in Jamaica and grew up in England. Another is a Cairo-born student who studied biochemistry and chemical engineering at the undergraduate and graduate level in the US. Several kilos of ammonium nitrate are found in one of his two apartments—a 'bomb factory' in Leeds. One suspect, Hasib Hussain is 18 yrs old, comes from a modest neighborhood in Leeds, was a cricket and soccer player, but was taken off the college track by his teachers and the cricket pitch on which he played with his team was shut down. He turned to Islam. Two bombers have made trips to Pakistan that apparently changed their lives. Another, 22-year-old Shehzad Tanweer, was born in Bradford, England, came from an upper middle-class family that owned a chip shop, was proud to be British, played cricket the week before the attack, but went to Pakistan to learn the Koran by heart and may have visited a militant Islamic private school for the wealthy and the planner of a Pakistani grenade attack that killed five." David Rising, "London Police Identify Bombings Suspects." Associated Press, July 26, 2005. Printed in London: *The Guardian* July 26, 2005 Retrieved July 26, 2005, from the World Wide Web www.guardian.co.uk/worldlatest/story/0,1280,-5168957,00.html BBC News, "Bombings police search seized car." Retrieved July 26, 2005, from the World Wide Web news.bbc.co.uk/1/hi/uk/4716535.stm. BBC News. "Failed bomb attacks: What we know." Retrieved July 26, 2005, from the World Wide Web news.bbc.co.uk/1/hi/uk/4717677.stm. BBC News. "Man 'saw Shepherd's Bush bomber.'" Retrieved July 26, 2005, from the World Wide Web news.bbc.co.uk/1/hi/uk/4705303.stm

1079. Angelique Chrisafis, "Charlie Hebdo attackers: born, raised and radicalised in Paris," *The Guardian*, Tuesday 13 January 2015, www.theguardian.com/world/2015/jan/12/-sp-charlie-hebdo-attackers-kids-france-radicalised-paris 2-4-2016

1080. Isaiah 2:4.

1081. Matthew 5:9.

1082. Adrian H. Bredero, *Christendom and Christianity in the Middle Ages*. Grand Rapids, Mich: William B. Eerdmans Publishing, 1994, pp. 109–110.

1083. Jonathan Simon Christopher Riley-Smith, *The First Crusade and Idea of Crusading*, London: Continuum, 2003, p. 4.

1084. Jonathan Simon Christopher Riley-Smith, *The First Crusade and Idea of Crusading*, London: Continuum, 2003, p. 4.

1085. Meredith Baldwin Weddle, *Walking in the Way of Peace: Quaker Pacifism in the Seventeenth Century*. New York: Oxford University Press, USA, 2001, p. 5.

1086. William Penn, *An Essay towards the Present and Future Peace of Europe by the Establishment of an European Dyet, Parliament, or Estates* (1693). The Danish Peace Academy, www.fredsakademiet.dk/library/penn.pdf 2-5-2016. David Cortright, *Peace: A History of Movements and Ideas*. Cambridge, UK: Cambridge University Press, Apr 24, 2008 p. 53.

1087. Peter van den Dungen, introduction, in William Penn, *An Essay Towards the Present and Future Peace of Europe: By the Establishment of an European Diet, Parliament, Or Estates*, New York: Georg Olms Verlag, 1944, p. xi.

1088. Immanuel Kant, "Perpetual Peace: A Philosophical Sketch" (1795), Slought Foundation, Philadelphia, slought.org/media/files/perpetual_peace.pdf 2-5-2016

1089. April Carter, *Peace Movements: International Protest and World Politics Since 1945*. London: Routledge, 2014, p. 3.

1090. Joel Myerson, *The Cambridge Companion to Henry David Thoreau*. Cambridge, UK: Cambridge University Press, 1995.

1091. Barbara L. Packer, *The Transcendentalists*. Athens, GA: University of Georgia Press, 2007, p. 188.

1092. Barbara L. Packer, *The Transcendentalists*. Athens, GA: University of Georgia Press, 2007, p. 188.

1093. Shannon L. Mariottie, *Thoreau's Democratic Withdrawal: Alienation, Participation, and Modernity*. Madison, Wis.: University of Wisconsin Press, 2010, p. 129.

1094. Rebecca Beatrice Brooks, "Henry David Thoreau Arrested For Nonpayment of Poll Tax," *History of Massachusetts*, July 14, 2012, historyofmassachusetts.org/henry-david-thoreau-arrested-for-nonpayment-of-poll-tax/ 2-6-2016

1095. Barbara L. Packer, *The Transcendentalists*. Athens, GA: University of Georgia Press, 2007, p. 188.

1096. Wendy McElroy, "Henry Thoreau and 'Civil Disobedience,'" *The Thoreau Reader*, thoreau.eserver.org/wendy.html, 1-6-2016

1097. Joel Myerson, *The Cambridge Companion to Henry David Thoreau*. Cambridge: Cambridge University Press, 1995.

1098. Anthony J. Parel, *Thoreau, Gandhi, and Comparative Political Thought, in A Political Companion to Henry David Thoreau*, ed. Jack Turner. Lexington, Ky.: University Press of Kentucky, May 1, 2010.

1099. John J. Ansbro, *Martin Luther King, Jr.: Nonviolent Strategies and Tactics for Social Change*. Lanham, Md.: Madison Books, 2000, p. 110.

1100. J. David Hacker, "A Census-Based Count of the Civil War Dead," *Civil War History*, Volume 57, Number 4, December 2011, pp. 307-348 | 10.1353/cwh.2011.0061, muse.jhu.edu/login? auth=0&type=summary&url=/journals/ civil_war_history/v057/57.4.hacker.html 3-10-2016

1101. John Keegan, *A History of Warfare*. New York: Random House, 1993.

1102. *The Sword of Islam*, David Darlow, producer/director, Brian Park and Fiona Moffitt, research, Rod Caird, executive producer, Granada TV, Manchester, England, 1987. This extraordinary documentary, one of the few to probe the hostile world of Islamic fundamentalism, was the result of an eighteen-month investigation in Beirut, Cairo and Iran.

1103. *Dābiq*, issue four, October 11, 2014.

1104. Ambrose Evans-Pritchard, "Dutch desert their changing country," *The Telegraph*, UK: filed 11/12/2004, www.telegraph.co.uk/news/main.jhtml?xml=/ news/2004/12/11/wneth11.xml&sSheet=/ portal/2004/12/11/ixportal.html

1105. Daisy Sindelar, "Netherlands: Week of Violence Leaves People Questioning Tradition of Tolerance," Radio Free Europe. www.rferl.org/featuresarticle/2004/11/ 4cf75cb4-c2fa-4a15-b977-d142d89acf89.html. Wikipedia, "Polder Model," en.wikipedia.org/wiki/Polder_Model

1106. Marcel Van De Hoef, "Muslim Schools Under Fire By Dutch," The Associated Press, AP-NY-03-18-2002

1107. Marcel Van De Hoef, "Muslim Schools Under Fire By Dutch," The Associated Press, AP-NY-03-18-2002

1108. Lorenzo Vidino, "The Muslim Brotherhood's Conquest of Europe," *Middle East Quarterly*, Winter 2005, pp. 25–34, www.meforum.org/687/ the-muslim-brotherhoods-conquest-of-europe

1109. The Muslim World League was founded by the Muslim Brotherhood's Said Ramadan, son-in-law of Hassan al-Banna, the Muslim Brotherhoods' founder.

1110. Pew Research Center, Muslim Networks and Movements in Western Europe, Muslim World League and World Assembly of Muslim Youth, September 15, 2010, www.pewforum.org/ 2010/09/15/muslim-networks-and-movements-in-westerneurope-muslim-world-league-and-world-assemblyof-muslim-youth/

1111. Lorenzo Vidino, "The Muslim Brotherhood's Conquest of Europe" *Middle East Quarterly*, Winter 2005, pp. 25–34, www.meforum.org/687/ the-muslim-brotherhoods-conquest-of-europe

1112. Soeren Kern, "Germany's New Islamic Centers Funded by Taxpayers," Gatestone Institute, January 19, 2012 at 5:00 am, www.gatestoneinstitute.org/ 2768/germany-islamic-centers

1113. For other Muslim organizations with government contact, see: "On the Deutsche Islam Konferenz: Muslim Organisations in Germany," www.deutsche-islam-konferenz.de/DIK/EN/Magazin/Moscheen/Organisationen/organisationen-node.html
And for a critical evaluation of these organizations and the dishonesty in the ways they present themselves, see: Soeren Kern,"Germany Aiming to Become More Muslim Friendly," February 6, 2014 at 5:00 a.m. www.gatestoneinstitute.org/4155/germany-muslim-friendly

1114. Lorenzo Vidino, "The Muslim Brotherhood's Conquest of Europe," *Middle East Quarterly*, Winter 2005, pp. 25-34, The Middle East Forum www.meforum.org/article/687

1115. Ursula Spuler-Stegemann, "Allah and the Occident: How Islam Came to Germany," "Part 2: The Founding of Germany's First Islamic Religious Communities," *Der Spiegel*, June 16, 2008, www.spiegel.de/international/germany/allah-and-the-occident-how-islam-came-to-germany-a-559927-2.html

1116. Ursula Spuler-Stegemann, "Allah and the Occident: How Islam Came to Germany," "Part 2: The Founding of Germany's First Islamic Religious Communities," *Der Spiegel*, June 16, 2008, www.spiegel.de/international/germany/allah-and-the-occident-how-islam-came-to-germany-a-559927-2.html

1117. Lorenzo Vidino, "The Muslim Brotherhood's Conquest of Europe" *Middle East Quarterly*, Winter 2005, pp. 25–34, www.meforum.org/687/the-muslim-brotherhoods-conquest-of-europe

1118. Wikipedia, "Muslim Brotherhood," en.wikipedia.org/wiki/Muslim_Brotherhood

1119. Lorenzo Vidino, "The Muslim Brotherhood's Conquest of Europe" *Middle East Quarterly*, Winter 2005, pp. 25–34, www.meforum.org/687/the-muslim-brotherhoods-conquest-of-europe.
Guido Steinberg, *Germany and the Muslim Brotherhood in The West and The Muslim Brotherhood After The Arab Spring*, Lorenzo Vidino, editor,, Al Mesbar Studies and Research Center, Dubai, in collaboration with
The Foreign Policy Research Institute, pp. 87-88 www.fpri.org/docs/chapters/201303.west_and_the_muslim_brotherhood_after_the_arab_spring.chapter5.pdf

1120. Soeren Kern, "The Islamization of Germany in 2013," Gatestone Institute, January 15, 2014 at 5:00 a.m. www.gatestoneinstitute.org/4130/islamization-germany

1121. "Terrorist cell found in Hamburg where 9/11 attacks conceived," *The Telegraph*, October 7, 2009, www.telegraph.co.uk/news/worldnews/europe/germany/6267615/Terrorist-cell-found-in-Hamburg-where-911-attacks-conceived.html
Joseph Lelyveld, "All Suicide Bombers Are Not Alike," New York Times Magazine, October 28, 2001 www.nytimes.com/2001/10/28/magazine/28TERRORIST.html?pagewanted=all

1122. Ambrose Evans-Pritchard, "Belgium is 'launch pad for terrorists,'" *The Telegraph*, UK: 04/06/2002, www.telegraph.co.uk/news/main.jhtml?xml=/news/2002/06/04/wbelg04. xml&sSheet=/news/2002/06/04/ixworld.html

1123. Ambrose Evans-Pritchard, "Belgium is 'launch pad for terrorists,'" *The Telegraph*, UK, filed 04/06/2002,
www.telegraph.co.uk/news/main.jhtml?xml=/news/2002/06/04/wbelg04. xml&sSheet=/news/2002/06/04/ixworld.html

1124. Ambrose Evans-Pritchard, "Belgium is 'launch pad for terrorists,'" Filed: 04/06/2002 www.telegraph.co.uk/news/main.jhtml?xml=/news/2002/06/04/wbelg04. xml&sSheet=/news/2002/06/04/ixworld.html

1125. Glen Ford, "Black Lives Matter Take Note: Apartheid Israel Targeting Everyone that Questions Its 'Legitimacy,'" Black Agenda Report, 02/24/2016 www.blackagendareport.com/apartheid_israel_targets_BDS 2015
Black Solidarity Statement with Palestine, www.blackforpalestine.com/read-the-statement.html
Kristian Davis Bailey, "Dream Defenders, Black Lives Matter & Ferguson Reps Take Historic Trip to Palestine — Leaders from American racial justice movements connect with Palestinians living under occupation," *Ebony*, January 09, 2015, www.ebony.com/news-views/dream-defenders-black-lives-matter-ferguson-reps-take-historic-trip-to-palestine#axzz43ybz5dw6.
Alex Kane, "The growing ties between #BlackLivesMatter and Palestine Activism," January 26, 2015 —
See more at: mondoweiss.net/2015/01/between-blacklivesmatter-palestine/#sthash.qJzUMFzo.dpuf

1126. In France, "asking people about their religious affiliation in a population census is forbidden. However, it is believed that between 4 and 5 million Muslims" live in France. Jean-Yves Camus, "Islam in France." May 10, 2004. Interdisciplinary Center Herzliya www.ict.org.il/articles/articledet.cfm?articleid=514 "approximately 4 to 6 million people of Islamic faith" en.wikipedia.org/wiki/Islam_in_France Hadi Yahmid of Islam Online uses two different figures for France's Islamic population—five million in one article and six million in another. As of 2005, he wrote, "Muslims make up some five million of France's 60 million people, the biggest Muslim minority in Europe." This statement appears in Hadi Yahmid, IOL Correspondent, "Paris Police Face Non-abating Immigrants Outrage," IslamOnline.net & News Agencies October 31, 2005 islamonline.net/English/News/2005-10/31/ article04.shtml In another Islam Online article, Yahmid wrote that France had "Six million Muslims, or 10 percent of the overall [French] population." Hadi Yahmid, "French Muslims Live In 'Ethnic Ghettos': Report." July 7, 2004 (IslamOnline.net) www.islamonline.net/English/News/2004-07/07/ article04.shtml As of 2014. But Yahmid's figures may have been exaggerated. By 2014, there were only 6.13 million. But that was 9.6% of France's total population. "Europe Muslim Population in 2014," *Muslim Population*, www.muslimpopulation.com/Europe/1127 Melissa Block, "French Riots Underscore Racial Inequity." National Public Radio. November 7, 2005. www.npr.org/templates/story/story.php?storyId=4993214 "Chirac promises tough response as riots continue," *Japan Today*. November 7, 2005 www.japantoday.com/e/?content=news&cat=8&id=354484 1128. John Leicester, "Violence in France Enters 10th Night—Security Tightens as Riots Spread Across the Country," AOL News, November 6, 2005, aolsvc.news.aol.com/news/article.adp?id=2005110322370999011&ncid=NWS00010000000001 1129. John Leicester, "Violence in France Enters 10th Night—Security Tightens as Riots Spread Across the Country," AOL News, November 6, 2005, aolsvc.news.aol.com/news/article.adp?id=2005110322370999011&ncid=NWS00010000000001

1130. Chris Burns, Hayat Mongodin, and Associated Press, "Unrest reaches French capital Riots, arson take new turn, spreads across country." CNN, Sunday, November 6, 2005. edition.cnn.com/2005/WORLD/europe/11/05/france.riots/ 1131. John Leicester, "Violence in France Enters 10th Night—Security Tightens as Riots Spread Across the Country," AOL News, November 6, 2005, aolsvc.news.aol.com/news/article.adp?id=2005110322370999011&ncid=NWS00010000000001. IslamOnline.net & Reuters, "France Getting Calmer After Weeks of Unrest." www.islamonline.net/English/News/2005-11/17/article03.shtml 1132. National Public Radio, Hourly Newscast, November 5, 2005, 3 p.m. EST, npr.org. 1133. Martin Walker, "EU aid as French riots slacken." UPI, Nov 14, 2005. news.monstersandcritics.com/europe/article_1062055.php/EU_aid_as_French_riots_slacken 1134. Tom Heneghan, "French youths riot again despite curfew threat." *Reuters*, November 8, 2005. www.washingtonpost.com/wp-dyn/content/article/2005/11/07/AR2005110700254_pf.html John Leicester, "Violence in France Enters 10th Night—Security Tightens as Riots Spread Across the Country," AOL News, November 6, 2005, aolsvc.news.aol.com/news/article.adp?id=2005110322370999011&ncid=NWS00010000000001 1135. Tom Hundley, "Riots could happen in rest of Europe." *Chicago Tribune*, November 20, 2005. www.chicagotribune.com/news/nationworld/chi-0511200308nov20,1,4542635.story?coll=chi-newsnationworld-hed chicagotribune.com 1136. Abigail R. Esman, "Fire and Fury on the Euro-Arab Street." *The Nation*, November 14, 2005. Retrieved November 23, 2005, from the World Wide Web news.yahoo.com/s/thenation/20051114/cm_thenation/20051128esman&printer=1;_ylt=ApLjoN.hYnXax_xl9G4rzy8__8QF;_ylu=X3oDMTA3MXN1bHEoBHNlYwNobWE

1137. Jean Chichizola, "A new jihad, according to Islamist sites." Paris: *Le Figaro*, November 14, 2005. Retrieved October 13, 2006, from the World Wide Web www.lefigaro.fr/cgi/edition/genimprime?cle=20051114.FIG0379.

n.a. Has an Intifada Begun in France? Assyrian International News Agency—News and Analysis of Assyrian and Assyrian-Related Issues Worldwide. November 18, 2005 Retrieved November 21, 2005, from the World Wide Web www.aina.org/news/20051118140740.htm.

1138. Tom Hundley, "Riots could happen in rest of Europe." *Chicago Tribune*, November 20, 2005. www.chicagotribune.com/news/nationworld/chi-0511200308nov20,1,4542635.story?coll=chi-newsnationworld-hed chicagotribune.com

1139. The French riots continued from October 27, 2005, to November 18, 2005. IslamOnline.net & Reuters, "France Getting Calmer After Weeks of Unrest—French policemen arrive at site of protest against government's handling of recent unrest in Paris." Reuters, Paris, November 17, 2005 (IslamOnline.net & News Agencies), www.islamonline.net/English/News/2005-11/17/article03.shtml

1140. Craig S. Smith with Ariane Bernard, "Immigrant Rioting Flares in France for Ninth Night." *The New York Times*, November 5, 2005. www.nytimes.com/2005/11/05/international/europe/05france.html?ei=5094&en=269c3943cbe7ce00&hp=&ex=1131166800&partner=homepage&pagewanted=print

1141. Hadi Yahmid, "Paris Police Face Non-abating Immigrants Outrage." October 31, 2005 (IslamOnline.net & News Agencies)

1142. "Muslims issue fatwa against riots Monday," Reuters, November 7, 2005 Posted: 0239 GMT (1039 HKT) edition.cnn.com/2005/WORLD/europe/11/06/france.riots.fatwa.reut/?section=cnn_latest

1143. Tom Heneghan, "The sight of imams and local Muslim leaders in the suburbs calming down angry teenagers who reject all other authority."

"RPT-Anti-riot fatwa sparks feud among French Muslims,"
Reuters Foundation AlertNet www.alertnet.org/thenews/newsdesk/L0775633.htm

1144. A. Savyon, "Reactions in the Arab and Muslim World to the Rioting in France." The Middle East Media Research Institute Inquiry and Analysis Series - No. 251 November 11, 2005. memri.org/bin/articles.cgi?Page=archives&Area=ia&ID=IA25105

1145. Chapter 2, verse 190, The Holy Qur'an. Translation by Abdullah Yusufali. Complete online text. www.wam.umd.edu/~stwright/rel/islam/ Retrieved November 19, 2001, from the World Wide Web

1146. Chapter 2, verse 191. The Holy Qur'an. Translation by Abdullah Yusufali. Complete online text. Retrieved November 19, 2001, from the World Wide Web
www.wam.umd.edu/~stwright/rel/islam/

1147. "war is guile." In *Sahih Bukhari, Virtues and Merits of the Prophet (pbuh) and his Companions*, Volume 4, Book 56, Number 808: USC-MSA Compendium of Muslim Texts. University of Southern California.
www.usc.edu/dept/MSA/fundamentals/hadithsunnah/bukhari/056.sbt.html#004.056.808
(Bukhari is one of the Islamic holy books, one of the Hadith.)
"When the Prophet (peace_be_upon_him) intended to go on an expedition, he always pretended to be going somewhere else, and he would say: War is deception." Book 14, Number 2631. Sunan Abu-Dawud. USC-MSA Compendium of Muslim Texts. University of Southern California.
www.usc.edu/dept/MSA/fundamentals/hadithsunnah/abudawud/014.sat.html#014.2631
Sunan Abu-Dawud is another of the Islamic holy books, the Hadith. Even God uses guile in Islam to deceive the enemy. Ishaq quotes Allah as saying, "I deceived them with My firm guile so that I delivered you from them." In fact, Ishaq says that when it comes to deception, "God is the best of plotters."A. Guillaume, *The Life of Muhammad: A Translation of Ibn Ishaq's Sirat Rasul Allah*. New York: Oxford University Press, 1955, p. 323.

1148. This blunt quote from Muhammad, "War is deceit," comes to us from Muhammad's first and most important biographer, Ibn Ishaq: A. Guillaume, *The Life of Muhammad: A Translation of Ibn Ishaq's Sirat Rasul Allah*. New York: Oxford University Press, 1955, eighteenth printing, 2004, p. 458.

1149. See the stories of the lies an Islamic agent sowed among the Jews and the Meccans during the Battle of the Trench. Muhammad told one of his men, Nu'aym, to "go and awake distrust among the enemy to draw him off us if you can, for war is deceit." Remember, Muhammad was talking to a man who must have been very aware of Muhammad's pronouncements on the use of lies in the murder of Ka'b the poet: "O apostle of God," said one of the brothers, "we shall have to tell lies." Muhammad answered with an uncaring, "Say what you like, for you are free in the matter." Nu'aym approached a group of Jews who had been his best friends from childhood, and "remind[ed] them of his affection for them and of the special tie between them." In reality, friendship was not Nu'aym's intention. His goal was the death of the Jews to whom he was pretending warmth and loyalty. With this bait, Nu'aym lured the Jews into a trap that would make them hated by their Meccan allies. One of Nu'aym's standard phrases for winning the trust of those he was about to betray went like this: "You are my stock and my family and the dearest of men to me." So when you hear a phrase of that sort from a militant Muslim who tells you he wants peace and friendship, be very, very careful. A. Guillaume, *The Life of Muhammad: A Translation of Ibn Ishaq's Sirat Rasul Allah.* New York: Oxford University Press, 1955, eighteenth printing, 2004: pp. 458–459.

1150. A. Savyon, "Reactions in the Arab and Muslim World to the Rioting in France." The Middle East Media Research Institute Inquiry and Analysis Series — No. 251 November 11, 2005. memri.org/bin/articles.cgi?Page=archives&Area=ia&ID=IA25105

1151. A. Savyon, "Reactions in the Arab and Muslim World to the Rioting in France." The Middle East Media Research Institute Inquiry and Analysis Series — No. 251 November 11, 2005. memri.org/bin/articles.cgi?Page=archives&Area=ia&ID=IA25105

1152. A. Savyon, "Reactions in the Arab and Muslim World to the Rioting in France." The Middle East Media Research Institute Inquiry and Analysis Series — No. 251 November 11, 2005. memri.org/bin/articles.cgi?Page=archives&Area=ia&ID=IA25105

1153. Ali, Ayaan Hirsi (2015-03-24). *Heretic: Why Islam Needs a Reformation Now* (p. 5). HarperCollins. Kindle Edition. Perry Chiaramonte, "US group CAIR named terrorist organization by United Arab Emirates," Fox News, November 17, 2014, www.foxnews.com/us/2014/11/17/us-group-cair-added-to-terror-list-by-united-arab-emirates.html

1154. UPI, "Foreign agitators in French riots?" United Press International, 11/18/2005 6:41:00 p.m., www.upi.com/SecurityTerrorism/view.php?StoryID=20051118-113424-7573r B. Raman. "Hizbut Tehrir Behind French Intifada," (SAAG-India), South Asia Analysis Group, South Asia Analysis Group Paper no. 1614, 16. 11. 2005 www.saag.org/%5Cpapers17%5Cpaper1614.html Retrieved July 9, 2005, from the World Wide Web.

1155. "Jamaat ul-Fuqra," South Asia Intelligence Review. www.satp.org/satporgtp/countries/pakistan/terroristoutfits/jamaat-ul-fuqra.htm

1156. BBC, "Who is Richard Reid?" BBC, Friday, 28 December, 2001, 13:32 GMT news.bbc.co.uk/1/hi/uk/1731568.stm

1157. Wikipedia. "Richard Reid (shoe bomber)," Wikipedia. en.wikipedia.org/wiki/Richard_Reid_%28shoe_bomber%29

1158. Michael Elliott, "The Shoe Bomber's World." *Time Magazine*—Web Exclusive. February 16, 2002. www.time.com/time/world/article/0,8599,203478,00.html

1159. Michael Elliott, "The Shoe Bomber's World." *Time Magazine*—Web Exclusive. February 16, 2002. www.time.com/time/world/article/0,8599,203478,00.html. Wikipedia, "Shoe Bomber." en.wikipedia.org/wiki/Shoe_bomber

1160. "Foreign agitators in French riots?" UPI, Nov. 18, 2005, www.upi.com/Business_News/Security-Industry/2005/11/18/Foreign-agitators-in-French-riots/75731132357284/

1161. UPI, "Foreign agitators in French riots?" United Press International, 11/18/2005 6:41:00 p.m., www.upi.com/SecurityTerrorism/view.php?StoryID=20051118-113424-7573r B. Raman. "Hizbut Tehrir Behind French Intifada," (SAAG-India), South Asia Analysis Group, South Asia Analysis Group Paper no. 1614, 16. 11. 2005 www.saag.org/%5Cpapers17%5Cpaper1614.html Retrieved July 9, 2005, from the World Wide Web.

1162. Mark Krikorian, Executive Director of the Center for Immigration Studies, Frank Gaffney, President of the Center for Security Policy, and Stephen Steinlight, Fellow at the Center for Immigration Studies, "The French Riots and U.S. Immigration Policy: Lessons for U.S. Lawmakers?" C-Span, November 14, 2005. 72.14.207.104/search?q=cache:EaT-eSGBbPMJ:www.cspan.org/VideoArchives.asp%3FCatCode-Pairs%3D,%26ArchiveDays%3D100%26Page%3D3+%22Stephen+Steinlight%22+2005&hl=en&client=googlet

1163. Mark Krikorian, Executive Director of the Center for Immigration Studies, Frank Gaffney, President of the Center for Security Policy, and Stephen Steinlight, Fellow at the Center for Immigration Studies, "The French Riots and U.S. Immigration Policy: Lessons for U.S. Lawmakers?" C-Span, November 14, 2005. 72.14.207.104/search?q=cache:EaT-eSGBbPMJ:www.cspan.org/VideoArchives.asp%3FCatCode-Pairs%3D,%26ArchiveDays%3D100%26Page%3D3+%22Stephen+Steinlight%22+2005&hl=en&client=googlet

1164. Khadija Abdul Qahaar, "An Important Message from the Publisher." Jihad Unspun, November 14, 2005. www.jihadunspun.net/home.php

1165. "Interview avec d'anciens terroristes (CN8)", CN8, Philadelphia, www.youtube.com/watch?v=NGJYT4t83CQ&search=shoebat%20CN8%20Islam%20Jihad%20Terrorism

1166. David G. Dalin, John F. Rothmann, Alan M. Dershowitz, Icon of Evil: Hitler's Mufti and the Rise of Radical Islam. Piscataway, NJ: Transaction Publishers, 2009, pp. 47–49.

1167. United States Holocaust Memorial Museum, "Hajj Amin Al-Husayni: Wartime Propagandist," www.ushmm.org/wlc/en/article.php?ModuleId=10007667

1168. United States Holocaust Memorial Museum, "Mobile Killing Squads," www.ushmm.org/outreach/en/article.php?ModuleId=10007710 United States Holocaust Memorial Museum, SS, www.ushmm.org/wlc/en/article.php?ModuleId=10007400

1169. United States Holocaust Memorial Museum, "Hajj Amin Al-Husayni: Wartime Propagandist," www.ushmm.org/wlc/en/article.php?ModuleId=10007667

1170. Saïd K. Aburish, Arafat: From Defender to Dictator. London: Bloomsbury Publishing, 1998, p. 16.

1171. Daniel Pipes, "How Many Muslims in the United States?" Apr. 22, 2003 updated Jan. 6, 2016, www.danielpipes.org/blog/2003/04/how-many-muslims-in-the-united-states

1172. CN8 Your Morning, Comcast, Pennsylvania, New Jersey, and New England cable channel. On the website of "Walid Shoebat—Former PLO Terrorist" www.shoebat.com/media/cn8_2006_01.wmv Shoebat has appeared on CNN News International, CNN USA, Fox News' O'Reilly Factor, has testified on Capitol Hill, and is author of Why I Left Jihad: The Root of Terrorism and the Return of Radical Islam, New York: Top Executive Media, 2005.

1173. Discover the Networks, COUNCIL ON AMERICAN-ISLAMIC RELATIONS (CAIR), www.discoverthenetworks.org/printgroupProfile.asp?grpid=6176

1174. Stephen Coughlin, (2015-05-04), Catastrophic Failure: Blindfolding America in the Face of Jihad (Kindle Locations 4452-13726). Center for Security Policy Press. Kindle Edition.

1175. Coughlin, Stephen (2015-05-04), Catastrophic Failure: Blindfolding America in the Face of Jihad (Kindle Location 6673). Center for Security Policy Press. Kindle Edition.

1176. As reported by the San Ramon Valley Herald. Cited in "CAIR: 'Moderate' friends of terror" by Daniel Pipes, New York Post April 22, 2002 www.danielpipes.org/article/394 Quotable Quotes, Clarion Project, www.clarionproject.org/content/omar-ahmad

1177. "CAIR, The American Muslim Council, MPAC, and the American Muslim Alliance work together under the name of the American Muslim Political Coordinating Council." Andrew Rippin, The Islamic World. New York: Routledge, 2013, p. 140.

1178. Coughlin, Stephen (2015-05-04), Catastrophic Failure: Blindfolding America in the Face of Jihad (Kindle Locations 10680-10682). Center for Security Policy Press. Kindle Edition.

1179. Human Rights Watch, January 2006, vol. 18, no. 1, p. 20.

1180. Ali, Ayaan Hirsi (2015-03-24), Heretic: Why Islam Needs a Reformation Now (p. 5). HarperCollins. Kindle Edition. "Why the U.A.E. is calling 2 American groups terrorists," by Adam Taylor, Washington Post, November 17, 2014, www.washingtonpost.com/news/worldviews/wp/2014/11/17/why-the-u-a-e-is-calling-2-american-groups-terrorists/ Perry Chiaramonte, "US group CAIR named terrorist organization by United Arab Emirates," Fox News, November 17, 2014, www.foxnews.com/us/2014/11/17/us-group-cair-added-to-terror-list-by-united-arab-emirates.html

1181. In The United States Court of Appeals for the Fourth Circuit, No. 07-4778, United States of America, Plaintiff-Appellee, V. Sabri Benkahla Defendant-Appellant on Appeal from The United States District Court for the Eastern District of Virginia Alexandria Division The Honorable James C. Cacheris, District Judge Brief for the United States, p. 58 www.investigativeproject.org/documents/case_docs/542.pdf

1182. The Muslim Brotherhood (author), "The Muslim Brotherhood. An Explanatory Memorandum On the General Strategic Goal for the Group In North America," 5/22/1991 www.investigativeproject.org/documents/misc/20.pdf

1183. Osama bin Laden, "Complete Text Of Sheikh Osama Bin Laden's Latest Message To Ummah May 12, 2004." Originally downloaded from Jihad Unspun, a militant Islamic website. www.mail-archive.com/tumpat@yahoogroups.com/msg00023.html

1184. Abu Abdullah Usama bin Laden, "Declaration Of War Against The Americans Occupying The Land Of The Two Holy Places," August 26, 1996. Retrieved from the World Wide Web May 05, 2004 www.intellnet.org/documents/300/080/382.htm

1185. The Muslim Brotherhood (author), "The Muslim Brotherhood. An Explanatory Memorandum On the General Strategic Goal for the Group In North America," 5/22/1991 www.investigativeproject.org/documents/misc/20.pdf

1186. Ali A. Mazrui, "Islamic Doctrine and the Politics of Induced Fertility Change: An African Perspective." *Population and Development Review*, Vol. 20, Supplement: The New Politics of Population: Conflict and Consensus in Family Planning, (1994), pp. 121–134.

1187. Belgium was consolidated as an independent nation in 1830. Wikipedia, "Belgium—History." en.wikipedia.org/wiki/Belgium#History. Germany was united as a nation in 1871. Wikipedia, "Germany—German Empire." en.wikipedia.org/wiki/Germany#German_Empire_.281871.E2.80.931918.29

1188. Dr. Ali Muhammad Naqvi, "Islam and Nationalism," Islamic Propagation Organization *Translated by:* Dr. Alaedin Pazargadi. al-islam.org/islamandnationalism/10.htm

1189. Sudinfo.be, "45% des détenus des prisons belges sont de confession musulmane" (45% of inmates in Belgian prisons are Muslim), May 18, 2013, www.sudinfo.be/726092/article/actualite/belgique/2013-05-17/45-des-detenus-des-prisons-belges-sont-de-confession-musulmane

1190. Sudinfo.be, "45% des détenus des prisons belges sont de confession musulmane" (45% of inmates in Belgian prisons are Muslim), May 18, 2013, www.sudinfo.be/726092/article/actualite/belgique/2013-05-17/45-des-detenus-des-prisons-belges-sont-de-confession-musulmane

1191. "Don't dismiss suicide bombers as madmen," *Daily Mail*, no date, www.dailymail.co.uk/news/article-179112/Dont-dismiss-suicide-bombers-madmen.html

1192. Theresa Perry, *Teaching Malcolm X: Popular Culture and Literacy*. Abingdon, Oxon, UK: Routledge, Jan 2, 2014

1193. "What Malcolm X read in prison," Tue 13 Jul 2010 by abagond, abagond.wordpress.com/2010/07/13/what-malcolm-x-read-in-prison/

1194. "What Malcolm X read in prison," Tue 13 Jul 2010 by abagond, abagond.wordpress.com/2010/07/13/what-malcolm-x-read-in-prison/

1195. Internet Movie Firearms Data Base, Malcolm X, www.imfdb.org/wiki/Malcolm_X#M2_Carbine

1196. Introduction by Imam Benjamin Karim, in Malcolm X, *The End of White World Supremacy: Four Speeches*. New York: Arcade Publishing, Inc., 2011.

1197. Wayne Drash, "Malcolm X killer freed after 44 years," CNN, April 28, 2010 9:02 a.m. EDT, www.cnn.com/2010/CRIME/04/26/malcolmx.killer/

1198. Dr. Wesley Muhammad—Guest Columnist, Master W. Fard Muhammad and FBI COINTELPRO, The Final Call, Jan 4, 2010 — 2:51:44 p.m., www.finalcall.com/artman/publish/perspectives_1/article_6699.shtml

1199. Kambiz GhaneaBassiri, *Competing Visions of Islam in the United States: A Study of Los Angeles*, Santa Barbara, CA: Greenwood Publishing Group, 1997, pp. 150–151.

1200. Federal Bureau of Investigation, Prison Radicalization: The Environment, the Threat, and the Response Testimony of Donald Van Duyn Deputy Assistant Director, Counterterrorism Division Federal Bureau of Investigation to the Senate Committee on Homeland Security and Governmental Affairs and Related Agencies, Washington, D.C. September 19, 2006, www.fbi.gov/news/testimony/prison-radicalization-the-environment-the-threatand-the-response

1201. Federal Bureau of Investigation, Prison Radicalization: The Environment, the Threat, and the Response Testimony of Donald Van Duyn Deputy Assistant Director, Counterterrorism Division Federal Bureau of Investigation to the Senate Committee on Homeland Security and Governmental Affairs and Related Agencies, Washington, D.C. September 19, 2006, www.fbi.gov/news/testimony/prison-radicalization-the-environment-the-threatand-the-response

1202. Federal Bureau of Investigation, Prison Radicalization: The Environment, the Threat, and the Response Testimony of Donald Van Duyn Deputy Assistant Director, Counterterrorism Division Federal Bureau of Investigation to the Senate Committee on Homeland Security and Governmental Affairs and Related Agencies, Washington, D.C. September 19, 2006, www.fbi.gov/news/testimony/prison-radicalization-the-environment-the-threatand-the-response

1203. Federal Bureau of Investigation, Prison Radicalization: The Environment, the Threat, and the Response Testimony of Donald Van Duyn Deputy Assistant Director, Counterterrorism Division Federal Bureau of Investigation to the Senate Committee on Homeland Security and Governmental Affairs and Related Agencies, Washington, D.C. September 19, 2006, www.fbi.gov/news/testimony/prison-radicalization-the-environment-the-threatand-the-response

1204. Stephen Levy, "Radical Muslims recruit criminals in U.S. prisons — Recent attempted attacks highlight the threat," *The Washington Times*, Wednesday, June 15, 2011, www.washingtontimes.com/news/2011/jun/15/radical-muslims-recruit-criminals-in-us-prisons/?page=all
For concrete examples of American prisoners who have traveled overseas to be trained in jihad, see: *The Hill*, June 15, 2011, 03:29 p.m. "The threat of Muslim radicalization in U.S. prisons," by Rep. Peter King (R-N.Y.), thehill.com/blogs/congress-blog/homeland-security/166557-the-threat-of-muslimradicalization-in-us-prisons#

1205. "al-Qaeda training manuals identify America's prisoners as candidates for conversion" This document is a research report submitted to the U.S. Department of Justice. This report has not been published by the Department. Opinions or points of view expressed are those of the author(s) and do not necessarily reflect the official position or policies of the U.S. Department of Justice. Document Title: Terrorist Recruitment in American Correctional Institutions: An Exploratory Study of Non-Traditional Faith Groups Final Report Author(s): Mark S. Hamm, Ph.D. Document No.: 220957 Date Received: December 2007 Award Number: Commissioned Report The author(s) shown below used Federal funds provided by the U.S. Department of Justice and prepared the following final report: www.ncjrs.gov/pdffiles1/nij/grants/220957.pdf See also: www.americanthinker.com/articles/2014/12/prisons_are_breeding_grounds_for_jihadists.html
American Thinker December 5, 2014 Prisons are breeding grounds for jihadists By Carol Brown. The idea that al-Qaeda targets American prison inmates for recruitment is also supported by: John Pistole Assistant Director Federal Bureau of Investigation Before the Senate Judiciary Committee, Subcommittee on Terrorism, Technology, and Homeland Security Washington D.C. October 14, 2003, www.fbi.gov/news/testimony/terrorist-recruitment-in-prisons-and-the-recent-arrests-related-to-guantanamo-bay-detainees

1206. Federal Bureau of Investigation, Prison Radicalization: The Environment, the Threat, and the Response Testimony of Donald Van Duyn Deputy Assistant Director, Counterterrorism Division Federal Bureau of Investigation to the Senate Committee on Homeland Security and Governmental Affairs and Related Agencies, Washington, D.C. September 19, 2006, www.fbi.gov/news/testimony/prison-radicalization-the-environment-the-threatand-the-response

1207. Joy Brighton, "U.S. Prisons Churning Out Thousands of Radicalized Inmates," *Daily Caller*, November 21, 2014, dailycaller.com/2014/11/21/u-s-prisons-churning-out-thousands-of-radicalized-inmates/

1208. Joy Brighton, "U.S. Prisons Churning Out Thousands Of Radicalized Inmates," *Daily Caller*, November 21, 2014, dailycaller.com/2014/11/21/u-s-prisonschurning-out-thousands-ofradicalized-inmates/
Joy Brighton is the author of the book *Sharia-ism is Here*.

1208. *Daily Caller*, "U.S. Prisons Churning Out Thousands Of Radicalized Inmates" Joy Brighton is the author of the book *Sharia-ism is Here*, 12:19 p.m. 11/21/2014 dailycaller.com/2014/11/21/u-s-prisonschurning-out-thousands-of-radicalized-inmates/

1209. Joy Brighton, "U.S. Prisons Churning Out Thousands of Radicalized Inmates," *Daily Caller*, November 21, 2014, dailycaller.com/2014/11/21/u-s-prisons-churningout-thousands-of-radicalizedinmates/

1210. Joy Brighton, "U.S. Prisons Churning Out Thousands of Radicalized Inmates," *Daily Caller*, November 21, 2014, dailycaller.com/2014/11/21/u-s-prisons-churningout-thousands-of-radicalizedinmates/

1211. Joy Brighton, "U.S. Prisons Churning Out Thousands of Radicalized Inmates," *Daily Caller*, November 21, 2014, dailycaller.com/2014/11/21/u-s-prisons-churningout-thousands-of-radicalizedinmates/

1212. "Coming to America: Saudi Hate TV," By STEVEN STALINSKY | October 26, 2005, New York: *The Sun*, www.nysun.com/foreign/coming-to-america-saudi-hate-tv/22097/

1213. After his "education" by Farrakhan, in May and June of 1989, Professor Griff, the "Minister of Information" of Public Enemy, "told the Washington Times, 'The Jews are wicked. And we can prove this.' He held the Jews responsible for 'the majority of wickedness that goes on across the globe.'" Anti-Defamation League, ADL Research Report, Louis Farrakhan: The Campaign to Manipulate Public Opinion, A Study in the Packaging of Bigotry, New York, Anti-Defamation League of B'nai B'rith, 1998, p. 21, archive.adl.org/issue_nation_of_islam/reports/packaging.pdf. For Farrakhan's testimony on his rap recruitment, see "Part 2 of the TSDtv Exclusive Interview with Minister Louis Farrakhan of the Nation of Islam, Farrakhan talks about hip-hop, NWA, the biopic *Straight Outta Compton*, the violent side effects of gangsta rap, and why he makes a point of reaching out to hip-hop artists." www.youtube.com/o28b6f6d-4e1a-4a6c-9d27-5f41525b1313
The protocols of the Elders of Zion is distributed in the United States by Louis Farrakhan's Nation of Islam according to: The "Protocols of the Elders of Zion" In the 21st Century Guest Publication by Arthur Wailer, Holocaust Education Archive Research Team, www.holocaustresearchproject.org/essays&editorials/protocols.html

1214. Esther Webman, *The Global Impact of the Protocols of the Elders of Zion: A Century-Old Myth*. London: Routledge, Mar. 29, 2012, p. 243. The "Protocols of the Elders of Zion" In the 21st Century Guest Publication by Arthur Wailer, Holocaust Education Archive Research Team, www.holocaustresearchproject.org/essays&editorials/protocols.html

1215. For Farrakhan's proud association with Henry Ford's virulent anti-Semitism, see: February 25, 2014, "Farrakhan Compares Himself To Henry Ford In Detroit," ADL, blog.adl.org/anti-semitism/farrakhan-saviours-day-henry-ford-jews-detroit. And for Chuck D's reliance on The International Jew, see: John Leland, "Do the Right Thing," *Spin* Magazine, September 1989, p. 72.

1216. Thomas Fuchs, *A Concise Biography of Adolf Hitler*. New York: Berkeley Books, 2000.

1217. Adam Parfrey, *Extreme Islam: Anti-American Propaganda of Muslim Fundamentalism*. Port Townsend, WA: Feral House, 2015.

1218. Qur'an, 2:65, 5:60, and 7:166, The Holy Qur'an. Translation by Abdullah Yusufali. Complete online text. Retrieved March 20, 2005, from the World Wide Web www.wam.umd.edu/~stwright/rel/islam/ and The Noble Qur'an, quran.com/search?q=apes "The Jews, who are the nation of pigs and monkeys, are nothing but a source of evil, corruption, tribulation and war. ...Our war against them is continuous." Abdul-Azeez Al-Qaari, "The Menace of the Jews." Translated by Hazem Ragab. Mecca: Alminbar.com—Alminbar.com—the Orator's garden and the Muslim's provision. Here you will find a variety of material to help you prepare for your sermons. Retrieved January 6, 2007, from the World Wide Web www.alminbar.com/khutbaheng/819.htm

1219. "Farrakhan abroad Rogues tour: Enemies of freedom are NOI leader's new friends." *Baltimore Sun*, February 18, 1996, articles.baltimoresun.com/1996-02-18/news/1996049002_1_farrakhan-sudan-islam.

1220. Reed Irvine and Cliff Kincaid, "The Nation of Islam And Violence," Accuracy in Media, November 12, 2002, www.aim.org/media-monitor/the-nation-of-islam-and-violence/

1221. Reed Irvine and Cliff Kincaid, "The Nation of Islam And Violence," Accuracy in Media, November 12, 2002, www.aim.org/media-monitor/the-nation-of-islam-and-violence/

1222. Reed Irvine and Cliff Kincaid, "The Nation of Islam And Violence," Accuracy in Media, November 12, 2002, www.aim.org/media-monitor/the-nation-of-islam-and-violence/

1223. Amy Kaslow, "Nation of Islam Extends Its Reach Behind Prison Walls—Followers preach provocative mix of discipline, separatism," *The Christian Science Monitor*, May 20, 1996, www.csmonitor.com/1996/0520/052096.feat.cover.1.html The Nation of Islam may have begun its practice of "fishing for the dead," seeking converts in prisons, as early as 1946, when NOI leader Elijah Muhammad was released from jail after a three-year term for draft evasion. Mattias Gardell, *In the Name of Elijah Muhammad: Louis Farrakhan and The Nation of Islam*. Durham, North Carolina: Duke University Press, 1996, pp. 63, 65, 102. In addition, The Nation of Islam has a full-time Nation of Islam Prison Reform Ministry.

1224. US Prison Culture, Black Muslims, the NOI and American Prisons..., usprisonculture.com, July 7, 2016, www.usprisonculture.com/blog/2012/07/16/black-muslims-and-american-prisons/

1225. Christiane Timmerman, *Faith-based Radicalism: Christianity, Islam and Judaism—Between Constructive Activism and Destructive Fanaticism*. New York: Peter Lang, 2007, p. 212.

1226. Matthew Holehouse, Henry Samuel, "Terrorist ringleader got into EU as 'refugee' Thousands of jihadists not being monitored," *The Telegraph*, London, 1:02AM GMT 20 Nov 2015, www.telegraph.co.uk/news/uknews/terrorism-in-the-uk/12006892/International-manhunt-underway-after-Frenchpolice-let-Paris-attacks-suspect-slip-throughtheir-fingers.html

1227. Elsa Buchanan, "Paris attacks: Ringleader Abdelhamid Abaaoud's 15 year-old brother Younes 'on his way back for revenge,'" IBT (International Business Times), December 3, 2015 09:42 GMT, www.ibtimes.co.uk/paris-attacks-ringleader-abdelhamid-abaaouds-brother-younes-his-way-back-revenge-1531616.

1228. Islamic State, "Urgent: Statement about the Blessed Paris Invasion on the French Crusaders," townhall.com/tipsheet/katiepavlich/2015/11/14/isis-claims-responsibility-for-paris-terror-attack-n2080755 downloaded November 14, 2015.

1229. The Muslim Brotherhood, An Explanatory Memorandum On the General Strategic Goal for the Group In North America 5/22/1991, p. 7, www.investigativeproject.org/documents/misc/20.pdf

1230. "It is not for a Prophet that he should have prisoners of war (and free them with ransom) until he had made a great slaughter (among his enemies) in the land." Qur'an, Verse (8:67), Mohsin Khan Translation, Quran: The Quranic Arabic Corpus, corpus.quran.com/translation.jsp?chapter=8&verse=67

1231. Declan Walsh, "Salmaan Taseer, Aasia Bibi and Pakistan's struggle with extremism," *The Guardian* January 8, 2011, last modified on Saturday 9 January 2016, www.theguardian.com/world/2011/jan/08/salmaan-taseer-blasphemy-pakistan-bibi 2-9-2016

1232. Asia Bibi, Anne-Isabelle Tollet, *Blasphemy: A Memoir: Sentenced to Death Over a Cup of Water*. Chicago: Chicago Review Press, 2013, pp. 77–78.

1233. Asia Bibi, Anne-Isabelle Tollet, *Blasphemy: A Memoir: Sentenced to Death Over a Cup of Water*. Chicago: Chicago Review Press, 2013, pp. 12–13.

1234. Asia Bibi, Anne-Isabelle Tollet, *Blasphemy: A Memoir: Sentenced to Death Over a Cup of Water*. Chicago: Chicago Review Press, 2013, p. 16.

1235. Mary Zeiss Stange, Carol K. Oyster, Jane E. Sloan, *The Multimedia Encyclopedia of Women in Today's World*. SAGE Publications, Jan 9, 2013, p. 94.

1236. Asher John, "No home for the 'impure' in Pakistan National," *Pakistan Today*, March 9, 2013, www.pakistantoday.com.pk/2013/03/09/national/no-home-for-the-impure-inpakistan/ 2-18-2016

1237. Ayatollah Khomeini, *Sayings of the Ayatollah Khomeini*. New York: Bantam Books, 1980, p. 51.

1238. Pakistan's Federal Interior Minister Chaudhry Nisar Ali Khan in 2015 called the use of the word kafir "hate speech." Mateen Haider, State will take action against those calling others infidels: Nisar, Dawn.com, September 07, 2015 09:55 PM,, www.dawn.com/news/1205480, 2-18-2016

1239. Bernardo Cervellera, Your signature to save Asia Bibi and Pakistan, AsiaNews.it, 11/15/2010, www.asianews.it/news-en/Your-signature-to-save-Asia-Bibi-and-Pakistan-19997.html 2-18-2016

1240. The calculation that Pakistan is 40% pluralist and 60% fundamentalist is a very, very rough approximation. Apparently, there have been no polls on the subject. Here are a few of the facts from which these numbers are derived. As of 2013, 84% of Pakistanis "favor enshrining sharia as official law." (Pew Research Center, April 30, 2013, "The World's Muslims: Religion, Politics and Society," p. 9, www.pewforum.org/files/2013/04/worlds-muslims-religion-politics-society-full-report.pdf 2-18-2016.) 64 percent of Pakistanis supported the death penalty for people who leave Islam. (Akhilesh Pillalamarri, "Blasphemy and Religious Intolerance in Pakistan—Recent violence against the Ahmadi minority is part of a disturbing trend," *The Diplomat*, August 07, 2014, thediplomat.com/2014/08/blasphemy-andreligious-intolerance-in-pakistan/ 2-19-2016.) Max Fisher, "Majorities of Muslims in Egypt and Pakistan support the death penalty for leaving Islam," *The Washington Post*, May 1, 2013, www.washingtonpost.com/news/worldviews/wp/2013/05/01/64-percent-of-muslims-in-egypt and-pakistan-support-the-death-penalty-for-leaving-islam/ 2-19-2016. On the other hand, 40% of Pakistanis "worry about Islamic extremism." (Pew Research Center, APRIL 30, 2013, "The World's Muslims: Religion, Politics and Society," p. 30, www.pewforum.org/files/2013/04/muslims-religion-politics-society-full-report.pdf 2-18-2016.) There's more from the Pew Research Center's 2013 report on The World's Muslims. On the liberal side, 96% of Pakistanis say it's good that others are free to practice their faith (p. 63). 70% say a woman should decide if she wears a veil p. 92. 64% say Sharia should apply to Muslims only (34% say it should apply to everyone) p. 48, and only 13% think suicide bombings against civilians are justified in defense of Islam, p. 70. Not bad, right? On the extremist side, 75% believe stoning should be the punishment for adultery p. 54. 81% of Pakistanis see "Sharia as the Revealed Word of God," p. 42. 61% of Pakistanis say that there is only one interpretation of Sharia p. 44. 91% think it's bad that the country's laws do not follow sharia closely p. 58. And 56% favor a strong leader over democracy. Only 29% prefer democracy p. 60. Most important is the role of the prophet as an absolute model of righteousness. 50% of Pakistanis say they follow the prophet's example as given in the hadith and in the sunnah a lot. Just 37% say they only follow Muhammad's example a little. P. 102. (Pew Research Center, "The World's Muslims: Religion, Politics and Society," April 30, 2013, p. 30, www.pewforum.org/files/2013/04/worldsmuslims-religion-politics-society-full-report.pdf 2-18-2016.) That's the founder effect.

1241. "Mumbai Terror Attacks Fast Facts," CNN Library, Updated 11:57 AM ET, Wed November 4, 2015, www.cnn.com/2013/09/18/world/asia/mumbai-terror-attacks/, 2-19-2016

1242. "Pakistan's high profile blasphemy cases in the last 63 years," Dawn, December 8, 2010, www.dawn.com/news/589587/high-profile-blasphemy-cases-in-the-last-63-years 2-10-2016

1243. "Gojra attack survivor recounts horror," Dawn, August 04, 2009 12:00 AM, www.dawn.com/news/963693/gojra-attacksurvivor-recounts-horror

1244. Marie Desnos, "La Mort N'est Pas Une Solution" Le Combat D'une Française Pour Une Pakistanaise, Paris Match, Le 08 mars 2015, www.parismatch.com/Actu/International/Seul-un-elan-international-pourra-sauver-Asia-Bibi-721332 2-19-2016

1245. Asia Bibi, Anne-Isabelle Tollet, Blasphemy: A Memoir: Sentenced to Death Over a Cup of Water. Chicago: Chicago Review Press, 2013, pp. 27-28.

1246. Asia Bibi, Anne-Isabelle Tollet, Blasphemy: A Memoir: Sentenced to Death Over a Cup of Water. Chicago: Chicago Review Press, 2013, pp. 11–12.

1247. Grewia asiatica 'Sherbet Berry,' Agri-Starts, www.agristarts.com/index.cfm/fuseaction/plants.plantDetail/plant_ID/312/index.htm

1248. Asia Bibi, Anne-Isabelle Tollet, Blasphemy: A Memoir: Sentenced to Death Over a Cup of Water. Chicago: Chicago Review Press, 2013, p. 11.

1249. Asia Bibi, Anne-Isabelle Tollet, Blasphemy: A Memoir: Sentenced to Death Over a Cup of Water. Chicago: Chicago Review Press, 2013, p. 16.

1250. Asia Bibi, Anne-Isabelle Tollet, Blasphemy: A Memoir: Sentenced to Death Over a Cup of Water. Chicago: Chicago Review Press, 2013, p. 17.

1251. Asia Bibi, Anne-Isabelle Tollet, Blasphemy: A Memoir: Sentenced to Death Over a Cup of Water. Chicago: Chicago Review Press, 2013, p. 17

1252. Asia Bibi, Anne-Isabelle Tollet, Blasphemy: A Memoir: Sentenced to Death Over a Cup of Water. Chicago: Chicago Review Press, 2013, pp. 20–21.

1253. Declan Walsh, "Salmaan Taseer, Aasia Bibi and Pakistan's struggle with extremism," The Guardian January 8, 2011, last modified on Saturday 9 January 2016, www.theguardian.com/world/2011/jan/08/salmaan-taseer-blasphemy-pakistan-bibi 2-9-2016

1254. According to Ibn Kathir, non-Muslims allowed to remain alive in Muslim territory must live in "humiliation, degradation and disgrace." Quoted in Coughlin, Stephen (2015-05-04), Catastrophic Failure: Blindfolding America in the Face of Jihad (Kindle Location 2776). Center for Security Policy Press. Kindle Edition. Keller, Reliance of the Traveller, Book O "Justice," at 011 "Non-Muslim Subjects of the Islamic State (Ahl Al-Dhimma)," at 011.5. "Nazir Bhatti said that its for information of Mufti Muneeb-ur-Rehman and all other Muslim groups and Islamic political parties in Pakistan that Christians are son of soil who voted for formation of Pakistan and deserve due share in resources of Pakistan not a treatment by Muslim majority towards them as 'Dhimmi' that Islamic laws which are for Muslims be enforced on them." Dr. Nazir S. Bhatti, "Implementation of blasphemy law on Asia Bibi is un-Islamic." Pakistan Christian Post, November 28, 2010, www.pakistanchristianpost.com/headlinenewsd.php?hnewsid=2453#sthash.yZSyZ7pk.dpuf Abdul-Kareem, "DHIMMI — Non-Muslims living in the Khilafah," Khilafah.com, 13th July 2015, www.khilafah.com/dhimmi-non-muslimsliving-in-the-khilafah-2/ 2-19-2016

1255. Says Asia Bibi, "Of course, when you're a Christian in Pakistan, you have to keep your head down. Some people see us as second-class citizens." Asia Bibi, Anne-Isabelle Tollet, Blasphemy: A Memoir: Sentenced to Death Over a Cup of Water. Chicago: Chicago Review Press, 2013, p. 3.

1256. "Christians have traditionally worked as cleaners and sweepers; many Muslims still consider them 'unclean.'" Declan Walsh, "Salmaan Taseer, Aasia Bibi and Pakistan's struggle with extremism," The Guardian January 8, 2011, Last modified on Saturday 9 January 2016, www.theguardian.com/world/2011/jan/08/salmaan-taseer-blasphemy-pakistan-bibi 2-9-2016

1257. "Haraam is that for which the one who does it will be punished and the one who abstains from it will be rewarded." "Islam Question and Answer," General Supervisor: Shaykh Muhammad Saalih al-Munajjid, 2000-09-25, islamqa.info/en/10887

1258. Asia Bibi, Anne-Isabelle Tollet, Blasphemy: A Memoir: Sentenced to Death Over a Cup of Water. Chicago: Chicago Review Press, 2013, pp. 19–20.

1259. Asia Bibi, Anne-Isabelle Tollet, *Blasphemy: A Memoir: Sentenced to Death Over a Cup of Water*. Chicago: Chicago Review Press, 2013, pp. 20-21.

1260. Declan Walsh, "Salmaan Taseer, Aasia Bibi and Pakistan's struggle with extremism," *The Guardian* January 8, 2011, last modified on Saturday 9 January 2016, www.theguardian.com/world/2011/jan/08/salmaan-taseer-blasphemy-pakistan-bibi 2-9-2016

1261. Qur'an 4:141, "never will Allah grant to the unbelievers a way (to triumph) over the believers." The Holy Qur'an. Translation by Abdullah Yusufali. Complete online text. Retrieved January 1998 from the Internet www.wam.umd.edu/~stwright/rel/islam/ Qur'an 9:33. "It is He who hath sent His apostle with guidance and religion of truth to proclaim it over all religions even though the pagans may detest (it)."
Qur'an 3:55. "I will make those who follow thee superior to those who reject Faith to the Day of Resurrection." The Holy Qur'an. Translation by Abdullah Yusufali. Complete online text. Retrieved January 1998 from the Internet www.wam.umd.edu/~stwright/rel/islam/

1262. Qur'an, 9:33, The Holy Qur'an. Translation by Abdullah Yusufali. Complete online text. Retrieved January 1998 from the Internet www.wam.umd.edu/~stwright/rel/islam/

1263. Syria crisis: ISIS imposes rules on Christians in Raqqa, 27 February 2014, www.bbc.com/news/world-middle-east-26366197 2-19-2016

1264. Qur'an 2:90. The Holy Qur'an. Translation by Abdullah Yusufali. Complete online text. Retrieved January 1998 from the Internet www.wam.umd.edu/~stwright/rel/islam/

1265. Take this statement from ISIS magazine *Dābiq* as an example: "And the Islamic State will continue to strike Russia until Shari'ah returns to all the lands of the Muslims usurped by the crusader Russians and until Russia pays the jizyah [the protection tax] in humiliation." The history of jihad in Bengal, *Dābiq*, issue 12, p. 84.

1266. Ayatollah Khomeini, *Sayings of the Ayatollah Khomeini*. New York: Bantam Books, 1980, p. 51.

1267. The Turks referred over and over again to Christians as "Christian dogs." It was not a flattering term. Especially once you realize that dogs, like unbelievers, are as impure as feces and urine in Allah's eyes. And that in the Hadith Muhammad ordered that nearly all dogs be killed. Thomas MacGill, "Travels in Turkey, Italy, and Russia during the Years 1803, 1804, 1805, and 1806, with an account of some of the Greek Islands," *The Annual Review*, and *History of Literature* for 1808, Volume 7, Issue 1, editor Arthur Aikin, London: Longman, Hurst, Rees, and Orme, 1809, p. 18. George Hunt, "Substance of a Speech delivered by Mr. George Hunt at the Ninth Anniversary of the Bristol Auxiliary Peace Society," *The Calumet: New Series of the Harbinger of Peace*, Volumes 1-2, Published under the direction of the American Peace Society, 1831–1834, New York: L.D. Dewey, 1831, p. 57.

1268. Qur'an 9:28, The Holy Qur'an. Translation by Abdullah Yusufali. Complete online text. Retrieved January 1998 from the Internet, www.wam.umd.edu/~stwright/rel/islam/

1269. Asia Bibi, Anne-Isabelle Tollet, *Blasphemy: A Memoir: Sentenced to Death Over a Cup of Water*. Chicago: Chicago Review Press, 2013, pp. 21–22.

1270. Declan Walsh, "Salmaan Taseer, Aasia Bibi and Pakistan's struggle with extremism," *The Guardian* January 8, 2011, last modified on Saturday 9 January 2016, www.theguardian.com/world/2011/jan/08/salmaan-taseer-blasphemy-pakistan-bibi 2-9-2016

1271. Web desk, "Report says over 35,000 madrassas operating in Pakistan," *Pakistan Today*, July 15, 2015, www.pakistantoday.com.pk/2015/07/31/national/report-says-over-35000-madrassasoperating-in-pakistan/ 2-19-2016 re: Umair Khalil, 'The Madrasa Conundrum — The state of religious education in Pakistan,' Umair Khalil is the lead researcher of the non-governmental research organisation, HIVE.

1272. David Rohde, "Pakistan's Terrorist Factory: Fact or Figment? Islamic schools resent and deny an official claim that they teach militancy to youth," Christian Science Monitor, April 14, 1995, www. csmonitor.com/1995/0414/14061.html 2-19-2016. See comment from sleepingnation, "Suicide Attack in Chakwal Kills 24," PK Politics, April 5, 2009, pkpolitics.com/2009/04/05/suicide-attack-in-chakwal-kills-24/ 2-19-2016
Sushant Sareen points out that Pakistan's state schools are even more effective at turning out suicide bombers than the Madrasas. ""Therefore [it] should come as no surprise that there are more jihadis coming out of the state school system than from the madrasas. A book on Jihad in Kashmir and Afghanistan by a young and very brave Pakistani journalist, Muhammad Amir Rana reveals some very startling facts about the jihad culture in Pakistan. Amir Rana's book unveils the impact of jihadi indoctrination of three generations of Pakistani children. He has examined the growth of madrasas inside Pakistan and has revealed statistics that show that the state schools are churning out far more jihadis than the madrasas. According to Amir Rana the list of martyrs from six jihadi organisations indicates that student martyrs from schools and colleges outnumbered those from madrasas by nearly five times. Amir Rana gives the example of the jihadi organisation Harkatul Mujahedin and writes: "It is a common impression about Harkatul Mujahedin that it is dominated by students of madrasas. My personal observation and the records of Harkatul Mujahedin indicate the opposite. I have met more than two dozen members of Harkatul Mujahedin in their offices at Kotli, Rawalakot, Dera Ghazi Khan and Karachi. Out of them, only 5 were from madrasas. Out of 800 martyrs of Harkatul Mujahedin, only 118 were from madrasas. Amir Rana has also interviewed some jihadis and their backgrounds only go to corroborate the role being played by the state schools in inculcating the spirit of jihad in children in Pakistan and indoctrinating them in the initial years to make sure that they turn into killing machines by the time they are out of school. The rest of the job is done by the jihadi organisations who impart them actual training and brainwash them to an extent that they turn into suicide bombers and fidayeen." Sushant Sareen, The Jihad Factory: Pakistan's Islamic Revolution in the Making. New Delhi: Har-Anand Publications, 2005, p. 36
1273. "Analysis: Madrassas, Saudi Time Bomb," Frontline, PBS, www.pbs.org/wgbh/pages/frontline/shows/saudi/analyses/madrassas.html 2-19-2016

1274. Wikipedia, "Hijackers in the September 11 attacks," en.wikipedia.org/wiki/Hijackers_in_the_September_11_attacks#Hijacked_aircraft, 2-23-2016.
1275. Sushant Sareen, The Jihad Factory: Pakistan's Islamic Revolution in the Making. New Delhi: Har-Anand Publications, 2005, p. 36.
1276. Declan Walsh, "Salmaan Taseer, Aasia Bibi and Pakistan's struggle with extremism," The Guardian January 8, 2011, last modified on Saturday 9 January 2016, www.theguardian.com/world/2011/jan/08/salmaan-taseer-blasphemy-pakistan-bibi 2-9-2016
1277. Rob Crilly in Islamabad and Aoun Sahi in Lahore, "Christian woman sentenced to death in Pakistan 'for blasphemy,'" The Telegraph, November 9, 2010, www.telegraph.co.uk/news/religion/8120142/Christian-woman-sentenced-to-death-in-Pakistan-for-blasphemy.html 2-12-2016
1278. Hal St. John, 'Ten million people now want to kill me,' Catholic Herald, June 4, 2012, www.catholicherald.co.uk/news/2012/06/14/ten-million-people-now-want-to-kill-me/ 2-12-2016
1279. Rob Crilly in Islamabad and Aoun Sahi in Lahore, "Christian woman sentenced to death in Pakistan 'for blasphemy,'" The Telegraph, November 9, 2010, www.telegraph.co.uk/news/religion/8120142/Christian-woman-sentenced-to-death-in-Pakistan-for-blasphemy.html 2-12-2016
1280. Rob Crilly in Islamabad and Aoun Sahi in Lahore, "Christian woman sentenced to death in Pakistan 'for blasphemy,'" The Telegraph, November 9, 2010, www.telegraph.co.uk/news/religion/8120142/Christian-woman-sentenced-to-death-in-Pakistan-for-blasphemy.html 2-12-2016
1281. Asia Bibi, Anne-Isabelle Tollet, Blasphemy: A Memoir: Sentenced to Death Over a Cup of Water. Chicago: Chicago Review Press, 2013, p. 33.
1282. Jason M. Breslow, "Outlawed In Pakistan— In Pakistan, a Delicate Balance Between Religious and Secular Law," Frontline, PBS, May 28, 2013 www.pbs.org/wgbh/frontline/article/in-pakistan-a-delicate-balance-between-religious-and-secular-law/ 2-19-2016
1283. Rachel Scott, The Challenge of Political Islam: Non-Muslims and the Egyptian State. Palo Alto, CA: Stanford University Press, 2010. Mark Walia, A Tale of Two Cultures: Islam and the West, Lee's Summit, MO: Father's Press LLC, 2012.

1284. [Bukhari 3,48,826] Muhammad asked, "Is not the value of a woman's eye-witness testimony half that of a man's?" A woman said, "Yes." He said, "That is because a woman's mind is deficient." quoted in *Sharia Law for Non-Muslims*, Dr. Bill Warner, CSPI International, Oct. 18, 2015 pp. 11-12. "If taken together, the laws discussed above point to a single demoralizing fact, namely the exclusion of women's evidence over a very wide field, tantamount to cutting women's worth by half. While women's testimony is not admissible for maximum punishment in theft, adultery and rape under the Hudood Ordinance, it is reduced to circumstantial evidence in matters relating to murder or bodily injury in the proposed Law of Qisas and Diyat. Finally, one woman alone cannot testify in matters implying financial and future obligation, according to the Law of Evidence. Which are the matters left (if any) ask women, where a woman's evidence will be acknowledged as that of a responsible human being?" *Encyclopaedia of Women in South Asia: Pakistan*, New Delhi: Gyan Publishing House, 2004, p. 50.

1285. Paul A. Marshall, Lela Gilbert, Nina Shea, *Persecuted: The Global Assault on Christians*. Nashville, TN: Thomas Nelson Inc., 2013, p. 195.

1286. Paul A. Marshall, Lela Gilbert, Nina Shea, *Persecuted: The Global Assault on Christians*. Nashville, TN: Thomas Nelson Inc., 2013, p. 195.

1287. Rob Crilly in Islamabad and Aoun Sahi in Lahore, "Christian woman sentenced to death in Pakistan 'for blasphemy,'" *The Telegraph*, November 9, 2010, www.telegraph.co.uk/news/religion/8120142/Christian-woman-sentenced-to-death-in-Pakistan-for-blasphemy.html 2-12-2016

1288. Hal St John, 'Ten million people now want to kill me,' *Catholic Herald*, June 14, 2012, www.catholicherald.co.uk/news/2012/06/14/ten-million-people-now-want-to-kill-me/ 2-12-2016

1289. Declan Walsh, Salmaan Taseer, "Aasia Bibi and Pakistan's struggle with extremism," *The Guardian* January 8, 2011, Last modified on Saturday 9 January 2016, www.theguardian.com/world/2011/jan/08/salmaan-taseer-blasphemy-pakistan-bibi 2-9-2016

1290. A. Guillaume, *The Life of Muhammad: A Translation of Ibn Ishaq's Sirat Rasul Allah*. New York: Oxford University Press, 1955, eighteenth printing, 2004, p. 369. See also al-Tabari, *The History of al-Tabari*: English translation of "at Tareekh al-Tabari." Albany: State University of New York Press. Volume VII, p. 97.

1291. Kunwar Khuldune Shahid, "Blasphemy and the Case of Mumtaz Qadri Can Pakistan's judiciary take a stand against religious extremism?" *The Diplomat*, March 02, 2015, thediplomat.com/2015/03/blasphemy-and-the-case-of-mumtaz-qadri/

1292. For Shehrbano Taseer's Tweets, see: twitter.com/shehrbanotaseer, 2-19-2016

1293. Declan Walsh, "Salmaan Taseer, Aasia Bibi and Pakistan's struggle with extremism," *The Guardian* January 8, 2011, Last modified on Saturday 9 January 2016, www.theguardian.com/world/2011/jan/08/salmaan-taseer-blasphemy-pakistan-bibi 2-9-2016

1294. Hassan Choudary, "Taseer's remarks about blasphemy law," *The Express Tribune*, Pakistan, January 5, 2011, tribune.com.pk/story/99277/taseers-remarks-about-blasphemy-law/, 2-23-2016

1295. Declan Walsh, "Salmaan Taseer, Aasia Bibi and Pakistan's struggle with extremism," *The Guardian* January 8, 2011, Last modified on Saturday 9 January 2016, www.theguardian.com/world/2011/jan/08/salmaan-taseer-blasphemy-pakistan-bibi 2-9-2016

1296. Declan Walsh, "Salmaan Taseer, Aasia Bibi and Pakistan's struggle with extremism," *The Guardian* January 8, 2011, Last modified on Saturday 9 January 2016, www.theguardian.com/world/2011/jan/08/salmaan-taseer-blasphemy-pakistan-bibi 2-9-2016

1297. "Religious leaders demand Taseer's dismissal," *Dawn*, December 30, 2010 11:38 p.m., www.dawn.com/news/595003/religious-leaders-demand-taseers-dismissal-2 2-19-2016. Mushtaq Bashar, Governor Punjab — Aasia Bibi Press Conference, Tune.pk, tune.pk/video/5674669/governor-punjab-aasia-bibi-press-conference 2-9-2016. Hassan Choudary, Taseer's remarks about blasphemy law, *The Express Tribune*, Pakistan, January 5, 2011 remarks-about-blasphemy-law/ 2-19-2016. Ayesha Tammy Haq, Interview: Salmaan Taseer, Governor of Punjab, *Newsline*, Pakistan, www.newslinemagazine.com/2010/12/interview-salmaan-taseer-governor-of-punjab/ 2-20-2016. Blasphemy convict gives mercy plea to Taseer, *Dawn*, November 20, 2010 09:52 PM, www.dawn.com/news/583850/blasphemy-convict-gives-mercy-plea-to-taseer-2 2-20-2016 For another video of the press conference, see: Governor Punjab — Aasia Bibi Press Conference, uploaded November 22, 2010, www.youtube.com/watch?v=HxvlLpSy4Bl 2-20-2016

1298. Reza Sayah, "Pakistan president urged not to pardon Christian woman," CNN, November 24, 2010 11:15 a.m. EST, www.cnn.com/2010/WORLD/asiapcf/11/24/pakistan.christian/ 2-12-2016

1299. Jibran Khan, "Lahore High Court issues stay order in Asia Bibi's appeal against blasphemy sentence," AsiaNews.it, Rome (says Wikipedia, AsiaNews.it is an official press agency of the Roman Catholic Pontifical Institute for Foreign Missions), www.asianews.it, 12/06/2010, www.asianews.it/news-en/Lahore-High-Courtissues-stay-order-in-Asia-Bibi%E2%80%99sappeal-against-blasphemy-sentence-20187.html 2-20-2016

1300. Declan Walsh, "Salmaan Taseer, Aasia Bibi and Pakistan's struggle with extremism," *The Guardian* January 8, 2011, Last modified on Saturday 9 January 2016, www.theguardian.com/world/2011/jan/08/salmaan-taseer-blasphemy-pakistan-bibi 2-9-2016

1301. Orla Guerin, "Pakistani Christian Asia Bibi 'has price on her head,'" BBC News, 7 December 2010, www.bbc.com/news/world-south-asia-11930849, 2-12-2016

1302. Hal St. John, 'Ten million people now want to kill me,' *Catholic Herald*, June 14, 2012, www.catholicherald.co.uk/news/2012/06/14/ten-million-people-now-want-to-kill-me/ 2-13-2016

1303. Carol Brown, "Who is Asia Bibi, and why should we care?" *American Thinker*, November 3, 2015, www.americanthinker.com/blog/2015/11/who_is_asia_bibi_and_why_should_we_care.html#ixzz405mCxrFi 2-13-2016

1304. "Sen. Rand Paul Speaks About Worldwide War On Christianity At 2013 Values Voter Summit," Real Clear Politics, October 11, 2013, www.realclearpolitics.com/video/2013/10/11/sen_rand_paul_speaks_about_worldwide_war_on_christianity_at_2013_values_voter_summit.html 2-13-2016

1305. Declan Walsh, "Salmaan Taseer, Aasia Bibi and Pakistan's struggle with extremism," *The Guardian* January 8, 2011, Last modified on Saturday 9 January 2016, www.theguardian.com/world/2011/jan/08/salmaan-taseer-blasphemy-pakistan-bibi 2-9-2016

1306. Declan Walsh, "Salmaan Taseer, Aasia Bibi and Pakistan's struggle with extremism," *The Guardian* January 8, 2011, Last modified on Saturday 9 January 2016, www.theguardian.com/world/2011/jan/08/salmaan-taseer-blasphemy-pakistan-bibi 2-9-2016

1307. "Pakistan minorities minister killed — Pakistani Taliban claim responsibility for the shooting attack that killed Shahbaz Bhatti, the only Christian minister," 02 Mar 2011, Al Jazeera, www.aljazeera.com/news/asia/2011/03/20113271659294319.html%5D 2-20-2016

1308. Orla Guerin, "Pakistani Christian Asia Bibi 'has price on her head,'" BBC News, 7 December 2010, www.bbc.com/news/world-south-asia-11930849 2-12-2016

1309. Julie McCarthy, "Christian's Death Verdict Spurs Holy Row In Pakistan," National Public Radio, December 14, 2010, www.scpr.org/news/2010/12/14/21884/christians-death-verdict-spurs-holyrow-in-pakista/, 2-21-2016

1310. Ashraf Khan, Associated Press, Thousands rally in Pakistan for blasphemy laws. The laws make insulting Islam a capital offense, NBCNews.com, 1/9/2011 1:09:35 p.m. ET, www.nbcnews.com/id/40989445/ns/world_news-south_and_central_asia/t/thousands-rally-pakistanblasphemy-laws/#.Vsj3DfkrJ5Q 2-20-2016

1311. Declan Walsh, Salmaan Taseer, Aasia Bibi and Pakistan's struggle with extremism, *The Guardian* January 8, 2011, Last modified on Saturday 9 January 2016, www.theguardian.com/world/2011/jan/08/salmaan-taseer-blasphemy-pakistan-bibi 2-9-2016

1312. Declan Walsh, Salmaan Taseer, Aasia Bibi and Pakistan's struggle with extremism, *The Guardian* January 8, 2011, Last modified on Saturday 9 January 2016, www.theguardian.com/world/2011/jan/08/salmaan-taseer-blasphemy-pakistan-bibi 2-9-2016. Fasi Zaka, "Someone Always to Kill," *The Express Tribune*, Pakistan, January 11, 2011, tribune.com.pk/story/101871/someone-always-to-kill/ 2-20-2016

1313. Supreme Court, Pakistan, Criminal Appeals No. 210 and 211 of 2015 (Against the judgment dated 09.03.2015 passed by the Islamabad High Court, Islamabad in Criminal Appeal No. 90 of 2011 and Capital Sentence Reference No. 01 of 2011), p. 16. www.supremecourt.gov.pk/web/user_files/File/Crl.A._210_2015.pdf 2-15-2016. For different accounts of the number of bullets fired into Salmaan Taseer, see: *The Express Tribune*, Pakistan, "Salmaan Taseer assassinated," published: January 4, 2011, tribune.com.pk/story/98988/salman-taseer-attacked-in-islamabad/ 2-13-2016. And Shehrbano Taseer, "27 bullets fired at my father, Salmaan Taseer," *The New York Times*, Updated: January 10, 2011 12:21 IST, reprinted by NDTV, India, www.ndtv.com/world-news/27-bullets-fired-at-my-father-salmaan-taseer-444544 2-13-2016

1314. Momina Sibtain, "Salmaan Taseer's assassination: Crime scene cleans out restaurants," *The Express Tribune*, Pakistan, January 14, 2011, tribune.com.pk/story/103488/salmaan-taseersassassination-crime-scene-cleans-out-restaurants/

1315. "Blasphemy law claims another life," *Dawn*, Pakistan, Published Jan 04, 2011 10:11pm, www.dawn.com/news/596195/salman-taseer-injured-in-attack

1316. Supreme Court, Pakistan, Criminal Appeals No. 210 and 211 of 2015 (Against the judgment dated 09.03.2015 passed by the Islamabad High Court, Islamabad in Criminal Appeal No. 90 of 2011 and Capital Sentence Reference No. 01 of 2011), p. 3. www.supremecourt.gov.pk/web/user_files/File/Crl.A._210_2015.pdf 2-15-2016

1317. "Punjab Governor Salman Taseer assassinated in Islamabad," 4 January 2011, BBC News, www.bbc.com/news/world-south-asia-12111831 2-13-2016

1318. "Salmaan Taseer Assassinated," *The Express Tribune*, Pakistan, January 4, 2011, tribune.com.pk/story/98988/salman-taseer-attacked-in-islamabad/ 2-24-2016

1319. "Blasphemy law claims another life," *Dawn*, JAN 04, 2011 10:11PM, Pakistan, www.dawn.com/news/596195/salman-taseer-injured-in-attack

1320. "No negotiations of blood money for Salman Taseer murder, says family," Dawn.Com, March 11, 2015 03:39 p.m., www.dawn.com/news/1168856 2-8-2016. BBC, "Punjab Governor Salman Taseer assassinated in Islamabad," BBC, 4 January 2011, www.bbc.com/news/world-south-asia-12111831 2-8-2016

1321. Supreme Court, Pakistan, Criminal Appeals No. 210 and 211 of 2015 (Against the judgment dated 09.03.2015 passed by the Islamabad High Court, Islamabad in Criminal Appeal No. 90 of 2011 and Capital Sentence Reference No. 01 of 2011), pp. 3, 8. www.supremecourt.gov.pk/web/user_files/File/Crl.A._210_2015.pdf 2-15-2016

1322. Your Daily Muslim #590: Malik Mumtaz Hussain Qadri, yourdailymuslim.com/2014/09/11/your-daily-muslim-590-malik-mumtaz-hussain-qadri/ 2-13-2016. Pak Politics Updates, "Death of Salmaan Taseer," pakpoliticsupdates.blogspot.com/2012_04_01_archive.html 2-13-2016

1323. "Blasphemy law claims another life," *Dawn*, Pakistan, January 04, 2011 10:11 p.m., www.dawn.com/news/596195/salman-taseer-injured-in-attack

1324. "Blasphemy law claims another life," *Dawn*, Pakistan, January 04, 2011 10:11 p.m., www.dawn.com/news/596195/salman-taseer-injured-in-attack

1325. Shehrbano Taseer, "My father's murder must not silence the voices of reason," in Paul Johnson, ed., The Bedside Guardian, 2011. Manchester, UK: Guardian Books, Dec. 6, 2011.

1326. Supreme Court, Pakistan, Criminal Appeals No. 2100 and 211 of 2015 (Against the judgment dated 09.03.2015 passed by the Islamabad High Court, Islamabad in Criminal Appeal No. 90 of 2011 and Capital Sentence Reference No. 01 of 2011), p. 6. www.supremecourt.gov.pk/web/user_files/File/Crl.A._210_2015.pdf 2-15-2016

1327. Supreme Court, Pakistan, Criminal Appeals No. 2100 and 211 of 2015 (Against the judgment dated 09.03.2015 passed by the Islamabad High Court, Islamabad in Criminal Appeal No. 90 of 2011 and Capital Sentence Reference No. 01 of 2011), p. 15. www.supremecourt.gov.pk/web/user_files/File/Crl.A._210_2015.pdf 2-15-2016

1328. In the Supreme Court of Pakistan, (Appellate Jurisdiction), Criminal Appeals No. 210 and 211 of 2015 (Against the judgment dated 09.03.2015 passed by the Islamabad High Court,Islamabad in Criminal Appeal No. 90 of 2011 and Capital Sentence Reference No. 01 of 2011), www.supremecourt.gov.pk/web/user_files/File/Crl.A._210_2015.pdf 2-16-2016, p. 17.

1329. Supreme Court, Pakistan, Criminal Appeals No. 210 and 211 of 2015 and 211 of 2015 (Against the judgment dated 09.03.2015 passed by the Islamabad High Court, Islamabad in Criminal Appeal No. 90 of 2011 and Capital Sentence Reference No. 01 of 2011), p. 8. www.supremecourt.gov.pk/web/user_files/File/Crl.A._210_2015.pdf, 2-15-2016. For different accounts of the number of bullets, see: "Salmaan Taseer assassinated," *The Express Tribune*, Pakistan, January 4, 2011, tribune.com.pk/story/98988/salman-taseer-attacked-in-islamabad/ 2-13-2016. And Shehrbano Taseer, "27 bullets fired at my father, Salmaan Taseer," *The New York Times*, January 10, 2011 12:21 IST, this story appeared on NDTV, India, www.ndtv.com/world-news/27-bullets-fired-atmy-father-salmaan-taseer-444544 2-13-2016

1330. Mohammad Nafees, "Blatant Misuse of Blasphemy Law," Center for Research & Security Studies, September 29, 2014, crss.pk/story/blatant-misuse-of-blasphemy-law/#sthash.frMdfZSU.dpuf

1331. Hasnaat Malik, "SC [Supreme Court] upholds death sentence for Salmaan Taseer's killer," *The Express Tribune*, Pakistan, October 7, 2015, tribune.com.pk/story/968851/sc-upholds-death-sentence-for-salmaan-taseers-killer/ 2-14-2016

1332. "Mumtaz Qadri admits killing Governor Salman Taseer," BBC News, 10 January 2011, www.bbc.com/news/world-south-asia-12149607 2-14-2016

1333. Supreme Court, Pakistan, Criminal Appeals No. 210 and 211 of 2015 (Against the judgment dated 09.03.2015 passed by the Islamabad High Court, Islamabad in Criminal Appeal No. 90 of 2011 and Capital Sentence Reference No. 01 of 2011), p. 3. www.supremecourt.gov.pk/web/user_files/File/Crl.A._210_2015.pdf 2-15-2016

1334. Supreme Court, Pakistan, Criminal Appeals No. 210 and 211 of 2015 (Against the judgment dated 09.03.2015 passed by the Islamabad High Court, Islamabad in Criminal Appeal No. 90 of 2011 and Capital Sentence Reference No. 01 of 2011), p. 8. www.supremecourt.gov.pk/web/user_files/File/Crl.A._210_2015.pdf 2-15-2016. For different accounts of the number of bullets, see: "Salmaan Taseer assassinated," *The Express Tribune*, Pakistan, January 4, 2011, tribune.com.pk/story/98988/salman-taseer-attacked-in-islamabad/ 2-13-2016. And Shehrbano Taseer, "27 bullets fired at my father, Salmaan Taseer," *The New York Times*, Updated: January 10, 2011, 12:21 IST, NDTV, India, www.ndtv.com/world-news/27-bullets-fired-at-my-father-salmaan-taseer-444544 2-13-2016

1335. Ghazi Malik Mumtaz Hussain Qadri reciting Naat [poetry in praise of the Prophet] in police custody, uploaded by Faizal, www.dailymotion.com/video/x20kuqf_ghazi-malik-mumtaz-hussain-qadri-reciting-naat-in-police-custody_news 2-14-2016

1336. "Salman Taseer murder: Killer's appeal denied," 7 October 2015, BBC News, www.bbc.com/news/world-asia-34467603 2-14-2016

1337. Supreme Court, Pakistan, Criminal Appeals No. 210 and 211 of 2015 (Against the judgment dated 09.03.2015 passed by the Islamabad High Court, Islamabad in Criminal Appeal No. 90 of 2011 and Capital Sentence Reference No. 01 of 2011), p. 5. www.supremecourt.gov.pk/web/user_files/File/Crl.A._210_2015.pdf 2-15-2016

1338. Supreme Court, Pakistan, Criminal Appeals No. 210 and 211 of 2015 (Against the judgment dated 09.03.2015 passed by the Islamabad High Court, Islamabad in Criminal Appeal No. 90 of 2011 and Capital Sentence Reference No. 01 of 2011), p. 5. www.supremecourt.gov.pk/web/user_files/File/Crl.A._210_2015.pdf 2-15-2016

1339. Supreme Court, Pakistan, Criminal Appeals No. 210 and 211 of 2015 (Against the judgment dated 09.03.2015 passed by the Islamabad High Court, Islamabad in Criminal Appeal No. 90 of 2011 and Capital Sentence Reference No. 01 of 2011), p. 3. www.supremecourt.gov.pk/web/user_files/File/Crl.A._210_2015.pdf 2-15-2016

1340. Masjid Abu Bakr, Halaqa of Hadees, Masjid Abu Bakr (Brookhaven Islamic Center), abubakrmasjid.org/programs/halaqa-of-hadees/ 2-15-2016

1341. Akhilesh Pillalamarri, "Blasphemy and Religious Intolerance in Pakistan — Recent violence against the Ahmadi minority is part of a disturbing trend." The Diplomat, August 07, 2014, thediplomat.com/2014/08/blasphemy-and-religious-intolerance-in-pakistan/ 2-19-2016

1342. Supreme Court, Pakistan, Criminal Appeals No. 210 and 211 of 2015 (Against the judgment dated 09.03.2015 passed by the Islamabad High Court, Islamabad in Criminal Appeal No. 90 of 2011 and Capital Sentence Reference No. 01 of 2011), p. 5. www.supremecourt.gov.pk/web/user_files/File/Crl.A._210_2015.pdf 2-15-2016

1343. Supreme Court, Pakistan, Criminal Appeals No. 210 and 211 of 2015 (Against the judgment dated 09.03.2015 passed by the Islamabad High Court, Islamabad in Criminal Appeal No. 90 of 2011 and Capital Sentence Reference No. 01 of 2011), p. 5. www.supremecourt.gov.pk/web/user_files/File/Crl.A._210_2015.pdf 2-15-2016

1344. Supreme Court, Pakistan, Criminal Appeals No. 210 and 211 of 2015 (Against the judgment dated 09.03.2015 passed by the Islamabad High Court, Islamabad in Criminal Appeal No. 90 of 2011 and Capital Sentence Reference No. 01 of 2011), p. 5. www.supremecourt.gov.pk/web/user_files/File/Crl.A._210_2015.pdf 2-15-2016

1345. Supreme Court, Pakistan, Criminal Appeals No. 210 and 211 of 2015 (Against the judgment dated 09.03.2015 passed by the Islamabad High Court, Islamabad in Criminal Appeal No. 01 of 2011 and Capital Sentence Reference No. 01 of 2011), p. 17. www.supremecourt.gov.pk/web/user_files/File/Crl.A._210_2015.pdf 2-15-2016

1346. Hasnaat Malik, "SC [Supreme Court] upholds death sentence for Salmaan Taseer's killer," The Express Tribune, Pakistan, October 7, 2015, tribune.com.pk/story/968851/sc-upholds-death-sentence-for-salmaan-taseers-killer/ 2-14-2016

1347. Hasnaat Malik, "Plea against death sentence: Defence says religious scholar influenced Qadri," The Express Tribune, Pakistan, October 6, 2015, tribune.com.pk/story/968054/plea-against-death-sentence-defence-says-religious-scholar-influenced-qadri/ 2-9-2016

1348. Supreme Court, Pakistan, Criminal Appeals No. 210 and 211 of 2015 (Against the judgment dated 09.03.2015 passed by the Islamabad High Court, Islamabad in Criminal Appeal No. 90 of 2011 and Capital Sentence Reference No. 01 of 2011), p. 33. www.supremecourt.gov.pk/web/user_files/File/Crl.A._210_2015.pdf 2-15-2016

1349. Declan Walsh, "Salmaan Taseer, Aasia Bibi and Pakistan's struggle with extremism," The Guardian January 8, 2011, Last modified on Saturday 9 January 2016, www.theguardian.com/world/2011/jan/08/salmaan-taseer-blasphemy-pakistan-bibi 2-9-2016

1350. "Salman Taseer: Thousands mourn Pakistan governor," BBC, 5 January 2011, www.bbc.com/news/world-southasia-12116764 2-10-2016

1351. Nazir Bhatti,"Pakistan where Judges or victims of blasphemy law are killed or forced to exile," Pakistan Christian Post, www.pakistanchristianpost.com/detail.php?hnewsid=3125#sthash.90NcjgsL.dpuf 2-20-2016. This quote also appears in: Ghazi Malik, "Mumtaz Qadri, Killer of Taseer Showered with Rose Petals, Lauded Before Court," Posted by Editor on Jan 5th, 2011, dailymuslims.com/2011/01/05/mumtaz-qadri-killer-of-taseer-showered-with-rose-petals-lauded-before-court/ 2-14-2016 "Pakistan governor's alleged killer lauded before court," CBC News Posted: Jan 05, 2011 6:59 AM ET Last Updated: Jan 05, 2011 3:43 p.m. ET, www.cbc.ca/news/world/pakistan-governor-s-alleged-killer-lauded-before-court-1.1067245 2-20-2016

1352. Jon Boone, "Pakistan's top court upholds death sentence in blasphemy murder case," The Guardian, October 7, 2015, www.theguardian.com/world/2015/oct/07/pakistan-supreme-court-mumtaz-qadri-blasphemy-murder 2-14-2016

1353. Kunwar Khuldune Shahid, "Blasphemy and the Case of Mumtaz Qadri — Can Pakistan's judiciary take a stand against religious extremism?", *The Diplomat*. March 02, 2015 thediplomat.com/2015/03/blasphemy-and-the-case-of-mumtaz-qadri/

1354. Jon Boone, "Pakistan's top court upholds death sentence in blasphemy murder case," *The Guardian*, October 7, 2015, www.theguardian.com/world/2015/oct/07/pakistan-supreme-court-mumtaz-qadri-blasphemy-murder 2-14-2016

1355. Associated Press, "Lawyers shower roses for governor's killer," *Dawn*, Pakistan, January 5, 2011, www.dawn.com/news/596300/lawyers-shower-roses-for-governors-killer 2-10-2016

1356. Associated Press, "Lawyers shower roses for governor's killer," *Dawn*, Pakistan, January 5, 2011, www.dawn.com/news/596300/lawyers-shower-roses-for-governors-killer 2-10-2016

1357. Associated Press, "Lawyers shower roses for governor's killer," *Dawn*, Pakistan, January 5, 2011, www.dawn.com/news/596300/lawyers-shower-roses-for-governors-killer 2-10-2016

1358. Associated Press, "Lawyers shower roses for governor's killer," *Dawn*, Pakistan, January 5, 2011, www.dawn.com/news/596300/lawyers-shower-roses-for-governors-killer 2-10-2016

1359. Associated Press, "Lawyers shower roses for governor's killer," *Dawn*, Pakistan, January 5, 2011, www.dawn.com/news/596300/lawyers-shower-roses-for-governors-killer 2-10-2016

1360. Declan Walsh, "Salmaan Taseer, Aasia Bibi and Pakistan's struggle with extremism," *The Guardian* January 8, 2011, last modified on Saturday 9 January 2016, www.theguardian.com/world/2011/jan/08/salmaan-taseer-blasphemy-pakistan-bibi 2-9-2016

1361. Wikipedia, "List of States with Nuclear Weapons," en.wikipedia.org/wiki/List_of_states_with_nuclear_weapons

1362. Jeremy Bender, "Pakistan successfully tested a nuclear-capable missile that can hit any point in India," *Business Insider*, Mar. 10, 2015, www.businessinsider.com/pakistan-tested-nuclear-missile-that-can-reach-israel-2015-3 2-21-2016

1363. "Mumtaz Qadri admits killing Governor Salman Taseer," 10 January 2011, BBC News, www.bbc.com/news/world-south-asia-12149607 2-14-2016

1364. "Thousands rally in Pakistan for blasphemy laws," January 9, 2011, *The Gazette*, gazette.com/thousands-rally-in-pakistan-for-blasphemy-laws/article/110845 2-10-2016

1365. "Mumtaz Qadri admits killing Governor Salman Taseer," 10 January 2011, BBC News, www.bbc.com/news/world-south-asia-12149607 2-14-2016

1366. Declan Walsh, "Salmaan Taseer, Aasia Bibi and Pakistan's struggle with extremism," *The Guardian*, January 8, 2011, Last modified on Saturday 9 January 2016, www.theguardian.com/world/2011/jan/08/salmaan-taseer-blasphemy-pakistan-bibi

1367. Declan Walsh, "Sherry Rehman, Pakistan's defiant prisoner of intolerance, vows to stay put," *The Guardian*, January 22, 2011, www.theguardian.com/world/2011/jan/23/sherry-rehman-pakistan-blasphemy

1368. Supreme Court, Pakistan, In the Supreme Court of Pakistan, (Appellate Jurisdiction), Criminal Appeals No. 210 and 211 of 2015 (Against the judgment dated 09.03.2015 passed by the Islamabad High Court, Islamabad in Criminal Appeal No. 90 of 2011 and Capital Sentence Reference No. 01 of 2011), www.supremecourt.gov.pk/web/user_files/File/Crl.A._210_2015.pdf 2-16-2016, p. 26.

1369. Declan Walsh, "Salmaan Taseer, Aasia Bibi and Pakistan's struggle with extremism," *The Guardian*, January 8, 2011, Last modified on Saturday 9 January 2016, www.theguardian.com/world/2011/jan/08/salmaan-taseer-blasphemy-pakistan-bibi

1370. Nasir Khan, "Salman Taseer's son Shahbaz Taseer released from Taliban captivity, family denies," *The News Tribe*, February 16, 2013, www.thenewstribe.com/2013/02/16/salman-taseers-son-shahbaz-taseer-released-from-taliban-captivity/ 2-21-2016

1371. "Salmaan Taseer's birthday celebrated at First Capital group," www.dailytimes.com.pk/national/01-Jun-2014/salmaan-taseer-s-birthday-celebrated-at-first-capital-group 2-21-2016

1372. "Shahbaz Taseer, Ali Haider Gilani in Afghanistan: Punjab home minister," Dawn.com, February 20, 2015 6:36 p.m., www.dawn.com/news/1164853 2-21-2016
"Slain Salman Taseer's son kidnapped," *Dawn*, Pakistan, August 26, 2011 10:03 p.m., www.dawn.com/news/654867/slain-salman-taseers-son-kidnapped 2-21-2016

1373. Declan Walsh, "Pak Taliban admit to holding Shahbaz Taseer for first time," *The New York Times*, Updated: March 16, 2012 15:04 IST, www.ndtv.com/world-news/pak-taliban-admit-to-holding-shahbaz-taseer-for-first-time-472028 2-21-2016

1374. "TTP Offers Exchange of Mumtaz Qadri with Shahbaz Taseer," *Awami Politics*, March 30, 2014, www.awamipolitics.com/ttp-offers-exchange-of-mumtaz-qadri-with-shahbaz-taseer-15713.html 2-21-2016. The TTP is the Taliban in Pakistan.

1375. Jon Boone, "Shahbaz Taseer: Pakistan's high-profile kidnap victim reunited with family," *The Guardian*, March 9, 2016, www.theguardian.com/world/2016/mar/09/shahbaz-taseer-man-held-five-years-pakistan-militants-reunited-family 3-21-2016
See the Twitter page of Shahbaz's wife, Maheen, twitter.com/maheentaseer 2-21-2016
1376. Indo-Asian News Service, IANS, India, "Pakistan: Salman Taseer'sassassin gets death sentence,"Daily.bhaskar.com October 01, 2011, 13:15 p.m. IST, daily.bhaskar.com/news/WOR-SAS-pakistan-salman-taseers-assassin-gets-death-sentence-2472142.html
"Former Governor of Pakistan's killer punished — A — पाकिस्तान के पूर्व गवर्नर के हत्यारे को सजा-ए-मौत". bhaskar.com. Wikipedia, "Salmaan Taseer," en.wikipedia.org/wiki/Salmaan_Taseer#cite_note-43 2-14-2016
1377. "The judge, who convicted Qadri to death, had to leave the country soon after passing the judgment for never to return." Mohammad Nafees, Senior Research Fellow, CRSS, "Blatant misuse of blasphemy law," Center for Research and Security Studies, September 29, 2014
1378. Raymond Ibrahim, *Crucified Again: Exposing Islam's New War on Christians*. Washington, DC: Regnery Publishing, 2013, p. 138.
1379. The Voice of the Martyrs, "More Asia Bibi Petitions Delivered," Persecution Blog, March 19, 2015, www.persecutionblog.com/asia-bibi/ 2-24-2016
Asia Bibi, A Pakistani Christian Woman Convicted of Blasphemy and Sentenced to Death, rescuechristians, YouTube, February 21, 2012, www.youtube.com/watch?v=zvwMfRsRpds 2-24-2016
1380. Wikipedia, "Asia Bibi blasphemy case," en.wikipedia.org/wiki/Asia_Bibi_blasphemy_case, 2-24-2016
1381. Maciej Grabysa and Michal Krol, filmmakers, *Freedom for Asia Bibi*. Saturday, April 18, 2015 "Television premiere of the film on Asia Bibi 'Freedom for ...'" — Infovaticana, newtelevisionss.blogspot.com/2015/04/television-premiere-of-film-on-asia.html 2-24-2016
1382. "1400 Cases of Blasphemy Registered in 2014," *Daily Times*, Pakistan, 15 October 2015, www.dailytimes.com.pk/national/15-Oct-2015/1400-cases-of-blasphemyregistered-in-2014 2-9-2016
1383. "1400 Cases of Blasphemy Registered in 2014," *Daily Times*, Pakistan, 15 October 2015, www.dailytimes.com.pk/national/15-Oct-2015/1400-cases-of-blasphemyregistered-in-2014 2-9-2016
1384. AFP, "Rights advocate Rashid Rehman Khan gunned down in Multan," Dawn.com, May 08, 2014 01:11 a.m. www.dawn.com/news/1104788 2-11-2016

1385. *Dābiq*, issue 12 implies that nationalism, minority rights, human rights, and all the beliefs of the unbelievers are false religions. Only Islam is the true religion. Here is one version of ISIS' disgust with all Western values: "So the kuffar—whether they are Catholic, Protestant, or Orthodox Christians, whether they are Orthodox, Conservative, or Progressive Jews, whether they are Buddhists, Hindus, or Sikhs, whether they are capitalists, communists, or fascists — they are ultimately allies of one another against Islam and the Muslims. This is because Islam — the religion of truth and fitrah — is the greatest threat to their religions of falsehood, all of which are at war with the inborn nature of man. This is also because the tawaghit and dajajilah (plural of dajjal) of these false religions fear losing control of their flocks of blind sheep and the wealth contained in their wooly pockets. This is also because the flocks of blind sheep fear losing their animalistic societies and carnal cultures that serve their lusts, desires, and doubts at the expense of reviving and nurturing the fitrah within their dead hearts." *Dābiq*, issue 12, p. 42.
1386. AFP, "Rights advocate Rashid Rehman Khan gunned down in Multan," Dawn.com, May 08, 2014 01:11 a.m. www.dawn.com/news/1104788 2-11-2016
1387. Wikipedia, "Asia Bibi Blasphemy Case," en.wikipedia.org/wiki/Asia_Bibi_blasphemy_case 2-21-2016. Pakistan: "Asia Bibi Case Delayed For Fifth Time, Court Seeks To Pardon TV Staff," *Global Dispatch*, May 28, 2014, www.theglobaldispatch.com/pakistan-asia-bibi-case-delayed-for-fifth-time-court-seeks-to-pardon-tv-staff-86305/ 2-21-2016
1388. Rafia Zakaria, "Mumtaz Qadri, Prison King," *Dawn*, Pakistan, November 01, 2014 12:19 a.m., www.dawn.com/news/1141574 2-14-2016
1389. Rafia Zakaria, "Mumtaz Qadri, Prison King," *Dawn*, Pakistan, November 01, 2014 12:19 a.m. www.dawn.com/news/1141574
1390. A. Guillaume, *The Life of Muhammad: A Translation of Ibn Ishaq's Sirat Rasul Allah*. New York: Oxford University Press, 1955, eighteenth printing, 2004, p. 369. See also al-Tabari, *The History of al-Tabari*: English translation of "at Tareekh al-Tabari." Albany: State University of New York Press. Volume VII, p. 97.
1391. Jon Boone, "Pakistan's top court upholds death sentence in blasphemy murder case — Supreme court says Mumtaz Qadri should be executed for shooting dead Punjab governor who backed reform of country's hardline blasphemy laws," Wednesday 7 October 2015 10.45 EDT, www.theguardian.com/world/2015/oct/07/pakistan-supreme-court-mumtaz-qadri-blasphemy-murder 2-14-2016
1392. Kunwar Khuldune Shahid, "Blasphemy and the Case of Mumtaz Qadri — Can Pakistan's judiciary take a stand against religious extremism?" *The Diplomat*, March 02, 2015, thediplomat.com/2015/03/blasphemy-and-thecase-of-mumtaz-qadri/

1393. Swords of Prophet Muhammad (SAW), Sirat Rasul Allah, seerah.hpage.ms/swords-of-prophet-muhammad_33232366.html#.VspT3PkrJ5Q 2-21-2016.
Sword of Hadrat Ali, Islam Helpline, www.islamhelpline.net/node/444 2-21-2016.

1394. Kunwar Khuldune Shahid, "Blasphemy and the Case of Mumtaz Qadri — Can Pakistan's judiciary take a stand against religious extremism?" *The Diplomat*, March 02, 2015, thediplomat.com/2015/03/blasphemy-and-thecase-of-mumtaz-qadri/

1395. Kunwar Khuldune Shahid, "Blasphemy and the Case of Mumtaz Qadri — Can Pakistan's judiciary take a stand against religious extremism?" *The Diplomat*, March 02, 2015, thediplomat.com/2015/03/blasphemy-and-thecase-of-mumtaz-qadri/

1396. Kunwar Khuldune Shahid, "Blasphemy and the Case of Mumtaz Qadri — Can Pakistan's judiciary take a stand against religious extremism?" *The Diplomat*, March 02, 2015, thediplomat.com/2015/03/blasphemy-and-thecase-of-mumtaz-qadri/

1397. Kunwar Khuldune Shahid, "Blasphemy and the Case of Mumtaz Qadri — Can Pakistan's judiciary take a stand against religious extremism?" *The Diplomat*, March 02, 2015, thediplomat.com/2015/03/blasphemy-and-thecase-of-mumtaz-qadri/

1398. Jon Boone, "Pakistan's top court upholds death sentence in blasphemy murder case — Supreme court says Mumtaz Qadri should be executed for shooting dead Punjab governor who backed reform of country's hardline blasphemy laws," 7 October 2015 10.45 EDT, www.theguardian.com/world/2015/oct/07/

1399. Jon Boone, "Pakistan's top court upholds death sentence in blasphemy murder case — Supreme court says Mumtaz Qadri should be executed for shooting dead Punjab governor who backed reform of country's hardline blasphemy laws," *The Guardian*, UK, 7 October 2015 10.45 EDT, www.theguardian.com/world/2015/oct/07/

1400. Kunwar Khuldune Shahid, "Blasphemy and the Case of Mumtaz Qadri — Can Pakistan's judiciary take a stand against religious extremism?" *The Diplomat*, March 02, 2015, thediplomat.com/2015/03/blasphemy-and-thecase-of-mumtaz-qadri/

1401. Kunwar Khuldune Shahid, "Blasphemy and the Case of Mumtaz Qadri — Can Pakistan's judiciary take a stand against religious extremism?" *The Diplomat*, March 02, 2015, thediplomat.com/2015/03/blasphemy-and-thecase-of-mumtaz-qadri/

1402. "Pakistan Court Overturns Asia Bibi's Death Sentence," CBN News, www1.cbn.com/cbnnews/world/2015/July/Pakistan-Court-Overturns-Asia-Bibis-Death-Sentence 07-24-2015

1403. Shaheryar Gill, "Christian Mom on Death Row Asia Bibi Forgives her Persecutors," ACLJ (American Center for Law and Justice), January 21, 2016, aclj.org/persecuted-church/christian-momon-death-row-asia-bibi-forgives-her-persecutors 2-21-2016

1404. Declan Walsh, "Salmaan Taseer, Aasia Bibi and Pakistan's struggle with extremism," *The Guardian*, January 8, 2011, Last modified on Saturday 9 January 2016, www.theguardian.com/world/2011/jan/08/salmaan-taseer-blasphemy-pakistan-bibi 2-9-2016

1405. Jon Boone, "Mumtaz Qadri supporters in Islamabad defy calls to disperse," *The Guardian*, March 30, 2016. "Asia Bibi, Tajani presenta interrogazione all'Ue," Avenire.it, March 30, 2016, www.avvenire.it/Politica/Pagine/tajani-interrogazione-mogherini-ue-fermi-esecuzione-asia-bibi.aspx

1406. IN THE SUPREME COURT OF PAKISTAN (Appellate Jurisdiction) PRESENT:
Mr. Justice Asif Saeed Khan Khosa
Mr. Justice Mushir Alam
Mr. Justice Dost Muhammad Khan
Criminal Appeals No. 210 and 211 of 2015 (Against the judgment dated 09.03.2015 passed by the Islamabad High Court,Islamabad in Criminal Appeal No. 90 of 2011 and Capital Sentence ReferenceNo. 01 of 2011) Malik Muhammad Mumtaz Qadri, www.supremecourt.gov.pk/web/user_files/File/Crl.A._210_2015.pdf 2-16-2016

1407. "Plea against death sentence: Defence says religious scholar influenced Qadri," Awaz.tv, Karachi, Pakistan, 06 October 2015, www.awaztoday.tv/News_Plea-againstdeath-sentence-Defence-says-religious-scholarinfluenced-Qadri_1_60719_Political-News.aspx 2-14-2016

1408. "verses of the Holy Qur'an including Surah At-Taubah: verse 12, Surah At-Taubah: verses 13, 14 & 15, Surah Al-Ma'idah: verse 33, Surah Al-Hujarat: verse 2, Surah AnNur: verse 63, Surah Al-Baqarah: verse 104, Surah Al-Ahzab: verse 57, Surah An-Nisa, verse 65, Surah At-Taubah: verses 64, 65 & 66, Surah Al-Mujadilah: verses 20 & 21 and Surah Al-Anfal: verses 12, 13 & 14...about thirty Ahadith (traditions) of the Holy Prophet Muhammad (peace be upon him) reported in different religious texts." In the Supreme Court of Pakistan, (Appellate Jurisdiction), Criminal Appeals No. 210 and 211 of 2015 (Against the judgment dated 09.03.2015 passed by the Islamabad High Court, Islamabad in Criminal Appeal No. 90 of 2011 and Capital Sentence Reference No. 01 of 2011), pp. 20-21. www.supremecourt.gov.pk/web/user_files/File/Crl.A._210_2015.pdf 2-16-2016

1409. In the Supreme Court of Pakistan, (Appellate Jurisdiction), Criminal Appeals No. 210 and 211 of 2015 (Against the judgment dated 09.03.2015 passed by the Islamabad High Court, Islamabad in Criminal Appeal No. 90 of 2011 and Capital Sentence Reference No. 01 of 2011), www.supremecourt.gov.pk/web/user_files/File/Crl.A._210_2015.pdf 2-16-2016

1410. In the Supreme Court of Pakistan, (Appellate Jurisdiction), Criminal Appeals No. 210 and 211 of 2015 (Against the judgment dated 09.03.2015 passed by the Islamabad High Court, Islamabad in Criminal Appeal No. 90 of 2011 and Capital Sentence Reference No. 01 of 2011), www.supremecourt.gov.pk/web/user_files/File/Crl.A._210_2015.pdf 2-16-2016

1411. In the Supreme Court of Pakistan, (Appellate Jurisdiction), Criminal Appeals No. 210 and 211 of 2015 (Against the judgment dated 09.03.2015 passed by the Islamabad High Court, Islamabad in Criminal Appeal No. 90 of 2011 and Capital Sentence Reference No. 01 of 2011), www.supremecourt.gov.pk/web/user_files/File/Crl.A._210_2015.pdf 2-16-2016, p. 2.
The verse from Muhammad that the judges cite is in the Qur'an, Chapter 49, verse 6.

1412. Rafia Zakaria, "Mumtaz Qadri, Prison King," *Dawn*, Pakistan, November 01, 2014 12:19 a.m., www.dawn.com/news/1141574 2-14-2016

1413. Rafia Zakaria, "Mumtaz Qadri, Prison King," *Dawn*, Pakistan, November 01, 2014 12:19 a.m., www.dawn.com/news/1141574 2-14-2016

1414. Rafia Zakaria, "Mumtaz Qadri, Prison King," *Dawn*, Pakistan, November 01, 2014 12:19 a.m., www.dawn.com/news/1141574 2-14-2016

1415. "Salman Taseer murder: Killer's appeal denied," BBC News, 7 October 2015, www.bbc.com/news/world-asia-34467603 2-14-2016

1416. "Mumtaz Qadri admits killing Governor Salman Taseer," 10 January 2011, www.bbc.com/news/world-south-asia-12149607

1417. "1400 cases of blasphemy registered in 2014," *Pakistan Daily Times*, October 15, 2015, www.dailytimes.com.pk/national/15-Oct-2015/1400-cases-of-blasphemy-registered-in-2014 2-21-2016. ASIA/PAKISTAN — "Over 1400 cases of blasphemy in a year," *Vatican News*, www.news.va/en/news/asiapakistan-over-1400-cases-of-blasphemy-in-a-yea [sic] 2-21-2016.
"In 2014 a record number of blasphemy cases were registered in Pakistan," Posted by Madeeha Bakhsh On October 16, 2015, *Christians in Pakistan*, www.christiansinpakistan.com/in-2014-a-record-number-of-blasphemy-cases-were-registered-in-pakistan/ 2-9-2016

1418. Christians in Pakistan News, "In 2014 a Record Number of Blasphemy Cases Were Registered in Pakistan," www.christiansinpakistan.com/in-2014-a-record-number-of-blasphemy-cases-wereregistered-in-pakistan/ 2-9-2016. Madeeha Bakhsh, "In 2014 a record number of blasphemy cases were registered in Pakistan," Official Vatican Network, October 16, 2015. www.news.va/en/news/asiapakistan-over-1400-cases-of-blasphemy-in-a-yea 2-9-2016. "Over 1400 cases of blasphemy in a year," *Daily Times*, Pakistan, October 15, 2015, www.dailytimes.com.pk/national/15-Oct-2015/1400-cases-of-blasphemy-registeredin-2014 2-9-2016

1419. Official Vatican news, Asia-Pakistan "Over 1400 Cases of Blasphemy in a Year," www.news.va/en/news/asiapakistan-over-1400-cases-of-blasphemy-in-a-yea 2-9-2016

1420. In the Supreme Court of Pakistan, (Appellate Jurisdiction), Criminal Appeals No. 210 and 211 of 2015 (Against the judgment dated 09.03.2015 passed by the Islamabad High Court, Islamabad in Criminal Appeal No. 90 of 2011 and Capital Sentence Reference No. 01 of 2011), www.supremecourt.gov.pk/web/user_files/File/Crl.A._210_2015.pdf 2-16-2016, p. 17.

1421. "Over 1400 cases of blasphemy in a year," *Daily Times*, Pakistan, October 15, 2015, www.dailytimes.com.pk/national/15-Oct-2015/1400-cases-of-blasphemy-registeredin-2014 2-9-2016.

1422. Angelina E. Theodorou, "Which countries still outlaw apostasy and blasphemy?" Pew Research Center, May 28, 2014, www.pewresearch.org/fact-tank/2014/05/28/which-countries-still-outlaw-apostasy-andblasphemy/ 2-24-2016.

1423. "Over 1400 cases of blasphemy in a year," *Daily Times*, Pakistan, October 15, 2015, www.dailytimes.com.pk/national/15-Oct-2015/1400-cases-of-blasphemy-registeredin-2014 2-9-2016 .

1424. "Mumtaz Qadri hanged to death," Nation.com, Pakistan, February 29, 2016, 5:44 a.m., nation.com.pk/national/29-Feb-2016/mumtaz-qadri-hangedto-death 2-28-2016

1425. "Violent protests erupt after hanging of Mumtaz Qadri," *Pakistan Today*, February 29, 2016, www.pakistantoday.com.pk/2016/02/29/city/lahore/violent-protests-erupt-after-hanging-of-mumtaz-qadri/ 3-2-2016

1426. "Violent protests erupt after hanging of Mumtaz Qadri," *Pakistan Today*, February 29, 2016, www.pakistantoday.com.pk/2016/02/29/city/lahore/violent-protests-erupt-after-hanging-of-mumtaz-qadri/ 3-2-2016.

1427. Aatish Taseer, "My Father's Killer's Funeral," *New York Times*, March 11, 2016, www.nytimes.com/2016/03/13/opinion/sunday/my-fathers-killers-funeral.html?_r=0

1428. "Quadri Finds Support in Thousands of Pakistanis on Funeral Day," *Business Standard*, Press Trust of India, March 1, 2016, www.business-standard.com/article/pti-stories/qadri-finds-support-in-thousands-of-pakistanison-funeral-day-116030100811_1.html 3-2-2016.

1429. Aatish Taseer, "My Father's Killer's Funeral," *New York Times*, March 11, 2016, www.nytimes.com/2016/03/13/opinion/sunday/my-fathers-killers funeral.html?_r=0

1430. Aatish Taseer, "My Father's Killer's Funeral," *New York Times*, March 11, 2016, www.nytimes.com/2016/03/13/opinion/sunday/my-fathers-killers funeral.html?_r=0

1431. Aatish Taseer, "My Father's Killer's Funeral," *New York Times*, March 11, 2016, www.nytimes.com/2016/03/13/opinion/sunday/my-fathers-killers funeral.html?_r=0

1432. AFP, "Fears grow for Aasia Bibi after Mumtaz Qadri's hanging," *The Express Tribune*, March 5, 2016 tribune.com.pk/story/1059784/fears-grow-forasia-bibi-after-mumtaz-qadris-hanging/

1433. MEMRI Turkish Media Blog, "PM Erdogan: The Term 'Moderate Islam' Is Ugly And Offensive; There Is No Moderate Islam; Islam Is Islam, Tayyip Recep Erdogan on Kanal D. TV's Arena Program," Source: Milliyet, Turkey, August 21, 2007 www.thememriblog.org/turkey/blog_personal/en/2595.htm

1434. Tom Heneghan, "West's free speech stand bars blasphemy ban — OIC" Reuters, Monday Oct 15, 2012, Istanbul, uk.reuters.com/article/uk-islam-blasphemyidUKBRE89E18W20121015

1435. Nadine Abdalla, "Protests in Egypt before and after the 25 January Revolution: Perspectives on the Evolution of their Forms and Features," The Awakening of Civil Society in the Mediterranean, Observatory of Euro-Mediterranean Policies, 2012, www.iemed.org/observatori-en/arees-danalisi/arxius-adjunts/anuari/med.2012/abdalla_en.pdf 1-20-2016, p. 86. Nicholas S. Hopkins, *Political and Social Protest in Egypt*. Cairo: American University in Cairo Press, 2009, p. 53

1436. Hamid Dabashi, *The Green Movement in Iran*. Piscataway, NJ: Transaction Publishers, Dec 31, 2011.

1437. Bahgat Korany, Rabab El-Mahdi, *The Arab Spring in Egypt: Revolution and Beyond*. Cairo: American University in Cairo Press, 2012. David Lesch, Mark Haas, *The Arab Spring: Change and Resistance in the Middle East*. Glendale, CA: Westview Press, 2012.

1438. David M. Faris, Babak Rahimi, *Social Media in Iran: Politics and Society After 2009*. Albany, NY: SUNY Press, 2015, p. 200.

1439. *Al-Ihsan*, Front Page, February 8, 2016, www.al-ihsan.net/ 2-27-2016

1440. Praveen Swami, "84 on hitlist, 8 killed: Dhaka's politics drives cycle of death," *The Indian Express*, Dhaka, April 17, 2015, indianexpress.com/article/india/india-others/84-on-hitlist-8-killed-dhakas-politics-drives-cycle-of-death/ 2-27-2016. Nilanjana S. Roy, "The hit list: Endangered bloggers of Bangladesh," www.aljazeera.com/indepth/opinion/2015/08/hit-list-endangered-bloggers-bangladesh-150813132059771.html 2-27-2016

1441. Mohammad Hossain, History at International Islamic University of Malaysia, "Myth of the 84 bloggers 'hit' list in Bangladesh: Busting the media narrative," *Turkey Agenda*, September 17, 2015, www.turkeyagenda.com/myth-of-the-84-bloggers-hit-list-in-bangladesh-busting-the-media-narrative-2842.html 2-27-2016.

1442. Nadeem F. Paracha, "Pakistani secularisms," *Dawn*, March 23, 2014 07:52 p.m., www.dawn.com/news/1094982 2-27-2016

1443. Vrushali Kadam, "9 From the 84 Atheist Blogger Hitlist in Bangladesh are Dead, Ananya Azad is Next," *The Bayside Journal*, baysidejournal.com/wp/9-from-the-84-atheist-blogger-hitlist-in-bangladesh-are-dead-ananya-azad-is-next/ 1-20-2016. Camila Domonoske, "Atheist Law Student Hacked To Death In Bangladesh," The Two-Way, Breaking News from NPR, www.npr.org/sections/thetwo-way/2016/04/07/473347159/atheist-law-student-hacked-to-deathin-bangladesh

1444. Compiled from wire services, "Bangladesh sentences 3 to death for killing atheist blogger," *Daily Sabah*, New Delhi, December 31, 2015, www.dailysabah.com/asia/2015/12/31/bangladesh-sentences-3-to-death-for-killing-atheist-blogger 1-20-2016

1445. N.a., "Bangladesh blogger Niloy Neel hacked to death in Dhaka," BBC News, August 7, 2015, www.bbc.com/news/world-asia-33819032 1-20-2016

1446. Syed Tashfin Chowdhury, "Al-Qaeda affiliate claims killing of secular publisher in Bangladesh," *Asia Times*, October 31, 2015, atimes.com/2015/10/blogger-avijit-roys-publisher-2-others-attacked-in-dhaka/

1447. Saeed Ahmed, "Washiqur Rahman: Another secular blogger hacked to death in Bangladesh," CNN, March 31, 2015, www.cnn.com/2015/03/31/asia/bangladesh-blogger-death/ 1-20-2016

1448. David Batty, "Saudi court sentences poet to death for renouncing Islam," *The Guardian*, November 20, 2015, www.theguardian.com/world/2015/nov/20/saudi-court-sentences-poet-to-death-for-renouncing-islam 1-20-2016

1449. Dr. Shahid Athar, Inner Jihad—Striving Toward Harmony, "Sufism: An Inquiry," sufismjournal.org/practice/practice.html

1450. Dr. Alan Godlas, "Sufism's Many Paths." University of Georgia. In *Overview Of World Religions*, Division of Religion and Philosophy, St. Martin's College, Lancaster, England. Retrieved October 14, 2006, from the World Wide Web www.uga.edu/islam/Sufism.html

1451. Dr. Alan Godlas, "The Qadiriyyah." In *Overview Of World Religions*, Division of Religion and Philosophy, St. Martin's College, Lancaster, England. Retrieved October 14, 2006, from the World Wide Web philtar.ucsm.ac.uk/encyclopedia/islam/sufi/qadir.html

1452. Shaykh Al-Islam Muhaddith Al A'zam Mission, Silsila Qadiriya-Chistiya-Ashrafiya. Muhaddith al A'zam Worldwide Mission. www.islam786.org/silsilaechistiya.htm Medieval Indian historian K.S. Lal says that the peaceful nature of the Sufis has been grossly exaggerated. "Chishtias are the most accommodative of the Sufi orders," he writes. "Suhrawardis and Naqshbandis are Sufis of a different kind. Shaikh Ahmad Sirhindi and Shah Walliullah were Sufis of this second sort. The latter considered Mahmud of Ghazni the greatest Muslim after the pious Caliphs. He invited Ahmad Shah Abdali to invade India to destroy the power of the Hindus. And he is considered by Muslims as a leading light of Islamic philosophy." Mahmud of Ghazni set records in bloodshed. To quote one of his Islamic admirers, "in more than 20 successful expeditions he amassed the wealth with which to lay the foundation of a vast empire that eventually included Kashmir, the Punjab, and a great part of Iran." n.a. "Mahmud Of Ghazni, 971 A.D.–1030 A.D." The Dynasties & Royal Governments of Afghanistan. *Afghan Network*. Toronto, Ontario, Canada. www.afghan-network.net/Rulers/ mahmud-ghazni.html.

1453. John S. Bowman, *Columbia Chronologies of Asian History and Culture*. New York: Columbia University Press, 2000, pp. 336, 340.

1454. John S. Bowman, *Columbia Chronologies of Asian History and Culture*. New York: Columbia University Press, 2000, p. 338.

1455. According to Wikipedia, Sufism is "the Islam of beauty and love.... Loving God & loving/helping every human being irrespective of his race, religion or nationality, and without consideration for any possible reward, is the key to ascension according to Sufis." en.wikipedia.org/wiki/Sufism#Origins

1456. Maitreya Sangha, "Life of Akbar the Great. Messengers of Light. Pantheon of the World Brotherhood of Light. A Tribute to the Memory of the Greatest Heros [Sic] in World History." sangha.net/messengers/akbar.htm# Life%20of%20Akbar%20th

1457. "Jainism: Jain Principles, Tradition and Practices," www.cs.colostate.edu/~malaiya/ jainhlinks.html

1458. "Religions And Religious Thoughts Of India. Zoroastrianism In India," Culturopedia: Treasure House of India's Culture and Heritage. India. www.culturopedia.com/Religions/ zoroastrianism.html

1459. Annemarie Schimmel, *The Empire of the Great Mughals: History, Art and Culture*. London: Reaktion Books, 2004, p. 38.

1460. Jean Jacques Waardenburg, *Muslims and Others*. Berlin: Walter de Gruyter, 2003, p. 119.

1461. *Merriam-Webster's Encyclopedia of World Religions by Merriam-Webster*. Springfield, MA: Merriam-Webster, 1999, p. 28.

1462. John S. Bowman, *Columbia Chronologies of Asian History and Culture*. New York: Columbia University Press, 2000, p. 410.

1463. Lyusi's full name was Abu Ali al-Yusi.

1464. David Robinson. *Muslim Societies in African History*. Cambridge, England: Cambridge University Press, 2004, pp. 99–100.

1465. Azyumardi Azra, Martin van Bruinessen, Julia Howell, "Sufism and the 'Modern' in Islam." An international conference organised by Griffith University (Brisbane), the International Institute for the Study of Islam in the Modern World (ISIM, Leiden), and the Centre for the Study of Islam and Society (PPIM, Jakarta) Jakarta, 4–7 September 2003. let.uu.nl/~martin.vanbruinessen/personal/ conferences/sufism_and_the_modern.html Willem A. Bijlefeld (professor emeritus at Hartford Seminary, Hartford, Conn.). "Sufism: General Information," BELIEVE Religious Information Source. Retrieved October 15, 2006, from the World Wide Web mb-soft.com/believe/txo/sufism.htm

1466. Elizabeth Sirriyeh, *Sufis and Anti-Sufis: The Defence, Rethinking and Rejection of Sufism in the Modern World*. Richmond, Surrey: Curzon Press, 1999. Neil Douglas-Klotz, *The Sufi Book of Life: 99 Pathways of the Heart for the Modern Dervish*. www.sufibookoflife.com/intro.html

1467. Charles McLean Andrews, *The Historical Development of Modern Europe: From the Congress of Vienna to the Present Time*. London: G.P. Putnam's Sons, 1898, p. 314. Art Biligisayar, "Discover the Ottomans." TheOttomans.org. www.theottomans.org/english/history/ history1700_7.asp and www.theottomans.org/ english/history/history1800_7.asp. Wikipedia, "List of Caliphs." en.wikipedia.org/wiki/List_of_caliphs

1468. Gail Minault, *The Khilafat Movement*. New York: Columbia University Press, 1982. Wikipedia, "Pan-Islamism," Retrieved August 12, 2005, from the World Wide Web en.wikipedia.org/ wiki/pan-Islamism

1469. Steven Runciman, *The Fall Of Constantinople: 1453*. Cambridge, UK: Cambridge University Press, 1965.

1470. Gail Minaoult, *The Khilafat Movement*. New York: Columbia University Press, 1982.

1471. John S. Bowman, *Columbia Chronologies of Asian History and Culture*. New York: Columbia University Press, 2000, p. 304.

1472. Some of the Khalifat Movement's leaders were pluralists, but not all. Writes Surya Prakash in *The Pioneer* of New Delhi, "Maulana Mohamed Ali, who presided over the All-India Khilafat Conference in 1921," made the following statement about Mahatma Gandhi. "However pure Mr Gandhi's character may be, he must appear to me from the point of view of religion inferior to any Mussalman." (Surya Prakash, "Muslim clergy's contempt for courts," *The Pioneer*, New Delhi 22 November 2005)

1473. Rahil Khan, "Abul Kalam Azad." In Vinay Lal, ed. *Manas: India and Its Neighbors.* www.sscnet.ucla.edu/southasia/History/Independent/Azad_indepindia.html. Pran Nath Chopra. *Encyclopaedia of India.* Delhi: Agam Prakashan, 1988.

1474. "Azad, (Maulana) Abul Kalam." In Sirajul Islam, ed. *Banglapedia. Asiatic Society of Bangladesh.* banglapedia.search.com.bd/HT/A_0376.htm

1475. I've used the portrait of Azad drawn by the Banglapedia. In fact, Azad may have been far less of a pluralist than the Banglapedia admits. His primary goal, according to another chronicler of the Khalifat movement, Gail Minault, was Muslim unity, Muslim obedience to the central authority of the Caliph, and, when necessary, jihad. Azad's interpretation of jihad was as peaceful struggle. But Minault feels Azad left the possibility of militant jihad—Holy War—open. Here is Minault's most pluralistic passage on Azad: "He then drew a contrast between those non-Muslims who (like the British) invade Muslim lands and threaten the Muslim religion, and those non-Muslims who (like the Hindus) live in peace with Muslims. The latter must be treated with friendship and trust, while all friendship with the former must be abandoned."
The Khilafat Movement by Gail Minault. New York: Columbia University Press, 1982, p. 95.

1476. "Muhammad ibn Abdul Wahhab," Iraq Museum International Open Encyclopedia. www.baghdadmuseum.org/ref/index.php?title=Muhammad_bin_Abdul_Wahhab
Azyumardi Azra, *Origins of Islamic Reformism in Southeast Asia: Networks of Malay-Indonesian and Middle Eastern 'Ulama" in the Seventeenth and Eighteenth Centuries.* Honolulu, HI, University of Hawaii Press, 2004. en.wikipedia.org/wiki/Muhammad_ibn_Abd_al_Wahhab

1477. Reza F. Safa, *Inside Islam—A Former Radical Shiite Muslim Speaks Out: Exposing and Reaching the World of Islam.* Lake Mary, Florida: Charisma House, 1997. Rachel Ehrenfeld, *Funding Evil, Expanded Edition: How Terrorism Is Financed — And How to Stop It.* Chicago: Bonus Books, 2003, pp. 25–26. Dore Gold, *Hatred's Kingdom: How Saudi Arabia Supports New Global Terrorism.* Washington, DC: Regnery Publishing, 2004, pp. 126, 149. *Militant Islam Monitor.org.* "The Islamisation of North America—The North American Islamic Trust and the Dow Jones Islamic Fund." January 12, 2006. www.militantislammonitor.org/article/id/1544

1478. Brian Viner, reviewer, "Last Night's TV: 'The Qur'an, Channel 4; Banged Up, Five: Man on a mission restores some faith,'" Monday 14 July 2008, www.independent.co.uk/arts-entertainment/tv/reviews/last-nights-tv-the-quran-channel-4-banged-up-five-867474.html 1-23-2016. Yousaf Butt, "How Saudi Wahhabism Is the Fountainhead of Islamist Terrorism," *The World Post* (the World Post is a partnership of the Huffington Post and the Berggruen Institute), 01/20/2015 06:01 p.m. ET | Updated Mar 22, 2015. Yousaf Butt is Visiting Senior Research Fellow at the Center for Technology and National Security Policy at the National Defense University. www.huffingtonpost.com/dr-yousaf-butt-/saudi-wahhabism-islam-terrorism_b_6501916.html. "Described in testimony before the US Senate Judiciary Committee, and listed on the late King Fahd's website, Saudi Arabia spent $4 billion per year on mosques, madrassas, preachers, students, and textbooks to spread the Wahhabi creed." Carol E.B. Choksy and Jamsheed K. Choksy, "The Saudi Connection: Wahhabism and Global Jihad," *World Affairs Journal,* May/June 2015 www.worldaffairsjournal.org/article/saudi-connection-wahhabism-and-global-jihad 1-23-2016.

1479. Cinnamon Stillwell, "Islam in America's public schools: Education or indoctrination?" 4:00 am, Wednesday, June 11, 2008, *SFGate,* www.sfgate.com/politics/article/Islam-in-America-s-public-schools-Educationor-2482820.php 1-23-2016

1480. Tokyo, Kamata Musolla, "Saitama Masjid (Saitama Muslim Cultural Association)," sites.google.com/site/smcajp/prayer/masjid-in-japan/tokyo 1-23-2016

1481. William Wager Cooper, Piyu Yue, *Challenges of the Muslim World: Present, Future and Past.* Bingley, UK: Emerald Group Publishing, 2008, p. 199.

1482. George Weigel, *Faith, Reason, and the War Against Jihadism: A Call to Action.* New York: Crown Publishing Group, 2009, p. 42.

1483. Theo Emery, "Debate Erupts Over Muslim School in Virginia," *New York Times,* June 10, 2009, www.nytimes.com/2009/06/11/us/11fairfax.html?_r=0

1484. Usama bin Ladin Abu Abdullah Usama bin Ladin, Declaration Of War Against The Americans Occupying The Land Of The Two Holy Places, "Expel the Infidels from the Arab Peninsula," A Message from Usama bin Muhammad bin Laden unto his Muslim Brethren all over the World generally, and in the Arab Peninsula specifically, retrieved from the World Wide Web May 05, 2004, www.intellnet.org/documents/300/080/382.htm

1485. Hasan Al-Banna, "Young Muslims in pursuit of Allah's Pleasure." www.youngmuslims.ca/biographies/display.asp?ID=8

1486. "The Roots of Violent Islamist Extremism and Efforts to Counter It: Hearing Before the Committee on Homeland Security and Governmental Affairs," United States Senate, One Hundred Tenth Congress, Second Session, July 10, 2008, p. 141. Sawad Hadi, *Looming Black Shadows: The Rise of Terrorist States and the New Generation al-Qaeda*. Gurgaon, India: Partridge Publishing, 2016, Joel C. Rosenberg, *Inside the Revolution*. Carol Stream, IL: Tyndale House Publishers, Inc., March 10, 2009, p. 36.

1487. American Society of Authors and Writers, "It Happened in History: Salman Rushdie." amsaw.org/amsaw-ithappenedinhistory-061904-rushdie.html

1488. The fatwa against Rushdie says: "In the name of God Almighty. There is only one God, to whom we shall all return. I would like to inform all intrepid Muslims in the world that the author of the book entitled *The Satanic Verses*, which has been compiled, printed, and published in opposition to Islam, the Prophet, and the Qur'an, as well as those publishers who were aware of its contents, have been sentenced to death. I call on all zealous Muslims to execute them quickly, wherever they find them, so that no one will dare insult the Islamic sanctions. Whoever is killed on this path will be regarded as a martyr, God willing. In addition, anyone who has access to the author of the book, but does not possess the power to execute him, should refer him to the people so that he may be punished for his actions. May God's blessing be on you all. Ruhollah Musavi Khomeini." Wikipedia, "Salman Rushdie—The Satanic Verses Controversy," en.wikipedia.org/wiki/Salman_rushdie# The_Satanic_Verses_controversy

1489. Wikipedia, "Salman Rushdie—The Satanic Verses Controversy," en.wikipedia.org/wiki/Salman_rushdie# The_Satanic_Verses_controversy

1489. en.wikipedia.org/wiki/Salman_rushdie# The_Satanic_Verses_controversy

1490. American Society of Authors and Writers, "It Happened in History: Salman Rushdie." amsaw.org/amsaw-ithappenedinhistory-061904-rushdie.html

1491. Edwin McDowell, "'Satanic Verses' Is Removed From Shelves by Book Chain," *New York Times*, February 17, 1989.

1492. "Cody's Books: An Historical Berkeley Landmark and Independent Bookstore Begins Archive at the Bancroft Library." *Bene Legere*— Newsletter of the Library Associates, number 53, Summer 1999. www.lib.berkeley.edu/LDO/bene53/codys.html

1493. Madalyn O'Hair, "Red Herring Rushdie, Part II," American Atheists. www.atheists.org/Islam/herring2.html

1494. Wikipedia, "Salman Rushdie—The Satanic Verses Controversy," en.wikipedia.org/wiki/Salman_rushdie#The_Satanic_Verses_controversy

1495. See Taslima Nasreen/Nasrin's website: www.taslimanasrin.com/

1496. Hinduism: Details about 'Taslima Nasrin,' hinduism-guide.com/hinduism/taslima_nasrin.htm 3-14-2016

1497. Wikipedia, "Taslima Nasrin," en.wikipedia.org/wiki/Taslima_Nasrin

1498. A. Guillaume, *The Life of Muhammad: A Translation of Ibn Ishaq's Sirat Rasul Allah*. New York: Oxford University Press, 1955, eighteenth printing, 2004, p. 676.

1499. Wikipedia, "World Trade Center Bombing—Before the Attacks," en.wikipedia.org/wiki/World_Trade_Center_bombing#Before_the_attacks Wikipedia, World Trade Center Bombing, en.wikipedia.org/wiki/World_Trade_Center_bombing Kentix Computing, *Dead or Alive*. "Omar Abdul Rahman."www.deadoraliveinfo.com/dead.nsf/rnames-nf/Rahman+Omar+Abdul

1500. Petri Liukkonen, "Naguib Mahfouz," *Books and Writers*, www.kirjasto.sci.fi/mahfouz.htm

1501. Mahfouz died August 30, 2006. Obituary: Naguib Mahfouz. December 11, 1911–August 30, 2006. *The Times*, London, August 31, 2006. www.timesonline.co.uk/article/0,,60-2335326,00.html

1502. Annie Brisibe, Miss World And Islam: "Fatwa" And Isioma Daniel A Nigerian "Fatwa," *Nigeria World*, November 26, 2002, nigeriaworld.com/columnist/brisibe/112602.html 8-18-2016

1503. CNN, Nigeria: Miss World, archives.cnn.com/2002/WORLD/africa/11/22/nigeria.missworld/

1504. Qur'an. chapter 33, verse 50. The Holy Qur'an. Translation by Abdullah Yusufali. Complete online text. www.wam.umd.edu/~stwright/rel/islam/

1505. John Paden, "Islam and Democratic Federalism in Nigeria," *Africa Notes*, Number 8, March 2002, Center for Strategic and International Studies, csis.org/files/media/csis/pubs/anotes_0203.pdf 3-14-2016. "Nigeria." *Encyclopædia Britannica*. 2006. Encyclopædia Britannica Online. Retrieved 2006, from the World Wide Web www.britannica.com/eb/article-55291.

1506. "Profile: Iranian academic facing death Hashem Aghajari." BBC, December 2, 2002, news.bbc.co.uk/2/hi/middle_east/2518835.stm

1507. Free Muslims Coalition, www.freemuslims.org/ 3-14-2016

1508. "Related by Abu Dawud in as-Sunan, vol. 4, p. 109 # 4291; al-Hakim in al-Mustadrak, vol. 4, pp. 567, 568 # 8592, 8593; and at-Tabarani in al-Mu'jam al-Awsat, vol. 7, p. 272 # 6523." Cited in the website of Muhammad Tahir-ul-Qadri's Minhaj-ul-Quran International, www.minhaj.org/english/tid/8718/A-Profile-of-Shaykh-ul-Islam-Dr-Muhammad-Tahir-ul-Qadri.html

1509. Minhaj ul quran, Facebook page, www.facebook.com/Minhaj-Ul-quran-248479055178833/ 3-4-2016

1510. "About PAT," *Pakistani Awami Tehreek*, www.pat.com.pk/english/tid/13644/About-PAT/ 3-4-2016

1511. "Dr Tahir-ul-Qadri launches Islamic Curriculum on Peace and Counter-Terrorism in UK," Dated: 23 June 2015, Minhaj-ul-Quran, www.minhaj.org/english/tid/33354/ Dr-Tahir-ul-Qadri-launches-anti-ISIS-Islamic-curriculum-peace-counter-terrorism-de-radicalisation-ideology-Jihad-elimination-extremism-UK.html 3-4-2016

1512. Minhaj ul Quran, "Dr. Tahir ul Qadri Launches Anti-ISIS Curriculum," www.minhaj.org/english/tid/ 33354/Dr-Tahir-ul-Qadri-launches-anti-ISIS-Islamic-curriculum-peace-counter-terrorism-de-radicalisation-ideology-Jihad-elimination-extremism-UK.html 8-18-2016

1513. Minhaj-ul-Quran International, www.minhaj.org/english/tid/1799/ Minhaj-ul-Quran-International.html 3-4-2016

1514. "Battle of Badr was an important one from the point of its consequences and impacts. In fact, it was the first instalment of punishment for atheists, from Allah, for denying the invitation to Islam. This battle made it clear as to who deserved the survival more? Islam or heathenism (certainly Islam) and how the things will take shape in future." Maulana A.S. Muhammad Abdul Hai (Rah.), *Holy Life of Hazrat Muhammad (Hayyat-E-Tayyaba)*. Delhi, India: Islami Academy, 1984. www.al-islamforall.org/litre/Englitre/Hmohd.htm

1515. Robert Spencer, "Robert Spencer in PJ Lifestyle: The Hypocrisy of the Fatwa Against Terrorism," *Jihad Watch*, December 25, 2013 2:38 p.m., www.jihadwatch.org/2013/12/ robert-spencerin-pj-lifestyle-thehypocrisy-of-the-fatwaagainst-terrorism 3-4-2016

1516. Muhammad Tahir-ul-Qadri, Fatwa On Terrorism, www.fatwaonterrorism.com/

1517. Ayaan Hirsi Ali, *Heretic: Why Islam Needs a Reformation Now*, New York: HarperCollins, 2015, p. 2.

1518. Ayaan Hirsi Ali (2015-03-24). *Heretic: Why Islam Needs a Reformation Now* (p. 177). HarperCollins. Kindle Edition.

1519. Ayaan Hirsi Ali (2015-03-24). *Heretic: Why Islam Needs a Reformation Now* (p. 177). HarperCollins. Kindle Edition.

1520. Ayaan Hirsi Ali (2015-03-24). *Heretic: Why Islam Needs a Reformation Now* (p. 42). HarperCollins. Kindle Edition.

1521. Ayaan Hirsi Ali (2015-03-24). *Heretic: Why Islam Needs a Reformation Now* (p. 42). HarperCollins. Kindle Edition.

1522. Ayaan Hirsi Ali (2015-03-24). *Heretic: Why Islam Needs a Reformation Now* (pp. 45–46). HarperCollins. Kindle Edition.

1523. Ayaan Hirsi Ali (2015-03-24). *Heretic: Why Islam Needs a Reformation Now* (p. 147). HarperCollins. Kindle Edition. For "four situations in which a husband is permitted to discipline his wife by hitting her," see Shaykh Muhammad Saalih al-Munajjid, Islam Question and Answer, 14 March 2016, Fiqh of the family » Rights of spouses. 10680: What are the rights of the husband and what are the rights of the wife? islamqa.info/en/10680 3-14-2016

1524. Ayaan Hirsi Ali (2015-03-24). *Heretic: Why Islam Needs a Reformation Now* (p. 6). HarperCollins. Kindle Edition.

1525. Ayaan Hirsi Ali (2015-03-24). *Heretic: Why Islam Needs a Reformation Now* (p. 3). HarperCollins. Kindle Edition.

1526. Samuel Smith, "Ayaan Hirsi Ali: America's Greatest 'Weakness' Against Radical Islamic Terrorism Is Political Correctness," *The Christian Post*, March 7, 2016, 4:06 pm, www.christianpost.com/news/ayaan-hirsi-aliradical-islamic-terrorism-cpac-america-weakness-against-jihadists-political-correctness-158996/

1527. The Muslim Brotherhood (author), An Explanatory Memorandum On the General Strategic Goal for the Group In North America 5/22/1991 www.investigativeproject.org/documents/ misc/20.pdf

1528. Tom Heneghan, "West's free speech stand bars blasphemy ban — OIC," Reuters, Monday Oct 15, 2012, Istanbul, uk.reuters.com/article/ uk-islam-blasphemyidUKBRE89E18W20121015

1529. Organization of Islamic Cooperation, "Organization of Islamic Cooperation, History," Webpage—Organization of Islamic Cooperation, www.oic-oci.org/oicv2/page/?p_id=52&p_ref= 26&lan=en

1530. Anti-Defamation League, "About the ADL," Anti-Defamation League website, www.adl.org/about-adl/

1531. Wikipedia, "Leo Frank," en.wikipedia.org/wiki/Leo_Frank

1532. Encyclopedia Judaica: "Anti-Defamation League (ADL)," The Jewish Virtual Library www.jewishvirtuallibrary.org/jsource/judaica/ ejud_0002_0002_0_01146.html

1533. Francis R. Nicosia, *Nazi Germany and the Arab World*, New York: Cambridge University Press, 2014. David G. Dalin, John F. Rothmann, Alan M. Dershowitz, *Icon of Evil: Hitler's Mufti and the Rise of Radical Islam*. Piscataway, NJ: Transaction Publishers, 2009, pp. 47–49. David Patterson, *Genocide in Jewish Thought*. New York: Cambridge University Press, Mar. 26, 2012, p. 209. Stefan Wild (1985). "National Socialism in the Arab near East between 1933 and 1939." *Die Welt des Islams*, New Series, Bd. 25, Nr. 1/4 (1985) p. 128. United States Holocaust Memorial Museum, Hajj Amin Al-Husayni: Wartime Propagandist, www.ushmm.org/wlc/en/article.php?ModuleId= 10007667

1534. Rachid Rahaoui, *L'islam des jeunes: entre contestation at normalisation*, edtions le manuscrit, 2006, *Le Manuscrit*, www.manuscrit.com p. 18.

1535. Etienne Dinet, Sliman Ben Ibrahim, *L'Orient vu de l'Occident*. Paris: Piazza-Geuthner, 1925.

1536. "Sliman ben Ibrahim Baâmer (1870-1953)," Bibliotheque National de France, data.bnf. fr/11891138/sliman_ben_ibrahim_baamer/

1537. "Slimane Ben Ibrahîm," Babelio, www.babelio. com/auteur/-Slimane-Ben-Ibrahim/322823

1538. Etienne Dinet and Sliman Ben Ibrahim, *The Project Gutenberg EBook of The Life of Mohammad*, www.gutenberg.org/cache/epub/39523/pg39523.txt

1539. Ruth Roded, *Modern Gendered Illustrations of The Life Of The Prophet Of Allah—Étienne Dinet And Sliman Ben Ibrahim* (1918), Arabica, Volume 49, Issue 3, 2002, pp. 325–359. Wikipedia, France, "Etienne Dinet," fr.wikipedia.org/wiki/%C3%89 tienne_Dinet#Biographie

1540. *Journal of the Royal Asiatic Society of Great Britain & Ireland (New Series)*, Volume 56, Issue January 1, 1924, pp. 130–131.

1541. Etienne Dinet, Sliman Ben Ibrahim, *L'Orient vu de l'Occident*. Paris: Piazza-Geuthner, 1925.

1542. Etienne Dinet, Sliman Ben Ibrahim, *The Life of Mohammad: The Prophet of Allah*. Paris: Paris Book Club: 1918.

1543. Etienne Dinet and Sliman Ben Ibrahim, *The Project Gutenberg EBook of The Life of Mohammad*, www.gutenberg.org/cache/epub/39523/pg39523.txt

1544. Asli Cirakman, *From the 'Terror of the World' to the 'Sick Man of Europe"—European Images of Ottoman Empire and Society from the Sixteenth Century to the Nineteenth*. New York: Peter Lang, 2002, p. 164.

1545. Felix Konrad, "From the 'Turkish Menace' to Exoticism and Orientalism: Islam as Antithesis of Europe (1453–1914)," *EGO*, European History Online, 2011-03-14, ieg-ego.eu/en/threads/models-and-stereotypes/ from-the-turkish-menace-to-orientalism/ felix-konrad-from-the-turkish-menace-to- exoticism-and-orientalism-1453-1914# TheImageofIslamintheEraoftheTurkishMenace 2-1-2016

1546. Peter O'Brien, *European Perceptions of Islam and America from Saladin to George W. Bush*. New York: Palgrave Macmillan, 2008, pp. 75–76.

1547. Quoted in Rachid Rahaoui, "L'islam des jeunes: entre contestation at normalisation," editions le manuscrit, 2006, *Le Manuscrit*, www.manuscrit.com p. 18.

1548. Edward W. Said, "The Phony Islamic Threat," *The New York Times Magazine*, November 21, 1993, p. 62.

1549. Edward W. Said, "Orientalism Reconsidered," *Race & Class*, 27, October 1985, pp. 1–15.

1550. Edward W. Said, "Orientalism Reconsidered," Cultural Critique. No. 1 (Autumn, 1985), pp. 89–107. Nasar Meer, *Racialization and Religion: Race, Culture and Difference in the Study of Antisemitism and Islamophobia*. Abingdon, Oxon, UK: Routledge, 2015, p. 34. Marc Helbling, *Islamophobia in the West: Measuring and Explaining Individual Attitudes*. Abingdon, Oxon, UK: Routledge, 2013.

1551. Edward W. Said, "Orientalism Reconsidered," *Cultural Critique*. No. 1 (Autumn, 1985), pp. 89–107, courses.arch.vt.edu/courses/wdunaway/gia5524/ said85.pdf

1552. Yvonne Yazbeck Haddad, *Muslims in the West: From Sojourners to Citizens*. Oxford, UK: Oxford University Press, 2002, p. 24.

1553. Muslim Museum Initiative, "Runnymede Trust Researches Islamophobia," Muslim Museum Initiative, muslimmuseum.org.uk/ runnymede-trust-researches-islamophobia/

1554. Yvonne Yazbeck Haddad, *Muslims in the West: From Sojourners to Citizens*. Oxford, UK: Oxford University Press, 2002, p. 24.

1555. Chris Allan co-authored the Summary Report on Islamophobia in the EU after 11 September 2001. Simon Sorgenfrei, "Islamophobia (review)," *Journal of Shi'a Islamic Studies*. Volume 5, Issue 2, Spring 2012, pp. 216-220, muse.jhu.edu/login?auth= 0&type=summary&url=/journals/ journal_of_shia_islamic_studies/v005/ 5.2.sorgenfrei.pdf

1556. Chris Allen, "The 'first' decade of Islamophobia," The Islamic Council of Western Australia, www.islamiccouncilwa.com.au/ wp-content/uploads/2014/05/ Decade_of_Islamophobia.pdf

1557. "Islamophobia: issues, challenges and action — A report by the Commission on British Muslims and Islamophobia," 2004. Chaired by Dr Richard Stone, Research by Hugh Muir and Laura Smith, Editor: Robin Richardson, Adviser: Imam Dr Abduljalil Sajid, 2002. www.insted.co.uk/islambook.pdf

1558. Koffi Annan, 7 December 2004 Sg/Sm/9637-Hr/4802-Pi/1627 Secretary-General, Addressing Headquarters Seminar On Confronting Islamophobia, Stresses Importance of Leadership, Two-Way Integration, Dialogue Secretary-General Press Release, United Nations, www.un.org/press/en/2004/sgsm9637.doc.htm

1559. Organization of Islamic Cooperation, Ten-Year Programme of Action to Meet The Challenges Facing The Muslim Ummah in the 21st Century, Report of The Third Extraordinary Session of the Islamic Summit, Mecca, December 7–8, 2005, www.oic-oci.org/ex-summit/english/ 10-years-plan.htm.

1560. Organization of Islamic Cooperation, TEN-YEAR PROGRAMME OF ACTION TO MEET THE CHALLENGES FACING THE MUSLIM UMMAH IN THE 21ST CENTURY, Report of The Third Extraordinary Session of the Islamic Summit, Mecca, December 7–8, 2005, www.oic-oci.org/ex-summit/english/10-years-plan.htm.

1561. Andrew E. Harrod, "Organization of Islamic Cooperation's 'Islamophobia' Campaign against Freedom," Religious Freedom Coalition, Middle East Forum, January 20, 2014, www.meforum.org/3721/oic-islamophobiacampaign 3-8-2016

1562. Toni Johnson, "The Organization of the Islamic Conference," Council for Foreign Relations, June 29, 2010, www.cfr.org/religion/organization-islamic-conference/p22563#p2

1563. Organization of Islamic Countries, Security Council Meeting on UN-OIC Cooperation, letter to the UN issued from Azerbaijan — 2013-10-28, www.oicun.org/oic_at_un/79/20131105042858831.html 3-6-2016

1564. Andrew E. Harrod of the Religious Freedom Coalition, "Organization of Islamic Cooperation's 'Islamophobia' Campaign against Freedom," Middle East Forum, January 20, 2014, www.meforum.org/3721/oic-islamophobia-campaign 3-8-2016

1565. "We cannot accept insults to Islam under the guise of freedom of thought," Turkish Prime Minister Tayyip Erdogan said about the OIC's anti-blasphemy efforts. Reuters, Mon Oct 15, 2012, Tom Heneghan, Reuters' Religion Editor, from Istanbul, "West's free speech stand bars blasphemy ban —OIC," Reuters, uk.reuters.com/article/uk-islam-blasphemyidUKBRE89E18W20121015

1566. Organization of Islamic Cooperation, Eight [sic] OIC Observatory Report on Islamophobia, May 2014–April 2015. Presented to the 42nd Council of Foreign Ministers, Organization of Islamic Cooperation, published May 25–28, 2015, p. 8. www.oic-oci.org/oicv2/upload/islamophobia/2015/en/reports/8th_ob_Rep_Islamophobia_Final.pdf 3-8-2016

1567. Organization of Islamic Cooperation, Eight [sic] OIC Observatory Report on Islamophobia, May 2014–April 2015. Presented to the 42nd Council of Foreign Ministers, Organization of Islamic Cooperation, published May 25–28, 2015, www.oic-oci.org/oicv2/upload/islamophobia/2015/en/reports/8th_ob_Rep_Islamophobia_Final.pdf 3-8-2016

1568. Organization of Islamic Cooperation, Eight [sic] OIC Observatory Report on Islamophobia, May 2014–April 2015. Presented to the 42nd Council of Foreign Ministers, Organization of Islamic Cooperation, published May 25–28, 2015, www.oic-oci.org/oicv2/upload/islamophobia/2015/en/reports/8th_ob_Rep_Islamophobia_Final.pdf 3-8-2016

1569. Stephen C. Poulson, Social Movements in Twentieth-century Iran: Culture, Ideology, and Mobilizing Frameworks. Lexington Books, 2006, pp. 55–56. Fuad I. Khuri, Imams and Emirs: State, Religion and Sects in Islam, London: Saqi, Feb. 1, 2014. Stephen Coughlin (2015-05-04), Catastrophic Failure: Blindfolding America in the Face of Jihad (Kindle Locations 4518-4519). Center for Security Policy Press. Kindle Edition.

1570. Sahih Bukhari. Book 52, Hadith pp. 176–177. Translated by M. Muhsin Khan. SearchTruth.com. "Search Truth is a non-profit organization aimed at utilizing the latest technologies available in order to spread the Word of Allah and the Sunnah of the Holy Prophet (pbuh) to as large an audience as possible." Retrieved January 18, 2016 February 18, 2007, from the World Wide Web www.searchtruth.com/searchHadith.php?keyword=There+is+a+Jew+hiding+behind+me&translator=1&search=1&book=&start=0&records_display=10&search_word=exact

1571. Kevin McCauley, "Saudis Bolster Spending at Qorvis," O'Dwyer's Inside News of PR & Marketing Communications, Mon., May 11, 2015, www.odwyerpr.com/story/public/4577/2015-05-11/saudis-bolster-spending-at-qorvis.html Fredreka Schouten, "Pakistan, Libyan rebels tap into lobbying firms," USA Today, Updated 5/12/2011 9:12 a.m. usatoday30.usatoday.com/news/washington/2011-05-11-Libya-lobbying-Pakistan-Washington_n.htm Kevin Bogardus, "Pakistan's $1M is up for grabs," The Hill, 11/13/13, thehill.com/business-a-lobbying/business-a-lobbying/190062-pakistans-1m-is-upfor-grabs Matt Hardigree, "How Bahrain Spends Millions To Spin The Press," Jalopnik, 4/09/12 2:00 p.m. jalopnik.com/5900113/how-bahrain-spendsmillions-to-spin-the-press Wikipedia, "Burston-Marsteller," en.wikipedia.org/wiki/Burson-Marsteller PR Watch, "Qorvis Communications: Relationship with Bahrain Government," Bahrain Watch, bahrainwatch.org/pr/qorvis.php

1572. Sheila Musaji, "The origins of the term 'Islamophobia'," The American Muslim, Posted May 20, 2015, updated 5/20/2015, theamericanmuslim.org/tam.php/features/articles/islamophobia-muslim-brotherhood/0019253 Discover the Networks, "Politics of 'Islamophobia,'" www.discoverthenetworks.org/viewSubCategory.asp?id=777 Discover the Networks describes itself as "a guide to the political left." Stephen Coughlin (2015-05-04), Catastrophic Failure: Blindfolding America in the Face of Jihad (Kindle Locations 5206–5208). Center for Security Policy Press. Kindle Edition.

1573. Ayaan Hirsi Ali, Heretic: Why Islam Needs a Reformation Now. New York: HarperCollins, 2015.

1574. Ayaan Hirsi Ali (2015-03-24), *Heretic: Why Islam Needs a Reformation Now* (p. 3). HarperCollins. Kindle Edition. pp. 3–4.

1575. S. Stern, *Saudi Arabia and the Global Islamic Terrorist Network: America and the West's Fatal Embrace*. New York: Palgrave Macmillan, 2011. Steven Emerson, The Council on American-Islamic Relations (CAIR), The Investigative Project, www.investigativeproject.org/profile/172/the-council-on-american-islamic-relations-cair. Steven Emerson, "The Council on American-Islamic Relations (CAIR)—CAIR Exposed," The Investigative Project, www.investigativeproject.org/documents/misc/122.pdf

1576. Michael Rubin, "Whitewashing Islamists," *Commentary Magazine*, October 1, 2012 www.aei.org/publication/whitewashing-islamists/

1577. Ayaan Hirsi Ali (2015-03-24), *Heretic: Why Islam Needs a Reformation Now* (p. 5). HarperCollins. Kindle Edition. Perry Chiaramonte, "US group CAIR named terrorist organization by United Arab Emirates," Fox News, November 17, 2014, www.foxnews.com/us/2014/11/17/us-group-cair-added-to-terror-list-by-united-arab-emirates.html

1578. Ayaan Hirsi Ali (2015-03-24), *Heretic: Why Islam Needs a Reformation Now* (p. 5). HarperCollins. Kindle Edition.

1579. *Isliamic Finder*, "Does Islam Allow Wife Beating?" www.islamicfinder.org/articles/article.php?id=307 The Religion of Peace, "What Does Islam Teach About Wife-Beating, What Makes Islam Different," www.thereligionofpeace.com/pages/quran/wife-beating.aspx IslamicFinder.org is a Muslim website for Muslims. Its description of itself: "IslamicFinder's mission is to help Muslims around the globe navigate their daily lives; we offer innovative products and services that are truly world-class and delight our users." The Religion of Peace website, on the other hand, is hostile to Islam. Here's how it describes itself: "TheReligionofPeace.com is a pluralistic, non-partisan site concerned with Islam's true political and religious teachings according to its own texts. The purpose is to underscore the threat that Islam poses to human dignity and freedom, as well as the violence and dysfunction that ensues as a direct consequence of this religion's supremacist teachings."

1580. Ayaan Hirsi Ali (2015-03-24), *Heretic: Why Islam Needs a Reformation Now* (p. 143). HarperCollins. Kindle Edition.

1581. Ayaan Hirsi Ali (2015-03-24), *Heretic: Why Islam Needs a Reformation Now* (pp. 26–27). HarperCollins. Kindle Edition.

1582. Asra Q. Nomani, Biography, www.asranomani.com/Biography.aspx 2-29-2016

1583. Qur'an, 2:65, 5:60, and 7:166, The Holy Qur'an. Translation by Abdullah Yusufali. Complete online text. Retrieved March 20, 2005, from the World Wide Web www.wam.umd.edu/~stwright/rel/islam/ and The Noble Qur'an, quran.com/search?q=apes "The Jews, who are the nation of pigs and monkeys, are nothing but a source of evil, corruption, tribulation and war. ...Our war against them is continuous." Abdul-Azeez Al-Qaari, *The Menace of the Jews*. Translated by Hazem Ragab. Mecca: Alminbar.com—Alminbar.com — the Orator's garden and the Muslim's provision. Here you will find a variety of material to help you prepare for your sermons. Retrieved January 6, 2007, from the World Wide Web www.alminbar.com/khutbaheng/819.htm

1584. Asra Q. Nomani, "Biography," Asra Nomani website, www.asranomani.com/Biography.aspx, 2-29-2016

1585. Asra Q. Nomani, "Biography," Asra Nomani website, www.asranomani.com/Biography.aspx, 2-29-2016

1586. Asra Q. Nomani, "Books description: Standing Alone in Mecca: An American Woman's Struggle for the Soul of Islam," asranomani.com, www.asranomani.com/books/standing.aspx

1587. Asra Nomani, "Islamic Feminist: Duke Students Tried To Cancel My Speech. That Made It Even More Important," *Time*, April 13, 2015, time.com/3818372/islamic-feminist-duke-speech/ 3-8-2016 .

1588. Asra Nomani, "Islamic Feminist: Duke Students Tried To Cancel My Speech. That Made It Even More Important," *Time*, April 13, 2015, time.com/3818372/islamic-feminist-duke-speech/ 3-8-2016

1589. The Investigative Project on Terrorism, Muslim Students Association, Dossier, www.investigativeproject.org/documents/misc/31.pdf. Edward E. Curtis, *Encyclopedia of Muslim-American History*. New York: Infobase Publishing, 2010 p. 572. Manning Marable, Hishaam D. Aidi, *Black Routes to Islam*. New York: Palgrave MacMillan, 2009, p. 53. S. Stern, *Saudi Arabia and the Global Islamic Terrorist Network: America and the West's Fatal Embrace*. New York: Palgrave Macmillan, 2011

1590. Itamar Marcus and Nan Jacques Zilberdik, "The Muslim Brotherhood — in its own words, PMW translation of Jihad is the way by Mustafa Mashhur, Leader of the Muslim Brotherhood in Egypt, 1996-2002," Palestine Media Watch, palwatch.org/main.aspx?fi=157&doc_id=4603 Federation of American Scientists, FAS Intelligence Resource Program, Muslim Brothers, fas.org/irp/world/para/mb.htm Foundation for Defense of Democracies, "The Muslim Brotherhood: Understanding its Roots and Impact," Foundation for Defense of Democracies, www.defenddemocracy.org/the-muslimbrotherhood-understanding-its-rootsand-impact/ #sthash.VI5KCCoj.dpuf. Lorenzo Vidino, "The Muslim Brotherhood's Conquest of Europe" Middle East Quarterly, Winter 2005, pp. 25–34, www.meforum.org/687/the-muslim-brotherhoods-conquest-of-europe 3-18-2016

1591. David Cameron, Written statement to Parliament Muslim Brotherhood review: statement by the Prime Minister From: Prime Minister's Office, 10 Downing Street, The Rt Hon David Cameron MP, Cabinet Office, Foreign & Commonwealth Office and + others. Delivered on: 17 December 2015, First published: 17 December 2015, www.gov.uk/government/speeches/muslim-brotherhood-review-statementby-the-prime-minister

1592. Manning Marable, Hishaam D. Aidi, Black Routes to Islam. New York: Palgrave MacMillan, 2009, p. 53.

1593. Jonathan Dowd-Gailey, "Islamism's Campus Club: The Muslim Students' Association," Middle East Quarterly, Spring 2004, pp. 63–72, www.meforum.org/603/islamisms-campusclub-the-muslim-students

1594. Carly Hoilman, "College's Muslim Student Association Demands 'Zero Tolerance Policy' Against 'Islamophobic Speech and Actions,'" The Blaze, Dec. 29, 2015 3:24 p.m., www.theblaze.com/stories/2015/12/29/colleges-muslim-student-association-demandszero-tolerance-policy-against-islamophobicspeech-and-actions/ Nikita Biryukov, "Rutgers Muslim Student Association hosts forum on Islamophobia," February 08, 2016, 10:09 p.m., The Daily Targum, www.dailytargum.com/article/2016/02/rutgers-muslim-student-association-hostsforum-on-islamophobia Jessica Mendoza, "Muslim students take on Islamophobia: Next protest movement in the making? Buoyed by both the Black Lives Matter movement and growing calls for safe spaces on campus, Muslim student groups across the country are pushing back against anti-Islamic sentiment," Christian Science Monitor, January 7, 2016, www.csmonitor.com/USA/Education/2016/0107/Muslim-students-take-on-Islamophobia-Next-protest-movement-in-the-making

1595. Manning Marable, Hishaam D. Aidi, Black Routes to Islam. New York: Palgrave MacMillan, 2009, p. 53.

1596. Wikipedia, "Montenegrin–Ottoman War (1861–62)", en.wikipedia.org/wiki/Montenegrin%E2%80%93 Ottoman_War_(1861%E2%80%9362)

1597. Ayatollah Khomeini, Sayings of the Ayatollah Khomeini, p. 5.

1598. Quoted in: Coughlin, Stephen (2015-05-04), Catastrophic Failure: Blindfolding America in the Face of Jihad (Kindle Locations 13313-13316). Center for Security Policy Press. Kindle Edition.

1599. John Keegan, A History of Warfare. Encore Booknotes. C-Span2 BookTV. May 27, 2006.

1600. Wikipedia, "Algerian War of Independence, War Dead," en.wikipedia.org/wiki/Algerian_War_of_Independence#War_dead

1601. I owe this phrase to Richard Kidd when he was at the State Department. Personal conversation, 2001.

1602. For a brief history of the rise of the protest industry, see: Howard Bloom, The Genius of the Beast: A Radical Re-Vision of Capitalism. Amherst, NY: Prometheus Books, 2010.

1603. Adam Hochschild, Bury the Chains: Prophets and Rebels in the Fight to Free an Empire's Slaves. Boston: Houghton Mifflin, 2005. "The Age of Abolition" is sometimes computed to have begun as early as 1748 with the criticism of slavery in Montesquieu's Esprit des Lois. But the idea that all men are born free appeared in Captain Johnson's History of the Pyrates, a book published in London in 1724 that some think was written by Daniel Defoe. And the first decree banning slavery appeared in Portugal in 1761. However it took time for the anti-slavery impulse to go from an idea that was occasionally bandied about to a mass movement. Robin Blackburn, The Overthrow of Colonial Slavery 1776–1848. New York: Verso, 1988, pp. 36, 45–46, 62. P.J. Marshall, Alaine Low, The Oxford History of the British Empire: Volume II: The Eighteenth Century. New York: Oxford University Press, 1998, p. xii. Wikipedia, "William Wilberforce." en.wikipedia.org/wiki/William_Wilberforce

1604. Wikipedia, "Anti-Slavery: National Abolition Dates," en.wikipedia.org/wiki/Anti-slavery#National_abolition_dates

1605. The industrialist and philanthropist Andrew Carnegie and the father of psychology William James founded the American Anti-Imperialist League in 1899. Modern History Sourcebook. Retrieved from the World Wide Web November 03, 2002 www.fordham.edu/halsall/mod/1899antiimp.html. Platform of the American Anti-Imperialist League (October 18, 1899) Retrieved from the World Wide Web November 02, 2002 www.boondocksnet.com/ai/ailtexts/ailplat.html

1606. Hadhrat Mirza Ghulam Ahmad, *Essence of Islam*. Volume One. Chapter 3. Islamic Books Library @ Alislam.org. Al Islam: The Official Website of the Ahmadiyya Muslim Community. www.alislam.org/books/essence1/chap3.htm

1607. Matthew 5: 7.

1608. The anti-war movement—and the entire protest industry—were given one of their most powerful techniques in 1849 when Henry David Thoreau protested the Mexican-American War and wrote his pamphlet on Resistance to Civil Government—a pamphlet that introduced the concept of Civil Disobedience. *Great American Essays* (Unabridged). Portsmouth, Rhode Island: Jimcin Recordings. nd. Wikipedia, "Civil Disobedience—Thoreau." en.wikipedia.org/wiki/Civil_Disobedience_%28Thoreau%29

1609. Thomas Jefferson and John Adams, "Declaration of Independence." 1776. These words were influenced by the creation myth of the Old Testament as seen through a deist Christian's eyes. To see how, take a peek at the following. The Wikipedia explains that "Avery Cardinal Dulles, a leading Roman Catholic theologian reports, 'he [Thomas Jefferson] saw Christianity as the highest expression of natural religion and Jesus as an incomparably great moral teacher." Avery Cardinal Dulles, "The Deist Minimum," *First Things: A Monthly Journal of Religion and Public Life* Issue: 149. (Jan 2005) pp.25+. Quoted in Wikipedia, "Thomas Jefferson—Religious views." en.wikipedia.org/wiki/Thomas_Jefferson#Religious_views.
See also Daniel J Boorstin, *The Lost World of Thomas Jefferson*. Chicago: The University of Chicago Press, 1981. Originally published 1948, p. 61. books.google.com/books?vid=ISBN0226064972&id=G3DkY0AOc6UC&pg=PA61&lpg=PA61&dq=boorstin+%22all+men+are+created+equal%22&sig=pp9s0InfGlzWHCoxRfhUY5u428Q

1610. Paul G. Kengor, Associate Professor, Grove City College, Political Science. Discussing *God and George W. Bush: A Spiritual Life* and *God and Ronald Reagan: A Spiritual Life*, both published by Regan Books. Paul Kengor. 2006 CPAC: Paul Kengor "God and Ronald Reagan" and "God and George W. Bush." C-Span2 BookTV May 28, 2006.

1611. Cathleen Falsani, "Obama on faith: The exclusive interview," transcript of a March 27, 2004, interview with Barack Obama, *Patheos*, www.patheos.com/blogs/thedudeabides/obama-on-faith-the-exclusive-interview/ 1-20-2016. Greg Jaffe, "The quiet impact of Obama's Christian faith: Why the president's convictions led him to believe he could unite a divided country — and why he failed," *Washington Post*, December 22, 2015 www.washingtonpost.com/sf/national/2015/12/22/obama-faith/ 1-20-2016

1612. Wikipedia, "Bosnia and Herzegovina: Modern Bosnia," en.wikipedia.org/wiki/Bosnia_and_Herzegovina#Modern_Bosnia

1613. Ismail Royer, Alija Izetbegovic, "Young Muslims in pursuit of Allah's Pleasure." www.iviews.com Published Wednesday June 14, 2000. www.youngmuslims.ca/biographies/display.asp?ID=2

1614. "Alija Izetbegović Islamic activist and former president of Bosnia and Herzegovina 1996-2000. In 1970, Izetbegović published a manifesto entitled *The Islamic Declaration*, a work which contributed greatly to his later portrayal as an Islamic fundamentalist. He highlighted the decayed state of Islam and called for an religious and political regeneration across the Muslim world, although the book made no reference to Bosnia. In two particularly controversial passages, he declared that 'there can be neither peace nor coexistence between the Islamic faith and non-Islamic social and political institutions' and that 'the Islamic movement must and can, take over political power as soon as it is morally and numerically so strong that it can not only destroy the existing non-Islamic power, but also to build up a new Islamic one.'" Wikipedia, Ali Izetbegović, en.wikipedia.org/wiki/Alija_Izetbegovi%C4%87
See also: Nebojsa Malic, Balkan Express, "The Real Izetbegovic: Laying to Rest a Mythical Autocrat." October 23, 2003. www.antiwar.com/malic/m102303.html

1615. Center for Peace in the Balkans, 7th Bosnian Muslim Brigade, based in Zenica—the international Islamic mercenary force known as the mujahideen. Centre For Peace In The Balkans, www.balkanpeace.org/temp/tmp13.html, reprinted in www.militantislammonitor.org/article/id/2088

1616. "The roots of Muslim mercenaries fighting for the Bosnians stretch back to World War II....the former Mufti of Jerusalem, Hajj Amine al-Husseini helped organize the Bosnian Muslims into several units under [Nazi] SS command, especially the largely Muslim 13th SS 'Handzar' division. ...The Bosnian Muslim units, including the Handzar division, joined the Ustashi forces in terror comapigns and ethnic cleansing against the Serbs in what is today western Bosnia-Herzegovina and the Krajina region. ...Bosnian president Isetbegovic's purpose in the wars against the Croats and the Serbs in the 1990 [sic] appeared to be to provoke the NATO intervention that preceded the Dayton peace accords of 1995. The building of the Bosnian Muslim army and the launching its campaigns was entrusted to Commander Ram Delic, whose plan was to precipitate Western intervention and enable the Muslim forces to conduct a major war against both Serbs and Croats. By 1993, Deleic, with help and encouragement from Muslim states abroad, and certainly with the knowledge if not the active help of the CIA, was importing foreign Muslim volunteers, especially moujahiddin veterans of the Afghan war. ...Iran, Syria, Turkey, Egypt and Saudi Arabia are believed to have pledged sophisticated weapons systems, including missiles, heavy artillery, and crews and ammunition. Iran delivered many of these supplies in C-130 cargo flights, detected by UN observers, to which the United States deliberately turned a blind eye." John K. Cooley in George Baravelle, editor. Rethink: Cause and Consequences of September 11. Millbrook, NY: [Publisher] De MO design.Method of Operation LTD. 2004

1617. n.a. "Blair: Nato united." BBC News Online Network. April 26, 1999. news.bbc.co.uk/1/hi/uk_politics/328677.stm

1618. Wikipedia, "Bosnia and Herzegovina: Modern Bosnia," en.wikipedia.org/wiki/Bosnia_and_Herzegovina#Modern_Bosnia

1619. Wikipedia, "UNPROFOR," en.wikipedia.org/wiki/UNPROFOR

1620. Wikipedia, "IFOR," en.wikipedia.org/wiki/IFOR and Wikipedia, SFOR, en.wikipedia.org/wiki/SFOR

1621. Larry K. Wentz, "Lessons From Bosnia: The IFOR Experience," Federation of American Scientists, www.fas.org/irp/ops/smo/docs/ifor/bosch02.htm.

1622. New York Times journalist Thomas Friedman reports that Assad's brother, Rifaat, who was responsible for the extermination, bragged that he'd killed 38,000. Wikipedia, "Hafez al-Assad: Rise to Power," en.wikipedia.org/wiki/Hafez_al-Assad#Rise_to_power. The New Encyclopaedia Britannica, Vol. I, p. 640 gives the figure of 10,000. British author David Pryce-Jones says the death toll was actually "several tens of thousands." (David Pryce-Jones, "SelfDetermination, Arab Style," Commentary, January 1989, p. 43.) Twenty thousand is the most commonly used estimate.

1623. Eyal Ziser, Commanding Syria: Bashar Al-Asad [sic] and the First Years in Power. London: I.B. Tauris, 2007. p. ii.

1624. Priyanka Boghani, "A Staggering New Death Toll for Syria's War— 470,000," Frontline, PBS: February 11, 2016, www.pbs.org/wgbh/frontline/article/a-staggering-new-death-toll-forsyrias-war-470000/

1625. "MercyCorps, Quick facts: What you need to know about the Syria crisis," MercyCorps, Iraq, Jordan, Lebanon, Syria, Turkey, February 5, 2016, www.mercycorps.org/articles/iraq-jordan-lebanon-syria-turkey/quick-facts-what-you-need-know-about-syria-crisis

1626. Wikipedia, "Black September in Jordan," en.wikipedia.org/wiki/Black_September_in_Jordan January 25, 2006. Quoted in: Black September in Jordan, Date 1970–1971, Location Jordan www.v-twinforum.com/forums/religion-politics/106735-37-years-ago.html and in www.democraticunderground.com/discuss/duboard.php?az=view_all&address=124x112844 Norvell De Atkine, Amman 1970, A Memoir, Rubin Center Research in International Affairs, December 7, 2002, www.rubincenter.org/2002/12/de-atkine-2002-12-07/ "Black September, The PLO's attempt to take over Jordan," EretzYisroel.org, www.eretzyisroel.org/~samuel/september.html Kamal S. Salibi, The Modern History of Jordan. London: I.B. Tauris, 1998, pp. 238–240 Beverley Milton-Edwards, Peter Hinchcliffe, Jordan: A Hashemite Legacy. London: Routledge, 2009, pp. 39–44. Wikipedia, "Black September in Jordan," en.wikipedia.org/wiki/Black_September_in_Jordan About News, "'Black September': The Jordanian-PLO Civil War of 1970 — King Hussein Crushes the PLO and Expels It from Jordan," middleeast.about.com/od/jordan/a/jordan-black-september.htm

1627. Eli E. Hertz, "Mandate for Palestine" — The Legal Aspects of Jewish Rights, Myths and Facts, www.mythsandfacts.com/conflict/mandate_for_palestine/mandate_for_palestine.htm Clifford A. Wright, Facts and Fables: The Arab-Israeli Conflict. London: Routledge, 2015. Gabriel G. Tabarani, Israeli-Palestinian Conflict: From Balfour Promise to Bush Declaration: The Complications and The Road for a Lasting Peace. Bloomington, IN: AuthorHouse, 2008, p. xxvi. Joseph Sambwa Mayuya, Politics & Crimes of Zambia. Rare Books, 1994, p. 96.

1628. The figure is as high as 20,000, says A. Gowers, T. Walker, *Behind the Myth: Yasser Arafat and the Palestinian Revolution*. London: W.H. Allen, 1990. Cited in Gemma Matheson, "The Significance of Black September," *CLIO*, a journal for students of history in the Australian Capital Territory, 2010, cliojournal.wikispaces.com/The+Significance+of+Black+September. "'Black September': The Jordanian-PLO Civil War of 1970 — King Hussein Crushes the PLO and Expels It from Jordan," About News, middleeast.about.com/od/jordan/a/jordan-black-september.htm

1629. Wikipedia, "Black September in Jordan," en.wikipedia.org/wiki/Black_September_in_Jordan

1630. Jay Nordlinger, *Peace, They Say: A History of the Nobel Peace Prize, the Most Famous and Controversial Prize in the World*. New York: Encounter Books, 2013, p. 6

1631. Mark Ensalaco, *Middle Eastern Terrorism: From Black September to September 11*. Philadelphia: University of Pennsylvania Press, Apr. 17, 2012, pp. 39–43.

1632. Wikipedia, "Benjamin Harrison," en.wikipedia.org/wiki/Benjamin%5FHarrison. Wikipedia, Wounded Knee Massacre, en.wikipedia.org/wiki/Wounded_Knee_Massacre. Wikipedia, "Indian Wars," en.wikipedia.org/wiki/Indian_wars.

1633. Wikipedia, "Utah War," en.wikipedia.org/wiki/Utah_War

1634. David Lipsky, *Absolutely American: Four Years at West Point*. Boston: Houghton Mifflin, 2003: p. 198.

1635. Church of God Evangel, Volume 81, Cleveland TN: Church of God Publishing House, 1991, p. 165. Mark Bradley, *Iran and Christianity: Historical Identity and Present Relevance*, New York: Bloomsbury Publishing, Oct. 27, 2011.

1636. Iran Human Rights Documentation Center, "Apostasy in the Islamic Republic of Iran," www.iranhrdc.org/english/publications/reports/1000000512-apostasy-in-the-Islamic-Republic-of-Iran.html#3.1.1 1-20-2016

1637. Muhammad H. Haykal, *The Life of Muhammad*. Translated by Isma'il Raji al-Faruqi. Kuala Lumpur, Malaysia: Islamic Book Trust, 2002, p. 300.

1638. Muhammad H. Haykal, *The Life of Muhammad*. Translated by Isma'il Raji al-Faruqi. Kuala Lumpur, Malaysia: Islamic Book Trust, 2002, p. 361.

1639. Muhammad H. Haykal, *The Life of Muhammad*. Translated by Isma'il Raji al-Faruqi. Kuala Lumpur, Malaysia: Islamic Book Trust, 2002, p. 361.

1640. Caroline Elkins won a Pulitzer Prize for general nonfiction for her book *Imperial Reckoning: The Untold Story of Britain's Gulag in Kenya*. For more on her point of view see: Caroline Elkins, Why Malaya Is No Model For Iraq: Royal Screwup, *The New Republic* Online December 19, 2005, www.tnr.com/doc.mhtml?i=20051219&s=elkins121905

1641. Arndt Graf, Susanne Schroter, Edwin Wieringa, "Aceh: History, Politics and Culture," Singapore: Institute of Southeast Asian Studies, 2010, pp. 182–183.

1642. "Islam," *Smithsonian World*, Program 305, Steve York, producer/director, Adrian Malone, executive producer, Sandra W. Bradley, senior producer, Michael Olmert, writer, coproduced by the Smithsonian Institution and WETA, Washington, D.C., first aired July 22, 1987.

1643. "Islam," *Smithsonian World*, Program 305, Steve York, producer/director, Adrian Malone, executive producer, Sandra W. Bradley, senior producer, Michael Olmert, writer, coproduced by the Smithsonian Institution and WETA, Washington, D.C., first aired July 22, 1987.

1644. "Saudi Cleric on American Democracy, Globalization, and Haircuts." Memri TV Monitor Project. www.memritv.org/Transcript.asp?P1=316

1645. www.almajdtv.net/index.asp

1646. Patrick Chovanec, "The $3 Trillion Question: Why China should not devalue its currency." *Foreign Policy*, February 1, 2016, foreignpolicy.com/2016/02/01/the-3-trillionquestion-china-rmb-yuan-economy/

1647. United Nations Development Programme and Arab Fund for Economic and Social Development, "Arab Human Development Report 2002: Creating Opportunites for Future Generations." New York: The Regional Bureau for Arab States, United Nations Development Programme, 2002.

1648. Richard Fletcher, *Moorish Spain*. Berkeley: University of California Press: 1993. Joseph F. O'Callaghan, *A History of Medieval Spain*. Ithaca: Cornell University Press, 1975. Wikipedia, "Caliph." en.wikipedia.org/wiki/Caliph

1649. Wikipedia, "Caliphate—The History of the Caliphate." en.wikipedia.org/wiki/Caliphate#The_history_of_the_caliphate

1650. One Cordoban (Spanish) Caliph's harem had 6,300 women. Alexander Murray, *Reason and Society in the Middle Ages*, Oxford, UK: Clarendon Press, 1978, p. 50. See also: Fatema Mernissi, *The Forgotten Queens of Islam*. Minneapolis: University of Minnesota Press, 1993. Leslie P. Peirce, *The Imperial Harem: Women and Sovereignty in the Ottoman Empire*. New York: Oxford University Press, 1993.

1651. Hitler received 37.3% in the Reichstag elections of July 31, 1932. David Nicholls, *Adolf Hitler: A Biographical Companion*. Santa Barbara, CA: ABC-CLIO, 2000 p. 76. Eberhard Jaeckel, *Hitler in History*. Lebanon, NH: University Press of New England, 2000, p. 17.

1652. Randall Law, *Terrorism: A History*. Cambridge, UK: Polity, 2009, p. 170.

1653. Randall Law, *Terrorism: A History*. Cambridge, UK: Polity, 2009, p. 174.

1654. Randall Law, *Terrorism: A History*. Cambridge, UK: Polity, 2009, p. 175.

1655. R.H.P. Mason, *A History of Japan*. Tokyo: Tuttle Publishing, 1997, p. 336.

1656. Abu Ja'far Muhammad al-Tabari, G.H.A. Juynboll, trans., *The History of al-Tabari: The Conquest of Iraq, Southwestern Persia, and Egypt*, vol. 2. Albany: State University of New York Press, p. 554. Nancy Hartevelt Kobrin, *The Banality of Suicide Terrorism: The Naked Truth about the Psychology of Islamic Suicide Bombing*. Sterling, VA: Potomac Books, Inc., 2010. Efraim Inbar, Hillel Frisch, *Radical Islam and International Security: Challenges and Responses*. London: Routledge, 2007, p. 46. Denis MacEoin, "Suicide Bombing as Worship—Dimensions of Jihad," *Middle East Quarterly*, Fall 2009, pp. 15–24. www.meforum.org/2478/suicide-bombing-asworship#_ftnref13

1657. Shaykh, Abu Qutaybah Ash-Shaml, *The Islamic Ruling on the Permissibility of Self-Sacrificial Operations* Based upon the book by the martyred Shaykh, Al-Hdfith, Mujdhid Shaykh Yusuf ibn Salih Al-'Uyayri May Allah have mercy upon him Originally translated by 'Azzam Publications Edited, revised, references added, and further expounded upon by At-Tibyan Publications Using the book *sll-hdbah FiTalab Ash-Shahddah* By the Shaykh, Abu Qutaybah Ash-Shaml May Allah have preserve him, *The Islamic Ruling on the Permissibility of Martyrdom Operations* www.religioscope.com/pdf/martyrdom.pdf also at archive.org/stream/ThePermissibilityOfMartyrdom Operations1005Dawla/The%20Permissibility%20 of%20Martyrdom%20Operations_djvu.txt

1658. "Islam," *Smithsonian World*, Program 305, Steve York, producer/director, Adrian Malone, executive producer, Sandra W. Bradley, senior producer, Michael Olmert, writer, coproduced by the Smithsonian Institution and WETA, Washington, D.C., first aired July 22, 1987.

1659. The Economic Freedom Network is a right-wing, conservative, free-market philosophy network with 91 international member organizations from Albania to Zambia. Free the World.com, website of the Economic Freedom Network, www.freetheworld.com/member.html

1660. "Ayn Rand Institute To Launch Ayn Rand Institute Europe," Voices for Reason, Ayn Rand Institute, ari.aynrand.org/blog/2015/01/27/ayn-rand-institute-to-launch-ayn-rand-instituteeurope

1661. Philip Jenkins, *The Next Christendom: The Coming of Global Christianity*. New York: Oxford University Press, 2002, pp. 3, 34.

1662. Stephen Ryan, "The Surprising Rise Of Christianity In Russia," December 21, 2015, *Patheos*, www.patheos.com/blogs/mysticpost/2015/12/21/the-surprising-rise-of-christianity-in-russia/ n.a. "Church In Siberia Grows. News About Religion In Russia," Zenit (an international news agency focused on Catholic Church issues), May 18, 1999. www.stetson.edu/~psteeves/relnews/9905b.html n.a. "A Russian Evangelical Alliance is Back on the Scene." *Pakistan Christian Post*. April 4, 2006, www.pakistanchristianpost.com/newsviewsdetails.php?newsid=131 "Yeltsin hands back new religion law —President Boris Yeltsin of Russia," *Christian Century*, August 13, 1997.

1663. Wes Granberg-Michaelson, "Think Christianity is dying? No, Christianity is shifting dramatically," *Washington Post*, May 20, 2015, www.washingtonpost.com/news/acts-of-faith/wp/2015/05/20/think-christianity-is-dyingno-christianity-is-shifting-dramatically/

1664. NAFTA Secretariat, North American Free Trade Agreement, full text, www.nafta-sec-alena.org/Home/Legal-Texts/North-American-Free-Trade-Agreement 10-2-2016

1665. Office of the United States Trade Representative, Executive Office of the President, CAFTA-TR, THE DOMINICAN REPUBLIC—CENTRAL AMERICA—UNITED STATES FREE TRADE AGREEMENT, ustr.gov/sites/default/files/uploads/agreements/cafta/asset_upload_file148_3916.pdf 10-2-2016

1666. Association of Southeast Asian Nations, asean.org

1667. Asia Pacific Economic Cooperation, www.apec.org

1668. World Muslim Congress, "World Muslim Congress—History." www.motamaralalamalislami.org/history.html

1669. Organisation for Islamic Cooperation, Homepage, www.oic-oci.org/

1670. S.R. "The Economist Explains Why China is creating a new 'World Bank' for Asia," *The Economist*, November 11, 2014, 23:50 www.economist.com/blogs/economist-explains/2014/11/economist-explains-6

1671. "CCTV, China, Biz Asia Special on China-ASEAN FTZ" english.cntv.cn/program/bizasia/special/ChinaASEAN_FTZ/ Fred Bergsten, "America's two-front economic conflict." *Foreign Affairs*, March/April 2001, pp. 16–17.

1672. Helen Wang, "China's Triple Wins: The New Silk Roads," *Forbes* January 15, 2016, www.forbes.com/sites/helenwang/2016/01/15/chinas-triple-wins-the-new-silk-roads/#4fd210ef520b

1673. Helen Wang, "China's Triple Wins: The New Silk Roads," *Forbes* January 15, 2016, www.forbes.com/sites/helenwang/2016/01/15/chinas-triple-wins-the-new-silk-roads/#4fd210ef520b

1674. Helen Wang, "China's Triple Wins: The New Silk Roads," *Forbes* January 15, 2016, www.forbes.com/sites/helenwang/2016/01/15/chinas-triple-wins-the-new-silk-roads/#4fd210ef520b

1675. Pepe Escobar, "China Is Building a New Silk Road to Europe, And It's Leaving America Behind — Today, 90% of the global container trade still travels by ocean, and that's what Beijing plans to change," *Mother Jones*, December 16, 2014 4:19 p.m. EST, www.motherjones.com/politics/2014/12/chinas-new-silk-road-europe-will-leaveamerica-behind

1676. Helen Wang, "China's Triple Wins: The New Silk Roads," *Forbes* January 15, 2016, www.forbes.com/sites/helenwang/2016/01/15/chinas-triple-wins-the-new-silk-roads/#4fd210ef520b

1677. For an example, see: George Staunton, *An Authentic Account of an Embassy from the King of Great Britain to the Emperor of China*. Volumes 1 and 2. Replica of 1797 edition by W. Bulmer and Co., London. Boston, MA: Adamant Media, 2005.

1678. Daniel J. Boorstin, *The Discoverers: A History of Man's Search To Know His World And Himself*. New York: Vintage Books, 1985. Dennis & Ching Ping Bloodworth, *The Chinese Machiavelli: 3,000 Years of Chinese Statecraft*. New York: Farrar, Straus and Giroux, 1976.

1679. Kevin Gray, "China Seeks Big Role on World Stage," The Associated Press Montevideo, Uruguay 04-16-2001. People's Daily, "Jiang: China Never Gives in to Outside Pressure — President Jiang Zemin said Monday in Buenos Aires that China 'never gives in to any outside pressure on principle issues related to China's state sovereignty and territorial integrity.'" *People's Daily*, April 10, 2001, english. peopledaily.com.cn/200104/10/eng20010410_67298.html downloaded 8/9/01

1680. Kerry Dumbaugh, Specialist in Asian Affairs, Mark P. Sullivan, Specialist in Latin American Affairs, "China's Growing Interest in Latin America," Congressional Research Service, Foreign Affairs, Defense, and Trade Division. CRS Report for Congress. April 20, 2005. fpc.state.gov/documents/organization/45464.pdf "President Hu Jintao Visit's Latin America; Attends APEC — A Special Press Summary." Virtual Information Center. November 24, 2004. www.vic-info.org/RegionsTop.nsf/0/78ec98f24a331ca20a256f56007dc031?OpenDocument See also: Ministry of Foreign Affairs of the People's Republica of China, Topics > Hu Jintao's Visit to the Four Latin-American Countries and His Attending of the Informal APEC Summit, www.fmprc.gov.cn/mfa_eng/topics_665678/huvisit_665888/

1681. Xinhua News Agency, "China, EU discuss strategic partnership," *China Daily*, Updated: 2005-05-18 21:05, www.chinadaily.com.cn/english/doc/2005-05/18/content_443745.htm

1682. European Union External Action Service, EU Relations with China, European Union External Action Service, eeas.europa.eu/china/index_en.htm

1683. European Union External Action Service, EU-China 2020 Strategic Agenda for Cooperation, European Union External Action Service, eeas.europa.eu/china/docs/20131123_agenda_2020__en.pdf

1684. Ministry of Foreign Affairs of the People's Republic of China, "Build a new international order on the basis of the Five Principles of Peaceful Coexistence," 11/17/2000. www.fmprc.gov.cn/eng/ziliao/3602/3604/t18016.htm

1685. U.S. Census Bureau. Historical Estimates of World Population. www.census.gov/ipc/www/worldhis.html

1686. "We can easily establish that fact that total Muslim Population in 2006 is 1.6 billion which is far greater than currently estimated 1.2 or 1.3 billion" says the homepage of the Islamic website Islamicpopulation.com. Muslim Population Worldwide. Islamicpopulation.com. June 7, 2013. Drew Desilver, "World's Muslim population more widespread than you might think," Pew Research, www.pewresearch.org/fact-tank/2013/06/07/worlds-muslim-population-more-widespreadthan-you-might-think/#comments www.islamicpopulation.com/ See also: The Ministry of Awqaf (Endowments) and Islamic Affairs in the State of Qatar's IslamicWeb, "Islam is the fastest growing religion and the second largest religion in the world." www.islamicweb.com/begin/results.htm

1687. China Population Information and Research Center, "China Population." www.cpirc.org.cn/en/eindex.htm. 1.357 billion 2013. Data from World Bank, Google Public Data, www.google.com/publicdata/explore?ds=d5bncppjof8f9_&met_y=sp_pop_totl&idim=country:CHN:IND&hl=en&dl=en

1688. The population of the European Union was 456 million in 2003. And the population of the U.S. in 2006 was 300 million, putting the Western world's population in 2005 at over 756 million. See: "European demography in 2003: EU25 population up by 0.4% to reach 456 million—One in 14 people in world live in EU25." Eurostat News Release 105/2004, August 31, 2004 epp.eurostat.cec.eu.int/cache/ITY_PUBLIC/3-31082004-BP/EN/3-31082004-BP-EN.PDF#search=%22european%20ounion%20population%22 U.S. Census Bureau. U.S. and World Population Clocks. www.census.gov/main/www/popclock.html

1689. The total human population of the planet in 1750 was roughly 629,000. By 1800 it had increased to 813,000. U.S. Census Bureau, "Historical Estimates of World Population." www.census.gov/ipc/www/worldhis.html

1690. Abu Bakr Naji, *The Management of Savagery: The Most Critical Stage Through Which the Umma Will Pass*. Translated by William McCants. Cambridge, MA: John M. Olin Institute for Strategic Studies at Harvard University, 23 May 2006.

1691. Candyce Kelshall, "Radical Islam and LNG [liquified natural gas] in Trinidad and Tobago," internet haganáh Confronting the Global Jihad. haganah.org.il/harchives/003378.html

1692. Ayatollah Khomeini, *Sayings of the Ayatollah Khomeini*, p. 4.

1693. Shaul Bakash, *The Reign of the Ayatollahs: Iran and the Islamic Revolution*, New York: Basic Books, 1990, p. 233. As R.K. Ramazani, the Harry Flood Byrd, Jr. professor of government and foreign affairs at the University of Virginia, put it, "Khomeini believes that the export of revolution is obligatory" in the interests of "an overarching concept of Islamic world order." Ramazani pointed out that Khomeini "rejected...the very idea of the [secular, non-Islamic] nation state.... In other words, in Khomeini's ideal Islamic world order there would be no room for the modern secular... international system." Khomeini, in Ramazani's words, felt "it is Iran that is uniquely qualified as a nation to pave the way for the ultimate founding of world government.... In Khomeini's words, '...the Iranian nation must grow in power and resolution until it has vouchsafed Islam to the entire world.'" (R.K. Ramazani, *Revolutionary Iran: Challenge and Respect in the Middle East*, Baltimore, MD: Johns Hopkins University Press, 1986, pp. 20–24.)

1694. Reuh Alleah Khumaynei (Ayatollah Khomeini), *Sayings of the Ayatollah Khomeini: Political, Philosophical, Social, and Religious*. New York: Bantam Books, 1980, p. 28.

1695. One example: "The Annihilation of the Infidels is a Divine Decree. ...Regardless of the norms of 'humanist' belief, which sees destroying the infidel countries as a tragedy requiring us to show some conscientious empathy and an atmosphere of sadness for the loss that is to be caused to human civilization — an approach that does not distinguish between believer and infidel. — I would like to stress that annihilating the infidels is an inarguable fact, as this is the [divine] decree of fate. ...the Qur'an places these tortures [to be inflicted on the infidels] in the solid framework of reward and punishment." MEMRI, An Al-Qa'ida-Affiliated Online Magazine: [Al-Ansar] On the Importance of Jihad as a Means of Destroying the 'Infidel Countries', Middle East Media Research Institute, Special Dispatch Series No. 418, September 4, 2002, www.memri.org/bin/articles.cgi?Page=archives&Area=sd&ID=SP41802

1696. "with His permission [you] were about to annihilate your enemy." Book 3, verse 152. The Holy Qur'an. Translation by Abdullah Yusufali. Complete online text. Retrieved November 19, 2001, from the World Wide Web www.wam.umd.edu/~stwright/rel/islam/

The Qur'an's one-time use of the phrase "with His permission [you] were about to annihilate your enemy" would seem insignifant on its own. But it's used over and over again by Muslim scholars like the Ayatollah to emphasize the importance of exterminating those who refuse to believe in Islam and who, through their unbelief, threaten to "corrupt" the ummah of Islam, the social body of Islam.

1697. MEMRI, An Al-Qa'ida-Affiliated Online Magazine: [Al-Ansar] On the Importance of Jihad as a Means of Destroying the 'Infidel Countries', Middle East Media Research Institute, Special Dispatch Series No. 418, September 4, 2002, www.memri.org/bin/articles.cgi?Page=archives&Area=sd&ID=SP41802

1698. Abdul Aziz Said, "Islamic Fundamentalism and the West," *Mediterranean Quarterly*, Fall 1992, pp. 21–36.

1699. John L. Esposito, *Islam and Politics*. Syracuse, NY: Syracuse University Press, 1998. Esposito's projects receive funding from the Organization of Islamic Cooperation, the OIC, the same group that brought you the anti-Islamophobia campaign, the crusade to muzzle your freedom of information and speech. For correspondence on a payment to underwrite one of Esposito's symposia at Georgetown University complete with "some ideas about the topic and list of invitees etc" from OIC Ambassador Abdul Wahab of the OIC, see docslide.us/documents/msa-oic.html.

1700. Edward W. Said, "The Phony Islamic Threat," *The New York Times Magazine*, November 21, 1993, p. 62.

1701. Phebe Marr, "The Islamic Revival: Security Issues," *Mediterranean Quarterly*, Fall 1992, pp. 37, 43–44.

1702. Here are the death tolls: 9/11: 2,996, Madrid train attack: 191, London: 56, Charlie Hebdo: 12, Jewish supermarket: 4, Paris attacks: 130

1703. murphthesurf3, "Dick Cheney — Neocon War Profiteer," *Daily Kos*, Wednesday Jun 18, 2014, 10:14 a.m. EDT, www.dailykos.com/story/2014/6/18/1307821/-Dick-Cheney-Neocon-War-Profiteer David Corn, Rand Paul Says Dick Cheney Pushed for the Iraq War So Halliburton Would Profit, As the ex-veep blasts Paul for being an isolationist, old video shows the Kentucky senator charging that Cheney used 9/11 as an excuse to invade Iraq and benefit his former company, *Mother Jones*, April 7, 2014, www.motherjones.com/politics/2014/04/rand-paul-dick-cheney-exploited-911-iraq-halliburton

1704. Antonia Juhasz, "Bechtel Takes a Hit for War Profiteering: Government auditors who canceled Bechtel's $50 million contract will soon find reasons to cancel the company's $2.85 billion in Iraq contracts," *Alternet*, August 3, 2006, www.alternet.org/story/39860/bechtel_ takes_a_hit_for_war_profiteering Institute for Southern Studies, Bechtel: The Biggest War Profiteer, www.southernstudies.org/reports/bechtel.pdf

1705. For opposing views on the profits won by Bechtel and Halliburton from the Afghan and Iraqi Wars, see: Daniel Drezner, "Fables of the Reconstruction — Bush isn't really favoring Halliburton and Bechtel." *Slate*, November 3, 2003. www.slate.com/id/2090636/ And see the report that this article critiques, "Windfalls of War: U.S. Contractors in Afghanistan & Iraq," The Center for Public Integrity: Investigative Journalism in the Public Interest. www.publicintegrity.org/wow/

1706. Angelo Young, "Cheney's Halliburton Made $39.5 Billion on Iraq War," *Business Insider*, March 20, 2013, www.businessinsider.com/halliburton-companygot-395billion-iraq-2013-3 Antonia Juhasz, "Bechtel Takes a Hit for War Profiteering," *Alternet*, August 3, 2006. www.alternet.org/story/39860/bechtel_takes_a_ hit_for_war_profiteering

1707. Jay M. Weiss, "Effects of coping behavior on development of gastrointestinal lesions in rats." *In Proceedings of the Annual Convention of the American Psychological Association*, 2 1967: 135–136. Jay M. Weiss, "Effects of coping responses on stress," *Journal of Comparative and Physiological Psychology*, 65, 251-260 (1968). Jay M. Weiss, "Effects of predictable and unpredictable shock on development of gastrointestinal lesions in rats." *In Proceedings of the Annual Convention of the American Psychological Association*, 3 1968: 263–264. Jay M. Weiss. "Effects of coping behavior in different warning signal conditions on stress pathology in rats." *Journal of Comparative & Physiological Psychology*, October 1971: 1–13. J.M. Weiss. "Influence of psychological variables on stress-induced pathology." In *Ciba Foundation Symposium*, 8 1972: 253–65. J.M. Weiss. "Psychological factors in stress and disease," *Scientific American*, June 1972: 104-13.

1708. "The Prophet sallallaahu 'alaihi wa sallam exerted maximum effort to instil the magnitude of Shahaadah [martyrdom] as well as the concept of Jihaad deep into the hearts of his companions and his followers who were to come after him." Usaamah Khayyaat, *The Virtues of Martyrdom*. Trans. Hazem Ragab. www.alminbar.com/khutbaheng/1478.htm

1709. Ceciel Shiraz Raj, "Who is killing dissent and diversity in Pakistan?" *MO Mondiaal Nieuws*, Holland, May 5, 2015, www.mo.be/en/analysis/who-killing-dissent-and-diversity-pakistan 2-7-2016 2-7-2016

1710. Ziauddin Ahmad, *Shaheed-e-Millat Liaquat Ali Khan, builder of Pakistan*. Karachi, Pakistan: Royal Book Co., 1990.

1711. AFP, "Islamic State leaflets found at shooting site of 'US national' in Karachi," *Express News*, Lahore, Pakistan, April 16, 2015, tribune.com.pk/story/870894/us-national-injured-after-being-shot-twice-in-the-head-in-karachi/ 2-7-2016

1712. "Usama bin Laden continues to be called Sheikh and held in high regard by many Muslims, even by the Arab media itself." "Nonie Darwish: Are Western Leaders Sellouts to Islam?" January 10, 2016, pamelageller.com/2016/01/nonie-darwish-are-western-leaders-sellouts-to-islam.html/

1713. Osama bin Laden, Complete Text Of Sheikh Osama Bin Laden's Latest Message To Ummah May 12, 2004. Originally downloaded from Jihad Unspun, a militant Islamic website. www.mail-archive.com/tumpat@yahoogroups.com/msg00023.html

1714. Osama Bin Laden, Complete Text Of Sheikh Osama Bin Laden's Latest Message To Ummah May 12, 2004. Retrieved from the World Wide Web May 14, 2004 www.jihadunspun.net/intheatre_internal.php?article=572&list=/home.php&

1715. Osama bin Laden. Full text: bin Laden's 'letter to America,' November 24, 2002. *The Observer*. November 24, 2002. *The Observer* points out that "The letter first appeared on the internet in Arabic and has since been translated and circulated by Islamists in Britain." Retrieved November 25, 2002, from the World Wide Web www.observer.co.uk/worldview/story/0,11581,845725,00.html

1716. Osama bin Laden, Complete Text Of Sheikh Osama Bin Laden's Latest Message To Ummah May 12, 2004. Originally downloaded from Jihad Unspun, a militant Islamic website. Retrieved once again September 15, 2006, from the World Wide Web www.mail-archive.com/tumpat@yahoogroups.com/msg00023.html

1717. Usama Bin Laden: Full Text of Message to Americans english.aljazeera.net english.aljazeera.net/NR/exeres/8E8EA580-943C-4FBF-9ABD- 21B47627FECD.htm Saturday, 18 October 2003.

1718. Osama Bin Laden. Full text: bin Laden's 'letter to America' Retrieved October 13, 2005, from the World Wide Web: observer.guardian.co.uk/worldview/story/0,11581,845725,00.html

1719. CNN, August 17, 2004. Retrieved August 18, 2004, from the World Wide Web demand1.stream.aol.com/ramgen/cnn/aolbb/world/2004/08/17/rodgers.militant.muslims.cnn.rv8.rm

1720. demand1.stream.aol.com/ramgen/cnn/aolbb/world/2004/08/17/rodgers.militant.muslims.cnn.rv8.rm CNN 8/17/2004

1721. BBC, "Gunman Kills Dutch Film Director." BBC News, November 2, 2004. news.bbc.co.uk/1/hi/world/europe/3974179.stm

1722. The man who describes modern jihadists as "knights" is Osama bin Laden. See; Foreign Broadcast Information Service, "FBIS Report: Compilation of Usama Bin Ladin Statements, 1994–January 2004," FBIS, Reston, VA: January 2004, pp. 210, 232, 266, 271. The FBIS was a component of the Central Intelligence Agency's Directorate of Science and Technology. It monitored media worldwide for the US government. See also: www.jihadunspun.com/intheatre_internal.php?article=88298&list=/home.php&

1723. Anthony Deutsch, "Dutch Vow Tough Measures After Death Threat Letter on Dead Filmmaker's Body Threatened Dutch Official," Associated Press, November 5, 2005, retrieved November 5, 2005, from the World Wide Web, aolsvc.news.aol.com/news/article.adp?id=20041105170509990006

1724. Sebastien Berger, "Teachers tote guns to arm against Muslim militants," New Zealand Herald, July 16, 2005, retrieved September 25, 2005,from the World Wide Web, www.nzherald.co.nz/category/print.cfm?c_id=340&objectid=10336080 Rungrawee C. Pinyorat, "Beheadings, arming of Buddhists raising tensions in Thailand's Muslim-dominated south," Associated Press, July 16, 2005, retrieved July 16, 2005, from the World Wide Web www.signonsandiego.com/news/world/20050716-0958-thailand-islamicviolence.html

1725. Reuters, "6 Die In Gun Battle At Rail Station," New York Times. January 3, 2004, www.nytimes.com/2004/01/03/world/world-briefing-asia-kashmir-6-die-in-gun-battle-at-rail-station.html?_r=0

1726. Kashmir Fast Facts. CNN Library www.cnn.com/2013/11/08/world/kashmir-fast-facts/ Amy Waldman, "Violence in Kashmir Invades a Most Sacred Space," New York Times, June 16, 2004. select.nytimes.com/gst/abstract.html?res=FB0B1EFB35540C758DDDAF0894DC404482

1727. "Kashmir Violence Erupts," CBSNews.com, April 8, 2004. www.cbsnews.com/stories/2004/04/08/world/printable610950.shtml

1728. SuperFerry Travel and Leisure—Aboitiz Transport System Corporation, Cebu, Philippines, www.superferry.com.ph/

1729. Wikipedia, "Abu Sayyaf," en.wikipedia.org/wiki/Abu_Sayyaf

1730. BBC, "In Depth: Madrid Train Attacks," BBC News, last updated Wednesday, 14 February 2007, 10:57 gmt, news.bbc.co.uk/2/hi/in_depth/europe/2004/madrid_train_attacks/default.stm Wikipedia, March 11, 2004 Madrid Attacks, en.wikipedia.org/wiki/March_11,_2004_Madrid_attacks

1731. CNN, "Video claims al Qaeda to blame. Spain arrests 5 in terror bombings," CNN, May 6, 2004, edition.cnn.com/2004/WORLD/europe/03/13/spain.blasts/

1732. Tewfik Cassis, "A brief history of ISIS," The Week, November 21, 2015, theweek.com/articles/589924/brief-history-isis

1733. "They call for a state of justice, law, and freedom, because they are embarrassed of Islam. They beautify and propagate the principles of the kuffar including nationalism, human rights, and minority rights." "The Muslims today have a loud, thundering statement, and possess heavy boots. They have a statement that will cause the world to hear and understand the meaning of terrorism, and boots that will trample the idol of nationalism, destroy the idol of democracy, and uncover its deviant nature. Dābiq, November 18, 2015, issue 12.

1734. Steven Stalinsky, "The Memri Report: Iranian Talk Of an Attack On America," The New York Sun, August 18, 2004, p. 9, daily.nysun.com/Repository/getmailfiles.asp?Style=OliveXLib:ArticleToMail&Type=text/html&Path=NYS/2004/08/18&ID=Ar00901

1735. Behrouz Mehri, "Iran successfully tests 'strategic missile,'" USA Today, September 24, 2004, retrieved October 15, 2005, from the World Wide Web www.usatoday.com/news/world/2004-09-25-iran-missile_x.htm. Ali Akbar Dareini, "Iran Says it Tested 'Strategic Missile,'" Associated Press, 25 September 2004. "Iran's Guards Commander Threatens to Hit US Bases in Retaliation," BBC, 1 October 2004. "Iran Has Missile With 2,000 km Range: Rafsanjani," Xinhua, 5 October 2004. "US Views Iran's Missile as Threat to American Interest," Xinhua, 6 October 2004. Nuclear Threat Intiative, Iran Profile: Missile Chronology 2004, August 2005, www.nti.org/e_research/profiles/Iran/Missile/1788_4594.html

1736. Nazila Fathi, "Iranian President Stands by Call to Wipe Israel Off Map," New York Times, October 28, 2005. www.nytimes.com/2005/10/29/international/middleeast/29iran.html?oref=login. Trita Parsi, "The Iran-Israel cold war," openDemocracy, October 28, 2005, www.opendemocracy.net/democracy-irandemocracy/israel_2974.jsp Safa Haeri, "Pakistan and Israel deal Iran a blow," Asia Times, September 3, 2005, www.atimes.com/atimes/South_Asia/GI03Df01.html. Safa Haeri, "The World Community Can Not Tolerate The Islamic Republic," Iran Press Service, March 1, 2005. www.iran-press-service.com/ips/articles-2005/march-2005/sholeh_1305.shtml The following inscription appeared on a Shahab 3 missile in the Holy Defense Week military parade in Iran's capital, Tehran, on September 22, 2003: "Israel must be uprooted and wiped off [the pages of history]." Intelligence and Terrorism Information Center at the Center for Special Studies (C.S.S.), Israel, SpecialInformation Bulletin, November 2003, www.intelligence.org.il/eng/bu/iran/shihab_11_03.htm Joshua Teitelbaum, What Iranian Leaders Really Say About Doing Away With Israel: A Refutation Of The Campaign To Excuse Ahmadinejad's Incitement To Genocide, Jerusalem: Jerusalem Center for Public Affairs, 2008, p. 13.

1737. Hannah Allam, "Iran's missiles a 'show of Words,'" Knight-Ridder News Service, *Lexington Herald Leader*, April 10, 2006, www.kentucky.com/mld/heraldleader/news/world/14306197.htm, "Iran continues to boast of its new weapons," *Midland Reporter-Telegram*, April 12, 2006, MyWestTexas.com. www.mywesttexas.com/site/news.cfm?newsid=16466550&BRD=2288&PAG=461&dept_id=475590&rfi=6

1738. Ali Akbar Dareini, "Iran: We have joined 'club' of nuclear nations," Associated Press, April 12, 2006, in IndyStar.com, www.indystar.com/apps/pbcs.dll/article?AID=/20060412/NEWS06/604120496/1012

1739. Wikipedia, "Pakistan," en.wikipedia.org/wiki/Pakistan

1740. Kathy Gannon, "New capability meant to bring pride to Islamic world—Pakistani Nuclear Testing," Associated Press, 31 May 1998.

1741. Wikipedia, "AQ Khan." en.wikipedia.org/wiki/Aq_khan

1742. Says *The Washington Post*'s Dafna Linzer, a meeting between the Iranians and the Pakistanis in Dubai concluded with a written sales agreement that, "kick-started Tehran's nuclear efforts and Khan's black market." Dafna Linzer, "Iran Was Offered Nuclear Parts," *The Washington Post*, Sunday 27 February 2005, http://www.washingtonpost.com/wp-dyn/articles/A56391-2005Feb26.html

1743. A.Q. Khan, Global Security.org. www.globalsecurity.org/wmd/world/pakistan/khan.htm

1744. "International investigators have uncovered evidence of a secret meeting 18 years ago between Iranian officials and associates of Pakistani scientist Abdul Qadeer Khan that resulted in a written offer to supply Tehran with the makings of a nuclear weapons program, foreign diplomats and U.S. officials familiar with the new findings said." Dafna Linzer, "Iran Was Offered Nuclear Parts," *The Washington Post*, Sunday 27 February 2005, http://www.washingtonpost.com/wp-dyn/articles/A56391-2005Feb26.html
Writes Douglas Frantz in the LA Times: "Khan started providing material to Iran in 1987 and continued as its primary nuclear supplier for at least a decade, recent reports by the International Atomic Energy Agency state." Douglas Frantz, "A High-Risk Nuclear Stakeout," *Los Angeles Times*, Sunday 27 February 2005, articles.latimes.com/2005/feb/27/world/fg-khan27

1745. "The CIA was told in 1989 that the Pakistani scientist was providing centrifuge designs and parts to Iran, said two former U.S. officials who read the reports." Douglas Frantz, "A High-Risk Nuclear Stakeout," *Los Angeles Times*, Sunday 27 February 2005, http://articles.latimes.com/2005/feb/27/world/fg-khan27

1746. Dafna Linzer, "Iran Was Offered Nuclear Parts," *The Washington Post*, Sunday 27 February 2005, http://www.washingtonpost.com/wp-dyn/articles/A56391-2005Feb26.html

1747. Douglas Frantz, "A High-Risk Nuclear Stakeout," *Los Angeles Times*, Sunday 27 February 2005, retrieved February 28, 2005, from the World Wide Web www.truthout.org/docs_2005/022705A

1748. B. Raman, "A.Q. Khan & Osama Bin Laden," South Asia Analysis Group. Paper no. 960. March 24, 2004. www.saag.org/papers10/paper960.html The writer is Additional Secretary (retd), Cabinet Secretariat, Govt. of India, New Delhi, and, presently, Director, Institute For Topical Studies, Chennai, and Distinguished Fellow and Convenor, Observer Research Foundation (ORF), Chennai Chapter. Graham Allison, "Tick, Tick, Tick Pakistan is a nuclear time bomb—perhaps the greatest threat to American security today. Here's how to defuse it," *Atlantic Monthly*, October 2004, www.theatlantic.com/doc/200410/allison1749 William J. Broad, David E. Sanger, "The Bomb Merchant: Chasing Dr. Khan's Network; As Nuclear Secrets Emerge, More Are Suspected," *New York Times*. December 26, 2004.

1750. William J. Broad and David E. Sanger, "The Bomb Merchant: Chasing Dr. Khan's Network; As Nuclear Secrets Emerge, More Are Suspected," *New York Times*. December 26, 2004.

1751. Nato School of Oberammergau, Germany, Pakistan launched a new Agosta B90, February 9, 2003, retrieved December 15, 2003, from the World Wide Web, www.natoschool-shape.de/text/site_polaris/Polaris_020903.doc

1752. Naval Technology - The Website for Defence Industries, SSK Agosta 90b Class Attack Submarine, France. Retrieved from the World Wide Web April 14, 2004 www.naval-technology.com/projects/agosta/

1753. Steve Crawford, *Twenty-First Century Submarines: Undersea Vessels of Today's Navies*. London: Zenith, 2003, pp. 36–37.

1754. Captain Iftikhar Riaz Qureshi PN, Ex Commanding Officer PNS/M Khalid & PNS/M Saad, "Saad's launching: Pakistan Navy Submarine Saad — Pride of Pakistan." *The Daily Mail*, Islamabad, Pakistan, December 12, 2003, Retrieved April 18, 2004, from the World Wide Web dailymailnews.com/200312/12/column.html This article was written by the Pakistani Naval Captain who helmed the first two Agosta 90B stealth submarines to enter the Pakistani Navy's arsenal—the Khalid and the Saad. DCN. Company History. Retrieved from the World Wide Web May 05, 2004 www.dcn.fr/us/entreprise/histoire.html DCN is the official, state-controlled French naval construction company responsible for developing and manufacturing state of the art ships for the French Navy and for export. In 1994, DCN completed a deal to sell its Agosta 90B attack submarine technology to Pakistan and to help Pakistan produce these submarines on its own at the Pakistani Navy's Karachi shipyard. Retrieved from the World Wide Web May 05, 2004 www.dcn.fr/us/entreprise/histoire.html. Naval-technology.com, Three Agosta 90Bs were ordered by the Pakistan Navy in September 1994, retrieved August 13, 2005, from the World Wide Web www.naval-technology.com/projects/agosta/ Naval-technology.com bills itself as "The Website for the defence industries."

1755. Nuclear Threat Initiative, NTI, Pakistan Active Duty Submarines, www.nti.org/media/pdfs/pakistan__active_duty_ submarines.pdf?_=1341271851&_=1341271851 B. Muralidhar Reddy, "Pak. plans to build four frigates with Chinese help," *The Hindu*, August 25, 2002, retrieved from the World Wide Web December 15, 2003. www.thehindu.com/2002/08/25/stories/ 2002082503191000.htm

1756. Originally these cruise missiles were Harpoon-style missiles with a range of 165 miles. But in August 2005, Pakistan launched a Pakistani-designed and Pakistani-built nuclear-capable missile with a range of 350 miles... a range that significantly upgrades the attack capacity of Pakistan's Agosta 90B submarines. Xinhuanet, Pakistan test-fires nuclear-capable cruise missile, retrieved August 11, 2005, from the World Wide Web www.chinaview.cn. Basque news and Information Channel, Pakistan to design and make cruise missiles after first test, retrieved August 11, 2005, from the World Wide Web www.eitb24.com/noticia_en.php?id=81849 The "Unofficial U.S. Navy Site," The Harpoon Missile, retrieved from the World Wide Web March 03, 2004, navysite.de/weapons/harpoon.htm

1757. Graham Allison, "National Security — Tick, Tick, Tick," *The Atlantic Monthly*, October 2004, retrieved May 21, 2005, from the World Wide Web, www.theatlantic.com/doc/200410/allison

1758. *Defence Journal*, SSK Agosta 90B Class Attack Submarine, retrieved from the World Wide Web March 03, 2004, www.defencejournal.com/2000/jan/ssk-agosta.htm. Fourays (Australian Army Aviation Association). Agosta Class Submarine, retrieved December 16, 2003, from the World Wide Web, www.fourays.org/submarine/agosta2.htm. SUB.net it@lia: the Submarine Portal. SSK — World Diesel-electric Submarines Archive Khalid Class-------- flag pakistan Navy, Retrieved from the World Wide Web April 07, 2004 www.subnetitalia.it/skkkhalid.htm.

1759. The following article is significant because it indicates how much of the U.S. population can be reached by sea-launched cruise missiles with a relatively short range—a range from 35 miles to 150 miles. Its key quote is this: "more than half of the nation's population lives in...673 coastal counties." Sid Perkins, "Coastal Surge: Ecosystems likely to suffer as more people move to the shores," *Science News Online*, Week of March 27, 2004, Vol. 165, No. 13.

1760. Department of the Navy, SURTASS LFA, retrieved August 16, 2004, from the World Wide Web www.surtass-lfa-eis.com/WhyNeed/index.htm Hwaa Irfan, "Sonar in Underwater Warfare Technology," IslamOnline, November 4, 2002, retrieved August 3, 2004, from the World Wide Web, www.islamonline.net/english/ Science/2002/04/article09.shtml

1761. Usman Ansari, "Pakistan, China Finalize 8-Sub Construction Plan," October 11, 2015, *Defense News*, www.defensenews.com/story/defense/ naval/submarines/2015/10/11/pakistan-china- finalize-8-sub-construction-plan/73634218/ Jeffrey Lin and P.W. Singer, "New Chinese Submarines To Pakistan — Why Do They Matter?" *Popular Science*, April 7, 2015, www.popsci.com/ new-chinese-submarinespakistan Ananth Krishnan, Chinese double barrel—Beijing has gone from being world's top arms importer to a huge supplier of military equipment, making deep inroads into India's traditional sphere of influence in South Asia, *India Today*, posted from Beijing, March 30, 2016, indiatoday.intoday.in/story/chinese-arms-military- beijing-peoples-liberation-army/1/631180.html

1762. C. Christine Fair, *Fighting to the End: The Pakistan Army's Way of War*. New York: Oxford University Press, 2014, pp. 68–80. C. Christine Fair, "Is Pakistan in ISIS' Crosshairs?" *Boston Review*, October 16, 2014, bostonreview.net/world/ c-christine-fair-isis-pakistan-militant-foreign-policy

1763. "Mapping Militant Organizations, Lashkar-e-Taiba," Stanford University, web.stanford.edu/group/mappingmilitants/cgi-bin/groups/view/79

1764. Rahul Bedi, "Vital intelligence on the Taliban may rest with its prime sponsor—Pakistan's ISI," *Jane's Defence Weekly*, October 1, 2001, www.janes.com/security/international_security/news/misc/janes011001_1_n.shtml

1765. Shamim-ur-Rahman, "Extremism biggest danger: Musharraf: Indigenously built Agosta inducted," *Dawn*, December 13, 2003, Shawwal 18, 1424 (*Dawn*—a mainstream Pakistani newspaper—in the case of this article has used the Islamic dating system). Retrieved August 13, 2005, from the World Wide Web December 13, 2003, www.dawn.com/2003/12/13/top1.htm

1766. Caroline Drees, "U.S general says militants eye seaborne attack," Reuters. Aug 26, 2004, www.swissinfo.org/sen/swissinfo.html?siteSect=143&sid=5171895. Timur Moon, "Anti-Islam axis goes nuclear," Al Jazeera, September 23, 2003, retrieved August 3, 2004, from the World Wide Web, english.aljazeera.net/NR/exeres/2D21761D-13C4-4921-8537-DF27AE41659D.htm.

1767. C. Christine Fair, "Pakistan's army is building an arsenal of 'tiny' nuclear weapons—and it's going to backfire," *Quartz*, December 21, 2015, qz.com/579334/pakistans-army-is-building-an-arsenal-of-tiny-nuclear-weapons-and-its-going-to-backfire/

1768. Franz-Stefan Gady, "Will Pakistan Soon Have the World's Third-Largest Nuclear Arsenal? Just how many nuclear weapons does Pakistan have?" *The Diplomat*, August 31, 2015, thediplomat.com/2015/08/will-pakistan-soon-have-the-worlds-thirdlargest-nuclear-arsenal/

1769. As early as 2004, the Israelis estimated the number of Hezbollah's missiles at 12,000. But Hassan Nasrallah, Hezbollah's leader, claimed the number was over 20,000. Fikret Ertan, "Nasrallah's Messages." Istanbul. *Zaman Online*, October 4, 2006, www.zaman.com/?bl=columnists&alt=&trh=20061004&hn=36830. Aaron Lerner, "12,000 Missiles covering much of Israel deters Action," *IMRA Newsletter*, January 21, 2004, Independent Media Review and Analysis, published in Kokhaviv Publications—Inter Net Press and Intelligence, Germany, www.kokhavivpublications.com/2004/israel/01/0401210720.html Jonathan Rosenblum, "Elul for All," *Cross-Currents* (an orthodox Jewish site), August 29, 2006, www.cross-currents.com/archives/2006/08/29/elul-for-all-2/.

1770. Here's a thread of postings on the website of the Lebanese Broadcasting Corporation, postings responding to a documentary showing what one viewer proudly called "the real power of hizbollah:"
How can we download the video
Now everyone can see the real power of hizbollah
houssam_d1
9/10/2006 1:01:49 p.m.
Posts: 1
Repeat
Please show us this program again because the time was late for us. Thanks, Sanaa
9/10/2006 5:07:00 a.m.
Posts: 1
I Really like this Documentary
I Really like this Documentary and i am just asking from where can we buy it or if you will put it again and when? Thank you, IO
9/8/2006 10:11:34 a.m.
Posts: 1
the video on the site
hope lbc would upload the video on the site
h
9/8/2006 12:44:01 a.m.
Posts: 1
Publish on Google....
If this is as good as I heard then we have a moral obligation to publish it and give the whole world a chnace to watch it. Although LBC is a business enterprise, I do believe that publishing this video on the internet (Google?) would be extremely rewarding to Lebanon and LBC in the long run.
to Israeli Site Vistors — Your errogance, ignorance, and sub-human moralities are not required. Go do what you do best when you're not slottering innocent civilians - stay within the boundaries of your gay porn sites...
Darweesh
9/8/2006 12:30:59 a.m.
Posts: 1
let us live in peace ...arrafouna
let us finish from all this games and let us live in peace ...arrafouna 9/7/2006
He (Nasralla) went to far, if you play with a fire, eventually you will be burn.
I will not be suprise that the Israeli will kill him. The problem is that he doesn't care from Lebanon an i will tell you why:
1) He built in south Lebanon bunkers, to be ready for a war when the Iranian will give him the order.
2) The aim of Hisbulla wepons was not to be put in the Museum.
It was a matter of time that this war will be open. LBC—The Lebanese Broadcasting Corporation. Forums. Topic:
المقايضة الكبرى- وثائقي عن عملية تبادل الأسرى بين حزب الله وإسرائيل
كيف ترى في رأيك توقيت بث هذه الحلقة؟
September 5, 2006–September 7, 2006. www.lbcgroup.tv/LBC/En/MainMenu/Forums/Thread+Posts?TID=19&FID=8

1771. "Our primary assumption in our fight against Israel states that the Zionist entity is aggressive from its inception, and built on lands wrested from their owners, at the expense of the rights of the Muslim people. Therefore our struggle will end only when this entity is obliterated. We recognize no treaty with it, no cease fire, and no peace agreements, whether separate or consolidated. We vigorously condemn all plans for negotiation with Israel, and regard all negotiators as enemies, for the reason that such negotiation is nothing but the recognition of the legitimacy of the Zionist occupation of Palestine. Therefore we oppose and reject the Camp David Agreements, the proposals of King Fahd, the Fez and Reagan plan, Brezhnev's and the French-Egyptian proposals, and all other programs that include the recognition (even the implied recognition) of the Zionist entity." The Hizballah Program. Translation of "Nass al-Risala al-Maftuha allati wajahaha Hizballah ila-l-Mustad'afin fi Lubnan wa-l-Alam," published February 16, 1985, in al-Safir (Beirut), and also in a separate brochure. In The Jerusalem Quarterly, number Forty-Eight, Fall 1988. www.ict.org.il/Articles/Hiz_letter.htm

1772. Associated Press, "Hezbollah hiding 100,000 missiles that can hit north, army says — If war breaks out, IDF warns, Israel will strike at south Lebanon's rocket arsenals, wherever they are placed," AP, May 13, 2015, www.timesofisrael.com/hezbollah-hiding-100000-missiles-that-canhit-north-army-says/

1773. Matthew Chance, Nic Robertson, Elise Labott and Karl Penhaul, "IDF: Hezbollah leaders' bunker hit," CNN.com, July 20, 2006. www.cnn.com/2006/WORLD/meast/07/19/mideast/index.html

1774. For a sense of Iran's practice of continually upgrading its missiles, see: n.a. "Iran Missile Milestones," January 2004, Iran Watch, www.iranwatch.org/wmd/wponac-missilemilestones.htm. And George Gedda, "Iran working to upgrade missile range," Milwaukee Journal Sentinel, May 12, 2002, www.findarticles.com/p/articles/mi_qn4196/is_20020512/ai_n10786562.

1775. Fredreka Schouten, "Pakistan, Libyan rebels tap into lobbying firms," USA Today, May 12, 2011, usatoday30.usatoday.com/news/washington/2011-05-11-Libya-lobbying-Pakistan-Washington_n.htm
Kevin Bogardus, "Pakistan's $1M is up for grabs," The Hill, November 13, 2013, thehill.com/business-a-lobbying/business-a-lobbying/190062-pakistans-1m-isup-for-grabs
Matt Hardigree, "How Bahrain Spends Millions To Spin The Press," Jalopnik, April 9, 2009, jalopnik.com/5900113/how-bahrain-spendsmillions-to-spin-the-press
Wikipedia, "Burston-Marsteller," en.wikipedia.org/wiki/Burson-Marsteller
PR Watch, "Qorvis Communications: Relationship with Bahrain Government," Bahrain Watch, bahrainwatch.org/pr/qorvis.php

1776. For a Sky News video showing these bunkers, see: "Israeli Golani Brigade Exposed Bunkers in Southern Lebanon 2006." This appears on the Israeli site 4law.co.il ("The 4Law website provides free Internet access to legal and security Internet materials.") www.4law.co.il/leb1.html and video.google.com/videoplay?docid=1055204675690374049. See also: Abraham Rabinovich, "Hezbollah trained for 6 years, dug deep bunkers," The Washington Times, July 21, 2006. www.washtimes.com/world/20060720-095532-3181r.htm. Associated Press, "IDF has razed Hezbollah bunkers in Lebanon within past 24 hours," September 1, 2006. From the Israeli newspaper Haaretz. www.haaretz.com/hasen/pages/ShArt.jhtml?itemNo=757688

1777. Jerusalem Post Staff, "Hezbollah bunkers under UN post," Jerusalem Post, August 27, 2006, www.jpost.com/servlet/Satellite?c=JPArticle&cid=1154525953897&pagename=JPost%2FJPArticle%2FShowFull. For additional information on Hezbollah's bunkers, see: David S. Cloud, Helene Cooper, "U.S. Speeds Up Bomb Delivery for the Israelis." New York Times, July 22, 2006, www.nytimes.com/2006/07/22/world/middleeast/22military.html?ex=1311220800&en=e256f1d8872a835d&ei=5088&partner=rssnyt&emc=
Seymour M. Hersh, "Watching Lebanon— Washington's interests in Israel's war," The New Yorker, August 8, 2006.

1778. Matthew Chance, Nic Robertson, Elise Labott and Karl Penhaul, "IDF: Hezbollah leaders' bunker hit," CNN.com, July 20, 2006, retrieved October 14, 2006, from the World Wide Web www.cnn.com/2006/WORLD/meast/07/19/mideast/index.html. Associated Press, Israeli Warplanes Target Suspected Hezbollah Bunker in Beirut, July 20, 2006, www.foxnews.com/story/0,2933,204482,00.html

1779. Chris Tinkler, "These are the pictures that damn Hezbollah: Graphic images smuggled out from Lebanon show how Hezbollah is waging war amid suburban homes," Sunday Mail, Adelaide, Australia, July 29, 2006, retrieved October 14, 2006, from the World Wide Web www.news.com.au/adelaidenow/story/0,22606,19960056-5006301,00.html

1780. Chris Tinkler, "These are the pictures that damn Hezbollah: Graphic images smuggled out from Lebanon show how Hezbollah is waging war amid suburban homes," Sunday Mail, Adelaide, Australia, July 29, 2006, retrieved October 14, 2006, from the World Wide Web www.news.com.au/adelaidenow/story/0,22606,19960056-5006301,00.html

1781. Chris Tinkler, "These are the pictures that damn Hezbollah: Graphic images smuggled out from Lebanon show how Hezbollah is waging war amid suburban homes," *Sunday Mail*, Adelaide, Australia, July 29, 2006, retrieved October 14, 2006, from the World Wide Web www.news.com.au/adelaidenow/story/0,22606,19960056-5006301,00.html

1782. Michael Martinez, "Is Hamas using human shields in Gaza? The answer is complicated," CNN, Wed July 23, 2014, www.cnn.com/2014/07/23/world/meast/human-shields-mideast-controversy/ Terrence McCoy, "Why Hamas stores its weapons inside hospitals, mosques and schools," *Washington Post*, July 31, 2014, www.washingtonpost.com/news/morning-mix/wp/2014/07/31/why-hamas-stores-itsweapons-inside-hospitals-mosques-and-schools/

1783. Tim Hume, Alireza Hajihosseini, "Iran fires ballistic missiles a day after test; U.S. officials hint at violation," CNN, Wed March 9, 2016, www.cnn.com/2016/03/09/middleeast/iran-missile-test/ retrieved from the World Wide Web 3-14-2016. "Iran fires ballistic missiles in new test: state media," *Dunya News*, Lahore, Pakistan, 09 March,2016, dunyanews.tv/en/World/326765-Iran-firesballistic-missiles-in-new-test-state-m 3-14-2016

1784. Ali A. Mazrui, "Islamic Doctrine and the Politics of Induced Fertility Change: An African Perspective," *Population and Development Review*, Vol. 20, Supplement: The New Politics of Population: Conflict and Consensus in Family Planning, (1994), p. 122.

1785. "Yousef Al-Qaradhawi and Other Sheikhs Herald the Coming Conquest of Rome," Middle East Media Research Institute (MEMRI), December 6, 2002 No. 447, retrieved June 22, 2005, from the World Wide Web: www.memri.de/uebersetzungen_analysen/themen/islamistische_ ideologie/isl_rom_18_12_02.pdf

1786. A. Guillaume, *The Life of Muhammad: A Translation of Ibn Ishaq's Sirat Rasul Allah*. New York: Oxford University Press, 1955, eighteenth printing, 2004, p. 452.

1787. Osama Bin Laden, Full text: bin Laden's 'letter to America,' retrieved October 13, 2005, from the World Wide Web observer.guardian.co.uk/worldview/story/0,11581,845725,00.html

1788. ISIS, "You Who Have Believed, Protect Yourselves And Your Families From Fire," in ISIS' magazine, *Dābiq*, November 18, 2015, issue 12.

1789. Osama Bin Laden, Full text: bin Laden's 'letter to America,' retrieved October 13, 2005, from the World Wide Web observer.guardian.co.uk/worldview/story/0,11581,845725,00.html

1790. Stephen Coughlin, *Catastrophic Failure: Blindfolding America in the Face of Jihad*, Washington, DC: Center for Security Policy Press, Kindle Edition. Stephen Coughlin is a Senior Fellow at the Center for Security Policy and a Lincoln Fellow at the Claremont Institute.

1791. Middle East Media Research Institute, Al-Qa'ida's 'Voice of Jihad' Magazine: Issue No. 9, Special Dispatch Series — No. 650 January 27, 2004, No. 650, www.memri.org/bin/latestnews.cgi?ID=SD65004.

1792. Barry Renfrew, "Al-Qaida Said to Have 18,000 Militants for Raids," AP, May 25, 2004, aolsvc.news.aol.com/news/article.adp?id=20040525060309990004

1793. Osama bin Laden, Full text: bin Laden's 'letter to America,' November 24, 2002, *The Observer*, November 24, 2002. *The Observer* points out, "The letter first appeared on the internet in Arabic and has since been translated and circulated by Islamists in Britain." Retrieved November 25, 2002, from the World Wide Web www.observer.co.uk/worldview/story/0,11581,845725,00.html

1794. Bernard Lewis, "At War: Does Iran have something in store?" *Wall Street Journal*, Tuesday, August 8, 2006.

1795. Bernard Lewis, "At War: Does Iran have something in store?" *Wall Street Journal*, Tuesday, August 8, 2006.

1796. "Allah will torture them [the Infidels] Himself at our Hands....The question now on the agenda is, how is the torture Allah wants done at our hands to be carried out?" Seif Al-Din Al-Ansari, On the Importance of Jihad as a Means of Destroying the 'Infidel Countries,'" article in the sixteenth issue of the al Qa'ida online magazine *Al-Ansar*, August 24, 2002, MEMRI, September 4, 2002 URL: www.memri.org/bin/articles.cgi?Page=archives&Area=sd&ID=SP41802 Also available at www.freerepublic.com/focus/news/744121/posts

1797. Qur'an, chapter 2,verse 24.

1798. On November 10, 2003, "Usama bin Laden got into the act and told the mass-circulation Dawn newspaper in Pakistan that his group possesses chemical and nuclear weapons," and, "In a letter dated in May of 1998, bin Laden said: 'We call for the Muslim brothers to imitate Pakistan as to the possession of nuclear, chemical and biological weapons.'" Steve Macko, "Laden And Al-Qaida Make More Threats," *Erri Daily Intelligence Report*, Saturday, November 10, 2001, Vol. 7, No. 316. As long ago as 1983, the Chinese had sold Muslim Pakistan the technology for building atomic bombs the size of soccer balls. Pakistan, in turn, had built facilities for mass-producing these weapons and was fully equipped with the ballistic missiles to deliver them. John Dikkenburg, "'Supermarket' in the Pacific," *Asia Magazine*, Hong Kong, reprinted in *World Press Review*, September, 1992, pp. 14–16. By 1993, there were active nuclear weapons development programs in Iraq, Iran, Libya, and several other Islamic states. According to Harvard University's Samuel P. Huntington, "a top Iranian official has declared that all Muslim states should acquire nuclear weapons...." (Samuel P. Huntington, "The Clash of Civilizations?" *Foreign Affairs*, Summer, 1993, p. 46.)

1799. n.a. "Nejad acknowledges diff. btwn Judaism and Zionism," September 24, 2006, Aljazeera.com. www.aljazeera.com/me.asp?service_ID=11990

1800. n.a. "Iranian leader: Wipe out Israel," CNN.com, Thursday, October 27, 2005, www.cnn.com/2005/ WORLD/meast/10/26/ahmadinejad/

1801. Franz-Stefan Gady, "Will Pakistan Soon Have the World's Third-Largest Nuclear Arsenal? Just how many nuclear weapons does Pakistan have?" *The Diplomat*, August 31, 2015, thediplomat.com/2015/08/will-pakistan-soon-havethe-worlds-third-largest-nuclear-arsenal/

1802. Raymond Case Kelly, *The Nuer Conquest: The Structure and Development of an Expansionist System*, Ann Arbor, MI: University of Michigan Press, 1985.

1803. Osama bin Laden, "al-Qaeda's Declaration in Response to the Saudi Ulema: It's Best You Prostrate Yourself in Secret," 2002, in Raymond Ibrahim, *The Al Qaeda Reader: The Essential Texts of Osama Bin Laden's Terrorist Organization*, New York: Crown/Archetype, 2007, p. 51.

1804. N.a., "From Hijrah to Khilafah," *Dābiq*, Issue 1, July 5, 2014, p. 34.

1805. The number of Prophets Muslims believe Allah sent varies widely, but the Qur'an is quite clear that there were "messengers whom We have mentioned to you before, and messengers whom We have not mentioned to you" (Al-Nisa, 4:164). The Institute of Islamic Information and Education says, "How many prophets has God sent to humanity? We do not know for sure. Some Muslim scholars have suggested 240 thousand prophets." *Prophethood in Islam*, Chicago, IL: The Institute of Islamic Information and Education, III&E Brochure Series; No. 3. Reprinted with the permission of World Assembly of Muslim Youth (WAMY), P.O. Box 10845, Riyadh 11443, Saudi Arabia. In USC-MSA (University of Southern California-Muslim Students' Association) Compendium of Muslim Texts. Retrieved January 12, 2007, from the World Wide Web, www.usc.edu/dept/MSA/fundamentals/prophet/prophethoodinislam.html. "It is obligatory, however, to believe in the 25 prophets mentioned by name in the Qur'an: Adam, Idris, Nuh (Noah), Hud (sent to the 'Aad people), Salih (sent to the Thamud), Ibrahim (Abraham), Lut (Lot), Isma'eel (Ishmael), Ishaq (Isaac), Ya'qub (Jacob) also known as Isra'eel (Israel), Yusuf (Joseph), Ayyub (Job), Shu'ayb (sent to Madyan), Musa (Moses), Harun (Aaron), Dhul-Kifl (Ezekiel), Dawud (David), Sulayman (Solomon), Al-Yas'a, Illyas (Elias), Yunus (Jonah), Zakariyya (Zacharias), Yahya (John), Isa (Jesus) and Muhammad (peace and blessings be upon them all)." Abu al-Hassan, "Prophets and messengers of Allah," *Gulf Times*, Doha, Qatar, August 11, 2006, www.gulf-times.com/site/topics/article.asp?cu_no=2&item_no=101919&version=1&template_id=47&parent_id=27

1806. "The Moral System of Islam," III&E Brochure Series; No. 6 (published by The Institute of Islamic Information and Education (III&E)). USC-MSA (University of Southern California-Muslim Students' Association) Compendium of Muslim Texts. www.usc.edu/dept/MSA/humanrelations/ moralsystem.html
Reprinted with the permission of World Assembly of Muslim Youth (WAMY), P.O. Box 10845, Riyadh 11443, Saudi Arabia.

1807. Khalid M. Baheyeldin, "Abu Bakr Muhammad ibn al-Walid al-Tartushi," in "The Baheyeldin Dynasty," 2002, baheyeldin.com/history/ abu-bakr-muhammad-ibn-al-walid-al-tartushi.html
Reuben Levy, The Social Structure of Islam: Being the Second Edition of the Sociology of Islam. Cambridge, UK: Cambridge University Press, 1957, p. 456.
Yassine Essid, "A Critique of the Origins of Islamic Economic Thought," Leiden: Brill Academic Publishers, 1995, pp 32–33.

1808. Say ye: "We believe in Allah and the revelation given to us and to Abraham Isma`il Isaac Jacob and the Tribes and that given to Moses and Jesus and that given to (all) Prophets from their Lord we make no difference between one and another of them and we bow to Allah (in Islam)." The Holy Qur'an, Chapter 2, verse 136. Translation by Abdullah Yusufali. Retrieved January 5, 2007, from the World Wide Web www.wam.umd.edu/~stwright/rel/islam/

1809. Muhammad H. Haykal, The Life of Muhammad. Translated by Isma'il Raji al-Faruqi. Kuala Lumpur, Malaysia: Islamic Book Trust, 2002.

1810. Syed Saeed Akhtar Rizvi, The Life of Muhammad The Prophet. Published by: Darul Tabligh North America Under the Patronage of World Federation of KSI Muslim Communities, Stanmore, Middlesex, UK. Reproduced with permission by the Ahlul Bayt Digital Islamic Library Project team. Retrieved January 5, 2007, from the World Wide Web www.al-islam.org/lifeprophet/10.htm.
The phrase, "There is no god but Allah and Muhammad is His Prophet," appears in translation in many other forms.

1811. For a typical use of the term "slave of god," try this: "Almighty God has bestowed on his servants the bounty of Islam, and liberated them from the yoke of slavery to be the slaves of God alone, slaves of the Almighty, the only divine power." Crown Prince Abdullah Bin Abdul Aziz, Deputy Prime Minister and Commander of the National Guard. Eid messages from King Fahd and the royal princes, February 18, 1996. Saudi Embassy Website. www.saudiembassy.net/1996News/News/ IslDetail.asp?cIndex=4230

1812. "Those who reject Our Signs We shall soon cast into the fire: as often as their skins are roasted through We shall change them for fresh skins that they may taste the penalty: for Allah is Exalted in Power Wise." Holy Qur'an, Chapter 4, verse 56. www.wam.umd.edu/~stwright/rel/islam/ Quran/4.html. English translations of the Qu'ran are available online from many Islamic sources, though these sources tend to appear and disappear rapidly. As of June 7, 2005, 625 online sources— primarily Islamic sources—included this quote.

1813. n.a., "The Battle Of Asadullah Al-Bilawi, A Historic Moment In The Fight To Unite The Muslim Lands: Smashing The Borders Of The Tawaghit," Islamic State News, June 1, 2014, archive.org/stream/IslamicStateNews/ Islamic-state-report-4_djvu.txt downloaded from the World Wide Web 1-4-2016

1814. A. Guillaume, The Life of Muhammad: A Translation of Ibn Ishaq's Sirat Rasul Allah. New York: Oxford University Press, 1955, eighteenth printing, 2004, p. 369. This blunt quote from Muhammad, "War is deceit," comes to us from Muhammad's first and most important biographer, Ibn Ishaq: A. Guillaume, The Life of Muhammad: A Translation of Ibn Ishaq's Sirat Rasul Allah. New York: Oxford University Press, 1955, eighteenth printing, 2004, p. 458.

1815. Adam Taylor, "These are America's 9 longest foreign wars," Washington Post May 29, 2014, www.washingtonpost.com/news/worldviews/ wp/2014/05/29/these-are-americas-9-longest-foreign-wars/

1816. "'The war is over': Last US soldiers leave Iraq," NBC News, Saturday Dec 17, 2011 8:43 p.m., worldnews.nbcnews.com/_news/2011/12/17/ 9528197-the-war-is-over-last-us-soldiers-leave-iraq

1817. Antonia Juhasz, "Bechtel Takes a Hit for War Profiteering: Government auditors who canceled Bechtel's $50 million contract will soon find reasons to cancel the company's $2.85 billion in Iraq contracts," Alternet, August 3, 2006, www.alternet.org/story/39860/bechtel_takes_ a_hit_for_war_profiteering
Institute for Southern Studies, "Bechtel: The Biggest War Profiteer," www.southernstudies.org/reports/bechtel.pdf

1818. murphthesurf3, "Dick Cheney — Neocon War Profiteer," Daily Kos, Wednesday Jun 18, 2014, 10:14 a.m. EDT, www.dailykos.com/story/2014/6/18/ 1307821/-Dick-Cheney-Neocon-War-Profiteer
David Corn, "Rand Paul Says Dick Cheney Pushed for the Iraq War So Halliburton Would Profit, As the ex-veep blasts Paul for being an isolationist, old video shows the Kentucky senator charging that Cheney used 9/11 as an excuse to invade Iraq and benefit his former company," Mother Jones, April 7, 2014, www.motherjones.com/politics/2014/04/ rand-paul-dick-cheney-exploited-911-iraq-halliburton

1819. "George W. Bush signs the Patriot Act," History.com, 2001. www.history.com/this-day-in-history/george-w-bush-signs-the-patriot-act

1820. Associated Press, "Wolfowitz Escapes Attack on Al Rashid Hotel," Fox News, October 27, 2003, www.foxnews.com/story/2003/10/27/wolfowitz-escapes-attack-on-al-rashid-hotel.html

1821. AP, "Bush Sr. Doormat in Baghdad Hotel Dismantled," Associated Press, April 11, 2003, www.foxnews.com/story/2003/04/11/bush-srdoormat-in-baghdad-hotel-dismantled.html

1822. Kenneth J. Bechtel, *The Iran Hostage Crisis.* University of Maryland, Baltimore County, UMBC Center for History Education, www.umbc.edu/che/tahlessons/lessondisplay.php?lesson=70 *American Experience*, "The Iranian Hostage Crisis," PBS, www.pbs.org/wgbh/americanexperience/features/general-article/carter-hostage-crisis/

1823. Elena Krieger, Michael Shank, Julia Trezona Peek, "Don't Let China Dominate—When it comes to renewable energy, China is trumping the U.S." U.S. News and World Report, September 18, 2014, www.usnews.com/opinion/blogs/world-report/2014/09/18/china-is-besting-the-us-on-renewable-energy

1824. Richard Curtiss,"Did Iran Delay Hostages Release To Ensure Reagan's Election?" Washington Report on Middle East Affairs, Special Report, October 1987, pp. 1, 16–17, www.wrmea.org/1987-october/did-iran-delay-hostages-release-to-ensure-reagan-s-election.html

1825. David C. Wills, *The First War on Terrorism: Counter-terrorism Policy during the Reagan Administration.* Lanham, MD: Rowman & Littlefield Publishers, 2004. Wikipedia, "1983 Beirut Barracks Bombing," en.wikipedia.org/wiki/1983_Beirut_barracks_bombings

1826. Micah Zenko, "When Reagan Cut and Run—The forgotten history of when America boldly abandoned ship in the Middle East," *Foreign Policy*, February 7, 2014, foreignpolicy.com/2014/02/07/when-reagan-cut-and-run

1827. Lee H. Hamilton, Daniel K. Inouye, "Report of the Congressional Committees Investigating the Iran/Contra Affair," Collingdale, PA: Diane Publishing, Nov. 1, 1995, p. 59. Ross Cheit, Sara Chimene-Weiss, Sol Eppel, Jeremy Feigenbaum, Seth Motel, Ingrid Pangandoyon, "Understanding the Iran-Contra Affairs," Brown University, www.brown.edu/Research/Understanding_the_Iran_Contra_Affair/documents.php www.pbs.org/wgbh/americanexperience/features/general-article/reagan-iran/

1828. United States History, "Iran-Contra Affair," www.u-s-history.com/pages/h1889.html

1829. Jonathan Marshall, Peter Dale Scott, Jane Hunter, *The Iran-Contra Connection: Secret Teams and Covert Operations in the Reagan Era.* Montreal: Black Rose Books Ltd., 1987.

1830. Efraim Karsh, *The Iran-Iraq War—1980–1988.* Oxford, UK: Osprey Publishing, 2002, p. 12.

1831. Wikipedia, "Iranian Constitution," en.wikipedia.org/wiki/Iranian_constitution

1832. Wikipedia, "Iranian Constitution," en.wikipedia.org/wiki/Iranian_constitution

1833. "The Islamic Revolutionary Guards Corps..will be responsible not only for guarding and preserving the frontiers of the country, but also for fulfilling the ideological mission of jihad in God's way; that is, extending the sovereignty of God's law throughout the world (this is in accordance with the Koranic verse "Prepare against them whatever force you are able to muster, and strings of horses, striking fear into the enemy of God and your enemy, and others besides them" [8:60]). Preamble to the 1979 Iranian Constitution, Hanover College history. hanover.edu/courses/excerpts/261ircon.html "The Constitution, taking into account the Islamic content of the Iranian revolution as a movement for the victory of all the oppressed and dispossessed over the rich and the powerful, will meet the needs for the prevalence of this revolution in Iran and outside of Iran. Outside of Iran, in cooperation with other Islamic and popular movements, it will spare no effort to strengthen the struggle for the victory of the oppressed and dispossessed people throughout the world and by so doing pave the way for the creation of a unique and just universal community. ...In so far as it relates to the creation and mobilization of the country's armed forces the prerequisites are that belief and ideology will constitute the principal driving force in their formation. In addition to safeguarding and preserving the country's frontiers they will have as their mission sacred battle in the name of god for the extension of the divine sovereignty of god in the world." Manouchehr Ganji, *Defying the Iranian Revolution: From a Minister to the Shah to a Leader of Resistance.* Westport, CT: Praeger Publishers, 2002, p. 130.

1834. Efraim Karsh, *The Iran-Iraq War—1980–1988*. Oxford, UK: Osprey Publishing, 2002, p. 13.

1835. In 1980, "the joint decision of the United States, Europe, and Japan to impose economic and technological sanctions on Iran...." Farhang Rajaee, *Iranian Perspectives on the Iran-Iraq War*. Gainesville, FL: University of Florida Press, 1997, p. 93. "[the U.S. and the Soviet Union], as well as other states, sought to preserve the Iran-Iraq balance both by bolstering Iraq and by tightening the embargo on the sale of weapons to Iran." Thomas L. McNaughter, *Arms and Oil: United States Military Strategy and the Persian Gulf*. Washington, DC: The Brookings Institution, 1985, p. 178.

"In February 1986...The balance of power was shifting in Iraq's favor. What tilted that balance was extensive U.S. efforts to prevent Iran from acquiring weapons, which seriously affected that country's maneuverability." Farhang Rajaee, *Iranian Perspectives on the Iran-Iraq War*. Gainesville, FL: University of Florida Press, 1997, p. 56.

1836. "The resulting tank battle, one of the largest of the war, destroyed approximately 100 of Iran's American-made tanks. Another 150 were captured. Iraq lost only 50 of its Soviet-made tanks." Edward C. Willett, *The Iran-Iraq War*. New York: The Rosen Publishing Group,2004, p. 24.

1837. Iran Chamber Society, "Iran-Iraq War 1980–1988," Iran Chamber Society, www.iranchamber.com/history/iran_iraq_war/iran_iraq_war1.php

1838. Iran Chamber Society, "Mohammad Reza Shah Pahlavi," History of Iran, Iran Chamber Society, www.iranchamber.com/history/mohammad_rezashah/mohammad_rezashah.php

1839. "Iran launched an arms development program during its 1980-88 war with Iraq to compensate for weapons shortages caused by a U.S. embargo. Since 1992, Iran has produced its own tanks, armored personnel carriers, missiles and a fighter plane." Ali Akbar Dareini, Iran Confirms Ballistic Missile Test, Associated Press, May 26, 2002. See also: Riyad Alam-al-Din, "Will War Break Out?," Al-Watan al-Arabi (Paris), 4 May 2001, pp. 18–21; in "Report on US-Iranian 'Deal,' Possibility of 'New' Iran-Iraq War," FBIS Document GMP20010503000175, 3 May 2001. "The...mission of the FBIS was to monitor, record, transcribe and translate intercepted radio broadcasts from foreign governments, official news services, and clandestine broadcasts from occupied territories."

"Iran launched an arms development program during its 1980–88 war with Iraq to compensate for a U.S. weapons embargo. Since 1992, Iran has produced its own tanks, armored personnel carriers, missiles and a fighter plane." Ali Akbar Dareini, "Iran calls test of new missile successful," AP, in *USA Today*, April 2, 2006, http://usatoday30.usatoday.com/news/world/2006-04-02-iran-missile_x.htm

1840. Iranian oil sold for $13.45 per barrel in 1979. By 1980, the price had skyrocketed to $30.37. The price remained lofty through most of the Iran-Iraq War, then, as the War died down, sank back from a high of $37 in 1981 to $12.75 in 1988, the year the Iran-Iraq War ended. Energy Information Administration.

Table 11.7 Crude Oil Prices by Selected Type, 1970–2006.

Table 11.7 Crude Oil Prices by Selected Type, 1970–2006
(Nominal Dollars per Barrel)

Year	Saudi Arabian Light-34° API	Iranian Light-34° API	Libyan [1] Es Sider-37° API	Nigerian [2] Bonny Light-37° API	Indonesian Minas-34° API	Venezuelan Tia Juana Light [3]	Mexico Maya-22° API	United Kingdom Brent Blend-38° API
1970	1.35	1.36	2.09	2.10	1.67	2.05	NA	NA
1971	1.75	1.76	2.80	2.65	2.18	2.45	NA	NA
1972	1.90	1.91	2.80	2.80	2.96	2.45	NA	NA
1973	2.10	2.11	3.10	3.10	2.96	2.60	NA	NA
1974	9.60	10.63	14.30	12.60	10.80	9.30	NA	NA
1975	10.46	10.67	11.98	11.80	12.60	11.00	NA	NA
1976	11.51	11.62	12.21	12.84	12.80	11.12	NA	NA
1977	12.09	12.81	13.74	14.33	13.55	12.72	NA	NA
1978	12.70	12.81	13.80	14.33	13.55	12.82	NA	NA
1979	13.34	13.45	14.52	14.80	13.90	13.36	15.45	15.70
1980	26.00	[4] 30.37	34.50	29.97	27.50	25.20	28.00	26.02
1981	32.00	37.00	40.78	40.00	35.00	32.88	34.50	39.25
1982	34.00	34.20	36.50	36.50	35.00	32.88	26.50	36.60
1983	34.00	31.20	35.10	35.50	34.53	32.88	25.50	33.50
1984	29.00	28.00	30.15	30.00	29.53	27.88	25.00	30.00
1985	29.00	28.00	30.15	28.00	29.53	27.88	25.50	28.65
1986	28.00	28.05	30.15	28.65	28.53	28.05	21.93	26.00
1987	16.15	16.14	16.95	17.13	16.28	15.10	14.00	18.25
1988	17.52	15.55	18.52	18.92	17.56	17.62	11.10	18.00
1989	13.15	12.75	15.40	15.05	15.50	12.27	10.63	15.80
1990	18.40	18.20	20.40	21.20	18.55	24.69	17.05	21.00
1991	24.00	23.65	26.90	27.80	26.50	28.62	20.00	27.20
1992	15.90	15.50	17.20	18.20	18.65	19.67	10.75	17.75
1993	16.80	16.70	17.55	18.50	19.10	17.97	12.50	17.90
1994	12.40	12.40	12.55	13.50	14.15	12.97	9.01	13.15
1995	16.63	16.18	16.05	16.15	16.95	16.57	13.77	16.15
1996	18.20	17.73	19.20	19.70	20.05	18.52	15.79	19.37
1997	22.98	22.63	24.10	24.65	24.95	26.62	19.33	24.05
1998	15.50	14.93	16.72	16.50	16.50	15.93	10.81	15.89
1999	10.03	9.83	10.65	10.60	9.95	9.45	6.38	10.44
2000	24.78	24.63	25.85	25.55	24.15	24.85	20.20	25.10
2001	20.30	20.20	22.40	22.00	22.80	22.13	15.82	22.50
2002	17.68	18.90	19.63	19.88	18.89	17.78	14.30	21.20
2003	27.39	27.85	30.40	31.16	35.03	30.25	26.29	31.36
2004	27.08	28.67	29.47	29.97	32.10	30.10	24.37	29.73
2005	31.86	33.84	38.00	38.21	35.86	35.98	26.16	39.43
2006	50.86	52.56	55.89	56.97	53.95	52.52	42.93	57.25

www.eia.doe.gov/emeu/aer/txt/ptb1107.html

1841. "After it became clear that the Iranian government was not going to take action against the students to free the hostages, President Carter initiated economic sanctions against Iran." Hossein G. Askari, John Forrer, Hildy Teegen, Jiawen Yang, *Case Studies of U.S. Economic Sanctions: The Chinese, Cuban, and Iranian Experience*. Westport, CT: Praeger Publishers, 2003, p. 173.

1842. Douglas Schoen, Melik Kaylan, *The Russia-China Axis: The New Cold War and America's Crisis of Leadership*. New York: Encounter Books, 2014.

1843. "Ukrainian President Viktor Yushchenko confirmed in 2005 that Iran illegally procured six Kh-55 cruise missiles from Ukraine four years earlier. ...China has also provided Iran with cruise missiles and technology."
Arms Control Association, "Arms Control and Proliferation Profile: Iran," Arms Control Association, October 2015, www.armscontrol.org/factsheets/iranprofile

1844. GlobalSecurity.org, Russia & Ukraine Military Industry, www.globalsecurity.org/military/world/russia/industry-ua.htm

1845. Anthony H. Cordesman, "Iran's Developing Military Capabilities," Center for Strategic and International Studies, CSIS, 2005, p. 20. Military Factory, DIO Zulfiqar Main Battle Tank (1999), February 13, 2015, www.militaryfactory.com/armor/detail.asp?armor_id=177

1846. Hossein Askari, Amin Mohseni, Shahrzad Daneshvar, *The Militarization of the Persian Gulf: An Economic Analysis.* Cheltenham, UK: Edward Elgar Publishing, Jan. 1, 2010, p. 89.

1847. Michael Elleman, "Iran's Ballistic Missile Program," The Iran Primer, United States Institute of Peace, updated August 2015, iranprimer.usip.org/resource/irans-ballistic-missile-program Iran Watch, "A History of Iran's Ballistic Missile Program," Iran Watch, the Wisconsin Project on Nuclear Arms Control, May 1, 2012, www.iranwatch.org/our-publications/weapon-program-background-report/history-irans-ballistic-missile-program "In response to Iranian missile attacks against Baghdad, some 190 missiles were fired by the Iraqis over a six week period at Iranian cities in 1988, during the 'War of the Cities.' The Iraqi missile attacks caused little destruction, but each warhead had a psychological and political impact — boosting Iraqi morale while causing almost 30 percent of Tehran's population to flee the city. The threat of rocketing the Iranian capital with missiles capable of carrying chemical warheads is cited as a significant reason why Iran accepted a disadvantageous peace agreement." Iran-Iraq War (1980–1988). *Persian Journal* — Latest Iran News & Iranian Culture Journal, www.iranian.ws/iran-online/iran-iraq_war/end.htm. In 1987, the Chinese delivered PL7 missiles modeled after the French Matra Magic R-550. These missiles were long-range, air-to-air missiles and could hit targets at up to 10km. China also assisted Iran in manufacturing a short-range, solid-fueled ballistic missile named Nazeat or Iran-130. Kenneth R. Timmerman, *Weapons of Mass Destruction: The Cases of Iran, Syria and Libya.* Los Angeles: Simon Wiesenthal Center, 1992, p. 25. In 1987, Iran launched 79 surface-to-surface missiles at Iraq; 18 of the missiles were Scuds. W. Seth Carus, "Ballistic Missiles Fired in the Iran-Iraq War, 1980–1988," unpublished document, 9 May 1988. "Iraq reportedly fired FROG-7 missiles against Iranian border towns as early as 1980 and escalated to longer-range Scud-B missiles against other targets in the mid-1980s. Iran responded by firing back 50 Scuds, purchased from Libya. Both countries revealed large ballistic missile inventories when they fired hundreds against each other in the 1988 'war of the cities.' For six weeks beginning on February 29, more ballistic missiles—some 570—were rained down on each country than had been fired since the German V2 attacks on England and Belgium during World War II. The missiles were obtained from the Soviet Union, North Korea, and China." Walker F. Paul, "High-tech killing power," *Bulletin of the Atomic Scientists,* 00963402, May 1990, Vol. 46, Issue 4.

1848. Wikipedia, "Iran-Iraq War." en.wikipedia.org/wiki/Iran-iraq_war#_note-2

1849. Wikipedia, "Iran-Iraq War." en.wikipedia.org/wiki/Iran-iraq_war#_note-2

1850. Quotes from the Iranian Islamic Revolutionary Constitution, in Manouchehr Ganji. *Defying the Iranian Revolution: From a Minister to the Shah to a Leader of Resistance.* Westport, CT: Praeger Publishers, 2002, p. 130.

1851. Reuben Levy, *The Social Structure of Islam: Being the Second Edition of the Sociology of Islam.* Cambridge, UK: Cambridge University Press, 1957, p. 456.

1852. Reuben Levy, *The Social Structure of Islam: Being the Second Edition of the Sociology of Islam.* Cambridge, UK: Cambridge University Press, 1957, p. 456.

1853. Reuben Levy, *The Social Structure of Islam: Being the Second Edition of the Sociology of Islam.* Cambridge, UK: Cambridge University Press, 1957, p. 456.

1854. Julian Borger, "US intelligence fears Iran duped hawks into Iraq war • Inquiry into Tehran's role in starting conflict • Top Pentagon ally Chalabi accused in Washington," *The Guardian,* May 25, 2004, retrieved from the World Wide Web May 26, 2004, www.guardian.co.uk/Iraq/Story/0,2763,1224075,00.html

1855. Douglas Mccollam, "How Chalabi Played the Press," *Columbia Journalism Review,* Issue 4: July/August, www.cjr.org/issues/2004/4/mccollam-list.asp

1856. "Some intelligence officials now believe that Iran used the hawks in the Pentagon and the White House to get rid of a hostile neighbour, and pave the way for a Shia-ruled Iraq. ... said an intelligence source in Washington yesterday. 'Iranian intelligence has been manipulating the US for several years through Chalabi.'" Julian Borger, "US intelligence fears Iran duped hawks into Iraq war • Inquiry into Tehran's role in starting conflict • Top Pentagon ally Chalabi accused in Washington," *The Guardian,* May 25, 2004, retrieved from the World Wide Web May 26, 2004, www.guardian.co.uk/Iraq/Story/0,2763,1224075,00.html

1857. Neil Best, "John Gilchrist, who played "Mikey" in TV ad, still likes it after all these years," November 22, 2012, 8:20 p.m., *Newsday,* www.newsday.com/sports/media/john-gilchrist-whoplayed-mikey-in-life-cereal-commercial-still-likesit-after-all-these-years-1.4253447

1858. Quaker Oats, Life Cereal Original, Quaker Oats, www.quakeroats.com/products/cold-cereals/life-cereal/regular.aspx

1859. John Dizard, "How Ahmed Chalabi conned the neocons," *Salon*, May 4, 2004, retrieved from the World Wide Web Wednesday, October 29, 2008, dir.salon.com/story/news/feature/2004/05/04/chalabi/index.html. For Chalabi's own views, see: Ma'ad Fayad, "Iraqi National Congress Leader Ahmad al-Chalabi Talks to Asharq Al-Awsat," September 15, 2007, retrieved from the World Wide Web Wednesday, October 29, 2008, www.aawsat.com/english/news.asp?section=3&id=10211

1860. Kevin Drum, "Ahmed Chalabi Timeline," *Washington Monthly*, May 24, 2004, retrieved from the World Wide Web Wednesday, October 29, 2008: www.washingtonmonthly.com/archives/individual/2004_05/003991.php

1861. Kevin Drum, "Ahmed Chalabi Timeline," *Washington Monthly*, May 24, 2004, www.washingtonmonthly.com/archives/individual/2004_05/003991.php

1861. Kevin Drum, "Ahmed Chalabi Timeline," *Washington Monthly*, May 24, 2004. www.washingtonmonthly.com/archives/individual/2004_05/003991.php

1862. Peter S. Goodman, "Ending Battle, Wolfowitz Resigns From World Bank," *Washington Post*, May 18, 2007, www.washingtonpost.com/wp-dyn/content/article/2007/05/17/AR2007051700216.html

1863. Sewell Channov, "Ahmad Chalabi, Iraqi Politician Who Pushed for U.S. Invasion, Dies at 71," *New York Times*, November 3, 2015, www.nytimes.com/2015/11/04/world/middleeast/ahmad-chalabi-iraq-dead.html?_r=0

1864. "Ahmed Chalabi Fast Facts," CNN, Updated 12:04 p.m. ET, Wed November 4, 2015, www.cnn.com/2013/08/05/world/meast/ahmed-chalabi-fast-facts/

1865. Robert Block, "Inside Failed Bank Run by Man U.S. Backs for Key Role in Iraq Chalabi's Bank Problem in Jordan Hurts Chances for Running Country," *Wall Street Journal*, May 22, 2003 12:01 a.m. ET, www.wsj.com/articles/SB105355075559908400

1866. Kevin Drum, "Ahmed Chalabi Timeline," *Washington Monthly*, May 24, 2004, retrieved from the World Wide Web Wednesday, October 29, 2008, www.washingtonmonthly.com/archives/individual/2004_05/003991.php

1867. BBC. Profile: Ahmed Chalabi. BBC, October 3, 2002. news.bbc.co.uk/1/hi/not_in_website/syndication/monitoring/media_reports/2291649.stm

1868. Tariq Alhomayed, "Iran's Conservatives Are Deceiving Themselves," *Asharq Alawsat*, April 24, 2008, retrieved from the World Wide Web Saturday, April 26, 2008, www.asharq-e.com/news.asp?section=2&id=12533

1869. Julian Borger, "Chalabi 'boasted of Iranian spy link'—Iraqi accused by CIA made claim in 1997, says former inspector," London: *The Guardian*, May 26, 2004, retrieved November 28, 2006, from the World Wide Web, www.guardian.co.uk/Iraq/Story/0,2763,1224916,00.html

1870. Julian Borger, "Chalabi 'boasted of Iranian spy link'—Iraqi accused by CIA made claim in 1997, says former inspector," London: *The Guardian*, May 26, 2004, retrieved November 28, 2006, from the World Wide Web, www.guardian.co.uk/Iraq/Story/individual/2004_05/003991.php

1871. Julian Borger, "Chalabi 'boasted of Iranian spy link'--Iraqi accused by CIA made claim in 1997, says former inspector," London: *The Guardian*, May 26, 2004, retrieved November 28, 2006, from the World Wide Web, www.guardian.co.uk/Iraq/Story/0,2763,1224916,00.html

1872. Joe Klein, "Searching for Saviors in Strange Places—Could Ahmad Chalabi end up running Iraq?" *Time Magazine*—Web Exclusive, October 22, 2005, content.time.com/time/magazine/article/0,9171,1122005,00.html

1873. Jane Mayer, "The Manipulator —Ahmad Chalabi pushed a tainted case for war. Can he survive the occupation?" *The New Yorker*, June 7, 2004, www.newyorker.com/magazine/2004/06/07/the-manipulator

1874. Seymour M. Hersh, "The Stovepipe," *The New Yorker*, October 27, 2003, www.newyorker.com/printables/fact/031027fa_fact

1875. Seymour M. Hersh, "The Stovepipe," *The New Yorker*, October 27, 2003, www.newyorker.com/printables/fact/031027fa_fact

1876. Seymour M. Hersh, "The Stovepipe," *The New Yorker*, October 27, 2003, www.newyorker.com/printables/fact/031027fa_fact

1877. Douglas McCollam, "How Chalabi Played the Press," *Columbia Journalism Review*, Issue 4: July/August, 2004, www.cjr.org/issues/2004/4/mccollam-list.asp

1878. Ma'ad Fayad, "Iraqi National Congress Leader Ahmad al-Chalabi Talks to Asharq Al-Awsat," September 15, 2007, retrieved from the World Wide Web Wednesday, October 29, 2008, www.aawsat.com/english/news.asp?section=3&id=10211

1879. Adam Taylor, "Deja vu? Neocons tout Ahmed Chalabi as Iraq's next leader," *The Washington Post*, July 8, 2014, www.washingtonpost.com/news/worldviews/wp/2014/07/08/deja-vu-neocons-toutahmed-chalabi-as-iraqs-next-leaader/

1880. The budget was last balanced by Bill Clinton in 1998. In fact, in 1998, the government ran a surplus.
Jim Dexter, CNN Fact Check: The last president to balance the budget, CNN, February 3, 2010, politicalticker.blogs.cnn.com/2010/02/03/cnn-fact-check-the-last-president-to-balancethe-budget/

1881. Wikipedia, "National Debt of the United States," en.wikipedia.org/wiki/National_debt_of_the_United_States

1882. Najaf is the center of Shia political power in Iraq. Religion Facts, "Najaf," www.religionfacts.com/najaf

1883. When the Ayatollah Khomeini was tossed out of Iran in 1964, he took up residence in Najaf, the headquarters of the Iraqi mosque system. He stayed in Najaf until 1978—developing a worldwide following for his religious and political ideas from an Iraqi base. (Wikipedia, "Saddam Hussein: Foreign Affairs," en.wikipedia.org/wiki/Saddam_hussein#Foreign_affairs)
In all probability, he influenced the Iraqi mosque leaders profoundly during his stay.

1884. Vali Nasr, "When the Shiites Rise," Foreign Affairs, Jul/Aug 2006, Vol. 85, Issue 4, pp. 58–74.

1885. Sistani.org, "Biography of Grand Ayatollah Sistani," The Official Website of Grand Ayatollah Sistani, www.sistani.org www.sistani.org/html/eng/main/ index.php?page=1&lang=eng&part=1. Wikipedia, "Sistani," en.wikipedia.org/wiki/Sistani. Tom Michael, "Sistani, Ali al-," Britannica Book of the Year, 2005. 2006, Encyclopædia Britannica Online, 9 Nov. 2006, www.britannica.com/eb/article-9398635 "Sistani, Ali al-" Year in Review 2004.

1886. The Iranians call their foreign operations the "extra-territorial activities of the IRGC"—Iranian Revolutionary Guard Corp, Iran Focus, "Iran Revolutionary Guards expect key changes in high command," Iran Focus, August 4, 2005, retrieved from the World Wide Web Monday, October 27, 2008, www.iranfocus.com/en/index.php?option=com_content&task=view&id=3169. See also: Associated Press, "Iran's stealth force—Accused of backing Iraqi militias, elite Quds corps deeply enmeshed in Iraq," Associated Press February 15, 2007, retrieved from the World Wide Web Monday, October 27, 2008, www.msnbc.msn.com/id/17175714/

1887. Ali Alfoneh, "Brigadier General Qassem Suleimani: A Biography," Middle Eastern Outlook, January 24, 2011, in AEI [American Enterprise Institute] Iran Tracker, www.irantracker.org/analysis/brigadier-general-qassem-suleimani-biography

1888. n.a. "Quds (Jerusalem) Force," GlobalSecurity.org, retrieved from the World Wide Web Monday, October 27, 2008: www.globalsecurity.org/intell/world/iran/qods.htm. "A primary focus for the Qods Force is training Islamic fundamentalist terrorist groups. Currently, the Qods Force conducts training activities in Iran and in Sudan. The Qods Force is also responsible for gathering information required for targeting and attack planning. The Pasdaran [the Qods Force] has contacts with underground movements in the Gulf region, and Pasdaran members are assigned to Iranian diplomatic missions, where, in the course of routine intelligence activities they monitor dissidents. Pasdaran influence has been particularly important in Kuwait, Bahrain, and the United Arab Emirates. ... The Pasdaran has also supported the establishment of Hizballah branches in Lebanon, Iraqi Kurdistan, Jordan and Palestine, and the Islamic Jihad in many other Muslim countries including Egypt, Turkey, Chechnya and in Caucasia." John Pike, Qods (Jerusalem) Force Iranian Revolutionary Guard Corps (IRGC — Pasdaran-e Inqilab), retrieved from the World Wide Web Saturday, June 21, 2008, www.globalsecurity.org/intell/world/iran/qods.htm

1889. Associated Press, "Iran's stealth force—Accused of backing Iraqi militias, elite Quds corps deeply enmeshed in Iraq," Associated Press February 15, 2007, retrieved from the World Wide Web Monday, October 27, 2008, www.msnbc.msn.com/id/17175714/

1890. n.a. "Qods (Jerusalem) Force," GlobalSecurity.org, retrieved from the World Wide Web Monday, October 27, 2008, www.globalsecurity.org/intell/world/iran/qods.htm

1891. Says Tariq Alhomayed, the editor of Asharq Al-Awsat, "Hamas has become a puppet in the hands of the Iranians and [their allies, the] Syrians." Tariq Alhomayed, "Iran and the Fearful Arabs," Asharq Al-Awsat, January 5, 2008, retrieved from the World Wide Web Tuesday, October 28, 2008, www.asharq-e.com/news.asp?section=2&id=12718

1892. Nima Adelkhah, "Iranian Perspectives on Yemen's Houthis," Terrorism Monitor, Volume: 13, Issue: 13, The Jamestown Foundation, June 26, 2015, 11:27 a.m. www.jamestown.org/regions/middleeast/single/?tx_ttnews%5Btt_news%5D=44082&tx_ttnews%5BbackPid%5D=674&cHash=4c53126c1dee3f2ea07148c93a7572ff#.VwLxp-IrKrY Bill Gertz, "U.S. Intelligence: Iran Sending More Fighters to Yemen—IRGC Quds Force, Hezbollah back pro-Iran Rebels," Washington Free Beacon, May 27, 2015 5:00 a.m., freebeacon.com/national-security/u-s-intelligence-iran-sending-more-fighters-to-yemen/ "Yemen: Classified document reveals extent of Iranian support for Houthis," Asharq Al-Awsat, July 6, 2015, 3:04 p.m. english.aawsat.com/2015/07/article55344262/yemen-classified-document-reveals-extent-of-iranian-support-for-houthis

1893. Tariq Alhomayed, editor of the leading Arab international newspaper *Asharq Al-Awsat*, is one of those who says that Muqtada al Sadr was an Iranian puppet. Writes Alhomayed, "Muqtada al Sadr is a mighty but reckless force; he is not as intelligent as Hassan Nasrallah and does not speak the language of politics, however he was an important factor in enforcing the Iranian influence at the moment in which Saddam Hussein's regime fell. Today, it appears that Tehran no longer needs al Sadr." Tariq Alhomayed, "Sadrists Under Fire," *Asharq Al-Awsat*, March 27, 2008, retrieved from the World Wide Web Tuesday, October 28, 2008, www.asharq-e.com/news.asp?section=2&id=12231

1894. Patrick Jackson, "Who are Iraq's Mehdi Army?" BBC News, May 30, 2007, retrieved from the World Wide Web Monday, October 27, 2008, news.bbc.co.uk/2/hi/middle_east/3604393.stm

1895. Lionel Beehner, Backgrounder—Iraq: Militia Groups, Council on Foreign Relations, retrieved from the World Wide Web Monday, October 27, 2008, www.cfr.org/publication/8175/#4 Abdul-Rahman Brent, Your Opinion Of Mahdi Army And Badr Organization, ShiaChat.com, retrieved from the World Wide Web Monday, October 27, 2008, www.shiachat.com/forum/lofiversion/index.php/t234935656.html

1896. n.a. "Badr Organization," NationMaster—Encyclopedia, retrieved from the World Wide Web Monday, October 27, 2008, www.nationmaster.com/encyclopedia/Badr-Organization

1897. Dahr Jamail, "State Sponsored Civil War," Dahr Jamail's Weblog, retrieved from the World Wide Web Monday, October 27, 2008, Google's cache of dahrjamailiraq.com/weblog/archives/2005_06_05.php. Dahr Jamail is a former writer for an Alaskan newspaper who planted himself in Iraq in 2003 to report on the unreported aspects of the Iraq War. He is a third-generation Lebanese-American who grew up in Houston.

1898. One hint that the answer is yes and that the Badr Organization still obeyed Iran comes the following: "In January 2003, before a planned meeting of Iraqi opposition leaders in London, Chalabi visited Tehran to meet with al-Hakim...U.S. aircraft flew [Ahmad] Chalabi from northern Iraq to the city of An Nasiriyah on April 6. It was a symbolic gesture, intended to demonstrate that the INC [Iraqi National Congress] was part of the fighting coalition. The problem was that Chalabi had trouble rounding up enough troops. The troops he used were drawn from the Badr Brigade, an Iranian-backed Shiite militia." n.a., "Ahmad Chalabi and His Iranian Connection," *Stratfor Weekly*, February 18, 2004, Global Policy Forum, www.globalpolicy.org/security/issues/iraq/justify/2004/0218chalabiconnection.htm

1899. Scott Peterson and Howard LaFranchi, "Iran Shifts Attention to Brokering Peace in Iraq," *Christian Science Monitor*, May 16, 2008, reprinted in Arab American News, retrieved from the World Wide Web Friday, June 20, 2008, www.arabamericannews.com/news/index.php?mod=article&cat=Iraq&article=1040. The Associated Press reported that in addition to Lebanon, Gaza, and Iraq, the Quds force was active in Bosnia, the Sudan, and in another location that will pop up in a minute—Afghanistan.

1900. Hussein Dakroub, "Beirut unity Cabinet gives Hezbollah veto power," Associated Press, July 11, 2008, in Cleveland.com, retrieved from the World Wide Web Wednesday, October 29, 2008, www.cleveland.com/world/index.ssf/2008/07/beirut_unity_cabinet_gives_hez.html

1901. Lionel Beehner, and Greg Bruno, Backgrounder: Iran's Involvement in Iraq, Council for Foreign Relations, March 3, 2008, www.cfr.org/iran/irans-involvement-iraq/p12521 Jim Michaels, "General says U.S. has proof Iran arming Iraqi militias— Bush vows to find, arrest suppliers," *USA Today*, April 10, 2011.

1902. Patrick Cockburn, "Baghdad: The bloodiest day," *The Independent*, London, September 15, 2005, retrieved from the World Wide Web Friday, October 31, 2008, www.independent.co.uk/news/world/middle-east/baghdad-the-bloodiest-day-506902.html

1903. Niko Price, "Iraq rebels used donkeys as missile launchers," Archives, *Irish Examiner*, November 22, 2008, retrieved from the World Wide Web Wednesday, October 29, 2008, archives.tcm.ie/irishexaminer/2003/11/22/story72888254.asp

1904. "Iranian 'Shape Charges' Discovered in Iraq," Voice of America, October 29, 2009 2:33 p.m., www.voanews.com/content/a-13-2005-08-06-voa5-67397622/275954.html Peter Spiegel, "U.S. Says Iran Is Aiding Iraq Rebels—The top commander, Gen. Casey, accuses the Shiite regime in Tehran of providing support and direction to fighters belonging to the sect," *Los Angeles Times*, June 23, 2006, articles.latimes.com/2006/jun/23/world/fg-usiran23 For a contrary view, a view that the connection drawn between Iran and improvised explosive devices was "phony," see the rabidly pro-Iranian and usually profoundly unreliable globalresearch.ca. Philip Giraldi, "Did Iranian Weapons Kill Americans? Another Phony Argument against a Deal with Iran," *Global Research*, August 20, 2015, www.globalresearch.ca/did-iranian-weapons-kill-americans-another-phony-argument-against-a-deal-with-iran/5470302?print=1

1905. I ran across the clues to Iran's peace blitz while doing research for four appearances on the Iranian government's world English-language service Press TV.

1906. The world press reported that Iran was hurt and disappointed by Syria's opening of negotiations with Israel. But there is strong reason to believe that this was a false front on Iran's part. One hint comes from the fact that Iran's President Ahmadinejad visited Turkey, host of the Israel-Syria talks, in August, 2008, not long after the Syria peace discussions began. One of the items on the agenda was the Israel-Syria talks. And there was no hint that Ahmadinejad wanted those talks stopped. For Ahmadinejad's visit, see: Hürriyet, "President Ahmadinejad meets Turkey's Gul, no energy deal," *Iran Press News*, August 18, 2008, retrieved from the World Wide Web Monday, October 27, 2008, www.iranpressnews.com/english/source/ 044776.html. For the standard view that Iran was wounded by Syria's Israel negotiations, see: Barak Ravid and Amos Harel, "Hamas: Olmert too weak to negotiate peace agreement with Syria," *Ha'aretz*. May 5, 2008.

1907. Press TV, "Hamas awaits Israel's truce response," Press TV, Iran, 26 Apr 2008. Press TV is Iran's worldwide English-language TV news station. It is wholly owned by the Iranian government.

1908. BBC News, "Hamas rejects truce plan," BBC News, January 17, 2003, retrieved from the World Wide Web Wednesday, October 29, 2008, news.bbc.co.uk/1/hi/world/middle_east/ 2668647.stm

1909. Hamas, Hamas Covenant 1988—The Covenant of the Islamic Resistance Movement, 18 August 1988, The Avalon Project at Yale Law School, retrieved from the World Wide Web Friday, April 25, 2008,www.yale.edu/lawweb/avalon/mideast/ hamas.htm

1910. Hamas, Hamas Covenant 1988—The Covenant of the Islamic Resistance Movement, 18 August 1988, The Avalon Project at Yale Law School, retrieved from the World Wide Web Friday, April 25, 2008, www.yale.edu/lawweb/avalon/mideast/ hamas.htm

1911. Tariq Alhomayed, "Nasrallah Has Been Ordered to Lie Down!" *Asharq Alawsat*, July 3, 2008, www.asharq-e.com/news.asp?section=2&id=13283 Tariq Alhomayed is the editor of *Asharq Alawsat*. Writes Alhomayed in *Asharq Alawsat*, Iran ordered Lebanon's Hezbollah to "lie down" and Hezbollah obeyed. Explains Alhomayed, the Lebanese "enforced calm cannot be isolated from the general calm that Iran is spreading throughout the region." Continues Alhomayed, "Iran's Supreme Leader [Ayatollah Ali Khamenei] issued a warning to the Iranians when he said, 'officials and political experts should avoid illogical, provocative statements,' and added, 'those who are acting against our interests want us to reject the offer made by major states which it is in our interest to accept.'" Then Alhomayed explains his conclusion: "The monumental efforts exerted by Hamas to impose calm as it called anyone who launched rockets from Gaza into Israel a traitor, brings the larger picture into focus. It appears as though the Iranians have issued instructions to their associates in Hezbollah and Hamas to stay put." Alhomayed is convinced that Iran got its proxy armies to feign peace in order to distract the United States from a preemptive strike at Iran's nuclear weapons development sites. If that's true, then the Iranians were trying to kill two flies with one blow. But it's very unlikely that Iran's Supreme Leader would see demands that Iran stop its nuclear weapons program as an "offer made by major states which it is in our interest to accept." And it is extremely likely that the Supreme Leader would see an American offer to withdraw from Iraq as very much in Iran's "interest to accept."

1912. Scott Peterson and Howard LaFranchi, "Iran Shifts Attention to Brokering Peace in Iraq," *Christian Science Monitor*, May 16, 2008, reprinted in *Arab American News*, retrieved from the World Wide Web Friday, June 20, 2008, www.arabamericannews.com/news/ index.php?mod=article&cat=Iraq&article=1040

1913. Bill Roggio, "US, Iraqi forces engage Mahdi Army in Baghdad, Rashidiyah, Hussaniyah," *Christian Science Monitor*, April 24, 2008, retrieved from the World Wide Web Wednesday, October 29, 2008, www.longwarjournal.org/archives/2008/ 04/us_iraqi_forces_enga.php

1914. Warren P. Strobel, "Iraq Forces Defeat A Blow to White House," *Miami Herald*, April 2, 2008, p. 1. Anthony H. Cordesman, Adam Mausner, Iraqi Force Development 2008, Washington, D.C.: Center for Strategic & International Studies, p. 6. Anthony H. Cordesman, Adam Mausner, "Withdrawal from Iraq: Assessing the Readiness of Iraqi Security Forces," Washington, D.C.: Center for Strategic and International Studies, 2009, pp. 20–23. "Moktada al-Sadr's militia's actions in Basra followed a pattern seen again and again: the Mahdi militia battles Iraqi government troops to a standstill and then retreats. Why his fighters have clung to those fight-then-fade tactics is unknown. But American military and civilian officials have repeatedly claimed that Mahdi Army units trained and equipped by Iran had played a major role in the unexpectedly strong resistance that government troops met in Basra." James Glanz, Alissa J. Rubin, "Iraqi Army Takes Last Basra Areas From Sadr Force," *New York Times*, April 20, 2008, www.nytimes.com/2008/04/20/world/middleeast/20iraq.html Thomas Harding, "Iraq: British 'abandoned Basra to terror,'" *London Telegraph*, 29 Sep 2010, www.telegraph.co.uk/news/worldnews/middleeast/iraq/8031642/Iraq-Britishabandoned-Basra-to-terror.html

1915. "Mehdi Army 'stop carrying arms,'" BBC News, 6 August 2008, news.bbc.co.uk/2/hi/middle_east/7545182.stm Leila Fadel, "In big concession, militia agrees to let Iraqi troops enter Sadr City," McClatchy Newspapers, May 9, 2006, retrieved from the World Wide Web Wednesday, October 29, 2008, www.mcclatchydc.com/251/story/36530.html *Telegraph*, "Mahdi Army to lay down arms," Telegraph.co.uk, August 6, 2008, retrieved from the World Wide Web Wednesday, October 29, 2008, www.telegraph.co.uk/news/worldnews/middleeast/iraq/2507701/Mahdi-Army-to-lay-down-arms.html James Hider, "Iraq: Al-Mahdi army offers to lay down its arms," *TimesOnline*, April 8, 2008. Retrieved from the World Wide Web Wednesday, October 29, 2008, www.timesonline.co.uk/tol/news/world/iraq/article3701511.ece

1916. "Nūrī al-Māliki," *Encyclopædia Britannica*, 2008, Encyclopædia Britannica Online, retrieved from the World Wide Web Monday, October 27, 2008, www.britannica.com/EBchecked/topic/1267089/Nuri-al-Maliki

1917. IRNA, "Iraqi Defense Ministry welcomes Iran-Iraq security pact," *The Tehran Times Daily*, June 21, 2008, retrieved from the World Wide Web Friday, June 20, 2008, www.tehrantimes.com/index_View.asp?code=170739. IRNA is Iran's Islamic Republic News Agency.

1918. Rajiv Chandrasekaran, *Imperial Life in the Emerald City: Inside Iraq's Green Zone*. New York: Vintage Books, 2007.

1919. Scott Peterson and Howard LaFranchi, "Iran Shifts Attention to Brokering Peace in Iraq," *Christian Science Monitor*, May 16, 2008, reprinted in *Arab American News*, retrieved from the World Wide Web Friday, June 20, 2008, www.arabamericannews.com/news/index.php?mod=article&cat=Iraq&article=1040

1920. Tariq Alhomayed, "Iran and the Fearful Arabs," *Asharq Al-Awsat*, January 5, 2008, retrieved from the World Wide Web Tuesday, October 28, 2008, www.asharq-e.com/news.asp?section=2&id=12718

1921. Osama bin Laden, Full text: bin Laden's 'letter to America', November 24, 2002, *The Observer*. London, November 24, 2002. *The Observer* points out that "The letter first appeared on the internet in Arabic and has since been translated and circulated by Islamists in Britain." Retrieved November 25, 2002, from the World Wide Web www.observer.co.uk/worldview/story/0,11581,845725,00.html Jason Burke, Osama issues new call to arms— Read the bin Laden letter in full, London, *The Observer*, Sunday November 24, 2002, www.observer.co.uk/worldview

1922. Ayatollah Khomeini, *Sayings of the Ayatollah Khomeini*, p. 5.

1923. Mahmoud Ahmadinejad, "Iranian President Mahmoud Ahmadinejad: As Soon as Iran Achieves Advanced Technologies, It Has the Capacity to Become an Invincible Global Power," The Middle East Media Research Institute, Video Clip No. 1288, 9/28/2006. Excerpts from an address delivered by Iranian President Mahmoud Ahmadinejad, which aired on the Iranian news channel (IRINN) on September 28, 2006. memritv.org/Transcript.asp?P1=1288

1924. Says *The Washington Post*'s Dafna Linzer, a meeting between the Iranians and the Pakistanis in Dubai concluded with a written sales agreement that "kick-started Tehran's nuclear efforts and Khan's black market." Dafna Linzer, "Iran Was Offered Nuclear Parts." *The Washington Post*, Sunday 27 February 2005.

1925. U.S. Department of the Treasury, Joint Plan of Action (JPOA) Archive, www.treasury.gov/resource-center/sanctions/Programs/Pages/jpoa_archive.aspx U.S. Department of State, Joint Comprehensive Plan of Action, www.state.gov/e/eb/tfs/spi/iran/jcpoa/

1926. Joint Comprehensive Plan of Action, Vienna, 14 July 2015, U.S. Department of State, www.state.gov/e/eb/tfs/spi/iran/jcpoa/ See also: Majlis Approval of JCPOA Inexpedient, Financial Tribune—First Iranian English Economic Daily, August 12, 2015, financialtribune.com/articles/national/23215/majlis-approval-jcpoa-inexpedient

1927. Joint Comprehensive Plan of Action, Vienna, 14 July 2015, U.S. Department of State, www.state.gov/e/eb/tfs/spi/iran/jcpoa/

1928. Press TV, "Iran nuclear agreement satisfactory not ideal: Salehi," Mon Feb 1, 2016 11:33 a.m., Press TV, Iran, www.presstv.ir/Detail/2016/02/01/448248/Iran-JCPOA-P51-Salehi-nuclear-agreement-/

1929. *Sahih Bukhari*, Volume 4, Book 54, Number 476: www.usc.edu/dept/MSA/fundamentals/hadithsunnah/bukhari/054.sbt.html#004.054.476

1930. "Jihad becomes Farde `Aain, obligatory on every individual, when the help of every individual is required. To fight in the cause of Allah (Qital) is one of the obligations that serves to fulfil the covenant between the faithful, and Allah. 'Allah has purchased, of the believers their lives and their properties, and in return gives the gardens of paradise. They fight in his cause. And slay and are slain. A promise binding on him in truth from the Torah . . .' (9:111)[9] Qital is a part of the bargain, and only if it is fulfilled, the promise of Allah's rewards to the believers will be fulfilled.

"Rank given for participating in Jihad:
"Those who have died in the way of Allah are given the title, Shahid (witness). They have given the ultimate sacrifice which is their life, as a witness unto the truth. 'Not equal are those believers who sit at home, and receive no hurt and those who fight in the cause of Allah with their goods and their persons . . . unto all in faith has Allah promised good: but those who strive and fight he has distinguished above those who sit at home.' (Qur'an 4:95-96)

"Treatment of those who do not participate in Jihad: "The treatment of those who do not participate in Jihad is outlined by Allah in Surah Tawbah, referring to the battle of Tabuk. 'Those who were allowed to stay behind rejoiced at remaining behind and not accompanying the messenger of Allah. They were adverse to striving in the cause of Allah with their belongings and their lives and told others; 'Do not go forth in this fierce heat. Tell them; the hell is far fiercer in heat." In "The Quranic Concept of Jihad (From a fundamentalist download — Young Muslim Organization (UK), abridged but otherwise unchanged): Aims and Objectives of Jihad," published in Human Rights Abuses in Islamic Countries, Left Shoe News, www.hraicjk.org/ the_quranic_concept_of_jihad.html

EXTREME ISLAM
ANTI-AMERICAN PROPAGANDA
OF MUSLIM FUNDAMENTALISM

EDITED BY ADAM PARFREY

EXTREME ISLAM
**Anti-American Propaganda
of Muslim Fundamentalism**

Edited by Adam Parfrey

0-922915-78-4

5½ × 8½ 318 pages

$16

"Every page of this book contains
interest. Parfrey has done another
outstanding trawl of data, presented
here in its bare face and without a
distorting commentary. With *Extreme
Islam*, Feral House maintains its
reputation as the most courageous
and incendiary publisher in the US."

— Jeremy Glover, *Headpress*